# Contents


Preface v

Introduction ix

Part 1 Organization 1

1. Business Organization 3
2. Tax Year and Accounting Methods 36
3. Recordkeeping for Business Income and Deductions 51

Part 2 Business Income and Losses 61

4. Income or Loss from Business Operations 63
5. Capital Gains and Losses 95
6. Gains and Losses from Sales of Business Property 113

Part 3 Business Deductions and Credits 125

7. Employee Compensation: Salary, Wages, and Employee Benefits 127
8. Travel, Meals, and Gift Expenses 164
9. Car and Truck Expenses 186
10. Repairs, Maintenance, and Energy Improvements 209
11. Bad Debts 225
12. Rents 236
13. Taxes and Interest 246

14. First-Year Expensing, Depreciation, Amortization, and Depletion 261
15. Advertising Expenses 294
16. Retirement Plans 300
17. Casualty and Theft Losses 339
18. Home Office Deductions 353
19. Medical Coverage 371
20. Deductions and Tax Credits for Farmers 391
21. Qualified Business Income Deduction 402
22. Miscellaneous Business Deductions 416
23. Roundup of Tax Credits 450

Part 4 Tax Planning for Your Small Business 463
24. Income and Deduction Strategies 465
25. Distributions from Your Business 479
26. Tax Strategies for Opening or Closing a Business 483
27. Tax Strategies for a Sideline Business 495
28. Tax Strategies for Multiple Businesses 499
29. Alternative Minimum Tax 504
30. Other Taxes 509
31. Filing Tax Returns, Paying Taxes, and Making Refund Claims 527
32. Retirement and Succession Planning 541
33. Working with CPAs and Other Tax Professionals 549
34. Handling Audits with the IRS 553
Appendix A. Information Returns 559
Appendix B. Tax Penalties 566
Appendix C. Checklist of Tax-Related Corporate Resolutions 572
Appendix D. List of Dollar Limits and Amounts Adjusted for Inflation 574
Index 577

# Preface

Many small businesses were adversely affected by COVID-19. Thousands closed temporarily or permanently while others stayed open but suffered significant revenue loss. Fortunately, many were able to hang on or even prosper. Various government programs, such as the Paycheck Protection Program (PPP), helped some in need. And a record number of new businesses sprung up in the wake of the pandemic. With the worst of COVID-19 behind us, small businesses are looking ahead to adapt to changes in the economy wrought by the pandemic, such as remote work arrangements, difficulties in hiring needed staff, shortages of certain items and materials, and inflation. Business policies are, or should be, under review.

With this in mind, tax changes and opportunities should not be overlooked. The American Rescue Plan Act of 2021 and other law changes altered many tax rules. Some of the changes apply only for 2021, some through 2022, others even longer, while still others are permanent. As a small business owner, you can't rely on the tax rules you've become accustomed to. You need to familiarize yourself with new rules to minimize your 2021 taxes, figure estimated taxes for 2022, and obtain tax refunds from certain prior years.

This book focuses primarily on federal income taxes. Businesses may be required to pay and report many other taxes, including state income taxes, employment taxes, sales and use taxes, and excise taxes. Some information about these taxes is included in this book to alert you to your possible obligations so that you can then obtain further assistance if necessary.

The book takes a holistic approach to taxes, showing you where applicable the ramifications that tax decisions can have on your business activities and your bottom line. Statistics, resources, and other materials are provided to help you better run your business by making good tax decisions and implementing sound business practices.

It is important to stay alert to future tax changes. Be sure to check on any final action before you take any steps that could be affected by these changes.

*For a free supplement on tax developments after October 1, 2021, affecting small businesses (available in February 2022), go to www.jklasser.com or www.BigIdeasForSmallBusiness.com.*

## How to Use This Book

The purpose of this book is to make you acutely aware of how your actions in business can affect your bottom line from a tax perspective. The way you organize your business, the accounting method you select, and the types of payments you make all have an impact on when you report income and the extent to which you can take deductions. This book is not designed to make you a tax expert. It is strongly suggested that you consult with a tax adviser before making certain important decisions that will affect your ability to minimize your taxes (and Chapter 33 tells you how to work with a tax professional). I hope that the insight you gain from this book will allow you to ask your adviser key questions to benefit your business.

In Part 1, you will find topics of interest to all businesses. First, there is an overview of the various forms of business organization and an explanation of how these forms of organization affect personal liability for an owner as well as reporting of income and claiming tax deductions. Part 1 also explains tax years and accounting methods that businesses can select. And it covers important recordkeeping requirements and suggestions to help you audit-proof your return to the extent possible and protect your deductions and tax credits.

Part 2 details how to report various types of income your business may receive. In addition to fees and sales receipts—the bread-and-butter of your business—you may receive other types of ordinary income such as interest income, royalties, and rents. You may have capital gain transactions as well as sales of business assets. But you may also have losses—from operations or the sale of assets. Special rules govern the tax treatment of these losses. The first part of each topic in a chapter discusses the types of income or loss to report and special rules that affect them. Then scan the second part of each topic in a chapter, which explains where on the tax return to report the income or claim the loss.

Part 3 focuses on specific deductions and tax credits. It provides you with guidance on the various types of deductions you can use to reduce your business income, including the qualified business income (QBI) deduction for owners of pass-through entities. In the first part of each topic in a chapter, you will learn what the write-off is all about and any dollar limits or other special requirements that may apply. As with the income chapters, the second part of each topic chapter explains where on the tax return you can claim the write-off based on your form of business organization. Also, in Chapter 22, Miscellaneous Business Deductions, you will find checklists that serve as handy reference guides on all business deductions. The checklists are organized according to your status: self-employed, employee, or small corporation. You will also find a checklist of business expenses that are not deductible.

Part 4 contains planning ideas for your business. You will learn about strategies for deferring income, boosting deductions, starting up or winding down a business, running a sideline business, owning multiple businesses, taking distributions, and avoiding audits. It also highlights the most common mistakes that business owners make in their returns, so by avoiding them you will not lose out on tax-saving opportunities. You will also find links to resources for tax assistance and planning purposes. And you will find information about other taxes on your business, including state income taxes, employment taxes, sales and use taxes, and excise taxes. Finally, you will see how to work with a tax professional and what to do if you are audited.

In Appendix A, you will find a listing of information returns you may be required to file with the IRS or other government agencies in conjunction with your tax obligations. These returns enable the federal government to crosscheck tax reporting and other financial information. Appendix B covers tax penalties that may apply if you fail to do something you were supposed to do, or if you do it wrong or do it late. Appendix C contains a checklist of tax-related corporate resolutions to help you keep your corporate minutes book up to date. Appendix D is a list of dollar limits and amounts for certain tax rules that are adjusted annually for inflation to help you plan ahead.

Several forms and schedules as well as excerpts from them have been included throughout the book to illustrate reporting rules. These forms are not to be used to file your return. (In many cases, the appropriate forms were not available when this book was published, and older or draft versions of the forms were included.) While most returns today are prepared and filed electronically, if you do not use software or a paid preparer to complete your return, you can obtain the forms you need from the IRS's website at https://www.irs.gov or where otherwise indicated.

Another way to stay abreast of tax and other small business developments that can affect your business throughout the year is by subscribing to *Barbara Weltman's Big Ideas for Small Business®*, a free online newsletter geared for small business owners and their professional advisers, and my "Idea of the Day®" (via e-mail) at www.BigIdeasForSmallBusiness.com. Again, the Supplement to this book, which covers developments after October 1, 2021, may be found at www.jklasser.com and my website www.BigIdeasForSmallBusiness.com.

This book has been in print for more than 25 years and has tracked dramatic changes in tax law and business operations. For those who are using it for the first time, the book is a resource guide for handling taxes effectively as well as for making financial decisions and using business practices to increase your bottom line. For those who are perennial readers, you will see that while much in the book is unchanged, it has been updated and expanded to reflect changes from new laws, court decisions, and IRS pronouncements as well as my additional comments on tax strategies and business practices. For tax practitioners, I recognize that there are no citations, and that there are some issues that are unsettled. I invite your comments on any areas in which you disagree with my presentation and for ways to make improvements in future editions (send comments to Barbara@BigIdeasForSmallBusiness.com). I also recognize that more small businesses are going global and have to contend with foreign taxes and the implications on their U.S. returns, but the subject of foreign taxes is not fully addressed in this book.

I would like to thank Sidney Kess, Esq. and CPA, for his valuable suggestions in the preparation of the original tax deduction book, Kenneth C. Laufer, CPA, for his careful review of the book, and Elliott Eiss, Esq., for his expertise and constant assistance with this and other projects.

Barbara Weltman
*October 2021*

# Introduction

Small businesses are vital to the U.S. economy despite the pounding they took from the pandemic. While tens of thousands of small businesses went out of business, many new ones started up. Small businesses account for 99.9% of all firms, employ nearly half of the country's private sector workforce, and contribute more than half of the nation's gross national product.

It's estimated there were more than 32 million small businesses—sole proprietorships, limited liability companies, partnerships, S corporations, and C corporations. While COVID-19 certainly hit many small businesses hard, the pandemic did not stop interest in entrepreneurship. The gig economy expanded and small businesses continued to be present on Main Street, farms, homes, and anywhere else that a business can be found.

Small businesses fall under the purview of the Internal Revenue Service's (IRS) Small Business and Self-Employed Division (SB/SE). This division services approximately 57 million tax filers, including 47 million individuals filing Schedules C, E, or F, as well as (3.8 million partnerships and 6.8 million corporations with assets of $10 million or less), more than 41 million of whom are full-time or partially self-employed, and about 7 million filers of employment, excise, and certain other returns. The SB/SE division accounts for about 40% of the total federal tax revenues collected. The goal of this IRS division is customer assistance to help small businesses comply with the tax laws.

There is also an IRS Small Business and Self-Employed Tax Center at https://www.irs.gov/Businesses/Small-Businesses-&-Self-Employed where you'll find links to topics of interest, such as stages of a business and free online learning opportunities.

As a small business owner, you work, try to grow your business, and hope to make a profit. What you can keep from that profit depends in part on the income tax you pay. The income tax applies to your net income rather than to your gross income or gross receipts. You are essentially taxed on what you keep after paying off the expenses of providing the services or making the sales that are the crux of your business. Deductions for these expenses operate to fix the amount of income that will be subject to tax. So deductions, in effect, help to determine the tax you pay and the profits you keep. And tax credits, the number of which has been expanded in recent years, can offset your tax to reduce the amount you ultimately pay.

## Special Rules for Small Businesses

Sometimes it pays to be small. The tax laws contain a number of special rules exclusively for small businesses. But what is a small business? The average size of a small business in the United States is one with fewer than 20 employees with annual revenue under $2 million. Different government departments and agencies, as well as different industries, use their own definitions of "small business." For federal tax purposes, the answer varies from rule to rule, as explained throughout this book. Sometimes, it depends on your revenues, the number of employees, or total assets. In Table I.1 are nearly 3 dozen definitions from the Internal Revenue Code on what constitutes a small business in 2021. You may be a small business for some tax rules but not for others.

**TABLE I.1** Examples of Tax Definitions of Small Business

| Tax Rule | Definition |
|---|---|
| Accrual method exception for small businesses (Chapter 2) | Average annual gross receipts of no more than $26 million in the 3 prior years (or number of years in business, if less) |
| Archer medical savings accounts (Chapter 19) | Fewer than 50 employees |
| Bad debts deducted on the nonaccrual-experience method (Chapter 11) | Average annual gross receipts for the 3 prior years of no more than $5 million |
| Building improvements safe harbor (Chapter 10) | Average annual gross receipts for the 3 prior years of no more than $10 million *and* building's unadjusted basis no greater than $1 million |
| Centralized audit regime for partnerships–election out (Chapter 33) | 100 or fewer partners |
| Disabled access credit (Chapter 10) | Gross receipts of no more than $1 million in the preceding year or no more than 30 full-time employees |
| Employer mandate exemption from providing affordable health coverage | Fewer than 50 full-time/full-time equivalent employees |
| Estimated tax for C corporations based on prior year's return (Chapter 30) | Taxable income of less than $1 million in any of the 3 preceding years |
| Employee retention income tax credit (Chapter 7) | Fewer than 100 employees |
| Employer differential wage payments credit (Chapter 7) | Fewer than 50 employees |
| First-year expensing election (Chapter 14) | Qualified property for 2021 of no more than $3.67 million |
| Golden parachute payments exemption (Chapter 7) | 100 or fewer shareholders |
| Independent contractor versus employee determination—shifting burden of proof to IRS (Chapter 7) | Net worth of business does not exceed $7 million |
| Interest deduction limit exemption (Chapter 13) | Average annual gross receipts of $26 million or less in the 3 prior years |
| Late filing penalty for failure to file information return—cap (Appendix B) | Average annual gross receipts of no more than $5 million for a 3-year period |

**TABLE I.1** *(Continued)*

| Tax Rule | Definition |
|---|---|
| Paid family leave employment tax credit (Chapter 7) | Fewer than 500 employees |
| Paid sick leave employment tax credit (Chapter 7) | Fewer than 500 employees |
| Qualified small employer health reimbursement arrangement (Chapter 19) | Fewer than 50 full-time and full-time equivalent employees |
| Reasonable compensation—shifting the burden of proof to the IRS (Chapter 7) | Net worth of business not in excess of $7 million |
| Recovery of legal fees from the government | Net worth less than $5 million and fewer than 500 employees at the time the action is filed |
| Repair regulations—deduction under safe harbor for items up to $2,500 per item or invoice (Chapter 10) | No applicable financial statement (SEC filing; audited financial statement) |
| Repair regulations—safe harbor not to capitalize improvements to buildings (Chapter 10) | Average annual gross receipts under $10 million and building has unadjusted basis under $1 million |
| Research credit–offset to AMT(Chapter 23) | Businesses with average annual gross receipts in the 3 prior years of $50 million or less |
| Research credit—offset to employer's Social Security taxes (Chapter 23) | Corporation or partnership with gross receipts of no more than $5 million for current year and no gross receipts during the 5-year period ending with the current year (similar for sole proprietors) |
| Retirement plan start-up credit (Chapter 16) | No more than 100 employees with compensation over $5,000 in the preceding year |
| Savings Incentive Match Plans for Employees (SIMPLE) plans (Chapter 16) | Self-employed or businesses with 100 or fewer employees who received at least $5,000 in compensation in the preceding year |
| Section 1244 losses (Chapter 5) | Equity of no more than $1 million at the time stock is issued |
| Simple cafeteria plans (Chapter 7) | 100 or fewer employees on business days during either of the 2 preceding years |
| Simplified change in accounting for repair safe harbors (Chapter 10) | Total assets less than $10 million or average annual gross receipts in 3 prior years less than $10 million |
| Small business/self-employed (SB/SE) division of IRS | Self-employed individuals, plus corporations and partnerships with assets under $10 million |
| Small employer automatic enrollment credit (Chapter 16) | No more than 100 employees with compensation over $5,000 in the preceding year |
| Small employer health care credit (Chapter 19) | No more than 25 full-time equivalent employees |
| Small business stock—exclusion of gain on sale (Chapter 5) | Gross assets of no more than $50 million when the stock is issued and immediately after |
| UNICAP small reseller exception (Chapter 2) | Average annual gross receipts of no more than $26 million for a 3-year period |
| UNICAP simplified dollar value last-in, first-out (LIFO) method (Chapter 2) | Average annual gross receipts of no more than $5 million for a 3-year period |

### Reporting Income

Generally, all of the income your business receives is taxable unless there is a specific tax rule that allows you to exclude the income permanently or defer it to a future time.

*When* you report income depends on your method of accounting. *How* and *where* you report income depends on the nature of the income and your type of business organization.

The IRS Commissioner said in 2021 that there's a "tax gap" (the spread between revenues that should be collected and what actually is collected) estimated to be $1 trillion per year and that a great portion of this can be traced to entrepreneurs who underreport or don't report their income, overstate their deductions, or fail to pay self-employment tax where warranted. While audit rates have recently been at historic lows due in part to budgetary issues, the SB/SE division wants to double the number of its examiners and plans to look carefully at self-employed individuals in an attempt to detect intentional or unintentional reporting errors.

### Claiming Deductions

You pay tax only on your profits, not on what you take in (gross receipts). In order to arrive at your profits, you are allowed to subtract certain expenses from your income. These expenses are called "deductions."

The law says what you can and cannot deduct (see below). Within this framework, the nature and amount of the deductions you have often vary with the size of your business, the industry you are in, where you are based in the country, and other factors. The most common deductions for businesses include car and truck expenses, salaries and wages, utilities, supplies, legal and professional services, insurance, depreciation, taxes, meals, advertising, repairs, travel, rent for business property and equipment, and in many cases, a home office.

### What Is the Legal Authority for Claiming Deductions?

Deductions are a legal way to reduce the amount of your business income subject to tax. But there is no constitutional right to tax deductions. Instead, deductions are a matter of legislative grace; if Congress chooses to allow a particular deduction, so be it. Therefore, deductions are carefully spelled out in the Internal Revenue Code (the Code).

The language of the Code in many instances is rather general. It may describe a category of deductions without getting into specifics. For example, the Code contains a general deduction for all *ordinary and necessary* business expenses, without explaining what constitutes these expenses. Over the years, the IRS and the courts have worked to flesh out what business expenses are ordinary and necessary. "Ordinary" means common or accepted in business and "necessary" means appropriate and helpful in developing and maintaining a business; it does not mean essential. The IRS and the courts often reach different conclusions about whether an item meets this definition and is deductible, leaving the taxpayer in a somewhat difficult position. If the taxpayer relies on a more favorable prior court position to claim a deduction, the IRS may very well attack the deduction in the event that the return is examined. This puts the taxpayer in the position of having to incur legal expenses to bring the matter to court. However, if the taxpayer simply follows the IRS approach, a good opportunity to reduce business income by means of a deduction will have been missed. Throughout this book, whenever unresolved questions remain about a particular deduction, both sides have been explained. The choice is up to you and your tax adviser.

Sometimes, the Code is very specific about a deduction, such as an employer's right to deduct employment taxes. Still, even where the Code is specific and there is less need for clarification, disputes about applicability or terminology may still arise. Again, the IRS and the courts may differ on the proper conclusion. It will remain for you and your tax adviser to review the different authorities for the positions stated and to reach your own conclusions based on the strength of the different positions and the amount of tax savings at stake.

A word about authorities for the deductions discussed in this book: There are a number of sources for these write-offs in addition to the Internal Revenue Code. These sources include court decisions from the U.S. Tax Court, the U.S. district courts and courts of appeal, the U.S. Court of Federal Claims, and the U.S. Supreme Court. There are also regulations issued by the Treasury Department to explain sections of the Internal Revenue Code. The IRS issues a number of pronouncements, including Revenue Rulings and Revenue Procedures, which are official IRS positions, as well as Notices, Announcements, and News Releases, which carry less weight. The IRS also issues private letter rulings, determination letters, field service advice, and technical advice memoranda. While these private types of pronouncements cannot be cited as authority by a taxpayer other than the one for whom the pronouncement was made, they are important nonetheless. They serve as an indication of IRS thinking on a particular topic, and it is often the case that private letter rulings on topics of general interest later get restated in revenue rulings. More recently, the IRS simply posts information on its website, in the form of Frequently Asked Questions (FAQs) or other pronouncement, which is helpful in understanding the IRS position on a matter.

### *What Is a Tax Deduction Worth to You?*

The answer depends on your tax bracket. The tax bracket is dependent on the way you organize your business. If you are self-employed and in the top tax bracket of 37% in 2021, then each $100 deduction will save you $37. Had you not claimed this deduction, you would have had to pay $37 of tax on that $100 of income that was offset by the deduction. For C corporations, there is a flat rate of 21%. This means that the corporation is in the 21% tax bracket. Thus, each $100 deduction claimed saves $21 of tax on the corporation's income. Deductions are even more valuable if your business is in a state that imposes income tax. The details of state income taxes are not discussed in this book. However, you should explore the tax rules in your state and ascertain their impact on your business income.

### *When Do You Claim Deductions?*

Like the timing of income, the timing of deductions—when to claim them—is determined by your tax year and method of accounting. Your form of business organization affects your choice of tax year and your accounting method.

Even when expenses are deductible, there may be limits on the timing of those deductions. Most common expenses are currently deductible in full. However, some expenses must be capitalized or amortized, or you must choose between current deductibility and capitalization. Capitalization generally means that costs can be written off ratably as amortized expenses or depreciated over a period of time. (Capitalized costs, such as for the purchase of machinery and equipment, are added to the balance sheet as company assets.) Amortized expenses include, for example, fees to incorporate a business and expenses to organize a new business. Certain capitalized costs may not be deductible at all, but are treated as an additional cost of an asset (*basis*).

Some expenses, even though related to business and not incurred but for business, are not deductible. The tax law specifically bars deductions for certain expenses (e.g., entertainment costs, transportation fringe benefits). And no deduction is allowed for personal expenses that are business-related, such as commuting costs. These nondeductible expenses are pointed out throughout the book.

### *Credits versus Deductions*

Not all write-offs of business expenses are treated as deductions. Some can be claimed as tax credits. A tax credit is worth more than a deduction since it reduces your taxes dollar for dollar. Like deductions, tax credits are available only to the extent that Congress allows. In a couple of instances, you have a choice between treating certain expenses as a deduction or a credit. In most cases, however, tax credits can be claimed for certain expenses for which no tax deduction is provided. Most business tax credits are offsets for income taxes, but some reduce employment taxes.

### *Tax Responsibilities*

As a small business owner, your obligations taxwise are broad. Not only do you have to pay income taxes and file income tax returns, but you must also manage payroll taxes if you have any employees. You may also have to collect and report on state and local sales taxes. Some businesses, such as farms, may have excise tax responsibilities. Finally, you may have to notify the IRS of certain activities on information returns.

It is very helpful to keep an eye on the tax calendar so you will not miss out on any payment or filing deadlines, which can result in interest and penalties. You might want to view the IRS's *Tax Calendar for Businesses and Self-Employed* (https://www.irs.gov/businesses/small-businesses-self-employed/irs-tax-calendar-for-businesses-and-self-employed).

Should you need them, you can obtain most federal tax forms online at https://www.irs.gov. Nonscannable forms, which cannot be downloaded from the IRS, can be ordered by calling toll free at 800-829-4933 during normal business hours.

PART 1

# Organization

# CHAPTER 1

# Business Organization


Sole Proprietorships 4
Partnerships and Limited Liability Companies 9
S Corporations and Their Shareholder-Employees 16
C Corporations and Their Shareholder-Employees 18
Benefit Corporations 26
Employees 27
Factors in Choosing Your Form of Business Organization 27
Forms of Business Organization Compared 33
Changing Your Form of Business 35


If you have a great idea for a product or a business and are eager to get started, do not let your enthusiasm be the reason you get off on the wrong foot. Take awhile to consider how you will organize your business. The form of organization your business takes controls how income and deductions are reported to the government on a tax return. Sometimes you have a choice of the type of business organization; other times, circumstances limit your choice. If you have not yet set up your business and do have a choice, this discussion will influence your decision on business organization. If you have already set up your business, you may want to consider changing to another form of organization.

According to the Tax Foundation, 92% of all businesses in the United States are organized as sole proprietorships, partnerships, limited liability companies (LLCs), or S corporations, all of which are "pass-through" entities. This means that the owners, rather than the businesses, pay tax on business income. The way in which you set up your business impacts the effective tax rate you pay on your profits. Taxes, however, are only one factor in deciding what type of entity to use for your business.

As you organize your business, consider which type of entity to use after factoring in taxes (federal and state) and other consequences. Also, as business activities and tax laws change, consider whether to change from your current form of business entity to a new one and what it means from a tax perspective, which is discussed later in this chapter. Finally, be sure to obtain your business's federal tax identification number or a new one when making certain entity changes (explained in Chapter 26).

## Sole Proprietorships

If you go into business for yourself and do not have any partners (with the exception of a spouse, as explained shortly), you are considered a *sole proprietor*, and your business is called a *sole proprietorship*. You may think that the term *proprietor* connotes a storekeeper. For purposes of tax treatment, however, proprietor means any unincorporated business owned entirely by one person. Thus, the category includes individuals in professional practice, such as doctors, lawyers, accountants, and architects. Those who are experts in an area, such as engineering, public relations, or computers, may set up their own consulting businesses and fall under the category of sole proprietor. The designation also applies to independent contractors. Other terms used for sole proprietors include freelancers, solopreneurs, and consultants. And it includes "dependent contractors": self-employed individuals who provide all (or substantially all) of their services for one company (often someone laid off or retired from a corporate job who is then engaged to provide nonemployee services for the same corporation). Further, it includes those working in the gig economy through such online platforms as Uber, Lyft, HopSkipDrive, TaskRabbit, Takl, and Upwork (although some workers for these companies may be employees under state law or court decisions).

Sole proprietorships are the most common form of business. The IRS reports that one in 6 Form 1040 or 1040-SR contains a Schedule C (the form used by sole proprietorships). Most sideline businesses are run as sole proprietorships, and many start-ups commence in this business form.

There are no formalities required to become a sole proprietor; you simply conduct business. You may have to register your business with your city, town, or county government by filing a simple form stating that you are doing business as the "Quality Dry Cleaners" or some other business name other than your own (a fictitious business name, or FBN). This is sometimes referred to as a DBA, which stands for "doing business as."

From a legal standpoint, as a sole proprietor, you are personally liable for any debts your business incurs. For example, if you borrow money and default on a loan, the lender can look not only to your business equipment and other business property but also to your personal stocks, bonds, and other property. Some states may give your house homestead protection; state or federal law may protect your pensions and even Individual Retirement Accounts (IRAs). Your only protection for your other personal assets is adequate insurance against accidents for your business and other liabilities and paying your debts in full.

Simplicity is the advantage to this form of business. This form of business is commonly used for sideline ventures, as evidenced by the fact that half of all sole proprietors earn salaries and wages along with their business income. For 2018 (the most recent year for statistics), more than 27.1 million taxpayers filed returns as sole proprietors.

### *Independent Contractors*

One type of sole proprietor is the *independent contractor*. To illustrate, suppose you used to work for Corporation X. You have retired, but X gives you a consulting contract under which you provide occasional services to X. In your retirement, you decide to provide consulting services not only to X, but to other customers as well. You are now a consultant. You are an independent contractor to each of the companies for which you provide services. Similarly, you have a full-time job but earn extra money by doing graphic design work through Fiverr. Here too you are an independent contractor.

More precisely, an independent contractor or freelancer is an individual who provides services to others outside an employment context. The provision of services becomes a business, an independent calling. In terms of claiming business deductions, classification as an independent contractor is generally more favorable than classification as an employee. (See "Tax Treatment of Income and Deductions in General," later in this chapter.) Therefore, many individuals whose employment status is not clear may wish to claim independent contractor status. Also, from the employer's perspective, hiring independent contractors is more favorable because the employer is not liable for employment taxes and need not provide employee benefits. (It costs about 30% more for a business to use an employee than an independent contractor after factoring in employment taxes, workers' compensation and other insurance, and benefits.) Federal employment taxes include Social Security and Medicare taxes under the Federal Insurance Contribution Act (FICA) as well as unemployment taxes under the Federal Unemployment Tax Act (FUTA).

You should be aware that the Internal Revenue Service (IRS) aggressively tries to reclassify workers as employees in order to collect employment taxes from employers. And states do so as well to see that workers are covered by unemployment insurance and workers' compensation. A discussion about worker classification may be found in Chapter 7.

There is a distinction that needs to be made between the classification of a worker for income tax purposes and the classification of a worker for employment tax purposes. By statute, certain employees are treated as independent contractors for employment taxes even though they continue to be treated as employees for income taxes. Other employees are treated as employees for employment taxes even though they are independent contractors for income taxes.

There are 2 categories of employees that are, by statute, treated as non-employees for purposes of federal employment taxes. These 2 categories are real estate salespersons and direct sellers of consumer goods. These employees are considered independent contractors (the ramifications of which are discussed later in this chapter). Such workers are deemed independent contractors if at least 90% of the employees' compensation is determined by their output. In other words, they are independent contractors if they are paid by commission and not a fixed salary. They must also perform their services under a written contract that specifies they will not be treated as employees for federal employment tax purposes.

### *Statutory Employees*

Some individuals who consider themselves to be in business for themselves—reporting their income and expenses as sole proprietors—may still be treated as employees for purposes of employment taxes. As such, Social Security and Medicare taxes are withheld from their compensation. These individuals include:

- Corporate officers
- Agent-drivers or commission-drivers engaged in the distribution of meat products, bakery products, produce, beverages other than milk, laundry, or dry-cleaning services
- Full-time life insurance salespersons
- Homeworkers who personally perform services according to specifications provided by the service recipient
- Traveling or city salespersons engaged on a full-time basis in the solicitation of orders from wholesalers, retailers, contractors, or operators of hotels, restaurants, or other similar businesses

Full-time life insurance salespersons, homeworkers, and traveling or city salespersons are exempt from FICA if they have made a substantial investment in the facilities used in connection with the performance of services. But they'll have to pay Social Security and Medicare taxes through self-employment tax on their net earnings.

### Day Traders

Traders in securities may be viewed as being engaged in a trade or business in securities if they seek profit from daily market movements in the prices of securities (rather than from dividends, interest, and long-term appreciation) and these activities are substantial, continuous, and regular. Calling yourself a day trader does not make it so; your activities must speak for themselves.

Being a trader means you report your trading expenses on Schedule C, such as subscriptions to publications and online services used in this securities business. Investment interest can be reported on Schedule C (it is not subject to the net investment income limitation that otherwise applies to individuals).

Being a trader means income is reported in a unique way—income from trading is *not* reported on Schedule C. Gains and losses are reported on Schedule D unless you make a mark-to-market election. If so, then income and losses are reported on Form 4797. The mark-to-market election is explained in Chapter 2.

Gains and losses from trading activities are not subject to self-employment tax (with or without the mark-to-market election).

### Spousal Joint Ventures

Usually when 2 or more people co-own a business, they are in partnership. However, spouses who co-own a business, file jointly, and conduct a joint venture can opt *not* to be treated as a partnership, which requires filing a partnership return (Form 1065) and reporting 2 Schedule K-1s (as explained later in this chapter). Instead, these "couplepreneurs" each report their share of income on 2 Schedule Cs attached to the couple's Form 1040 or 1040-SR. To qualify for this election, each must materially participate in the business (neither can be a silent partner), and there can be no other co-owners. Making this election simplifies reporting while ensuring that each spouse receives credit for paying Social Security and Medicare taxes.

### One-Member Limited Liability Companies

Every state allows a single owner to form a limited liability company (LLC) under state law. From a legal standpoint, an LLC gives the owner protection from personal liability (only business assets are at risk from the claims of creditors) as explained later in this chapter. But from a tax standpoint, a single-member LLC is treated as a "disregarded entity." If the owner is an individual (and not a corporation), all of the income and expenses of the LLC are reported on Schedule C of the owner's Form 1040 or 1040-SR. In other words, for federal income tax purposes, the LLC is treated just like a sole proprietorship.

The owner may elect to have the LLC taxed as a corporation, but this is not typical. An election made to be taxed as a corporation can be followed by an S election, so that the owner can make tax payments through wage withholding rather than making estimated tax payments, as well as minimize Social Security and Medicare taxes.

### Tax Treatment of Income and Deductions in General

Sole proprietors, including independent contractors and statutory employees, report their income and deductions on Schedule C, see *Profit or Loss From Business* (Figure 1.1). The net amount (profit or loss after offsetting income with deductions) is then reported on Schedule 1 of Form 1040 or 1040-SR. Individuals engaged in farming activities report business income and deductions on Schedule F, *Profit or Loss from Farming*, the net amount of which is then reported on Schedule 1 of Form 1040 or 1040-SR. Individuals who are considered employees

**SCHEDULE C (Form 1040)**
Department of the Treasury Internal Revenue Service (99)

# Profit or Loss From Business
(Sole Proprietorship)

▶ Go to *www.irs.gov/ScheduleC* for instructions and the latest information.
▶ Attach to Form 1040, 1040-SR, 1040-NR, or 1041; partnerships must generally file Form 1065.

OMB No. 1545-0074
**2021**
Attachment Sequence No. **09**

Name of proprietor | **Social security number (SSN)**

**A** Principal business or profession, including product or service (see instructions) | **B** Enter code from instructions ▶

**C** Business name. If no separate business name, leave blank. | **D** Employer ID number (EIN) (see instr.)

**E** Business address (including suite or room no.) ▶
City, town or post office, state, and ZIP code

**F** Accounting method: (1) ☐ Cash (2) ☐ Accrual (3) ☐ Other (specify) ▶

**G** Did you "materially participate" in the operation of this business during 2021? If "No," see instructions for limit on losses . ☐ Yes ☐ No

**H** If you started or acquired this business during 2021, check here . . . ▶ ☐

**I** Did you make any payments in 2021 that would require you to file Form(s) 1099? See instructions . . . ☐ Yes ☐ No

**J** If "Yes," did you or will you file required Form(s) 1099? . . . ☐ Yes ☐ No

## Part I Income

| | |  | |
|---|---|---|---|
| 1 | Gross receipts or sales. See instructions for line 1 and check the box if this income was reported to you on Form W-2 and the "Statutory employee" box on that form was checked . . . ▶ ☐ | 1 | |
| 2 | Returns and allowances . . . | 2 | |
| 3 | Subtract line 2 from line 1 . . . | 3 | |
| 4 | Cost of goods sold (from line 42) . . . | 4 | |
| 5 | **Gross profit.** Subtract line 4 from line 3 . . . | 5 | |
| 6 | Other income, including federal and state gasoline or fuel tax credit or refund (see instructions) . . . | 6 | |
| 7 | **Gross income.** Add lines 5 and 6 . . . ▶ | 7 | |

## Part II Expenses. Enter expenses for business use of your home **only** on line 30.

| | |  | | | |  | |
|---|---|---|---|---|---|---|---|
| 8 | Advertising . . . | 8 | | 18 | Office expense (see instructions) | 18 | |
| 9 | Car and truck expenses (see instructions) . . . | 9 | | 19 | Pension and profit-sharing plans . | 19 | |
| 10 | Commissions and fees . | 10 | | 20 | Rent or lease (see instructions): | | |
| 11 | Contract labor (see instructions) | 11 | | a | Vehicles, machinery, and equipment | 20a | |
| 12 | Depletion . . . | 12 | | b | Other business property . . . | 20b | |
| 13 | Depreciation and section 179 expense deduction (not included in Part III) (see instructions) . . . | 13 | | 21 | Repairs and maintenance . . . | 21 | |
| | | | | 22 | Supplies (not included in Part III) . | 22 | |
| | | | | 23 | Taxes and licenses . . . | 23 | |
| | | | | 24 | Travel and meals: | | |
| 14 | Employee benefit programs (other than on line 19) . . | 14 | | a | Travel . . . | 24a | |
| 15 | Insurance (other than health) | 15 | | b | Deductible meals (see instructions) . . . | 24b | |
| 16 | Interest (see instructions): | | | 25 | Utilities . . . | 25 | |
| a | Mortgage (paid to banks, etc.) | 16a | | 26 | Wages (less employment credits) . | 26 | |
| b | Other . . . | 16b | | 27a | Other expenses (from line 48) . . | 27a | |
| 17 | Legal and professional services | 17 | | b | **Reserved for future use** . . . | 27b | |

| | |  | |
|---|---|---|---|
| 28 | **Total expenses** before expenses for business use of home. Add lines 8 through 27a . . . ▶ | 28 | |
| 29 | Tentative profit or (loss). Subtract line 28 from line 7 . . . | 29 | |
| 30 | Expenses for business use of your home. Do not report these expenses elsewhere. Attach Form 8829 unless using the simplified method. See instructions.<br>**Simplified method filers only:** Enter the total square footage of (a) your home: ________<br>and (b) the part of your home used for business: ________ . Use the Simplified Method Worksheet in the instructions to figure the amount to enter on line 30 . . . | 30 | |
| 31 | **Net profit or (loss).** Subtract line 30 from line 29.<br>• If a profit, enter on both **Schedule 1 (Form 1040), line 3,** and on **Schedule SE, line 2.** (If you checked the box on line 1, see instructions). Estates and trusts, enter on **Form 1041, line 3.**<br>• If a loss, you **must** go to line 32. | 31 | |
| 32 | If you have a loss, check the box that describes your investment in this activity. See instructions.<br>• If you checked 32a, enter the loss on both **Schedule 1 (Form 1040), line 3,** and on **Schedule SE, line 2.** (If you checked the box on line 1, see the line 31 instructions.) Estates and trusts, enter on **Form 1041, line 3.**<br>• If you checked 32b, you **must** attach **Form 6198.** Your loss may be limited. | 32a ☐ All investment is at risk.<br>32b ☐ Some investment is not at risk. | |

**For Paperwork Reduction Act Notice, see the separate instructions.** Cat. No. 11334P **Schedule C (Form 1040) 2021**

**FIGURE 1.1** Schedule C, Profit or Loss From Business

Schedule C (Form 1040) 2021 Page 2

**Part III** **Cost of Goods Sold** (see instructions)

33 Method(s) used to value closing inventory: **a** ☐ Cost **b** ☐ Lower of cost or market **c** ☐ Other (attach explanation)

34 Was there any change in determining quantities, costs, or valuations between opening and closing inventory? If "Yes," attach explanation . . . ☐ **Yes** ☐ **No**

| | | | |
|---|---|---|---|
| 35 | Inventory at beginning of year. If different from last year's closing inventory, attach explanation | **35** | |
| 36 | Purchases less cost of items withdrawn for personal use | **36** | |
| 37 | Cost of labor. Do not include any amounts paid to yourself | **37** | |
| 38 | Materials and supplies | **38** | |
| 39 | Other costs | **39** | |
| 40 | Add lines 35 through 39 | **40** | |
| 41 | Inventory at end of year | **41** | |
| 42 | **Cost of goods sold.** Subtract line 41 from line 40. Enter the result here and on line 4 | **42** | |

**Part IV** **Information on Your Vehicle.** Complete this part **only** if you are claiming car or truck expenses on line 9 and are not required to file Form 4562 for this business. See the instructions for line 13 to find out if you must file Form 4562.

43 When did you place your vehicle in service for business purposes? (month/day/year) ▶ / /

44 Of the total number of miles you drove your vehicle during 2021, enter the number of miles you used your vehicle for:

**a** Business ______ **b** Commuting (see instructions) ______ **c** Other ______

45 Was your vehicle available for personal use during off-duty hours? . . . ☐ **Yes** ☐ **No**

46 Do you (or your spouse) have another vehicle available for personal use?. . . ☐ **Yes** ☐ **No**

47a Do you have evidence to support your deduction? . . . ☐ **Yes** ☐ **No**

**b** If "Yes," is the evidence written? . . . ☐ **Yes** ☐ **No**

**Part V** **Other Expenses.** List below business expenses not included on lines 8–26 or line 30.

| | |
|---|---|
| | |
| | |
| | |
| | |
| | |
| | |
| | |
| | |
| **48** **Total other expenses.** Enter here and on line 27a | **48** |

**Schedule C (Form 1040) 2021**

**FIGURE 1.1** ***(Continued)***

cannot use Schedule C to report their income and claim deductions. See page 11 for the tax treatment of income and deductions by employees.

In effect, a sole proprietor pays tax on business profits using tax rates for individuals; there is no separate tax rate for a sole proprietorship. The top rate for an individual in 2021 is 37%, although the sole proprietor may be able to claim a 20% qualified business income deduction on his or her personal return to reduce the effective tax rate on their profits (see Chapter 21).

## Partnerships and Limited Liability Companies

If you go into business with others, then you cannot be a sole proprietor (with the exception of a spousal joint venture, explained earlier). You are automatically in a *partnership* if you join together with one or more people to share the profits of the business, even if you take no formal action. Owners of a partnership are called *partners*.

There are 2 types of partnerships: *general partnerships* and *limited partnerships*. In general partnerships, all of the partners are personally liable for the debts of the business. Creditors can go after the personal assets of any and all of the partners to satisfy partnership debts. In limited partnerships (LPs), only the general partners are personally liable for the debts of the business. Limited partners are liable only to the extent of their investments in the business plus their share of recourse debts and obligations to make future investments. Some states allow LPs to become limited liability limited partnerships (LLLPs) to give general partners personal liability protection with respect to the debts of the partnership.

**Example**

**If a partnership incurs debts of $10,000 (none of which are recourse), a general partner is liable for the full $10,000. A limited partner who initially contributed $1,000 to the limited partnership is liable only to that extent. He or she can lose the $1,000 investment, but creditors cannot go after personal assets.**

General partners are jointly and severally liable for the business's debts. This means that a creditor can go after any one partner for the full amount of the debt. That partner can seek to recoup a proportional share of the debt from other partner(s).

Partnerships may be informal agreements to share profits and losses of a business venture. More typically, however, they are organized with formal partnership agreements. These agreements detail how income, deductions, gains, losses, and credits are to be split (if there are any special allocations to be made) and what happens on the retirement, disability, bankruptcy, or death of a partner. A limited partnership must have a partnership agreement that complies with state law requirements.

Another form of organization that may be used by those joining together for business is a limited liability company (LLC). This type of business organization is formed under state law in which all owners are given limited liability. Owners of LLCs are called *members*. Every state has LLC statutes to permit the formation of an LLC within its boundaries. Most states also permit limited liability partnerships (LLPs)—LLCs for accountants, attorneys, doctors, and other professionals—which are easily established by existing partnerships filing an LLP election with the state. A partner in an LLP has personal liability protection with respect to the firm's debts, but remains personally liable for his or her professional actions.

Alabama, Arkansas, Delaware, District of Columbia, Illinois, Indiana, Iowa, Kansas, Missouri, Montana, Nebraska, Nevada, North Dakota (to a limited extent), Oklahoma, Tennessee, Texas, Utah, Virginia, Wisconsin (to a limited extent), and Wyoming permit multiple LLCs to operate under a single LLC umbrella called a "series LLC" (each LLC is called a "cell"). (California and some other states don't allow the formation of a series LLC but permit one formed in another state to register and do business in the state.) The rules are not uniform in all of these states. If you are in a state that does not have a law for series LLC, in most but not all states you can form the series in Delaware, for example, and then register to do business in your state. The debts and liabilities of each LLC remain separate from those of the other LLCs, something that is ideal for those owning several pieces of real estate—each can be owned by a separate LLC under the master LLC as long as each LLC maintains separate bank accounts and financial records. At present, state law is evolving to determine the treatment of LLCs formed in one state but doing business in another.

As the name suggests, the creditors of LLCs can look only to the assets of the company to satisfy debts; creditors cannot go after members and hope to recover their personal assets.

### *Tax Treatment of Income and Deductions in General*

Partnerships are *pass-through* entities. They are not separate taxpaying entities; instead, they pass income, deductions, gains, losses, and tax credits through to their owners. (Partnerships only become taxpayers if they are audited under the Bipartisan Budget Act regime explained in Chapter 34 and don't opt to push out tax resulting from the audit to partners.) Nearly 4.5 million partnership returns were filed in the government's 2020 fiscal year. Of these, more than two-thirds were limited liability companies, representing the most prevalent type of entity filing a partnership return; more common than general partnerships or limited partnerships. The owners report these amounts on their individual returns. Owners may be able to claim a 20% qualified business income deduction on their personal returns to reduce the effective rate levied on business profits.

While the entity does not pay taxes (except to the extent of certain adjustments following an audit as explained in Chapter 33), it must file an information return with IRS Form 1065, *U.S. Return of Partnership Income*, to report the total pass-through amounts. Even though the return is called a *partnership return*, it is the same return filed by LLCs with 2 or more owners who do not elect to be taxed as a corporation. The entity also completes Schedule K-1 of Form 1065, see Figure 1.2, a copy of which is given to each owner to allocate the share of partnership/LLC amounts. Like W-2 forms used by the IRS to match employees' reporting of their compensation, the IRS employs computer matching of Schedules K-1 to ensure that owners are properly reporting their share of their business's income.

> **NOTE**
>
> **K-1s can be distributed to partners electronically if the partnership has the partners' consent. Obtain consent by sending instructions to partners on how to obtain, complete, and submit a consent form to the partnership.**

For 2021 returns, there are 2 new schedules that apply to partnerships with certain foreign interests and activities: Schedule K-2, *Partners' Distributive Share Items—International* and Schedule K-3, *Partner's Share of Income, Deductions, Credits, Etc.,—International.* Because these relate to foreign matters, which are not discussed in detail in this book, these schedules are not covered here. Note that the IRS has provided penalty relief for 2021 Schedule K-2s and K-3s as long as a good faith effort has been made to complete these schedules correctly.

For federal income tax purposes, LLCs with more than one member are treated like partnerships unless the members elect to have the LLCs taxed as corporations. This is done on IRS Form 8832, *Entity Classification Election*. See Figure 1.3. For purposes of our discussion throughout this book, it will be assumed that multi-member LLCs have not chosen corporate tax treatment and so are taxed the same way as partnerships.

651121

☐ Final K-1 ☐ Amended K-1 OMB No. 1545-0123

**Schedule K-1 (Form 1065)** **2021**
Department of the Treasury
Internal Revenue Service

For calendar year 2021, or tax year

beginning / / 2021 ending / /

## Partner's Share of Income, Deductions, Credits, etc.

▶ See back of form and separate instructions.

**Part I Information About the Partnership**

A Partnership's employer identification number

B Partnership's name, address, city, state, and ZIP code

C IRS center where partnership filed return ▶

D ☐ Check if this is a publicly traded partnership (PTP)

**Part II Information About the Partner**

E Partner's SSN or TIN (Do not use TIN of a disregarded entity. See instructions.)

F Name, address, city, state, and ZIP code for partner entered in E. See instructions.

G ☐ General partner or LLC member-manager ☐ Limited partner or other LLC member

H1 ☐ Domestic partner ☐ Foreign partner

H2 ☐ If the partner is a disregarded entity (DE), enter the partner's:

TIN ______ Name ______

I1 What type of entity is this partner?

I2 If this partner is a retirement plan (IRA/SEP/Keogh/etc.), check here ▶ ☐

J Partner's share of profit, loss, and capital (see instructions):

| | Beginning | Ending |
|---|---|---|
| Profit | % | % |
| Loss | % | % |
| Capital | % | % |

Check if decrease is due to sale or exchange of partnership interest . ▶ ☐

K Partner's share of liabilities:

| | Beginning | Ending |
|---|---|---|
| Nonrecourse . . . | $ | $ |
| Qualified nonrecourse financing . . . | $ | $ |
| Recourse . . . | $ | $ |

Check this box if Item K includes liability amounts from lower tier partnerships ▶ ☐

L **Partner's Capital Account Analysis**

| | |
|---|---|
| **Beginning capital account** . . . | $ |
| Capital contributed during the year . . | $ |
| Current year net income (loss) . . . | $ |
| Other increase (decrease) (attach explanation) | $ |
| Withdrawals and distributions . . . | $( ) |
| **Ending capital account** . . . . | $ |

M Did the partner contribute property with a built-in gain (loss)?
☐ **Yes** ☐ **No** If "Yes," attach statement. See instructions.

N **Partner's Share of Net Unrecognized Section 704(c) Gain or (Loss)**
Beginning . . . . . . . . . $
Ending . . . . . . . . . . $

**Part III Partner's Share of Current Year Income, Deductions, Credits, and Other Items**

| | | | |
|---|---|---|---|
| 1 | Ordinary business income (loss) | 14 | Self-employment earnings (loss) |
| 2 | Net rental real estate income (loss) | | |
| 3 | Other net rental income (loss) | 15 | Credits |
| 4a | Guaranteed payments for services | | |
| 4b | Guaranteed payments for capital | 16 | Schedule K-3 is attached if checked . . . . ▶ ☐ |
| 4c | Total guaranteed payments | 17 | Alternative minimum tax (AMT) items |
| 5 | Interest income | | |
| 6a | Ordinary dividends | | |
| 6b | Qualified dividends | 18 | Tax-exempt income and nondeductible expenses |
| 6c | Dividend equivalents | | |
| 7 | Royalties | | |
| 8 | Net short-term capital gain (loss) | | |
| | | 19 | Distributions |
| 9a | Net long-term capital gain (loss) | | |
| 9b | Collectibles (28%) gain (loss) | | |
| | | 20 | Other information |
| 9c | Unrecaptured section 1250 gain | | |
| 10 | Net section 1231 gain (loss) | | |
| 11 | Other income (loss) | | |
| 12 | Section 179 deduction | 21 | Foreign taxes paid or accrued |
| 13 | Other deductions | | |

22 ☐ More than one activity for at-risk purposes*

23 ☐ More than one activity for passive activity purposes*

*See attached statement for additional information.

For IRS Use Only

For Paperwork Reduction Act Notice, see the Instructions for Form 1065. www.irs.gov/Form1065 Cat. No. 11394R Schedule K-1 (Form 1065) 2021

**FIGURE 1.2** Schedule K-1, Partner's Share of Income, Deductions, Credits, etc.

Form **8832**
(Rev. December 2013)
Department of the Treasury
Internal Revenue Service

## Entity Classification Election

► Information about Form 8832 and its instructions is at *www.irs.gov/form8832*.

OMB No. 1545-1516

| Type or Print | Name of eligible entity making election | Employer identification number |
|---|---|---|
| | Number, street, and room or suite no. If a P.O. box, see instructions. | |
| | City or town, state, and ZIP code. If a foreign address, enter city, province or state, postal code and country. Follow the country's practice for entering the postal code. | |

► Check if: ☐ Address change ☐ Late classification relief sought under Revenue Procedure 2009-41
☐ Relief for a late change of entity classification election sought under Revenue Procedure 2010-32

**Part I Election Information**

1 **Type of election** (see instructions):

a ☐ Initial classification by a newly-formed entity. Skip lines 2a and 2b and go to line 3.
b ☐ Change in current classification. Go to line 2a.

2a Has the eligible entity previously filed an entity election that had an effective date within the last 60 months?

☐ **Yes.** Go to line 2b.
☐ **No.** Skip line 2b and go to line 3.

2b Was the eligible entity's prior election an initial classification election by a newly formed entity that was effective on the date of formation?

☐ **Yes.** Go to line 3.
☐ **No.** Stop here. You generally are not currently eligible to make the election (see instructions).

3 Does the eligible entity have more than one owner?

☐ **Yes.** You can elect to be classified as a partnership or an association taxable as a corporation. Skip line 4 and go to line 5.
☐ **No.** You can elect to be classified as an association taxable as a corporation or to be disregarded as a separate entity. Go to line 4.

4 If the eligible entity has only one owner, provide the following information:

a Name of owner ► ____________
b Identifying number of owner ► ____________

5 If the eligible entity is owned by one or more affiliated corporations that file a consolidated return, provide the name and employer identification number of the parent corporation:

a Name of parent corporation ► ____________
b Employer identification number ► ____________

**For Paperwork Reduction Act Notice, see instructions.** Cat. No. 22598R Form **8832** (Rev. 12-2013)

**FIGURE 1.3 Form 8832, Entity Classification Election**

Form 8832 (Rev. 12-2013) Page 2

**Part I** **Election Information** (Continued)

6 **Type of entity** (see instructions):

a ☐ A domestic eligible entity electing to be classified as an association taxable as a corporation.
b ☐ A domestic eligible entity electing to be classified as a partnership.
c ☐ A domestic eligible entity with a single owner electing to be disregarded as a separate entity.
d ☐ A foreign eligible entity electing to be classified as an association taxable as a corporation.
e ☐ A foreign eligible entity electing to be classified as a partnership.
f ☐ A foreign eligible entity with a single owner electing to be disregarded as a separate entity.

7 If the eligible entity is created or organized in a foreign jurisdiction, provide the foreign country of organization ▶ ______

8 Election is to be effective beginning (month, day, year) (see instructions) . . . . . . . . . . . . . ▶ ______

| 9 Name and title of contact person whom the IRS may call for more information | 10 Contact person's telephone number |
|---|---|
| | |

**Consent Statement and Signature(s) (see instructions)**

Under penalties of perjury, I (we) declare that I (we) consent to the election of the above-named entity to be classified as indicated above, and that I (we) have examined this election and consent statement, and to the best of my (our) knowledge and belief, this election and consent statement are true, correct, and complete. If I am an officer, manager, or member signing for the entity, I further declare under penalties of perjury that I am authorized to make the election on its behalf.

| Signature(s) | Date | Title |
|---|---|---|
| | | |
| | | |
| | | |
| | | |
| | | |
| | | |
| | | |
| | | |
| | | |
| | | |
| | | |
| | | |
| | | |
| | | |
| | | |

Form **8832** (Rev. 12-2013)

**FIGURE 1.3** ***(Continued)***

As explained earlier, a single-member LLC is treated for tax purposes like a sole proprietor if it is owned by an individual who reports the company's income and expenses on his or her Schedule C. Like multi-member LLCs, a single-member LLC may choose to be taxed as a corporation.

Under regulations proposed in 2010 and not yet finalized, for federal tax purposes a series LLC is treated as an entity formed under local law, whether or not local law treats the series as a separate legal entity. The tax treatment of the series is then governed by the check-the-box rules.

There are 2 types of items that pass through to an owner: trade or business income or loss and separately stated items. A partner's or member's share is called the *distributive share*. Trade or business income or loss takes into account most ordinary deductions of the business—compensation to employees (non-partners), rent, taxes, interest, and so forth. Guaranteed payments to an owner are also taken into account when determining ordinary income or loss. From an owner's perspective, deductions net out against income from the business, and the owner's allocable share of the net amount is then reported on the owner's Schedule E of Form 1040 or 1040-SR. Figure 1.4 shows Part II of Schedule E on which a partner's or member's distributive share is reported.

Separately stated items are stand-alone items that pass through to owners apart from the net amount of trade or business income. These are items that are subject to limitations on an individual's tax return and must be segregated from the net amount of trade or business income. They are reported along with similar items on the owner's own tax return.

**Example**

**A charitable contribution deduction made by a partnership passes through separately as a charitable contribution. The partner adds the amount of the pass-through charitable contribution to his or her other charitable contributions. Since an individual's cash contributions in 2021 are deductible only to the extent of 100% of adjusted gross income (after reduction for all other charitable donations), the partner's allocable share of the partnership's charitable contribution is subject to his or her individual adjusted gross income limit.**

Other items that pass through separately to owners include capital gains and losses, Section 179 (first-year expensing) deductions, investment interest deductions, and tax credits.

When a partnership or LLC has substantial expenses that exceed its operating income, a loss is passed through to the owner. A number of different rules operate to limit a loss deduction. The owner may not be able to claim the entire loss. The loss is limited by the owner's *basis*, or the amount of cash and property contributed to the partnership, in the interest in the partnership.

**Example**

**You contributed $12,000 to the AB Partnership. In 2021, the partnership had sizable expenses and only a small amount of revenue. Your allocable share of partnership loss is $13,000. You may deduct only $12,000 in 2021, which is the amount of your basis in your partnership interest. You may deduct that additional $1,000 of loss when you have additional basis to offset it.**

There may be additional limits on your write-offs from partnerships and LLCs. If you are a passive investor—a silent partner—in these businesses, your loss deduction is further limited by the passive activity loss rules. In general, these rules limit a current deduction for losses from

Schedule E (Form 1040) 2021 Attachment Sequence No. 13 Page 2

| Name(s) shown on return. Do not enter name and social security number if shown on other side. | Your social security number |
|---|---|
| | |

**Caution:** The IRS compares amounts reported on your tax return with amounts shown on Schedule(s) K-1.

**Part II** **Income or Loss From Partnerships and S Corporations** – **Note:** If you report a loss, receive a distribution, dispose of stock, or receive a loan repayment from an S corporation, you **must** check the box in column **(e)** on line 28 and attach the required basis computation. If you report a loss from an at-risk activity for which **any** amount is **not** at risk, you **must** check the box in column **(f)** on line 28 and attach **Form 6198.** See instructions.

27 Are you reporting any loss not allowed in a prior year due to the at-risk or basis limitations, a prior year unallowed loss from a passive activity (if that loss was not reported on Form 8582), or unreimbursed partnership expenses? If you answered "Yes," see instructions before completing this section . . . . . . . . . . . . . . . . . . ☐ **Yes** ☐ **No**

| 28 | **(a)** Name | **(b)** Enter **P** for partnership; **S** for S corporation | **(c)** Check if foreign partnership | **(d)** Employer identification number | **(e)** Check if basis computation is required | **(f)** Check if any amount is not at risk |
|---|---|---|---|---|---|---|
| **A** | | | ☐ | | ☐ | ☐ |
| **B** | | | ☐ | | ☐ | ☐ |
| **C** | | | ☐ | | ☐ | ☐ |
| **D** | | | ☐ | | ☐ | ☐ |

| | **Passive Income and Loss** | | **Nonpassive Income and Loss** | | |
|---|---|---|---|---|---|
| | **(g)** Passive loss allowed (attach **Form 8582** if required) | **(h)** Passive income from **Schedule K-1** | **(i)** Nonpassive loss allowed (see **Schedule K-1**) | **(j)** Section 179 expense deduction from **Form 4562** | **(k)** Nonpassive income from **Schedule K-1** |
| **A** | | | | | |
| **B** | | | | | |
| **C** | | | | | |
| **D** | | | | | |
| **29a** Totals | | | | | |
| **b** Totals | | | | | |

| | | | |
|---|---|---|---|
| **30** | Add columns (h) and (k) of line 29a. . . . . . . . . . . . . . . . | **30** | |
| **31** | Add columns (g), (i), and (j) of line 29b. . . . . . . . . . . . . . . | **31** | ( ) |
| **32** | **Total partnership and S corporation income or (loss).** Combine lines 30 and 31 . . . . | **32** | |

**Part III** **Income or Loss From Estates and Trusts**

| 33 | **(a)** Name | **(b)** Employer identification number |
|---|---|---|
| **A** | | |
| **B** | | |

| | **Passive Income and Loss** | | **Nonpassive Income and Loss** | |
|---|---|---|---|---|
| | **(c)** Passive deduction or loss allowed (attach **Form 8582** if required) | **(d)** Passive income from **Schedule K-1** | **(e)** Deduction or loss from **Schedule K-1** | **(f)** Other income from **Schedule K-1** |
| **A** | | | | |
| **B** | | | | |
| **34a** Totals | | | | |
| **b** Totals | | | | |

| | | | |
|---|---|---|---|
| **35** | Add columns (d) and (f) of line 34a . . . . . . . . . . . . . . . . | **35** | |
| **36** | Add columns (c) and (e) of line 34b . . . . . . . . . . . . . . . . | **36** | ( ) |
| **37** | **Total estate and trust income or (loss).** Combine lines 35 and 36 . . . . . . . . . | **37** | |

**Part IV** **Income or Loss From Real Estate Mortgage Investment Conduits (REMICs)—Residual Holder**

| 38 | **(a)** Name | **(b)** Employer identification number | **(c)** Excess inclusion from **Schedules Q,** line 2c (see instructions) | **(d)** Taxable income (net loss) from **Schedules Q,** line 1b | **(e)** Income from **Schedules Q,** line 3b |
|---|---|---|---|---|---|
| | | | | | |

| | | | |
|---|---|---|---|
| **39** | Combine columns (d) and (e) only. Enter the result here and include in the total on line 41 below | **39** | |

**Part V** **Summary**

| | | | |
|---|---|---|---|
| **40** | Net farm rental income or (loss) from **Form 4835.** Also, complete line 42 below . . . . . . | **40** | |
| **41** | **Total income or (loss).** Combine lines 26, 32, 37, 39, and 40. Enter the result here and on Schedule 1 (Form 1040), line 5 ▶ | **41** | |
| **42** | **Reconciliation of farming and fishing income.** Enter your **gross** farming and fishing income reported on Form 4835, line 7; Schedule K-1 (Form 1065), box 14, code B; Schedule K-1 (Form 1120-S), box 17, code AD; and Schedule K-1 (Form 1041), box 14, code F. See instructions . . **42** | | |
| **43** | **Reconciliation for real estate professionals.** If you were a real estate professional (see instructions), enter the net income or (loss) you reported anywhere on Form 1040, Form 1040-SR, or Form 1040-NR from all rental real estate activities in which you materially participated under the passive activity loss rules . . . . . . **43** | | |

Schedule E (Form 1040) 2021

**FIGURE 1.4** Part II of Schedule E

passive activities to the extent of income from passive activities. Additionally, losses are limited by the individual's economic risk in the business. This limit is called the *at-risk rule*. The passive activity loss and at-risk rules are discussed in Chapter 4. For a further discussion of the passive activity loss rules, see IRS Publication 925, *Passive Activity and At-Risk Rules*.

## S Corporations and Their Shareholder-Employees

There were over 5 million S corporations in the government's 2020 fiscal year, making these entities the most prevalent type of corporation. Over 79% of all corporations file a Form 1120-S, the return for S corporations. The vast majority of S corporations have only 1, 2, or 3 shareholders.

**NOTE**

**State laws vary on the tax treatment of S corporations for state income tax purposes. Be sure to check the laws of any state in which you do business.**

*S corporations* are like regular corporations (called *C corporations*) for business law purposes. They are separate entities in the eyes of the law and exist independently from their owners. For example, if an owner dies, the S corporation's existence continues. S corporations are formed under state law in the same way as other corporations. The only difference between S corporations and other corporations is their tax treatment for federal income tax purposes (and state income taxes where applicable).

For the most part, S corporations are treated as pass-through entities for federal income tax purposes. This means that, as with partnerships and LLCs, the income and loss pass through to owners, and their allocable share is reported by S corporation shareholders on their individual income tax returns. The tax treatment of S corporations is discussed more fully later in this chapter.

S corporation status is not automatic. A corporation must elect S status in a timely manner. This election is made on Form 2553, *Election by Small Business Corporations to Tax Corporate Income Directly to Shareholders*. It must be filed with the IRS no later than the 15th day of the 3rd month of the corporation's tax year. The National Taxpayer Advocate has recommended that an election be permitted with the filing of the first tax return for a new corporation; see the Supplement for any update.

**Example**

**A corporation (on a calendar year) that has been in existence for a number of years wants to elect S status. It had to file an election no later than March 15, 2021, to be effective for its 2021 tax year. If a corporation is formed on August 1, 2021, and wants an S election to be effective for its first tax year, the S election must be filed no later than November 15, 2021.**

If an S election is filed after the deadline, it is automatically effective for the following year. A corporation can simply decide to make a prospective election by filing at any time during the year prior to that for which the election is to be effective. However, if you want the election to be effective now but missed the deadline, you may qualify for relief under Rev. Proc. 2013–30 (see the instructions to Form 2553 for making a late election).

**Example**

**A corporation (on a calendar year) that has been in existence for a number of years wants to elect S status for its 2022 tax year. It can file an election at any time during 2021.**

To be eligible for an S election, the corporation must meet certain shareholder requirements. There can be no more than 100 shareholders. For this purpose, all family members (up to 6 generations) are treated as a single shareholder. Only certain types of trusts are permitted to be shareholders. There can be no nonresident alien shareholders as direct shareholders; nonresidents can be indirect shareholders if they become beneficiaries of Electing Small Business Trusts (ESBTs). A complete discussion of ESBTs and their taxation is beyond the scope of this book.

An election cannot be made before the corporation is formed. The board of directors of the corporation must agree to the election and should indicate this assent in the minutes of a board of directors meeting.

Once the election is made, it remains in effect until it is revoked or is terminated because the corporation fails to meet S corporation requirements (e.g., more than 100 shareholders own the stock, a nonresident alien becomes a direct shareholder, or the corporation creates a second class of stock). If an election is revoked, a new one cannot be made for 5 years unless the IRS agrees to it.

Remember, if state law also allows S status, a separate election may have to be filed with the state. Check with all state law requirements.

### *Tax Treatment of Income and Deductions in General*

For the most part, S corporations, like partnerships and LLCs, are pass-through entities. They are generally not separate taxpaying entities. Instead, they pass through to their shareholders' income, deductions, gains, losses, and tax credits. The shareholders report these amounts on their individual returns. This means owners pay tax on their business profits using individual tax rates. They may be able to claim a 20% qualified business income deduction on their personal return (see Chapter 21). The S corporation files a return with the IRS—Form 1120-S, *U.S. Income Tax Return for an S Corporation*—to report the total pass-through amounts. The S corporation also completes Schedule K-1 of Form 1120-S, a copy of which is given to each shareholder. The K-1 tells the shareholder his or her allocable share of S corporation amounts. The K-1 for S corporation shareholders is similar to the K-1 for partners and LLC members (as shown in Figure 1.2). For 2021 returns, there are 2 new schedules that apply to S corporations with certain foreign interests and activities: Schedule K-2, *Shareholders' Pro Rata Share Items—International* and Schedule K-3, *Shareholder's Share of Income, Deductions, Credits, Etc.,—International.* Because these relate to foreign matters, which are not discussed in detail in this book, these schedules are not covered here. Note that the IRS has provided penalty relief for 2021 Schedule K-2s and K-3s.

S corporations may become taxpayers if they have certain types of income. There are only 3 types of income that result in a tax on the S corporation. These 3 items cannot be reduced by any deductions:

1. *Built-in gains*. These are gains related to appreciation of assets held by a C corporation that converts to S status. Thus, if a corporation is formed and immediately elects S status, there will never be any built-in gains to worry about. The built-in gains tax ends once the S corporation has held the appreciated assets for more than 5 years.
2. *Passive investment income*. This is income of a corporation that has earnings and profits from a time when it was a C corporation. A tax on the S corporation results only when this passive investment income exceeds 25% of gross receipts. Again, if a corporation is formed and immediately elects S status, or if a corporation that converted to S status does not have any earnings and profits at the time of conversion, then there will never be any tax from this source.

3. *LIFO recapture*. When a C corporation using last-in, first-out or LIFO to report inventory converts to S status, there may be recapture income that is taken into account, partly on the C corporation's final return, but also on the S corporation's return. Again, if a corporation is formed and immediately elects S status, there will not be any recapture income on which the S corporation must pay tax.

To sum up, if a corporation is formed and immediately elects S status, the corporation will always be solely a pass-through entity and there will never be any tax at the corporate level. If the S corporation was, at one time (other than momentarily), a C corporation, there may be some tax at the corporate level.

## C Corporations and Their Shareholder-Employees

A *C corporation* is an entity separate and apart from its owners; it has its own legal existence. Though formed under state law, it need not be formed in the state in which the business operates. Many corporations, for example, are formed in Delaware or Nevada because the laws in these states favor the corporation, as opposed to the investors (shareholders). However, state law for the state in which the business operates may still require the corporation to make some formal notification of doing business in the state. The corporation may also be subject to tax on income generated in that state.

Until now, C corporations primarily were used by big businesses, even though there was nothing technically barring even a one-person company from being a C corporation. According to IRS data for its 2020 fiscal year, there were more than 1.8 million C corporations, the vast majority of which were small or midsize companies (with assets of $10 million or less). But with the corporate tax rate at 21% (at least through 2021), there is some interest in C corporations by small businesses. Changing your form of business is discussed later in this chapter.

For federal tax purposes, a C corporation is a separate taxpaying entity. It files its own return (Form 1120, *U.S. Corporation Income Tax Return*) to report its income or losses. Shareholders do not report their share of the corporation's income. The tax treatment of C corporations is explained more fully later in this chapter.

### Personal Service Corporations

Professionals who incorporate their practices are a special type of C corporation called **personal service corporations (PSCs)**.

***Personal service corporation (PSC)*** **A C corporation that performs personal services in the fields of health, law, accounting, engineering, architecture, actuarial science, performing arts, or consulting and meets certain ownership and service tests.**

Personal service corporations are subject to special rules in the tax law. Some of these rules are beneficial; others are not. Personal service corporations:

- Are generally required to use the same tax year as that of their owners. Typically, individuals report their income on a calendar year basis (explained more fully in Chapter 2), so their

PSCs must also use a calendar year. However, there is a special election that can be made to use a fiscal year.

- May use the cash method of accounting. Other C corporations cannot use the cash method and instead must use the accrual method unless they meet a gross receipts test (explained more fully in Chapter 2).
- Are subject to the passive loss limitation rules (explained in Chapter 4).
- May have their income and deductions reallocated by the IRS between the corporation and the shareholders if it more correctly reflects the economics of the situation.
- Have a smaller exemption from the accumulated earnings penalty than other C corporations. This penalty imposes an additional tax on corporations that accumulate their income above and beyond the reasonable needs of the business instead of distributing income to shareholders.

### Tax Treatment of Income and Deductions in General

The C corporation reports its own income and claims its own deductions on Form 1120, *U.S. Corporation Income Tax Return*. Shareholders in C corporations do not have to report any income of the corporation (and cannot claim any deductions of the corporation). Figure 1.5 shows a sample copy of Form 1120.

C corporations have a flat corporate tax rate of 21% for 2021 (check the Supplement if there is an increase in the tax rate after 2021). Thus, a small business that operates as a C corporation and a multinational corporation pay the same tax rate on their profits.

Distributions from the C corporation to its shareholders are personal items for the shareholders. For example, if a shareholder works for his or her C corporation and receives a salary, the corporation deducts that salary against corporate income. The shareholder reports the salary as income on his or her individual income tax return. If the corporation distributes a dividend to the shareholder, again, the shareholder reports the dividend as income on his or her individual income tax return. In the case of dividends, however, the corporation may not claim a deduction. This, then, creates a 2-tier tax system, commonly referred to as *double taxation*. First, earnings are taxed at the corporate level. Then, when they are distributed to shareholders as dividends, they are taxed again, this time at the shareholder level. There has been sentiment in Congress over the years to eliminate the double taxation, but as of yet there has been no legislation to accomplish this end other than the relief provided by capping the rate on dividends (zero for individuals with taxable income below a threshold amount; 20% for those with taxable income above a threshold amount; and 15% for those with taxable income above the lower threshold but below the upper threshold).

### Other Tax Issues for C Corporations

In view of the favorable corporate rate tax structure (compared with the individual tax rates), certain tax penalties prevent businesses from using this form of business organization to optimum advantage.

- *Personal holding company penalty*. Corporations that function as a shareholder investment portfolio rather than as an operating company may fall subject to the personal holding corporation (PHC) penalty tax of 20% on certain undistributed corporate income. The tax rules strictly define a PHC according to stock ownership and adjusted gross income. The penalty may be avoided by *not* triggering the definition of PHC or by paying out certain dividends.

Form **1120**
Department of the Treasury
Internal Revenue Service

# U.S. Corporation Income Tax Return

For calendar year 2021 or tax year beginning ________, 2021, ending ________, 20 ____

▶ Go to *www.irs.gov/Form1120* for instructions and the latest information.

OMB No. 1545-0123

2021

**A Check if:**
1a Consolidated return (attach Form 851) . ☐
b Life/nonlife consolidated return . . . ☐
2 Personal holding co. (attach Sch. PH) . ☐
3 Personal service corp. (see instructions) . ☐
4 Schedule M-3 attached ☐

**TYPE OR PRINT**
Name
Number, street, and room or suite no. If a P.O. box, see instructions.
City or town, state or province, country, and ZIP or foreign postal code

**B** Employer identification number
**C** Date incorporated
**D** Total assets (see instructions) $

**E** Check if: (1) ☐ Initial return (2) ☐ Final return (3) ☐ Name change (4) ☐ Address change

|  |  |  |  |  |
|---|---|---|---|---|
| Income | 1a | Gross receipts or sales | 1a | |
| | b | Returns and allowances | 1b | |
| | c | Balance. Subtract line 1b from line 1a | | 1c |
| | 2 | Cost of goods sold (attach Form 1125-A) | | 2 |
| | 3 | Gross profit. Subtract line 2 from line 1c | | 3 |
| | 4 | Dividends and inclusions (Schedule C, line 23) | | 4 |
| | 5 | Interest | | 5 |
| | 6 | Gross rents | | 6 |
| | 7 | Gross royalties | | 7 |
| | 8 | Capital gain net income (attach Schedule D (Form 1120)) | | 8 |
| | 9 | Net gain or (loss) from Form 4797, Part II, line 17 (attach Form 4797) | | 9 |
| | 10 | Other income (see instructions—attach statement) | | 10 |
| | 11 | **Total income.** Add lines 3 through 10 ▶ | | 11 |
| Deductions (See instructions for limitations on deductions.) | 12 | Compensation of officers (see instructions—attach Form 1125-E) ▶ | | 12 |
| | 13 | Salaries and wages (less employment credits) | | 13 |
| | 14 | Repairs and maintenance | | 14 |
| | 15 | Bad debts | | 15 |
| | 16 | Rents | | 16 |
| | 17 | Taxes and licenses | | 17 |
| | 18 | Interest (see instructions) | | 18 |
| | 19 | Charitable contributions | | 19 |
| | 20 | Depreciation from Form 4562 not claimed on Form 1125-A or elsewhere on return (attach Form 4562) | | 20 |
| | 21 | Depletion | | 21 |
| | 22 | Advertising | | 22 |
| | 23 | Pension, profit-sharing, etc., plans | | 23 |
| | 24 | Employee benefit programs | | 24 |
| | 25 | Reserved for future use | | 25 |
| | 26 | Other deductions (attach statement) | | 26 |
| | 27 | **Total deductions.** Add lines 12 through 26 ▶ | | 27 |
| | 28 | Taxable income before net operating loss deduction and special deductions. Subtract line 27 from line 11. | | 28 |
| | 29a | Net operating loss deduction (see instructions) | 29a | |
| | b | Special deductions (Schedule C, line 24) | 29b | |
| | c | Add lines 29a and 29b | | 29c |
| Tax, Refundable Credits, and Payments | 30 | **Taxable income.** Subtract line 29c from line 28. See instructions | | 30 |
| | 31 | Total tax (Schedule J, Part I, line 11) | | 31 |
| | 32 | 2020 net 965 tax liability paid (Schedule J, Part II, line 12) | | 32 |
| | 33 | Total payments, credits, and section 965 net tax liability (Schedule J, Part III, line 23) | | 33 |
| | 34 | Estimated tax penalty. See instructions. Check if Form 2220 is attached ▶ ☐ | | 34 |
| | 35 | **Amount owed.** If line 33 is smaller than the total of lines 31, 32, and 34, enter amount owed | | 35 |
| | 36 | **Overpayment.** If line 33 is larger than the total of lines 31, 32, and 34, enter amount overpaid | | 36 |
| | 37 | Enter amount from line 36 you want: **Credited to 2021 estimated tax ▶** Refunded ▶ | | 37 |

**Sign Here**

Under penalties of perjury, I declare that I have examined this return, including accompanying schedules and statements, and to the best of my knowledge and belief, it is true, correct, and complete. Declaration of preparer (other than taxpayer) is based on all information of which preparer has any knowledge.

▶ Signature of officer | Date | ▶ Title

May the IRS discuss this return with the preparer shown below? See instructions. ☐ Yes ☐ No

**Paid Preparer Use Only**

| Print/Type preparer's name | Preparer's signature | Date | Check ☐ if self-employed | PTIN |
|---|---|---|---|---|
| Firm's name ▶ | | | Firm's EIN ▶ | |
| Firm's address ▶ | | | Phone no. | |

**For Paperwork Reduction Act Notice, see separate instructions.** Cat. No. 11450Q Form **1120** (2021)

**FIGURE 1.5** Form 1120, U.S. Corporation Income Tax Return

Form 1120 (2021) Page 2

| Schedule C | Dividends, Inclusions, and Special Deductions (see instructions) | (a) Dividends and inclusions | (b) % | (c) Special deductions (a) × (b) |
|---|---|---|---|---|
| 1 | Dividends from less-than-20%-owned domestic corporations (other than debt-financed stock) | | 50 | |
| 2 | Dividends from 20%-or-more-owned domestic corporations (other than debt-financed stock) | | 65 | |
| 3 | Dividends on certain debt-financed stock of domestic and foreign corporations | | See instructions | |
| 4 | Dividends on certain preferred stock of less-than-20%-owned public utilities | | 23.3 | |
| 5 | Dividends on certain preferred stock of 20%-or-more-owned public utilities | | 26.7 | |
| 6 | Dividends from less-than-20%-owned foreign corporations and certain FSCs | | 50 | |
| 7 | Dividends from 20%-or-more-owned foreign corporations and certain FSCs | | 65 | |
| 8 | Dividends from wholly owned foreign subsidiaries | | 100 | |
| 9 | **Subtotal.** Add lines 1 through 8. See instructions for limitations | | See instructions | |
| 10 | Dividends from domestic corporations received by a small business investment company operating under the Small Business Investment Act of 1958 | | 100 | |
| 11 | Dividends from affiliated group members | | 100 | |
| 12 | Dividends from certain FSCs | | 100 | |
| 13 | Foreign-source portion of dividends received from a specified 10%-owned foreign corporation (excluding hybrid dividends) (see instructions) | | 100 | |
| 14 | Dividends from foreign corporations not included on line 3, 6, 7, 8, 11, 12, or 13 (including any hybrid dividends) | | | |
| 15 | Section 965(a) inclusion | | See instructions | |
| 16a | Subpart F inclusions derived from the sale by a controlled foreign corporation (CFC) of the stock of a lower-tier foreign corporation treated as a dividend (attach Form(s) 5471) (see instructions) | | 100 | |
| b | Subpart F inclusions derived from hybrid dividends of tiered corporations (attach Form(s) 5471) (see instructions) | | | |
| c | Other inclusions from CFCs under subpart F not included on line 15, 16a, 16b, or 17 (attach Form(s) 5471) (see instructions) | | | |
| 17 | Global Intangible Low-Taxed Income (GILTI) (attach Form(s) 5471 and Form 8992) | | | |
| 18 | Gross-up for foreign taxes deemed paid | | | |
| 19 | IC-DISC and former DISC dividends not included on line 1, 2, or 3 | | | |
| 20 | Other dividends | | | |
| 21 | Deduction for dividends paid on certain preferred stock of public utilities | | | |
| 22 | Section 250 deduction (attach Form 8993) | | | |
| 23 | **Total dividends and inclusions.** Add column (a), lines 9 through 20. Enter here and on page 1, line 4 | | | |
| 24 | **Total special deductions.** Add column (c), lines 9 through 22. Enter here and on page 1, line 29b | | | |

Form **1120** (2021)

**FIGURE 1.5** ***(Continued)***

Form 1120 (2021) Page 3

**Schedule J — Tax Computation and Payment** (see instructions)

**Part I—Tax Computation**

| | | | | | |
|---|---|---|---|---|---|
| 1 | Check if the corporation is a member of a controlled group (attach Schedule O (Form 1120)). See instructions ▶ ☐ | | | | |
| 2 | Income tax. See instructions | | | 2 | |
| 3 | Base erosion minimum tax amount (attach Form 8991) | | | 3 | |
| 4 | Add lines 2 and 3 | | | 4 | |
| 5a | Foreign tax credit (attach Form 1118) | 5a | | | |
| b | Credit from Form 8834 (see instructions) | 5b | | | |
| c | General business credit (attach Form 3800) | 5c | | | |
| d | Credit for prior year minimum tax (attach Form 8827) | 5d | | | |
| e | Bond credits from Form 8912 | 5e | | | |
| 6 | **Total credits.** Add lines 5a through 5e | | | 6 | |
| 7 | Subtract line 6 from line 4 | | | 7 | |
| 8 | Personal holding company tax (attach Schedule PH (Form 1120)) | | | 8 | |
| 9a | Recapture of investment credit (attach Form 4255) | 9a | | | |
| b | Recapture of low-income housing credit (attach Form 8611) | 9b | | | |
| c | Interest due under the look-back method—completed long-term contracts (attach Form 8697) | 9c | | | |
| d | Interest due under the look-back method—income forecast method (attach Form 8866) | 9d | | | |
| e | Alternative tax on qualifying shipping activities (attach Form 8902) | 9e | | | |
| f | Interest/tax due under Section 453A(c) and/or Section 453(l) | 9f | | | |
| g | Other (see instructions—attach statement) | 9g | | | |
| 10 | **Total.** Add lines 9a through 9g | | | 10 | |
| 11 | **Total tax.** Add lines 7, 8, and 10. Enter here and on page 1, line 31 | | | 11 | |

**Part II—Section 965 Payments** (see instructions)

| | | | |
|---|---|---|---|
| 12 | 2020 net 965 tax liability paid from Form 965-B, Part II, column (k), line 4. Enter here and on page 1, line 32 | 12 | |

**Part III—Payments, Refundable Credits, and Section 965 Net Tax Liability**

| | | | | | |
|---|---|---|---|---|---|
| 13 | 2019 overpayment credited to 2020 | | | 13 | |
| 14 | 2020 estimated tax payments | | | 14 | |
| 15 | 2020 refund applied for on Form 4466 | | | 15 | ( ) |
| 16 | Combine lines 13, 14, and 15 | | | 16 | |
| 17 | Tax deposited with Form 7004 | | | 17 | |
| 18 | Withholding (see instructions) | | | 18 | |
| 19 | **Total payments.** Add lines 16, 17, and 18 | | | 19 | |
| 20 | Refundable credits from: | | | | |
| a | Form 2439 | 20a | | | |
| b | Form 4136 | 20b | | | |
| c | Reserved for future use | 20c | | | |
| d | Other (attach statement—see instructions) | 20d | | | |
| 21 | **Total credits.** Add lines 20a through 20d | | | 21 | |
| 22 | 2020 net 965 tax liability from Form 965-B, Part I, column (d), line 4. See instructions | | | 22 | |
| 23 | **Total payments, credits, and section 965 net tax liability.** Add lines 19, 21, and 22. Enter here and on page 1, line 33 | | | 23 | |

Form **1120** (2021)

**FIGURE 1.5** ***(Continued)***

Form 1120 (2021) Page **4**

**Schedule K** **Other Information** (see instructions)

| | | Yes | No |
|---|---|---|---|
| 1 | Check accounting method: **a** ☐ Cash **b** ☐ Accrual **c** ☐ Other (specify) ▶ | | |
| 2 | See the instructions and enter the: | | |
| a | Business activity code no. ▶ | | |
| b | Business activity ▶ | | |
| c | Product or service ▶ | | |
| 3 | Is the corporation a subsidiary in an affiliated group or a parent–subsidiary controlled group? If "Yes," enter name and EIN of the parent corporation ▶ | | |
| 4 | At the end of the tax year: | | |
| a | Did any foreign or domestic corporation, partnership (including any entity treated as a partnership), trust, or tax-exempt organization own directly 20% or more, or own, directly or indirectly, 50% or more of the total voting power of all classes of the corporation's stock entitled to vote? If "Yes," complete Part I of Schedule G (Form 1120) (attach Schedule G) | | |
| b | Did any individual or estate own directly 20% or more, or own, directly or indirectly, 50% or more of the total voting power of all classes of the corporation's stock entitled to vote? If "Yes," complete Part II of Schedule G (Form 1120) (attach Schedule G) | | |
| 5 | At the end of the tax year, did the corporation: | | |
| a | Own directly 20% or more, or own, directly or indirectly, 50% or more of the total voting power of all classes of stock entitled to vote of any foreign or domestic corporation not included on **Form 851,** Affiliations Schedule? For rules of constructive ownership, see instructions. If "Yes," complete (i) through (iv) below. | | |

| **(i)** Name of Corporation | **(ii)** Employer Identification Number (if any) | **(iii)** Country of Incorporation | **(iv)** Percentage Owned in Voting Stock |
|---|---|---|---|
| | | | |
| | | | |
| | | | |

| | | Yes | No |
|---|---|---|---|
| b | Own directly an interest of 20% or more, or own, directly or indirectly, an interest of 50% or more in any foreign or domestic partnership (including an entity treated as a partnership) or in the beneficial interest of a trust? For rules of constructive ownership, see instructions. If "Yes," complete (i) through (iv) below. | | |

| **(i)** Name of Entity | **(ii)** Employer Identification Number (if any) | **(iii)** Country of Organization | **(iv)** Maximum Percentage Owned in Profit, Loss, or Capital |
|---|---|---|---|
| | | | |
| | | | |
| | | | |

| | | Yes | No |
|---|---|---|---|
| 6 | During this tax year, did the corporation pay dividends (other than stock dividends and distributions in exchange for stock) in excess of the corporation's current and accumulated earnings and profits? See sections 301 and 316. If "Yes," file **Form 5452,** Corporate Report of Nondividend Distributions. See the instructions for Form 5452. If this is a consolidated return, answer here for the parent corporation and on Form 851 for each subsidiary. | | |
| 7 | At any time during the tax year, did one foreign person own, directly or indirectly, at least 25% of the total voting power of all classes of the corporation's stock entitled to vote or at least 25% of the total value of all classes of the corporation's stock? For rules of attribution, see section 318. If "Yes," enter: **(a)** Percentage owned ▶ and **(b)** Owner's country ▶ **(c)** The corporation may have to file **Form 5472,** Information Return of a 25% Foreign-Owned U.S. Corporation or a Foreign Corporation Engaged in a U.S. Trade or Business. Enter the number of Forms 5472 attached ▶ | | |
| 8 | Check this box if the corporation issued publicly offered debt instruments with original issue discount ▶ ☐ If checked, the corporation may have to file **Form 8281,** Information Return for Publicly Offered Original Issue Discount Instruments. | | |
| 9 | Enter the amount of tax-exempt interest received or accrued during the tax year ▶ $ | | |
| 10 | Enter the number of shareholders at the end of the tax year (if 100 or fewer) ▶ | | |
| 11 | If the corporation has an NOL for the tax year and is electing to forego the carryback period, check here (see instructions) ▶ ☐ If the corporation is filing a consolidated return, the statement required by Regulations section 1.1502-21(b)(3) must be attached or the election will not be valid. | | |
| 12 | Enter the available NOL carryover from prior tax years (do not reduce it by any deduction reported on page 1, line 29a.) ▶ $ | | |

Form **1120** (2021)

**FIGURE 1.5** ***(Continued)***

Form 1120 (2021) Page **5**

**Schedule K** **Other Information** *(continued from page 4)*

| | | Yes | No |
|---|---|---|---|
| 13 | Are the corporation's total receipts (page 1, line 1a, plus lines 4 through 10) for the tax year **and** its total assets at the end of the tax year less than $250,000? | | |
| | If "Yes," the corporation is not required to complete Schedules L, M-1, and M-2. Instead, enter the total amount of cash distributions and the book value of property distributions (other than cash) made during the tax year ▶ $ | | |
| 14 | Is the corporation required to file Schedule UTP (Form 1120), Uncertain Tax Position Statement? See instructions | | |
| | If "Yes," complete and attach Schedule UTP. | | |
| 15a | Did the corporation make any payments in 2020 that would require it to file Form(s) 1099? | | |
| b | If "Yes," did or will the corporation file required Form(s) 1099? | | |
| 16 | During this tax year, did the corporation have an 80%-or-more change in ownership, including a change due to redemption of its own stock? | | |
| 17 | During or subsequent to this tax year, but before the filing of this return, did the corporation dispose of more than 65% (by value) of its assets in a taxable, non-taxable, or tax deferred transaction? | | |
| 18 | Did the corporation receive assets in a section 351 transfer in which any of the transferred assets had a fair market basis or fair market value of more than $1 million? | | |
| 19 | During the corporation's tax year, did the corporation make any payments that would require it to file Forms 1042 and 1042-S under chapter 3 (sections 1441 through 1464) or chapter 4 (sections 1471 through 1474) of the Code? | | |
| 20 | Is the corporation operating on a cooperative basis? | | |
| 21 | During the tax year, did the corporation pay or accrue any interest or royalty for which the deduction is not allowed under section 267A? See instructions | | |
| | If "Yes," enter the total amount of the disallowed deductions ▶ $ | | |
| 22 | Does the corporation have gross receipts of at least $500 million in any of the 3 preceding tax years? (See sections 59A(e)(2) and (3)) | | |
| | If "Yes," complete and attach Form 8991. | | |
| 23 | Did the corporation have an election under section 163(j) for any real property trade or business or any farming business in effect during the tax year? See instructions | | |
| 24 | Does the corporation satisfy one or more of the following? See instructions | | |
| a | The corporation owns a pass-through entity with current, or prior year carryover, excess business interest expense. | | |
| b | The corporation's aggregate average annual gross receipts (determined under section 448(c)) for the 3 tax years preceding the current tax year are more than $26 million and the corporation has business interest expense. | | |
| c | The corporation is a tax shelter and the corporation has business interest expense. | | |
| | If "Yes," complete and attach Form 8990. | | |
| 25 | Is the corporation attaching Form 8996 to certify as a Qualified Opportunity Fund? | | |
| | If "Yes," enter amount from Form 8996, line 15 ▶ $ | | |
| 26 | Since December 22, 2017, did a foreign corporation directly or indirectly acquire substantially all of the properties held directly or indirectly by the corporation, and was the ownership percentage (by vote or value) for purposes of section 7874 greater than 50% (for example, the shareholders held more than 50% of the stock of the foreign corporation)? If "Yes," list the ownership percentage by vote and by value. See instructions | | |
| | Percentage: By Vote By Value | | |

Form **1120** (2021)

**FIGURE 1.5** ***(Continued)***

Form 1120 (2021) Page 6

**Schedule L Balance Sheets per Books**

| Assets | Beginning of tax year (a) | (b) | End of tax year (c) | (d) |
|---|---|---|---|---|
| 1 Cash | | | | |
| 2a Trade notes and accounts receivable | | | | |
| b Less allowance for bad debts | ( ) | | ( ) | |
| 3 Inventories | | | | |
| 4 U.S. government obligations | | | | |
| 5 Tax-exempt securities (see instructions) | | | | |
| 6 Other current assets (attach statement) | | | | |
| 7 Loans to shareholders | | | | |
| 8 Mortgage and real estate loans | | | | |
| 9 Other investments (attach statement) | | | | |
| 10a Buildings and other depreciable assets | | | | |
| b Less accumulated depreciation | ( ) | | ( ) | |
| 11a Depletable assets | | | | |
| b Less accumulated depletion | ( ) | | ( ) | |
| 12 Land (net of any amortization) | | | | |
| 13a Intangible assets (amortizable only) | | | | |
| b Less accumulated amortization | ( ) | | ( ) | |
| 14 Other assets (attach statement) | | | | |
| 15 Total assets | | | | |
| **Liabilities and Shareholders' Equity** | | | | |
| 16 Accounts payable | | | | |
| 17 Mortgages, notes, bonds payable in less than 1 year | | | | |
| 18 Other current liabilities (attach statement) | | | | |
| 19 Loans from shareholders | | | | |
| 20 Mortgages, notes, bonds payable in 1 year or more | | | | |
| 21 Other liabilities (attach statement) | | | | |
| 22 Capital stock: a Preferred stock | | | | |
| b Common stock | | | | |
| 23 Additional paid-in capital | | | | |
| 24 Retained earnings—Appropriated (attach statement) | | | | |
| 25 Retained earnings—Unappropriated | | | | |
| 26 Adjustments to shareholders' equity (attach statement) | | | | |
| 27 Less cost of treasury stock | | ( ) | | ( ) |
| 28 Total liabilities and shareholders' equity | | | | |

**Schedule M-1 Reconciliation of Income (Loss) per Books With Income per Return**

**Note:** The corporation may be required to file Schedule M-3. See instructions.

| | | | |
|---|---|---|---|
| 1 Net income (loss) per books | | 7 Income recorded on books this year not included on this return (itemize): | |
| 2 Federal income tax per books | | Tax-exempt interest $ | |
| 3 Excess of capital losses over capital gains | | | |
| 4 Income subject to tax not recorded on books this year (itemize): | | | |
| 5 Expenses recorded on books this year not deducted on this return (itemize): | | 8 Deductions on this return not charged against book income this year (itemize): | |
| a Depreciation $ | | a Depreciation $ | |
| b Charitable contributions $ | | b Charitable contributions $ | |
| c Travel and entertainment $ | | | |
| | | 9 Add lines 7 and 8 | |
| 6 Add lines 1 through 5 | | 10 Income (page 1, line 28)—line 6 less line 9 | |

**Schedule M-2 Analysis of Unappropriated Retained Earnings per Books (Schedule L, Line 25)**

| | | | |
|---|---|---|---|
| 1 Balance at beginning of year | | 5 Distributions: a Cash | |
| 2 Net income (loss) per books | | b Stock | |
| 3 Other increases (itemize): | | c Property | |
| | | 6 Other decreases (itemize): | |
| | | 7 Add lines 5 and 6 | |
| 4 Add lines 1, 2, and 3 | | 8 Balance at end of year (line 4 less line 7) | |

Form **1120** (2021)

**FIGURE 1.5** ***(Continued)***

- *Accumulated earnings tax*. Corporations may seek to keep money in corporate accounts rather than distribute it as dividends to shareholders with the view that an eventual sale of the business will enable shareholders to extract those funds at capital gain rates. Unfortunately, the tax law imposes a penalty on excess accumulations at 20%. Excess accumulations are those above an exemption amount ($250,000 for most businesses, but only $150,000 for PSCs) *plus* amounts for the reasonable needs of the business. Thus, for example, amounts retained to finance planned construction costs, to pay for a possible legal liability, or to buy out a retiring owner are reasonable needs not subject to penalty regardless of amount.

## Benefit Corporations

As of February 2021, more than 40 states and the District of Columbia permit benefit corporations in their jurisdications (with Alabama and Georgia effective January 1, 2021) or are considering it. Benefit corporations are for for-profit companies committed to having a positive impact on employees, the environment, the community, and society; officers and directors must consider these stakeholders in their business decisions. Companies incorporate as benefit corporations, which protects officers and directors from certain investor lawsuits and tells the public that they're committed to societal benefit programs. The key attributes of a benefit corporation are:

- Public benefit programs to create a material impact on society and the environment
- Transparency and reporting to provide an annual review of its conduct. When no audit is required, performance is measured against a third-party standard to assess their creation of a general public benefit.
- Benefit enforcement to entitle shareholders to sue in order to hold the corporation accountable for its public purpose.

Benefit corporations do not have any special tax treatment. Thus, they may be an S corporation or a C corporation, with the tax treatment that follows these entities. There are state filing fees for becoming a benefit corporation.

Instead of "inc," "corp," or "ltd," a benefit corporation uses the designation PBC (public benefit corporation). They can be public or privately held; there's no asset or revenue limits or requirements. A well-known PBC is Kickstarter (www.kickstarter.com/blog/kickstarter-is-now-a-benefit-corporation).

Do not confuse benefit corporations with B corporations. B corporations are corporations certified by B Lab, a non-profit organization, to show they meet standards for social and environmental performance, accountability, and transparency. The "b" stands for benefits. This certification can be used by a corporation in any state, whether or not it incorporated as a benefit corporation. The cost for B certification ranges from $500 to $50,000, depending on the business's revenue.

There are also "social enterprises," which are for-profit (or non-profit) businesses using any legal structure that has a business model addressing unmet basic needs in society. More information about these businesses can be found from the Social Enterprise Alliance at https://socialenterprise.us/.

Some states (e.g., Delaware, Kansas, Illinois, Maryland, Oregon, Pennsylvania, and Utah) allow for benefit LLCs, which are limited liability companies obtaining the same opportunities that the state's benefit corporations enjoy.

## Employees

Whether or not you own any interest in a business, if you are employed by one, you still have income and business expenses. Your salary or other compensation is reported as wages on page 1 of your Form 1040 or 1040-SR.

Generally, your business expenses are not deductible. In 2018 through 2025, employees cannot deduct their unreimbursed employee business expenses, other than were noted throughout the book. In the past they were able to deduct them all as miscellaneous itemized deductions on Schedule A of Form 1040 or 1040-SR.

**Example**

**You are the owner-employee of an S corporation. You drive your personal car on company business. You cannot take any deduction in 2021 for this business driving on your personal return. (There is a better way to handle this expense, as explained in Chapter 9).**

## Factors in Choosing Your Form of Business Organization

Throughout this chapter, the differences of how income and deductions are reported have been explained for different entities, but these differences are not the only reasons for choosing a form of business organization. When you are deciding on which form of business organization to choose, tax, financial, and many other factors come into play, including:

- Personal liability
- Access to capital
- Lack of profitability
- Fringe benefits
- Nature and number of owners
- Tax rates
- Social Security and Medicare taxes
- Restrictions on accounting periods and account methods
- Owner's payment of company expenses
- Multistate operations
- Audit chances
- Filing deadlines and extensions
- Exit strategy

Each of these factors is discussed below.

### *Personal Liability*

If your business owes money to another party, are your personal assets—home, car, investments—at risk? The answer depends on your form of business organization. You have personal liability—your personal assets are at risk—if you are a sole proprietor or a general partner in a partnership. In all other cases, you do not have personal liability. Thus, for example, if you are a shareholder in an S corporation, you do not have personal liability for the debts of your corporation.

Of course, you can protect yourself against personal liability for some types of occurrences by having adequate insurance coverage. For example, if you are a sole proprietor who runs a store, be sure that you have adequate liability coverage in the event someone is injured on your premises and sues you.

Even if your form of business organization provides personal liability protection, you can become personally liable if you agree to it in a contract. For example, some banks may not be willing to lend money to a small corporation unless you, as a principal shareholder, agree to guarantee the corporation's debt. For instance, SBA loans usually require the personal guarantee of any owner with a 20% or more ownership interest in the business. In this case, you are personally liable to the extent of the loan to the corporation. If the corporation does not or cannot repay the loan, then the bank can look to you, and your personal assets, for repayment.

There is another instance in which corporate or LLC status will not provide you with personal protection. Even if you have a corporation or LLC, you can be personally liable for failing to withhold and deposit payroll taxes, which are called trust fund taxes (employees' income tax withholding and their share of FICA taxes, which are held in trust for them) to the IRS. This liability is explained in Chapter 29.

### *Access to Capital*

Most small businesses start up using an owner's personal resources or by turning to family and friends. However, some businesses need outside capital—equity and/or debt—to get started properly. A C corporation may make it easier to raise money, especially now. For example, access to equity crowdfunding, which allows businesses to raise small amounts from numerous investors, is effectively limited to C corporations (S corporations cannot have more than 100 investors unless Congress changes the law; partnerships and LLCs would have difficulty in divvying up ownership among an ever-changing number of owners). Equity crowdfunding for accredited investors (net worth more than $1 million, excluding a principal residence or income exceeding $300,000) obviously works best for C corporations. As of March 15, 2021, there is no dollar limit on investments by accredited investors.

For non-accredited investors (those who do not qualify as accredited investors because they don't have annual income of $200,000, or $300,000 with a spouse), equity crowdfunding investments are capped at up to 10% of annual income for those with income over $100,000, or up to $2,000 or 5% of annual income, whichever is greater, for investors with annual income under $100,000.

### *Lack of Profitability*

All businesses hope to make money. But many sustain losses, especially in the start-up years and during tough economic times. The way in which a business is organized affects how losses are treated.

Pass-through entities allow owners to deduct their share of the company's losses on their personal returns (subject to limits discussed in Chapter 4). If a business is set up as a C corporation, only the corporation can deduct losses. Thus, when losses are anticipated, for example, in the start-up phase, a pass-through entity generally is a preferable form of business organization. However, once the business becomes profitable, the tables turn. In that situation, C corporations can offer more tax opportunities, such as a lower tax rate and fringe benefits for owners working in the business. Companies that suffer severe losses may be forced into bankruptcy. The bankruptcy rules for corporations (C or S) are very different from the rules for other entities (see Chapter 25).

### *Fringe Benefits*

The tax law gives employees of corporations the opportunity to enjoy special fringe benefits on a tax-free basis. They can receive employer-provided group term life insurance up to $50,000, health insurance coverage, dependent care assistance up to $10,500 in 2021, education assistance up to $5,250, adoption assistance, and more. They can also be covered by certain medical reimbursement plans. This same opportunity is not extended to sole proprietors. Remember that sole proprietors are not employees, so they cannot get the benefits given only to employees. Similarly, partners, LLC members, and even S corporation shareholders who own more than 2% of the stock in their corporations (and are not considered employees) are not eligible for fringe benefits.

If the business can afford to provide these benefits, the form of business becomes important. All forms of business can offer tax-favored retirement plans. Corporations make it possible to give ownership opportunities to employees. Corporations—both C and S—can offer employee stock ownership plans (ESOPs) in which employees receive ownership interests through a plan that is much like a qualified retirement plan (see Chapter 16). Certain C corporations can offer employees an income tax exclusion opportunity for stock they buy or receive as compensation. For 2021, 50%, 75%, or 100% of the gain on the sale of qualified small business stock (explained in Chapter 5) is excludable from gross income, depending on when the stock was acquired, as long as the stock has been held for more than 5 years. C corporations may also offer incentive stock option (ISO) plans and nonqualified stock option (NSO) plans (see Chapter 7). The tax law does not bar S corporations from offering stock option plans, but because of the 100-shareholder limit (discussed earlier in this chapter), it becomes difficult to do so.

### *Nature and Number of Owners*

With whom you go into business affects your choice of business organization. For example, foreign individuals are not permitted to own S corporation stock directly (resident aliens are permitted to own S corporation stock). But a nonresident alien may be a potential current income beneficiary of an electing small business trust (ESBT). An S corporation also cannot be used if investors are partnerships or corporations. In other words, in order to use an S corporation, all shareholders must be individuals who are not nonresident aliens (there are exceptions for estates, certain trusts, and certain exempt organizations).

The number of owners also presents limits on your choice of business organization. If you are the only owner, then your choices are limited to a sole proprietorship or a corporation (either C or S). All states allow single-member LLCs. If you have more than one owner, you can set up the business in just about any way you choose. S corporations cannot have more than 100 shareholders, but this number provides great leeway for small businesses.

If you have a business already formed as a C corporation and want to start another corporation, you must take into consideration the impact of special tax rules for multiple corporations. These rules apply regardless of the size of the business, the number of employees you have, and the profit the businesses make. Multiple corporations are corporations under common control, meaning they are essentially owned by the same parties. The rules for multiple corporations are explained in Chapter 28. If you want to avoid restrictions on multiple corporations, you may want to look to LLCs or some other form of business organization.

### Tax Rates

If a business is highly profitable, tax rates may become a consideration in entity choice. C corporations pay a flat 21% rate on their profits. Owners of pass-through entities may pay up to a 37% tax rate on their share of profits. While there is a 20% qualified business income (QBI) deduction for owners of pass-through entities designed to lower the effective tax rate on business profits, there are various limitations that may restrict or bar the use of this write-off. For example, an accountant or attorney with taxable income in 2021 over $429,800 on a joint return, $214,925 for married persons filing separately, or $214,900 for singles and heads of households cannot claim this deduction. The 20% QBI deduction is explained in Chapter 21.

But remember, even though the C corporation has a lower tax rate, there is a 2-tier tax structure with which to contend if earnings are paid out to you as dividends—tax at the corporate level and again at the shareholder level. While the so-called double taxation for C corporations is lessened by having a lower tax rate on dividends for individuals, there is still some double tax because dividends remain nondeductible at the corporate level. The rate on qualified dividends for most taxpayers is 15% (it may be zero or 20%, depending upon taxable income).

The tax rates on capital gains also differ between C corporations and other taxpayers. This is because capital gains of C corporations are not subject to special tax rates (they are taxed the same as ordinary business income), while owners of other types of businesses may pay tax on the business's capital gains at no more than zero, 15%, or 20%, depending on taxable income). Of course, tax rates alone should not be the determining factor in selecting your form of business organization. At the time of publication, Congress was considering a hike in the capital gains rate for transactions after September 13, 2021; check the Supplement for any update.

### Social Security and Medicare Taxes

Owners of businesses organized any way other than as a corporation (C or S) are not employees of their businesses. As such, they are personally responsible for paying Social Security and Medicare taxes (called *self-employment* taxes for owners of unincorporated businesses). This tax is made up of the employer and employee shares of Social Security and Medicare taxes. The deduction for one-half of self-employment taxes is explained in Chapter 13.

However, owners of corporations have these taxes applied only against their salary and taxable benefits. Owners of unincorporated businesses pay self-employment tax on net earnings from self-employment. This essentially means profits, whether they are distributed to the owners or reinvested in the business. The result: Owners of unincorporated businesses may wind up paying higher Social Security and Medicare taxes than comparable owners who work for their corporations. On the other hand, in unprofitable businesses, owners of unincorporated businesses may not be able to earn any Social Security credits, while corporate owners can have salary paid to them on which Social Security credits can be generated.

There have been proposals to treat certain S corporation owner-employees like partners for purposes of self-employment tax. To date, these proposals have failed, but could be revived in the future. Check the Supplement for any update.

The additional Medicare surtaxes on earned income and net investment income (NII) are yet another factor to consider. The 0.9% surtax on earned income applies to taxable compensation (e.g., wages, bonuses, commissions, and taxable fringe benefits) of shareholders in S or C corporations; it applies to all net earnings from self-employment for sole proprietors, partners, and limited liability company members. At present, the 3.8% NII tax applies to business income passed through from an entity in which the owner does not materially participate (i.e., one in which the owner is effectively a silent investor).

### Restrictions on Accounting Periods and Accounting Methods

As you will see in Chapter 2, the tax law limits the use of fiscal years and the cash method of accounting for certain types of business organizations. For example, partnerships and S corporations in general are required to use a calendar year to report income.

Also, C corporations generally are required to use the accrual method of accounting to report income. There are exceptions to both of these rules. However, as you can see, accounting periods and accounting methods are considerations in choosing your form of business organization.

### Owner's Payment of Company Expenses

In small businesses it is common practice for owners to pay certain business expenses out of their own pockets—either as a matter of convenience or because the company is short of cash. The type of entity dictates where owners can deduct these payments.

A partner who is not reimbursed for paying partnership expenses can deduct his or her payments of these expenses as an above-the-line deduction (on a separate line on Schedule E of the partner's Form 1040 or 1040-SR, which should be marked as "UPE"), as long as the partnership agreement requires the partner to pay specified expenses personally and includes language that no reimbursement will be made.

A shareholder in a corporation (S or C) is an employee, so that unreimbursed expenses paid on behalf of the corporation cannot be deducted in 2018 through 2025 because the deduction for itemized miscellaneous expenses has been suspended. However, shareholders can avoid this deduction problem by having the corporation adopt an accountable plan to reimburse their out-of-pocket business expenses. An accountable plan allows the corporation to deduct the expenses, while the shareholders do not report income from the reimbursement (see Chapter 8).

### Multistate Operations

Each state has its own way of taxing businesses subject to its jurisdiction. The way in which a business is organized for federal income tax purposes may not necessarily control for state income tax purposes. For example, some jurisdictions do not recognize S corporation elections and tax such entities as regular corporations.

A company must file a return in each state in which it does business and pay income tax on the portion of its profits earned in that state. Income tax liability is based on having a *nexus*, or connection, to a state. This is not always an easy matter to settle. Where there is a physical presence—for example, a company maintains an office—then there is a clear nexus. But when a company merely makes sales to customers within a state or offers goods for sale from a website, there is generally no nexus. However, a growing number of states are liberalizing the definition of nexus in order to get more businesses to pay state taxes so they can increase revenue; some states are moving toward "a significant economic presence," meaning taking advantage of a state's economy to produce income, as a basis for taxation.

Assuming that a company does conduct multistate business, then its form of organization becomes important. Most multistate businesses are C corporations because only one corporate income tax return needs to be filed in each state where they do business. Doing business as a pass-through entity means that each owner would have to file a tax return in each state the company does business. More on multistate operations is in Chapter 28.

### Audit Chances

Each year, the IRS publishes statistics on the number and type of audits it conducts. The rates for the government's fiscal year 2020, the most recent year for which statistics are available, show a very low overall audit activity of business returns. The IRS said in early 2021 that it's planning to

**TABLE 1.1 Percentage of Returns Audited**

| | FY 2020* | FY 2019* |
|---|---|---|
| Partnerships | 0.05 | 0.07 |
| S corporations | 0.1 | 0.1 |
| C corporations (based on assets) | | |
| Under $250,000 | 0.1 | 0.16 |
| $250,000 to under $1 million | 0.3 | 0.48 |
| $1 million to under $5 million | 0.6 | 0.57 |
| $5 million to under $10 million | 1.4 | 0.63 |

*Fiscal year from October 1 to September 30.
*Source:* IRS Data Book.

increase by 50% the number of audits of small businesses but hasn't indicated what triggers (e.g., income level, type of deductions, industry) will be used to select taxpayers for audit.

The chances of being audited vary with the type of business organization, the amount of income generated by the business, and the geographic location of the business. While the chance of an audit is not a significant reason for choosing one form of business organization over another, it is helpful to keep these statistics in mind.

Table 1.1 sheds some light on the chances of an S corporation, partnership, or C corporation being audited, based on the most recently available statistics. The IRS no longer provides a breakdown of audits for Schedule C or F filers.

Many tax experts agree that your location can impact your audit chances. Some IRS offices are better staffed than others. There have been no recent statistics identifying these high-audit locations.

### *Filing Deadlines and Extensions*

How your business is organized dictates when its tax return must be filed, the form to use, and the additional time that can be obtained for filing the return. Pass-throughs (partnerships and S corporations) reporting on a calendar year must file by March 15; they can obtain a 6-month filing extension. Calendar year C corporations don't have to file until April 15 (the same deadline for individuals, including Schedule C filers); they too have an extended due date of October 15. The September 15 extended due date gives S corporations, limited liability companies, and partnerships time to provide a Schedule K-1 to owners so they can file their personal returns by their extended due date of October 15. The filing deadlines and extensions may be longer for owners and businesses within federally-declared disaster areas (see disaster relief at https://www.irs.gov/newsroom/tax-relief-in-disaster-situations).

Table 1.2 lists the filing deadlines for calendar-year businesses, the available automatic extensions, and the forms to use in filing the return or requesting a filing extension. Note that these dates are extended to the next business day when a deadline falls on a Saturday, Sunday, or legal holiday.

### *Exit Strategy*

The tax treatment on the termination of a business is another factor to consider. While the choice of entity is made when the business starts out, you cannot ignore the tax consequences that this choice will have when the business terminates, is sold, or goes public. The liquidation of a C corporation usually produces a double tax—at the entity and owner levels. The liquidation of

**TABLE 1.2 Filing Deadlines, Extensions, and Forms for 2021 Returns**

| Type of Entity | Return Due Date | Income Tax Return | Automatic Filing Extension | Form to Request Filing Extension |
|---|---|---|---|---|
| Sole proprietorship | April 18 | Schedule C of Form 1040 or 1040-SR | October 17 | Form 4868 |
| Partnership/LLC | March 15 | Form 1065 | September 15 | Form 7004 |
| S corporation | March 15 | Form 1120-S | September 15 | Form 7004 |
| C corporation | April 18 | Form 1120 | October 17 | Form 7004 |

an S corporation produces a double tax *only* if there is a built-in gains tax issue—created by having appreciated assets in the business when an S election is made. However, the built-in gains tax problem disappears a certain number of years after the S election, so termination after that time does not result in a double tax.

If you plan to sell the business some time in the future, again your choice of entity may have an impact on the tax consequences of the sale. The sale of a sole proprietorship is viewed as a sale of the underlying assets of the business; some may produce ordinary income while others trigger capital gains. In contrast, the sale of qualified small business stock, which is stock in a C corporation, may result in tax-free treatment under certain conditions. Sales of business interests are discussed in Chapter 5.

Another exit strategy is using an Employee Stock Ownership Plan (ESOP) to have a trust-a ready marketplace for privately held stock-acquire the owner's stock; the employees who participate in the ESOP effectively becomes owners. Obviously, because ESOPs are based on stock, only C and S corporations can use them. ESOPs are discussed in greater detail in Chapter 31.

If the termination of the business results in a loss, different tax rules come into play. Losses from partnerships and LLCs are treated as capital losses (explained in Chapter 5). A shareholder's losses from the termination of a C or S corporation may qualify as a Section 1244 loss—treated as an ordinary loss within limits (explained in Chapter 5).

If the business goes bankrupt, the entity type influences the type of bankruptcy filing to be used and whether the owners can escape personal liability for the debts of the business. Bankruptcy is discussed in Chapter 26.

## Forms of Business Organization Compared

So far, you have learned about the various forms of business organization. Which form is right for your business? The answer is really a judgment call based on all the factors previously discussed. You can, of course, use different forms of business organization for your different business activities. For example, you may have a C corporation and personally own the building in which it operates— directly or through an LLC. Or you may be in partnership for your professional activities, while running a sideline business as an S corporation.

Table 1.3 summarizes 2 important considerations: how the type of business organization is formed and what effect the form of business organization has on where income and deductions are reported.

**TABLE 1.3** Comparison of Forms of Business Organization

| Type of Business | How It Is Formed | Where Income and Deductions Are Reported |
|---|---|---|
| Sole proprietorship | No special requirements | On owner's Schedule C (Schedule F for farming) |
| Partnership | No special requirements | Some items taken into account in figuring trade or business income directly on Form 1065 (allocable amount claimed on partner's Schedule E); separately stated items are passed through to partners and claimed in various places on partner's tax return. |
| Limited special partnership | Some items taken into account in figuring partnership under state law | Trade or business income directly on Form 1065 (allocable amount claimed on partner's Schedule E); separately stated items passed through to partners and claimed in various places on partner's tax return |
| Limited liability company | Organized as such under state law | Some items taken into account in figuring trade or business income directly on Form 1065 (allocable amount claimed on member's Schedule E); separately stated items passed through to members and claimed in various places on member's tax return |
| Limited liability partnership | Organized as such under state law | Some items taken into account in figuring trade or business income directly on Form 1065 (allocable amount claimed on member's Schedule E); separately stated items passed through to members and claimed in various places on member's tax return |
| S corporation | Formed as corporation under state law; tax status elected by filing with IRS | Some items taken into account in figuring trade or business income directly on Form 1120-S (allocable amount claimed on shareholder's Schedule E); separately stated items passed through to shareholders and claimed in various places on shareholder's tax return |
| C corporation | Formed under state law | Claimed by corporation in figuring its trade or business income on Form 1120 |
| Employee | No ownership interest | Income reported as wages; no deduction for unreimbursed employee business expenses |
| Independent contractor | No ownership interest in a business | Claimed on individual's Schedule C |

## Changing Your Form of Business

The lowering of the corporate tax rate to 21% sparked discussion about whether other entities should become C corporations. But tax rates which may change, aren't the only reason for making a change in entity choice.

Suppose you have a business that you have been running as a sole proprietorship. Now you want to make a change. Your new choice of business organization is dictated by the reason for the change. If you are taking in a partner, you would consider these alternatives: partnership, LLC, S corporation, or C corporation. If you are not taking in a partner, but want to obtain limited personal liability, you would consider an LLC (if your state permits a one-person LLC), an S corporation, or a C corporation. If you are looking to take advantage of certain fringe benefits, such as certain medical reimbursement plans, you would consider only a C corporation.

If you project that the tax rate on your business profits would be greatly reduced by becoming a C corporation, then you'd need to revoke an S election or incorporate an unincorporated business. Keep in mind that if you revoke an S election, a new one cannot be made for 5 years. Also, if an S corporation revoked its election and became a C corporation, any adjustment to income resulting from a change in accounting method attributable to the conversion during the 2-year period beginning December 22, 2017, is taken into account ratably over a 6-year period beginning with the year of the change. This means some of the adjustment is reported on a 2021 return. This rule applies if the business was an S corporation on December 21, 2017, made the revocation by December 22, 2019, and it had the same shareholders on December 22, 2017, and on the day of revocation.

Whatever your reason, changing from a sole proprietorship to another type of business organization generally does not entail tax costs on making the changeover. You can set up a partnership or corporation, transfer your business assets to it, obtain an ownership interest in the new entity, and do all this on a tax-free basis. You may, however, have some tax consequences if you transfer your business liabilities to the new entity.

But what if you now have a corporation or partnership and want to change your form of business organization? This change may not be so simple. Suppose you have an S corporation or a C corporation. If you liquidate the corporation to change to another form of business organization, you may have to report gains on the liquidation. In fact, gains may have to be reported both by the business and by you as owner.

Partnerships can become corporations and elect S corporation status for their first taxable year without having any intervening short taxable year as a C corporation if corporate formation is made under a state law formless conversion statute or under the check-the-box regulations mentioned earlier in this chapter.

Before changing your form of business organization, it is important to review your particular situation with a tax professional. In making any change in business, consider the legal and accounting costs involved.

CHAPTER 2

# Tax Year and Accounting Methods


| | | | |
|---|---|---|---|
| Accounting Periods | 36 | Uniform Capitalization Rules | 49 |
| Accounting Methods | 40 | Change in Accounting Method | 50 |


Once you select your form of business organization, you must decide how you will report your income. There are 2 key decisions you must make: What is the time frame for calculating your income and deductions (called the tax year or accounting period), and what are the rules that you will follow to calculate your income and deductions (called the accounting method). In some cases, as you will see, your form of business organization restricts you to an accounting period or accounting method. In other cases, however, you can choose which method is best for your business. Depending upon circumstances, you may want or need to change your accounting method. Sometimes making a change is easy, with automatic procedures; other situations require IRS consent, as you will see later in this chapter.

For a further discussion on tax years and accounting methods, see IRS Publication 538, *Accounting Periods and Methods*. Inventory rules are discussed in Chapter 4.

## Accounting Periods

You account for your income and expenses on an annual basis. This period is called your *tax year*. There are 2 methods for fixing your tax year: *calendar* and *fiscal*. Under the calendar year, you use a 12-month period ending on December 31. Under the fiscal year, you use a 12-month period ending at the end of any month other than December.

When you start your business and don't select a fiscal year, you automatically have a calendar year. You don't need to file any form or obtain IRS approval. If you commence your business in the middle of the tax year you have selected, your first tax year will be short.

**Example**

**You start your S corporation in May 2021. It uses a calendar year to report expenses. The corporation will have a short tax year ending December 31, 2021, for its first tax year. Then, for 2022, it will have a full 12-month tax year.**

A short tax year may occur in the final year of business.

**Example**

**If you closed the doors to your business on May 31, 2021, even though you operated on a calendar year, your final tax year is a short year because it is only 5 months.**

You do not have to apportion or prorate deductions for this short year merely because the business was not in existence for the entire year. Different rules apply if a short year results from a change in accounting period.

### *Seasonal Businesses*

Seasonal businesses should use special care when selecting their tax year. It is often advisable to select a tax year that will include both the period in which most of the expenses as well as most of the income is realized. For example, if a business expects to sell its products primarily in the spring and incurs most of its expenses for these sales in the preceding fall, it may be best to select a fiscal year ending just after the selling season, such as July or August. In this way, the expenses and the income that are related to each other will be reported on the same return.

### *Limits on Use of the Fiscal Year*

C corporations, other than personal service corporations (PSCs), can choose a calendar year or a fiscal year, whichever is more advantageous. Other entities, however, cannot simply choose a fiscal year, even though it offers tax advantages to its owners. In general, partnerships, limited liability companies (LLCs), S corporations, and PSCs must use a **required year**. Since individuals typically use a calendar year, their partnership or LLC must also use a calendar year.

***Required year*** **For S corporations, this is a calendar year; for partnerships and LLCs, it is the same year as the tax year of the entity's owners. When owners have different tax years, special rules determine which owner's tax year governs.**

### *Business Purpose for Fiscal Year*

The entity can use a fiscal year even though its owners use a calendar year if it can be established to the satisfaction of the IRS that there is a business purpose for the fiscal year. The fact that the use of a fiscal year defers income for its owners is not considered to be a valid **business purpose** warranting a tax year other than a required tax year.

***Business purpose*** **This is shown if the fiscal year is the natural business year of the entity. For a PSC, for example, a fiscal year is treated as a natural business year if 25% or more of its gross receipts for the 12-month period ending on the last month of the requested tax year are received within the last 2 months of that year.**

While the vast majority of small businesses use a calendar year, some companies may use a fiscal year because it is the natural year of the type of business they are in. The end of the fiscal year coincides with the close of the business cycle. For example, a ski shop may close out its year on June 30 after running end-of-season sales. They do not have to use this fiscal year, however, and many such businesses use a calendar year.

### Section 444 Election for Fiscal Year

If an entity wants to use a fiscal year that is not its natural business year, it can do so by making a Section 444 election. The only acceptable tax years under this election are those ending September 30, October 31, and November 30. Use of these fiscal years means that at most there can be a 3-month deferral for the owners. The election is made by filing Form 8716, *Election to Have a Tax Year Other Than a Required Tax Year*, by the earlier of the due date of the return for the new tax year (without regard to extensions) or the 15th day of the 6th month of the tax year for which the election will be effective.

If the election is made, then partnerships, LLCs, and S corporations must make certain *required payments*. These essentially are designed to give to the federal government the tax that has been deferred by reason of the special tax year. This payment can be thought of as simply a deposit, since it does not serve to increase the tax that is otherwise due. The payment is calculated using the highest individual income tax rate plus one percentage point. Therefore, the rate for 2021 is 38%. The required payment is made by filing Form 8752, *Required Payment or Refund Under Section 7519 for Partnerships and S Corporations*, by May 15 of the calendar year following the calendar year in which the election begins. For example, if the election begins on October 1, 2021, the required payment must be made no later than May 15, 2022. In view of the high required payment and the complications involved in making and maintaining a Section 444 election, most of these entities use a calendar year.

Personal service corporations that make a Section 444 election need not make a required payment. Instead, these corporations must make *required distributions*. They must distribute certain amounts of compensation to employee-owners by December 31 of each year for which an election is in effect. The reason for the required elections is to ensure that amounts will be taxed to owner-employees as soon as possible and will not be deferred simply because the corporation uses a fiscal year. Required distributions are figured on Part I of Schedule H of Form 1120, *Section 280H Limitations for a Personal Service Corporation*.

### Pass-Through Business on a Fiscal Year

Owners in pass-through entities who are on a calendar year report their share of the business's income, deductions, gains, losses, and credits from the entity's tax year that ends in the owners' tax year.

**Example**

**You are in a partnership that uses a fiscal year ending October 31. The partnership's items for its 2021 fiscal year ending October 31, 2021, are reported on your 2021 return. The portion of the partnership's income and deductions from the period November 1, 2021, through December 31, 2021, are part of its 2022 fiscal year, which will be reported on your 2022 return.**

### *Short Tax Years*

You may have a year that is less than a full tax year. This results most commonly in the year you start or end a business.

**Example**

**You start an LLC on August 1, 2021, and use a calendar year to report your income and expenses. The LLC's first tax year is a short tax year, running from August 1, 2021, through December 31, 2021.**

A short tax year can also result when a C corporation that had been reporting on a fiscal year elects S status and adopts a calendar year. The tax year of the C corporation ends on the date the S election becomes effective.

Alternatively, if an S election is terminated within the year or there is a substantial change in ownership (50% or more), then the corporation can have 2 short tax years in this case.

**Example**

**A C corporation with a fiscal year ending on June 30 elects to become an S corporation and adopts a calendar year. The election is effective on January 1, 2022. The C corporation has a short tax year starting on July 1, 2021, and ending on December 31, 2021.**

**Example**

**An S corporation reporting on a calendar year has its election involuntarily terminated on July 31, 2021, when another corporation becomes a shareholder. The corporation has 2 short tax years: the S tax year running from January 1, 2021, through July 31, 2021, and the C tax year running from August 1, 2021, through December 31, 2021.**

**The IRS says that an unincorporated entity converting to a corporation under a state law formless conversion statute or check-the-box rules and which is eligible for S corporation status as of the first day of its first year does *not* have any short tax year for the momentary period it was a C corporation.**

### Change in Tax Year

If your business has been using a particular tax year and you want to change to a different one, you must obtain IRS approval to do so. Depending on the reason for the change, approval may be automatic or discretionary. You can request a change in your tax year by filing Form 1128, *Application to Adopt, Change, or Retain a Tax Year*. There is a user fee (an amount set by the IRS) for this request.

## Accounting Methods

An accounting method is a set of rules used to determine when and how to record income and expenses on your books and for tax-reporting purposes. In some cases, how items are treated may differ for tax reporting purposes and financial accounting purposes. What is included in this chapter are the accounting method rules for tax reporting purposes.

There are 2 overall methods of accounting: *cash basis* and *accrual basis*. Use of a particular method determines when income is reported and a deduction can be claimed. However, restrictions apply for both methods of accounting. Also, the form of business organization may preclude the use of the cash method of accounting even though it may be the method of choice.

### Cash Method

Cash method is the simpler overall accounting method. Income is reported when it is actually or constructively received, and a deduction for an allowable deductible expense can be claimed when and to the extent the expense is paid.

**Example**

**You are a consultant. You perform services and send a bill. You report the income when you receive payment. Similarly, you buy business cards and stationery. You can deduct this expense when you pay for the supplies.**

Actual receipt is the time when income is in your hands. Constructive receipt occurs when you have control over the income and can reduce it to an actual receipt.

**Example**

**You earn a fee for services rendered but ask your customer not to pay you immediately. Since the customer was ready and able to pay immediately, you are in constructive receipt of the fee at that time.**

Payments received by check are income when the check is received even though you may deposit it some time later. However, if the check bounces, then no income results at the time the check was received. You report income only when the check is later honored.

Sole proprietors and independent contractors on the cash method (and reporting on a calendar year basis) can run into a problem with respect to Form 1099-NEC for year-end payments. A company may send a payment late in December 2021 and include it on Form 1099-NEC for 2021; the contractor may receive the payment in January 2022. While this income is not taxable to the contractor until 2022, he or she must report the income on the return as it is reported by the company (because of IRS computer matching of information returns with income reported by recipients on their returns) and then make a subtraction to eliminate this amount from income. The payment is then included in income in 2022 even though it is not reflected on a Form 1099-NEC for 2022.

Expenses are usually fully deductible when paid. Payments by a general credit card, such as Mastercard or Visa, are deductible in the year they are charged, even if you pay the credit card bill in the following year. Payments using "pay by phone" with your bank are deductible when the bank sends the payment (check your bank account statement). There has been no IRS guidance on deductibility when using PayPal, Amazon Payments, or other electronic payment methods, but it appears that payments are deductible when you instruct PayPal or other provider to make them because that is when the funds are taken from your account. Bitcoin and other digital currencies are not treated by the IRS as currency (they're treated as property), so this complicates the deduction process (payments in cryptocurrency are discussed in Chapter 4).

You may not be able to deduct all expenses when they are paid because there are some limitations that come into play. Generally, you cannot deduct advance payments (so-called prepaid expenses) that relate to periods beyond the current tax year. However, under a 12-month rule, you can deduct amounts paid for a benefit that does not extend beyond the earlier of 12 months after the benefit begins or the end of the tax year after the tax year in which payment is made.

**Example**

**You pay a $10,000 insurance policy on July 1, 2021, that is effective for one year. Because you meet the 12-month rule, you can deduct the full $10,000 in 2021. You take out a 3-year subscription to a business journal and pay the 3-year subscription price this year. Because the 12-month rule does not apply, you can deduct only ⅓ of the payment—the amount that relates to the current year. You can deduct another ⅓ next year, and the final ⅓ the following year.**

Prepayments may occur for a number of expenses. You may prepay rent, insurance premiums, or subscriptions. Generally, prepayments that do not extend beyond 12 months are currently deductible.

In the case of interest, no deduction is allowed for prepayments by businesses. For example, if you are required to pay points to obtain a mortgage on your office building, these points are considered to be prepaid interest. You must deduct the points ratably over the term of the loan.

**Example**

**If the mortgage on the office building runs for 30 years (or 360 months) and you pay the points on July 1, you can deduct 6/360 of the points in the first year. In each succeeding year you would deduct 12/360 of the points. In the final year, you would again deduct 6/360.**

Deposits you make, such as an extra month's rent, may be called advances. If they are refundable, then they cannot be deducted when paid. If they are nonrefundable, they can be deducted when made.

If you pay off the mortgage before the end of the term (you sell the property or refinance the loan), you can then write off any points you still have not deducted.

### RESTRICTIONS ON THE USE OF THE CASH METHOD

The tax law requires the use of the accrual method of accounting for certain taxpayers. Generally, a business must be on an accrual basis for its overall accounting method if it maintains inventory, is a large farming corporation, or if it is a C corporation, a partnership with a C corporation as a partner, or a tax shelter. However, key exceptions listed below permit small businesses to use the cash method of accounting.

*Small Business Exception.* Businesses can use the cash method of accounting if they are considered to be *small businesses*. A small business for this purpose in 2021 is one that has average annual **gross receipts** of $26 million or less for the 3-year period ending in the prior year. This is referred to as the gross receipts test.

***Gross receipts*** **All the income taken in by the business without offsets for expenses. For example, if a consultant receives fees of $25,000 for the year and has expenses of $10,000, gross receipts are $25,000.**

In figuring gross receipts, noncorporate taxpayers—owners of pass-through entities—must aggregate gross receipts from the all the businesses they own. If you've been using the accrual method because you failed the gross receipts test but meet it in the current year, you must obtain IRS consent before changing to the cash method if you previously changed from the cash method during any of the preceding 5 years ending with the current tax year.

*Farming Corporations Exception.* Farming corporations and farming partnerships in which a corporation is a partner usually must use the accrual method. However, the farming business is exempt from this rule if it meets the $26 million gross receipts test. A farming business includes any business that operates a nursery or sod farm or that raises or harvests trees bearing fruit, nuts, or other crops and ornamental trees.

*PSC Exception.* A **qualified personal service corporation** (PSC) can use the cash method of accounting without regard to gross receipts.

***Qualified personal service corporation*** **A corporation (other than an S corporation) with a substantial number of activities involving the performance of personal services in the fields of medicine, law, accounting, architecture, actuarial sciences, performing arts, or consulting by someone who owns stock in the corporation (or who is retired or the executor of the estate of a deceased former employee).**

*Small Inventory-Based Business Exception.* Even though you have inventory, you are permitted to use the cash method if you meet the $26 million gross receipts test.

You can use the cash method of accounting even though you use the accrual method for financial accounting purposes (for example, on profit and loss statements). However, you do not qualify for this exception if your principal business activity is retailing, wholesaling, manufacturing (other than custom manufacturing), mining, publishing, or sound recording. (Principal business activity is based on the largest percentage of your gross receipts using the North American Industry Classification System [NAICS], published by the U.S. Department of Commerce and which can be found in instructions to Schedule C of Form 1040 or 1040-SR.) NAICS codes are also used for government contracting purposes, so be sure that you use the correct code if you want to work with the government. You can get help determining which NAICS code is most appropriate for your business by using an online tool at www.naics.com/search.htm. Alternatively, you can contact the U.S. Census Bureau for help by calling 888-75NAICS.

**NOTE**

**If you use the small business exception or small inventory-based business exception, you account for inventoriable items as non-incidental materials and supplies (see Chapter 4).**

## *Accrual Method of Accounting*

Under the accrual method, you report income when it is earned rather than when it is received, and you deduct expenses when they are incurred rather than when they are paid. There are 2 tests to determine whether there is a fixed right to receive income so that it must be accrued and whether an expense is treated as having been incurred for tax purposes.

### ALL EVENTS TEST

All events that fix the income and set the liability must have occurred. Also, you must be able to determine the amount of the income or expense with reasonable accuracy.

### ECONOMIC PERFORMANCE TEST

In order to report income or deduct an expense, economic performance must occur. In most cases, this is rather obvious. If you provide goods and services, economic performance occurs when you provide the goods or services. By the same token, if goods or services are provided to you, economic performance occurs when the goods or services are provided to you. Thus, for example, if you buy office supplies, economic performance occurs when the purchase is made and the bill is tendered. You can accrue the expense at that date even though you do not pay the bill until a later date.

If you sell gift cards to customers, do not report the income until the cards are redeemed.

**Example**

**If you sell a gift card to a customer in December 2021, and the customer gives the card to a friend who redeems it in January 2022, under the all-events test, the income from the sale of the gift card is deferred until 2022.**

If you give gift cards to customers in exchange for returns of merchandise, you can treat the card as a payment of a cash refund and a sale of a gift card, allowing you to defer the income to be received through the gift cards. This is treated as a change in accounting method for which automatic consent is provided, but you must file for a change in accounting method as explained later in this chapter.

***Advance payments.*** When a business receives advance payments, the revenue can only be deferred to the year after the year of receipt, and only if the deferral is consistent with the business's financial statement. This rule does not apply to long-term contracts and installment sale reporting explained later in this chapter. But there is a special rule explained earlier for gift cards.

***Recurring items.*** There is an exception to the economic performance test for certain recurring items (items that are repeated on a regular basis). A deduction for these items can be accrued even though economic performance has not occurred.

***Real estate taxes.*** There is a special rule for real estate taxes. An election can be made to ratably accrue real property taxes that are related to a definite period of time over that period of time.

**Example**

**You own a building in which you conduct your business. Real property taxes for the property tax year ending June 30 are $12,000. You are an accrual method taxpayer on a calendar year of reporting. You can elect to ratably accrue the taxes. If the election is made, you deduct $6,000 in the current year, the amount of taxes that relates to the period for your tax year. The balance of the taxes is deductible next year.**

Any real property taxes that would normally be deductible for the tax year that apply to periods prior to your election are deductible in the year of the election.

The election must be made for the first tax year in which real property taxes are incurred. It is made simply by attaching a statement to the return for that tax year. The return must be filed on time (including any extensions) in order for the election to be valid. Include on the statement the businesses to which the election applies and their methods of accounting, the period of time to which the taxes relate, and the computation of the real property tax deduction for the first year of the election.

Once you make this election, it continues indefinitely unless you revoke it. To revoke your election, you must obtain the consent of the IRS. However, there is an automatic procedure rule that allows you to elect or revoke an election by attaching a statement to your return. Under this method, you may assume you have IRS consent; you do not have to request it and wait for a reply.

If you have been accruing real property taxes under the general rule for accrual, you must file for a change in accounting method, which is explained later in this chapter.

You can make an election to ratably accrue real property taxes over the period to which they relate for each separate business you own.

### TWO-AND-A-HALF-MONTH RULE

If you pay salary, interest, or other expenses to an unrelated party, you can accrue the expense only if it is paid within 2½ months after the close of the tax year.

**Example**

**You declare a year-end bonus for your manager (who is not related to you under the rules discussed). You are on the calendar year. You can accrue the bonus in the year in which you declare it if you actually pay it no later than March 15.**

*Related Parties.* If expenses are paid to related parties, a special rule applies. This rule, in effect, puts an accrual taxpayer on the cash basis so that payments are not deductible until actually paid. Related parties include:

- Members of an immediate family (spouses, children, brothers and sisters of whole or half blood, grandchildren, and grandparents).
- An individual and a C corporation (other than a PSC) in which he or she owns more than 50% of the corporation's outstanding stock (based on the stock's value). Stock ownership may be *direct* or *indirect*. Direct means that the individual holds the stock in his or her name. Indirect ownership means the stock is owned by a member of the individual's immediate family (listed above) or by a corporation, partnership, estate, or trust owned in full or in part by the individual. If the individual has only a partial ownership interest, that same proportion of stock owned by the entity is treated as owned by the individual. Thus, if an individual owns 75% of stock in Corporation X and X owns 100% of the stock in Corporation Y, the individual is treated as owning 75% of the stock in Y for purposes of this accrual method limitation.
- An individual and an S corporation in which he or she owns any of the corporation's outstanding stock. The Tax Court has said that this includes employees who are participants in an S corporation's ESOP and an appellate court has agreed.
- A PSC and any owner-employee (regardless of the amount of stock ownership). Thus, if an individual owns 10% of the stock in Corporation X (a PSC), and X owns 100% of the stock in Y, the individual is treated as owning 100% of the stock in Y.
- Other categories of related parties (e.g., 2 corporations that are members of a controlled group—they have certain owners in common).

If you fall under this related party rule, you cannot deduct the expense until payment is actually made and the related party includes the payment in his or her income.

**Example**

**You have an accrual business in which your child is an employee. Your business is on the calendar year. On December 31, 2021, you declare a year-end bonus of $5,000 for your child. You may not accrue the bonus until you pay the $5,000 to your child and your child includes the payment as income. Therefore, if you write a check on January 15, 2022, for the bonus and your child cashes it that day, you can accrue the expense in 2022.**

### *Accounting Methods for Long-Term Contracts*

For businesses involved in building, constructing, installing, or manufacturing property where the work cannot be completed within one year, special accounting rules exist. These rules do not affect the amount of income or expenses to be reported—they merely dictate the timing of the income or expenses.

Generally, you must use the percentage-of-completion method to report income and expenses from these long-term contracts. Under this method, you must estimate your income and expenses while the contract is in progress and report a percentage of these items relative to the portion of the contract that has been completed. However, income and expenses are not fully accounted for until the earlier of either the completion of the job and acceptance of the work or the buyer starts to use the item and 5% or less of the total contract costs remain to be completed.

You may also have to use a *look-back method* (discussed later) to compensate for any inaccuracies in your estimates for income or expenses.

#### EXCEPTIONS FROM THE PERCENTAGE-OF-COMPLETION METHOD

Under this method you account for your income and expenses when, as the name implies, the contract has been completed. You can account for income and expenses using the completed-contract method if:

1. The contracts are small construction contracts that will be completed within 2 years and average annual gross receipts for the 3 preceding years from the start of the contract do not exceed $26 million.
2. The contracts are for the construction of homes containing 4 or fewer dwelling units and 80% or more of the estimated total costs of the contract must be for these homes plus any related land improvements.
3. The contracts are for the construction of residential apartments (80% or more of the total contract costs are attributable to these buildings).

You can account for your income and expenses using the completed-contract method if you meet either of the first 2 exceptions. If you meet the third exception, you account for your income and expenses under a special method called the percentage-of-completion/capitalized-cost method. Under this hybrid method, 70% of income and expenses are reported under the percentage-of-completion method while 30% of income and expenses are reported under the completed-contract method.

Manufacturing contracts are treated as long-term contracts only if they involve the manufacture of unique items that cannot be completed within a 12-month period. Thus, income and expenses relating to most manufacturing contracts are reported under the company's usual method of accounting.

#### LOOK-BACK METHOD

At the end of the contract period, you must look back to each year that the contract was in progress and recalculate the income using the correct contract price and costs. These revised numbers determine whether the business owes additional interest on the taxes it should have paid or it is entitled to receive interest on the taxes already paid. Interest for this purpose is hypothetical interest on the overpayment and underpayment for each of the years in issue. This interest is calculated on Form 8697, *Interest Computation Under the Look-Back Method for Completed Long-Term Contracts*.

Small business owners, however, may escape the application of the look-back method. This method is *not* required if the contract is completed within a 2-year period and the contract's gross sale price does not exceed the lesser of $1 million or 1% of the business' average annual gross receipts for the 3 years preceding the tax year in which the contract is completed. The gross receipts test used for construction contracts in general does not apply for the exception to the look-back method.

Even if the exception for small businesses cannot be met, it is still possible to avoid the look-back method and its complications. You can elect not to use the look-back method if the estimated income and expenses are within 10% of the actual income and expenses. Once this election is made, it applies to all future contracts. In order to make the election, you must make the recalculations of the actual income and expenses for the prior years to see if the 10% threshold has been satisfied.

## *Other Accounting Methods*

The cash and accrual methods of accounting are the most commonly used methods. There are, however, other accounting methods.

### INSTALLMENT METHOD ACCOUNTING

If you sell property and receive payments over time, you generally can account for your gain on the *installment method*, whether you use the cash or accrual method for reporting your other income and expenses. More specifically, the installment method applies if one or more payments are received after the year of the sale. *Gain* is reported when payments are received. The capital gain rate applicable to the gain on the installment received in the current year is the rate to which the taxpayer is now subject. For example, say a sole proprietor makes an installment sale in 2015, with a payment term of 10 years. In 2021, the sole proprietor has taxable income that makes her capital gain rate 20%. This is the rate imposed on the gain from the installment received in 2021, even though this taxpayer had a 15% capital gain tax rate in the year of the sale. This method can be used by taxpayers who report other income and expenses on the cash or accrual method.

**Example**

**You sell business property and figure your gain to be $10,000. Under the terms of sale you receive $5,000 in 2021, the year of sale, and $5,000 in 2022. You report one-half of your gain, or $5,000, in 2021 and the other half of your gain, $5,000, in 2022.**

However, if the sale involves depreciable property, the recapture rules trigger the immediate reporting of this portion of the gain—without regard to payments received. Recapture rules are discussed in Chapter 6.

The installment method applies only to gains on certain sales; it generally cannot be used for inventory sales even though payment is received over time. The installment method does not apply to losses. It cannot be used by dealers in personal property or for real estate held for resale to customers.

You can elect *not* to report on the installment basis and instead report all of the gain in the year of sale. The election is made simply by reporting all of the gain on the appropriate tax form or schedule. Once made, however, this election is generally irrevocable. The election out of installment reporting may make sense, for example, if an owner is subject to the 15% capital gains rate in the year of the installment sale but expects to be a high-income taxpayer subject to the 20% capital gains rate in one or more of the years in which installment payments will be received. Of course, potential tax law changes occurring after the year of an installment sale complicates the election out decision.

#### MARK-TO-MARKET ACCOUNTING

Traders in securities (often referred to as "day traders") can use a special accounting method that enables them to report paper transactions rather than waiting for actualized gains and losses, and losses no longer are limited to the extent of capital gains and up to $3,000 of ordinary income. Under mark-to-market accounting, gains and losses are reported on Form 4797 (rather than on Schedule D). These include completed trades throughout the year as well as paper gains and losses in securities held at the end of the year (these are treated as if they had been sold on December 31).

A trader is someone who seeks to profit from daily market swings rather than long-term appreciation, interest, or dividends. The trader's activities must be substantial and carried on with continuity and regularity.

Make the mark-to-market election by filing a statement attached to your return for the prior year, stating you are making the election under Code Sec. 475(f) and the year for which it is effective. For example, if you want the election to start in 2022, you must attach this statement to your 2021 income tax return. Those who are not required to file a return for 2021 should place such statement in their books and records no later than March 15, 2022, and then attach a copy to the 2022 return. The election is treated as a change in accounting method.

A revocation in order to return to the realization method (reporting gains and losses when realized) may be made using the automatic change in accounting method, which merely requires a notification of revocation statement to be attached to the tax return (or the filing extension request) for the year preceding the year of the change. Details about what the notification statement must include are in Revenue Procedure 2015–14.

#### OTHER ACCOUNTING METHODS

These include, for example: Special Accounting for Multi-Year Service Warranty Contracts and Special Rules for Farmers.

### *Accounting for Discounts*

#### DISCOUNTS YOU RECEIVE

When vendors or other sellers give you cash discounts for prompt payment, there are two ways to account for this discount, regardless of your method of accounting. They are:

1. Deduct the discount as a purchase in figuring the cost of goods sold.
2. Credit the discount to a special discount income account you set up in your records. Any balance in this account at the end of the year is reported as other income on your return.

Trade discounts are not reflected on your books or tax returns. These discounts are reductions from list price or catalog prices for merchandise you purchase. Once you make the choice, you must continue to use it in future years to account for all cash discounts.

#### DISCOUNTS YOU GIVE

When you reduce the price of your goods and services, you cannot deduct the price reduction. Your gross receipts are reduced accordingly, so you simply report less income.

## Uniform Capitalization Rules

Regardless of your method of accounting, special tax rules limit your ability to claim a current deduction for certain expenses. These are called the *uniform capitalization rules*, referred to as the UNICAP rules for short. The uniform capitalization rules are a form of accounting method that operates in coordination with the accrual method, but overrides it. In essence, these rules require you to add to the cost of property certain expenses—instead of currently deducting them. The cost of these expenses, in effect, are recovered through depreciation or amortization, or as part of the costs of goods sold when you use, sell, or otherwise dispose of the property. The uniform capitalization rules are complex. Important things to recognize are whether you may be subject to them and that expenses discussed throughout this book may not be currently deductible because of the application of the uniform capitalization rules.

### *Capitalization Required*

Unless one of the exceptions is applicable, you must use the uniform capitalization rules and add certain expenses to the basis of property if you:

- Produce real property or tangible personal property for use in your business or for sale to customers (producers), or
- Acquire property for resale (resellers).

#### EXCEPTIONS TO THE UNICAP RULES

There are many exceptions to the uniform capitalization rules. Small businesses may be able to escape application of the uniform capitalization rules by relying on one of these exceptions.

- You do not have to capitalize costs if the property you produce is for your personal or non-business use.
- You do not have to capitalize costs if you meet the gross receipts test discussed earlier in this chapter. Again, in applying this test, you must aggregate gross receipts from all businesses you own. The gross receipts of a C corporation partner are included in the gross receipts of a partnership if the aggregation rules apply to the C corporation partner and the partnership.
- Creative expenses incurred by freelance authors, photographers, and artists are not subject to the uniform capitalization rules. According to the IRS, this exception does not apply to a musician's demo tape or other sound recording.
- There is a de minimis exception for certain producers who use a simplified method and whose total indirect costs are $200,000 or less.
- There are other exceptions not detailed here, for certain farming businesses and other types of businesses.

#### CAPITALIZED COSTS

If you are subject to the uniform capitalization rules, you capitalize all direct costs of your production or resale activities. Direct costs for producers include direct material costs and direct labor costs. Direct costs for resellers mean acquisition costs.

You also capitalize a portion of indirect costs. Indirect costs for producers and resellers include costs of purchasing, handling, and storage, as well as taxes, interest, rent, insurance, utilities, repairs, engineering and design costs, quality control, tools and equipment, licensing, and more.

## Change in Accounting Method

Law changes or new business practices may warrant a change in accounting method. If you want to change your method of accounting (for example, from the accrual method to the cash method), you must file Form 3115, *Application for Change in Accounting Method (Rev. Dec. 2018)*, during the year for which the change is to be effective. (Instructions on how and where to file this form are included in instructions to the form.) Some changes are automatic—just by filing you are ensured that your change is recognized; other changes require the consent of the IRS.

Periodically, the IRS modifies its list of automatic changes (see Revenue Procedure 2019–43 for the latest list of automatic changes). These include changing to a required accounting method from an incorrect one, switching to the cash method by an eligible small business, implementing depreciation changes pursuant to a cost segregation study, changing the treatment of repair and maintenance costs from capitalized to currently deductible, deducting the cost of "smallwares" (such as dishes and glassware) in the year they are first put to use by restaurants, and applying the de minimis rule for certain repairs. Form 3115 cannot be filed electronically; it must be submitted on paper. However, the IRS permitted the use of a digital signature on the form through December 31, 2021. Whether this continues to be permissible remains to be seen; check the Supplement for any update.

# CHAPTER 3

# Recordkeeping for Business Income and Deductions


General Recordkeeping 51
Specific Substantiation Requirements for Certain Expenses 54
Records for Depreciation, Basis, Carryovers, and Prepaid Expenses 56
How Long You Should Maintain Records 59


Recordkeeping is a tiresome and time-consuming task. Still, you have little choice but to do it. Records show whether your business is producing a profit or a loss, enabling you to change your business strategies to optimize results. The information in your records enables you to prepare financial statements, such as profit and loss statements and balance sheets, which may be required by your lenders or investors. From a tax perspective, you are required to maintain books and records for a business. You need records to report all you income correctly, including determining your gain or loss when you sell property. And as a general rule, you must be able to back up your deductions with certain clear proof, such as receipts, canceled checks, and other documentation. If you do not have this proof, your deductions may be disallowed or force you to litigate in order to win your position (a costly and time-consuming activity). Certain deductions require specific evidence. Other deductions are based on more general means of proof.

For further information on recordkeeping, see IRS Publication 334, *Tax Guide for Small Business (for Individuals Who File Schedule C)*; IRS Publication 552, *Recordkeeping for Individuals*; and IRS Publication 583, *Starting a Business and Keeping Records*.

## General Recordkeeping

The tax law does not require you to maintain books and records in any particular way. It does, however, require you to keep an accurate and complete set of books for each business you operate. Statistics show that this can be an awesome task.

According to the IRS, it takes a mere 3 hours and 36 minutes for recordkeeping to prepare a Schedule C for a sole proprietor. But business owners know that recordkeeping is a year-round activity that consumes many hours and effectively costs a significant sum.

Set up your books when you begin your business. Your books are based on your choice of tax year and accounting method, as explained in Chapter 2. In the past, when you kept your books in paper ledgers, you needed to choose a bookkeeping method—single-entry or double-entry. If you were a service business, single-entry bookkeeping may have been sufficient. Today, with software, online accounting solutions, and mobile apps, you don't need to know about bookkeeping methods; you merely input income and expense items, and the program does the rest.

Your books should be set up with various accounts in order to group your income and expenses. The broad categories of accounts include income, expenses, assets, liabilities, and equity (or net worth). Within these accounts you can keep various subaccounts. For example, in an account called Expenses you may have subaccounts for advertising, bad debts, interest expense, taxes, rents, repairs, and more. In fact, your subaccounts should reflect the various income and deduction topics discussed throughout this book.

***Books for multiple businesses.*** Generally, you must maintain separate books and records for each business you own. Regulations specify that "no trade or business will be considered separate and distinct unless a complete and separable set of books and records are kept." In other words, you may use one set of books as long as the income and expenses of each are separable. To clarify, separable does not mean separate or multiple sets of books, merely distinct entries to track the income and expenses of each business.

If a business conducts multiple activities, one or more of which is a specified service trade or business (SSTB) and one or more of which is a non-specified SSTB (SSTB is explained in Chapter 21), you may keep one set of books for the activities as long as they are a "complete and *separable* set of books and records."

**Example**

**A veterinary practice treats animals. It also manufactures and sells dog food. Each unit has separate employees. The veterinary practice is an SSTB; the dog food sales unit is a non-SSTB. Here separate books can be maintained for each business or one set of books for both businesses as long as income and expenses can be separated to determine the taxable income of each business.**

### *Technology for Recordkeeping*

Most businesses today use computers, tablets, and smartphones to maintain books and records rather than having bookkeepers make handwritten entries. Computer-generated records save time—an important commodity for the small business owner—and generally are more accurate than handwritten entries.

The IRS accepts computer-generated records if they are legible and provide all the necessary information. You are required to keep a description of the computerized portion of your accounting system. You must keep this documentation as long as you keep the records themselves. Your document should show:

- Applications being performed
- Procedures used in each application

- Controls used to ensure accurate and reliable processing
- Controls used to prevent the unauthorized addition, alteration, or deletion of retained records

Use recordkeeping software that facilitates recordkeeping both for tax purposes as well as for financial matters. Using software and cloud-based solutions such as Intuit's Quickbooks Online, Online Simple Start, Quickbooks Pro, and QuickBooks Self-Employed; Sage 50cloud and other Sage products; FreshBooks; GoDaddy; Sunrise; Xero; Wave; or Zoho Books enables you to forward data to your tax professional as well as transfer information into tax return preparation programs at tax time, saving you both time and money. Many accounting options integrate seamlessly with your sales activities, eliminating the need to input data more than once. For example, Shopify is integrated with QuickBooks and Xero, Avalara's sales tax product is integrated with QuickBooks, and Bigcommerce has also partnered with QuickBooks. There are also stand-alone apps and apps accompanying accounting solutions to facilitate mobile accounting (including the ability to invoice and process payments on the go). For example, Botkeeper is an app that mines your bank account and credit card to automate your bookkeeping. Similar options are Bench, Pilot, and Scalefactor; prices vary considerably. As your business grows (and the number of users for your accounting solution exceeds your current licensing limit), you will likely move to more a sophisticated accounting product that can better accommodate your needs.

Your books alone do not fully substantiate deductions; you need supporting evidence. This evidence includes sales slips, invoices, canceled checks, paid bills, time sheets for part-time help, duplicate deposit slips, brokerage statements on stock purchases and sales, and other documents that help to explain a particular entry in your books. Certain deductions—travel expenses and charitable contributions—require specific types of supporting evidence, as explained later in this chapter. The IRS considers your own memoranda or sketchy records to be inadequate when claiming deductions. However, you can upgrade these records by backing them up with a photo on your smartphone. For example, if you buy a business publication at the newsstand and cannot obtain a paper receipt, consider taking a photo (which is timestamped) to accompany your own memoranda. Keep these records and documentation in an orderly fashion. Use files or other storage facilities to retain receipts and other evidence.

Keep your files in a safe place. Data breaches can lead to identity theft and the need for data reconstruction, both of which are very costly problems. If you use desktop solutions, be sure to back up files regularly (online solutions do not require backup because data is automatically stored in the cloud). Consider using a service that enables you to automate your backup (e.g., every day at 2 a.m.). For paper files, store them in a fireproof safe or use a service, such as Neat, Receipts by Wave, and Shoeboxed, that will sort and store receipts for you. If you lose files with receipts because they were not stored safely, you may lose deductions and face penalties as well. If you "lose" records before or during an audit, you may be charged with a hefty negligence or accuracy-related penalty. If, despite your best efforts, files and records that are not stored in the cloud are lost or destroyed by a casualty (such as a fire, storm, earthquake, or flood), you may be permitted to reconstruct records if you can prove those records existed before the casualty. Of course, reconstruction takes considerable time, and it is probably impossible to reconstruct all of your expenses. Therefore, take special care to safeguard your records.

### *Electronic Records*

Storage of receipts and other records in paper form makes retrieval of wanted items difficult. This is especially so for large companies, but it can be problematic for smaller businesses as well.

You can use an electronic storage system for preparing or keeping records. An electronic system includes an **electronic imaging system** and transfers to electronic storage media.

---

***Electronic imaging system*** **Any system for preparing or keeping records either by electronic imaging or by transfer to an electronic storage media.**

---

If an electronic imaging system is used, it must ensure accurate and complete transfer of the hard copy or the computerized books and records. It must include:

- Reasonable controls to ensure the integrity, accuracy, and reliability of the system
- Reasonable controls to prevent and detect the unauthorized creation of, addition to, alteration of, deletion of, or deterioration of records
- An inspection and quality assurance program evidenced by regular evaluations of the electronic storage system
- A retrieval system that includes an indexing system
- The ability to reproduce legible hard copies of electronically stored books and records

Once an electronic storage system has been tested to make sure that hard copies are being reproduced in compliance with the requirements above, the original hard copy books and records can be destroyed.

## Specific Substantiation Requirements for Certain Expenses

The law requires businesses to maintain books and records, and to provide special substantiation for certain deductions. There is a negligence penalty that may be imposed for 20% of an underpayment resulting from the failure to keep adequate books and records or to substantiate items properly.

### *Travel Expenses*

The tax law imposes special substantiation requirements for claiming travel expenses. If you fail to satisfy these requirements, your deduction for these business expenses may be disallowed. There are 2 types of records you need in order to claim deductions for your travel expenses:

- *Written* substantiation in a diary, log book, or other notation system containing certain specific information, and
- *Documentary evidence* (receipts, canceled checks, or bills) to prove the amount of the expense.

There are a number of elements to substantiate for each business expense. In general, to substantiate each item you must show the amount, time, place, and business purpose for the travel expense or the business relationship with the person or persons you provide gifts to and, in some cases, a description of the item. The exact substantiation requirements depend on the type of business expense.

In all cases, you are strongly advised to use a written or electronic daily log or diary to record expenses. As you will see, you need written proof of your expenses (or an electronic log that can be turned into written proof), and this proof must be recorded "contemporaneously" with the expenses—generally meaning at the time you incur the expense or as soon as is practical thereafter to record it. Use a separate credit card for business expenses. The monthly statement from the credit card company is also useful in substantiating these expenses.

### TRAVEL

You must show the amount of each separate expense for travel, lodging, meals, and incidental expenses. You can total these items in any reasonable category. For example, you can simply keep track of meals in a category called Daily Meals. You must also note the dates you left for the trip and returned, as well as the days spent on the trip for business purposes. You must list the name of the city or other designation of the place of the travel, along with the reason for the trip or the business benefit gained or expected to be gained from it.

While this may sound like a great deal of recordkeeping, as a practical matter, hotel receipts may provide you with much of the information necessary. For example, a hotel receipt typically shows the dates you arrived and departed, the name and location of the hotel, and separate charges for lodging, meals, telephone calls, and other items. A sample log for travel expenses is in Chapter 8.

### GIFTS

Show the cost of the gift, the date it was given, and a description of the gift. Also show the business reason for the gift or the business benefit gained or expected to be gained from providing it. Include the name of the person receiving the gift, his or her occupation or other identifying information, and his or her business relationship to you.

A canceled check, along with a bill, generally establishes the cost of a business item. However, the check alone does not prove a business expense without other evidence of its business purpose.

If you do not have adequate records and your return is questioned, you may still be able to deduct an item if you can prove by your own statement or other supporting evidence an element of substantiation. Where receipts have been destroyed, you may be able to reconstruct your expenses. You must, of course, show that you actually maintained records and how the records were destroyed (for example, in a fire, storm, or flood). The IRS may require additional information to prove the accuracy or reliability of the information contained in your records.

### VEHICLE EXPENSES

Show the number of miles driven for business purposes (starting and ending odometer readings), the destination, the purpose of the trip, and the name of the party visited (if relevant). Simply jot down the odometer reading on January 1 to start a good recordkeeping habit. Or use an app that simplifies recordkeeping for your vehicle mileage. Include notations of expenses for gas, oil, parking, tolls, and other expenses. Recordkeeping shortcuts and tips, and a sample log for keeping track of vehicle expenses, can be found in Chapter 9.

### RECORDKEEPING RELIEF

You do not need receipts, canceled checks, bills, or other proof of the cost of a travel expense in the following situations:

- You use a standard rate (such as a standard mileage rate for car use or a per diem rate for meals and lodging). Per diem rates are explained in Chapter 8; the standard mileage rate is explained in Chapter 9.

- The expense is less than $75 (such as a light rail fare from your hotel to a customer's facility). However, you cannot use this exception for lodging (you must have documentary evidence for lodging regardless of amount).
- You have a transportation expense (such as a taxi fare) for which a receipt is not readily available.

#### THE COHAN RULE

While the IRS says that deductions will be disallowed if you do not have adequate substantiation, you may be able to rely on a special rule developed by the courts. The *Cohan rule*, named after noted songwriter/showman George M. Cohan, is based on approximation. A court may agree to approximate your expenses if your records are inadequate to establish actual expenses and you have some way to show your approximate expenses. A court cannot be compelled to use the Cohan rule; it must be persuaded to do so because of special circumstances. And the Tax Court has repeatedly rejected "guestimates" for expenses where there is no basis on which to compute them. The Cohan rule is only a last resort for claiming unsubstantiated travel expenses. The Cohan rule has been used for some expenses other than travel expenses (e.g., research expenses, licensing fees, and building sign replacements).

### *Charitable Contributions*

Cash contributions of any amount must be substantiated by a written acknowledgment from the charity, a bank statement, or other permissible method (which depends on the amount of the donation). Presumably, a credit card statement showing the date of a contribution and the amount is also acceptable proof. Cash contributions of $250 or more require a written acknowledgment from the charity (the bank or credit card statement is not sufficient).

If a property donation is valued at over $5,000, you may also be required to obtain an appraisal by a certified appraiser and keep a record of this appraisal.

## Records for Depreciation, Basis, Carryovers, and Prepaid Expenses

For some tax items you must keep a running account, because deductions will be claimed not only in the current year but also in years to come.

### *Depreciation*

*Depreciation* allows you to recover the cost of property over the life of that property by deducting a portion of the cost each year. In order to claim your annual deductions, you must keep certain records:

- Costs and other information necessary to calculate your depreciation
- Capital improvements to depreciable assets
- Depreciation deductions already claimed
- Adjustments to basis as a result of depreciation deductions

This information not only is necessary for depreciation purposes but will also be needed to calculate gain or loss and any depreciation recapture on the sale or other disposition of a depreciable asset. For full details on claiming depreciation, see Chapter 14.

The same recordkeeping rules apply not only to depreciation but also to amortization and depletion deductions.

### Basis

*Basis* is the cost of property or some other value assigned to property. Basis is used for several purposes: It is the amount on which depreciation deductions are based, as well as the amount used to determine gain or loss on the sale or other disposition of property. And it is a factor in figuring the qualified business income deduction (Chapter 21).

The basis of property can vary from its basis upon acquisition. Some items increase basis; others decrease it. Keep track of changes in basis. These can result from:

- Depreciation deductions or first-year expensing
- Casualty deductions relating to the property
- Certain tax credits
- Capitalized costs, such as capital improvements. One court has said that proof of capital improvements to increase basis includes such items as written records, canceled checks, construction permits, and before-and-after pictures.

One of the most important records that must be kept for shareholders and partners is their basis in their entities, which is explained in Chapter 4.

### Carryovers

A number of deductions may be limited in a current year, but you may be able to carry over any unused portion to other years. In order to take advantage of carryover opportunities, you must keep records of deductions you have already taken and the years in which they were taken. What is more, you must maintain relevant records for the carryover periods. The following list details the types of carryovers for which records should be maintained and limits on the carryover period, if any:

- *At-risk losses.* Losses disallowed because of the application of the at-risk rules (see Chapter 4) can be carried over indefinitely.
- *Capital losses.* There is no limit on the carryover period for individuals. There is a 5-year limit on carryover losses for C corporations.
- *Charitable contributions.* Individuals who cannot fully use current charitable contributions because of adjusted gross income limits can carry over the unused deductions for a period of 5 years. C corporations that cannot fully use current charitable contributions because of the taxable income limit can carry over the unused deductions for a period of 5 years. If the deductions cannot be used within that 5-year period (there is insufficient taxable income to offset the deduction in the carryover years), the deductions are lost forever.
- *Farm losses.* Farm losses barred because of a limitation (explained in Chapter 4) that has been suspended for 2018 through 2025 can still be carried forward and used starting in 2026.
- *Home office deductions.* Individuals who maintain an office in their home and whose actual home office deductions are limited in the current year by gross income earned in the home office can carry forward unused deductions indefinitely. The unused deductions can be used in a future year if there is gross income from the home office activity to offset it. (There is no carryover if the simplified method is used to figure the home office deduction as explained in Chapter 18.)

- *Interest expense.* Businesses with average annual gross receipts over $26 million for the 3 prior years are subject to the 50% interest limitation (explained in Chapter 13), although farming and real estate businesses may elect to be exempt. Any disallowed interest because of this limit can be carried forward and treated as business interest in the succeeding taxable year.
- *Investment interest.* Individuals (including partners, LLC members, and S corporation shareholders) may be limited in their current deduction for investment interest by the amount of their net investment income. Excess investment interest can be carried forward indefinitely. There is no limitation on corporations, so there is no carryover.
- *Net operating losses.* When operating losses cannot be used in full in the current year, they may be applied against income in certain other years. NOLs arising in 2021 cannot be carried back (other than a 2-year carryback for farming businesses), but can be carried forward indefinitely. NOLs arising in 2018, 2019, and 2020 had a 5-year carryback; unused amounts can be carried forward indefinitely. NOLs arising before 2018 had a 2-year carryback and a 20-year carryforward. Good recordkeeping is necessary to track these carrybacks and apply them in the correct order (see Chapter 4).
- *Passive activity losses.* Losses disallowed because of the application of the passive activity loss rules (*suspended losses*) can be carried forward indefinitely. The same rules apply to credits from passive activities.
- *Cash basis and prepayment.* Depreciation and carryovers are not the only tax items that may run beyond the current tax year. If you are on the cash basis and prepay certain expenses, you may not be allowed a current deduction for your outlays. You may be required to deduct the expenses ratably over the period of time to which they relate. Some examples of commonly prepaid expenses that may have to be deducted ratably include:

  *Insurance premiums.* If your insurance premiums cover a period of more than 12 months, you may be required to deduct them over the term covered by the policy.

  *Prepaid interest.* If you pay points or other amounts treated as prepaid interest to obtain financing to acquire real estate for your business, you deduct the prepaid interest ratably over the term of the loan. If you dispose of the property or refinance the loan before the end of the term, you can then deduct any unused portion of the prepaid interest in that final year.

  *Rents.* If you prepay rents for a period of more than 12 months, you may be required to deduct the rents over the term of the lease.

  *Subscriptions.* If you pay for subscriptions running more than 12 months, you generally have to deduct the cost over the term of the subscriptions. For example, if you pay in full the cost of a 3-year subscription to a business journal, you generally must deduct the cost over the same 3-year period.

You need to keep a running record of Section 1231 losses—losses on the sale of certain business assets. This is because of a special recapture rule that applies to net ordinary losses from Section 1231 property. A net Section 1231 gain is treated as ordinary income to the extent it does not exceed nonrecaptured net Section 1231 losses taken in prior years. *Nonrecaptured losses* are the total of net Section 1231 losses for the 5 most recent years that have not yet been applied (recaptured) against any net Section 1231 gains in those same years. In order to determine this recapture, you must retain information on Section 1231 gains and losses. Section 1231 losses are explained in more detail in Chapter 6.

You also need to keep track of tax credits that are not completely used in the current year. Tax credits that are part of the general business credit (such as the work opportunity credit, research credit, and the disabled access credit) are subject to a carryback and carryforward period depending on the year in which the excess credits result. Excess credits are carried back one year and forward for up to 20 years. No election can be made to forgo this carryback period.

If you own a pass-through entity that has negative qualified business income (QBI) for the year, you must also keep track of this information (the QBI deduction is explained in Chapter 21). While it does not impact your business income, it affects your QBI deduction going forward. The negative QBI is carried forward and treated as negative QBI from a separate business for purposes of determining the QBI component in the next taxable year (i.e., it is an offset to positive QBI in the next taxable year).

## How Long You Should Maintain Records

Your books and records must be available at all times for inspection by the IRS. You should keep these books and records at least until the time when the IRS's ability to question your deductions runs out. This time period is called the *statute of limitations*. In general, the statute of limitations is either 3 years after the due date of your return or 2 years after the date the tax was paid—whichever is later. Some records must be kept even longer. You need to keep records to support the basis in property owned by the business. You also need to keep records for depreciation and carryovers, as discussed earlier.

### *Tax Returns*

Keep copies of tax returns to help you prepare future returns, as well as to help you if your return is questioned by the IRS. While you can obtain old returns from the IRS, this entails unnecessary time and expense. Although you may only need information on an old return for 3 additional years (or 6 years if you omit more than 25% of your gross income from your return), it is a good idea to keep old tax returns indefinitely. If the IRS claims you never filed a return, it has an unlimited number of years in which to audit you. But if you have your old return along with proof that you filed it (for example, a certified receipt or an acknowledgment of efiling from the IRS), the IRS has only 3 years, in most cases, to start an audit.

Keep a record of the basis of property used in your business for as long as you own the property, plus the statute of limitations on filing the return for the year in which property is sold or otherwise disposed of.

**Example**

**If in 2021 you buy equipment that you will sell in 2022, keep records on the basis of the property at least until 2026 (3 years from the due date of the return for the year in which the property was sold).**

### *Employer Records*

If you have employees, special recordkeeping rules apply. For tax purposes, you are required to keep records on employment taxes for at least 4 years after the due date of the return or after the tax is paid, whichever is later. Keep copies of all returns you have filed and the dates and amount of tax deposits you have made. Your records should also show your employer identification number

(EIN). Every business type (sole proprietorship, partnership, and corporation) must have one if wages are paid (see Chapter 26).

You may also need to retain certain employee records for purposes other than taxes. For example, OSHA requires an employer to keep certain employee medical records for at least the duration of employment plus 30 years.

**NOTE**

**The IRS is not the only government agency to require record retention related to employees. Be sure to check on recordkeeping requirements of the Equal Employment Opportunity Commission (EEOC), the Occupational Safety and Health Administration (OSHA), as well as other federal and state agencies.**

### *Income Tax Withholding*

You must keep records of each employee's name, address, and Social Security number, the amount of each wage payment, the amount of each payment subject to income tax withholding, and the amount of income tax withheld. You must also keep copies of all employees' withholding certificates (Form W-4).

### *Other Employment Taxes*

Similar records must be kept for each employee for Social Security and Medicare taxes, as well as for federal unemployment taxes (FUTA).

### *Other Tax Records*

Certain documents should be retained indefinitely. These include IRS letters and private rulings you've obtained. For corporations, retain all corporation resolutions related to taxes and other matters. And, of course, retain all accounting records, annual financial statements, and audit reports forever.

## *How to Dispose of Tax Records*

Gone are the days when you could simply toss your old files in the garbage. Today, because of the potential for identity theft affecting both individuals and businesses, proper disposal is essential. For tax records containing Social Security numbers, bank accounts (the business's or employees' accounts if paychecks use direct deposit) or credit card information, be sure to follow federal and state laws regarding disposal. Shredding documents on paper or CDs and DVDs is a good way to prevent unwanted eyes from viewing confidential information. Be sure to wipe tax and other confidential information off computers, tablets, and smartphones being disposed of. Physically destroy thumb drives containing tax records by smashing them or submerging them in water.

PART 2

# Business Income and Losses

# CHAPTER 4

# Income or Loss from Business Operations


| | | | |
|---|---|---|---|
| Business Income | 64 | State Income Taxes on Business Income | 76 |
| Income for Service Businesses | 65 | Noncorporate Excess Business Losses | 76 |
| Income from the Sale of Goods | 66 | Net Operating Losses | 77 |
| Income from Farming | 68 | Other Limitations on Business Losses | 80 |
| Income from Commercial Fishing | 70 | Income Earned Abroad | 89 |
| Income from Rentals | 71 | | |
| Income from Government Programs | 71 | | |
| Investment-Type Income | 72 | | |
| Miscellaneous Business Income | 74 | | |


The fees you earn for your services or the receipts you collect from the sale of goods are the bread-and-butter income of your business. Hopefully, your pricing policies are realistic and you have a strong customer or client base so that you can make a profit.

Even if sales are healthy, expenses can outrun receipts, resulting in a loss for the business. You will not know whether you have a net income or loss until all of the expenses discussed throughout this book have been taken into account. Income and loss for accounting purposes (referred to as "book income"), which reflects the actual money in and out of the business, may not be the same as income and loss for tax purposes. The reason: Some income may be treated as tax free or tax deferred, so it is not counted currently, while some expenses may not be fully or even partially deductible. For example, the business pays a $1,000 governmental fine, which reduces its profits for accounting purposes by $1,000; for tax purposes, the fine is not deductible (see Chapter 22), so it cannot be used to offset income on a tax return. For tax purposes, if there is a net loss, then limitations may come into play on when and the extent to which business losses can be deducted.

The 20% qualified business income (QBI) deduction isn't a business deduction; it's a personal one. This write-off is explained in Chapter 21.

It is now harder for businesses to hide income (not report it) because of reporting requirements for transactions made on credit and debit cards. The processors must report to the IRS and to merchants the annual transactions, although there is an exception for small merchants (see Appendix A).

Special rules apply to sideline businesses that are considered to be hobbies, and in 2018 through 2025, no losses from these activities can be deducted; hobby activities are discussed in Chapter 27.

For further information about business income and losses, see IRS Publication 225, *Farmer's Tax Guide*; IRS Publication 334, *Tax Guide for Small Business*; IRS Publication 536, *Net Operating Losses—Individuals, Trusts & Estates*; IRS Publication 541, *Partnerships*; and IRS Publication 542, *Corporations*. A further discussion of the hobby loss rules may be found in IRS Publication 535, *Business Expenses*. For information on the at-risk rules and passive activity loss limitations, see IRS Publication 925, *Passive Activity and At-Risk Rules*.

## Business Income

Whether you work full-time or part-time, income received for your business activity is part of your business income. How you report it depends on your accounting method (explained in Chapter 2).

Where you report it depends on how your business is organized. For example, sole proprietors report income on Schedule C or on Schedule F if the business is farming. Partnerships and LLCs (in most cases) report income on Form 1065, S corporations use Form 1120-S, and C corporations report income on Form 1120. Where to report business income is explained at the end of this chapter.

### *Payment Methods*

Most business transactions are in cash. For tax purposes the term *cash* includes coins and currency of the U.S. and foreign countries, checks, credit card charges, PayPal and other electronic payments, and smart cards. However, in some cases, payments may take a different form.

**CAUTION**

**Bartering does not avoid sales taxes. For example, if you barter your goods to dispose of excess inventory, be sure to follow the same sales tax rules that you would if you had been paid in cash. See Chapter 29.**

#### PAYMENTS IN KIND

If you exchange your goods or services for property, you must include the fair market value of the property you received in income. While bartering is a good cash flow strategy, it does not avoid the requirement to report income. This is true whether you barter directly—one-on-one—or receive property through a barter exchange that gives you credit for the goods or services you provide. Bartering through a barter exchange is reported to the IRS on Form 1099-B, *Proceeds from Broker and Barter Exchange Transactions*.

#### PAYMENTS IN CRYPTOCURRENCY

There are about 3,000 virtual or digital currencies being traded today. According to a 2020 survey by HBS, 36% of small and mid-sized businesses in the U.S. accept payment in Bitcoin or other cryptocurrency. This percentage is likely to increase with PayPal now facilitating payments in certain cryptocurrency to merchants.

If you are paid in a digital currency, it's treated like property, not currency. It is income when received based on the fair market value of the Bitcoin or other digital currency, which may be determined by an exchange on which it is traded. The IRS warns that because transactions in virtual currencies can be difficult to trace and have an inherently pseudo-anonymous aspect, there is temptation to not report this income, but severe penalties can result if the IRS catches the omissions. And there are proposals for third-party reporting on information returns; see the Supplement for any update.

#### PAYMENTS IN SERVICES

If you exchange your goods or services for someone else's services, you are also taxed on the value of the services you receive. If services are exchanged for services, you both can agree to the value of the services you report as income.

**Example**

**You are a house painter who paints the offices of an attorney who handles a legal matter for you in exchange for your work. You must include the value of the attorney's services in your income. You may value this according to what the attorney would have charged you if you had paid cash for the work. Or you can both agree to the value of the services, assuming that value is reasonable.**

#### CONSIGNMENTS

If items owned by others are consigned to you for sale, do not include these items in your inventory. Instead, report income from any commissions or profits you are entitled to upon sale.

If you consign your goods to others, do not report this arrangement as a sale. You report income from the sale of consigned goods when they are sold by the consignee. Do not remove the items from your inventory until there is a sale by the consignee.

#### KICKBACKS

Amounts you receive as kickbacks are included in income. However, do not include them as a separate income item if you properly treat these amounts as a reduction to the cost of goods sold, a capital expenditure, or an expense item.

#### LOANS

If you obtain business loans, do not include the proceeds in income. They are funds that must be repaid according to the terms of the loan agreement unless there is loan forgiveness (e.g., loan forgiveness under the Paycheck Protection Program discussed later in this chapter).

## Income for Service Businesses

If your main business activity is providing services to customers, clients, or patients, you are in a service business. As such, reporting business income is generally a simple matter. You report as income all of your revenues from performing services according to your method of accounting. Since most service businesses are on the cash basis, income usually is reported when fees are collected.

### *1099 Income*

If you are an independent contractor, your clients or customers who are in business are required to report income paid to you on Form 1099-NEC, *Nonemployee Compensation*. This informs the IRS of income you have received. Income is required to be reported on Form 1099-NEC if annual payments are at least $600, but you are required to report on your tax return *all* income you receive (even if no form has been issued). Form 1099-NEC must also be given by businesses to incorporated attorneys and law firms for payments of $600 or more. Certain other types of business income may be reported on Form 1099-MISC. These include (but are not limited to):

- Rents
- Royalties
- Fish boat proceeds
- Prizes won by the business

**Example**

**An author receives royalties on a book of $2,749, which is reported on Form 1099-MISC. Assuming the author is a sole proprietor, the royalty income is reported on Schedule C.**

### *Advances and Prepayments*

If you receive income for services to be performed in the future, you usually report the income if you have free and unrestricted use of the money.

However, if you use the accrual method, the revenue can only be deferred to the year after the year of receipt, and only if the deferral is consistent with the business's financial statement (see Chapter 2). This rule does not apply to long-term contracts and installment sale reporting, explained later in this chapter. But there is a special rule for gift cards.

## Income from the Sale of Goods

Reporting income from the sale of goods involves a 2-step process. First you must figure your *gross receipts*—amounts received from sales (determined by your method of accounting). Then you must subtract from gross receipts your **cost of goods sold.** This is not a separate deduction, but an adjustment to what you report as income from sales.

***Cost of goods sold*** **The cost of buying raw materials and producing finished goods. Essentially, it is the cost of buying inventory or manufacturing inventory.**

### *Cost of Goods Sold*

Cost of goods sold (COGS) is determined each year by adjusting beginning inventory for changes made during the year. Schedule C of Form 1040 or 1040-SR (used by sole proprietors) has a separate portion of the schedule (Part III) for figuring the cost of goods sold. For Forms 1065, 1120, and 1120-S, the cost of goods sold is figured on Form 1025-A (rather than on a schedule on the return).

Start with your opening inventory, which is usually the same as the closing inventory from the previous year. For merchants, this is the cost of merchandise on hand at the beginning of the year that is for sale to customers. For manufacturers, opening inventory includes the total cost of raw materials, work in process, finished goods, and materials and supplies used in manufacturing those goods.

Increase opening inventory for purchases during the year (less any items withdrawn for your personal use). For manufacturers, purchases include the cost of all raw materials or parts purchased for manufacture into a finished product. Use the prices you pay after any trade discounts you receive.

Subtract all returns and allowances you make during the year. Also, if you are a manufacturer, subtract labor costs properly allocable to the cost of goods sold, which includes both the direct and indirect labor used in fabricating the raw material into a finished, saleable product. Also, if you are a manufacturer, subtract materials and supplies, such as hardware and chemicals, used in manufacturing goods charged to cost of goods sold, as well as other costs (e.g., containers; freight-in, overhead expenses allocable to the cost of goods sold).

After increasing your opening inventory and then making certain subtractions, find your cost of goods sold (COGS). Again, by reducing your gross receipts for the year by COGS, you determine your gross profit (explained in detail next).

To know what your opening inventory and closing inventory is, you need to take a physical inventory. A physical inventory must be taken at reasonable intervals, and the actual count must be used to adjust the inventory figures you have been maintaining all along. Generally, a physical inventory is taken at year-end. You are permitted to estimate year-end inventory by factoring in a reasonable allowance for shrinkage. Inventory shrinkage, which is the difference between what a business shows as the inventory count in its records versus an actual physical count of items on hand, can result from a casualty event, theft by employees or others, or just miscounts and can be handled on your return in 2 ways as explained in Chapter 17. If you make such an estimate, then you must take a physical count on a consistent basis and adjust—upward or downward—the actual inventory count.

There are 4 methods for reporting inventory. They are:

1. Cost
2. Lower of cost or market method
3. Write-down of subnormal goods
4. Other inventory methods

Retailers can use a retail inventory method (see Revenue Procedure 2014-48 for instructions on how to change to this method if the business is currently using a different method).

Resellers—those who buy items for sale to others—use certain rules and methods to assign the cost of these items to those sold during the year:

- *First-in, First-out (FIFO)*. An item sold is deemed to be the first item booked into inventory. For example, if you bought 10 widgets on 3 occasions at a cost of 10¢ each, 15¢ each, and 20¢ each and you sell 15, under FIFO you have sold 10 at 10¢ each and 5 at 15¢ each.
- *Last-in, First-out (LIFO)*. An item sold is deemed to be the last item booked into inventory. In the widget example, you have sold 10 at 20¢ each and 5 at 15¢ each.
- *Specific identification method*. The actual cost of the items is used. This method generally is used when a business owns large or unique items (for example, an antique store would use this method for its objects since items are not identical and cannot be commingled).

Small businesses (small but not small enough to meet the gross receipts test) are allowed to use a simplified value LIFO method that makes it easier to determine the value of inventory. If you elect FIFO, you must use the lower of cost or market method to report inventory. If you elect LIFO, you must use cost to report inventory.

***Small businesses treating inventory as materials and supplies.*** If you meet the gross receipts test that allows you use the cash method (explained in Chapter 2), then instead of treating purchases as part of COGS you can treat inventoriable items as non-incidental materials and supplies. This means the costs are deductible when purchased or consumed (i.e., items are sold), whichever is later. Non-incidental materials and supplies are items for which a record of consumption or physical inventory is kept.

In determining the amount of materials and supplies to be deducted, you can use specific identification, first-in first-out (FIFO), or average cost (discussed earlier in this chapter). You cannot use last-in first-out (LIFO) and lower-of-cost-or-market methods.

### Gross Profits

*Gross profits* from the sale of goods is the difference between the gross receipts (sales revenues) and the cost of goods sold (as well as other allowances). If you remove items from inventory for your personal use, be sure to adjust your figures accordingly.

You generally cannot use the installment method of accounting to report the sale of inventory items—even if you receive payment on an installment plan. You report the sale according to your usual method of accounting so that on the accrual basis you pick up the income in full in the year of sale even though the full payment will not be received at that time.

### Other Income for Direct Sellers

In addition to income from sales of products to customers, direct sellers may receive income in other ways:

- Commissions, bonuses, or percentages you receive for sales and the sales of others who work under you.
- Prizes, awards, and gifts resulting from your sales activities.

## Income from Farming

When a business earns its income from sales of livestock and produce, payments from agricultural programs and farm rents and other similar sources, it is considered a farming business. Since most small farms use the cash method of accounting to report income and expenses, the following discussion is limited to this method of accounting. However, if items regularly produced in the farming business or used in the farming business are sold on an installment basis, the sale can be reported on the installment method, deferring income until payment is received.

While many income items of farms are similar to nonfarm businesses, there are a number of income items unique to farming. These include:

- *Agricultural payments* (cash, materials, services, or commodity certificates) from government programs are generally included in income. If you later refund or repay a portion of the payments, you can deduct these amounts at that time. For details on how to treat specific government payments, see IRS Publication 225, *Farmer's Tax Guide*.
- *Conservation Reserve Program (CRP) payments*. If you own or operate highly erodible or other specified cropland and have entered into a long-term contract with the USDA, agreeing to convert to a less intensive use of that cropland, include the annual rental payments and any onetime incentive payment you receive under the program as ordinary income (there is a special line on Schedule F for reporting Agricultural Program Payments). Cost-share payments may qualify for the cost-sharing exclusion.
- *Crop insurance and crop disaster payments* received as a result of crop damage. This type of income is generally included in income in the year received. Farmers can request federal

income tax withholding at the rate of 7%, 10%, 12%, or 22% by filing Form W-4V, *Voluntary Withholding Request*.

- *Feed assistance and payments*. If you receive partial reimbursement for the cost of purchased feed, certain transportation expenses, and/or the donation or sale at a below-market price of feed owned by the Commodity Credit Corporation, include in income (1) the market value of the donated feed, (2) the difference between the market value and the price you paid for feed you buy at below-market prices, and (3) any cost reimbursement you receive.
- *Forest health protection payments*. Payments to landowners who voluntarily participate in the FHPP are tax free.
- *Market Facilitation Program (MFP) payments*. Payments to farmers under the USDATrade Aid Package for producers of crops impacted from tariffs are viewed as income replacements includible in gross income.
- *Patronage dividends* from farm cooperatives through which you purchase farm supplies and sell your farm products are included in income.
- *Rents, including crop shares*. Generally, rents are not treated as farm income but as rental income, and these rents are not part of your net income or loss from farming. However, rents are treated as farm income if you materially participate in the management or operations of the farm (material participation is explained later in this chapter).
- *Sales of livestock caused by drought, flood, or other weather conditions*. While such sales are generally reported in the current year, you can opt to report them in the following year if you can show that you would not have sold the livestock this year but for the weather conditions *and* you are eligible for federal assistance because of the weather conditions. You must file a separate election with your tax return for the year of the weather conditions for each class of animals (e.g., cattle, sheep). Alternatively, deferral is indefinite, if proceeds are reinvested in similar livestock, until the end of the first tax year ending after the first "drought-free year" (assuming the drought-free year ends in or after the last year of a 4-year replacement period). The IRS listed affected counties between September 1, 2020, and August 31, 2021, in Notice 2021-55. The counties for the balance of 2021 won't be known until September 22.
- *Sales of livestock (including poultry) and produce*. The sale of livestock classified as Section 1231 property may result in Section 1231 gain or loss (explained in Chapter 6). If crops are sold on a deferred payment contract, you report the income when payment is received.
- *Sales of timber*. Outright sales of timber qualify for capital gain treatment if the timber was held for more than one year before the date of disposal and you elect this tax treatment.

Income from marijuana activities must be reported as income, even though marijuana is a controlled substance under federal law. Restrictions on deductions for these activities are explained in Chapter 20.

### Commodity Credit Corporation Loans

Loan proceeds are generally not income. However, farmers who pledge part or all of their production to secure a Commodity Credit Corporation (CCC) loan can make a special election to treat the loan proceeds as income in the year received and obtain a basis in the commodity for the amount reported as income. The election is made by including the loan proceeds as income on Schedule F and attaching a statement to the return showing the details of the loan. Then the amount you report as income becomes your basis in the commodity, so that when you later repay the loan, redeem the pledged commodity, and sell it, you report as income the sale proceeds minus the basis in the commodity. A forfeiture of pledged crops is treated as a sale for this purpose. Farmers who do not make this election must report market gain as income.

The repayment amount is generally based on the lower of the loan rate or the prevailing world market price of the commodity on the date of repayment. If the world price is lower when the loan is repaid, the difference between the repayment amount and the original loan amount is market gain. Whether cash or CCC certificates are used to repay the loan, Form 1099-CCC is issued to show the market gain. Market gain is included in income in the year of repayment if the CCC loan was not included in income in the year received.

Not all income received by farmers and ranchers is includable in gross income. Income from federal or state cost-sharing conservation, reclamation, and restoration programs can be excluded in whole or in part (depending on the program and other factors). Qualifying programs include, but are not limited to, small watershed programs as well as the water bank program under the Water Bank Act, emergency conservation measures program under Title IV of the Agricultural Credit Act of 1978, and the Great Plains conservation program authorized by the Soil Conservation and Domestic Policy Act.

### *Farm Income Averaging*

You can choose to figure the tax on your farming income (*elected farm income*) by averaging it over the past 3 years. If you make this election, it will lower the tax on this year's income if income was substantially lower in the 3 prior years. However, it does not always save taxes to average your farming income—it is a good idea to figure your tax in both ways (the usual way and averaging) to determine which method is more favorable to you.

## Income from Commercial Fishing

Income from commercial fishing activities is usually fully taxable. However, under a special rule, you can opt to defer certain income. This deferral rule applies if you set up a Capital Construction Fund (CCF) account and make deposits to it. You are eligible to do this if you own or lease one or more eligible vessels. An eligible vessel is a U.S.-built vessel weighing more than 2 tons. Technically, deposits to your account are not deductible, but do reduce taxable income. Also, income earned on the account is tax deferred.

To use this deferral rule, you must enter into an agreement with the Secretary of Commerce through the National Marine Fisheries Service (NMFS). The agreement names the vessels that will be the basis for income tax deferral and the planned use of withdrawals from your account to acquire, build, or rebuild a vessel.

You can deposit up to a set ceiling (100% of income, plus annual depreciation and certain other amounts). You must make minimum annual deposits (2% of your estimated objectives listed on your agreement).

Details about the accounts and other aspects of this special rule are in IRS Publication 595. Special reporting with respect to a CCF account is explained at the end of this chapter.

### *Income Averaging from Fishing*

The income averaging rules applicable to farmers, explained earlier, apply to commercial fishermen.

## Income from Rentals

Income from rentals is taxable. Rentals may be the core of the business activity or merely an ancillary one. For example, a business may rent out its equipment on a short-term basis through an online platform, such as Kwipped.com and EquipmentShare.com.

Rent payments may be classified as business or mere rental (passive) income. For an individual, this means the difference between reporting the rent payments on Schedule C of Form 1040 or 1040-SR as business income or on Schedule E of Form 1040 or 1040-SR as passive income. If profitable, the income tax results may be the same, but reporting rents on Schedule C means that net income from rents become subject to self-employment tax. If unprofitable, the passive activity loss limitation discussed in this chapter may apply.

When renting out residential realty, the rents are business income if substantial services for the benefit of tenants are provided, such as in the case of a motel. Substantial services include changing linens, maid service, and regular cleaning. Substantial services do not include cleaning common areas, providing heating/cooling/lighting, and trash collection.

## Income from Government Programs

It's a general rule that income from government programs is taxable. For example, any direct contributions to the capital of a corporation are taxable income (although these are typically only made to large corporations). So too are state grants to businesses whose property is damaged or destroyed in a disaster (but gain on the resulting income may be postponed under the rules for involuntary conversions discussed in Chapter 6).

State and local governments may provide relocation subsidies and various tax breaks (discussed later). Typically, they are enjoyed by large corporations promising to bring jobs and business to a particular area. However, some small businesses may qualify for special grants that afford them similar tax subsidies.

However, in response to COVID-19, federal, state, and local governments offered a variety of programs to help small businesses survive and recover. These are in addition to existing programs, such as those for farmers discussed earlier in this chapter. The following are treated as nontaxable:

- Forgiveness of loans under the Paycheck Protection Program
- SBA's Shuttered Venue Operators Grants (live venue operators or promoters; theatrical producers; live performing arts organization operators; relevant museum, zoo, and aquarium operators who meet specific criteria; motion picture theater operators; talent representatives; and each business entity owned by an eligible entity that also meets eligibility requirements specified at https://www.sba.gov/funding-programs/loans/coronavirus-relief-options/shuttered-venue-operators-grant)
- SBA's Restaurant Revitalization Fund grants
- SBA's Economic Injury Disaster Loans program's $10,000 advance payment

**NOTE**

**In addition to tax-free treatment for PPP loan forgiveness, businesses may deduct expenses for which loan proceeds were used.**

Certain other COVID-19-related programs trigger taxable income:

- Treasury's Coronavirus Economic Relief for Transportation Services (CERTS) Program
- USDA's Coronavirus Food Assistance Program (CFAP)
- USDA's Pandemic Livestock Indemnity Program

### Location Tax Incentives

If you receive a state or local location tax incentive, in the form of an abatement, credit, deduction, rate reduction, or exemption, in order to attract your company to a particular area, the incentive is not taxable income. Of course, only the amount of state and local tax you are liable for, after reduction by any location tax incentives, is deductible (you can't deduct what you aren't required to pay) (see Chapter 13).

## Investment-Type Income

Operating income from a business may include certain investment-type income, such as interest on business bank accounts and rents from leasing property. Pass-through entities segregate investment-type income and, in most cases, report these separately to owners. How to report this income can be found later in this chapter. Also included at the end of this chapter are rules for reporting certain foreign assets that may generate investment-type income. Capital gains are discussed in Chapter 5, and other gains from the sale of business property are discussed in Chapter 6.

### Interest Income

Interest received on business bank accounts and on accounts or notes receivable in the ordinary course of business is a common type of ordinary business income. If the business lends money, interest received on business loans is business income. Deductions for business loans that go sour are explained in Chapter 22.

If you've made an installment sale with little or no interest provided for in the contract, you must report a portion of each installment as unstated interest. Figuring the amount of unstated interest can be complicated (there's a lengthy explanation in IRS Publication 537).

Businesses that make below-market or interest-free loans may be deemed to receive interest, called *imputed interest*. Below-market loan rules from the deduction perspective are discussed in Chapter 13.

### Dividends

Businesses that own stock in a corporation may receive dividends. C corporations report the dividends as ordinary income. Pass-through entities report the dividends as separately stated items to enable owners to apply favorable tax rates on their personal returns. For example, if the dividends are "qualified," owners may pay tax at no more than 15% on their share of the dividends (those with taxable income above a threshold amount pay no more than 20% on their share of dividends).

#### DIVIDENDS-RECEIVED DEDUCTION

C corporations that receive dividends from domestic (U.S.) corporations can effectively exclude some or all of these dividends by claiming a special dividends-received deduction. The amount of the dividends-received deduction depends on the percentage of ownership in the corporation paying the dividend. This special write-off for C corporations is discussed in Chapter 22.

### Rents

Rents can be generated from leasing personal property items such as equipment, formal wear, or vehicles. Rents can also be generated from leasing out real property.

#### REAL ESTATE RENTS

A business that provides services in conjunction with rentals reports rents as business income. For example, if you own a motel, you report your rentals as business income because you provide maid service and other services to your business guests.

If your tenant pays expenses on your behalf in lieu of making rental payments to you, these payments to third parties are part of your business income. For example, if your tenant pays your property taxes, you report the payment of taxes as rental income.

#### PREPAID RENT

Advances, including security deposits, must be reported as income if you have unrestricted right to them. If you are required by law or contract to segregate these payments, you do not have to report them as income until you are entitled to enjoy them (the restrictions no longer apply).

#### LEASE BONUS OR CANCELLATION PAYMENTS

Amounts your tenant pays to secure a lease (lease bonus payments) or to get out of a lease early (cancellation payments) are income to you.

### Cancellation of Debt

If you owe money and some or all of your debt is forgiven by the lender, you generally must include this debt forgiveness in income. However, you do not have to include debt forgiveness in income if any of the following conditions apply:

- You file for bankruptcy under Title 11 of the U.S. Code.
- You are insolvent at the time of the cancellation. Your exclusion is limited to the extent of your insolvency.
- The canceled debt is a qualified farm debt. This is a debt incurred by a business that received at least 50% of its gross receipts in the prior 3 years from farming activities. This debt must be owed to one who is regularly engaged in lending money, including the U.S. Department of Agriculture.
- The canceled debt is qualified real property business debt—secured by the property and incurred before January 1, 1993, or after December 31, 1992, if incurred or assumed to acquire, construct, or substantially improve real property used in the business. You must elect this exclusion for the year in which the cancellation occurs. The exclusion cannot exceed certain amounts.
- The canceled debt is for a loan under the Paycheck Protection Program (PPP).

Instead of recognizing income from the cancellation of indebtedness (referred to as COD income), you can choose to reduce certain **tax attributes**. This has the effect of limiting your future write-offs with respect to these tax attributes. Generally, the amount excluded from income reduces the tax attributes (in a certain order) on a dollar-for-dollar or 33 cents basis. As follows:

- Net operating loss (NOL) for the year of the COD (dollar-for-dollar)
- General business credit carryover to or from the year of COD (33⅓¢ per dollar)
- Minimum tax credit as of the beginning of the tax year immediately after the year of COD (33⅓¢ per dollar)
- Net capital loss for the year of COD (dollar-for-dollar)
- Basis of property (dollar-for-dollar)

- Passive activity loss (dollar-for-dollar) and credit (33 ⅓¢ per dollar) carryovers from the year of COD
- Foreign tax credit carryover to or from the year of COD

However, a corporation can elect to adjust the basis of property in a manner that is different from the general rule described in Reg. §1.1082-3(b).

---

***Tax attributes*** **These are tax aspects that provide a tax benefit in the current year or future years. They include the basis of depreciable real property, the basis of other depreciable property, net operating losses and loss carryovers, general business credit carryovers, minimum tax credit, capital losses and loss carryovers, passive activity loss and credit carryovers, and foreign tax credit carryovers.**

---

The election to reduce tax attributes instead of recognizing COD income is made on Form 982, *Reduction of Tax Attributes Due to Discharge of Indebtedness*.

***Cancellation of debt income for S corporations.*** When corporate debt is forgiven and the S corporation opts not to report the cancellation of debt income but rather to reduce tax attributes, special rules apply. Any disallowed losses or deductions, including those of a shareholder who transferred all stock during the year, are included in an S corporation's deemed NOL (it is "deemed" because technically NOLs are reported only at the shareholder level, but adjustments to the NOL are made at the corporate level). If the deemed NOL exceeds the discharged cancellation of debt income, the excess deemed NOL is allowed to the shareholders as disallowed losses and deductions that shareholders can later take into account.

The character of the excess deemed NOL that is allocated to shareholders will consist of a proportionate amount of each item of the shareholder's loss or deduction that is disallowed for the year of the debt discharge. The corporations are required to provide information to shareholders regarding these suspended losses.

### *Damages and Other Recoveries*

If you receive damages for patent, copyright or trademark infringement, breach of contract, or other business-related injuries, you report the damages as business income.

## Miscellaneous Business Income

Almost any type of income earned by a business is considered to be business income. This is so whether the income is legal or illegal (e.g., bribes, kickbacks) In addition to the types of income already discussed, the following are other examples of business income you must report:

- Credit for federal tax paid on gasoline or other fuels claimed on the prior year return
- Finance reserve income
- Income adjustments resulting from a change in accounting method
- Income under the tax benefit rule of Section 111 (recoveries of previously deducted items)
- Kickbacks (unless you treat them as a reduction to an expense item, a capital expenditure, or the cost of goods sold)
- Prizes and awards for the business
- Recapture of first-year expensing deduction (first-year expensing is explained in Chapter 14)

- Recapture of depreciation for so-called luxury cars if business use drops below 50% (figure recapture amount on Form 4797 in Chapter 4)
- Recovery of bad debts previously deducted under the specific charge-off method or any other item deducted in a prior year
- Scrap sales
- State gasoline or fuel tax refunds received in the current year
- Taxable income from insurance proceeds (such as key person insurance)

Trade discounts provided to a retailer by a manufacturer or wholesaler are *not* taken into income; they are subtracted from the invoice price to figure inventory cost.

### *Special Income Items for S Corporations*

If a corporation operated as a C corporation and then converted to S status, certain unique income items may result. These items are taxed to the S corporation; they are not pass-through items taxed to the shareholders:

- *Last-in, first-out inventory recapture on the conversion from C status to S status*. It can also result from the transfer of LIFO inventory by a C corporation to the S corporation in a transaction in which no income was recognized. Recapture results in an income adjustment payable in 4 equal installments, one reported on the final return of the C corporation (or the year of the transfer), and one-fourth each in the first, second, and third years of the S corporation's life (or the year of the transfer and the 2 successive years).
- *Excess net passive income*. If there were accumulated earnings and profits (E&P) from the time when the corporation was a C corporation *and* it has passive income for the year in excess of 25% of gross receipts, then tax is due at the rate of 21%. The S corporation must have taxable income for the year to be subject to this special tax.
- *Built-in capital gains*. If the corporation has appreciated property when it converts, the appreciation to the date of conversion is reported as built-in gains if the property is sold or otherwise disposed of within 5 years of conversion. The tax on the net recognized built-in gains is 21%.

If a corporation elects S status for its first year of existence, it need not be concerned with any of these income items; they will never arise.

### *Special Income Items for C Corporations*

If a C corporation converts to S status and reports inventory using LIFO, it must recapture one-fourth of the resulting income adjustment, reporting it as income on its final return (the year of conversion).

If the corporation receives a tax refund of taxes deducted in a prior year, the refund must be reported as income to the extent that it produced a tax benefit for the corporation.

***Income from conversion of S corporation to C corporation***. If you are an S corporation and revoke the election in order to be taxed as a C corporation, any adjustment under Code Sec. 481(a) of an **eligible terminated S corporation** is reported ratably over 6 tax years beginning with the year of the change. For example, a change from the cash method to the accrual method, which requires an adjustment under Code Sec. 481(a), is subject to this reporting rule for an eligible terminated S corporation.

***Eligible terminated S corporation*** **A C corporation that was an S corporation on December 21, 2017. During the 2-year period beginning on December 22, 2017 (before December 22, 2019), the S election was revoked, and all of the owners on the date of revocation were the same owners in identical proportions to the owners on December 22, 2017.**

**Example**

**A calendar year S corporation revoked its election effective January 1, 2018. It must report 1/6th of any resulting adjustment each year for 2018 through 2023 (a total of 6 years).**

## State Income Taxes on Business Income

Federal income taxes on your business income may not be your only concern. You may also be subject to state income taxes. For corporations, this may be a corporate income tax or a gross receipts tax. This liability depends on whether you do business within the state. Generally, this means having a nexus (connection) to the state. This is based on having a physical presence there, which may be evidenced by maintaining an office or sending a sales force into the state; merely shipping goods into the state without some additional connection is not enough to prove a business presence within the state. You may have a nexus to more than one state, no matter how small your business is.

If there is a business connection, the business income is apportioned among the states in which you do business. Apportionment is based on a sales factor, a payroll factor, and a property factor (the states have different apportionment rules). The rules are highly complex, but there is some wiggle room to shift income into the state with the lowest tax rates.

For more information about state income taxes, contact the tax or revenue departments of each state in which you do business.

## Noncorporate Excess Business Losses

You run your business with the expectation of making a profit, but things happen that may trigger a loss. If your business is not a C corporation, there is a limitation on deducting losses through 2026. Essentially, any "excess" is treated as a net operating loss (discussed next). And you must apply the passive activity loss rules before you get to this noncorporate excess business loss limitation. An excess business loss is the excess, if any, of:

- Your aggregate deductions for the year from all your businesses (figured without regard to whether deductions are disallowed for this excess business loss limitation), over
- Your aggregate gross income or gain from all your businesses, plus $262,000 ($524,000 if married filing jointly) in 2021.

**Example**

**You are a one-member LLC with $1 million of gross income for 2021 (you are single and have no other businesses). Deductions for the LLC are $1.4 million. You are treated as having an excess business loss of $138,000 ($1.4 million deductions – [$1 million income + $262,000]).**

### *Partnerships and S corporations*

You figure this limitation at the owner level. This means you compute the limitation based on your distributive share of income from partnerships and S corporations in which you own interests. Schedule K-1 contained relevant information for this limitation in the "Other Information" section.

## Net Operating Losses

If deductions and losses from your business exceed your business income, you may be able to use the losses to offset income in other years. Net losses from the conduct of your business are *net operating losses (NOLs)*. There are no statistics on the amount of net operating losses that resulted from the pandemic, but it's probable they were claimed by millions of C corporations and owners of pass-through entities and totaled in the billions of dollars.

Net operating losses are not an additional loss deduction. Rather, they are the result of your deductions exceeding the income from your business. The excess deductions are not lost; they are simply used in certain other years.

You have an NOL if you have deductions from a trade or business, deductions from your work as an employee, or deductions from casualty and theft losses.

Only individuals and C corporations can claim NOLs. Partnerships, limited liability companies (LLCs), and S corporations cannot have NOLs, since their income and losses pass through to owners. However, partners, LLC members, and S corporation shareholders can have NOLs on their individual returns. These NOLs are created by their share of the business's operating losses.

### *Calculating NOLs*

After you have completed your tax return for the year, you may find that you have an NOL. If you are an individual, you may have an NOL if your adjusted gross income, reduced by itemized deductions or the standard deduction, is a negative figure. C corporations may have an NOL if taxable income is a negative figure. This negative figure merely indicates a possibility of an NOL; then you must determine whether, in fact, there actually is one. This is due to the fact that certain adjustments must be made to that negative figure in arriving at an NOL. Individuals and corporations calculate NOLs in a slightly different manner.

#### INDIVIDUALS

An NOL does not include net capital losses, nonbusiness losses, or nonbusiness deductions. The NOL can be computed on Schedule A of Form 1045, which was an application for a tentative refund for an individual. This form adds back to taxable income any of these items claimed on the return and makes other adjustments required to compute the NOL. Nonetheless, individuals must add back to taxable income any deductions for Individual Retirement Account (IRA) contributions, deductible alimony, the standard deduction, and charitable contributions. More specifically, nonbusiness deductions in excess of nonbusiness income get added back. Do not add back business-related deductions for:

- Deductible portion of self-employment tax
- State income tax on business profits
- Interest and litigation expenses on state or federal income taxes related to business
- Payments by a federal employee to buy sick leave

- Loss on rental property
- Loss on the sale or exchange of business real estate or depreciable business property
- Loss on the sale of accounts receivable if you are on the accrual method
- Loss on the sale or exchange of stock in a small business company or small business investment company if the loss is treated as an ordinary loss (such as loss on Section 1244)

#### CORPORATIONS

The NOL for corporations generally is calculated by reducing gross income by deductions. Special rules then apply to adjust the NOL. They are:

- A full dividends-received deduction is taken into account in calculating the NOL. For example, the 50% or 65% limit is ignored.
- NOLs from other years are not taken into account in calculating a current NOL.
- Losses that fall under the passive activity rules cannot be used to calculate an NOL.

If a corporation's ownership changes hands, limits apply on the use of NOL carryforwards. The tax law does not want one corporation to acquire another for the purpose of using NOLs of the target corporation to offset the income of the acquiring corporation. These rules are highly complex.

S corporations do not have net operating losses. Instead, losses are passed through to owners who figure their NOLs on their individual returns. NOL carryovers of a C corporation cannot be claimed after the conversion to S corporation status (they remain in limbo and can be used by the corporation if it terminates its S status and returns to being a C corporation). However, the S corporation can use the C corporation's NOL carryover as a deduction to offset any net recognized built-in gain (built-in gain is explained earlier in this chapter).

### *Carrybacks and Carryovers*

Carrybacks present a refund opportunity. The carryback and carryforward periods depend on the year in which the NOL arose. Keep careful track of your NOLs so you can take full advantage of them.

**NOTE**

**For partnerships, limited liability companies, and S corporations, the election of the longer carryback period was made at the entity level even though the carryback was claimed by owners on their personal returns.**

***Pre-2018 NOLs.*** Generally, there was a 2-year carryback and a 20-year carryforward period. However, for small businesses (those with average annual gross receipts of $5 million or less during a 3-year period), a 3-year carryback applied to NOLs arising from government-declared disasters, and for farmers and ranchers and certain specified disaster victims, there was a 5-year carryback for all NOLs. There was a 10-year carryback for NOLs arising from product liability. Carryforwards may offset 100% of taxable income.

***NOLs in 2018, 2019, and 2020.*** For NOLs in these years, there was a 5-year carryback of net operating losses that can offset 100% of taxable income. There is an unlimited carryforward, but it can only offset 80% of taxable income.

***Post-2020 NOLs.*** In general, no carryback is allowed, but there is an unlimited carryforward. The exception: farmers who have a 2-year carryback. Carryforwards may only offset 80% of taxable income in the carryforward years.

The carryback is applied to the oldest carryback year to offset taxable income in that year. If it is not used up, the remaining NOL is net applied to the next year, and so forth.

**Example**

**In 2021, you are a farmer with a $150,000 net operating loss. You can carry it back to offset 80% of taxable income in 2019. If taxable income in 2019 was $120,000, then the remaining NOL of $30,000 is applied against 80% of 2020 taxable income. Any unused NOL is then carried forward, year by year, until it is used up.**

For 2018, 2019, and 2020, personal service corporations (PSCs) were not allowed to carry back an NOL to any year in which there was a Section 444 election in effect to use a tax year other than a required tax year.

If your marital status in the carryback or carryover years differs from your status in the NOL year, only the spouse who has the NOL can claim it. If you file a joint return, the NOL deduction is limited to the income of the spouse who had the NOL. Special rules apply for carrybacks where applicable to a year involving a different marital status from the status in the year the NOL arises.

If your NOL is greater than the taxable income for the year to which you carried it, you must make certain modifications to taxable income to see how much of the NOL is used up in that carryback/carryover year and how much is still available as a *carry over*. The carryover is the excess of the NOL deduction over modified taxable income for the carryback/carryforward year. Modified taxable income is taxable income without regard to the NOL and with no deduction for net capital losses. Also, you must recalculate items affected by a change in adjusted gross income. Your modified taxable income cannot be less than zero. You can determine your modified taxable income using Schedule B of Form 1045 for any carryback years and for carryovers from those years. If you have carry overs from more than one year, you use the carry overs in the order in which they were incurred. Thus, if you have a carryforward from 2019 and 2020, first use the amounts from 2019; if income is not fully offset, then use the 2020 carry forward.

While the NOL carryforward reduces income in the carryforward years for income tax purposes, it does *not* affect income for self-employment tax purposes in the carryforward years.

### *Election to Forgo Carryback*

A farmer eligible to take an NOL carryback can elect to forgo it and just carry the loss forward indefinitely. You make this election in the NOL year by attaching a statement to your return if you are an individual, or by checking the appropriate box on the corporate return for C corporations. Once the election is made, it cannot be changed. If you incur another NOL in a subsequent year, you must make a separate election if you also want to forgo the carryback. Farming businesses were given flexibility with respect to net operating losses that arose in 2018 and 2019. They could retain the 2-year carryback even though the CARES Act introduced a 5-year carryback for NOLs arising in 2018, 2019, and 2020. However, they could opt to waive the 2-year carryback, or if they previously waived it, revoke the waiver and use the 5-year carryback or simply carry NOLs forward indefinitely. Bottom line: for 2021 returns, check on what was done with farming NOLs from 2018, 2019, and 2020.

Some taxpayers prefer to forgo the carryback because they are afraid of calling attention to prior tax years and risking an audit. While this is certainly a possibility, claiming a carryback will not necessarily result in an audit of a prior year.

The election by individuals to forgo the NOL carryback applies not only to regular income tax purposes but also to alternative minimum tax purposes.

### *Quick Refunds from Carrybacks*

If your farming business is struggling, you can use an NOL carryback to generate quickcash flow. The carryback will offset income in the carryback years, and you will receive a refund of taxes paid in those years. Filing for refunds is explained in Chapter 31.

## Other Limitations on Business Losses

Once you figure whether your business has sustained operating losses, you must then determine the extent to which you can deduct these losses. A number of limits apply that restrict full and immediate write-offs of business losses. The noncorporate excess business losses limitation was explained earlier in this chapter, but there are other limitations that can apply. For example, the hobby loss rules bar deductions from certain business activities, as explained in Chapter 26. Not all of the rules that follow apply to all types of businesses, so only review those rules applicable to your company.

### *Basis*

If you own a pass-through entity, business losses claimed on your personal return cannot exceed your tax basis in the company. Losses in excess of basis can be carried forward and used in future years to the extent of basis at that time. There is no time limit on these carryforwards.

#### PARTNERSHIPS AND LLCS

When it comes to partnerships, there is "inside basis" and "outside basis." Inside basis is the partnership's basis in each of its assets. This is used by the partnership to determine gain or loss on the disposition of partnership assets.

Outside basis is the partner's basis in his or her interest in the partnership. Different calculations go into each type of basis.

Outside basis is determined, in part, by the way in which you as a partner or member acquire your interest in the entity.

- If the interest is acquired by contributing directly to the entity (typically in the start-up of the business), then basis is the cash and owner's basis of the property contributed to the entity.
- If the interest is purchased from an owner (for example, a retiring partner), then basis is the cash and value of the property paid.
- If the interest is acquired by performing services for the business, then basis is the amount of compensation reported. However, the receipt of an interest in the profits of the business (and not a capital interest) is not taxable under certain conditions and so does not give rise to any basis.
- If the interest is inherited from a deceased owner, then basis is the value of the interest for estate tax purposes (typically the value of the interest on the date of the owner's death).

If property transferred to the entity is subject to liabilities, owners increase their basis by their share of the liabilities.

After the initial determination of basis, it may be increased or decreased annually. Basis is increased by the following items (determined on a per-share, per-day basis):

- The owner's distributive share of entity income
- The owner's share of tax-exempt income (such as life insurance proceeds)
- Excess of depletion deductions over the basis of depletable property
- Additional capital contributions
- Share of new partnership liabilities (limited partners in limited partnerships do not increase their basis by a share of liabilities assumed by the general partners.)

Basis is decreased (on a per-share, per-day basis), but not below zero, by:

- The owner's distributive share of entity losses (including capital losses)
- The owner's share of expenses that are not deductible in figuring entity income
- Distributions to the owner by the entity

**NOTE**

**For 2020 returns, the IRS did not impose penalties due to incorrect information in a partner's beginning capital accounts if the partnership took ordinary and prudent care in following IRS instructions to Form 1065. Whether there is similar relief for 2021 returns is unclear; check the Supplement for any update.**

As a partner or LLC member can use a worksheet in the instructions to Schedule K-1 to figure basis of a partner's interest in a partnership. (Figure 4.1).

Keep in mind that the partnership is not responsible for keeping track of a partner's basis in his or her interest in the partnership. The partnership is required to report on the partner's capital account based on the partnership's books and records. For tax years beginning on or after January 1, 2020, the capital account must be reported on the tax basis method. Compliance with this requirement may necessitate the partnership going back years to reconstruct the capital account.

### S CORPORATIONS

Basis for the purpose of deducting pass-through losses means your basis in your S corporation stock—what you contributed to the corporation to acquire your shares—plus the amount of any money you loaned to the corporation. If S corporation stock is acquired by inheritance, the basis, which is generally the value of the stock on the date of the owner's death, is reduced by the portion of the value attributable to income in respect of a decedent. This is income earned by the owner prior to death that is received by and reported by the person who inherits the stock.

Guaranteeing corporate debt, which is a common practice for bank loans to S corporations, does *not* give rise to basis. However, if you are called on to make good on your guarantee so that you have an "economic outlay," then you can increase your basis by the amount you pay to the bank on the corporation's behalf. A better strategy: Talk to third-party lenders so that outstanding loans are reworked to make you primarily liable on the debt, which allows you to increase your basis. It's as if the third party loaned money to you and then you loaned it to your S corporation. Be sure that the corporation repays you, and then you repay the third-party lender. One federal appellate court allows a shareholder who guarantees a third-party loan to the corporation to increase basis if it can be shown that the lender looks to the shareholder as the primary obligor.

## Worksheet for Adjusting the Basis of a Partner's Interest in the Partnership

*Keep for Your Records* 

| | | |
|---|---|---|
| **1.** | Your adjusted basis at the end of the prior year. Do not enter less than zero. Enter -0- if this is your first tax year | **1.** ______ |
| | Increases: | |
| **2.** | Money and your adjusted basis in property contributed to the partnership less the associated liabilities (but not less than zero) | **2.** ______ |
| **3.** | Your increased share of or assumption of partnership liabilities. (Subtract your share of liabilities shown in item K of your 2019 Schedule K-1 from your share of liabilities shown in item K of your 2020 Schedule K-1 and add the amount of any partnership liabilities you assumed during the tax year (but not less than zero)) | **3.** ______ |
| **4a.** | Your share of the partnership's income or gain (including tax-exempt income) reduced by any amount included in interest income with respect to the credit to holders of clean renewable energy bonds ........ 4a.______ | |
| **4b.** | Enter the amount of business interest expense included on 4a ........ 4b.______ | |
| **4c.** | Subtract line 4b from line 4a. If the result is less than zero, include this amount on line 10 | **4c.** ______ |
| **5.** | Any gain recognized this year on contributions of property. Do not include gain from transfer of liabilities | **5.** ______ |
| **6.** | Your share of the excess of the deductions for depletion (other than oil and gas depletion) over the basis of the property subject to depletion | **6.** ______ |
| | Decreases: | |
| **7.** | Withdrawals and distributions of money and the adjusted basis of property distributed to you from the partnership. Do not include the amount of property distributions included in the partner's income (taxable income) | **7.** ______ |
| | **Caution:** A distribution may be taxable if the amount exceeds your adjusted basis of your partnership interest immediately before the distribution. | |
| **8.** | Your decreased share of partnership liabilities and any decrease in your individual liabilities because they were assumed by the partnership. (Subtract your share of liabilities shown in item K of your 2020 Schedule K-1 from your share of liabilities shown in item K of your 2019 Schedule K-1 and add the amount of your individual liabilities that the partnership assumed during the tax year (but not less than zero)) | **8.** ______ |
| **9.** | Your share of the partnership's nondeductible expenses that are not capital expenditures (excluding business interest expense) | **9.** ______ |
| **10.** | Your share of the partnership's losses and deductions (including capital losses). However, include your share of the partnership's section 179 expense deduction for this year even if you cannot deduct all of it because of limitations. Include business interest expense subject to section 163(j) limitations as a separate loss class. See Note below. | **10.** ______ |
| **11.** | The amount of your deduction for depletion of any partnership oil and gas property, not to exceed your allocable share of the adjusted basis of that property | **11.** ______ |
| **12.** | Your adjusted basis in the partnership at the end of this tax year. (Add lines 1 through 6 and subtract lines 7 through 11 from the total. If zero or less, enter -0-.) | **12.** ______ |

**Caution.** The deduction for your share of the partnership's losses and deductions is limited to your adjusted basis in your partnership interest. If you entered zero on line 12 and the amount figured for line 12 was less than zero, a portion of your share of the partnership losses and deductions may not be deductible. (See *Basis Limitations*, earlier, for more information.) Also see *Part III. Partner's Share of Current Year Income, Deductions, Credits, and Other Items.*

**Note.** Include in line 10 business interest expense that was removed from the amount in line 4a. Business interest expense is considered a separate loss class under Proposed Regulations section 1.163(j)-6(h)(1). However, to the extent basis is proportionately allocated to this loss class, interest expense is absorbed by applying currently deductible business interest expense to basis first. Excess business interest expense is applied to basis second. Excess business interest expense is only applicable to partnerships subject to section 163(j). In addition, if a partnership has negative section 704(d) expense (interest expense that is limited by basis), negative section 704(d) expense becomes excess business interest expense in the year that the basis limitation no longer applies. This is effective for tax years beginning after November 12, 2020.

**FIGURE 4.1 Computation of Partner's Basis in Partnership Interest**

A shareholder's basis is not affected by the corporation's liabilities. Unlike a partner who can increase his basis by his share of partnership liabilities, an S corporation shareholder may not increase his basis by his share of corporate liabilities.

After the initial determination of basis, it may be increased or decreased annually. Basis is increased by:

- The shareholder's share of the corporation's ordinary income
- The shareholder's share of separately stated items reported on the Schedule K-1 (including tax-exempt income)
- Excess of depletion deductions over the basis of depletable property
- Additional capital contributions

Basis is decreased (but not below zero) by:

- The shareholder's share of the corporation's losses
- The shareholder's share of expenses and losses that are not deductible in figuring ordinary income
- Noncapital and nondeductible corporate expenses reported on the Schedule K-1 (e.g., 50% of meal costs and nondeductible penalties)
- Distributions not includible in the shareholder's income (e.g., dividends in excess of basis)

**NOTE**

**The IRS is developing Form 7203, *S Corporation Shareholder Stock and Debt Basis Limitations*. The form essentially replaces the worksheets in Figures 4.2 and 4.3. It is not clear whether this form will be used for 2021 returns. Check the Supplement for any update.**

If an S corporation donates appreciated property to charity, the shareholder reduces his or her basis by the allocable share of the corporation's basis in the property (not the corporation's charitable contribution, which is based on the property's fair market value).

As an S corporation owner, if you received a distribution or loan repayment, or you disposed of stock in the corporation, you are required to attach to your return a basis computation. Check the box on line 28 of Schedule E to indicate that a basis statement is required. At present you may use a shareholder stock worksheet (Figure 4.2) and shareholder debt basis worksheet (Figure 4.3).

### *At-Risk Rules*

In the past, it was not uncommon for someone to invest in a business by contributing a small sum of cash and a large note on which there was no personal liability. The note increased the investor's basis against which tax write-offs could be claimed. If the business prospered, all was well and good. If the business failed, the individual lost only the small amount of cash invested. Congress felt this arrangement was unreasonably beneficial to investors and created *at-risk rules*. At-risk rules operate to limit your losses to the extent of your at-risk amounts in the activity. Your at-risk amounts are, in effect, your economic investment in the activity. This is the cash you put into a business. It also includes the adjusted basis of other property you contribute and any debts secured by your property or for which you are personally liable for repayment.

You are not considered at risk if you have an agreement or arrangement that limits your risk. As a practical matter, if you set up and conduct an active business operation, you probably do not

**Worksheet for Figuring a Shareholder's Stock and Debt Basis**

**Part I—Shareholder Stock Basis**

| | | | |
|---|---|---|---|
| **1.** | Stock basis at the beginning of the corporation's tax year | | **1.** ______ |
| **2.** | Basis from any capital contributions made or additional stock acquired during the tax year | | **2.** ______ |
| **3a.** | Ordinary business income (enter losses in Part III) | **3a.** ______ | |
| **b.** | Net rental real estate income (enter losses in Part III) | **3b.** ______ | |
| **c.** | Other net rental income (enter losses in Part III) | **3c.** ______ | |
| **d.** | Interest income | **3d.** ______ | |
| **e.** | Ordinary dividends | **3e.** ______ | |
| **f.** | Royalties | **3f.** ______ | |
| **g.** | Net capital gains (enter losses in Part III) | **3g.** ______ | |
| **h.** | Net section 1231 gain (enter losses in Part III) | **3h.** ______ | |
| **i.** | Other income (enter losses in Part III) | **3i.** ______ | |
| **j.** | Excess depletion adjustment | **3j.** ______ | |
| **k.** | Tax-exempt income | **3k.** ______ | |
| **l.** | Recapture of business credits | **3l.** ______ | |
| **m.** | Other items that increase stock basis | **3m.** ______ | |
| **4.** | Add lines 3a through 3m | | **4.** ______ |
| **5.** | Stock basis before distributions. Add lines 1, 2, and 4 | | **5.** ______ |
| **6.** | Distributions (excluding dividend distributions) | | **6.** ______ |
| | **Note.** If line 6 is larger than line 5, subtract line 5 from line 6 and report the result as a capital gain on Form 8949 and Schedule D. See instructions. | | |
| **7.** | Stock basis after distributions. Subtract line 6 from line 5. If the result is zero or less, enter -0-, skip lines 8 through 14, and enter -0- on line 15 | | **7.** ______ |
| **8a.** | Nondeductible expenses | **8a.** ______ | |
| **b.** | Depletion for oil and gas | **8b.** ______ | |
| **c.** | Business credits (sections 50(c)(1) and (5)) | **8c.** ______ | |
| **9.** | Add lines 8a through 8c | | **9.** ______ |
| **10.** | Stock basis before loss and deduction items. Subtract line 9 from line 7. If the result is zero or less, enter -0-, skip lines 11 through 14, and enter -0- on line 15 | | **10.** ______ |
| **11.** | Allowable loss and deduction items. Enter the amount from Part III, line 13, column (c) | | **11.** ______ |
| **12.** | Debt basis restoration (see net increase in instructions for Part II, line 8) | | **12.** ______ |
| **13.** | Other items that decrease stock basis | | **13.** ______ |
| **14.** | Add lines 11, 12, and 13 | | **14.** ______ |
| **15.** | **Stock basis at the end of the corporation's tax year.** Subtract line 14 from line 10. If the result is zero or less, enter -0- | | **15.** ______ |

**FIGURE 4.2 S Corporation Shareholder Basis in Stock**

have to be concerned with the at-risk rules. First, you may qualify for an exception to the at-risk rules for closely held C corporations (discussed later). Also, in all probability, your investment is what has started and sustained the business. But, if you are an investor, your contribution may be limited, and your losses may be limited as well.

**Part II—Shareholder Debt Basis**

| Description | Debt 1 ☐ Formal note ☐ Open account debt | Debt 2 ☐ Formal note ☐ Open account debt | Debt 3 ☐ Formal note ☐ Open account debt | Total |
|---|---|---|---|---|
| **Section A—Amount of Debt (If more than three debts, see instructions.)** | | | | |
| 1. Loan balance at the beginning of the corporation's tax year | | | | |
| 2. Additional loans (see instructions) | | | | |
| 3. Loan balance before repayment. Combine lines 1 and 2 | | | | |
| 4. Principal portion of debt repayment (this line doesn't include interest) | ( ) | ( ) | ( ) | ( ) |
| 5. Loan balance at the end of the corporation's tax year. Combine lines 3 and 4 | | | | |
| **Section B—Adjustments to Debt Basis** | | | | |
| 6. Debt basis at the beginning of the corporation's tax year | | | | |
| 7. Enter the amount, if any, from line 2 | | | | |
| 8. Debt basis restoration (see instructions) | | | | |
| 9. Debt basis before repayment. Combine lines 6, 7, and 8 | | | | |
| 10. Divide line 9 by line 3 | | | | |
| 11. Nontaxable debt repayment. Multiply line 10 by line 4 | | | | |
| 12. Debt basis before nondeductible expenses and losses. Subtract line 11 from line 9 | | | | |
| 13. Nondeductible expenses and oil and gas depletion deductions in excess of stock basis | | | | |
| 14. Debt basis before losses and deductions. Subtract line 13 from line 12. If the result is zero or less, enter -0- | | | | |
| 15. Allowable losses in excess of stock basis. Enter the amount from Part III, line 13, column (d) | | | | |
| 16. **Debt basis at the end of the corporation's tax year.** Subtract line 15 from line 14. If the result is zero or less, enter -0- | | | | |
| **Section C—Gain on Loan Repayment** | | | | |
| 17. Repayment. Enter the amount from line 4 | | | | |
| 18. Nontaxable repayments. Enter the amount from line 11 | | | | |
| 19. **Reportable gain.** Subtract line 18 from line 17 | | | | |

**FIGURE 4.3** S Corporation Shareholder Basis in Debt

**Example**

**You invest in a partnership to distribute a motion picture. You invest $1,000 cash and sign a promissory note for $9,000. The note is nonrecourse (you are not personally liable for the debt). Your at-risk amount is $1,000, the cash you invested. You cannot deduct losses from this activity in excess of $1,000.**

If you are subject to the at-risk rules, you do not lose your deductions to the extent they exceed your at-risk amounts; you simply cannot claim them currently. The losses can be carried forward and used in subsequent years if your at-risk amount increases. There is no limit on the carryover period. If the activity is sold, your gain from the disposition of property is treated as income from the activity, and you can then offset the gain by the amount of your carried-over losses.

At-risk rules do not apply to investments in closely held C corporations that meet active business tests and that do not engage in equipment leasing or any business involving master sound recording, films, videotapes, or other artistic, literary, or musical property. Partners and S corporation shareholders subject to the at-risk rules must check a box indicating this on Schedule E of Form 1040 or 1040-SR.

### CALCULATING YOUR AT-RISK LIMITATION

Your at-risk amounts—cash, adjusted basis of property contributed to the activity, and recourse loans—form your *at-risk basis*. It is this basis that is used to limit your losses. Your at-risk basis is calculated at the end of the year. Losses allowed reduce your at-risk basis. Thus, once you have offset your entire at-risk basis, you cannot claim further losses from the activity until you increase your at-risk basis.

Partners and LLC members are treated as at risk to the extent that basis in the entity is increased by their share of the entity's income. If the partnership or LLC makes distributions of income, the amount distributed reduces the partner's or LLC member's at-risk amount.

If you are subject to the at-risk rules, you must file Form 6198, *At-Risk Limitations*, to determine the amount of loss you can claim in the current year. You file a separate form for each activity. If you have an interest in a partnership, LLC, or S corporation that has more than one investment in any of the 4 categories listed, you can aggregate these activities. The 4 categories subject to these aggregation rules are:

1. Holding, producing, or distributing motion picture films or videotapes
2. Exploring for or exploiting oil and gas properties
3. Exploring for or exploiting geothermal deposits
4. Farming (but not forestry)

For example, if your S corporation distributes films and videotapes, you can aggregate these activities and treat them as one activity. In addition, all leased depreciable business equipment is treated as one activity for purposes of the at-risk rules.

You may also aggregate activities that you actively manage. This allows you to use losses from one activity as long as there is sufficient at-risk basis from another. If you invest in a partnership, LLC, or S corporation, the activities of the entity can be aggregated if 65% or more of the losses for the year are allocable to persons who actively participate in the management of the entity.

### SPECIAL RULE FOR REAL ESTATE FINANCING

You can treat nonrecourse financing from commercial lenders or government agencies as being at risk if the financing is secured by the real estate. This special rule does not apply to financing from related parties, seller financing, or financing from promoters. It does apply to real property placed in service after 1986. However, if you acquire an interest in a partnership, LLC, or S corporation after 1986, you can use this special rule regardless of when the entity placed the realty in service.

### *Passive Activity Loss Rules*

If you work for your business full-time, you need not be concerned with the **passive activity loss (PAL)** rules. These rules apply only to a business in which you have an ownership interest but do not work in the day-to-day operations or management (i.e., there is no **material participation**) as well as rental real estate activities. If an owner is subject to the PAL rules, then deductions from the activity for the year are limited (see under How the Passive Activity Loss Rules Limit Deductions for Expenses). If you fall under the PAL rules, you may also be subject to the 3.8% tax on net investment income (NII). But the passive activity loss rules do not affect the qualified business income deduction (Chapter 21).

Limited partners can never materially participate because they are barred by their status from making day-to-day operating decisions in their business.

Under regulations proposed, limited liability company (LLC) members would be treated like limited partners only if:

- The LLC is treated like a partnership, and
- The member does not have rights to manage the LLC at all times during the LLC's tax year under the law of the jurisdiction in which the LLC was organized and under the LLC governing agreement. Rights to manage include the power to bind the entity to a contract.

However, some courts have decided that LLC members are not treated the same as limited partners because they can participate in daily activities; their **material participation** determines whether they are subject to the PAL rules. The IRS has acquiesced in these cases.

---

***Passive activity loss (PAL)*** **Any activity involving the conduct of a business in which you do not materially participate and all rental activities. These rules operate to limit a current deduction for losses from these activities unless certain exceptions, discussed later in this chapter, apply.**

***Material participation*** **Participation in a passive activity that satisfies 1 of 7 tests set forth in the tax law. The basic test requires a minimum of 500 hours of participation during the year. Material participation may be allowed for as little as 100 hours of participation during the year if no other owner in the activity participates more.**

---

The 7 tests for proving material participation include:

1. You participate in the activity for more than 500 hours during the year. You need only participate for a mere 10 hours a week for 50 weeks in the year to satisfy this test.
2. Your participation is substantially all of the participation in the activity of all individuals for the year, including the participation of individuals who did not own any interest in the activity. This means that if you are a sole proprietor and do not hire someone else to run the business, you meet this participation test, even if you work only 5 hours each week.
3. You participate in the activity for more than 100 hours during the tax year, and you participate at least as much as any other individual (including individuals who do not own any interest in the activity) for the year.

**NOTE**

**Material participation is taken into account in determining whether the net investment income tax applies.** **See Chapter 30.**

4. The activity is a *significant participation activity*, and you participate in all significant participation activities for more than 500 hours. A significant participation activity is any business in which you participate for more than 100 hours during the year and in which you did not materially participate under any of the other material participation tests.
5. You materially participated in the activity for any 5 (whether or not consecutive) of the 10 preceding tax years. This rule can be useful to someone who retires from the business while continuing to own an interest but who materially participated prior to retirement.
6. The activity is a personal service activity in which you materially participated for any 3 (whether or not consecutive) preceding tax years.
7. Based on all the facts and circumstances, you participate in the activity on a regular, continuous, and substantial basis. At a minimum, you must have participated during more than 100 hours. Managing the activity is not treated as participation if any person other than you received compensation for managing it or any individual spent more hours during the year managing the activity than you (regardless of whether such individual was compensated).

#### RENTAL REAL ESTATE EXCEPTIONS

There are 2 special rules for rental real estate activities that may allow you to claim losses in excess of rental income. Rule 1 allows a limited amount of loss in excess of income to be deducted if participation is considered to be active (**active participation**). This limited loss deduction is called the $25,000 allowance and can be claimed by individuals whose adjusted gross income does not exceed $100,000. The allowance is phased out for those with adjusted gross income over $100,000 and is entirely eliminated when adjusted gross income is $150,000 or more. Married couples must file jointly to claim this allowance unless they lived apart for the entire year. In this case, up to $12,500 in losses can be deducted on a separate return (with a phase-out of the allowance for adjusted gross income over $50,000).

***Active participation*** **Participation in a rental real estate activity that is less than the material participation standard. Participation in decision making may be sufficient. For example, if you set the rents, screen tenants, and review expenses, you may satisfy the active participation test. Having a managing agent to collect rents and see to property repairs does not prevent active participation by an owner.**

Rule 2 allows real estate professionals to escape the PAL limitations altogether for purposes of deducting losses from their rental real estate activities. Individuals can be considered real estate professionals if they meet certain tests regarding their participation in real estate activities in general, including real estate construction, conversion, management, or brokerage activities, as well as rental real estate. If a qualifying real estate professional then meets material participation tests with respect to the rental real estate, losses from the rental real estate activity escape PAL restrictions. (Details of these rules are in the instructions to Form 8582.)

The PAL rules are very complicated. Determine whether you may be subject to the rules or whether you can ignore them. If you are subject to the rules, be sure you understand the potential impact that they can have on deducting expenses of an activity.

#### HOW THE PASSIVE ACTIVITY LOSS RULES LIMIT DEDUCTIONS FOR EXPENSES

If you run a business or work full time, you usually need not be concerned with the PAL rules. You probably meet the tests for material participation, although Schedule C for sole proprietors asks "Did you 'materially participate' in the operation of this business during 2021?" If you are a silent partner in a partnership, LLC, or S corporation, you should be concerned that you may be subject to the PAL rules. However, you may fall within an exception to the PAL rules in order to deduct losses in excess of income from the activity (for example, you may be able to eke out enough participation to be considered a material participant). Keep a diary or log book noting the time you put into the business and the types of activities you perform for the business.

If the rules apply, your losses from passive activities that exceed income from all other passive activities cannot be deducted in the current year. You can carry over your unused deductions to future years. These are called *suspended losses*, for which there is no limit on the carryover period.

You can claim all carryover deductions from an activity in the year in which you dispose of your entire interest in the activity. A disposition includes a sale to an unrelated party, abandonment of the business, or the business becoming completely worthless. Simply giving away your interest does not amount to a disposition that allows you to deduct your suspended losses.

The PAL limitation for noncorporate taxpayers is computed on Form 8582, *Passive Activity Loss Limitations*. Closely held C corporations subject to the PAL rules must file Form 8810, *Corporate Passive Activity Loss and Credit Limitations*. Similar rules apply to tax credits from passive activities. The limitation on tax credits from passive activities for noncorporate taxpayers is computed on Form 8582-CR, *Passive Activity Credit Limitations*.

#### COORDINATION WITH AT-RISK RULES

At-risk rules are applied first. Any amounts that are deductible after applying your at-risk loss limitation are then subject to the passive activity loss rules. Complete Form 6198 first; then complete Form 8582.

### *Limits on Farm Losses*

Prior to 2018, losses on Schedule F by those receiving certain subsidies were limited in how much could be used to offset nonfarm income. The limit was the greater of $300,000 ($150,000 for married persons filing separately) or the net farm income received over the past 5 years. This limitation on the use of farm losses is suspended for 2018 through 2025.

Pre-2018 losses limited by this rule are not lost forever; they can be carried forward and used after 2025 to the extent allowed by this rule. The limit for pre-2018 losses applies to farmers (other than those operating as C corporations) who received any direct or countercyclical payments under Title I of the Food, Conservation, and Energy Act of 2008, or Commodity Credit loans. For partnerships and S corporations, the pre-2018 limit applied at the partner or shareholder level, based on the year in which the entity's tax year ends.

## Income Earned Abroad

U.S. citizens and residents are subject to federal income tax on their worldwide income. However, if you live and work abroad, you may be able to exclude net income up to a set dollar amount each year. In other words, this income is tax free for federal income tax purposes (it may be subject to income taxes in which you work).

The foreign earned income exclusion for 2021 is up to $108,700. If you are married and both you and your spouse have foreign income, you may each be eligible for an exclusion. If your foreign earned income is more than $108,700, you are taxed only on amounts in excess of $108,700. This exclusion is not automatic; you must elect it.

To qualify for the foreign earned income exclusion, you must meet 2 conditions:

1. Your tax home is in a foreign country.
2. You meet either a foreign residence test (you live abroad for an uninterrupted period that includes one full year) or a physical presence test (you live abroad for 330 days during a 12-month period). However, the time requirements are waived for some countries. Due to the global health emergency caused by COVID-19, the minimum time requirements necessary to meet the bona fide residence test or physical presence test for the foreign earned income exclusion have been waived if leaving the foreign country was required. This applies to leaving:
   - The People's Republic of China (excluding Hong Kong and Macau) on or after December 1, 2019, but on or before July 15, 2020; or
   - Another foreign country on or after February 1, 2020, but on or before July 15, 2020 (unless the IRS provides additional relief).

If you qualify under the foreign residence or physical presence test for only part of the year, you can prorate the exclusion. Proration is made on a daily basis.

**Example**

**On January 1, 2020, you move to England and reside there until you move back to the United States on July 1, 2021. Since you have satisfied the foreign residence test (you lived abroad for an uninterrupted one-year period) and you lived abroad in 2021 for 181 days, you can exclude 181/365 of $108,700, or $53,903.**

If you receive payment this year for foreign earned income earned last year, you can exclude this amount this year to the extent that you did not use up your exclusion in the prior year. No exclusion can be claimed for a payment received this year for work done before the prior year.

**Example**

**In 2020, you had net earnings of $110,000 but were paid only $95,000, which you excluded. In 2021, you had net earnings of $140,000 and received the $15,000 owed for 2020. In 2021, you can exclude a total of $121,300 ($12,600 for 2020 because you did not use up your 2020 exclusion of $107,600, plus $108,700 exclusion for 2021). You are taxable on $18,700 of your 2021 earnings.**

If, while you are living abroad, you receive earned income in the United States, you cannot exclude this income.

What happens if you haven't met the foreign residence or physical presence test by the time your return is due? You cannot claim the exclusion before you have met either test, but you have a choice: You can ask for a filing extension if you expect to meet either test within the extension period.

**Example**

**Your return for 2021 is due June 15, 2022, but you request a filing extension to October 17, 2022, because you expect to satisfy the 330-day test in July 2021. You can claim the exclusion on your 2021 return.**

Alternatively, you can file your return to report the foreign earned income and then file an amended return to claim the exclusion once you satisfy either test.

**Example**

**Same as the preceding facts except that you won't satisfy the 330-day test until after October 17, 2022. You file your 2021 return and pay tax on the foreign income. Once the test is met, you file an amended return to receive a refund.**

Once you make the election to exclude foreign earned income, it remains in effect for subsequent years unless you revoke it. You revoke the election by attaching a statement to your return indicating revocation. Weigh carefully whether you want to revoke the election to claim the foreign earned income exclusion. Following a revocation you may not use the exclusion for 5 years unless the IRS grants you permission to do so. The IRS may grant permission under these circumstances:

- You return to the United States for a period of time.
- You move to a different foreign country that has different tax rates.
- You change employers.
- There is a change in the tax law of the foreign country in which you reside.

If you qualify for the foreign earned income exclusion, you may also take a deduction for foreign housing expenses (see Chapter 22). However, unlike employees qualifying for the foreign earned income exclusion, self-employed individuals cannot use the foreign housing exclusion, only the foreign housing deduction.

Taking the foreign earned income exclusion, which is electable and not mandatory, has an impact on other tax rules:

- You cannot reduce your net earnings from self-employment by the foreign earned income exclusion for purposes of self-employment tax.
- You cannot base IRA or Roth IRA contributions on excluded income, but must factor this income into account in determining whether you qualify for contributions if you have earned income above the excluded foreign earned income limit.
- You cannot take the foreign tax credit or deduction for foreign taxes related to the excludable foreign earned income. If you claimed the foreign earned income exclusion in the past and claim a foreign tax credit this year, this revokes your election to claim the exclusion. You cannot claim the exclusion for at least 5 years unless the IRS grants you permission to claim the exclusion.

## Where to Report Business Income or Loss

### *Self-Employed (Including Independent Contractors)*

Business income is generally reported on Schedule C, *Profit or Loss from Business*. The results from this schedule are part of your personal income tax return, Form 1040 or 1040-SR.

If you maintain inventory, you must complete Part III of Schedule C to figure your cost of goods sold.

Business-related investment-type income may be reported on Schedule C or on your personal return, depending on what's involved. Interest on a business bank account is reported on Schedule C. Similarly, if the business's activity is lending money, then interest income from customers is reported on Schedule C. Dealers in securities also report dividends received on stock as business income on Schedule C. Other investment-type income is reported directly on Form 1040 or 1040-SR.

NOL carryforwards are reported as a negative amount entered on Schedule 1 of Form 1040 or 1040-SR as other income.

### *Foreign Earned Income Exclusion*

Self-employed individuals electing the foreign earned income exclusion file Form 2555, *Foreign Earned Income*.

### *Farmers*

If you are a sole proprietor operating a farming business, instead of using Schedule C to report your income, you use Schedule F, Profit or Loss from Farming. The section of the schedule used to report your farm income depends on your method of accounting. Cash basis farmers use Part I of Schedule F to report income. Accrual basis farmers use Part III of Schedule F to report farm income.

If you received rental income based on farm production or crop shares and you did not materially participate in the management or operation of the farm, use Form 4835, *Farm Rental Income and Expenses*, to report this rental income. Since you did not materially participate, this income is not part of your farming income on which self-employment tax is assessed. If you elect to income-average your farm income, you must file Schedule J, *Farm Income Averaging*.

Net operating losses that you carryback are computed on Form 1045, *Application for Tentative Refund*. You use this form or Form 1040-X to claim an NOL carryback. If you are carrying forward an NOL, you claim the loss as a negative amount entered as other income on Schedule 1 of Form 1040 or 1040-SR.

### *Partnerships and LLCs*

Operating income of a partnership or LLC, called *total income* (loss), is reported on Form 1065, *U.S. Return of Partnership Income*. For inventory-based partnerships and LLCs, the cost of goods sold is figured on Form 1125-A, *Cost of Goods Sold*.

Miscellaneous income items discussed in this chapter are reported separately from the gross profit, fees, and sales. Miscellaneous items are detailed on a separate schedule attached to the return. Partners and members in LLCs then report their share of net income or loss from the business on Schedule E, *Supplemental Income and Loss*, as part of their personal return.

Other income items are separately stated items that pass through to partners and members apart from the business' total income, and are reported on Schedule K-1, *Partner's Share of*

*Income, Credits, Deductions, Etc.* Owners then report these separate items on the appropriate place on their personal returns. For example, items considered to be portfolio income—income other than that derived in the ordinary course of business—are separately stated items.

If the partnership or LLC passes through losses to the partners and members, they may be able to claim an NOL deduction on their personal returns. Refer to the earlier discussion of "Self-Employed."

### S Corporations

Operating income of an S corporation is reported on Form 1120-S, *U.S. Income Tax Return for an S Corporation*. For inventory-based S corporations, the cost of goods sold is figured on Form 1125-A, *Cost of Goods Sold*.

Miscellaneous income items discussed in this chapter are reported separately from the gross profit from fees and sales. These miscellaneous items are detailed on a separate schedule attached to the return. Shareholders then report their share of net income or loss from the business on Schedule E, *Supplemental Income and Loss*.

Income taxed to the S corporation for LIFO recapture, excessive passive income, or built-in gains is explained on a separate schedule. The tax on this income is then reported on Form 1120-S.

Other income items are separately stated items that pass through to shareholders apart from the corporation's total income and are reported on Schedule K-1, *Shareholder's Share of Income, Credits, Deductions, Etc*. Shareholders then report these separate items on the appropriate place on their personal returns. For example, items considered to be portfolio income—income other than income derived in the ordinary course of business—are separately stated items.

If the S corporation passes through losses to the shareholders, they may be able to claim an NOL deduction on their personal returns. Refer to the earlier discussion of "Self-Employed."

### C Corporations

C corporations report their income on Form 1120, *U.S. Corporation Income Tax Return*. For inventory-based corporations, the cost of goods sold is figured on Form 1125-A, *Cost of Goods Sold*. Dividends are reported on Schedule C of Form 1120 to enable the corporation to figure its dividends-received deduction. Tax-exempt interest received or accrued is reported on Schedule K of Form 1120.

Miscellaneous income items, such as recoveries of bad debts deducted in prior years or recapture of the first-year expense deduction, are detailed on a separate schedule attached to the return.

Net operating losses carried from other years to the current year are deducted on the specific line provided for this item on Form 1120.

### All Taxpayers

**Merchant Income on Credit Cards.** Merchant card and third-party payment providers must report transactions on Form 1099-K that total more than $20,000 for at least 200 transactions. (For transactions settled after December 31, 2021, the threshold drops to $600, regardless of the number of transactions.) Include the income from these transactions along with other gross receipts. Adjust the income reported by any returns, refunds, allowances, cash-backs, or other amounts that reduced the revenue from these transactions. No reconciliation with 1099-K amounts is required.

**At-Risk Loss Limits and Passive Loss Rules.** Taxpayers subject to the PAL rules and the at-risk rules must figure any limitations on business losses on specific tax forms. Figure the at-risk loss limits first. Then compute the PAL limits.

Only individuals and pass-through entities must figure the at-risk loss limits (closely held C corporations that are active companies are exempt from these rules). The limits are figured on Form 6198, *At-Risk Limitations*.

Noncorporate taxpayers compute their PAL limits on Form 8582, *Passive Activity Loss Limitations*. Closely held C corporations subject to the PAL rules must file Form 8810, *Corporate Passive Activity Loss and Credit Limitations*.

**Commercial Fishermen.** For federal income tax reporting purposes, report all income from commercial fishing activities, without regard to the deferral rule explained earlier in this chapter. The amount contributed to your CCF account is entered as a negative number on the line for taxable income on Form 1040 or 1040-SR. Write "CCF" next to the line and the amount deposited.

Beginning with the tax year in which you establish a CCF agreement with the Department of Commerce, you must report annual deposit activities—even if there is no activity. Reporting is made on NMFS Form 34-82 (at https://www.fisheries.noaa.gov/national/funding-and-financial-services/capital-construction-fund-documents-and-forms) to the National Oceanic and Atmospheric Administration Fisheries, at CCF Program, 1315 East-West Highway, Silver Springs, MD 20910-3282, within 30 days of the day you file your federal income tax return.

**Foreign Investments.** Special reporting rules apply for foreign assets and accounts. Form 8938, *Statement of Specified Foreign Financial Assets,* must be filed with a taxpayer's income tax return if the aggregate value of specified foreign assets exceeds $50,000 on the last day of the year, or $75,000 at any time during the year. This applies to an individual as well as to a specified domestic entity, which includes a domestic corporation or partnership formed or used to hold, directly or indirectly, specified foreign assets. Such a domestic entity is (1) an entity closely held by a specified individual and (2) at least 50% of the entity's gross income is passive income, or 50% of its assets are assets that produce passive income. For further clarification on this reporting requirement, see regulations (T.D. 9752).

There may be additional (separate) reporting to the Treasury. This is explained in Appendix A.

# CHAPTER 5

# Capital Gains and Losses


| | | | |
|---|---|---|---|
| What Are Capital Gains and Losses? | 95 | Loss Limitations | 103 |
| Tax Treatment of Capital Gains and Losses for Pass-Through Entities | 101 | Sales of Business Interests | 105 |
| Tax Treatment of Capital Gains for C Corporations | 103 | Opportunity Zone Investments | 106 |
| | | Special Situations | 107 |


Companies may sell assets other than inventory items. These sales may result in gains or losses that are classified as *capital gains or losses*. Similarly, companies may exchange assets, also producing capital gains or losses unless tax-free exchange rules apply. Furthermore, owners may sell their interests in the business for gain or loss.

Capital gains generally are treated more favorably than other types of income. However, C corporations do not realize any significant tax benefit from capital gains. What's more, capital losses are subject to special limitations.

The treatment of gains and losses from Section 1231 property and income resulting from depreciation recapture are discussed in Chapter 6.

For further information about capital gains and losses, see IRS Publication 537, *Installment Sales*; IRS Publication 544, *Sales and Other Dispositions of Assets*; and IRS Publication 550, *Investment Interest and Expenses*.

## What Are Capital Gains and Losses?

The tax law generally looks more favorably on income classified as capital gains than on other types of income—at least for pass-through entities. On the flip side, the tax law provides special treatment for capital losses. To understand how capital gains and losses affect your business income, you need to know what items are subject to capital gain or loss treatment and how to determine gains and losses.

### Capital Assets

If you own property used in or owned by your business (other than Section 1231 property, discussed in Chapter 6, or Section 1244 stock, discussed later in this chapter), gain or loss on the disposition of the property generally is treated as capital gain or loss. *Capital gains and losses* are gains and losses taken on **capital assets**.

> ***Capital assets*** **Property held for investment and other property not otherwise excluded from capital asset treatment. For example, your interest in a partnership or stocks and securities is treated as a capital asset.**

Most property is treated as capital assets. Excluded from the definition of capital assets are:

- Property held for sale to customers or property that will physically become part of merchandise for sale to customers (inventory)
- Accounts or notes receivable generated by your business (e.g., accounts receivable from the sale of inventory)
- Depreciable property used in your business, even if already fully depreciated (e.g., telephones)
- Real property used in your business (e.g., your factory)
- A copyright; literary or artistic composition; a letter or memorandum; or other similar property (e.g., photographs, tapes, manuscripts) created by your personal efforts or acquired from the creator by gift or in another transaction entitling you to use the creator's basis
- A patent, invention, model or design, or secret formula or process created by you
- U.S. government publications

Under a special rule, self-created musical works qualify for capital asset treatment, if the musician so elects. A separate election must be made for each musical composition or copyright for the musical work in the year it is sold or exchanged. The election is made simply by reporting capital gain or the sale or exchange (there's a 6-month window to revoke the election). Similarly, the cutting of standing timber may be treated as eligible for capital gain treatment as Section 1231 property (explained in Chapter 6).

### Determining the Amount of Your Gain or Loss

The difference between the **amount received** for your property on a sale, exchange, or other disposition, and your **adjusted basis** in the property is your gain or loss.

> ***Amount received*** **The cash, fair market value of property, and relief of liability you get when you dispose of your property. For example, if you own a computer system for your business and you upgrade with a new system and sell your old system to another business, any cash you receive is considered an amount received. Upon the sale, you receive $5,000 cash, plus the buyer agrees to pay the remaining balance of $2,000 on a bank loan you took to buy the system; your amount received is $7,000 ($5,000 cash, plus $2,000 liability relieved).**

***Adjusted basis*** **This is your basis in the property, adjusted for certain items. Start with the original cost if you bought the property (the cash and other property you paid to acquire it). Even if the cash did not come out of your pocket—for example, if you took a loan—the cash you turn over to the seller is part of your basis. Adjust the basis by reducing it for any depreciation claimed (or that could have been claimed) and any casualty loss you claimed with respect to the property. For example, if your original computer system cost you $10,000, and you claimed $2,000 depreciation, your adjusted basis is $8,000.**

You adjust basis—upward or downward—for certain items occurring in the acquisition of the asset or during the time you hold it. Amounts that *increase* basis include:

- Improvements or additions to property.
- Legal fees to acquire property or defend title to it.
- Unharvested crops sold with the land.

Amounts that *decrease* basis include:

- Amortized bond premiums.
- Cancellation of income adjustments (e.g., debt forgiveness because of bankruptcy or insolvency or on farm or business real property).
- Casualty losses that have been deducted (e.g., insurance awards and other settlements).
- Deductions for energy-efficient commercial buildings.
- Depletion allowances with respect to certain natural resources.
- Depreciation, amortization, first-year expensing, and obsolescence. (You must reduce the basis of property by the amount of depreciation that you were entitled to take even if you failed to take it.)
- Investment credit claimed with respect to the property. (The full credit decreases basis but one-half of the credit claimed after 1982 is added back for a net reduction of one-half of the credit.)
- Return of capital. (Dividends on stock that are paid out of capital or out of a depletion reserve instead of earnings and profits or surplus.)
- Tax credit for alternative fuel vehicles and plug-in electric vehicles.

You do not adjust basis for selling expenses and related costs. These amounts are factored into the amount received (they reduce the amount received on the transaction).
Examples of selling expenses that reduce the amount received include:

- Advertising
- Appraisal fees
- Attorneys fees to close a sale
- Document preparation costs
- Escrow fees

- Overnight delivery costs for mailing a mortgage satisfaction check in a real estate transaction
- Recording fees for real estate transactions (if paid by the seller)
- Title search fees for real estate transactions
- Transfer or stamp taxes

**NOTE**

**Overstating (inflating) the adjusted basis to minimize gain can result in tax penalties and extends the statute of limitations for audits to 6 years (from the usual 3 years) if the omission from gross income is more than 25%.**

**DETERMINING BASIS ON ASSETS TRANSFERRED BETWEEN YOU AND YOUR ENTITY**

The entity takes over your basis in any assets you contribute in a nontaxable transaction. Thus, if you contribute property to your partnership, the partnership assumes your basis in the property. Similarly, if you contribute property to your corporation as part of a tax-free incorporation, the corporation takes over your basis in the property. The rules for determining the basis in interests in pass-through entities are explained in Chapter 4.

**FIGURING GAIN OR LOSS**

When the amount received exceeds the adjusted basis of the property, you have a gain. When the adjusted basis exceeds the amount received, you have a loss.

### *Sale or Exchange Requirement*

In order to obtain capital gain or loss treatment on the disposition of a capital asset, you usually must sell or exchange property. Typically, you sell your property, but other transactions may qualify for sale or exchange treatment. For example, if your corporation redeems some or all of your stock, you may be able to treat the redemption as a sale or exchange. Capital losses are subject to limitation on current deductibility as explained later in this chapter.

If you dispose of property in some way other than a sale or exchange, gain or loss is generally treated as ordinary gain or loss. For example, if you abandon business property, your loss is treated as ordinary loss, even though the property is a capital asset. However, if the property is foreclosed on or repossessed, your loss may be a capital loss. If stock becomes worthless, this is treated as a capital loss. Ordinary losses are deductible without regard to the results from other transactions and can be used to offset various types of income (such as interest income).

### *Holding Period*

Whether gains and losses are short-term or long-term depends on how long the asset disposed of has been held. If the holding period is more than 1 year, then gain or loss is long-term. If the holding period is 1 year or less, then the gain or loss is short-term.

If the business buys an asset, the holding period commences at that time (technically on the day after the acquisition date). If you transfer property to your business and the transfer is viewed as a nonrecognition transaction (for example, a tax-free incorporation), the company's holding period includes your holding period.

**Example**

**You form a corporation and transfer ownership of your truck and other items to the corporation in exchange for all of its stock. You acquired your truck on June 1, 2020, and transfer it to the corporation on July 1, 2021. On November 1, 2021, the corporation sells the truck. Its gain or loss on the sale of the truck is long-term because the holding period for the truck is more than one year—measured from the time you acquired it.**

If a partnership makes an in-kind (property) distribution to you, include the partnership's holding period in your holding period. However, if the distribution is from the partnership's inventory, then you cannot add the partnership's holding period to yours if you sell the property within 5 years.

#### TRANSFERS TO A PARTNERSHIP OR LIMITED LIABILITY COMPANY

If you transfer an asset to your company, the company takes on your holding period since this is a nontaxable transaction. If you sell an asset to your company, the company starts its own holding period since the sale generally is a taxable transaction (the company obtains a stepped-up basis for the property).

### Tax-Free Exchanges

Gain need not be immediately reported as income if the transaction qualifies as a tax-free exchange. The term *tax free* is not an entirely apt description because the tax rules for these transactions merely *postpone* the reporting of gain rather than make gain permanently tax free. You reduce the basis of the property you acquire in the exchange by the gain you realized on the trade but did not have to report. Then, when you later sell the replacement property in a taxable transaction, you will report the gain on both initial exchange and the later disposition (if any).

The tax-free exchange rules apply only for real property; exchanges of other types of property (e.g., vehicles; livestock; intangibles) do not qualify.

Real property includes land and improvements to land, unsevered crops and other natural products of land, and water and air space superjacent to land. Improvements to land include inherently permanent structures (e.g., buildings) and the structural components of inherently permanent structures. Local law definitions may be used to determine the meaning of the term "real property" for purposes of like-kind exchanges.

Under an incidental rule, personal property may be treated as part of real property qualifying for like-kind exchange treatment. Personal property is incidental to real property acquired in an exchange if, in standard commercial transactions, the personal property is typically transferred together with the real property, and the aggregate fair market value of the incidental personal property transferred with the real property does not exceed 15% of the aggregate fair market value of the replacement real property.

**Example**

**You exchange one office building for another of equal value. Your building is worth $175,000, but has a basis of $100,000. The value of the new building is $175,000. You have a gain of $75,000, which may be postponed because of the tax-free exchange rules. The basis in the new building is $100,000 ($175,000 minus $75,000 gain not recognized). If you sell the new building in the future for $225,000, you will recognize gain of $125,000 ($75,000 deferred from the initial exchange, plus $50,000 from the appreciation of the replacement building).**

To qualify for the tax-free exchange treatment, both the old property (the property you are giving up, called *relinquished property*) and the new property (the property you are acquiring, called *replacement property*) must be business or investment property (certain property cannot be exchanged tax free). And both of the properties must be of *like kind*. This means they must be of the same class of property. Examples of like-kind property include:

- Vacant lot for a factory building
- Factory building for an office complex
- City property for farmland
- Real estate owned outright for real estate subject to a lease of 30 years or more

If non-like-kind property is also received in the exchange, you must recognize gain to the extent of this other property, called *boot*.

**Example**

**Use the example of the building, except that the replacement building is only valued at $150,000 and you receive $25,000 cash to make the exchange of equal value. You must recognize gain of $25,000, the extent of the boot received. The basis of the replacement building in this case is reduced by only $50,000, and the gain is not recognized.**

#### TIMING

Like-kind exchanges must be completed within set time limits. The new property must be identified within 45 days after you transfer the old property. This identification applies to up to 3 properties (or any number where the value of the properties is not more than double the value of the property given up). To identify the property, a good description of it must be put in writing. *Incidental property*, property valued at not more than 15% of the total value of the other property, is disregarded; it need not be identified. Then, the exchange must be completed (you must receive the new property) within 180 days after you transfer the old property or the due date of your return (including extensions) for the year you gave up the old property if this is earlier than 180 days after the transfer. For 2020, as a result of COVID-19, the IRS had granted more time to meet the time tests for like-kind exchanges. Whether similar relief will be available for 2021 is uncertain. Check the Supplement for any update.

Since it is not always easy to locate appropriate exchange property, you may work with a qualified intermediary to locate the property, acquire it, and then exchange it with you. A *qualified intermediary* is someone (other than your attorney, accountant, broker, employee, or a related person) who makes a written agreement to acquire the property you are giving up and to transfer replacement property to you. The agreement must limit your rights to receive, pledge, borrow, or otherwise obtain the benefits of money or other property held by the qualified intermediary.

### *Installment Sales*

Gain need not be reported all at once if the sale is structured as an installment sale. This generally allows you to report gain as payments are received. An *installment sale* occurs when at least one payment is received after the year of sale.

Under the installment method, a portion of each payment received represents a return of your investment (part of your adjusted basis), and another part represents your profit (gain). You figure the amount of gain reported each year by a ratio:

$$\text{Gross profit percentage (reportable gain)} = \frac{\text{Gross profit}}{\text{Selling price (contract price)}}$$

### ELECTION OUT OF INSTALLMENT REPORTING

You can opt out of installment reporting and elect to report the entire gain in the year of sale (even though payments will be received at a later time). The election does not require any special forms. You simply report your entire gain in the year of sale. But once you do so, you generally cannot change your mind later on, even if your choice proved to be the wrong one taxwise.

**Example**

**You sell property worth $100,000 for 5 annual installments of $20,000, plus 8% interest. Your adjusted basis in the property is $60,000 so your gross profit is $40,000 ($100,000 – $60,000). Your gross profit percentage is 40% ($40,000 ÷ $100,000). This means that 40% of each installment represents your gain while 60% is a return of your investment. Thus, in the first year, $8,000 of the $20,000 payment is gain while $12,000 is a return of your investment.**

Why would you want to report all of your gain in one year when you can spread it out over a number of years? Reporting the entire gain in the year of sale may be wise, for example, if you have a capital loss carryforward that can be used to offset the gain.

### INTEREST ON DEFERRED PAYMENTS

Payments must bear a reasonable rate of interest. If you fail to fix a reasonable rate of interest, then a portion of each payment is deemed to represent interest rather than capital gain. *Reasonable rate of interest* usually is the applicable federal rate (AFR) of interest for the term of the installment sale. (Applicable federal rate is explained in Chapter 7.)

If the seller finances the purchase, the required minimum interest rate is the lower of 9% ("safe harbor rate") compounded semiannually or the AFR (even if it's higher than 9%), provided the financed amount (the stated principal) does not exceed $6,099,500 in 2021. With interest rates running below the 9% safe harbor rate, charging the AFR will produce a lower allowable interest rate. If the deferred amount exceeds $6,099,500, then the required minimum interest rate is 100% of the AFR.

### DEPRECIABLE PROPERTY

If you sell depreciable property on the installment basis, any depreciation recapture must be reported in full in the year of sale regardless of when payments are actually received. In other words, gain resulting from depreciation recapture may exceed the cash payments received in the year of the installment sale but must be reported as income anyway. Installment sales are also discussed in Chapter 2.

## Tax Treatment of Capital Gains and Losses for Pass-Through Entities

Capital gains and losses are separately stated items that pass through separately to owners. They are not taken into account in figuring the entity's total income (or loss). The reason for this distinction is to allow individual owners to apply the capital gain and loss rules on individual tax returns.

The impact of pass-through treatment of capital gains and losses is that owners may have favorable capital gains rates applied to their share of the business's capital gains. Similarly, they may offset pass-through gains and losses from their business against their personal gains and losses.

**Example**

**In 2021, a shareholder in an S corporation has a pass-through capital loss from his corporation of $10,000. He also has a $10,000 capital gain distribution from a mutual fund he owns in his personal investment account. He can offset the business loss by his personal gain on his individual income tax return.**

### *Tax Rates on Capital Gains*

Owners of pass-through entities who are individuals pay tax on their share of capital gains as they would on their gains from personal investments. Thus, long-term capital gains are generally subject to a basic capital gains rate of 15%. However, owners may have a 0% or 20% tax rate, depending on their taxable income, including their capital gains. The taxable income breakpoints for the zero, 15%, and 20% tax rates on long-term capital gains for individuals can be found in Table 5.1. At the time of publication, Congress was considering a hike in the capital gains rate for transactions after September 13, 2021; check the Supplement for any update.

Owners who are "high income taxpayers" may also pay the 3.8% tax on net investment income (although gains from the sale of business property may not be treated as investment income). The capital gains rates apply to sales and exchanges in 2021 as well as to payments received in 2021 on installment sales made in prior years.

#### SHORT-TERM GAIN

This type of gain is subject to the same tax rates as ordinary income. Owners in a pass-through entity may pay different tax rates on the same share of short-term capital gain.

**Example**

**An LLC with 2 equal owners sells at a profit a capital asset held for 2 years. In 2021, one owner may be above the 20% threshold for capital gains while another is below the 20% threshold. Even though each owner receives an equal share of the gain, one owner pays a greater amount of tax on that gain than the other according to each owner's taxable income.**

#### UNRECAPTURED GAIN

Gain from the sale of real property on which straight line depreciation was taken results in unrecaptured gain (the amount of straight line depreciation). This portion of capital gain is taxed at the maximum rate of 25%.

If property with unrecaptured gain is sold on the installment basis (discussed earlier in this chapter), then the first payment is deemed to reflect unrecaptured gain. When this amount has

**TABLE 5.1 2021 Taxable Income Breakpoints for Capital Gains Rates***

| Rate | Married Filing Jointly | Head of Household | Single | Married Filing Separately |
|---|---|---|---|---|
| 0% | Up to $80,800 | Up to $54,100 | Up to $40,400 | Up to $40,400 |
| 15% | $80,800–$501,600 | $54,100–$473,750 | $40,400–$445,850 | $40,400–$250,800 |
| 20% | Over $501,600 | Over $473,750 | Over $445,850 | Over $250,800 |

*Rates may be changed for transactions after September 13, 2021; see the Supplement for any update.

been fully reported, all additional amounts are capital gains subject to the lower rates detailed above.

#### SECTION 1202 GAIN

Gain on the sale of Section 1202 stock (referred to as "small business stock"), which is stock in a C corporation that meets certain requirements, is partly or fully excludable. The exclusion depends on when the stock was acquired. Later in this chapter there is more on the sale of small business stock. If there is a portion that isn't excludable, it is taxed at a maximum 28% capital gain rate.

#### CAPITAL LOSSES

Special rules determine how capital losses of individuals may be used. These rules are discussed later in this chapter.

## Tax Treatment of Capital Gains for C Corporations

C corporations must follow the rules discussed throughout this chapter on reporting capital gains and losses separately from their other income. These gains and losses are detailed on the corporation's Schedule D. However, C corporations realize no benefit from capital gains. *Net gains*, capital gains in excess of capital losses, are simply added to other business income. In effect, capital gains are taxed at the same rate as the corporation's other income.

While there are no benefits from capital gains, capital losses of C corporations are subject to special limitations discussed later in this chapter. Thus, in order to apply the capital loss limitation, capital gains must be segregated from ordinary income.

## Loss Limitations

In some cases, even if you sell or exchange property at a loss, you may not be permitted to deduct your loss. If you sell, exchange, or even abandon a Section 197 intangible (see Chapter 14 for a complete discussion of the amortization of Section 197 intangibles), you cannot deduct your loss if you still hold other Section 197 intangibles that you acquired in the same transaction. Instead, you increase the basis of the Section 197 intangibles that you still own. This means that instead of deducting your loss in the year you dispose of one Section 197 intangible, you will deduct a portion of the loss over the remaining recovery period for the Section 197 intangibles you still hold.

Similarly, you cannot deduct losses on sales or exchanges of property between related parties (defined later). This related party rule prevents you from deducting a loss if you sell a piece of equipment to your spouse. However, the party acquiring the property from you (the original transferee, or in this case, your spouse) can add to the basis the amount of loss you were not allowed to deduct in determining gain or loss on a subsequent disposition of the property.

**Example**

**You sell your partnership interest to your daughter for $7,500. Your basis in the interest is $10,000. You cannot deduct your $2,500 loss. However, if your daughter then sells the partnership interest for $12,000, her gain is minimized to the extent of your nondeductible loss. Her tentative gain is $4,500 ($12,000 amount received less basis of $7,500). The amount of gain she must report is $2,000 ($4,500 tentative gain less $2,500 nondeductible loss).**

### Related Parties

The tax law defines who is considered a *related party*. This includes not only certain close relatives (spouses, siblings, parents, children, grandparents, and grandchildren), but also certain businesses you control. A *controlled entity* is a corporation in which you own, directly or indirectly, more than 50% of the value of all outstanding stock, or a partnership in which you own, directly or indirectly, more than 50% of the capital interest or profits interest.

Businesses may be treated as related parties. These relationships include:

- A corporation and partnership if the same persons own more than 50% in the value of the outstanding stock of the corporation and more than 50% of the capital interest or profits interest in the partnership.
- Two corporations that are members of the same controlled group (one corporation owns a certain percentage of the other, or owners own a certain percentage of each corporation).
- Two S corporations if the same persons own more than 50% in value of the outstanding stock in each corporation.
- Two corporations, one of which is an S corporation, if the same person owns more than 50% in value of the outstanding stock of each corporation.
- Special rules are used to determine control. These rules not only look at actual ownership but also take into account certain constructive ownership (ownership that is not actual but has the same effect in the eyes of the tax law). For example, for purposes of the related-party rule, you are treated as constructively owning any stock owned by your spouse.

Special rules also apply to transactions between partners and their partnerships. It is important to note that what you may view as a related party may not be treated as such for tax purposes. Thus, for example, your in-laws and cousins are not treated as related parties. If you sell property to an in-law or cousin at a loss, you are not prevented from deducting the loss.

### Capital Loss Limits on Individuals

You can deduct capital losses against capital gains without limit. Short-term losses from sales of assets held one year or less are first used to offset short-term gains otherwise taxed up to 37%. Similarly, long-term losses from sales of assets held more than one year offset long-term gains otherwise taxed as low as 15% (it's unlikely that the zero rate would apply because capital gains are taken into account in determining taxable income, which in turn dictates the capital gains rate). Losses in excess of their category are then used to offset gains starting with those taxed at the highest rates. For example, short-term losses in excess of short-term capital gains can be used to offset long-term capital gains from the sale of qualified small business stock acquired before February 18, 2009, and held more than 5 years, 50% of such gain of which is otherwise taxed at up to 28% (for an effective tax rate of 14%). However, if your capital losses exceed your capital gains, you can deduct only $3,000 of losses against your other income (such as salaries, dividends, and interest income).

If married persons file separate returns, the capital loss offset to other income is limited to $1,500. If you do not use up all of your capital losses, you can carry over any unused amount and claim it in future years. There is no limit on the carryover period for individuals.

### Capital Loss Limits on C Corporations

If your C corporation realizes capital losses, they are deductible only against capital gains. Any capital losses in excess of capital gains can be carried back for 3 years and then, if not used up, carried forward for up to 5 years. If they are not used within the 5-year carryover period, they are lost forever.

The carryback may entitle your corporation to a refund of taxes from the carryback years. The corporation can apply for this refund by filing Form 1120-X, *Amended U.S. Corporation Income Tax Return*. A corporation cannot choose to forgo the carryback in order to simply carry forward the unused capital losses.

Special rules apply in calculating the corporation's carryback and carryforward. You do not use any capital loss carried from another year when determining the corporation's capital loss deduction for the current year. If you have losses from more than one year carried to another year, you use the losses as follows: First, deduct the loss from the earliest year. After that is fully deducted, deduct the remaining loss from the next earliest year. You cannot use a capital loss carried from another year to produce or increase a net operating loss (NOL) in the year to which you carry it.

## Sales of Business Interests

The type of interest you own governs the tax treatment accorded to the sale of your interest (more details about the tax treatment of distributions on the sales of business interests are discussed in Chapter 25).

### *Sole Proprietorship*

If you sell your unincorporated sole proprietorship, you are viewed as selling the assets of the business. The sale of all the assets of a business is discussed in Chapter 6.

### *Partnerships and LLCs*

#### PARTNERSHIPS

Gain or loss on the sale of your partnership interest is treated as capital gain *except* to the extent any gain relates to **unrealized receivables** and inventory items. Gain in this case is ordinary income.

***Unrealized receivables*** **These are amounts not previously included in income that represent a right to payments for noncapital assets, which include inventory, services rendered, and services to be rendered.**

If you receive items that were inventory to the partnership, they may be treated as capital assets to you. However, if you dispose of the items within 5 years, then any gain with respect to these items is ordinary income, not capital gain.

#### LLCS

Generally, the rules governing the sale of a partnership interest apply with equal force to the sale of an interest in an LLC. However, there are 2 special situations to consider:

1. *Sale of multiple-owner LLC to a single buyer*. The entity is treated as hypothetically making a liquidating distribution of all of its assets to the sellers, followed by a deemed purchase by the single buyer of all the assets now hypothetically held by the sellers. The sellers then recognize gain or loss (depending on their basis in the LLC interests).
2. *Sale of a single-member LLC to multiple buyers*. This entity is treated as hypothetically selling its assets and then contributing them to the new entity composed of multiple buyers (treated as a partnership). You recognize gain or loss on the deemed sale of your interest to the buyers. There is no gain or loss recognition upon the contribution of the assets to the new entity.

### *S and C Corporations*

When you sell your stock in a corporation, you recognize capital gain or loss. The amount of your gain or loss is the difference between your adjusted basis in the stock and the amount received in exchange.

If another corporation acquires 80% or more of the stock in your corporation within a 12-month period, it can elect to treat the stock purchase as if it had purchased the underlying asset. If so, your corporation must recognize gain or loss as if it had sold its assets for fair market value. From the buyer's perspective, this enables the corporation to step up the basis of its assets as if it were a new corporation. The purchase price is allocated to the assets as explained in Chapter 6.

## Opportunity Zone Investments

Regardless of where your business is located, if it invests in a Qualified Opportunity Fund (QOF), which is a fund required to invest at least 90% of its funds in low-income communities designated by the U.S. Treasury, then special tax rules apply to gains from these holdings. The rules for being a Qualified Opportunity Zone Business are discussed in Chapter 6.

### *Tax Deferral*

If the business has capital gains and invests the proceeds in QOF within 180 days of the sale (with special relief for COVID-19 for 2020 explained in Notice 2020–39), the gain is deferred. There is no monetary limit on the amount of gain that can be deferred. The deferred gain is recognized on the earlier of an inclusion event for shares in the QOF or December 31, 2026.

- *Inclusion events*: A sale of a QOF interest, gift of a QOF interest, transfer to a spouse incident to divorce, loss of QOF status (a decertification of the fund as qualified, either voluntarily or involuntarily), a partnership distribution of a QOF to the extent that cash or the fair market value exceeds the partner's outside basis in the QOF; a QOF becomes worthless.
- *Non-inclusion events*: Death (but heirs do not get a stepped-up basis; they recognize the deferred gain in 2026 or when they have an inclusion event, whichever is earlier), contribution to a partnership.

**NOTE**

**Not all states allow for QOF tax breaks. California and Massachusetts, for example, have specifically decoupled from the QOF tax rules. (Out-of-state investors in a QOF that has projects in California may also be subject to California income tax; it's not yet clear.)**

For Section 1231 gains (discussed in Chapter 6), the 180-day period begins on the date of the sale (not the end of the year in which Section 1231 gains are netted against Section 1231 losses). The gross amount of the Section 1231 gain (not the next amount after offsetting them by Section 1231 losses) qualify for deferral.

Gains from installment sales can be deferred through an investment in an Opportunity Zone. This is so even if the original sale took place prior to 2018 when the Opportunity Zone rules went into effect.

The deferral election can be made by a partnership or S corporation or its owners. So, for example, if a partnership realizes a gain, the partnership can make a Qualified Opportunity Zone (QOZ) election; gain is not included in the partners' distributive share. Similar but not identical rules apply for S corporations. At the owner's election, the 180-day period begins on any of these dates:

1. The date that the entity would have used (i.e., usually the date of sale)
2. The final day of the entity's tax year (e.g., December 31 for a calendar-year entity)
3. The due date of the entity's tax return without extensions.

### *Stepped-Up Basis*

Capital gains reinvested in a QOF get a step up in basis. This is 10% if the investment is held at least 5 years and an additional 5% if held at least 7 years (total step up of 15%). This minimizes the gain recognized on the deferred income explained above.

### *Exclusion of Gain*

All capital gain from the sale or exchange of an investment in a QOF is excludable from gross income if the investment is held at least 10 years. The exclusion applies only to gains accrued after the investment is made, not to prior capital gains that have been deferred as explained above.

## Special Situations

### *Sale of Qualified Business Stock*

Tax laws encourage investments in small businesses by offering a unique tax incentive. If you own stock in a corporation treated as a **small business**, you may be able to exclude somc or all of your gain. Stock in such a small business is called Section 1202 stock after the section in the Tax Code that governs it.

***Small business*** **For purposes of excluding gain on the sale of stock, a small business is a C corporation with gross assets of no more than $50 million when the stock is issued. The small business must be an active business and not a mere holding company. The stock must have been issued after August 10,1993.**

There are many conditions surrounding this exclusion:

- It applies only to stock issued by a small business after August 10, 1993.
- As of the date the stock was issued, the corporation was a qualified small business (see definition).
- The company must be a C corporation (not an S corporation).
- You must have acquired the stock at its original issue, either in exchange for money or other property, or as pay for services.
- During substantially all of the time you held the stock:
  - The corporation was a C corporation. However, the IRS has ruled privately that the stock does not lose its qualification when a C corporation converts to a limited liability company under state law in a Sec. 368(f) reorganization; the original stockholders who continue to own the stock can exclude gain on its sale if other conditions are met.
  - At least 80% of the value of the corporation's assets were used in the active conduct of one or more qualified businesses.
  - The corporation was engaged in any business *other than*: the performance of services in the fields of health, law, engineering, architecture, accounting, actuarial science, performing arts, consulting, athletics, financial services, brokerage services, or any trade or business where the principal asset of such trade or business is the reputation or skill of one or more of its employees; banking, insurance, financing, leasing, investing, or similar business; farming business (including the business of raising or harvesting trees); mining; or operating a hotel, motel, restaurant, or similar business. Which types of businesses *do* qualify? Manufacturing, retail and wholesale, and technology companies are the types of companies that can qualify as a small business for purposes of the exclusion. Insurance brokers may also qualify.

- The corporation was not a foreign corporation, domestic international sales corporation (DISC), former DISC, regulated investment company, real estate investment trust, real estate mortgage investment conduit (REMIC), financial asset securitization investment trust (FASIT), cooperative, or a corporation that has made a Section 936 election.

**CAUTION**

**The partially excluded gain is a tax preference for the alternative minimum tax (AMT). This means that individuals subject to the AMT lose part of the exclusion, unless the 100% exclusion applies. See Chapter 28.**

You must own the stock for more than 5 years to claim an exclusion. The amount of the exclusion depends on *when* the stock is acquired, and to some extent *where* the corporation is located.

- *50% exclusion.* Stock acquired before February 18, 2009.
- *60% exclusion.* Stock acquired in a corporation in an empowerment zone business where the 50% exclusion would otherwise apply.
- *75% exclusion.* Stock acquired after February 17, 2009, and before September 29, 2010.
- *100% exclusion.* Stock acquired after September 28, 2010.

**Example**

**In 2021, an individual sells small business stock that she acquired in 2009 for $10,000; it is now worth $100,000. Of her $90,000 gain ($100,000 – $10,000), 50%, or $45,000, is excludable. If she acquired the stock on July 17, 2010, and sold it in 2021, the exclusion would be $67,500, or 75% of her gain; only $22,500 would be includible in income. If the stock was acquired on October 1, 2011, and sold in 2021, *all* of the gain is excludable. It is the date that the stock was acquired, not the date it is sold, that governs the exclusion amount.**

**NOTE**

**Gain on the sale of qualified small business stock (Sec. 1202 stock) held more than 6 months can be deferred by acquiring other Section 1202 stock within 60 days of the sale.**

The amount of the exclusion related to stock from a particular company is limited to the greater of 10 times your basis in the stock or $10 million ($5 million if married filing separately) minus any gain on stock from the same company excluded in a prior year.

### Zero Percent Gain from Community Renewal Property

If you own a business that invested in business assets within a specially designated renewal community before January 1, 2010, and hold the assets for more than 5 years, you do not have to pay *any* tax on your gain (40 authorized community renewal areas were designated by the Secretaries of Housing and Urban Development and Agriculture). However, any portion of the gain attributable to periods before January 1, 2002, is ineligible for this special treatment and is taxed in the usual way.

### Section 1244 Losses

If you own stock in a company considered to be a small business (whether it is a C or an S corporation) and you realize a loss on this stock, you may be able to treat the loss as an ordinary loss (within set limits). This loss is referred to as a *Section 1244 loss* because it is this section in the Internal Revenue Code.

Ordinary loss treatment applies to both common stock issued at any time and preferred stock issued after July 18, 1984. You can claim an ordinary loss if you sell or exchange the stock or if it becomes worthless. This special tax rule for small business stock presents another win-win situation for owners. If the company does well and a disposition of the stock produces a gain, it is treated as capital gain. If the company does not do well and the disposition of the stock results in a loss, the loss is treated as ordinary loss, which is fully deductible against your other income (such as salary, dividends, and interest income).

#### QUALIFYING FOR ORDINARY LOSS TREATMENT

The corporation issuing the stock must be a small business. This means that it can have equity of no more than $1 million at the time the stock is issued. This equity is the amount of cash or other property invested in the company in exchange for the stock. The stock must be issued for cash and property other than stock and securities. This definition of small business stock applies only to the loss deduction under Section 1244. Other definitions of small business stock apply for other purposes under the tax law.

You must acquire the stock by purchase. The ordinary loss deduction is allowed only to the original purchaser of the stock. If you inherit stock in a small business, receive it as a gift, or buy it from someone who was the original purchaser of the stock, you do not qualify for ordinary loss treatment.

Most important, the corporation must have derived over half its gross receipts during the 5 years preceding the year of your loss from business operations, and not from passive income. If the corporation is in business for fewer than 5 years, then only the years in which it is in business are considered. If the corporation's deductions (other than for dividends received and NOL) exceed gross income, the 5-year requirement is waived.

#### LIMIT ON ORDINARY LOSS DEDUCTION

You can treat only the first $50,000 of your loss on small business stock as an ordinary loss. The limit is raised to $100,000 on a joint return, even if only one spouse owned the stock. Losses in excess of these dollar limits can be treated as capital losses, as discussed earlier in this chapter.

The ordinary loss deduction can be claimed only by individuals. If a partnership owns Section 1244 stock and sustains a loss, an ordinary loss deduction can be claimed by individuals who were partners when the stock was issued. If the partnership distributes stock to partners and the partners then realize a loss on the stock, they cannot treat the loss as an ordinary loss.

If an S corporation owns Section 1244 stock and sustains a loss, it cannot pass the loss through to its shareholders in the same way that partnerships can pass the loss through to their partners. Even though S corporation shareholders receive tax treatment similar to that of partners, one court that has considered this question concluded that the language of the tax law results in a difference in this instance. The denial of an ordinary loss deduction for Section 1244 stock is one important way in which the tax treatment differs between partnerships and S corporations.

### *Worthless Securities*

If you buy stock or bonds (collectively called *securities*) in a corporation and they become worthless, special tax rules apply. In general, loss on a security that becomes worthless is treated as a capital loss. If the stock is Section 1244 stock, you can claim an ordinary loss deduction, as explained earlier.

To claim a deduction, you must be able to show that the securities are completely worthless. If they still have some value, you cannot claim a loss. You must show that there is no reasonable possibility of receiving repayment on a bond or any value for your stock. Insolvency of the corporation issuing the security is certainly indicative of worthlessness. However, even if a corporation is insolvent, there may still be some value to your securities. The corporation may be in a bankruptcy restructuring arrangement designed to make the corporation solvent again someday. In this instance, the securities are not considered to be worthless.

A deduction for worthless securities is also allowed if the securities are "abandoned" (the owner permanently relinquishes all rights without receiving any payment; gives up ownership).

You can claim a deduction for worthless securities only in the year in which worthlessness occurs. Since it is difficult to pinpoint when worthlessness occurs, you have some flexibility. The tax law allows you 7 years to go back and amend a prior return to claim a deduction for worthless securities.

**Example**

**In December 2021, you learn that stock you owned in a business became worthless in 2017. In general, you have 7 years from the due date of your 2016 return, or April 15, 2025, to amend your 2017 return to claim the loss deduction.**

If you own stock in a publicly held corporation, it is advisable to check with a securities broker to see whether there has been some definite event to fix the time of worthlessness. If you are unsure whether a security actually became worthless in a particular year, consider claiming it anyway. You can renew your claim in a subsequent year if the facts show worthlessness did, in fact, occur in that subsequent year. If you fail to claim the loss in the earlier year and that year proves to be the year of worthlessness, your claim may be lost forever.

If you own stock in an S corporation that becomes worthless, you must first adjust the basis in the stock for your share of corporate items of income, loss, and deductions. If there is any excess basis remaining, you can then claim the excess as a loss on worthless securities.

## Where to Report Capital Gains and Losses

### *Employees*

Employees may buy stock in their employer (or acquire it through stock options or as compensation). When this stock is disposed of at a loss (or it becomes worthless), the loss may be a capital loss or an ordinary loss on Section 1244 stock. Capital losses are reported on Form 8949 and then on Schedule D and are carried over to Form 1040 or 1040-SR. An ordinary loss on Section 1244 stock is reported in Part II of Form 4797. The results of Form 4797 are then reported on Form 1040 or 1040-SR. If you need to amend a tax return to claim a deduction for worthless securities, file Form 1040-X, *Amended U.S. Individual Income Tax Return*.

### *Self-Employed*

Self-employed individuals report any capital gains and losses on their personal Form 8949 and then on Schedule D—there is no special reporting for the business since these assets are viewed as personal assets, not business assets, even if acquired with business profits.

### Partnerships and LLCs

Capital gains and losses are separately stated items that are not taken into account in calculating ordinary business income or loss. However, the entity figures the net amount of capital gains or losses on its own Schedule D. The net amount is then entered on Schedule K, and the partners' or members' allocable share of the capital gains or losses is reported to them on Schedule K-1.

Gain on the sale of qualified small business stock is passed through as such. Partners and members must have held their interest in the entity on the date that the pass-through entity acquired the qualified small business stock *and* at all times until the stock was sold in order to qualify for the exclusion.

### S Corporations

Capital gains and losses are separately stated items that are not taken into account in figuring the S corporation's ordinary income or loss. However, the corporation figures its net amount of capital gain or loss on its own Schedule D. The net amount is entered on Schedule K, and the shareholder's allocable share of the gain or loss is reported to them on Schedule K-1.

Gain on the sale of qualified small business stock is passed through as such. Shareholders must have held their interest in the corporation on the date that it acquired the qualified small business stock *and* at all times until the stock was sold in order to qualify for the exclusion.

Built-in capital gains of the S corporation, however, are *not* passed through to shareholders since they are taxed to the corporation. They are reported on a separate part of Schedule D. The computation of built-in gains is made on a separate attachment (of your own making). If there is an excess of recognized built-in gain over recognized built-in losses for the year and this net amount exceeds taxable income (figured without regard to this net gain), the tax is figured on the net amount. It can be reduced by the general business credit and minimum tax credit carryforwards from years in which the corporation was a C corporation. The tax is then entered on Form 1120-S. The amount of the built-in gains tax is treated as a loss sustained by the corporation (so that shareholders can report their share of this loss on their personal returns). Deduct the tax attributable to an ordinary gain as a deduction for taxes on page 1 of Form 1120-S; for tax attributable to short-term or long-term capital gain, report the loss as a short-term or long-term capital loss on Schedule D.

### C Corporations

Capital gains and losses are reported on the corporation's Schedule D. The net amount of gain or loss is entered on Form 1120 on the line provided for capital gain net income. If there is a net loss, then the corporation must apply its own limitations on capital losses, as explained in this chapter. If the corporation discovers that it suffered a loss from worthless securities in a prior year and wants to file an amended return, use Form 1120-X, *Amended U.S. Corporation Income Tax Return*.

### Tax-Free Exchanges

Regardless of your form of business organization, all tax-free exchanges are reported on Form 8824, *Like Kind Exchanges*. Any taxable gain resulting from the exchange is picked up from Form 8824 and then carried to the appropriate tax schedule or form for the entity. For example, if your C corporation makes a tax-free exchange of capital gain property (other than Section 1231) that results in a gain (because boot is received), the gain is then reported on the corporation's Schedule D. Any taxable gain from a like-kind exchange involving Section 1231 property is picked up from From 8824 and reported on Form 4797, *Sales of Business Property*, discussed in Chapter 6.

### *Installment Sales*

Regardless of your form of business organization, all installment sales are reported on Form 6252, *Installment Sales*. The gain reported in the current year is then carried to the appropriate tax schedule or form for the entity. For example, if your C corporation makes an installment sale of capital gain property (other than Section 1231) that results in a gain, the gain is then reported on the corporation's Schedule D. Installment sales involving Section 1231 property are reported on Form 4797, *Sales of Business Property*, discussed further in Chapter 6.

### *Opportunity Zone Investments*

A taxpayer who holds an investment in a qualified opportunity fund at any point during the year must file Form 8997, *Initial and Annual Statement of Qualified Opportunity Fund (QOF) Investments*.

CHAPTER 6

# Gains and Losses from Sales of Business Property


| | | | |
|---|---|---|---|
| Section 1231 Gains and Losses | 113 | Abandonment, Foreclosure, and Repossession of Property | 119 |
| Sale-Leasebacks | 115 | Sale of All the Assets of the Business | 121 |
| Installment Sales | 116 | Opportunity Zone Business Transactions | 122 |
| Recapture | 116 | | |
| Involuntary Conversions | 117 | | |


Businesses hold a unique category of assets called *Section 1231 property*. This category is named after the section in the Internal Revenue Code that created them. Upon the disposition of these assets, you can realize the best of both possible worlds—capital gain treatment for profitable sales and ordinary loss treatment for sales that result in a loss. Gain may be recognized all at once or spread out through an installment sale.

You may also realize gains or losses from other transactions involving business property, including involuntary conversions, abandonment or repossession of property, or the sale of all of the assets of the business. And your business may become an Opportunity Zone business and enjoy special tax breaks.

Complex rules govern the overall treatment of these transactions. (The treatment of capital gains and losses from other property is also discussed in Chapter 5.) The purpose of this chapter is to alert you to the basic rules governing certain sales of business property. If any transaction applies to your business, you may wish to delve deeper with the assistance of a tax professional.

For further information about capital gains and losses, see IRS Publication 537, *Installment Sales*, and IRS Publication 544, *Sales and Other Dispositions of Assets*.

## Section 1231 Gains and Losses

Certain assets used in business are granted special tax treatment. This treatment seeks to provide a win-win situation for a business. If a sale or other disposition of these assets (called **Section 1231 property**) results in a net gain, the gain can be treated as capital gain. If a net loss results, the loss is an ordinary loss.

***Section 1231 property*** **Property held for more than one year and used in a business or held for the production of rents or royalties.**

Examples of Section 1231 property include:

- Real property and depreciable personal property (such as equipment)
- Leaseholds
- Timber, coal, and iron ore
- Certain livestock and unharvested crops

Gains or losses due to casualty, theft, or condemnation may also be treated as Section 1231 gains or losses if the property was held for more than one year. Also, the payment from a manufacturer to a distributor to cancel the distributor agreement is treated as a long-term capital gain, provided the distributor made a substantial capital investment in the distributorship and the investment is reflected in physical assets.

Section 1231 property does *not* include:

- Inventory or other property held for sale to customers
- Copyrights; literary, musical (unless a special election is made, as explained in Chapter 5), or artistic compositions; letters or memoranda; or similar property created by your efforts
- Patents, inventions, models or designs (whether or not patented), secret formulas, or processes
- Government publications

### *Determining Section 1231 Gains or Losses*

You must use a *netting process* to determine your Section 1231 gains or losses. This means combining all gains and losses from the sale or other disposition of Section 1231 property. If your Section 1231 gains exceed your Section 1231 losses, then all of your gains and losses are treated as capital gains and losses. In contrast, if your Section 1231 losses equal or exceed your Section 1231 gains, all of your gains and losses are treated as ordinary gains and losses.

If you sell appreciated Section 1231 property to a *related party*, gain that would otherwise be capital gain is recharacterized as ordinary income if the property is depreciable property in the hands of the buyer. Related parties for this purpose means a person and all entities that are controlled entities. A *controlled entity* is:

- A corporation with more than 50% of the value of the outstanding stock that is owned, directly or indirectly, by you.
- A partnership with more than 50% of the capital interest or profit interest that is owned, directly or indirectly, by you.
- Two corporations that are members of a controlled group.
- A corporation and a partnership if the same person owns more than 50% of the value of the stock and more than 50% of the capital interest or profit interest in the partnership.
- An S corporation and another S corporation where the same person owns more than 50% of each.

#### LOSSES

The fact that your Section 1231 losses for the year equal or exceed Section 1231 gains does not automatically ensure ordinary loss treatment. You must check to see whether a special recapture rule applies. Under the recapture rule, net Section 1231 gain is treated as ordinary income to the extent it does not exceed **nonrecaptured** net Section 1231 **losses** taken in prior years.

***Nonrecaptured losses*** **Total of net Section 1231 losses for the 5 most recent preceding tax years that have not been applied (recaptured) against any net Section 1231 gains in those years.**

The recapture rules for Section 1231 gains and losses are extremely complex. They are designed to prevent you from being able to time gains and losses from year to year so that you take your gains as capital gains and your losses as ordinary losses. (Do not confuse these recapture rules with those that apply to depreciation, which are discussed later in this chapter.) The recapture rules, in effect, treat your gains and losses as occurring in the same year so that what would ordinarily have been treated as capital gains is partially or fully treated as ordinary income.

Losses are recaptured beginning with the earliest year subject to recapture.

## Sale-Leasebacks

A sale-leaseback is an arrangement in which an owner of business realty sells the property to a buyer or transfers it to a trust and then leases the property back for use in the business. The lease usually runs long term (e.g., 10 or 15 years); however, a lease term of 20 years or more can trigger unwanted tax results. The following information relates solely to a sale (transfers to a trust are not considered here). The arrangement is not new but has garnered considerable media attention in recent years with many large public corporations, including Darden Restaurants (operator of Olive Garden, LongHorn Steakhouse, Capital Grille, and other restaurants), Bob Evans Farms (owner of Bob Evans restaurants), Tiffany's, and various Verizon operation centers and certain newspaper properties, using it.

**NOTE**

**An alternative to a sale-leaseback for unleashing the value of the property is to mortgage the realty or refinance an existing mortgage based on the current value of the property. There are no immediate tax consequences for mortgaging the property, in contrast to having to recognize gain on a sale-leaseback.**

### *Seller Perspective*

The arrangement is largely viewed as a financing arrangement because the seller unleashes the otherwise illiquid equity that has been built up. The funds are then used to pay down debt on the property, other business debt, or for any other purpose. Aside from the financial aspects of the arrangement, disposing of the realty allows the company to focus on its core business rather than have to divert some attention to maintaining the property.

From a tax point of view, the sale of the realty usually qualifies for Section 1231 treatment, explained earlier in this chapter. It is a way to generate capital gain that can be used to offset capital losses that have been realized from other transactions.

### *Buyer Perspective*

For the buyer, the lease payments usually are structured to closely match the costs of ownership, including debt service and other expenses. The lease may be set up so that the seller pays taxes on the property. The buyer becomes a landlord, and can deduct rental-related expenses (including depreciation on the realty as explained in Chapter 14).

## Installment Sales

If you sell property and receive at least one payment after the year of sale, you have automatically transacted an installment sale. You report your gain over the period in which you receive payment *unless* you elect to report all of the gain in the year of sale. Installment reporting does not apply to losses. This is called the installment method. You can use it regardless of your other accounting method for reporting income. Installment reporting does not affect the amount of gain you report, nor the characterization of that gain. It merely affects the timing of reporting the gain.

Installment reporting is explained in greater detail in Chapter 5.

### *Recapture*

If part of the gain on an installment sale relates to depreciation recapture, this gain must be reported up front, regardless of the payments received.

## Recapture

Certain write-offs you may take can come back to haunt you. The benefit you enjoy now may have to be repaid at a later time. For instance, if you claim certain *depreciation* on business assets (explained in Chapter 14)—a write-off of the cost of the assets over a set time—you must *recapture* the benefit when you dispose of the assets. Recapture in some instances is merely a matter of recharacterizing gain—instead of capital gain, the recapture amount is treated as ordinary income. However, in other instances, recapture means reporting income that would not otherwise be due.

Most of the following discussion about recapture applies only to businesses other than C corporations. The reason: C corporations do not have favorable tax rates on capital gains. There is, however, one recapture rule specifically for C corporations, which is explained later in this chapter.

### *Recaptured Depreciation*

If you claim accelerated depreciation on realty (generally, this applies to realty placed in service before 1987), then you must recapture (report as ordinary income) the portion of gain relating to the excess of accelerated depreciation.

- For equipment and other personal property, recapture all of depreciation claimed (to the extent of gain).
- For nonresidential realty depreciated under the Accelerated Cost Recovery System (ACRS) (placed in service after 1981 and before 1987), recapture the excess of ACRS depreciation in excess of straight-line depreciation. Different rules apply to pre-ACRS property.

### *Unrecaptured Depreciation*

If you claim a home office deduction for business use of a portion of your home (these rules are explained in Chapter 18), you do *not* have to apportion your gain; in effect, you can apply the home sale exclusion to your entire gain. However, all depreciation claimed on a home office after May 6, 1997, is unrecaptured depreciation—it must all be reported as gain upon the sale of the home. This gain is taxed at a maximum of 25%.

### *Recapture on Installment Reporting*

When to report recapture on an installment sale depends on the type of recapture involved:

- *For recaptured depreciation*—All of the depreciation must be reported in full in the year of sale. This recapture is reported without regard to the proceeds received in the year of sale.
- *For unrecaptured depreciation*—The gain, with respect to each installment payment received, is reported first at a maximum 25% rate. Once unrecaptured depreciation has been fully reported, the balance of any gain is reported at the basic capital gains rate (generally 15% for owners of pass-through entities, but 20% for owners with taxable income over a threshold amount listed in Chapter 5; check the Supplement for any rate changes which may apply for 2021).

**Example**

**You purchased realty for $100,000 that you depreciated by $20,000 (for a basis of $80,000). In July 2021, you then sell the property for $130,000, payable in 5 equal annual installments. Of these installments, $10,000 of gain must be reported each year. (Gain is the difference between $130,000 received for the property and $80,000 basis.) Thus, gain on the first 2 installments is taxed at 25%. Gain on the 3 remaining installments will be taxed at 15% (assuming you're not subject to the 20% rate).**

## Involuntary Conversions

If business property is destroyed or stolen, condemned or disposed of through threat of condemnation and you receive insurance proceeds or other funds to compensate you for your loss, you have suffered an *involuntary conversion*. *Condemnations* are the taking of your property for public purposes, such as building roads or putting up utility poles—in effect, a forced sale. Threat of condemnation occurs when you learn from a government official or other authorized person that the government intends to take your property. If you do not sell it to the government, it will be condemned.

If the funds you receive for the involuntary conversion of your property exceed your **adjusted basis** in the involuntarily converted property, you have a gain that is currently taxable unless you qualify to postpone your gain (explained later). If the funds you receive are less than your adjusted basis in the involuntarily converted property, you have a loss that is currently deductible (subject to usual loss limitation rules discussed in this chapter and in Chapter 5).

***Adjusted basis*** **This is your basis in the property, adjusted for certain items. Start with your original cost if you bought the property (the cash and other property you paid to acquire it). Even if the cash did not come out of your pocket, for example, if you took a loan, the cash you turn over to the seller is part of your basis. Then, adjust the basis by reducing it for any depreciation claimed (or that could have been claimed) and any casualty loss you claimed with respect to the property. For example, if your original computer system cost you $10,000 and you claimed $2,000 depreciation, your adjusted basis is $8,000. (Other basis adjustments are explained in Chapter 5.)**

In reporting condemnation awards, you can reduce your receipts by any legal fees or other expenses you incurred to obtain the payment as well as any special assessments levied against the part of the property if only a portion of the property was condemned. If amounts are withheld from the award to pay off your mortgage or outstanding taxes, you treat these amounts as payment you receive. Also add to the amount any severance payments you receive for the decrease in the value of the property you retain if only a portion of the property was condemned. The portion of gain relating to severance damages can be postponed in the same way as direct payments for the condemned property.

In figuring your gain or loss from an involuntary conversion, certain payments related to the event are not taken into account (they are treated separately):

- *Relocation payments from the federal government or an assistance program*. If you are displaced from your business (including a home in which you maintain a home office) or farm, you may be eligible for these funds. These amounts are tax-free payments.
- *Interest on a condemnation award*. The municipality may pay you out over time, plus interest. This interest is reported separately as interest income (see Chapter 4).

### *Election to Postpone Gain*

You make the election to postpone gain by acquiring replacement property within set time limits. In deciding whether or not to postpone gain, keep in mind that you do not have to use the insurance proceeds or other funds to acquire the replacement property—you need only invest a similar amount. You can, for example, spend the proceeds and take a loan to buy the replacement property. First, consider the advantage and disadvantage to help you decide whether or not you want to postpone gain.

- *Advantage*—Postponing gain allows you to use the proceeds undiminished by taxes on your gain.
- *Disadvantage*—You must reduce the basis of the replacement property by the amount of gain not immediately recognized. This results in a lower basis for purposes of figuring depreciation on the replacement property as well as for determining gain or loss on the disposition of the property.

#### REPLACEMENT PROPERTY

*Replacement property* is property that is similar or related in service or use to the involuntarily converted property. *Similar or related* means that the functions of the old and replacement properties are related. For example, if one piece of machinery is destroyed in a storm and you buy a new machine to perform the same work in your business, the new machine is clearly replacement property.

You need not buy the property directly. You are treated as acquiring replacement property if you buy at least an 80% interest in a corporation that owns property similar or related in service or use to the involuntarily converted property. However, you cannot buy replacement property from a *related party*—a business you control or a close relative—if the gain is more than $100,000. You can buy replacement property from a related party if the gain is $100,000 or less.

If your business property is destroyed in a disaster within an area qualifying for federal disaster relief, acquiring *any* tangible property for your business is treated as similar or related, even if the functions of the old and new property are entirely different.

#### REPLACEMENT TIME LIMITS

You must decide whether or not to postpone gain by acting with set time limits to place replacement property in service for your business. Generally, you have until the end of the 2 years following the close of the year in which gain from the involuntary conversion was realized to acquire replacement property. For property involuntarily converted after certain major catastrophes, the replacement period may be extended to 5 years. Check the IRS's Tax Relief in Disaster Situations at https://www.irs.gov/uac/Tax-Relief-in-Disaster-Situations.

If business property has been condemned (or sold under threat of condemnation), the replacement period is 3 years from the close of the year in which the gain from condemnation (or threat of condemnation) was realized. However, if you buy replacement property by acquiring a controlling interest in a corporation, then the 2-year replacement period applies.

**Example**

**In February 2021, a machine is destroyed by a storm, and the insurance proceeds you receive produce a gain. You can postpone the reporting of this gain by obtaining replacement property no later than December 2023.**

If you decide you want to postpone gain but time is running out on buying replacement property, you can request an extension. For example, if you have already found property but have yet to close on the sale, ask for more time to do so. Address your request to the local district director of the IRS. Do not let the replacement period expire without submitting your extension request—it may be almost impossible to obtain an extension at this late date.

## Abandonment, Foreclosure, and Repossession of Property

Disposing of business property by abandonment, foreclosure, or repossession generally produces taxable results.

### *Abandonment*

If you abandon business property, you *automatically* have a loss that is treated as an ordinary loss. The amount of your loss is the adjusted basis of the abandoned property. However, if you effectively abandon inventory that has become unsalable because it is obsolete or defective, you do not report it as a loss. Instead, you adjust your inventory valuation to reflect the actual value of the items, which may be merely their scrap value.

If the property you are abandoning is subject to a debt for which you are personally liable and the debt is canceled, you have ordinary income to the extent of this debt cancellation. Report this income separately from the abandonment loss—do not net one against the other. (Income from the cancellation of debt is discussed in Chapter 4.)

### *Foreclosure or Repossession*

If you cannot pay a loan or the mortgage on your business property, the lender will recoup this amount by *foreclosing* on the property or *repossessing* it. Foreclosure and repossession are treated as a sale or exchange for tax purposes, producing a gain or loss on the transaction. This is the case even if you voluntarily transfer the property back. The amount realized usually is the debt you no longer have to pay. The difference between this amount and the adjusted basis in the property is the amount of your gain or loss.

- *If the debt is recourse debt* (you are personally liable for it)—do not include the debt cancellation in the amount realized (you report the debt cancellation separately as income as explained in Chapter 4). *Exception:* If the value of the property is less than the canceled debt, then the amount realized includes the debt cancellation to the extent of the value of the property.
- *If the debt is nonrecourse debt* (you are not personally liable for it)—include the full debt cancellation in the amount realized, regardless of the property's value.

**Example**

**The business bought a car for $30,000, financing $25,000 of the purchase price. The business stops paying the loan when there is still $20,000 outstanding and the adjusted basis of the car is $22,040. The lender repossesses the car and walks away from the remaining debt. If the debt is nonrecourse, report $2,040 as a loss (the difference between the amount realized of $20,000 and the adjusted basis of the car, $22,040).**

**Example**

**Continuing with the car example, except that the debt is recourse. The value of the car at the time of the repossession is $19,000. In this instance, report a loss of $3,040 (the difference between the amount realized of $19,000 less $22,040). But you must also report income of $1,000 (the amount of the canceled debt in excess of the value of the car).**

### *Lender's Perspective*

If you are the lender and foreclose or repossess property because of nonpayment, you recognize gain or loss on the transaction. This is so whether or not the debtor cooperates and voluntarily transfers the property back to you.

#### REAL PROPERTY

Generally, your gain is the difference between the total payments you have already received for the property and the gain you already reported as income. However, your reportable gain on a foreclosure or repossession is limited to the gross profit on your original gain minus any gain already reported. Reduce your profit by any costs related to the foreclosure or repossession, such as legal fees, court costs, and costs of recording or clearing title to the property.

**Example**

**You foreclose on an office building for nonpayment of the mortgage you hold on the property you sold. (It was a seller-financed mortgage that you had agreed to in order to swing the sale.) You figure your basis in the building as follows:**

| | |
|---|---|
| Original basis | $200,000 |
| Plus: Gain reported on principal received | +18,000 |
| Plus: Gain on foreclosure | +27,000 |
| Less: Principal received | (−90,000) |
| New basis | $155,000 |

Your basis in the reacquired property is your original basis in the property, increased by any gain recognized on the receipt of principal and foreclosure/ repossession, and decreased by any principal payments received.

#### EQUIPMENT AND OTHER PERSONAL PROPERTY

If you sold property on the installment method and repossess it for nonpayment, report gain or loss on the transaction. In review, gain or loss is the difference between your basis in the installment obligations and the value of the property you repossess. Reduce the basis in the installment obligations by any costs for the repossession. Increase the value of the property by anything you receive from the debtor upon the repossession, such as a partial payment.

What is your basis in the installment obligations? This depends on how you originally opted to report the sale. If you used the installment method, your basis in the installment obligations is the unpaid balance of the installment obligations divided by your gross profit percentage.

## Sale of All the Assets of the Business

If you sell your business, such as a sole proprietorship, by selling all of its assets, the rules for reporting gain or loss are really no different from a single-asset sale. You allocate the purchase price of the sale to each of the assets, including goodwill or going concern value, in order to determine your gain or loss. You usually arrive at this allocation through negotiations between you and the buyer.

Asset classes reported on Form 8594, *Asset Acquisition Under Section 1060,* include the following:

- *Class I assets*—Cash, and savings and checking accounts.
- *Class II assets*—Certificates of deposit, government securities, publicly traded stock or securities, and foreign currency.
- *Class III assets*—Mark-to-market assets.
- *Class IV assets*—Stock in trade and inventory.

- *Class V assets*—All assets that do not fall within another class. Furniture and fixtures, buildings, land, vehicles, and equipment generally fall within this class.
- *Class VI assets*—Section 197 assets (other than goodwill and going concern value) such as patents, copyrights, licenses, permits, franchises, trademarks, and covenants not to compete. Section 197 assets are discussed in Chapter 14.
- *Class VII assets*—Goodwill and going concern value.

The sale price is allocated in descending order—first to Class I assets, then Class II assets, and so on. There is no debate on allocating part of the purchase price to assets in the first 2 classes since the value of the assets is not in dispute. But as a seller, you generally want to allocate as much of the remaining purchase price to assets that will produce the most favorable tax results to you. For example, if you can allocate an amount to goodwill, you will achieve capital gain treatment.

In contrast, if such an amount is allocated to inventory, you have ordinary income. However, the buyer has competing interests and wants to allocate as much as possible to depreciable assets. That would give him or her the opportunity to maximize depreciation deductions. Ultimately, the price you receive for the assets will reflect negotiations that include the allocation process.

Corporations that acquire stock in another corporation may, under certain circumstances, elect to treat the stock purchase as an asset sale (see Chapter 5).

## Opportunity Zone Business Transactions

An investor in a Qualified Opportunity Zone Fund (QOF) may obtain various tax benefits (explained in Chapter 5). However, you may be able to use business property to not just be an investor but benefit from being an Opportunity Zone business.

### BEING A QUALIFIED OPPORTUNITY ZONE BUSINESS

A QOF invests in Qualified Opportunity Zone Businesses (QOZBs). If you are a QOZB, you may receive capital investments through a QOF; the QOF invests in you. To be a QOZB, you must derive at least 50% of your gross income from the active conduct of business within an OZ (there are more than 8,700 OZ designations). Under a safe harbor, the 50% requirement is met if:

- The management, operations, and tangible property needed to produce 50% or more of the gross income of the business is located within an OZ, or
- 50% or more of the services performed for the business-by employees or independent contractors-are performed in the OZ. This is determined by either hours worked or compensation paid.

**Example**

**In 2021, a business starts up in an OZ. Because its management, operations, and tangible property needed to produce more than 50% of the gross income of the business are within the OZ, it's a Qualified Opportunity Zone Business.**

"Sin businesses," such as massage parlors, strip clubs, liquor stores, and casinos, cannot be treated as QOZBs, even if they meet the 50% test. It is unsettled whether cannabis businesses within a QOZ could be a qualified business. Given that cannabis is still a controlled substance under federal law, it is unlikely that the IRS will permit cannabis businesses to be QOZBs. Check the Supplement for any update.

#### SELLING BUSINESS PROPERTY TO A QOF

Even if you don't qualify as a QOZB, you can sell business property to a QOF. In effect, depending on where you're located, you may be able to sell real property to a QOF at handsome profits. However, doing this may only result in part of the investment being eligible for tax breaks explained in Chapter 5. In other words, not all of your gain may be deferred.

## Where to Report Gains and Losses on Business Property

### *For All Taxpayers*

Section 1231 gains and losses are reported on Form 4797, *Sales of Business Property*, regardless of the type of entity. The results from Form 4797 are carried over and reported on the business's tax return. For individuals, Form 4797 gains and losses are reported on Schedule 1 of Form 1040 or 1040-SR.

Installment sales are figured on Form 6252, *Installment Sale Income*. The results are carried over to Form 4797 (installment sales of nonbusiness property are explained in Chapter 5). Use a separate Form 6252 for each installment sale you transact. Do not complete the form if you elect out of installment reporting—instead, simply report your entire gain on Form 4797.

A sale of all the assets of the business is reported on Form 8594, *Asset Acquisition Statement*. This form is used to allocate the purchase price to specific assets.

### *Self-Employed*

Gains and losses on Section 1231 property are reported on Form 4797. The results are carried over to Form 1040 or 1040-SR. Do not enter the results on Schedule C (or on Schedule F, in the case of farming operations).

If you elect to postpone gain on a casualty, theft, or condemnation, make your election on the return for the year in which you realized gain. If you acquired replacement property before filing your return, attach a statement to the return showing the amount realized, how you computed your gain, and any gain reported. If you have not yet acquired replacement property by the time you must file your return, simply attach a statement to your return showing the circumstances of the casualty, theft, or condemnation giving rise to the gain, how you calculated your gain, and that you intend to acquire replacement property within the replacement period. Then, when you do buy replacement property, attach another statement to the return for the year of the replacement purchase explaining the replacement.

If the replacement period expires before you acquire replacement property (and you do not obtain an extension for the replacement period), you must file an amended return for the year in which you realized gain. You report your full gain on this amended return. You must also file an amended return if you buy replacement property and the cost is not sufficient to postpone the reporting of all of your gain. You report the portion of the gain not covered by the replacement property on this amended return.

Once you have designated certain property as your replacement property, you cannot later substitute other property for it. However, if your replacement property is found to be unsuitable, you can then substitute other qualified property, provided the replacement period has not expired.

### Partnerships and LLCs

Section 1231 gains and losses are calculated on Form 4797 and then entered on Schedule K and allocated to partners on Schedule K-1.

If there is a gain as a result of a casualty or theft to business property, the partnership or LLC must elect to defer the recognition of gain and buy the replacement property. The individual partners or LLC members cannot make sa separate election. Each partner or LLC member reports his or her distributive share of business income or loss on his or her personal income tax return.

### S Corporations

Section 1231 gains and losses are computed on Form 4797 and then entered on Schedule K and allocated to shareholders on Schedule K-1.

If there is a gain as a result of a casualty or theft to business property, the S corporation must elect to defer the recognition of gain and buy the replacement property. The individual shareholders cannot make a separate election. Each shareholder reports his or her distributive share of S corporation income or loss on his or her personal income tax return.

### C Corporations

Section 1231 gains and losses are computed on Form 4797 and then entered on Form 1120. Both capital losses and Section 1231 losses are part of the corporation's taxable income.

### All Businesses

Businesses that discover worthless securities take the loss on the return for the year of worthlessness. This means filing an amended return for the year of worthlessness.

- Sole proprietorship: Form 1040-X.
- Partnership: Small partnerships that have opted out of the Bipartisan Budget Act (BBA) audit rules report the worthlessness on an amended return use Form 1065, check box (G5) on page 1 and attach a statement identifying the line item change with an explanation for it. Then, file a corrected Schedule K-1, checking the "Amended K-1" box at the top of the schedule and give a copy to the partners. BBA partnerships file Form 1065-X.
- S corporation: Report the worthlessness on an amended return (use Form 1120-S, check box (H4) on page 1), and attach a statement identifying the line item change and an explanation for it. Then, file a corrected Schedule K-1, checking the "Amended K-1" box at the top of the schedule and give a copy to the shareholder(s).
- C corporation: Form 1120-X.

PART 3

# Business Deductions and Credits

# Employee Compensation

## Salary, Wages, and Employee Benefits


| | | | |
|---|---|---|---|
| Worker Classification | 128 | Disallowance Repayment Agreements | 139 |
| Temporary Workers and Outsourced HR | 130 | Golden Parachute Payments | 140 |
| Deductible Employee Compensation | 131 | Fringe Benefits | 141 |
| Compensation to Owners | 135 | Cafeteria Plans | 154 |
| Stock Options and Restricted Stock | 136 | Employment Tax Credits | 155 |
| Deferred Compensation | 139 | | |


As the economy emerges from the effects of the pandemic, the number one concern for many small businesses is finding and retaining employees. The tight labor market has required many businesses to change their compensation packages by increasing wages and offering a variety of benefits. Business considerations, such as a company's budget, drive decisions on pay and benefits. But the tax implications of what is given to employees should not be ignored.

If you are an employee of someone else's business, you do not pay compensation to another individual. You can skip most of this chapter and go on to look at other deductible expenses. However, you might want to review the areas covered to understand your employer's burdens and responsibilities for the wages and benefits paid to you. You may also be interested in a couple of tax credits to which you may be entitled by virtue of working.

If you are the owner of a sole proprietorship, partnership, or limited liability company, you are not an employee and cannot receive employee compensation. Money you take out of your business is a "draw," but it is not a deductible expense for the business (you already pay tax on your share of business income, whether or not it is distributed to you). However, your business may have employees, and payments to them are deductible according to the rules discussed in this chapter. According to the Spring 2021 *Statistics of Income Bulletin*, salary and wages plus commissions was the second largest deduction type for sole proprietorships (other than cost of goods sold and depreciation).

As a business owner, you need to understand a number of matters related to compensation: how to properly classify workers, the rules for deducting compensation to employees, the rules for claiming employment-related tax credits, and payroll obligations for employers. You also need to understand the effect of W-2 wages on the 20% qualified business income (QBI) deduction calculation (Chapter 21).

Compensation to employees is not limited to salaries, wages, and bonuses. Likely compensation to employees includes various fringe benefits. Some may be taxable, such as vacation and sick days, while others are tax free, such as health coverage and retirement plan contributions. Some benefits are tax free up to set limits, such as dependent care assistance and adoption assistance. Obviously, fringe benefits are an important way to attract and retain good employees, but offerings are limited to what you can afford. And some benefits may be tax free to employees but aren't deductible by the business. Even with tight budgets, however, small businesses can offer valued benefits such as flex time, mentoring, and better job titles. You can't put a price on these benefits and they're tax free to employees.

Besides deductions for compensation and some fringe benefits you provide, you may be eligible for certain tax credits related to employment. For example, there is an income tax credit for paying wages to an employee on family and medical leave if your state doesn't require you to do it (separate from COVID-19-related paid leave). Also discussed in this chapter are the *earned income credit* and the *dependent care credit*. These are not business credits; rather, they are personal credits that arise by virtue of employment. The earned income credit is a refundable credit for low-income workers, and the dependent care credit is designed to offset the costs of babysitting and other dependent-related expenses incurred to allow parents to work.

Employment taxes on compensation you pay to your employees, including federal income tax withholding, FICA (Social Security and Medicare taxes), FUTA (federal unemployment tax), and state taxes (income, unemployment, and disability), are discussed in Chapter 30.

Providing retirement plans for your staff is another valued employee benefit. These plans are covered in Chapter 16. Medical coverage is also an important facet of employee compensation. It is also a necessary item for self-employed individuals. Medical coverage for you and your employees is explained in Chapter 19.

For further information about employee compensation, see IRS Publication 334, *Tax Guide for Small Business*; IRS Publication 15, *Circular E, Employer's Tax Guide*; IRS Publication 15-A; *Employer's Supplemental Tax Guide*; and IRS Publication 15-B, *Employer's Guide to Fringe Benefits*.

## Worker Classification

In order to know whether payments to workers are wages, you must first determine whether the workers are employees or independent contractors. This is a hot issue for the IRS because there are substantial tax dollars at stake. While no one has exact figures, most estimates suggest that billions of tax dollars are lost from the underpayment of income taxes by independent contractors as well as the underpayment of employment taxes by companies and workers. The issue, however, goes beyond the IRS and concerns the Department of Labor (because wage and hour laws apply to employees but not to independent contractors) and the National Labor Relations Board (because only employees can be unionized). The DOL had issued a final rule on the definition of independent contractor for purposes of wage and hour laws, but it was withdrawn on May 6, 2021. State labor departments are also concerned with correct worker classification because only employees can claim unemployment benefits and workers' compensation.

According to the IRS, a worker is treated as an employee if your company exercises sufficient control over when, where, and how the work gets done. If you control only the final results, the worker may be an independent contractor. The key to worker classification is control. In order to prove independent contractor status, you, as the employee, must show that you do not have the right to control the details and means by which the work is to be accomplished. You may also want to show that the worker has an economic stake in the work (that the worker stands to make a profit or loss depending on how the work turns out). It is helpful in this regard for the worker to supply tools and place of work, although working from home, using his or her own computer, and even setting hours (flex time) are not conclusive factors that preclude an employee classification. Various behavioral, financial, and other factors can be brought to bear on the issue of whether a worker is under your control. You can learn more about worker classification in IRS Publication 15-A, *Employer's Supplemental Tax Guide* and at https://www.irs.gov/Businesses/Small-Businesses-&-Self-Employed/Independent-Contractor-Self-Employed-or-Employee.

Some states use a different test for determining worker classification for unemployment insurance, wage and hour rules, and state income taxes. Several states, including California, Massachusetts, and New Jersey, use an ABC test. Under this test, a worker is considered an independent contractor for certain state law purposes only if the company engaging the worker can show that:

(A) The worker is free from the control and direction of the hirer in connection with the performance of the work, both under the contract for the performance of such work and in fact;

(B) The worker performs work that is outside the usual course of the hiring entity's business; and

(C) The worker is customarily engaged in an independently established trade, occupation, or business of the same nature as the work performed for the hiring entity.

The real challenge is in (B). For example, under this test, if a company that does web design engages a web designer, the worker would be treated under state law as an employee because the work is not outside the usual course of the company's business. But if the same company engaged a bookkeeper, the worker could be an independent contractor, assuming tests (A) and (C) were satisfied.

Note: A federal appeals court said that federal law does not preempt state law, allowing California's ABC test to control the worker classification of long-haul truckers in the state. Other court challenges are in the works against this test. And a proposed federal law—the PRO Act—would adopt the ABC test for federal tax and other law purposes; check the Supplement for any update.

### *Misclassifying Workers*

From a federal tax perspective it is critical to note that the consequences for misclassifying workers can be dire for an employer. If you fail to treat a worker as an employee when you should do so, you are penalized for not withholding income taxes on wages and paying employment taxes. Penalties and interest in this regard can, in some instances, be enough to bankrupt your company. Misclassification can also wreak havoc with employee benefit plans, including retirement plans. If the IRS successfully reclassifies workers as employees, you will be required to provide back benefits (medical, retirement plan contributions, and other benefits you provided to your correctly classified employees).

You may be able to rely on a "safe harbor" rule (called Section 530 relief) to avoid employment tax penalties. (This relief provision is not in the Internal Revenue Code; it's from the Revenue Act of 1978.) At a minimum, if you want to treat workers as independent contractors, make sure you do so consistently and that you have a reasonable basis for doing so. The tax law considers these situations to be a reasonable basis:

- You relied on a court case about federal taxes or a ruling issued to you by the IRS.
- You have already gone through an IRS audit in which the issue of worker classification was raised and your workers were not reclassified.
- A significant segment of your industry (at least 25%) treats such workers as independent contractors.

Require your independent contractors to complete Form W-9, *Request for Taxpayer Identification Number and Certification*, a form on which they accept responsibility for paying their required taxes.

Also make sure you file Form 1099-NEC for independent contractors if the worker earned at least $600 (see Appendix A for details).

If the IRS questions your worker classification and you cannot prove your position on audit or resolve it through the classification settlement program, you can now bring your case to Tax Court for a determination. This means you do not have to pay the taxes up front to have your case reviewed in court.

***VCSP.*** The IRS has a Voluntary Classification Settlement Program (VCSP) that allows companies to reclassify workers as employees with nominal penalties. To qualify, you must not be under an audit by the IRS, must have issued required 1099s, and must meet other qualifications. You can choose to reclassify one group of workers while not reclassifying another. Before you request participation in this program, be sure to talk with a tax adviser. Participation protects you only from IRS audit on worker classification; it provides no protection from challenges by other government agencies (e.g., state labor departments examining a worker's claim for unemployment benefits or workers' compensation), third parties, or workers.

## Temporary Workers and Outsourced HR

There are other ways to obtain workers who are not independent contractors and also are not your employees:

- ***Temporary workers.*** If you engage someone through a temporary agency, such as Kelly Services or Manpower, the worker is the employee of the agency. The agency, and not you, is responsible for all employer obligations. You merely pay the agency a fee for the services (the deduction for this fee is explained in Chapter 22).
- ***Outsourced HR.*** You may continue using existing employees, but shift employer obligations to an outside source. For example, a professional employer organization (PEO) effectively creates a co-employer situation. You have the right to hire and fire, but the PEO is responsible for all HR functions, including payroll taxes and insurance. Again, the PEO fee is deductible (see Chapter 22). IRS-approved CPEO are listed at https://www.irs.gov/tax-professionals/cpeo-public-listings.

## Deductible Employee Compensation

Compensation you pay to your employees can take many forms. In general, most types of compensation are fully deductible by you. *Deductible compensation* includes the more common forms, such as salary, wages, signing and retention bonuses, bonuses for services performed, vacation pay, sick pay (not otherwise paid by insurance), pay for personal days, and fringe benefits, whether or not they are tax free to your employee. In setting compensation, determine what you can afford and what your competitors are paying their workers. Understand that federal law does not require you to offer paid leave for federal or state holidays, vacation, sick days, personal days, or other time off. The average number of paid holidays at firms with under 100 employees is less than the number of federal holidays. A handful of states require some paid sick leave or time off for certain activities (e.g., attending school events; voting). And, due to COVID-19, small employers may continue to offer paid sick leave and paid family leave to employees impacted by the virus. Such paid leave is funded through refundable employment tax credits through September 30, 2021 (this paid leave had been mandatory in 2020), while such compensation remains deductible.

> **NOTE**
> **Obtaining forgiveness of a loan under the Paycheck Protection Program does not bar a deduction for compensation. Similarly, payments of compensation with funds from the SBA's Shuttered Venue Operators grants and Restaurant Revitalization Program grants are also deductible.**

The deduction for compensation must be reduced, however, by any employment-related tax credits claimed as offsets to income tax. These tax credits are discussed later in this chapter. The timing of when to deduct year-end bonuses paid after the end of the year is discussed in Chapter 2.

### *General Rules for Deductibility of Compensation*

To be deductible, compensation must meet 5 tests. **Test 1** requires that the compensation be an **ordinary and necessary business expense**. The payments must be directly connected to the conduct of your business, and they also must be necessary for you to carry on your business.

> ***Ordinary and necessary business expense*** **An *ordinary expense* is one that is common and accepted in your business. A *necessary expense* is one that is helpful and appropriate to your business (but not necessarily essential).**

For **test 2,** the compensation must be reasonable. For most employees, this issue never comes up; it is assumed that pay to rank-and-file employees is reasonable. The question of reasonableness typically arises in connection with pay to owners and top executives. There are no absolute guidelines for determining what is reasonable—it depends on the individual facts and circumstances. Ask yourself: "Would another business pay the same compensation under your circumstances?" If you are confident that the answer is yes, most likely the compensation is reasonable. To get an idea of what other companies are paying for comparable work, go to Indeed.com (https://www.indeed.com/salaries/Indeed-Salaries).

The IRS uses a number of factors to determine whether compensation is reasonable. These factors include:

- *The job description of the employee*. What duties must the employee perform? How much responsibility does the employee shoulder? How much time is required to perform the job? How much business is handled by the employee?

- *The nature of the business*. What are the complexities of your business? What has been your pay policy for all employees? What is the pay to a particular employee as compared with the gross and net profit of the business and distributions to shareholders?
- *The general cost of living in your locality*. Formula-based compensation (such as a percentage of sales or some other fixed arrangement) may be reasonable if it is an industrywide practice to use these formulas.

Courts have also used a hypothetical independent investor standard to test reasonableness. Under this test, courts decide whether a disinterested investor would approve the compensation level in light of the dividends and return on equity. In determining reasonableness, you must look at the total compensation package and not merely the base salary. Also, each employee's pay package must be reasonable by itself. The fact that your total payroll is reasonable is not sufficient.

Remember, if compensation paid to an employee who is also an owner of the corporation is not reasonable, then it may be viewed as a **constructive dividend** to such an owner-employee. As such, the payment is not deductible by the corporation even though it is fully taxable to the owner. However, the owner-employee and corporation can enter into a disallowance repayment agreement to preserve deductibility. Such agreements are discussed later in this chapter.

***Constructive dividend*** **The transfer to a shareholder of an economic benefit with no expectation of reimbursement.**

Generally, it is up to you to prove the reasonableness of compensation. However, if the issue goes to court, the burden of proof shifts to the IRS once you have presented credible evidence of reasonableness. Only small businesses (corporations and partnerships whose net worth does not exceed $7 million) can shift the burden of proof to the IRS.

There are dollar limits on the deduction for reasonable compensation for certain types of executives, as explained in "Audit Strategies" later in this chapter. These dollar limits do not apply for small businesses.

**Test 3** requires that the payment be for services actually performed. This issue does not generally arise for ordinary employees. However, in a family situation, the IRS may pay closer attention to see that work has actually been performed for the compensation paid. Thus, for example, if you employ your spouse, children, or parent, be sure to document their work hours and duties should your return be questioned. In one case, a parent was able to deduct salary paid to his 7-year-old son because he showed that the child performed meaningful tasks for his business. In another case, a parent who had her 3 children perform services in her home office, including photocopying, stuffing envelopes, and shredding, could not deduct their wages because she never actually paid them; merely buying things they wanted did not establish that they were paid. In several cases, a deduction for equal pay to both spouses was denied where one spouse was a professional (e.g., an engineer or a doctor) and the other performed administrative and secretarial duties. The compensation to the professional might have been reasonable, but the same pay to the spouse was not.

Guaranteed annual wages may be deductible as salary even though work is not performed. The deduction is limited to full-time guaranteed wages paid under a collective bargaining agreement.

**Test 4** is that you must actually have paid the compensation if you are on the cash basis, or incurred the expense if you are on the accrual basis. Incurring the expense means that economic performance has occurred. For a complete discussion on economic performance, see Chapter 2.

Again, a mother whose 3 children did office work at her law office could not deduct their pay because she couldn't show there had been any payment (no checks for payments were given to them and no W-2s were issued).

**Test 5** applies to year-end bonuses and other payments by accrual basis businesses. Bonuses accrued before year-end cannot be deducted unless they are actually paid within a certain time. The time limit depends upon who is receiving the payment.

- *Rank-and-file employees*—payment must be completed within 2 ½ months after the close of the year. For example, a bonus declared on December 24, 2021, by an accrual basis corporation for an employee who is not a shareholder must be paid by March 15, 2022, in order to be deductible in 2021. If you create a pot for bonuses to be divvied up among employees, you can deduct the lump sum as long as bonuses are paid within the 2 ½ month rule. However, if you reserve the right to alter bonus amounts or which employees are eligible to receive them, you cannot deduct the bonuses until actually paid.
- *Shareholders in C corporations*—payments to those owning more than 50% of the stock cannot be deducted until actual payment is made. Shareholders who own 50% or less are considered rank-and-file employees for purposes of this rule.
- *Owners of pass-through entities*—payments cannot be deducted until actual payment is made, regardless of the percentage of ownership. For example, a year-end bonus paid to an S corporation shareholder by an accrual basis corporation is not deductible until the bonus is actually paid. The Tax Court has said that an accrual basis S corporation cannot deduct accrued wages to employees who are participants in the company's ESOP because the employees are viewed as related persons; the wages are deductible when paid (i.e., when includible in the employees' income).

### *Other Types of Deductible Compensation*

Here are some less common, but equally deductible, compensation items:

- *Outplacement services provided to workers you have laid off*. The types of outplacement services that are deductible include career counseling, resume assistance, skills assessment, and even the cost of renting equipment to facilitate these services.
- *Black Lung benefit trust contributions made by coal mine operators*, provided the contributions are paid no later than the filing of the return (including extensions). The contribution must be made in cash (check) or property; a promissory note is not currently deductible.
- *Interest-free or below-market loans to employees*. The amount of interest not charged that is less than the applicable federal interest rate (a rate that changes monthly and depends on whether the loan is short-term, mid-term, or long-term) is treated as compensation. The employer includes that same amount as taxable interest.
- *Severance pay*. If you are forced to downsize your workforce or otherwise let employees go, you may offer them some benefits package. The IRS has acknowledged that severance pay generally is deductible as an ordinary and necessary business expense even though an argument could be made that it provides some future benefit (which would suggest capitalizing the cost). However, if severance pay is part of a plan, method, or arrangement deferring the receipt of income, then it is deductible only when it is included in the worker's income (whether or not the employer is on the cash or accrual method of reporting).
- *Salary continuation*. If you want to continue paying wages to an owner-employee who becomes disabled and to claim a deduction for such payments, do so under a salary

continuation plan that you set up for this purpose. Without such a plan in place, you risk having the IRS label the payments as dividends or withdrawals of capital, neither of which are deductible by the company.

- *Director's fees*. A corporation's payment of fees to its directors is deductible, but such fees are not treated as compensation even if the director is also an officer or other employee of the corporation. The fees are deductible as other business expenses (see Chapter 22).
- *Employment agency fees*. If you pay a fee to an employment agency or headhunter to hire an employee, you may deduct the cost as another business expense.
- *Sustainability perk*. If you offer employees a cash payment or other incentive so they buy a hybrid or electric vehicle rather than a standard vehicle, the amount is treated as additional compensation; it is deductible by you and taxable to the employee. Other taxable sustainability perks are bonuses to employees who move closer to your facility and grants to employees who shrink their carbon footprints.
- *Tax return preparation fees*. If you pay for your employees' tax return preparation, the cost is deductible by you and taxable to them.

### Other Limits on Deducting Compensation

Besides the reasonable compensation and other tests discussed earlier, there are several limitations on deducting compensation.

- *Deferred compensation*. If your employee agrees to defer compensation to some future date, such as retirement, you cannot claim a deduction until such time as the employee includes the compensation in his or her income. This is true for accrual method businesses as well as cash basis businesses.
- *Prizes and awards*. You can deduct prizes and awards you pay to employees, but only certain ones are tax free to them. An *employee achievement award* is tangible personal property given for an employee's length of service or safety achievement, which is awarded as part of a meaningful presentation and under conditions and circumstances that do not create a significant likelihood of disguising the award as compensation. No deduction is allowed for awards of cash, gift cards, coupons, vacations, meals and lodging, tickets to theater or sporting events, or securities (e.g., U.S. Savings bonds). An award is not considered a length-of-service award if made within the first 5 years of employment. An award is not considered a safety achievement award if it is given to a manager, administrator, clerical employees, or other professional employee, or if it is given to more than 10% of employees (other than those just listed). Awards can be qualified or nonqualified; the difference impacts what is tax free to employees. A *qualified achievement award* is one given under a written plan that does not discriminate in favor of highly compensated employees as to eligibility or benefits; it is fully tax free. A *nonqualified achievement award,* which does not meet the definition of a qualified achievement award, is tax free to an employee as long as it does not exceed $400 per year and total awards (qualified and nonqualified) made to any one employee do not exceed $1,600.
- *Vacation pay by accrual basis employers*. Vacation pay earned by an employee is deductible in the current year only if you actually pay it out by the close of the year or within 2 ½ months of the close of the year. If you fail to pay it out within this time frame, it becomes deductible in the year it is actually paid out. Of course, for cash basis employers, vacation pay is deductible as wages when it is paid to an employee.

### *Noncash Payments*

In some cases, you may pay your employees with property instead of cash. What is the amount you deduct? Your cost for the property (*basis*), or its value at the time it is paid to employees? You may deduct only your basis in the property, even though its value is included in the employee's income as compensation and employment taxes are based on this value.

**Example**

**Your company owns a car with a basis (after depreciation deductions) of $8,000. The car is worth $22,000. You give the car to your top salesperson as a bonus. You may deduct $8,000, the basis of the car. On the employee's W-2 form you include $22,000 as compensation.**

Payments in virtual or digital currency (e.g., Bitcoin and BitcoinCash) are treated as payments in property, not cash. You have to determine the value of the cryptocurrency in order to claim a deduction for making the payment; check the value on a cryptocurrency exchange for a particular type.

### *Restricted Property*

If you transfer stock or other property that is subject to restrictions to an employee in payment for services, you generally cannot deduct the expense until such time as the stock or other property is no longer subject to restrictions. Restrictions include limits on transferring the stock or property. The term also covers property that is not **substantially vested** in the employee.

***Substantially vested*** **A person can transfer the property and is not subject to a risk of forfeiture (is not likely to be forced to give up rights in the future).**

When and how much you can deduct for this type of compensation depends on a number of factors, such as the kind of property transferred and when the property is included in the employee's gross income. In the past, an employer could deduct restricted property only when such property was subject to withholding. Sometimes this was impossible, because a worker was no longer in the employer's employment. The IRS has eased its position and has dropped the withholding requirement. The property must still be included in the worker's income in order for the employer to claim a deduction. According to the IRS, the worker will be deemed to have included the amount in income in the year for which an employer complies with W-2 reporting requirements.

## Compensation to Owners

How much should you pay yourself? What are the tax ramifications? The answers depend on your business's financial situation, your personal needs, how the business is organized, and more.

### *Employee versus Self-Employed*

If your business is a corporation, whether C or S, you are an employee if you provide services for the corporation. Compensation is deductible by the corporation and taxable to you. Compensation is subject to Social Security and Medicare (FICA) taxes as well as the additional Medicare tax of 0.9% if compensation exceeds a threshold amount for your filing status ($200,000 for singles; $250,000 for joint filers; $125,000 for married persons filing separately) (see Chapter 30). And it can affect the 20% qualified business income deduction (see Chapter 21).

In contrast, if you are a self-employed person because your business is a sole proprietorship, partnership, or limited liability company, you do not receive compensation. Instead, you can take a *draw*, which can be fixed to appear like a salary. The draw is not deductible by the company; it is not separately taxable to you (it is part of the net earnings from the business on which you are taxed). The draw is not separately subject to self-employment tax (which is effectively the employer and employee share of Social Security and Medicare taxes). Instead, self-employment tax is paid on all of the net earnings allocated to the owner (with some modifications), regardless of whether earnings are paid out (as draw or otherwise) or retained by the business. Net earnings from self-employment over your applicable threshold amount (the same threshold that applies to employees described earlier) is subject to the 0.9% additional Medicare tax; the amount of your draw has no impact on whether and to what extent this tax applies to you.

*Guaranteed payments* to partners are different from a draw. These payments are made for services without regard to the income of the partnership. The payments are deductible by the partnership (before determining partnership profit or loss), are treated as ordinary income to the recipient-partner, and generally are subject to self-employment tax.

### Audit Strategies

The compensation payment strategy varies for C and S corporations.

- *C corporations*. The general approach is to maximize compensation to create large tax deductions for the business. Deductible compensation cannot exceed what is reasonable under the circumstances; what is reasonable is a highly litigated issue in tax law. Whereas public corporations can deduct compensation to certain employees only up to $1 million and up to $500,000 for compensation paid to service providers of a covered health insurance provider (CHIP), privately-held C corporations do not have any dollar limit on deductible compensation.
- *S corporations*. The general approach is to minimize compensation to reduce FICA taxes for the corporation and owner. The owner pays income tax on all of the net earnings allocated to him or her, but FICA tax applies only to amounts distributed as compensation. Some owners have opted to take *no* compensation in order to avoid any FICA tax, but courts have said that owners must receive at least some compensation for work performed (essentially what the corporation would have to pay a third party to do the same work). The IRS has identified the lack of compensation to S corporation owner-employees as a key audit target. And, with the 20% qualified business income deduction, taking compensation to increase W-2 wages (a factor in determining the extent of this deduction, if any) should be considered by owner-employees with taxable income on their personal returns likely to exceed the applicable taxable income threshold (in 2021, it's $329,800 for joint filers, $164,925 for married persons filing separately, and $164,900 for all other filers).

## Stock Options and Restricted Stock

If your business is incorporated, you can give or sell to employees (including owner-employees) the right to buy shares in the corporation. They can be a useful form of compensation when the business does not have cash on hand. Of course, when the options are exercised and employees obtain stock, this dilutes the ownership interests of previously existing shareholders.

There are 2 types of options: (1) qualified stock options, which are **incentive stock options (ISOs)** and options granted under an **employee stock purchase plan** (usually used only in large corporations and not discussed any further here), and (2) **nonqualified employee stock options**.

***Incentive stock options (ISOs)*** **These are stock options meeting certain statutory requirements and that are granted to employees.**

***Employee stock purchase plan*** **This is a plan meeting statutory requirements to grant options to employees.**

***Nonqualified employee stock options*** **These are stock options granted to employees who do not meet statutory requirements.**

***ISOs.*** From the employee perspective, income is recognized *not* when the option is granted or exercised, but only when the stock acquired pursuant to the option is sold (provided certain holding periods are met). However, the exercise of an ISO may be an adjustment for purposes of the alternative minimum tax (see Chapter 28).

From the employer perspective, because employees do not have income from the ISO at the time it is granted or exercised, there is no compensation deduction at that time. However, if there is a disqualifying disposition of the stock acquired, the disposition creates compensation income for the employee, which is the difference between the strike price and the stock's fair market value (FMV) at the time of exercise. A disqualifying disposition is a disposition of the stock within either 2 years from the date that the option is granted or one year from the date that the option is exercised.

***Nonqualified employee stock options.*** From the employee perspective, the nonqualified stock option is taxable to the employee at the time it is granted *if* it has a "readily ascertainable fair market value." For closely held corporations, this means the option can be transferred and/or exercised immediately, without restrictions or conditions. If there is no such value, then the employee is taxed when the option is exercised.

The employee can make what is called a Section 83(b) election to report the income when the option is exercised but the stock is not vested (there are restrictions or conditions to transferring the stock), even if he or she is not otherwise required to do so. This election allows an employee to convert what would be ordinary income into capital gain; by reporting some ordinary income now, all future appreciation becomes capital gain. The election must be made within 30 days of receipt of the restricted stock. The election can be on the IRS sample form (Form 7.1) or on the employee's own statement (there is no IRS form for this), which is filed with the IRS service center in which the employee files his or her return; provide a copy to the employer-corporation.

From the corporation's perspective, a deduction for the value of the nonqualified stock option can be claimed when the option is included in the employee's gross income as compensation. This occurs when the option is granted *if* the option has a readily ascertainable value (something very rare in closely held corporations). If the option does not have a readily ascertainable value, the corporation's deduction is postponed until the employee exercises the option, provided the employee's rights in the stock are vested. If rights in the stock are not vested, then the deduction is further postponed until such rights are vested. The deduction at this time is the amount of income that the employee recognizes (i.e., the value of the stock minus the strike price and any amount paid by the employee, or the net amount received by the employee in exchange for the option).

When an employee exercises the option, you as the employer must report to the employee and the IRS the excess of the fair market value of the stock over the amount that the employee paid for the stock. This reporting is done on the employee's W-2 form.

***Qualified equity grants.*** Privately held corporations can enable employees to defer the income resulting from the acquisition of stock pursuant to stock options or restricted stock units (RSUs) (collectively called "qualified equity grants" under Code Section 83(i)). The corporation must provide an escrow arrangement to hold the shares until the proper amount of income tax is withheld from the employees at the end of the deferral period.

Employees who wish to defer income recognition must make an election within 30 days from the time the stock becomes substantially vested or transferable, whichever is earlier. The sample election form (Form 7.1) that is used for making a Section 83(b) election can be modified and used to make a Section 83(i) election.

***Section 83(b) Election***

*The undersigned taxpayer hereby elects, pursuant to § 83(b) of the Internal Revenue Code of 1986, as amended, to include in gross income as compensation for services the excess (if any) of the fair market value of the shares described below over the amount paid for those shares.*

1. *The name, taxpayer identification number, address of the undersigned, and the taxable year for which this election is being made are:*

   *TAXPAYER'S NAME: ______________________*
   *TAXPAYER'S SOCIAL SECURITY NUMBER: ____________*
   *ADDRESS: ______________________*
   *TAXABLE YEAR: Calendar Year 20__*

2. *The property which is the subject of this election is _________ shares of common stock of _____________.*

3. *The property was transferred to the undersigned on* ***[DATE].***

4. *The property is subject to the following restrictions:* ***[Describe applicable restrictions here.]***

5. *The fair market value of the property at the time of transfer (determined without regard to any restriction other than a nonlapse restriction as defined in § 1.83-3(h) of the Income Tax Regulations) is: $______ per share x _______ shares = $_________.*

6. *For the property transferred, the undersigned paid $______ per share x ________ shares = $____________.*

7. *The amount to include in gross income is $____________.* ***[The result of the amount reported in Item 5 minus the amount reported in Item 6.]***

*The undersigned taxpayer will file this election with the Internal Revenue Service office with which taxpayer files his or her annual income tax return not later than 30 days after the date of transfer of the property. A copy of the election also will be furnished to the person for whom the services were performed. Additionally, the undersigned will include a copy of the election with his or her income tax return for the taxable year in which the property is transferred. The undersigned is the person performing the services in connection with which the property was transferred.*

*Dated:* ______________________ ______________________
*Taxpayer*

**FIGURE 7.1 Sample Form for Section 83(b) Election**

## Deferred Compensation

Owners (and certain employees) may wish to defer the receipt of compensation to a future date. Deferral is often used for bonuses or special payments above a base salary. If the deferred compensation arrangement is done properly, the compensation is not taxed until it is received, postponing the tax on the earnings. Deferred compensation is also used as a way to create retirement income, since receipt is usually postponed until the person retires or leaves the company. The company generally cannot deduct the deferred compensation until it is paid to the employee, although a special rule applies to year-end bonuses paid by accrual-based companies within 2½ months after the close of the year, as explained earlier in this chapter.

**NOTE**

**Deferred compensation that fails to pass muster results in immediate taxation (even though the employee may not yet be able to touch the funds) as well as a 20% penalty.**

Deferred compensation can be created under an agreement, arrangement, or plan set up by the company. Key points to making deferred compensation plans work for maximum tax advantage:

- The employee must agree to defer the compensation before it is earned. Once earned, any deferred payments are immediately treated as taxable.
- Receipt of deferred compensation must be postponed to a fixed date, such as separation from service.
- The employer cannot segregate the deferred amounts; they must remain an unfunded promise of payment by the company and subject to the claims of the company's creditors.

It should be noted that even though compensation is deferred for income tax purposes, it may be subject to payroll taxes when earned (see Chapter 29). There is uncertainty about tax rates for individuals in the future. From a planning perspective, owners may not want to defer compensation at this time if they believe tax rates will be higher when they expect to receive the deferred amounts.

## Disallowance Repayment Agreements

If you are an employee of a corporation you own and a portion of your salary is viewed by the IRS as unreasonable, the corporation loses its deduction for the payment. You are taxed on the payment in any event—either as compensation or as a constructive dividend. However, there is a way you can ensure that the corporation does not lose out if the IRS later characterizes its compensation deduction as partially unreasonable: You can enter into a *disallowance repayment agreement*.

The repayment agreement, which may be a stand-alone agreement or part of an employment contract, provides that if certain payments to you by the corporation are disallowed by the IRS, you are required to repay such amounts to your corporation. The agreement must be in writing and enforceable under local law. The agreement should be reflected not only in a separate written agreement between you and your corporation, such as part of your employment contract with the corporation, but also in the corporate minutes as a resolution of the board of directors. The bylaws of the corporation should also reflect the ability of the board to enforce the agreement.

### *Effect of the Repayment Agreement*

The repayment agreement is a way for you to offset dividend income you are required to report if the IRS considers payments to you to be constructive dividends. By virtue of the repayment agreement, you would have been entitled to deduct the amounts you are contractually required to repay to your corporation as a miscellaneous itemized deduction on your personal return in the year repayment was made if miscellaneous itemized deductions subject to the 2%-of-adjusted-gross-income threshold were not suspended through 2025. However, some tax experts do not think that a repayment agreement is a good idea. Having one could be viewed as an admission that the corporation expects to pay an unreasonable salary.

## Golden Parachute Payments

When a C corporation merges or is acquired by another corporation, special compensation may be paid to key people, such as owners and top managers ("disqualified individuals") who are forced out of the business. These payments are called golden parachutes. Typically, they arise in large publicly traded corporations, but can occur in privately held businesses as well.

### *Overview*

When there is a "change in control" and special compensation is paid to a "disqualified person" (these terms are explained further on), the compensation is treated as a golden parachute. The results: There is a 20% excise tax on *excess* parachute payments on the recipient. The corporation loses its tax deduction for the payments and must withhold the 20% excise tax. Only *excess* payments receive this adverse tax treatment. "Excess" for this purpose means 3 times the individual's base amount, which is his or her average annual compensation for the past 5 years.

A change in control means any of the following:

- A change in the ownership of corporate stock
- A change in the ownership of a substantial portion of corporate assets
- A change in the effective control of the corporation

A disqualified person includes:

- A more-than-1% shareholder
- Officers of the corporation
- Highly compensated employees

A disqualified person can also be an independent contractor, such as a corporate director.

### *Small Business Exemption*

If the corporation is a "small business corporation," it is exempt from the golden parachute rules. To be exempt, the corporation must be an S corporation, which means that all of the following conditions must be met:

- There are 100 or fewer shareholders
- There is one class of stock
- All shareholders are individuals, estates, trusts, and certain tax-exempt organizations
- The corporation is a domestic (U.S.) corporation and is not an excluded entity (e.g., financial institution, insurance company, or former DISC)

## Fringe Benefits

### In General

Employers usually are not required by federal law to offer any specific types of employee benefits. (There is the employer mandate for health coverage explained in Chapter 19 and there may be some state law requirements for certain fringe benefits.) However, in today's tighten job market, employers may want to offer various *fringe benefits* (also called perks or perquisites) as a way of attracting and retaining a good workforce. Businesses may also want to provide these benefits because owners want such benefits for themselves as well.

If you pay certain expenses for an employee, you can usually claim a deduction. This is so even though the benefits may be excluded from the employee's gross income. If you are a sole proprietor, partner, or LLC member, you are not an employee and cannot receive these benefits on a tax-free basis. For purposes of this rule, employees who are more than 2% shareholders in their S corporations are treated the same as partners and cannot get these benefits on a tax-free basis. Limits on benefits for sole proprietors, partners, LLC members, and more-than-2% S corporation shareholders are discussed later in this chapter.

The benefits provided to an employee must be ordinary and necessary business expenses. The cost of the benefits must be reasonable in amount. And, in most cases, the benefits must be provided on a nondiscriminatory basis; they cannot be extended only to owner-employees and highly paid workers. The following is a review of the various types of fringe benefits that may be offered to employees.

#### NO-COST FRINGE BENEFITS

Some desirable benefits may be offered to employees at no cost to employers. Obviously, because there is no cost involved, no-cost benefits do not generate any tax deductions. Examples of no-cost benefits include:

- Better job titles (without any increase in pay)
- Bringing pets to work
- "Emotional compensation" (personally supporting each employee's individual concerns and providing a culture of connection in your company)
- Flexible work schedules
- Job sharing
- Mentoring among employees
- Remote work arrangements

#### MEDICAL INSURANCE AND BENEFITS

In general, medical insurance coverage, along with any reimbursements of medical expenses, is excluded from an employee's gross income. You deduct the cost of the medical insurance premiums. If you are *self-insured* (you reimburse employees for medical costs out of your operating expenses under a written medical reimbursement plan), you deduct reimbursements to the employees when and to the extent made. Medical coverage, including health savings accounts (HSAs), long-term care coverage, and medical reimbursement plans, is discussed more fully in Chapter 19.

#### SMARTPHONES

If you give smartphones to employees, you can deduct the cost of the phone and monthly service charges without employees reporting their business usage to you.

Personal usage of employer-provided phones to employees is not taxed to the employees if there is a noncompensatory reason for providing the phones. Examples of noncompensatory reasons:

- The employer needs to contact the employee at all times for work-related emergencies.
- The employer requires that the employee be available to speak with customers or clients at times when the employee is away from the office.
- The employee needs to speak with customers or clients located in other time zones at times outside of the employee's normal workday.

Providing a phone to promote the morale or goodwill of an employee, to attract a prospective employee, or as a means of furnishing additional compensation to an employee is *not* providing the phone primarily for noncompensatory business purposes.

### DEPENDENT CARE ASSISTANCE

Up to $10,500 ($5,250 for a married person filing separately) may be excluded from an employee's gross income for 2021; your outlays are fully deductible. You must set up a program to provide this benefit—a plan that makes clear to your employees what they may be entitled to. You do not have to fund the plan (set money aside); instead you can pay as you go. Special rules apply for dependent care assistance plans for 2021 regarding employee elections and carryovers of unused amounts. For example, unused amounts from 2021 may be carried over and used by employees in 2022 if the plan allows it. There's more information about these special rules in IRS Notices 2021-15 and 2021-26.

However, as a practical matter, this benefit may not make sense for all small businesses since nondiscrimination rules intended to make sure that the plan does not favor owners prevents more than 25% of the amounts paid by the plan from benefiting owners (their spouses or dependents) who own more than 5% of the business.

You may allow your employees to pay for their own dependent care on a pretax basis by setting up a flexible spending arrangement (FSA) discussed later in this section.

For information about building child care facilities or offering child care referral services, see Chapter 23.

### GROUP-TERM LIFE INSURANCE

You deduct the cost of providing this benefit, which is the cost of the premiums. Typical coverage runs 2 times or more of the annual salary of the employee. The cost for up to $50,000 of coverage is excludable from an employee's gross income. If coverage over $50,000 is provided, an *imputed income* amount for excess coverage is includible in the employee's gross income. The imputed income is calculated according to an age-based IRS table; it is not based on the actual cost of premiums. While you deduct the actual cost of providing this benefit, your employees will be pleased to learn that the income from excess coverage may be modest. Use Table 7.1 to figure employee income from excess coverage that is reported on the employee's Form W-2. The amount shown is the cost per $1,000 of excess coverage *each month*.

The amount of coverage up to $2,000 for spouses and dependents is also excludable from an employee's gross income as a de minimis fringe benefit. If the amount of coverage exceeds $2,000, then all is taxable using Table 7.1 (not just the amount over $2,000).

If a group insurance plan is considered to be discriminatory, key employees (owners and top executives) will have income from the coverage and will not be able to exclude the cost for the first $50,000 of coverage. In this instance, income to them is the greater of the actual cost of

**TABLE 7.1 Employee Income from Excess Coverage**

| Age | Imputed Income ($) |
|---|---|
| Under age 25 | 0.05 |
| 25–29 | 0.06 |
| 30–34 | 0.08 |
| 35–39 | 0.09 |
| 40–44 | 0.10 |
| 45–49 | 0.15 |
| 50–54 | 0.23 |
| 55–59 | 0.43 |
| 60–64 | 0.66 |
| 65–69 | 1.27 |
| 70 and older | 2.06 |

the coverage, or the imputed amount calculated according to the age-based IRS tables. Special insurance coverage arranged on an individual basis (for example, split-dollar life insurance) is discussed later in this chapter.

### EDUCATIONAL ASSISTANCE

If the courses are job related, your payments are deductible as noncompensatory business expenses with no dollar limit. If the courses are not job related, your expenses are deductible as wages. If you lay off workers and pay for their retraining, you may also deduct your payments.

There is a special exclusion of up to $5,250 for employer-financed education assistance, including graduate-level courses, under a qualifying plan. This applies even if the education is not job related. It also applies to student loan repayment assistance through 2025–directly to the employee or to the lender.

Amounts you pay for an employee under the plan can be excluded from the employee's income even if the courses are not job related. In that case, your payments under the plan would be deductible as noncompensatory business expenses.

As a practical matter, it is generally not advisable for most owners of small businesses to set up educational assistance plans for the same reason that dependent care assistance programs may not make sense—no more than 5% of benefits can go to owner-employees or their spouses or dependents.

### ADOPTION ASSISTANCE

You may deduct the cost of adoption assistance you provide to your employees. If you set up a special assistance program (a separate written plan to provide adoption assistance), your employees can exclude up to $14,440 per child in 2021. However, in 2021, the exclusion is phased out for those with adjusted gross income (AGI) between $216,660 and $256,660 (regardless of your filing status as married or single).

As in the case of educational assistance plans, adoption assistance plans do not make sense for small employers in most cases, since no more than 5% of benefits can go to owner-employees.

### RETIREMENT PLANNING ADVICE

If you maintain a qualified retirement plan, you can pay for expert advice for your employees and their spouses with respect to retirement planning, and they are not taxed on this benefit. There is no dollar limit to the exclusion. However, it does *not* apply to tax preparation, accounting, legal, or brokerage services. If you pay for these services on behalf of your employees, they are taxed on this amount, although you can deduct your payments.

### HEALTH SAVINGS ACCOUNTS

If you maintain a high-deductible health insurance plan and contribute to a Health Savings Account (HSA) for an employee, you can deduct your contributions. Contribution limits and other rules for Health Savings Accounts are discussed in Chapter 30. Contributions are not taxed to employees and are exempt from payroll taxes. You must complete contributions by April 18, 2022, in order to deduct them on your 2021 return (even if you obtain a filing extension).

HSAs and MSAs are discussed more fully in Chapter 19.

**NOTE**

**If you are a small business or a self-employed individual, you can contribute to an Archer Medical Savings Account (MSA), assuming the account was set up prior to 2008.**

### HEALTH REIMBURSEMENT ACCOUNTS (HRAs)

These are plans under which an employee can draw up to a dollar limit fixed by the employer to cover out-of-pocket medical expenses. HRAs are used to supplement employer-provided health coverage. In addition, there are special types of reimbursement arrangements. One is called, called a Qualified Small Employer Health Reimbursement Arrangement (QSEHRA), to reimburse employees for their individually obtained health coverage but no other out-of-pocket costs. Another is an Individual Coverage Health reimbursement Arrangement (ICHRA), which also reimburses employees for their individually obtained health insurance. These plans are discussed more fully in Chapter 19.

### CAFETERIA PLANS AND FLEXIBLE SPENDING ACCOUNTS

If you make contributions to cafeteria plans, you can claim a deduction as an employee benefit expense. Cafeteria plans are designed to offer employees choices among benefits on a nondiscriminatory basis. Simple cafeteria plans for small employers are explained later in this chapter.

Flexible spending accounts (FSAs) are also nondiscriminatory plans but are funded primarily with employee contributions. Flexible spending accounts are intended to cover medical costs or dependent care costs on a pretax basis. Employees agree to salary reductions (within limits set by law) that are then contributed to the FSA to be used for medical costs or dependent care costs. The dollar limit in 2021 on elective deferrals is $2,750 to health FSAs and $10,500 for dependent care FSAs.

As a result of COVID-19, Congress created some relief for employees in 2021 if the employer's plan permits this:

- Employees may be allowed to make mid-year election changes in 2021 (as was permitted in 2020). This means opting to participate, opting out of participation, or changing the salary reduction contribution. A change only applies going forward.
- Employees can carry over unused contributions in FSAs to the following year if the plan allows it. This means that any of the used contribution in 2020 (up to the annual limit of

$2,750 for health FSAs and $5,000 for dependent care FSAs) may be carried over to 2021, and any unused contribution in 2021 (up to the annual limit of $2,750 for health FSAs and $10,500 for dependent care FSAs) may be carried over to 2022.

- The grace period for using up contributions from health FSAs, which normally runs only to March 15, has been extended for the entire year. This applies for 2020 and 2021. Thus, unused contributions for 2020 may be used at any time in 2021.
- The age for a covered dependent in dependent care FSAs is increased from under age 13 to under age 14 for 2021.
- Employees who cease participation during the year because they've left the job (e.g., they've been laid off) can be reimbursed for unused amounts. This applies for 2020 and 2021.

***Reminder***: A health FSA may offer a carryover option or a grace period, but not both. An FSA is not required to offer either option.

From your perspective, however, you may be on the hook for payments if the plan pays out more than the employee has paid in and the employee then terminates employment. The reason: The plan must pay out benefits equal to the employees' annual commitment for salary reduction contributions, even if they have not been fully paid.

**Example**

**An employee agrees to contribute $100 at the end of each month to an FSA. In January 2021, the employee submits a claim of $1,200 for dependent care payable to an agency to cover the next 6 months. The employee quits the job in the first week of February 2021. The business is out $1,100.**

Be sure you observe cafeteria plans compliance rules. This includes having written plan documents, providing employees with a summary plan description within 90 days of their becoming covered by the plan, and furnishing plan documents to all participants every 10 years if the plan has not been updated, or every 5 years if it has been updated.

### *Other Employee Benefits*

In addition to the various employee benefit plans just discussed, there are other types of benefits you may provide for employees for which you can claim a deduction for your expenses.

**NOTE**

**You may incur costs to administer these employee benefit plans. If you handle them internally (e.g., with your company bookkeeper), there is no additional cost; it is part of wages you already pay. If you use outside companies to administer these plans, you may separately deduct the costs.**

#### SUPPLEMENTAL UNEMPLOYMENT BENEFITS

If you make contributions to a welfare benefit fund to provide supplemental unemployment benefits for your employees, you may deduct your contributions as ordinary and necessary business expenses. The deduction is claimed as an employee benefit expense, not as a compensation cost. Your deduction cannot exceed the fund's qualified cost for the year. *Qualified cost* is the amount you could have claimed had you provided the benefits directly and been on the cash basis, plus the amount estimated to be actually necessary to build the fund to cover claims incurred but not yet paid and administrative costs for such claims.

### MEALS AND LODGING

In general, the costs of providing meals and lodging to your employees are deductible as an expense of operating your business. The costs may or may not be taxable to your employees. The tax treatment of this benefit to your employees affects the amount and how you claim a deduction. Usually, you may deduct only 50% of the cost of providing meals. A 100% limit applies in 2021 and 2022 for business meals furnished at restaurants (explained in Chapter 8).

The usual 50% limit on deducting meals does not apply if:

- Your employees must include the benefit in income. In this case, you may deduct 100% of the cost as compensation.
- You operate a restaurant or catering business and provide meals to your employees at your restaurant or work site. However, in this case, the full cost of the meals is not deductible as compensation; instead, it is treated as part of the cost of goods sold.

**Example**

**You pay your employee's meal costs when she attends a ballgame with a client (assuming the food for the employee and client are separately billed from the tickets). (Assume proper substantiation and reimbursement arrangements, as explained in Chapter 8.) The meal costs are not included in your employee's gross income. You deduct 50% of the meal costs (the 100% limit does not apply because the meal costs were not furnished at a restaurant).**

**Example**

**You give your employee a $200 meal allowance because of seniority. The $200 is included in your employee's gross income. You deduct 100% of the $200 meal allowance.**

**NOTE**

**Under a safe harbor rule, meals provided to all your employees are treated as furnished for your convenience (and fully deductible) if more than half of the employees to whom such meals are provided are treated as having been furnished meals for your convenience.**

- You provide the meals as part of the expense of providing recreational or social activities. For example, the cost of a company picnic is fully deductible.

You may deduct the full amount of meal costs if your employees are able to exclude this amount from their gross income. They do this if the meals are furnished on your premises and for your convenience, or if the meals qualify as a de minimis fringe benefit.

Special rules apply for valuing the meals provided at an employer-operated eating facility. An *employer-operated eating facility* is a lunchroom or other facility that you own or lease and operate directly or by a contract to provide meals on or near your business premises during or immediately before or after your employees' workday. Meals provided at an eating facility on or near your business premises are treated as a de minimis fringe benefit. As such, they are excluded from your employee's income and you can claim a full deduction.

If you provide your employees with lodging on your premises (for example, if you run a motel, nursing home, or rental property and the employee must live on the premises in order to manage it), you may deduct your full expenses according to the particular expense involved. For example, you deduct the cost of heating and lighting as part of your utilities, the cost of bedding as part of your linen expenses, and the use of the room as a depreciation item.

However, if you are a self-employed individual, you cannot make your living costs tax deductible. You may not exclude them even if you live at your business (e.g., you own a motel and live in it) since you are *not* an employee of your business.

**Looking Ahead**

**After 2025, no deduction will be allowed for meals excludable from an employee's income (e.g., provided for your convenience on your premises) and any food, beverage, and facility expenses for meals that are treated as de minimis fringe benefits. This will not bar a deduction for company cafeterias or executive dining rooms.**

### HOUSING RELOCATION COSTS

While this may be rare, a small business may provide relocation assistance to an employee by helping with the sale of the employee's home. The business may deduct as "compensation" the payment of expenses related to the home where the employee retains the right to negotiate for a final sale price. Before 2018, if you paid for employees' moving expenses, you could deduct your costs and treat them as a tax-free fringe benefit. Through 2025, if the business pays moving costs, they are taxable compensation to the employee (and deductible as compensation by the company).

### TRAVEL COSTS

If you pay for travel costs, you may deduct your outlays, subject to certain limits. These expenses are explained in Chapter 8.

### EMPLOYEE USE OF A COMPANY CAR

An employer may choose to treat all use by an employee of a company-owned car as personal use and include an appropriate amount in the employee's gross income. For 2018 through 2025, this places a serious burden on employees who are taxed on their business use but are unable to deduct it on their personal returns. If personal use of a company car is de minimis, then nothing need be included in the employee's gross income. As a practical matter, when the employee is an owner, the decision on how to value personal use of a company car is a mutual decision. Both the employer and employee in this case agree on which method is preferable. Keep in mind that when valuing personal use for an owner, only the fair market value or ALV methods can be used.

If you want to treat only personal use as a noncash fringe benefit, there are several methods you can use. You can use a method described below on a vehicle-by-vehicle basis (other than for the fleet valuation method). You must notify employees about the method used no later than the start of the year or 30 days after providing the benefit, whichever is later. This notice must be given in a "manner reasonably expected to come to the attention of all affected employees" (e.g., a notice mailed to each employee; a posting on the employee notice board).

***Fair market value.*** One method is based on the actual fair market value (FMV) of the personal use. This is determined by looking at the cost of leasing a comparable car at a comparable price for a comparable period of time in the same geographical area.

***Annual lease value.*** Another method is based on the car's annual lease value (ALV). The ALV is set by the IRS and depends on the FMV of the car on the date the car is first used for personal purposes (see Table 7.2).

**TABLE 7.2** Annual Lease Value (ALV) Table for Cars

| FMV | ALV |
|---|---|
| $0 to 999 | $ 600 |
| 1,000 to 1,999 | 850 |
| 2,000 to 2,999 | 1,100 |
| 3,000 to 3,999 | 1,350 |
| 4,000 to 4,999 | 1,600 |
| 5,000 to 5,999 | 1,850 |
| 6,000 to 6,999 | 2,100 |
| 7,000 to 7,999 | 2,350 |
| 8,000 to 8,999 | 2,600 |
| 9,000 to 9,999 | 2,850 |
| 10,000 to 10,999 | 3,100 |
| 11,000 to 11,999 | 3,350 |
| 12,000 to 12,999 | 3,600 |
| 13,000 to 13,999 | 3,850 |
| 14,000 to 14,999 | 4,100 |
| 15,000 to 15,999 | 4,350 |
| 16,000 to 16,999 | 4,600 |
| 17,000 to 17,999 | 4,850 |
| 18,000 to 18,999 | 5,100 |
| 19,000 to 19,999 | 5,350 |
| 20,000 to 20,999 | 5,600 |
| 21,000 to 21,999 | 5,850 |
| 22,000 to 22,999 | 6,100 |
| 23,000 to 23,999 | 6,350 |
| 24,000 to 24,999 | 6,600 |
| 25,000 to 25,999 | 6,850 |
| 26,000 to 27,999 | 7,250 |
| 28,000 to 29,999 | 7,750 |
| 30,000 to 31,999 | 8,250 |
| 32,000 to 33,999 | 8,750 |
| 34,000 to 35,999 | 9,250 |

**TABLE 7.2** ***(Continued)***

| FMV | ALV |
|---|---|
| 36,000 to 37,999 | 9,750 |
| 38,000 to 39,999 | 10,250 |
| 40,000 to 41,999 | 10,750 |
| 42,000 to 43,999 | 11,250 |
| 44,000 to 45,999 | 11,750 |
| 46,000 to 47,999 | 12,250 |
| 48,000 to 49,999 | 12,750 |
| 50,000 to 51,999 | 13,250 |
| 52,000 to 53,999 | 13,750 |
| 54,000 to 55,999 | 14,250 |
| 56,000 to 57,999 | 14,750 |
| 58,000 to 59,999 | 15,250 |

**Example**

**During all of 2021, your employee uses a company car 50% of the time for personal purposes and 50% for business purposes. The fair market value of the car as of January 1, 2021, is $15,000. The ALV is $4,350. The amount included in the employee's gross income is $2,175 ($4,350 × .50).**

For cars over $59,999, calculate the ALV as follows: Multiply the fair market value of the car by 25% and add $500. The ALV figures apply for a 4-year period starting with the year of the ALV election. Thereafter, the ALV for each subsequent 4-year period is based on the car's then fair market value.

If the car is used continuously for personal purposes for at least 30 days but less than the entire year, you must prorate the value of personal use.

**Example**

**Using the company car example, except that the employee uses the car from May 1 through September 30, 2021. The $2,175 is prorated for the 153 days of personal use. The amount included in the employee's gross income is $911.71 ($2,175 × [153 ÷ 365]).**

The ALV method already takes into account maintenance and insurance costs. Fuel provided by an employer is not included in the ALV. Fuel provided in kind can be valued at FMV or 5.5¢ per mile for purposes of including it in the employee's gross income. If fuel is paid by a company credit card, the actual charges are used to compute personal use included in the employee's gross income.

***Cents-per-mile rule.*** Another valuation method for personal use of a company vehicle is the cents-per-mile special rule. This rule can be used only if a vehicle is valued in 2021 at no more than $51,100 and the vehicle is regularly used in the business (at least 50% of total annual mileage is for the business, or the vehicle is used each workday to drive at least 3 employees to and from work in a carpool) or for a vehicle driven by employees at least 10,000 miles during a calendar year. And the employee cannot be a control employee (see below). If the vehicle is owned or leased for less than a full year, the 10,000 miles are prorated accordingly. The value of personal use is based on the standard mileage rate. The standard mileage rate for 2021 is 56¢ per mile.

***Fleet valuation method.*** There is another method for valuing personal use of company vehicles called the fleet valuation method. This applies to companies with a fleet of 20 or more vehicles, something that small businesses usually do not have; this method is not explained further in this book.

***Commuting rule.*** If you allow your employees to use company cars to commute to and from work because of unsafe conditions, a special valuation rule is used to determine the amount includable in the employee's gross income. The car must be owned or leased by the employer for use in the business, and the employer must have genuine noncompensatory business reasons for requiring an employee to commute in the vehicle. Also, the employer must have a written policy preventing use of the vehicle for personal purposes other than commuting (or de minimis personal use). The employee cannot be a *control employee* (an employee who is a board-appointed, shareholder-appointed, confirmed, or elected officer with compensation of at least $115,000, a director, a 1% or greater owner, or someone who receives compensation of $235,000 or more in 2021). If the special commuting vehicle rule is met, then the value of commuting is $1.50 each way ($3.00 round trip), regardless of the length of the commute. The same flat rate applies to each employee even if more than one employee commutes in the vehicle. While the commuting vehicle rule is optional at the employer's election, it must be used for valuing all commuting if it is used for valuing any commuting.

The deduction for vehicle expenses—depreciation, insurance, gas, oil, and repairs—is explained in Chapter 9. This chapter covers only business use of a company car.

***Reimbursement methods.*** There are reimbursement methods you can use to help employees cover the cost of business driving. One is mileage reimbursement based on the IRS-set standard mileage rate (56¢ per mile in 2021). Another is the fixed and variable rate (FAVR) allowance. This is a reimbursement amount that includes a combination of payments covering fixed and variable costs, such as the cents-per-mile rate for variable operating costs (e.g., oil and gasoline) and a flat amount for fixed costs (e.g., depreciation or lease payments). The FAVR allowance is based on a vehicle cost in 2021 that cannot exceed $51,100.

Both the mileage reimbursement and FAVR allowance can be tax free to employees.

### COUNTRY CLUB DUES

If you pay the cost of membership at a golf or other country club, the dues are not deductible.

### FLIGHTS ON EMPLOYER-PROVIDED AIRCRAFT

Special rules are used to determine the value of personal use of flights provided on employer aircraft. A discussion of these rules is beyond the scope of this book.

### LIFE INSURANCE PROVIDED ON AN INDIVIDUAL BASIS

Businesses may provide owners and other top employees with coverage on an individual basis. This coverage may be term insurance or permanent insurance (e.g., a whole life policy). This coverage is taxable to the individual and does not have to be provided on a nondiscriminatory basis.

Under a split-dollar life insurance plan, the cost of coverage is shared between the business and the insured. Here is how the plan usually works.

A cash value life insurance policy is used for a split-dollar arrangement, with the business paying some or all of the premiums. At the death of the employee, the business recoups its outlay, and the balance of the proceeds is payable to the insured's beneficiary (typically his or her spouse or child). Under final regulations, how the employee is taxed on this benefit depends on who owns the policy:

- *If the employee owns the policy*, premiums paid by the business are treated as loans, with imputed interest taxed to the employee.
- *If the business owns the policy*, the employee is taxed on the value of the life insurance protection (which is the 1-year term cost of this protection).

In view of income tax being imposed on split-dollar life insurance arrangements, they are no longer favored as wealth builders for business owners.

#### IDENTITY THEFT PROTECTION

If your company's computer data has been hacked, you may offer employees identity theft protection services (e.g., credit reports and credit monitoring, identity theft protection insurance, identity theft restoration services). The benefit is deductible by you and is tax free to employees.

If you offer these benefits in the absence of having data compromised (e.g., you do it to attract and retain valued employees), you can still deduct the benefit, but it is taxable to employees and subject to employment taxes.

#### NO-ADDITIONAL-COST SERVICE

Don't include in your employee's gross income the value of a service you offer to customers in the ordinary course of the business in which your employee works (e.g., if you run a ferry line and allow employees to ride for free on scheduled runs). In the case of no-additional-cost service, you generally do not have any expense to deduct by virtue of providing the benefit to the employee. You have already deducted costs related to providing the service.

#### QUALIFIED EMPLOYEE DISCOUNT

Don't include in your employee's gross income a price reduction you give on certain property or services you offer to customers in the ordinary course of your business in which the employee performs services (e.g., if you own a clothing boutique and give your salespersons a 15% discount on your merchandise). A qualified employee discount cannot exceed the price at which the item is ordinarily sold to customers multiplied by your *gross profit percent* (total sales price of property less cost of property, divided by total sales price of property) or 20% in the case of services.

A qualified employee discount does not include any discount on real property. A deduction for the goods or services provided as a qualified employee discount is not taken into account as a compensation expense but rather as some other item. Goods provided to employees at a discount are part of the cost of goods sold.

#### WORKING CONDITION FRINGE BENEFIT

Don't include in your employee's gross income a benefit provided to your employee if the employee could have claimed his or her own deduction had he or she paid for the benefit. The fact an employee cannot deduct business expenses as a miscellaneous itemized deduction in 2018 through 2025 does not change this rule. For example, if you paid for a job-related course that would have been deductible by your employee under pre-2018 rules had the employee paid for it, the course is a working condition fringe benefit. Other examples of working condition fringe benefits include employer-provided vehicles for business driving and outplacement services.

### DE MINIMIS (MINIMAL) FRINGE

Don't include in your employee's gross income the value of any benefit that is so little in value as to make accounting for it unreasonable or administratively impracticable, such as the typing of a personal letter by a company secretary or the occasional use of the company copying machine for personal matters. Holiday gifts of nominal value, such as turkeys and hams, are considered de minimis fringes. However, cash of any amount is not a de minimis fringe and must be included in the employee's gross income. Other examples of de minimis fringes include:

- Group term life insurance for spouses and dependents up to $2,000 (discussed earlier in this chapter).
- Meals furnished at an eating facility on or near your premises.
- Coffee or soft drinks and donuts or apples furnished to employees in the break room.
- Flowers or fruit baskets for special occasions.
- Occasional tickets to sporting or entertainment events.
- Occasional meal money or transportation fare for employees working overtime.
- Company events (such as parties or picnics) for employees and their guests.

It may be possible to treat some costs as de minimis even though they are substantial. The Tax Court allowed the Boston Bruins hockey team to treat meals provided to players, coaches, and other personnel at away games as a de minimis fringe benefit. The deduction for meals is explained in greater detail in Chapter 8.

### QUALIFIED TRANSPORTATION FRINGE BENEFIT

If you provide your employee with a transit pass for mass transit, transportation in a commuter highway vehicle, or qualified parking, you cannot deduct the cost (see Chapter 12 on determining limits on a rent deduction covering employee parking), but you do not include the benefit in your employee's gross income. For 2021, the monthly exclusion for qualified parking is $270 and the monthly exclusion for commuter highway vehicle transportation and transit passes is $270.

The value of parking is based on what a person would have to pay for space in an arm's-length transaction. If you provide parking space to employees that is primarily available to customers, then the parking has no value. If you give employees who carpool preferential parking, the value of the space must be taken into consideration. The fact that you offer an employee a choice between a qualified transportation fringe benefit and cash does not make the benefit taxable if the employee chooses the benefit. The employee is, of course, taxed on cash received in lieu of the transportation fringe benefit. Employer-paid parking at a temporary job assignment—one expected to last one year or less that does in fact last that period—is deductible by you and fully excludable for an employee as paid under an accountable plan (explained in Chapter 8); there is no dollar limit in this situation.

If you pay for bicycle commuting in 2018 through 2025, you cannot deduct this benefit and the employee is taxable on it. Companies may allow employees to pay for transportation fringe benefits, such as monthly transit passes, through salary reductions. Due to COVID-19, many employees work remotely, while some employees opt to drive to work rather than take public transportation. Informally, the IRS has said that unused compensation reduction amounts may be carried over to the subsequent period and used for future commuting expenses. What's more, the unused amounts can be applied to a different type of commuter expense, such as qualified parking instead of transit passes, as long as the employer plan covers all such options. Of course, all this depends on the terms of the employer's transportation fringe benefit plan. If your business offers transportation fringe benefits, consider redesigning your plan to permit this type of flexibility going forward.

### CERTAIN ATHLETIC FACILITIES

You need not include in your employee's gross income the value of an on-site gym or other athletic facilities for use by employees, their spouses, and children. However, if you pay for a membership to an outside health club or athletic facility open to the general public, you must include the benefit in the employee's gross income. No deduction can be claimed for club dues (see Chapter 8).

### FREQUENT FLYER MILES

Some companies allow employees to use business-generated frequent flyer mileage for personal purposes. This benefit defies classification and, to date, the IRS has not figured out a way to tax it without causing an administrative nightmare. However, the IRS has said it was going to take another look at taxing frequent flyer miles; to date it has not, but check the Supplement for any update.

### LIMITS ON FRINGE BENEFITS FOR OWNERS

Benefits for sole proprietors, partners, LLC members, and more-than-2% S corporation shareholders that are otherwise excludable by rank-and-file employees are taxable to sole proprietors, partners, LLC members, and more-than-2% S corporation shareholders. For example, if the business pays for their health insurance (which may include long-term care insurance), the coverage is taxable to them. The business can deduct the costs as guaranteed payments to partners or as compensation to S corporation shareholders. Owners can then deduct the amount directly from gross income on Schedule 1 of Form 1040 or 1040-SR.

The balance can be treated as a deductible medical expense, which is taken as an itemized deduction subject to the 7.5%-of-adjusted-gross-income floor. Medical coverage for these owners is discussed in Chapter 19. In the case of monthly transit passes, the excludable amount is limited to $21 per month. If the value of the pass exceeds $21 per month, then the entire amount is includible in gross income for the owner. For free parking, there is no exclusion; the entire value of free parking for an owner is includible in gross income.

### REIMBURSEMENTS OF CERTAIN COSTS

Some business costs are paid by employees. Because of the suspension of the deduction for unreimbursed employee business expenses for 2018 through 2025, employers may want to cover their business-related expenses. If this is done through an accountable plan (explained in Chapter 8), then the employee is not taxed on the reimbursement while the company can deduct the payment without incurring any employment taxes. Examples of costs that can be reimbursed through an accountable plan include:

- Dues
- Home office expenses (e.g., internet access fees)

- Professional licenses
- Smartphones and tablets
- Subscriptions
- Tools and supplies
- Training and development
- Travel expenses (explained in Chapter 8)

## Cafeteria Plans

A cafeteria plan is a written plan that allows your employees to choose to receive cash or taxable benefits instead of certain tax-free benefits. If an employee chooses to receive a tax-free benefit under the plan, the fact that the employee could have received cash or a taxable benefit instead will not make the tax-free benefit taxable. The plan must be set up and operated on a nondiscriminatory basis; complicated testing rules apply unless it's a simplified cafeteria plan described later.

Benefits allowed to be offered under a cafeteria plan:

- Health and accident insurance
- Adoption assistance
- Dependent care assistance
- Group-term life insurance
- Health savings accounts

Benefits *not* allowed to be offered under a cafeteria plan:

- Educational assistance
- Meals and lodging
- Moving expense reimbursements
- Transportation (commuting) benefits

### *Simple Cafeteria Plans*

Small employers may offer cafeteria plans without any complicated testing rules to ensure that the plans are nondiscriminatory. A small employer is one with 100 or fewer employees. However, once a plan is established, it can continue as a simple cafeteria plan until there are 200 employees.

What distinguishes the simple cafeteria plan from a regular cafeteria plan is mandatory employer contributions. These must be made regardless of whether employees make salary reduction contributions to the plan.

There are 2 contribution formulas that an employer can choose to use:

1. A uniform percentage (not less than 2%) of the employee's compensation, or
2. An amount not less than 6% of the employee's compensation or twice the employee's salary reduction contribution.

A cafeteria plan must cover all employees (other than certain S corporation shareholder-employees). The plan *cannot* include sole proprietors, partners, members of LLCs (in most cases), or more-than-2% S corporation shareholder-employees. The plan *can* exclude those under age 21, those with less than one year of service, those covered by a collective bargaining agreement, and nonresident aliens working outside the United States whose income did not come from U.S. sources.

**NOTE**

**As yet, the IRS has not issued any guidance on simple cafeteria plans beyond information in Publication 15-B.**

Small business owners need to decide whether the benefits of offering a cafeteria plan for employees make sense when the owners cannot participate.

## Employment Tax Credits

*Tax credits* are even better than tax deductions. A tax deduction is worth only as much as the tax bracket you are in. For example, if you are in the top federal income tax bracket for individuals, 37% in 2021, a $100 deduction saves $37 in taxes. For a C corporation, a $100 deduction only saves $21 in taxes. Tax credits that offset income taxes reduce your taxes dollar-for-dollar. A $100 tax credit saves $100 in taxes. Thus, the credit results in only a $63 savings for the individual (without regard to the impact on self-employment tax where applicable) and a $79 savings for a C corporation. Some tax credits offset employment taxes as explained later.

### *Employer's Employment-Related Tax Credits*

There are a number of tax credits related to the employment of workers. Tax credits that offset income tax reduce your deduction for compensation dollar-for-dollar. For example, if your deduction for compensation is $40,000 and you are entitled to claim a $2,000 employment tax credit that reduces your income tax, you may deduct only $38,000.

The following credits are income tax offsets (and reductions to the deduction for compensation). Special COVID-19-related tax credits that reduce employment taxes for 2021 are discussed later.

#### WORK OPPORTUNITY CREDIT

To encourage employers to hire certain individuals from specially targeted groups, there is a tax credit called the work opportunity credit. A top credit of up to $9,600 applies to certain veterans, but smaller credits are allowed for hiring other individuals.

The credit applies for hiring an employee from one of the following targeted groups:

1. Member of a family receiving Temporary Assistance for Needy Families (TANF)
2. Qualified veteran (there are 5 subcategories)
3. Qualified ex-felon
4. Designated community resident
5. Vocational rehabilitation referral
6. Summer youth employee
7. Recipient of SNAP benefits (food stamps)
8. SSI recipient

9. Long-term family assistance recipient
10. Long-term unemployed (someone who has been unemployed for at least 27 consecutive weeks and received government unemployment benefits)

The amount of the credit varies with the targeted group category and, in some cases, the term of employment. The basic credit amount is 40% of first year wages up to $6,000, for a top credit of $2,400. This basic amount applies for those who work at least 400 hours. For those who are retained on the job for at least 120 hours but not more than 400 hours, the credit percentage drops to 25%, for a top credit of $1,500. However, the credit for summer youth is limited to 40% of wages up to $3,000, for a top credit of $1,200. And the credit for veterans with service-connected disabilities who are employed for at least 6 months is 40% of wages up to $24,000, for a top credit of $9,600.

There is no limit on the number of employees who can be hired to generate the work opportunity credit. What's more, some states have their own work opportunity programs, so check with your state revenue department.

If you employ an eligible worker, be sure to obtain the necessary certification from your state employment security agency. This is done by having the employee sign IRS Form 8850, *Pre-Screening Notice and Certification Request for the Work Opportunity Credit,* on the first day of work and submitting it to your state workforce agency within 28 days of the new employee's starting work, along with the Department of Labor's Employment and Training Administration (ETA) Form 9061, *Individual Characteristics Form* or Form 9062, *Conditional Certification*. Without having submitted Form 8850, you cannot claim the credit, but if you make a timely submission, you claim the credit even if the state agency fails to respond to you. It is highly advisable to get a new employee to sign the form and timely submit it to the state workforce agency if the agency is willing to accept it. (The IRS had provided an extension for submitting Form 8850 for some workers through November 8, 2021; see Notice 2021-43 for details.)

### EMPLOYER CREDIT FOR FICA ON TIPS

Owners of restaurants and beverage establishments can claim a credit for the employer portion of FICA paid on tips related to the furnishing of food and beverages on or off the premises. This is 7.65% of tips in excess of those treated as wages for purposes of satisfying the minimum wage provisions of the Fair Labor Standards Act (FLSA).

### INDIAN EMPLOYMENT CREDIT

You can claim a credit if you employ part-time or full-time workers who receive more than 50% of their wages from services performed on an Indian reservation. The employee must be an enrolled member of an Indian tribe or a spouse of an enrolled member. The employee must also live on or near the reservation on which the services are performed. The credit is 20% of the first $20,000 of excess wages and the cost of health insurance. Excess wages and health insurance costs are such costs over amounts paid or incurred during 1993. However, wages paid to any employee earning more than $30,000 are not taken into account; such employee is not a qualified employee.

#### Looking Ahead

**The Indian employment credit expires at the end of 2021, unless Congress extends it.**

### EMPLOYER DIFFERENTIAL WAGE PAYMENTS CREDIT FOR ACTIVATED RESERVISTS

If you continue some or all of the wages of employees called to active duty (called a differential wage payment), you can take a tax credit of 20% of the differential that does not exceed $20,000 (a top credit of $4,000).

This credit applies only to small employers (on average fewer than 50 employees on business days during the year) that have a written plan to provide the wage differential. No deduction for compensation can be claimed if the compensation is a differential wage payment used to determine this credit. The differential wage payment is not treated as "wages" for purposes of FICA and FUTA taxes. For income tax withholding, they are treated as supplemental wages (discussed in Chapter 29).

### CREDIT FOR PAID FAMILY AND MEDICAL LEAVE

Federal law does not require you to continue paying wages to employees who take family and medical leave (there had been a requirement related to COVID-19 in 2020). In fact, only companies with 50 or more employees are required to offer unpaid leave time.

States and localities may have their own rules. For example, California, New Jersey, New York, Massachusetts (as of January 1, 2021), Rhode Island, and the District of Columbia have paid family-leave requirements (and additional locations are considering this).

If you aren't required by state or local law to provide paid family and medical leave but choose to do so, you may qualify for a tax credit.

The minimum credit percentage is 12.5% of wages paid during the leave time to eligible employees. The percentage is increased by 0.25% for each percentage point by which payments to a qualifying employee exceed 50% of his or her wages, up to a maximum credit percentage of 25%.

An eligible employee in 2021 is someone who has been with the company for at least a year, earned no more than $78,000 in 2020, and receives wages during leave time under a written policy that requires full-time employees to receive at least 2 weeks of paid leave and part-timers to receive a pro rata amount.

You must pay the employee at least 50% of preleave wages in order to claim the credit. The credit must be subtracted from deductible compensation and is part of the general business credit.

### GENERAL BUSINESS CREDIT

Some employment tax credits are part of the general business credit. As such, they not only reduce your deduction for wages but are also subject to special limitations. The general business credit is the sum of employment tax credits and certain other business-related credits. The general business credit cannot exceed your net tax liability (tax liability reduced by certain personal and other credits), reduced by the greater of:

- Tentative minimum tax (the alternative minimum tax before the foreign tax credit), or
- 25% of regular tax liability (without regard to personal credits) over $25,000.

The amount of the general business credit in excess of this limit can be carried back for one year. Any additional excess amount can then be carried forward for up to 20 years. You cannot elect to forgo the carryback.

**Example**

**Your 2021 tax liability (without regard to personal credits) is $15,000, and you have no alternative minimum tax liability. Your general business credit from eligible small business credits is $17,000. In 2021, you can claim a general business credit of $15,000 (your net tax liability reduced by your tentative minimum tax liability of zero). The $2,000 unused credit is carried back 1 year. If it cannot be fully used on the amended return for the prior year, it is carried forward for up to 20 years starting on your 2022 return.**

## *Covid-19 Related Credits Offsetting Employment Taxes*

Due to the pandemic, special tax credits have been created to offset certain employment taxes. These credits do not reduce income tax, do not reduce the deduction for compensation, and are not part of the general business credit.

### EMPLOYEE RETENTION CREDIT

An employee retention credit applies for employers that continue to pay employees despite full or partial cessation of business or a significant decline in gross receipts. The credit applies for wages paid from January 1, 2021, through December 31, 2021 (or only through September 30, 2021, if pending legislation is enacted; see the Supplement for an update). The credit is 70% of the first $10,000 of qualified wages (a credit of up to $7,000 per employee for each quarter). This includes group health costs even if no other wages are paid. The credit limit is $28,000 per employee in 2021.

***Eligible employer***. The credit applies only to eligible employers, which means employers that meet either of the following tests:

- Having a trade or business fully or partially suspended due to a government order limiting commerce, travel, or group meetings as a result of COVID-19, or
- Having gross receipts for any such quarter or for the immediately preceding quarter that are less than 80% of its gross receipts for the same quarter in 2019.

For Q3 and Q4 in 2021, an eligible employer also includes:

- Recovery startup businesses, which are those that began carrying on a business after February 15, 2020, and had average annual gross receipts for up to a 3-year period before the applicable quarter of no more than $1 million.
- Severely financially distressed employers, which are those with gross receipts for a quarter that are less than 10% of the gross receipts for the same quarter in 2019 (i.e., a gross receipts reduction of 90%).

***Qualified wages***. The credit applies only to wages paid to an employee who has been employed by the employer for at least 30 days. However, it does not include wages paid to an individual related to the owner. A related individual includes:

- A child or descendant of a child
- A brother, sister, stepbrother, or stepsister
- The father or mother, or ancestor of either

- A stepfather or stepmother
- A niece or nephew
- An aunt or uncle
- A son-in-law, daughter-in-law, father-in-law, mother-in-law, brother-in-law, or sister-in-law

If the eligible employer is a corporation, then a related individual is any person that bears a relationship described above with an individual owning, directly or indirectly, more than 50% in value of the outstanding stock of the corporation. If the eligible employer is an entity other than a corporation, then a related individual is any person that bears a relationship described above with an individual owning, directly or indirectly, more than 50% of the capital and profits interests in the entity.

The amount of qualified wages depends for 2021 on the number of employees that an eligible employer had in 2019.

- If the employer had more than 500 full-time employees in 2019, qualified wages are wages paid when employee services are not provided and qualified wages are limited to the amount the employee would have been paid for working an equivalent duration during the 30 days preceding the non-service period.
- If the employer had 500 or fewer full-time employees in 2019, all employee wages paid by eligible employers are eligible for the credit.

A full-time employee is anyone who in any calendar month, had an average of at least 30 hours of service per week or 130 hours of service in the month (130 hours of service in a month is treated as the monthly equivalent of at least 30 hours of service per week). If you own more than one business, you have to aggregate the number of employees for purposes of the 500-employee rule.

The employee retention credit is not allowed with respect to wages paid with proceeds from PPP loans or grants under the Shuttered Venue Operators or Restaurant Revitalization programs.

The credit is an offset to payroll taxes. This includes federal income tax withholding plus the employer and employee share of FICA. It does not include FUTA tax or any state employment taxes.

### COVID-19 PAID SICK LEAVE CREDIT

Small businesses (fewer than 500 employees) may but are not required to provide certain paid sick leave to employees that's COVID-19 related from January 1, 2021, through September 30, 2021.

The amount of the credit depends on the reason for the sick leave:

1. The employee is under a Federal, State, or local quarantine or isolation order related to COVID-19.
2. The employee has been advised by a health care provider to self-quarantine due to concerns related to COVID-19.
3. The employee is experiencing symptoms of COVID-19 and seeking a medical diagnosis.
4. The employee is caring for an individual who is subject to a federal, state, or local quarantine or isolation order related to COVID-19, or has been advised by a health care provider to self-quarantine due to concerns related to COVID-19.
5. The employee is caring for the child of such employee if the school or place of care of the child has been closed, or the child care provider of such child is unavailable, due to COVID-19 precautions.

6. The employee is experiencing any other substantially similar condition specified by the U.S. Department of Health and Human Services.
7. The employee is receiving the COVID-19 vaccine.
8. The employee is recovering from a condition, illness, or disability related to the COVID-19 vaccine.
9. The employee is seeking or awaiting the results of a COVID-19 test or diagnosis.

If the reason for the sick leave is 1, 2, 3, 7, 8, or 9 above, then the maximum credit is up to $511 per day, or $5,110 in the aggregate for each employee. If the reason for the sick leave is 4, 5, or 6, then the maximum credit is up to $200 per day, or $2,000 in the aggregate for each employee. From April 1, 2021, through September 30, 2021, an additional 80 hours of paid sick leave may be taken into account for the credit.

If this credit is taken, then the employer cannot use the employee retention credit discussed earlier.

**NOTE**

**Self-employed individuals can take comparable sick leave and family leave credits. Such credits are claimed on the 2021 income tax return; they effectively reduce estimated tax payments. See Chapter 23.**

The credit for paid sick leave is refundable and payable in advance. It is taken into account on the employers' quarterly tax return, Form 941.

#### COVID-19 PAID FAMILY LEAVE CREDIT

If an employee is unable to work from January 1, 2021, through September 30, 2021, including telework, because of the need to care for a child whose school or place of care is closed, or whose child care provider is unable to work because of condition number 5 listed above, the employer can claim a tax credit equal to two-thirds of the employee's regular pay, up to $200 per day and $10,000 in the aggregate. Up to 12 weeks of qualifying leave can be counted towards the family leave credit.

If this credit is taken, then the employer cannot use the employee retention credit discussed earlier.

The credit for COVID-19 paid sick leave is refundable and payable in advance. It is taken into account on the employers' quarterly tax return, Form 941. Even though this paid leave is taxable compensation reported as such on employees' Forms W-2, additional reporting in box 14 is needed to identify this pay.

**NOTE**

**Self-employed individuals who had a bad year in business may be eligible for the earned income credit. Find more details about this personal refundable tax credit in IRS Publication 596, *Earned Income Credit (EIC)*.**

### *Employee's Employment-Related Tax Credits*

An employee may be entitled to claim certain credits by virtue of working. These include the earned income credit and the dependent care credit. They are personal tax credits, not business credits. They are in addition to any child tax credit to which a person may be entitled ($3,600 for a child age 5 or under, $3,000 for a child age 6 through 17, and $500 for a qualifying dependent if the employee's income is below a threshold amount).

#### EARNED INCOME CREDIT

If you employ an individual whose income is below threshold amounts, the employee may be eligible to claim an earned income credit. This is a special type of credit because it can exceed tax liability. It is called a refundable credit, since it can be paid to a worker even though it more than offsets tax liability.

### DEPENDENT CARE CREDIT

Whether you are an employee or a business owner, if you hire someone to look after your children under age 13 or a disabled spouse or child of any age so that you can go to work, you may claim a tax credit. This is a personal tax credit, not a business tax credit. You claim the credit on your individual tax return. The credit is fully refundable.

The credit is 50% of qualified expenses. The full credit applies only for those with modified adjusted gross income (MAGI) under $125,000. The 50% maximum credit is reduced by one percentage point for each $2,000 of MAGI (or fraction thereof) over $125,000 until MAGI reaches $185,000. Then a credit of 20% applies until MAGI reaches $400,000. The credit percentage is again reduced by one percentage point for each $2,000 of MAGI (or fraction thereof) over $400,000; no credit may be claimed once MAGI reaches $440,000.

For 2021, the percentage is applied to certain employment-related expenses up to $8,000 per year for one dependent, or $16,000 per year if you have 2 or more qualifying dependents. Employment-related expenses include household expenses to care for your dependent—housekeeper, babysitter, or nanny—and out-of-the-house expenses for the care of dependents, such as day-care centers, preschools, and day camps. Not treated as qualifying expenses are the costs of food; travel to and from day care, preschool, or day camp; education; and clothing. Also, the cost of sleep-away camp does not qualify as an eligible expense.

The dependent care credit must be coordinated with the dependent care FSA, the limit of which is $10,500 in 2021.

If you hire someone to work in your home, be sure to obtain their tax identification number (Social Security number) and pay the nanny tax. This is the employment taxes (Social Security, Medicare, and FUTA taxes) on compensation you pay to your housekeeper, babysitter, or other in-home worker. You must pay Social Security and Medicare taxes if annual payments to a household worker in 2021 exceed $2,300. If you paid cash wages of $1,000 or more in any calendar quarter to a household employee during the current tax year or the previous year, you also must pay federal unemployment tax (FUTA) on the first $7,000 of wages. You do not pay these taxes separately but instead can report them on Schedule H and include them on your Form 1040 or 1040-SR. You should increase your withholding or estimated tax to cover your liability for them to avoid estimated tax penalties. You cannot deduct employment taxes on household workers as a business expense. However, the tax itself is treated as a qualifying expense for the dependent care credit.

**Looking Ahead**

**The increases and refundability of the dependent care credit apply only for 2021, unless Congress extends them.**

## Where to Deduct Compensation Costs

### *Self-Employed (Including Independent Contractors and Statutory Employees)*

Compensation paid to employees and employee benefits paid or provided to/for them are deductible on the appropriate lines of Schedule C. The deduction for wages must be reduced by any employment credits paid. Self-employed farmers deduct compensation costs on Schedule F.

If you maintain a cafeteria plan for employees, you must file an information return, Form 5500, annually. If you personally incur dependent care costs for which a credit can be claimed, you must file Form 2441, *Child and Dependent Care Expenses*. The credit is then entered on Schedule 3 of Form 1040 or 1040-SR.

Self-employed individuals claiming a benefit equivalent to credits for COVID-19 related sick leave and family leave (explained in Chapter 23) file Form 7202, *Credits for Sick Leave and Family Leave for Certain Self-Employed Individuals*.

### Partnerships and LLCs

Compensation paid to employees and employee benefits paid or provided to them are a trade or business expense taken into account in determining the profit or loss of the partnership or LLC on Form 1065, *U.S. Return of Partnership Income*. Report these items on the specific lines provided on Form 1065. Be sure to offset them by employment tax credits. Salaries and wages paid to employees and employee benefits are not separately stated items passed through to partners and members. Partners and members in LLCs report their net income or loss from the business on Schedule E of Form 1040 or 1040-SR; they do not deduct compensation and employee benefit costs on their individual tax returns.

Guaranteed payments to partners are also taken into account in determining trade or business profit or loss. There is a specific line on Form 1065 for reporting guaranteed payments to partners. They are also reported on Schedule K-1 as a separately stated item passed through to partners and LLC members as net earnings from self-employment. This will allow the partners and LLC members to calculate their self-employment tax on the guaranteed payments. If the partnership or LLC maintains a cafeteria plan for employees, the business must file an information return, Form 5500, annually. Partners and LLC members who personally incur dependent care costs for which a credit can be claimed must file Form 2441 with their Form 1040 or 1040-SR.

### S Corporations

Compensation paid to employees and employee benefits paid or provided to them are trade or business expenses that are taken into account in determining the profit or loss of the S corporation on Form 1120-S, *U.S. Income Tax Return for an S Corporation*. They are not separately stated items passed through to shareholders. This applies as well to compensation paid to owners employed by the corporation. Note that compensation to officers is reported on a separate line on the return from salary and wages paid to nonofficers. Be sure to reduce salary and wages by employment tax credits.

Shareholders report their net income or loss from the business on Schedule E of Form 1040 or 1040-SR; they do not deduct compensation and employee benefit costs on their individual tax returns. If the corporation maintains a cafeteria plan for employees, it must file an information return, Form 5500, annually. Shareholders who personally incur dependent care costs for which a credit can be claimed must file Form 2441 with their Form 1040 or 1040-SR.

### C Corporations

Compensation and employee benefits paid to employees are trade or business expenses taken into account in determining the profit or loss of the C corporation on Form 1120, *U.S. Corporation Income Tax Return*. Compensation paid to officers is segregated from salaries and wages paid to employees. Be sure to reduce salary and wages by employment tax credits. Total compensation exceeding $500,000 paid to officers of the corporation is explained in greater detail on Form 1025-E, *Compensation of Officers*, which accompanies Form 1120. Remember that the corporation then pays tax on its net profit. Shareholders do not report any income (or loss) from the corporation. If the corporation maintains a cafeteria plan for employees, it must file an information return, Form 5500, annually.

### *Employment Tax Credits for All Businesses*

Employment tax credits that offset income taxes are figured on separate forms, with the results in most cases entered on Form 3800, *General Business Credit*. Form 3800 need not be completed if you are claiming only one business credit, you have no carryback or carryover, and the credit is not from a passive activity.

The separate forms for employment taxes are the following:

- Employer differential wage payments credit for activated reservists: Form 8932
- Empowerment zone credit: Form 8844
- Paid family and medical leave credit: Form 8994
- Indian employment credit: Form 8845*
- Social Security tax credit on certain tips: Form 8846
- Work opportunity credit: Form 5884 (and Form 8850 for certification from the state workforce agency)

### *Tax Credits Offsetting Employment Taxes*

Generally, all employers take into account the employee retention credit, the qualified sick leave credit, and the qualified family leave credit on quarterly Form 941, *Employer's Quarterly Federal Tax Return*. Employers that requested an advance of these credits file Form 7200, *Advance Payment of Employer Credits Due to COVID-19*. The amounts claimed on Form 7200 are then taken into account on Form 941. Any credits erroneously refunded or credited to an employer are treated as underpayments of taxes, which can be administratively assessed and collected just like any other underpayments of employment taxes.

*This credit expires at the end of 2021, but could be extended; see the Supplement for details.

CHAPTER 8

# Travel, Meals, and Gift Expenses


| | | | |
|---|---|---|---|
| Local Transportation Costs | 164 | Meal and Entertainment Expenses | 175 |
| Travel within the United States | 166 | Business Gifts | 178 |
| Foreign Travel | 170 | Reimbursement Arrangements | 179 |
| Conventions | 172 | Recordkeeping Requirements | 182 |
| Living Away from Home on Temporary Assignments | 174 | | |


Technology has enabled small business owners to market their goods and services in a manner similar to that of larger companies and expand beyond the general area in which their office are located. To service these expanding markets, remote meetings via Zoom or otherwise may not be sufficient. You may have to travel to see clients, customers, vendors, suppliers, and others who are part of your business operations. If you do, you may be able to deduct a number of expenses.

Entertainment costs for clients, customers, vendors, and other business associates are not deductible, but wining and dining such people remains deductible as long as certain conditions are met. The ban on deducting entertainment costs does not apply to office-related events. Also, the cost of business gifts is deductible up to a set limit.

For further information about travel costs, see IRS Publication 463, *Travel, Gift, and Car Expenses*. Business use of your car for travel purposes is discussed in Chapter 9.

## Local Transportation Costs

Do you travel from your office to see clients or customers? Do you have more than one business location? Do you have an office in your home but go into the field to transact business? If the answer to any of these questions is yes and you are self-employed, you may be able to deduct local transportation costs. (Employees cannot deduct business-related expenses as miscellaneous itemized deductions subject to a 2%-of-adjusted-gross-income floor; this deduction has been suspended through 2025.) More specifically, local transportation costs include the cost of work-related travel within the area of your **tax home**.

***Tax home*** **In general, your tax home is the entire city or general area of your regular place of business. If you have more than one business interest, then it is the location of your main business interest based on the comparative time spent in each location and the income derived from each business interest. If you do not have a regular place of business, you are considered an itinerant without any tax home.**

**NOTE**

**If you do not have a regular place of business but work at temporary work sites in the metropolitan area of your home, you cannot deduct your transportation costs. Thus, according to the IRS, a lumberjack who worked at a number of temporary cutting sites was not allowed to deduct the cost of transportation to those sites. The entire area of the cutting sites was considered his regular place of business. However, the Tax Court has allowed a deduction for transportation costs in this instance, so the issue is not yet settled.**

### Deductible Costs

Local transportation costs include the cost of driving and maintaining your car (including tolls and parking) or the cost of taxis, bus fare, train fare, or airfare. Computing the cost of driving and maintaining your car is discussed in Chapter 9.

### Commuting Costs

As a general rule, the costs of commuting between your home and workplace are not deductible. Thus, your bus or train fare, taxi or Uber/Lyft fare, gas for your car, bridge and highway tolls, and parking fees are nondeductible. This rule does not change merely because the commute is unusually long or you do work on the way (e.g., reading reports on the train, talking to clients on your car phone, or displaying advertising on your car). Commuting costs are considered nondeductible personal expenses. This is so despite the distance or time it takes to commute. Even if there is no public transportation to the worksite or any lodging nearby, commuting costs remain nondeductible personal expenses.

However, there are a few exceptions that make certain commuting expenses deductible:

1. If you have one or more regular places of business but work at different locations on a temporary basis (as defined under the following exception), you can deduct the daily cost of travel between your home and the other work site.
2. If you travel from your home to a temporary work site outside the metropolitan area where you live and normally work, you can deduct the daily cost of travel between your home and the temporary work site, regardless of the distance. *Temporary* means that work is realistically expected to last for one year or less. If it turns out to last longer, the period up until the realistic expectation change is treated as temporary.

**Example**

**You have a medical practice with an office across the street from the hospital in which you practice. You sometimes stop to see patients in their homes before going to the office or the hospital. You can deduct the cost of travel from your home to the patients' homes, as well as the cost of travel from their homes to your office or the hospital.**

**Example**

**You have an office downtown but work on a 2-month project at a client's facilities in the next city. You can deduct the cost of travel from your home (which is in the same metropolitan area as your office) to the client's facilities (and back) each day.**

If you travel outside your **metropolitan area**, both the IRS and courts agree that the costs of traveling between your home and a temporary work site outside your area are deductible.

***Metropolitan area*** **The area within a city and its surrounding suburbs.**

3. If you have a home office that is the principal place of business for the activity conducted there (see Chapter 18), the cost of traveling from your home to your clients or customers or to other business locations is deductible.

**Example**

**You run a tax return preparation business from your home and generally meet clients in your home office. Occasionally, you go to clients' homes to do your work. You may deduct the cost of traveling between your home and the clients' homes and back again.**

4. If you must haul tools or equipment to your jobsite and you use a trailer or have to make other special arrangements, the additional cost of commuting with the tools is deductible. The basic transportation costs are still treated as nondeductible commuting expenses.

**Example**

**You rent a trailer to haul tools to and from home and business. You may not deduct the expenses of using your car; however, you can deduct the cost of renting the trailer that you haul with your car.**

### *Local Overnight Stays*

The IRS has liberalized the rules for deducting the cost of local overnight stays. As long as this is not a compensatory benefit, but done for a business purpose, the employee is not taxed on the overnight stay(s), and the employer can deduct the cost. For example, an employer may require its employees to stay at a local hotel for the bona fide purpose of facilitating training or team building directly connected with the employer's trade or business.

## Travel within the United States

If you travel on business away from home and you are self-employed or the business pays for the travel, a deduction can be claimed not only for the cost of transportation but also personal costs, such as your food, lodging, and incidentals. You must be away from your tax home (defined earlier) for more than the day. You usually must be required, because of the distance or the length of the business day, to get sleep or rest away from home in order to meet the demands of your work. This is called the *sleep or rest* rule. The *away from home* rule is being eased in certain cases. The IRS has said that the *sleep or rest* rule will not apply to an employee if the lodging is necessary to participate in or be available for a bona fide business meeting or function of the employer and the expense would otherwise be deductible by the employee if he or she had paid it (being away from home is not mandatory). And the Tax Court has allowed a ferryboat captain who had layovers of between one and 6 hours to deduct meals and incidental expenses even though he docked at his home port (it was impractical to go home during layovers, and sleep or rest on the company cot was necessary for him to do his job).

And your travel away from home must be considered **temporary** (discussed later in this chapter).

***Temporary*** **Travel that is expected to last for no more than one year and does in fact last no more than one year. Travel expected to last for more than a year or that actually lasts for more than a year is considered to be indefinite, not temporary.**

**Example**

**You fly from New York to San Francisco to meet with a business client. You stay for 5 days, after which time you return to New York. In this case, your travel expenses are deductible.**

### *Deductible Costs*

Travel costs include transportation costs, lodging, meals, and other related expenses.

#### TRANSPORTATION COSTS

The cost of a ticket to travel by air, train, or bus between your home and a business destination is deductible. However, if you receive the fare for free because of frequent flyer miles or otherwise, the cost is not deductible. The cost of travel by ship may not be fully deductible (see the section on Conventions later in this chapter).

Transportation costs also include local costs once you arrive at your business destination. Thus, the cost of taxi fare between the airport and your hotel is deductible. Local transportation costs at the business location, such as taxi fare from your hotel to the location of clients or customers, are also deductible. Other deductible local transportation costs include bus fare and limousine fare. Transportation costs for personal travel—sightseeing, visiting relatives, shopping, and other nonbusiness activities—are not deductible.

If you use your car for travel, see Chapter 9. If you rent a car for travel to or at your business destination, the rental charges, as well as gas, parking, and tolls, are deductible. However, if the rental exceeds 30 days and the value of the car exceeds a dollar limit, there may be income to include, called *inclusion amount*. This concept is also explained in Chapter 9.

#### LODGING COSTS

The cost of hotel, motel, or other accommodations is deductible if the nature of the business trip requires an overnight stay in order for you to sleep or properly perform your job. If you are self-employed, you must keep track of all costs and deduct these actual costs. You cannot use a per diem rate as explained below.

For other businesses, you have a choice when deducting lodging costs: (1) keep track of all costs and deduct these actual costs, or (2) use a standard daily allowance that covers lodging, meals, and incidental expenses. There are 2 standard allowances—the per diem rates for the continental United States set by the General Services Administration (GSA) or 2 rates under a high-low method (a high rate applies to high-cost areas and the other rate applies to all other areas in the continental United States) set by the IRS. The rates for the IRS's high-low method are listed later in this chapter. Other per diem rates may be found at https://www.gsa.gov.

**NOTE**

**Using the standard allowance eliminates the need to keep receipts for cost but does not eliminate the need for other recordkeeping, as explained later in this chapter.**

Each year, the GSA sets the per diem rates for the 48 contiguous United States (CONUS), which are the maximum allowances that federal employees are reimbursed for expenses incurred while on official travel. Employees in private companies can use these rates as well to substantiate their travel costs.

Most of the CONUS (about 2,600 counties) are covered by the standard CONUS per diem rate in the government's 2021 fiscal year ending September 30, 2021, of $151 ($96 for lodging and $55 meals and incidental expenses). There are about 400 non-standard areas (NSAs) that have per diem rates higher than the standard CONUS rate. For example, the rate for travel to San Francisco can be as high as $299 (it depends on the time of year for that travel). The rates for the 2022 fiscal year, which includes rates for October 1, 2021, through December 31, 2021, are $155 ($96 and $59 for meals and incidental expenses).

In addition to the federal per diem rates, the IRS has a simplified high-low substantiation method that is similar. Under this method, there are only 2 basic rates: those for high-cost areas (as defined by the IRS) and those for all other areas within CONUS. The per diem rate for high-cost areas from October 1, 2020, through September 30, 2021, is $292 (of which $71 is for meals and incidental expenses); the rate for all other areas in CONUS is $198 (of which $60 is for meals and incidental expenses). The per diem rates for the 2022 fiscal year, which includes rates for October 1, 2021, through December 31, 2021, are $296 (of which $74 is for meals and incidental expenses) in high-cost areas and $202 (of which $64 is for meals and incidental expenses) in all other CONUS areas. Workers in the transportation industry who are subject to the Department of Transportation's hours of service limitations have a special per diem rate for meals in CONUS ($66 for fiscal year 2021; $69 for fiscal year 2022).

### MEALS

The cost of your meals on a trip away from home is deductible (subject to a percent limit, explained later). The cost of meals includes food, beverages, taxes, and tips. However, if the meals are considered to be lavish or extravagant, the deductible portion is limited to the amount that is reasonable. What is considered reasonable is based on the facts and circumstances of the situation. Lavish or extravagant is not automatically the conclusion when the cost of meals exceeds the standard meal allowance rate or when meals are eaten in deluxe hotels, restaurants, nightclubs, or resorts.

**NOTE**

**Using the standard meal allowance does not eliminate the need for other recordkeeping, as explained later in this chapter.**

You have a choice when deducting meal costs: (1) keep track of all costs and deduct these actual costs, or (2) use a standard meal allowance (after the federal rate on the IRS's high-low rate). The Tax Court has said that self-employed individuals can use a standard meal allowance even though they cannot use the per diem rates for lodging. The daily dollar amount of the standard meal allowance is fixed by the government and is adjusted each year for inflation. The adjustment is made on the government's fiscal year beginning October 1 of each year. For your calendar year, you may use the rates in effect on January 1 (that became effective the previous October 1) throughout the year. Or you may use the actual rates in effect from January 1 through September 30 and the new rates that commence on October 1.

The dollar amount you can deduct using a standard meal allowance depends on where your business takes you. In most of the United States, the daily amount is $55 (for October 1, 2020, through September 30, 2021). In non-standard areas designated by the GSA's federal per diem rate, the daily amount is slightly higher ($55, $56, $61, $66, $71, or $76). The GSA rates for October 1, 2021, through September 30, 2022, are $59, $64, $69, $74, or $79. The IRS's high-low substantiation rates for meals and incidental expenses are listed earlier.

### OTHER DEDUCTIBLE TRAVEL COSTS

While you are away from home on business, you may incur a number of miscellaneous or incidental travel expenses. These expenses are deductible in full. They include, for example, the reasonable cost of cleaning and laundering your clothes and tips you pay for services rendered in connection with any deductible expenses (such as a taxi ride or a bellhop). However, if you use a per diem travel rate covering lodging, meals, and incidental expenses, then these items are not separately deductible. Or you can use a per diem rate solely for incidental expenses, which is $5 per day. You may also incur any number of miscellaneous expenses that are deductible, such as various services through a hotel's business service center. These costs are not considered part of incidental expenses for purposes of per diem allowances, explained later in this chapter.

#### *Travel with Another Person*

If you take your spouse, child, or another person on a business trip, the costs related to that person are generally not deductible. The only way in which the costs are deductible is if that person works for you, there is a bona fide business reason for the travel, and the costs would have been deductible had they been incurred by someone who was not accompanying you. If the person provides only incidental services (such as taking notes or acting as assistant), his or her travel expenses are not deductible.

How do you distinguish between expenses that are yours (and deductible) from those of your companion (not deductible)? Clearly, the full cost of the other person's travel fare and meals is not deductible. In the case of lodging costs, if you are sharing a room, you must determine what you would have paid for a single, rather than a double, accommodation. For the most part, this is not simply half the cost. You may be able to deduct two-thirds or more of the cost of lodging.

There is a way for a business to turn nondeductible spousal travel costs into deductible costs. If your corporation treats spousal travel costs as additional compensation to you as an employee, then the corporation can claim a deduction for the costs as compensation rather than as travel costs. In most cases, this alternative does not make much sense from your perspective, since it only shifts the tax burden from your corporation to you. However, if your personal tax picture is such that additional compensation will not result in much additional tax, consider this alternative.

#### *Major and Minor Job Locations*

Some individuals work in more than one location. They may, for example, have a major job in one city and conduct some minor business in another. The cost of travel between the 2 business activities is deductible.

#### *Part Business–Part Pleasure*

If you combine business with pleasure, only part of your costs may be deductible. If your trip was primarily for business, then the portion of the travel costs related to business are deductible.

This means that the full amount of airfare may be deductible. Meals and lodging for the days spent on business are also deductible.

**Example**

**An airline pilot based in Minneapolis also flew for the National Guard out of Sioux Falls, South Dakota. His family lived in Sioux Falls. The IRS disallowed his travel expenses from Minneapolis to Sioux Falls, but a district court allowed the deduction. The fact that he derived some pleasure from the trip to Sioux Falls was secondary to the business nature of the trip. He deducted travel costs to that city only when he was required to fly there for Guard Duty.**

Whether the time spent is primarily for business is determined by the facts and circumstances. There is no hard-and-fast rule.

**Example**

**You travel from New York to San Diego for 5 days of business. You spend 2 more days sightseeing at the zoo and other attractions before returning to New York. All of your airfare is deductible. Five-sevenths of your lodging and food costs are also deductible. Any incidental expenses related to business are deductible. The cost of sightseeing and other personal expenses is not deductible.**

If you stay over on a Saturday at a business location in order to obtain a reduced airfare, the stay is treated as business, and the cost of lodging for that stay is fully deductible. This is so even though you spend the time on personal matters. If the trip is primarily for personal reasons but you do conduct some business, you can deduct the direct costs of the business activities but no part of the travel costs.

**Example**

**You spend a week at a resort location. One afternoon you make a business appointment and take a client out to lunch. None of your airfare to the resort or your lodging costs is deductible. You may, however, deduct the cost of the business lunch (assuming the IRS determines that such business meals are still deductible; see the discussion later in this chapter).**

## Foreign Travel

### *Entirely for Business*

If you travel abroad entirely on business, all of your travel costs are deductible. (Meal costs are still subject to the 50% limit.) If your trip is considered to be entirely business, then even if some time is spent sightseeing or on other personal activities, all of your transportation expenses are still deductible. There are special rules for determining whether your trip is considered to be *entirely* for business. You are treated as having spent your entire trip on business if you meet any of the following 4 rules.

1. You do not have substantial control over arranging your trip; travel is presumed to be entirely for business. You do not have control if you are an employee who is reimbursed for travel and are not related to your employer nor a managing executive (someone whose actions are not subject to veto by another). As a small business owner, it is virtually impossible to satisfy this rule. However, you can still fall within one of the other rules.
2. You are outside the United States for a week or less (7 or fewer consecutive days). In counting days, do not count the day you leave the United States, but do count the day of your return.

**Example**

**You fly from Washington, D.C., to Tokyo on Sunday, arriving at Narita Airport on Monday morning. You work until Friday morning, then spend Friday and Saturday sightseeing and shopping. You fly out on Saturday night, arriving back in Washington on Sunday morning. You are considered to have been abroad for 7 days (Monday through Sunday). All of your airfare is deductible. The cost of lodging, meals, and incidentals for the business days is also deductible, but meals may be subject to the 50% limit explained later in this chapter.**

3. You spend less than 25% of the time outside the United States on personal activities, regardless of the length of the stay abroad. In counting days for this rule, count both the day you leave and the day you return.

**Example**

**You fly on Sunday from Chicago to Paris, where you spend 14 days on business and 5 days on personal matters. You spend 1 day flying in each direction. Your total time abroad is 21 days (14 days for business, 5 days for personal activities, and 2 days for travel). Since the time spent on nonbusiness activities is less than 25% of the total travel time abroad (5 days personal/21 days total), you may treat the trip as entirely business. Thus, the entire cost of the airfare is deductible. You may treat the days of travel as business days so that 16/21 of the lodging and meal costs (subject to the 50% limit on meals) are deductible.**

4. You can show that a personal vacation or another personal reason was not the major consideration in arranging the trip. You can use this rule even though you do have substantial control over arranging the trip.

### *Primarily for Business*

If your travel abroad is not treated as entirely business (because you do not meet any of the 4 rules), you may still deduct some business expenses if the trip is *primarily* business. There is no mechanical rule to establish that the trip is primarily business. However, if you can show a valid business reason for the trip, you can deduct the portion of business expenses allocable to the business part of the trip, including the allocable portion of transportation costs.

**Example**

**You fly from Boston to Rome, where you spend 10 days on business and 5 days on personal matters. You spend 1 day flying in each direction. Your total time abroad is 17 days (10 days for business, 5 days for personal activities, and 2 days in travel time). You had substantial control over arranging your trip, spent more than a week abroad, more than 25% of your time on personal activities, and cannot establish that a personal vacation was not a major consideration. Thus, you cannot show the trip was entirely for business. However, you can show the trip was primarily for business. You spent the greater part of the time on business and arranged the trip accordingly. In this instance, 12/17 of the costs of the airfare and other expenses are deductible business costs; the balance is treated as nondeductible personal expenses.**

#### COUNTING BUSINESS DAYS

In counting days for business when travel is primarily for that purpose, travel days are treated as business days. However, extra days of travel for personal activities, such as side trips, are not counted. You can also treat any day your presence is required at a business meeting or activity as a business day even if you spend the greater part of the day on personal activities. You can also treat as business days any days you wanted to spend on business but were prevented from doing so by circumstances beyond your control (such as weather, strikes, or civil unrest). Saturday, Sunday, and holidays are treated as business days if they fall between two business days. Thus, if you work on Friday and Monday, you count the weekend days as business days. Weekends following the close of your business activities are not treated as business days if you choose to stay on for personal purposes. However, overnight Saturday stays to obtain a reduced airfare are treated as business even when the time is spent on personal activities.

### *Primarily for Vacation*

If you travel abroad primarily for vacation but attend some business or professional seminar, you may not deduct any portion of the trip as a business expense. You may, however, deduct the cost of the seminar (registration fees and other related expenses) as a business expense.

**Example**

**Your professional association sponsors a 2-week trip abroad. It holds two 3-hour seminars during the trip and awards a Certificate in Continuing Education to those who attend the seminars. The entire cost of the trip is a nondeductible personal expense, as it is viewed as primarily for vacation. However, the registration fees for the seminars are deductible.**

## Conventions

COVID-19 put a damper on holding conventions. Nonetheless, if they were held, then travel expenses to conventions held within the United States are deductible if you can show that your attendance benefits your business. The fact that you are appointed or elected to be a delegate to the convention does not, by itself, mean you can deduct expenses; you must show that attendance is connected to your business. You can do this by showing that the convention agenda is related to the active conduct of your business. The same rule applies to both employees and self-employed persons.

**TABLE 8.1 North American Area**

| | |
|---|---|
| American Samoa | Jarvis Island |
| Antigua and Barbuda | Johnston Island |
| Aruba | Kingman Reef |
| Bahamas | Marshall Islands |
| Baker Island | Mexico |
| Barbados | Micronesia |
| Bermuda | Midway Islands |
| Canada | Northern Mariana Islands |
| Costa Rica | Palau |
| Curacao | Palmyra Atoll |
| Dominica | Panama |
| Dominican Republic | Puerto Rico |
| Grenada | St. Lucia |
| Guam | Trinidad and Tobago |
| Guyana | United States |
| Honduras | U.S. Virgin Islands |
| Howland Island | Wake Island |
| Jamaica | |

### *Foreign Conventions*

The expenses of attending a convention outside the North American area (see Table 8.1) are not deductible unless the meeting is directly related to your business and it is reasonable to hold it outside the North American area.

A number of facts and circumstances are taken into account in showing that it is reasonable to hold the convention outside the North American area. They are:

- The purpose of the meeting and the activities taking place at the meeting
- The purposes and activities of the sponsoring organizations or groups
- The residences of the active members of the sponsoring organization and the places at which the meetings of the sponsoring organizations or groups have been held or will be held
- Other relevant factors

### *Cruise Ships*

The cost of business conventions or meetings held on a cruise ship is limited. The maximum deduction per year is $2,000 per employee for each individual attending the convention on the cruise ship. In order to get this deduction, a number of requirements must be met:

1. The meeting must be directly related to your business.
2. The cruise ship must be a vessel registered in the United States. (All ships that sail are considered cruise ships.)

3. All of the ship's ports of call must be located in the United States or in U.S. possessions.
4. You must attach a written statement to your return showing the days of the cruise, the number of hours devoted to business, and a program of scheduled business activities.
5. You must also attach a written statement to your return signed by an officer of the organization or group sponsoring the meeting that shows the schedule of the business activities of each day of the meeting and the number of hours you attended.

As a practical matter, the only cruises that qualify for this $2,000 limit for business conventions or meetings while cruising are those in Hawaii, the Great Lakes, and some on the Mississippi River. However, the cost of business travel by sea that is not for a convention or meeting is deductible at twice the highest federal per diem rate (the daily living rate paid to a federal employee) at the time of the travel.

## Living Away from Home on Temporary Assignments

If you are self-employed, work in a location other than your regular place of business, and are forced to live away from your home (because the distance is too great to reasonably expect that you would travel back and forth each day), then not only the cost of your transportation to the **temporary assignment** but also living expenses are deductible. If you are an employee, you cannot deduct your unreimbursed employee business expenses in 2018 through 2025.

---

***Temporary assignment*** **An assignment away from the area of your tax home that is realistically expected to last for no more than a year and does, in fact, end at that time.**

---

An assignment that is expected to last for more than a year, or one that does in fact last for more than a year, is considered indefinite. Also, a series of short assignments in the same location that, taken together, last more than a year are considered an indefinite assignment. Probationary work is also treated as indefinite. Thus, for example, if you relocate with the understanding that your assignment will be permanent if your work is satisfactory, the engagement is considered indefinite. Transportation to the location of the indefinite assignment from your general area of your tax home is deductible; personal living expenses are not.

### *Change in Work Assignments*

Suppose your assignment gets extended or shortened. How does this affect whether the assignment is treated as temporary or indefinite?

**SITUATION 1**

You go out of town on an assignment expected to last for 10 months but it is extended and, in fact, lasts for 14 months. As long as the initial expectation of 10 months was reasonable, your living expenses are deductible until the time that the expectation changed. Thus, if at the end of 10 months the assignment projection changed, expenses for the first 10 months are deductible.

If, however, at the end of 6 months, the assignment projection changed, only expenses for the first 6 months are deductible.

**SITUATION 2**

You go out of town on an assignment expected to last 14 months, but in fact it is shortened and lasts only 10 months. Since the original expectation of the work length exceeded one year, no part of the living expenses is deductible. The entire assignment is treated as indefinite even though it did in fact end within a year.

Remember, you must have a tax home to be away from when deducting living expenses on temporary assignments. If all of your assignments are away and you have no tax home, no living expenses will be allowed.

**Example**

**An engineering consultant in Florida took temporary engineering assignments for a period of 3 years in 5 states as well as in his home state. During this time, he maintained a home office in his apartment, where he returned after each assignment for periods of 4 to 6 months at a time, and he continued to seek permanent employment there. The IRS argued that he was an itinerant, so his expenses were not deductible. The Tax Court disagreed and found his Florida home to be his tax home. He needed to maintain a permanent address and business number to obtain consulting jobs. He always returned there between assignments and never stopped seeking permanent employment there.**

### *What Expenses Are Deductible?*

If a job assignment is temporary, then personal living expenses—rent, utilities, food, and other expenses—are deductible. The reason for this rule: Congress recognized that if you are required to be away from home on a temporary basis, you will have to incur duplicative living expenses, since it would be unreasonable to expect you to relocate for that short period of time.

However, if the assignment is indefinite, it would be reasonable to expect you to relocate, and there would be no need for duplicative living expenses. Unfortunately, you cannot deduct the cost of your personal moving expenses in 2018 through 2025.

If you are on a temporary assignment and return home on weekends, holidays, or visits, the time at home is not treated as away from home, and the cost of your lodging at home is not deductible. The cost of your lodging at the temporary work site, however, continues to be deductible. Thus, for example, if you are living away from home in a motel and return home on a weekend but must pay for the motel room anyway, that cost is deductible. The cost of meals on a return trip home is deductible only to the extent that the cost of meals away would have been deductible. The cost of travel from the temporary assignment home and the return trip is also deductible.

## Meal and Entertainment Expenses

Entertainment costs, such as tickets to ballgames and the theater, are not deductible. But meal costs, which can come in a variety of forms, are usually deductible.

### Meal Costs 100% Deductible

You can fully deduct the cost of:

- *Business meals in 2021 and 2022 provided at restaurants*. This includes meals consumed by those traveling away from home on business as well as in-town meals with customers, clients, and other business associates. The IRS defines restaurants to include businesses that prepare and sell food or beverages to retail customers for immediate on-premises and/or off-premises consumption. However, restaurants do not include businesses that primarily sell pre-packaged goods not for immediate consumption, such as grocery stores, liquor stores, and convenience stores.
- *Meal expenses treated as compensation to employees*. This would occur, for example, if you reimburse employee business travel expenses under a nonaccountable plan (explained later in this chapter).
- *Company recreational, social, or similar activities for the benefit of employees*. This would include the cost of company picnics, barbeques, and similar events that provide food and beverages to staff and other attendees (e.g., employees' spouses and children).
- *Items available to the public*. This would include complimentary coffee that you provide in your lobby or waiting room. It also includes meals furnished as part of promotional activities.
- *Shift meals for employees in the restaurant industry*. Meals furnished to employees before or after their shifts is fully deductible, according to the Joint Committee on Taxation's Blue Book (December 20, 2018).

**Example**

**A real estate broker selling vacation property gave potential investors a free meal if they agreed to sit through a sales presentation. The IRS allowed the broker to deduct the full cost of the meals in this case, since they were made available to the general public as part of promotional activities.**

### Meal Costs 80% Deductible

Workers in the transportation industry who are subject to the Department of Transportation's hours of service limitations, such as self-employed longhaul drivers, can deduct 80% of the cost of food and beverages consumed while away from home where the meals are not provided at restaurants. If they are provided at restaurants, then the 100% limit applies.

### Meal Costs 50% Deductible

You can deduct only half of the cost of:

- *De minimis fringe benefits*. This includes food and beverages, such as donuts, fruit, coffee, and sodas, furnished in your company break room. It also includes occasional meals or meal money provided to enable an employee to work overtime. De minimis fringe benefits must be furnished on the employer's premises.

**Example**

**The Tax Court said the de minimis fringe benefit rule includes meals furnished by the Boston Bruins to its team and staff in "meal rooms" (a hotel space used for this purpose). This was treated as being on the employer's premises. The IRS acquiesced in the results only.**

- *Meals at entertainment events*. While you can't deduct the cost of attending an entertainment event, you may deduct the cost of food and beverages at such events if:
  1. The expense is an ordinary and necessary expense paid or incurred during the taxable year in carrying on any trade or business;
  2. The expense is not lavish or extravagant under the circumstances;
  3. The business owner or an employee of the taxpayer is present at the furnishing of the food or beverages;
  4. The food and beverages are provided to a current or potential business customer, client, consultant, or similar business contact; and
  5. The food and beverages are purchased separately from the entertainment.

**Example**

**You take a client to a baseball game and purchase the tickets to attend. While at the game you buy hot dogs and beer for both of you. The cost of the food and beverages is deductible.**

**Example**

**Your company has a suite for basketball games, the price of which includes food and beverages. In this situation, there is no deduction allowed for meal costs.**

- *Meals away from home*. Half the cost of meals incurred while traveling away from home on business is deductible if the meals are not provided at restaurants. This is so whether deducting the actual cost of the meals or relying on a per diem rate (discussed earlier in this chapter).
- *Meals for the convenience of the employer on the employer's business premises*. This applies to meals where there is a substantial noncompensatory business reason for the employer to provide the meals. Such a reason includes the need to restrict an employee's meal time, lack of easy access to food in the area, or being on hand at all times in case of emergency. Caution: In a 2019 technical advice memorandum, the IRS intimated that having access to food through a delivery service (e.g., DoorDash, GrubHub, and UberEats) may counter a claimed substantial noncompensatory business reason of lack of easy access to food in the area.

- *Employer-operated eating facility for employees*. As long as this is not restricted to highly compensated employees (i.e., it's not an executive dining room), you can deduct operating costs. This includes food, beverages, and labor (including employment taxes for employees of the facility).

The fact that the company deducts only 50% of its costs for meals in some situations does not affect the tax treatment for employees. For example, employees are not taxed on the nondeductible portion of meal costs even though they receive a full reimbursement or an advance for these expenses under an accountable plan.

### Nondeductible Meal Costs

Even if a business meal has a business connection, you may not be able to deduct any of your costs. Nondeductible meal costs include:

- *Personal meals*. This includes your morning coffee, your lunch at the noon hour, or a drink after work. The reason: These are inherently personal in nature.

**Example**

**In one case, attorneys met for lunch each day to discuss clients' matters. The Tax Court said their meal costs were nondeductible. They were not away from home and there were no clients present at the meals.**

- *Unsubstantiated meal costs*. If you fail to meet substantiation requirements, you can lose the write-offs for legitimate business meals.

**Looking Ahead**

**Starting in 2026, no deduction is allowed for:**

- **De minimis fringe benefits (e.g., donuts in the break room)**
- **Meals for the convenience of the employer (e.g., meals to employees on hand for emergencies)**
- **Food and beverages provided at a company eating facility (see the example discussed earlier in this chapter involving pre-game meals to Bruins)**

### Club Dues

Dues to clubs organized for pleasure, recreation, or other social purposes (e.g., airline clubs, country clubs) are not deductible. However, dues to certain business, professional, and civic organizations (e.g., professional associations, chambers of commerce) are still deductible.

## Business Gifts

In the course of your business, you may give gifts to your dealers, distributors, customers, clients, and employees. The cost of business gifts is deductible, within limits. You may deduct only up to

$25 per person per year (the dollar limit that was set back in 1962). This rule applies to both *direct* and *indirect* gifts. An indirect gift includes a gift to a company that is intended for the eventual personal use of a particular person or a gift to a spouse or child of a business customer or client.

In using the $25 limit, do not count incidental costs, such as wrapping, insuring, or shipping the gifts. Also, do not count engraving on jewelry.

**Example**

**You give a $30 gift to client A. You may deduct $25. You give a $20 gift to client B. You may deduct $20.**

### *Exceptions*

Certain gifts are not subject to the $25 limit. These include gifts of nominal value ($4 or less) with your company name imprinted on them that you distribute to a number of clients or customers. These gifts would include, for example, pens, plastic bags, kitchen magnets, and calendars. Thus, if you give a customer a $25 gift and also send a calendar, the value of the calendar (assuming it is below $4) is not taken into account. Both gifts are deductible. Another exception to the $25 rule includes signs, display racks, or other promotional material used on business premises. Thus, if you give a dealer a display rack to hold your items, the gift is a deductible business expense, regardless of cost.

**NOTE**

**Expect the IRS to continue to challenge any gifts in excess of the $25 limit so, if you want to make larger gifts, be sure to have a business rationale for doing so.**

In one case, the Tax Court recognized another exception to the $25 limit for gifts to employees—gifts designated as an *employee relations expense* rather than as a gift or compensation. The court allowed a deduction in this case of almost $1,500 (the cost of a set of golf clubs) given as incentive for continued good performance by a top salesperson. Of course, "gifts" to employees are taxable compensation to them and subject to payroll taxes.

## Reimbursement Arrangements

If an employer reimburses an employee for travel expenses, how you arrange the reimbursement affects what the employer and employee can deduct.

### *No Reimbursement Arrangement*

If an employee on salary has no reimbursement arrangement and is expected or required to pay for travel costs by himself or herself, the employee cannot deduct the costs. This is due to the suspension in 2018 through 2025 of the miscellaneous itemized deduction for costs exceeding 2% of adjusted gross income. The reimbursement is taxable to the employee.

### *Accountable Plans*

If an employer maintains an *accountable plan*, the employer pays for and deducts all costs. No reimbursements are reported as income to the employee, and the reimbursements are not subject to payroll taxes. Thus, an accountable plan is a tax saver for both the employer and employee. In view of the suspension of the miscellaneous itemized deduction for employees, a company would be well advised to consider using an accountable plan; it eliminates taxable compensation for employees and avoids employment taxes for the company. Typically, accountable plans are used for travel, but can be used for any purpose (e.g., reimbursing Internet access fees for employees required to work at home or tools of the trade).

A reimbursement arrangement is treated as an accountable plan if:

- *The expenses have a business connection.* This means the expenses must have been incurred while performing services as an employee for an employer.
- *The employee must adequately account to the employer for expenses within a reasonable time.* Accounting within 60 days after paying or incurring the expenses is considered a reasonable time. The employee must supply the employer with documentary evidence (canceled checks, receipts, or bills) of mileage, travel, and other business expenses unless reimbursement is made at a per diem rate. All employees must provide the employer with a statement of expense, an account book or diary, or a similar record (including computer logs) in which expenses are entered at or near the time at which they were incurred. All amounts received from an employer must be documented. This includes not only cash advances but also amounts charged to an employer by credit card or other method.
- *The employee must return to the employer within a reasonable period of time any excess reimbursements.* Thus, for example, if an employer advances an employee $400 for a business trip and expenses totaled only $350, the employee must return the excess $50 within a reasonable period of time. A reasonable period of time depends on the facts and circumstances. However, it is automatically treated as reasonable if an advance is made within 30 days of the expense, adequate accounting of the expense is made to the employer within 60 days after it was paid or incurred, and any excess reimbursement is refunded to the employer within 120 days after the expense was paid or incurred. It is also automatically treated as reasonable if an employer furnishes an employee with a periodic (at least quarterly) statement requesting reimbursement of excess amounts and reimbursement is in fact made within 120 days after receipt of the statement.

If the employer maintains an accountable plan but an employee does not meet all the rules (for example, the employee fails to return excess amounts or is reimbursed for nonbusiness expenses), then those expenses are treated as paid under a nonaccountable plan. The remaining expenses are treated as paid under an accountable plan.

**Example**

**An employer maintains an accountable plan. During the year, an employee is reimbursed for business travel expenses and also receives reimbursement for meals eaten while working late for the employer. The meals are nonbusiness expenses. The employer is treated as having 2 plans in this instance: an accountable plan for the travel expenses and a nonaccountable plan for the personal meal expenses.**

It is advisable for the company to formally adopt an accountable plan by putting the action into corporate minutes (see Appendix B) or in other written form.

### *Nonaccountable Plans*

If an employer maintains a reimbursement arrangement but it does not qualify as an accountable plan (for example, excess reimbursements need not be returned, or reimbursements cover nondeductible personal expenses), the plan is considered a nonaccountable plan. In this case, the employer must report the reimbursements on an employee's Form W-2. For 2018 through 2025, the employee cannot deduct the expenses on his or her individual income tax return.

### *Reimbursement at Per Diem Rates*

Reimbursing employees for travel and related expenses at a per diem rate simplifies things for all concerned; employees need not keep track of every expense and retain receipts for all of them, and employers can make reimbursements at a flat rate, easing accounting procedures. If an employer pays for business expenses using a per diem rate, special rules apply. If the rate used by the employer is the same as or lower than the federal per diem rate for the area of travel, reimbursements are not reported on an employee's Form W-2. If an employee's actual expenses exceeded the reimbursement at or below the federal rate, the employee can deduct the excess expenses on his or her individual income tax return. However, if the rate used by the employer is higher than the federal rate, the amounts are reported on Form W-2. The amount of the federal rate is not included in an employee's gross income, though excess reimbursements are included in the employee's gross income. The employee cannot claim business deductions for these excess amounts in 2018 through 2025.

There are several acceptable federal rates that an employer can use to make reimbursements, including the federal per diem rate, high-low method, standard meal allowance, and the incidental rate.

There are several types of per diem or standard rates that can be used for substantiating travel costs (the rates are listed earlier in this chapter). The rules and amounts for each of these rates have been discussed previously in this chapter. These rates include:

- Federal per diem rate
- High-low substantiation rate
- Standard meal allowance

You cannot use the standard meal allowance if you are related to your employer. You are considered related if your employer is your brother, sister (half or whole), spouse, parent, grandparent, child, or grandchild. You are also considered related if you own, directly or indirectly, more than 10% of the value of your employer's stock. Indirect ownership arises when you have an interest in a corporation, partnership, trust, or estate that owns stock in your employer's corporation or if family members own stock in your employer's corporation. Again, you can use the standard meal allowance if you are self-employed.

**NOTE**

**Self-employed individuals cannot use the standard rates covering lodging, meals, and incidental expenses to substantiate their travel costs. They can, however, use the standard meal allowance to substantiate meal costs during business travel.**

#### INCIDENTAL RATE

There is a $5 per day rate for incidental expenses, such as tips and transportation between the hotel and place of business. This modest rate can be used to cover incidental expenses only if no meal costs are incurred on such a day (for example, it is a day of personal travel).

#### PARTIAL DAYS OF TRAVEL

If the federal per diem rate or high-low method is used for any day of travel that does not include a full 24-hour period, the per diem amount must be prorated. The full rate is allocated on a quarterly basis for each 6-hour period in the day (midnight to 6 a.m.; 6 a.m. to noon; noon to 6 p.m.; 6 p.m. to midnight).

## Recordkeeping Requirements

Business expenses can be disallowed unless there is adequate substantiation for the expenses claimed. For travel expenses, there are 2 main ways to prove costs: actual substantiation or reliance on a per diem rate. First look at actual substantiation; then consider how recordkeeping can be simplified with the use of per diem rates.

There are a number of elements to substantiate for each business expense. In general, to substantiate each item, you must show the amount, the time, the place, the business purpose for the travel or the business relationship with the persons you entertain or provide gifts to, and, in some cases, a description of the item. The exact type of substantiation required depends on the item of business expense.

### *Travel*

You must show the amount of each separate expense for travel, lodging, meals, and incidental expenses. You can total these items in any reasonable category. For example, you can simply keep track of meals in a category called daily meals. You must also note the dates you left for the trip and returned, as well as the days spent on the trip for business purposes. You must list the name of the city or other designation of the place of the travel, along with the reason for the travel or the business benefit gained or expected to be gained from it.

While this may sound like a great deal of recordkeeping, as a practical matter, hotel receipts may provide you with much of the information necessary. For example, a hotel receipt typically shows the dates you arrived and departed; the name and location of the hotel; and separate charges for lodging, meals, telephone calls, and other items. The IRS says that a charge slip for hotel costs is no substitute for the hotel receipt itself. You must have documentary evidence for the cost of lodging. You do not need documentary evidence if the item (other than lodging) is less than $75 or, in the case of transportation costs, if a receipt is not readily available. Thus, if a cab ride is $9 and the driver does not provide you with a receipt, you are not required to show documentary evidence of this expense.

### *Meals*

If the deduction is for a business meal, you must note that you or your employer was present at the meal. Again, a restaurant receipt typically will supply much of the information required. It will show the name and location of the restaurant, the number of people served, and the date and amount of the expense. Be sure to jot down the business aspect of the meal, such as asking a client for a referral or trying to sell your services.

### *Gifts*

Show the cost of the gift, the date given, and a description. Also show the business reason for the gift or the business benefit gained or expected to be gained from providing it. Indicate the name of the person receiving the gift, his or her occupation or other identifying information, and his or her business relationship to you.

A canceled check, along with a bill, generally establishes the cost of a business item. A canceled check alone does not prove a business expense without other evidence to show its business purpose.

### *Using a Diary, Log, or App*

Enter your expenses in a diary (see Table 8.2) or log (e.g., in writing or with an app) at or near the time of the event giving rise to the expenses. Computer-generated records are acceptable. Be sure to include all the elements required for the expense (especially the business reason for it).

It is a good idea to total expenses on a monthly basis and then use a recap form to put annual figures together.

**NOTE**

**There are various apps that you can use to track your travel expenses to record expenses and create reports.**

### *Other Substantiation Methods*

The IRS has recognized various substantiation methods. For example, if each employee has a company credit card, electronic reports from the credit card company can be used to substantiate charged expenses (paper receipts of expenses in excess of $75 are still required).

There are a growing number of apps that can be used for keeping track of travel expenses that turn smartphones into timely recordkeepers. Some are free; some have a modest cost. Each has different features (e.g., customization, mileage tracking, links to credit cards, whether limited to iPhone/Android, whether they are stand-alone or tied into software). Some apps to consider: Certify, Expensify, Rydoo, webexpenses, and Zoho Expense.

### *Missing, Lost, or Inadequate Records*

If you do not have adequate records, you may still be able to deduct an item if you can prove by your own statement or other supporting evidence an element of substantiation. A court may even allow an estimation of expenses under the "Cohan rule," under certain circumstances (the Cohan rule is named after entertainer George M. Cohan's case in the last century). Where receipts have been destroyed, you may be able to reconstruct your expenses. You must, of course, show how the records were destroyed (fire, storm, flood). The IRS may require additional information to prove the accuracy or reliability of the information contained in your records. Recordkeeping alternatives are discussed in more detail in Chapter 3.

**TABLE 8.2** Sample Expense Diary

| Date | Description | Fares | Lodging | Meals | Entertainment | Other |
|---|---|---|---|---|---|---|
| 1/10 | Breakfast with Sue Smith, CEO, X Corp., discussed sales | | | $21.50 | | |
| 1/11 | Sales trip to Buyers in NYC | $408.00 | $455.00 | $105.00 | | $28.00 |
| 1/14 | Lunch with Mark Hess after sales call | | | $38.75 | | |
| 1/15 | Gift for John Jones (customer) | | | | | $22.00 |

### Per Diem Rates

If you receive reimbursement using one of the per diem rates discussed earlier, you need not retain documentary evidence of the amount of an expense. The per diem rate is deemed to satisfy the proof of the amount of the expense. However, use of the per diem rate does not prove any of the other elements of substantiation. For example, if an employee is reimbursed for business travel using the high-low method, the employee still must show the time, the place, and the business purpose for business travel.

## Where to Deduct Travel, Meals, and Gift Expenses

### Employees

Because no deduction for these costs can be claimed by employees in 2018 through 2025, no reporting is required unless one of the exceptions below applies.

***Disabled employees.*** If you have a physical or mental disability, your impairment-related work expenses are deductible as an itemized deduction, which is not subject to the 2%-of-AGI floor. Impairment-related work expenses include expenses for attendant care at your place of work as well as other expenses that are necessary to enable you to work (e.g., the cost of an attendant traveling with you on business). These expenses must be entered on Form 2106 and then on Schedule A of Form 1040 or 1040-SR.

***Reservists.*** If you are a reservist who travels more than 100 miles away from home in connection with the performance of duties, enter your travel expenses on Form 2106 and then on Schedule 1 of Form 1040 or 1040-SR.

***Fee-based government officials.*** If you are a fee-based official employed by a state or local government, enter your travel expenses on Form 2106 and then on Schedule 1 of Form 1040 or 1040-SR.

***Special rule for performing artists.*** If you meet certain requirements, you can deduct all of your travel expenses as an adjustment to gross income on Schdule 1 of Form 1040 or 1040-SR instead of claiming them as miscellaneous itemized deductions on Schedule A. You are treated as a qualified performing artist (QPA) if you meet all of the following tests:

1. You perform services in the performing arts for at least 2 employers in the year.
2. You receive at least $200 each from any 2 of these employers.
3. Your related performing arts business expenses are more than 10% of your income from the performance of such services.
4. Your adjusted gross income from *all* sources does not exceed $16,000 (before deducting business expenses from your performing arts). The $16,000 limit is fixed by law and has not changed since 1987.
5. If you are married and you file a joint return (unless you lived apart from your spouse for the entire year).

You figure tests 1, 2, and 3 based on your separate experience. However, the adjusted gross income in test 4 is based on the combined adjusted gross income of you and your spouse.

If you meet these criteria, you deduct your performing arts business expenses as an adjustment to gross income on Schedule 1 of Form 1040 or 1040-SR.

### Self-Employed (Including Independent Contractor and Statutory Employee)

You enter travel and meal expenses on Schedule C, *Profit and Loss from Business* of Form 1040 or 1040-SR. On Schedule C, there are separate lines for travel and meals. Business gifts are reported as other expenses, which are explained on page 2 of Schedule C.

Self-employed farmers deduct travel and meal expenses on Schedule F of Form 1040 or 1040-SR.

### Partnerships and LLCs

Travel and meal expenses are reported on Form 1065 and are taken into account in arriving at the business's ordinary income (or loss). They are entered in the category of Other Deductions on the form. A schedule is attached to the return explaining the deductions claimed in this category. Be sure to apply the 50% limit to meals where applicable. Travel and meal expenses are not separately stated items; they are part of ordinary business income (or loss). The partner's share of ordinary income (or loss) is reported on Schedule K-1.

### S Corporations

Travel and meal expenses are reported on Form 1120-S and are taken into account in arriving at the corporation's ordinary income (or loss). They are entered in the category of Other Deductions on the form. A schedule is attached to the return explaining the deductions claimed in this category. Be sure to apply the 50% limit to meals where applicable. Travel and meal expenses are not separately stated items; they are part of ordinary business income (or loss). The shareholder's share of ordinary income (or loss) is reported on Schedule K-1.

### C Corporations

Travel and meal expenses are reported on Form 1120 and are taken into account in arriving at the corporation's taxable income (or loss). They are entered in the category of Other Deductions on the form. A schedule is attached to the return explaining the deductions claimed in this category. Be sure to apply the 50% limit on meals where applicable.

CHAPTER 9

# Car and Truck Expenses


| | |
|---|---|
| Deducting Car and Truck Expenses in General | 186 |
| Actual Expense Method | 188 |
| Standard Mileage Allowance | 195 |
| Leasing a Vehicle for Business | 196 |
| Arranging Vehicle Ownership | 199 |
| Nonpersonal Use Vehicles | 200 |
| Credit for Plug-In Electric Vehicles | 200 |
| Dispositions of a Vehicle | 201 |
| Reimbursement Arrangements | 202 |
| Recordkeeping for Vehicle Expenses | 203 |


Americans are highly mobile, with 286.9 million vehicles registered in the U.S. in 2020, according to automotive research agency Hedges & Company. Businesses and self-employed individuals may write off various costs. For 2018 through 2025, employees who use their personal vehicles for business driving cannot deduct driving costs. The IRS reported that on 2018 returns (the most recent year for statistics), car and truck expenses were a significant category of deductions on Schedule C (Form 1040) for sole proprietors (only salaries and wages was larger). In order to nail down deductions for these expenses, you must carefully observe certain recordkeeping rules. There are 2 methods for deducting costs: the actual expense method and the standard mileage allowance. In order to use either method, you must maintain proper records for business driving.

For further information about deductions with respect to business use of your car, see IRS Publication 463, *Travel, Gift, and Car Expenses*.

## Deducting Car and Truck Expenses in General

The discussion in this chapter usually refers to **cars** used partly or entirely for business. For 2021, the same rules apply to light trucks and vans.

***Car*** **Any 4-wheel vehicle made primarily for use on public streets, roads, and highways that has an unloaded gross vehicle weight of 6,000 pounds or less (the manufacturer can provide this information). A truck or van is a "light" truck or van if its unloaded gross weight is 6,000 pounds or less and is subject to rules for passenger cars. Excluded from the definition is an ambulance, hearse, or combination thereof used in business and any vehicle used in business for transporting people or for compensation or hire.**

The law allows you to choose between two methods for deducting business-related expenses of a car: the actual expense method or the standard mileage allowance fixed by the IRS, both of which are detailed in this chapter. Again, the same rules apply to light trucks and vans. For convenience, they will collectively be referred to as vehicles.

### *Choosing between the Actual Expense Method and the Standard Mileage Allowance*

Read over the rules on the *actual expense method* and the *standard mileage allowance*. For the most part, the choice of method is yours. The choice applies whether you own or lease the vehicles. In some cases, however, you may not be able to use the standard mileage rate. Where you are not barred from using the standard mileage rate and can choose between the methods, which is better? Obviously, it is the one that produces the greater deduction. However, there is no easy way to determine which method will produce the greater deduction. Many factors will affect your decision, including the number of miles you drive each year and the extent of your actual expenses. See the example's comparison.

**Example**

**You are self-employed and buy a car in January 2021 for $25,000; you use it 100% for business. In 2021, the first year the car is in service, you drive 1,500 miles per month. If you use the standard mileage allowance, your car deduction for 2021 is $10,080 (18,000 miles × 0.56). If your actual costs exceed this amount, it may be advisable to use the actual expense method. If they are less than $10,080, the standard mileage allowance may be better.**

In making your decision, bear in mind that the standard mileage allowance simplifies record-keeping for business use of the vehicle.

You should make the decision in the first year you own the vehicle. This is because a choice of the actual expense method for the first year will forever bar the use of the standard mileage allowance in subsequent years. If you use the standard mileage rate, you can still use the actual expense method in later years. However, if the vehicle has not yet been fully depreciated (using the deemed depreciation rates discussed later), then, for depreciation purposes, you must use the straight-line method over what you estimate to be the vehicle's remaining useful life.

## Actual Expense Method

The *actual expense method* allows you to deduct all of your out-of-pocket costs for operating your vehicle for business, plus an allowance for depreciation if you own the vehicle. Actual expenses include:

| | | |
|---|---|---|
| Car washes | Lease fees | Repairs |
| Depreciation | Licenses | Tires |
| Garage rent | Loan interest | Tolls |
| Gas | Oil | Towing |
| Insurance | Parking fees | Vehicle registration fees |

For individuals, whether interest on a loan to buy the vehicle is deductible depends on employment status. If you are an employee who uses a vehicle for business, you cannot deduct interest on the loan; the interest is treated as nondeductible personal interest. However, if you are self-employed, the interest may be treated as business interest. For corporations, interest on a loan to buy a vehicle is fully deductible (subject to interest deduction limits explained in Chapter 13).

If you pay personal property tax on a vehicle used for business, the tax is deductible by an employee as an itemized deduction for personal property tax, subject to the overall limit on state and local taxes.

If your vehicle is damaged, destroyed, or stolen, the part of the loss not covered by insurance may be deductible. If the vehicle was used entirely for business, the loss is treated as a fully deductible casualty or theft loss. If it was used partly for personal purposes, the personal portion of the loss is deductible as an itemized deduction, but is only deductible if it resulted from a federally declared disaster. See Chapter 17 for a discussion of casualty and theft losses.

Not all vehicle-related expenses are deductible. Luxury and sales taxes cannot be separately deducted even if a vehicle is used entirely for business; these taxes are treated as part of the cost of the vehicle and are added to the basis of the vehicle for purposes of calculating depreciation, as well as gain or loss on the future sale of the vehicle.

Fines for traffic violations, including parking violations, are not deductible, even when they were incurred in the course of business-related travel.

### *Depreciation*

If you own your vehicle and use it for business, you may recoup part of the cost of the vehicle through a deduction called *depreciation*. The amount of depreciation depends on a great many factors. First, it depends on whether you use the depreciation allowance or claim a Section 179 deduction (discussed later in this chapter). It also varies according to the year in which you begin to use your vehicle for business, the cost of the vehicle, and the amount of business mileage for the year as compared with the total mileage for the year. Depreciation is covered in Chapter 14 as well.

### *Business Use versus Personal or Investment Use*

Whether you claim a depreciation allowance or a Section 179 deduction, you can do so only with respect to the portion of the vehicle used for business. For example, if you use your car 75% for business and 25% for personal purposes, you must allocate the cost of the car for purposes of calculating depreciation. The allocation is based on the number of miles driven for business compared to the total number of miles driven for the year.

**Example**

**In 2021, you buy a car for $26,000 and drive it 20,000 miles. Of this mileage, 15,000 miles were for business; 5,000 miles were personal. For purposes of depreciation, you must allocate $19,500 for business use. It is this amount on which you figure depreciation.**

If you use a vehicle for investment purposes (e.g., to visit rental properties held for investment), you can add the miles driven for investment purposes when making an allocation for depreciation.

### *Depreciation Allowance*

A depreciation allowance is simply a deduction calculated by applying a percentage to the **basis** of the car. Cars, light trucks, and vans are treated as 5-year property under the Modified Accelerated Cost Recovery System (MACRS), the depreciation system currently in effect, as discussed in Chapter 14. As such, you would think that the cost of the vehicle could be recovered through depreciation deductions over a period of 5 years. However, this is generally not the case because of a number of different rules that exist. These rules all operate to limit the amount of depreciation that can be claimed in any one year and to extend the number of years for claiming depreciation.

***Basis*** **Generally, this is the original cost of the vehicle. If a vehicle was bought in part with the trade-in of an old car prior to 2018, the basis of the new vehicle was the adjusted basis of the old vehicle plus any cash payment you make. Basis is reduced by any first-year expense deduction and any qualified electric vehicle tax credit. It is also adjusted downward for any depreciation deductions.**

Depreciation can take several forms. There is *accelerated depreciation* under MACRS, which results in greater deductions in the early years of ownership and smaller deductions in the later years. There is *straight line depreciation*, which spreads depreciation deductions evenly over the years the car is expected to last (the fixed number of years may, in fact, have no relation to the actual number of years the car is in operation). Tables 9.1 and 9.2 provide the percentage for depreciation under both methods. There is the *first-year expense deduction*, discussed later in this chapter, which is in lieu of depreciation. It takes the place of depreciation for the first year. Any part of the cost of the vehicle not recovered through the first-year expense deduction can then be recovered through depreciation deductions in subsequent years.

### *Business Use*

In order for you to claim an accelerated depreciation deduction or a first-year expense, the vehicle must be used more than 50% for business. Compare the miles driven during the year for business with the total miles driven. If more than 50% of the mileage represents business use, accelerated depreciation (or the first-year expense deduction below) can be claimed.

If you satisfy the 50% test, you may also add to business mileage any miles driven for investment purposes when calculating the depreciation deduction. You may not add investment mileage in order to determine whether you meet the 50% test. If you fail the 50% test (you use the car 50% or less for business), you can deduct depreciation using only the straight-line method. Your deduction is limited to the rates listed in the section on "Conventions."

What if the percentage of business use changes from year to year? You may use your vehicle 75% for business in one year but only 40% the next. Where business use in the year the vehicle is placed in service is more than 50% but drops below 50% in a subsequent year, you must also change depreciation rates. Once business use drops to 50% or below, you can use only the straight-line method thereafter. The depreciation rate is taken from the table for the straight-line method (Table 9.1) as if the vehicle had not qualified for accelerated depreciation in a prior year.

Where business use drops to 50% or less, you may have to include in income an amount called *excess depreciation*. This is the amount of depreciation (including the first-year expense deduction) claimed when the vehicle was used more than 50% for business over the amount of depreciation that would have been allowable had the car not been used more than 50% in the year it was placed in service. In addition to including excess depreciation in income, you must increase the basis of your car by the same amount.

**Example**

**In 2019, you placed in service a car costing $37,000. (Assume the car was used 100% for business, you did not elect first-year expensing or use bonus depreciation, and the half-year convention applied.) In 2021, business use drops to 40%. The depreciation claimed for 2019 and 2020 totaled $19,240 using MACRS. Had the straight-line method been used (see Table 9.1), depreciation would have been $11,100. Thus, the excess of $8,140 ($19,240 – $11,100) must be included in income. Your new adjusted basis for the car is $25,900 ($37,000 – $19,240 + $8,140).**

### Conventions

There are special rules that operate to limit write-offs for depreciation, called *conventions*. Two conventions apply to depreciation for vehicles: the half-year convention and the mid-quarter convention.

The *half-year convention*, in effect, assumes that the vehicle was placed in service in the second half of the year. Thus, in the first year you are allowed to claim only one-half the normal rate of depreciation, regardless of when in the year the car was placed in service. Thus, even if the vehicle was placed in service on January 1, the half-year convention must still be used.

You can see in Table 9.1 how the half-year convention operates to limit depreciation in the first year. By the same token, the amount of depreciation denied in the first year will ultimately be allowed in the sixth year. Still, the half-year convention means that even though the car is classified as 5-year property, its cost will be recovered only over a period of 6 years. If the half-year convention applies to property used 50% or less for business, the depreciation rate is in Table 9.1. If the half-year convention applies to property used more than 50% for business, the depreciation rate is in Table 9.2.

**TABLE 9.1 Straight-Line Half-Year Convention***

| Year | Rate (Percent) |
|---|---|
| 1 | 10 |
| 2 | 20 |
| 3 | 20 |
| 4 | 20 |
| 5 | 20 |
| 6 | 10 |

*Depreciation may not exceed a dollar limit (see page 193).

**TABLE 9.2 MACRS Half-Year Convention***

| Year | Rate (Percent) |
|---|---|
| 1 | 20.00 |
| 2 | 32.00 |
| 3 | 19.20 |
| 4 | 11.52 |
| 5 | 11.52 |
| 6 | 5.76 |

*Depreciation may not exceed a dollar limit (see page 193).

**Example**

In March 2021, you buy and place in service a new pickup truck for your business (assume it's used entirely for business and not for personal driving). It cost $34,000. Assume that the half-year convention (see Table 9.2) applies and that the pickup continues to be used in the business. The depreciation allowances are:

For 2021: $6,800 (20% of $34,000)
For 2022: $10,880 (32% of $34,000)
For 2023: $6,528 (19.2% of $34,000)
For 2024: $3,917 (11.52% of $34,000)
For 2025: $3,917 (11.52% of $34,000)
For 2026: $1,958 (5.76% of $34,000)

Over this 6-year period, the cost of the pickup can be fully written off (assuming you own it for this long).

The other convention, the *mid-quarter convention*, applies if more than 40% of all the depreciable property you place in service during the year is placed in service in the last quarter of the year.

If the mid-quarter convention applies to property used 50% or less for business, the rate is in Table 9.3.

**Example**

In 2021, you place in service a computer costing $5,000 in January and a used car costing $15,000 in December. The mid-quarter convention applies because more than 40% of the depreciable property you placed in service during the year was placed in service during the last quarter of the year ($15,000 is 75% of the total of $20,000 of depreciable property placed in service in 2021).

**TABLE 9.3** Straight-Line Mid-Quarter Convention*

| Year Placed in Service | 1st Quarter | 2nd Quarter | 3rd Quarter | 4th Quarter |
|---|---|---|---|---|
| 1 | 17.5% | 12.5% | 7.5% | 2.5% |
| 2 | 20.0 | 20.0 | 20.0 | 20.0 |
| 3 | 20.0 | 20.0 | 20.0 | 20.0 |
| 4 | 20.0 | 20.0 | 20.0 | 20.0 |
| 5 | 20.0 | 20.0 | 20.0 | 20.0 |
| 6 | 2.5 | 7.5 | 12.5 | 17.5 |

*Depreciation may not exceed a dollar limit (see page 193).

**Example**

**The circumstances are the same, except the car was placed in service in January and the computer was placed in service in December. The mid-quarter convention does not apply because only 25% of the depreciable property was placed in service in the last quarter of the year ($5,000 is 25% of the total of $20,000 of depreciable property placed in service in 2021).**

If the mid-quarter convention applies to property used more than 50% for business, the rate is in Table 9.4.

**Example**

**In December 2021, you place in service a used car costing $14,000. You use the car 40% for business and 60% for personal purposes. Assume that this is the only depreciable property you place in service in 2021, so the mid-quarter convention applies. Your depreciation deduction for the first year is $140 (2.5% of $5,600 [40% of $14,000]).**

**TABLE 9.4** MACRS Mid-Quarter Convention*

| Year Placed in Service | 1st Quarter | 2nd Quarter | 3rd Quarter | 4th Quarter |
|---|---|---|---|---|
| 1 | 35.00% | 25.00% | 15.00% | 5.00% |
| 2 | 26.00 | 30.00 | 34.00 | 38.00 |
| 3 | 15.60 | 18.00 | 20.40 | 22.80 |
| 4 | 11.01 | 11.37 | 12.24 | 13.68 |
| 5 | 11.01 | 11.37 | 11.30 | 10.94 |
| 6 | 1.38 | 4.26 | 7.06 | 9.58 |

*Depreciation may not exceed a dollar limit (see page 193).

**Example**

**In December 2021, you place in service a used car costing $14,000. You use the car 100% for business. Assume that this is the only depreciable property you place in service in 2021, so the mid-quarter convention applies. Your depreciation deduction for the first year is $700 (5% of $14,000).**

### *Section 179 Deduction*

The *Section 179 deduction*, also called the first-year expense allowance, is a one-time write-off for the cost of the car. The maximum amount of the Section 179 deduction in 2021 is $1,050,000. However, this may not be the limit that applies to the deduction for the purchase of a vehicle, because there are other limits that supersede this cap:

- Dollar limits (discussed later) for the purchase of passenger vehicles, light trucks, and vans
- A special limit of $26,200 for the purchase of heavy SUVs

### *Dollar Limit on Depreciation Deduction*

The law sets a *dollar limit* on the amount of depreciation that can be claimed on a vehicle used for business (see Table 9.5). The dollar limit is intended to limit depreciation that can be claimed on a luxury vehicle. In essence, the government does not want to underwrite the cost of buying high-priced cars and trucks.

For a luxury vehicle means one costing more than $90,000. The dollar limit isn't triggered by buying a vehicle costing less than this amount.

**Example**

**In March 2021, you place in service a used car costing $30,000 that is used 100% for business and weighs 3,500 pounds. In 2021, you can deduct $6,000 (regular depreciation of 20% of $30,000) because this is less than the dollar limit ($18,200, or $10,200 if bonus depreciation is not used).**

**TABLE 9.5 Dollar Limit on Depreciation of Passenger Cars (including Light Trucks and Vans)**

| Date Car Placed in Service | 1st Year | 2nd Year | 3rd Year | 4th and Later Years |
|---|---|---|---|---|
| 2021 | $18,200* | $16,400 | $9,800 | $5,860 |
| 2019 and 2020 | 18,100* | 16,100 | 9,700 | 5,760 |
| 2018 | 18,000* | 16,000 | 9,600 | 5,700 |
| 2012 through 2017 | 11,160** | 5,100 | 3,050 | 1,875 |

*$8,000 less if bonus depreciation is not claimed.

**$3,160 if the car did not qualify for bonus depreciation (i.e., it was a used car). Different limits applied to light trucks and vans.

**Example**

Same as the previous example, except the car costs $95,000. Regular depreciation would be $19,000 (20% of $95,000), but you are limited to the cap. In 2021, you can deduct $18,200, or $10,200 if you do not use bonus depreciation.

***Safe harbor method when bonus depreciation was previously claimed.*** If you claim bonus depreciation for a vehicle, you can continue to claim depreciation on it if you follow the rules set forth in Rev. Proc. 2019-13. Essentially, this means figuring depreciation for years following the placed-in-service year using Table 9.2 if the half-year convention applies or Table 9.3 if the mid-quarter convention applies. The depreciation claimed each year is the lower of the amount figured using the applicable table or the dollar limit in Table 9.5.

**Example**

In 2020, you placed in service a car costing $60,000, for which 100% bonus depreciation was used (assume no Section 179 deduction was claimed and the mid-quarter convention did not apply). As a result, $18,100 was deducted in 2020, leaving a remaining adjusted depreciable basis for the car of $41,900 ($60,000 – $18,100). For 2021 through 2025, figure depreciation using the annual rate in Table 9.2. For 2021, the depreciation allowance is $13,408 (32% x $41,900), which is less than the dollar limit of $16,100 for 2021 for a car placed in service in 2020 (from Table 9.5). Total depreciation allowed for the vehicle through its recovery period will be $51,620, as follows:

| Taxable year | Dollar Limit | Depreciation |
|---|---|---|
| 2020 | $18,100 | $18,100 |
| 2021 | $16,100 | $13,408 ($41,900 x 32%) |
| 2022 | $ 9,700 | $ 8,045 ($41,900 x 19.2%) |
| 2023 | $ 5,760 | $ 4,827 ($41,900 x 11.52%) |
| 2024 | $ 5,760 | $ 4,827 ($41,900 x 11.52%) |
| 2025 | $ 5,760 | $ 2,413 ($41,900 x 5.76%) |
| TOTAL | | $51,620 |

For 2026, the depreciation deduction is $5,760, which is the lesser of the adjusted depreciable basis of $8,380 ($60,000 – $51,620) or the dollar limit of $5,760. The remaining basis of $2,620 is deducted in 2027, assuming the vehicle is still owned at that time.

The dollar limit applies only to vehicles with a gross vehicle weight (the manufacturer's maximum weight rating when loaded to capacity) of 6,000 pounds or less. Most cars, light trucks, and vans fall into this category.

#### HEAVY SUVS

If you use an SUV as your business vehicle, check the manufacturer's specifications to see if the weight exceeds 6,000 pounds (but not 14,000 pounds). If so, the dollar limits in Table 9.5 do not apply and the cost of the vehicle bought and placed in service in 2021 can be expensed up to $26,200. In addition, bonus depreciation can be claimed, allowing the full cost of the vehicle written off in 2021.

**Example**

**In 2021, you buy an SUV weighing more than 6,000 pounds that costs $85,000 and use it entirely for business. You can use bonus depreciation to write off the balance of the purchase price in 2021. If you elect out of bonus depreciation, you can deduct $26,200 plus regular depreciation to write off the remainder of the cost over time.**

As a practical matter, for 2021, bonus depreciation can be used to write off the full cost of a heavy SUV and there is no need to elect the $26,200 first-year expensing allowance. The same is true through 2022. When bonus depreciation begins to phase out in 2023 through 2026, then the first-year expensing allowance may come into play.

These dollar amounts apply to cars used 100% for business. If you use your car for personal purposes as well as for business, you must allocate the dollar limit. The method for allocating this limit is the same method used for allocating the cost of the vehicle for purposes of depreciation, as described earlier.

**Example**

**In July 2021, you place in service a car costing $100,000 that is used 75% for business and 25% for personal purposes. The full dollar limit of $18,200 is allocated 75% for business. Thus, the 2021 dollar limit for this car is $13,650 (75% of $18,200).**

## Standard Mileage Allowance

Instead of keeping a record of all your expenses and having to calculate depreciation, you can use a *standard mileage allowance* fixed by the IRS to determine your deduction for business use of your car, light truck, or van (referred to throughout as "car" for simplicity purposes. You can use the standard mileage allowance in 2021 whether you own or lease the car. The standard mileage allowance takes the place of a deduction for gasoline, oil, insurance, maintenance and repairs, vehicle registration fees, and depreciation (if you own the car) or lease payments (if you lease the car). Towing charges for the car are separately deductible in addition to the standard mileage allowance. Parking fees and tolls, interest to purchase the vehicle, and personal property tax to register are also allowed in addition to the standard mileage allowance. Deductible parking fees include those incurred when visiting clients and customers or while traveling away from home on business. Fees to park your car at home or at your place of work are nondeductible personal expenses.

**TABLE 9.6** Sample Deductions under the Standard Mileage Allowance for 2021

| Miles Driven | Deduction | Miles Driven | Deduction |
|---|---|---|---|
| 5,000 | $2,800 | 30,000 | $16,800 |
| 10,000 | 5,600 | 35,000 | 19,600 |
| 15,000 | 8,400 | 40,000 | 22,400 |
| 20,000 | 11,200 | 45,000 | 25,200 |
| 25,000 | 14,000 | 50,000 | 28,000 |

The standard mileage allowance for business use of a car in 2021 is 56¢ per mile. The IRS standard mileage rate can be adjusted annually for inflation. See Table 9.6 for mileage allowances based on the amount of driving.

### *Standard Mileage Rate Barred*

You cannot use the standard mileage rate when:

- You operate more than 4 cars at the same time (such as in a fleet operation). This limit does not apply to the use of more than 4 cars on an alternate basis. For example, if you own cars and vans and alternate the use of these vehicles for business use, then you are not barred from using the standard mileage rate to account for the expenses of the business use for the vehicles.
- You have already claimed MACRS or the first-year expense deduction on the car.

### *Standard Mileage Rate or Actual Expense Method?*

As discussed earlier in this chapter, which method is preferable for you depends on a number of variables. The most important is the number of business miles you drive each year. As a rule of thumb, those who drive a great number of miles each year frequently find the standard mileage rate offers the greater deduction. However, the rate may not adequately reflect your actual driving costs. It is also important to note that the standard mileage rate is not dependent on the price of the car. Less expensive cars can claim the same deduction as more expensive cars, assuming each is driven the same number of business miles. Certainly, those with heavy SUVs can claim a greater deduction with the actual expense method.

## Leasing a Vehicle for Business

Leasing a business car is a popular alternative to buying one. If you use the car entirely for business, the cost of leasing is fully deductible. If you make advance payments, you must spread these payments over the entire lease period and deduct them accordingly. You cannot depreciate a car you lease, because depreciation applies only to property that is owned. However, you can choose to deduct the standard mileage rate in lieu of actual expenses (including lease payments).

### *Lease with an Option to Buy*

When you have this arrangement, are you leasing or buying the car? The answer depends on:

- The intent of the parties to the transaction.
- If any equity results from the arrangement.

- If any interest is paid.
- If the fair market value of the car is less than the lease payment or option payment when the option to buy is exercised.

When the factors support a lease arrangement, the payments are deductible. If, however, the factors support a purchase agreement, the payments are not deductible.

### *Inclusion Amount*

If the car price exceeds a certain amount and you deduct your actual costs (you do not use the standard mileage rate), you may have to include in income an *inclusion amount* (technically, you merely reduce the deduction for vehicle lease payments by the inclusion amount). This is because the law seeks to equate buying with leasing. Since there is a dollar limit on the amount of depreciation that can be claimed on a luxury car that is owned, the law also requires an amount to be included in income as an offset to high lease payments on a car that is leased. In essence, the inclusion amount seeks to limit your deduction for lease payments to what it would be if you owned the car and claimed depreciation. The inclusion amount, applies if a car is leased for more than 30 days and its value exceeds a certain amount. Amounts are adjusted annually for inflation. The inclusion amount is taken into account as long as you lease the car, but the amount taken into account each year is based on the year that the lease begins (i.e., you are unaffected by future inflation adjustments). If the capitalized cost of the car is specified in the lease agreement, that amount is considered to be the fair market value of the car. At the start of the lease, you can see what your inclusion amount will be for that year and for all subsequent years. The inclusion amount is based on a percentage of the **fair market value** of the car at the time the lease begins.

***Fair market value*** **The price that would be paid for the property when there is a willing buyer and seller (neither being required to buy or sell) and both have reasonable knowledge of all the necessary facts. Evidence of fair market value includes the price paid for similar property on or about the same date.**

The inclusion amount applies only if the fair market value of the car when the lease began was more than $18,500 in 2011 and 2012, $19,000 in 2013, $18,500 in 2014, $17,500 in 2015, $19,000 in 2016 and 2017, $50,000 in 2018, 2019, and 2020, and $51,000 in 2021.

Inclusion amounts for 2021 in Table 9.9 are taken from IRS tables in Rev. Proc. 2021-31; inclusion amounts for cars placed in service before 2021 can be found in the appendix to IRS Publication 463, *Travel, Gift, and Car Expenses*. The full amount in the table applies if the car is leased for the full year and used entirely for business. If the car is leased for less than the full year, or if it is used partly for personal purposes, the inclusion amount must be allocated to business use for the period of the year during which it was used. The allocation for part-year use is made on a day-by-day basis.

**Example**

**The inclusion amount for your car in 2021 is $12. You used your car only 6 months of the year. You must include $6 in income (183/365 of $12).**

**TABLE 9.7** Dollar Amounts for Passenger Automobiles with a Lease Term Beginning in Calendar Year 2021

| Fair Market Value of Passenger Automobile | | Tax Year during Lease | | | | |
|---|---|---|---|---|---|---|
| **Over** | **Not Over** | **1st** | **2nd** | **3rd** | **4th** | **5th & Later** |
| $51,000 | $52,000 | 0 | 0 | 1 | 0 | 1 |
| 52,000 | 53,000 | 1 | 1 | 1 | 2 | 2 |
| 53,000 | 54,000 | 1 | 2 | 2 | 3 | 4 |
| 54,000 | 55,000 | 1 | 3 | 3 | 5 | 5 |
| 55,000 | 56,000 | 2 | 3 | 5 | 6 | 6 |
| 56,000 | 57,000 | 2 | 4 | 6 | 7 | 8 |
| 57,000 | 58,000 | 2 | 5 | 7 | 8 | 10 |
| 58,000 | 59,000 | 3 | 5 | 8 | 10 | 11 |
| 59,000 | 60,000 | 3 | 6 | 9 | 11 | 13 |
| 60,000 | 62,000 | 3 | 7 | 11 | 13 | 15 |
| 62,000 | 64,000 | 4 | 9 | 13 | 15 | 18 |
| 64,000 | 66,000 | 5 | 10 | 15 | 18 | 21 |
| 66,000 | 68,000 | 5 | 12 | 17 | 21 | 24 |
| 68,000 | 70,000 | 6 | 13 | 20 | 23 | 27 |
| 70,000 | 72,000 | 7 | 14 | 22 | 26 | 30 |
| 72,000 | 74,000 | 7 | 16 | 24 | 29 | 33 |
| 74,000 | 76,000 | 8 | 18 | 26 | 31 | 36 |
| 76,000 | 78,000 | 9 | 19 | 28 | 34 | 39 |
| 78,000 | 80,000 | 9 | 21 | 30 | 37 | 42 |
| 80,000 | 85,000 | 11 | 23 | 34 | 41 | 48 |
| 85,000 | 90,000 | 12 | 27 | 40 | 47 | 55 |
| 90,000 | 95,000 | 14 | 30 | 45 | 55 | 62 |
| 95,000 | 100,000 | 16 | 34 | 50 | 61 | 70 |
| 100,000 | 110,000 | 18 | 40 | 58 | 71 | 81 |
| 110,000 | 120,000 | 21 | 47 | 70 | 83 | 97 |
| 120,000 | 130,000 | 25 | 54 | 81 | 96 | 112 |
| 130,000 | 140,000 | 28 | 62 | 91 | 110 | 127 |
| 140,000 | 150,000 | 31 | 69 | 103 | 123 | 141 |
| 150,000 | 160,000 | 35 | 76 | 114 | 136 | 157 |
| 160,000 | 170,000 | 38 | 84 | 124 | 149 | 172 |
| 170,000 | 180,000 | 41 | 91 | 135 | 163 | 187 |
| 180,000 | 190,000 | 45 | 98 | 146 | 176 | 202 |
| 190,000 | 200,000 | 48 | 106 | 157 | 188 | 218 |

**TABLE 9.7** ***(Continued)***

| Fair Market Value of Passenger Automobile | | Tax Year during Lease | | | | |
|---|---|---|---|---|---|---|
| Over | Not Over | 1st | 2nd | 3rd | 4th | 5th & Later |
| 200,000 | 210,000 | 51 | 113 | 168 | 202 | 232 |
| 210,000 | 220,000 | 55 | 120 | 179 | 215 | 247 |
| 220,000 | 230,000 | 58 | 128 | 190 | 227 | 263 |
| 230,000 | 240,000 | 61 | 135 | 201 | 241 | 278 |
| 240,000 | and over | 65 | 142 | 212 | 254 | 293 |

Remember that if you use your car for commuting or other nonbusiness purposes, you cannot deduct that allocable part of the lease; there is no inclusion amount for this portion.

### *Should You Lease or Buy?*

The decision to lease or buy a vehicle used for business is not an easy one. There are many financial advantages to leasing. Most important is that you need not pay more than a small amount of up-front cash to lease, whereas a purchase generally requires a significant down payment. So leasing can enable you to drive a more expensive vehicle than you could afford to buy. However, as a practical matter, if a car is driven extensively (more than 15,000 miles per year), leasing may not make sense because of the annual mileage limit and the charge for excess mileage. In such cases, owning may be preferable. Take into consideration that at the end of the lease term you own nothing, whereas at the end of the same period of time with a purchased vehicle, you own an asset that can be sold or traded in for a newer model. And, if you want to get out of the lease before the end of the lease term, there may be substantial penalties and fees (although there may also be ways to avoid them).

Whether there are any tax advantages is difficult to say. With leasing, you deduct the entire lease charge; with a purchase, you generally deduct depreciation, subject to dollar limits. While the inclusion amount is designed to offset this differential, it is not sufficient to make leasing and depreciation equate.

The only way to know whether leasing or buying is more advantageous tax-wise is to run the numbers. Project your deductible costs of leasing versus your costs of purchasing the car, truck, or van for your business.

## Arranging Vehicle Ownership

If you have a corporation, should you or your corporation own the vehicle you will use for business? From a tax standpoint, it is generally wise to have the corporation own the vehicle because the corporation can fully deduct the expenses of the vehicle (subject, of course, to the dollar limit on depreciation). If you own the vehicle, as an employee you cannot deduct vehicle expenses in 2018 through 2025 due to the suspension of miscellaneous itemized deductions.

For insurance purposes, coverage for business-owned vehicles can be more expensive than personal coverage. However, in some cases, it may still be more advantageous to have the corporation own the vehicle. If the corporation owns several vehicles, it can command better insurance rates than an individual who owns only one vehicle. Also, if the vehicle is involved in an accident, the corporation's insurance rates are not affected. If you drive your personal vehicle for business, be sure your insurance policy covers this use or you may not be protected.

Finally, if there is a lawsuit involving the vehicle, it is generally preferable to have the corporation sued rather than you personally, since a recovery against the corporation is limited to corporate assets.

## Nonpersonal Use Vehicles

Trucks (including SUVs) and vans that are configured in such a way as to be used for personal purposes only minimally are not subject to the dollar limits on depreciation that apply to passenger cars weighing no more than 6,000 pounds. These trucks and vans are referred to as qualified nonpersonal use vehicles.

Modifications likely to render a truck or van a qualified nonpersonal use vehicle include having a front jump seat, permanent shelving that fills the cargo area, and advertising or a company name printed on the side. However, attaching a nonpermanent sign to the vehicle does not make it a qualified nonpersonal use vehicle.

## Credit for Plug-In Electric Vehicles

There are certain tax credits applicable to certain electric vehicles.

### *4-Wheel Vehicles*

There is a credit for a new plug-in highway-ready electric vehicle (EV) purchased and placed in service in 2021. The credit is up to $7,500, regardless of the weight of the vehicle.

The full $7,500 credit for such 2021 models as the Pacifica Plug-In Hybrid, Ford Mustang Mach-E, Jaguar I-Pace, and many more. The credit applies only to 200,000 cars per manufacturer; there is a partial credit for up to a year after this limit is reached. The U.S Department of Energy lists all the vehicles that qualify for a full or partial credit at https://fueleconomy.gov/feg/taxevb.shtml.

If the vehicle is purchased for business, it is part of the general business credit (see Chapter 23).

The credit can be claimed for both regular tax and alternative minimum tax purposes (see Chapter 28).

### *2-Wheel Vehicles*

There is also a credit for a 2-wheel electric vehicle (electric motorcycle). The credit is 10% of the cost of the motorcycle, for a maximum credit of $2,500. The motorcycle must have a battery capacity of at least 2.5 kilowatt-hours, be manufactured primarily for use on public streets, roads, and highways, and be capable of achieving speeds of at least 45 miles per hour.

**Looking Ahead**

**The credit for 2-wheel electric vehicles expires at the end of 2021, but could be extended by Congress.**

## Dispositions of a Vehicle

### SALE

If you sell your vehicle, your gain or loss is the difference between what you receive for the vehicle and your adjusted basis. Your adjusted basis is your original basis reduced by any first-year expensing or depreciation (up to the dollar limit each year). If the vehicle has been fully depreciated, anything you receive for the vehicle is all gain.

If you used the standard mileage allowance, you are considered to have claimed depreciation even though you did not have to figure a separate depreciation deduction. The standard mileage allowance automatically takes into account a deduction for depreciation. You figure your *deemed depreciation* according to the number of miles you drove the vehicle for business each year and the years in which it was used (see Table 9.8).

**Example**

**You bought a vehicle and placed it in service at the beginning of 2018. You drove the vehicle 20,000 miles each year for business. You sell it at the end of 2021. You must adjust the basis of the vehicle for purposes of determining gain or loss on the sale by deemed depreciation of \$20,800 (20,000 miles × 25¢/mile + 40,000 miles × 26¢/mile + 20,000 × 27¢). You reduce your original basis by the total of deemed depreciation but do not reduce the basis below zero.**

If you use the actual expense method and sell the vehicle before the end of its recovery period, you can claim a reduced depreciation deduction in the year of disposition. Calculate what the depreciation deduction would have been had you held the vehicle for the full year. Then, if you originally placed your vehicle in service during the first three-quarters of the year (January 1 through September 30), you can deduct 50% of the amount that would have been allowed. If you originally placed your vehicle in service in the last quarter of the year (October 1 through December 31), you can deduct an amount calculated by applying the percentage in Table 9.9 to what would have been allowed.

### TRADE-IN

Before 2018, when you traded in your vehicle, you had an option to treat it as a tax-free exchange, so that the basis of the new vehicle was the remaining basis of the old vehicle, plus any cash paid

**TABLE 9.8 Deemed Depreciation**

| Year | Cents per Mile |
|---|---|
| 2021 | 26 |
| 2020 | 27 |
| 2019 | 26 |
| 2017–2018 | 25 |
| 2015–2016 | 24 |
| 2014 | 22 |
| 2012–2013 | 23 |

**TABLE 9.9 Depreciation in Year of Sale***

| Month Car Sold** | Percentage |
|---|---|
| January, February, March | 12.5 |
| April, May, June | 37.5 |
| July, August, September | 62.5 |
| October, November, December | 87.5 |

*Table is not for fiscal-year taxpayers.
**Car placed in service October 1–December 31.

toward the new vehicle. Or you could treat the trade-in as a sale, recognizing gain or loss on the transaction. After 2017, tax-free exchange treatment for a trade-in does not apply. You must use what had only been a second option: a sale of the old vehicle.

In 2021, when you trade in your old vehicle, your gain or loss is the difference between the basis of the old vehicle and the amount you receive for it. If the basis is less than what you receive, you have a taxable gain. If the basis is more (a very unusual situation), you have a loss.

**Example**

**You bought a truck in 2018 that you trade in for a new one on January 2, 2021. The old truck cost you $35,000, but you claimed depreciation on it of $16,150 ($7,000 in 2018, $5,700 in 2019, and $3,450 in 2020). Your basis in the old truck is $18,850 ($35,000 – $16,150). If the dealer gives you anything more than $18,850 toward the purchase of a new truck, you have taxable gain.**

#### CASUALTY OR THEFT

If your vehicle is damaged or stolen and insurance or other reimbursements exceed the adjusted basis of the vehicle, you have a tax gain. However, if you use the reimbursements to buy another vehicle for business or to repair the old vehicle within 2 years of the end of the year of the casualty or theft, then no gain is recognized. The basis of the new vehicle for purposes of depreciation is its cost less any gain that is not recognized.

## Reimbursement Arrangements

If you are an employee who is reimbursed by your employer for the business use of your car, you do not claim depreciation.

### *Accountable Plan*

If your employer maintains an arrangement that reimburses you for business-related use of the car, requires you to adequately account to the employer for these expenses, and also requires you to return within a reasonable time any advances or reimbursements in excess of these expenses, then the plan is treated as an *accountable plan*. (For details on adequate accounting under accountable plans and returning excess amounts within a reasonable time, see Chapter 8.) If your employer maintains an accountable plan for reimbursement of business expenses and the amount of reimbursement does not exceed the standard mileage allowance, the reimbursements are not reported on your W-2. If the reimbursements exceed the standard mileage allowance, only the excess over the standard mileage allowance is included on your W-2. You may not deduct your actual expenses that exceed the standard mileage rate due to the suspension of the miscellaneous itemized deduction subject to the 2% of AGI floor.

### *Nonaccountable Plan*

Your employer must include on your W-2 form all reimbursements made under a nonaccountable plan. But you cannot deduct your costs because of the suspension of miscellaneous itemized deductions subject to the 2% of AGI floor in 2018 through 2025.

## Recordkeeping for Vehicle Expenses

Regardless of whether you use the actual expense method or the standard mileage allowance for your car (or a car that your employer provides you with), certain recordkeeping requirements apply. You must keep track of the number of miles you drive each year for business, as well as the total miles driven each year. You must also record the date of the business mileage, the destination of the business travel, and the business reason for the car expense. An unsubstantiated deduction for business driving is one of the most common audit issues. Even though you drive your vehicle for business, without the proper records your deduction may be limited or denied entirely.

It is advisable to maintain a daily travel log or diary in which you record the date, the destination, the business purpose of the trip, and the number of miles driven (use the odometer readings at the start and end of the trip, and then total the miles for each trip). Be sure to note the odometer reading on January 1 each year (Table 9.10).

If you use the actual expense method, you must also keep a record of the costs of operating the car. These include the cost of gasoline and oil, car insurance, interest on a car loan (if you are self-employed), licenses and taxes, and repairs and maintenance. Record these amounts in your expense log or diary.

If you lease a car, you must keep track of the amount of the lease payments, in addition to the number of miles driven (and the number of business miles), the dates of travel, the destinations, and the purpose for the travel.

Use a diary or log to keep track of your business mileage and other related costs. You can buy a car expense log in stationery and business supply stores or reproduce the blank log in Table 9.10. Table 9.11 is a model of an IRS sample daily business mileage and expense log.

You can also use your smartphone to keep mileage records. Examples of these apps include MileIQ, SherpaShare, TripLog, Hurdlr, and Everlance. Check pricing; some offer free versions. Consider printing out your year-end statement from an app to keep with your tax records.

It is essential that you keep a written record of the business use of your car. You must note on your tax return whether you have such a record. Remember that your return is signed under penalty of perjury.

### *Proving Expenses with a Mileage Allowance*

Generally, required recordkeeping includes tracking the odometer at the start and end of each business trip (as well as the date, destination, and purpose of the trip). However, the IRS permits "sampling" in some situations. You are treated as having adequate substantiation if you keep records for a representative portion of the year and can demonstrate that the period for which records are kept is representative of use for the entire year.

**TABLE 9.10** Business Mileage Log

| | | | Odometer Readings | | | Expenses | |
|---|---|---|---|---|---|---|---|
| **Date** | **Destination** | **Business Purpose** | **Start** | **Stop** | **Miles This Trip** | **Type** | **Amount** |
| | | | | | | | |
| | | | | | | | |
| | | | | | | | |
| | | | | | | | |
| | | | | | | | |
| | | | | | | | |
| | | | | | | | |
| | | | | | | | |
| | | | | | | | |
| | | | | | | | |
| | | | | | | | |
| | | | | | | | |
| | | | | | | | |
| | | | | | | | |
| | | | | | | | |
| | | | | | | | |
| | | | | | | | |
| | | | | | | | |
| | | | | | | | |
| | | | | | | | |
| | | | | | | | |
| | | | | | | | |
| | | | | | | | |
| | | | | | | | |
| | | | | | | | |
| | | | | | | | |

Sampling may not be used unless you can show a consistent pattern of car use. Also, not all substantiation shortcuts are acceptable. For instance, one taxpayer used mileage figured by a computer atlas to substantiate his car expenses. Unfortunately, the Tax Court rejected this method, observing that he failed to keep track of his odometer readings at the time the expenses were incurred.

**TABLE 9.11** Sample Log

| Date | Destination | Business Purpose | Odometer Readings | | | Expenses | |
|---|---|---|---|---|---|---|---|
| | | | Start | Stop | Miles This Trip | Type | Amount |
| 5/4/21 | Local—St. Louis | Sales calls | 8,097 | 8,188 | 91 | Gas | $38.00 |
| 5/5/21 | Indianapolis | Sales calls | 8,211 | 8,486 | 275 | Parking | 5.00 |
| 5/6/21 | Louisville | Bob Smith (potential client) | 8,486 | 8,599 | 113 | Gas Repair<br>Flat tire | 37.80<br>10.00 |
| 5/7/21 | Return to St. Louis | | 8,599 | 8,875 | 276 | Gas | 38.25 |
| 5/8/21 | Local—St. Louis | Sales calls | 8,914 | 9,005 | 91 | | |
| Weekly total | | | 8,097 | 9,005 | 846 | | 129.05 |
| Year-to-date total | | | | | 5,883 | | $1,074.75 |

**Example**

**An interior designer who runs her sole proprietorship from home visits clients using her personal car for this business driving. She records her mileage for the first 3 months of the year, which shows that the car is used 75% for business and 25% for personal driving. Invoices from her business show that business activity was nearly constant throughout the year, indicating that her driving pattern remained the same. Under these facts, she can extrapolate that 75% of her car expenses for the year are business-related.**

**Example**

**The same interior designer instead records her mileage for the first week of every month, showing 75% business use. Invoices show that business continued at the same rate throughout the month so that the first week's record was representative of the full month. Under these facts, she can extrapolate that 75% of her car expenses for the balance of the month (and throughout the year) are business-related.**

**Example**

**You use your car to visit the offices of clients, meet with suppliers and other subcontractors, and pick up and deliver items to clients. There is no other business use of the car, although you use the car for personal purposes. You keep adequate records during the first week of each month that show that 75% of the use of the car is for business. Invoices and bills show that your business use continues at the same rate during the later weeks of each month. Your weekly records are representative of the use of the car each month and are sufficient evidence to support the percentage of business use for the year. Thus 75% of the miles driven during the year are for business (you need the odometer reading for the first and last day of the year to determine total miles driven).**

## Where to Deduct Car Expenses

### *Employees*

Unless you are in a special category of employee as explained next, you cannot deduct vehicle expenses in 2018 through 2025 because of the suspension of miscellaneous itemized deductions subject to the 2%-of-adjusted-gross-income floor.

***Disabled employees.*** If you have a physical or mental disability, your impairment-related work expenses are deductible as an itemized deduction but the 2% floor does not apply. Impairment-related work expenses include costs of attendant care at your place of work and those that are necessary to enable you to work (such as the cost of a driver to bring you to business locations). General medical expenses, however, are not impairment-related work expenses; they are simply personal medical expenses and are deductible as such.

***Special rule for performing artists.*** If you meet certain requirements, you can deduct all of your car expenses as an adjustment to income on Schedule 1 of Form 1040 or 1040-SR. You are treated as a performing artist if you meet *all* of the following 5 tests:

1. You perform services in the performing arts for at least 2 employers during the year.
2. You receive at least $200 each from any 2 of these employers.
3. Your related performing arts business expenses are more than 10% of your adjusted gross income from the performance of such services.
4. Your adjusted gross income (and not merely performing arts income) does not exceed $16,000 (before deducting business expenses from your performing arts).
5. If you are married, you file a joint return (unless you lived apart from your spouse for the entire year).

You perform tests 1, 2, and 3 based on your individual experience. However, the adjusted gross income in test 4 is the combined adjusted gross income of you and your spouse. If you meet these tests, you deduct your performing arts business expenses as an adjustment to gross income on Schedule 1 of Form 1040 or 1040-SR.

***Reservists.*** If you are a reservist who travels more than 100 miles away from home in connection with the performance of duties and use your vehicle for the travel, enter your expenses on Form 2106 and then on Schedule 1 of Form 1040 or 1040-SR.

***Fee-based government officials.*** If you are a fee-based official employed by a state or local government, enter your vehicle expenses on Form 2106 and then on Schedule 1 of Form 1040 or 1040-SR.

### Self-Employed

You enter your car expenses on Schedule C, *Profit and Loss from Business*. If you are not required to complete Form 4562, *Depreciation and Amortization*, because you did not place any depreciable or amortizable property in service in 2021, then use Part IV of Schedule C to report information on your car. You need to know and provide when the car was placed in service and the number of miles driven for business, commuting, or other purposes; whether there is another car available for personal use and whether your business car was available during off-duty hours; evidence to support your deductions and whether this evidence is written. If you are otherwise required to complete Form 4562, then report the information about your car on this form and not on Schedule C.

Farmers who are self-employed deduct their car expenses on Schedule F. Also complete Part IV of Form 4562, to provide information about car use.

### Partnerships and LLCs

Expenses of business-owned cars are reported on the business's Form 1065 as part of the business's ordinary income (or loss). They are entered in the category of Other Deductions. A schedule is attached to the return explaining the deductions claimed in this category. Car expenses are not separately stated items. The owner's share of ordinary income (or loss) is reported on Schedule K-1.

### S Corporations

Car expenses of business-owned cars are reported on the corporation's Form 1120-S as part of the S corporation's ordinary income (or loss). They are entered in the category of Other Deductions. A schedule is attached to the return explaining the deductions claimed in this category. Car expenses are not separately stated items. The shareholder's share of ordinary income (or loss) is reported on Schedule K-1.

### C Corporations

Car expenses are reported on the corporation's Form 1120 as part of its taxable income (or loss). They are entered in the category of Other Deductions. A schedule is attached to the return explaining the deductions claimed in this category.

### All Businesses

If you claim depreciation for a vehicle used in business, you must complete Form 4562, *Depreciation and Amortization*. Generally, this form must be filed every year in which the IRS mileage allowance or actual vehicle expenses (including depreciation) are claimed to provide certain requested information. Those filing Schedule C can include this information on Part IV of the schedule; they do not have to file Form 4562 unless they are otherwise required to do so (e.g., have placed depreciable property in service this year).

The credit for purchasing a plug-in electric vehicle or converting a conventional-fuel vehicle to electric power is computed on Form 8836, *Qualified Plug-in Electric and Electric Vehicle Credit*. For business-owned vehicles, the credit is part of the general business credit, figured on Form 3800, *General Business Credit*.

# CHAPTER 10

# Repairs, Maintenance, and Energy Improvements


| | | | |
|---|---|---|---|
| Ordinary Repairs | 209 | Special Rules for Improvements for the Elderly and People with Disabilities | 216 |
| Rehabilitation Plans | 212 | Lists of Deductible Repairs and Capital Improvements | 220 |
| Qualified Improvement Property | 213 | Energy Improvements | 221 |
| Small Business Safe Harbors | 214 | | |
| Rotable Spare Parts | 215 | | |
| Change in Accounting Method | 216 | | |


Property and equipment generally need constant repairs to keep them in working order. Preventative maintenance—regular servicing of equipment—can cut down on replacement costs by allowing you to keep your current equipment longer. When your computer goes down, a service person is required to make repairs. When the air-conditioning system in your office building stops working, again, servicing is necessary. If you have property or equipment to which you make repairs, you can deduct these expenses. The only hitch is making sure that the expenses are not *capital expenditures*. As a general rule, the cost of capital expenditures cannot be currently deducted but instead are added to the basis of property and recovered through depreciation or upon the disposition of the property. But there are several important exceptions to this rule, which were created by what tax pros call the "repair regulations" issued several years ago.

For further information about deducting repairs, see IRS Publication 535, *Business Expenses*.

## Ordinary Repairs

### *Deducting Incidental Repairs in General*

The cost of repairing property and equipment used in your business is a deductible business expense. In contrast, expenditures that materially add to the value of the property, prolong its life, or adapt the property to a new or different use must be capitalized (added to the basis of the property and recovered through depreciation). In most cases, the distinction is clear. If you pay a repair person to service your copying machine because paper keeps getting jammed, the cost of the service call is a repair expense and is currently deductible. If you put a new roof on your office building, you usually must capitalize the expenditure and recover the cost through depreciation. Sometimes, however, the classification of an expense as a repair or a capital expenditure is not clear. For example, in one case the cost of a new roof was currently deductible where it was installed merely to repair a leak and did not change the structure of the building or add to its value.

### Guidelines on Distinguishing Between a Repair and a Capital Item

Repairs are expenses designed to keep property in good working condition. This includes the replacement of short-lived parts. Typically, the cost of repairs is small compared with the cost of the property itself.

Capital items, on the other hand, are akin to original construction. Costs are usually substantial. Table 10.1 includes some common examples of repairs and capital improvements. Under the repair regulations, there are many favorable safe harbors and de minimis rules that allow otherwise capitalized costs to be currently deductible.

Even though repairs add to the length of a property's useful life, this does not automatically make them capital improvements. It can be argued that *all* repairs produce this result. For example, one business owner with a fleet of tug boats made substantial engine repairs each year. The IRS said that the repairs should be capitalized because they added to the life of the boats, but the Tax Court said no. Despite the cost of the repairs—over $100,000 per tug—and the fact that the repairs kept the tugs afloat longer—they were still ordinary repairs that were currently deductible.

To distinguish repairs from capital improvements, there are no bright line tests; the determination is based on facts and circumstances. Capital improvements include a betterment to or restoration of the unit of property, or an adaptation of the unit of property to a new or different use. A "unit of property" is functionally interdependent on components such as a machine or a building. However, certain major building systems (e.g., HVAC, plumbing, and electrical) are treated as separate units of property; they are also viewed as qualified improvement property (defined later in this chapter for which a Section 179 deduction up to $1,050,000 may be claimed in 2021 (see later in this chapter and in Chapter 14). The cost (no matter how minor) of restoring property after a casualty loss is not a deductible repair cost if a casualty loss deduction is taken. For more guidance on determining a betterment, restoration, or adaption, see IRS questions and answers at https://www.irs.gov/Businesses/Small-Businesses-&-Self-Employed/Tangible-Property-Final-Regulations.

The cost of routine maintenance is currently deductible if it is done to keep property in its ordinarily efficient operating condition. This maintenance safe harbor rule applies to buildings as long as the owner expects to perform the maintenance more than once over a 10-year period. The safe harbor applies to property other than buildings if expected to be done more than once

**TABLE 10.1 Examples of Repairs versus Capital Items**

| Repairs | Capital Items |
|---|---|
| Painting the outside of office building | Vinyl siding the outside of office building |
| Replacing missing shingles on roof | Replacing entire roof unless strictly for repair purposes |
| Replacing compressor for air conditioner | Adding air-conditioning system |
| Cleaning canopy over restaurant entrance | Adding canopy over restaurant entrance |
| Resurfacing office floor | Replacing office floor |

during the class life (essentially, the recovery period for depreciation purposes) of the unit of property (the terms "class life" and "recovery period" are defined in Chapter 14). However, you can elect to capitalize repair and maintenance costs for tangible personal property (not realty) if you treat the costs as such on your books and records. The election is made on your tax return (not on an amended return) and, once made, the costs become depreciable. For partnerships and S corporations, the election is made by the entity and not by the individual owners.

The fact that certain repairs are necessitated by governmental directives does not change the character of the expense. If it is a required repair, it is currently deductible; if it substantially improves the property, it is a capital expenditure. For example, in one case, rewiring ordered by local fire prevention inspectors was a capital expenditure. The same is true for capital expenditures ordered by the U.S. Public Health Service and state sanitary or health laws.

**Example**

**Various assets of a business are damaged by a storm; some are nearly destroyed while others suffer less damage. If the business claims a casualty loss deduction, the cost of repairs to any assets in this case must be capitalized.**

### Special Rules

If things weren't confusing enough when differentiating between repairs and capital improvements, the IRS has created 2 special rules:

1. *Repairs and remodeling of restaurants and retail establishments*. Because these expenditures typically occur every 5 to 7 years, the IRS lets a business elect to treat 75% of the costs to remodel and refresh their premises as an ordinary repair cost that is currently deductible. The balance of 25% of such costs must be capitalized. A listing of qualified expenses may be found in Revenue Procedure 2015-56. However, this safe harbor currently applies only if a business has an applicable financial statement (AFS), which includes an SEC filing, an audited financial statement, or a filing with a government agency other than the SEC or IRS. Most small businesses don't have an AFS and cannot use this write-off option. But, the IRS may extend the remodel-refresh rule to small businesses in the future.
2. *Routine maintenance safe harbor*. This rule allows you to deduct certain repairs and maintenance that would otherwise have to be capitalized if such actions are reasonably expected to occur at least once every 10 years. The rule, which can be used by any business, is discussed later in this chapter.

### Environmental Cleanup Costs

If you are forced to take certain actions to comply with Environmental Protection Agency (EPA) requirements, such as encapsulating or removing asbestos, understand which expenses are currently deductible and which expenses must be capitalized. Environmental remediation costs can be currently deducted. For instance, the cost of replacing mold-contaminated drywall in a nursing home was a deductible remediation cost that merely restored the building to its precontamination condition. The costs of cleanups to comply with environmental laws that effectively restore property to its original (precontamination) condition may be deductible. But the cost of capital improvements, even though required to comply with environmental laws, must be capitalized.

**Example**

**The cost of encapsulating asbestos in a warehouse is currently deductible. The cost of removing asbestos from a boiler room must be capitalized. (The removal makes the property substantially more attractive to potential buyers.)**

## Rehabilitation Plans

In the past, there was a rehabilitation doctrine created by case law, which had required property owners to capitalize the cost of ordinary repairs incurred as part of a plan of rehabilitation, modernization, or improvement to property. The "repair regulations" make this doctrine obsolete.

However, if you improve property in a building by changing structural components (e.g., windows, HVAC units, or the roof), you are not required to continue depreciating the old component along with the new component. Instead, you can do either of the following (for details see Reg. §1.168(i)-8):

- Continue depreciation under the old rule, which required you to continue depreciating the old component along with the new component.
- Make a partial disposition election. Under this option, you take a current deduction for the remaining undepreciated basis of the old component. The cost of the new component is then subject to depreciation (even if it could have been treated as a currently deductible repair). The election must be made on a timely filed return for the year of the replacement.

### *Tax Credits for Rehabilitation*

While rehabilitation costs generally must be capitalized, in special instances you can claim a tax credit for your expenditures. If you rehabilitate a certified historic structure (a building that is listed in the National Register or located in a registered historic district), the credit is 20% of costs. The credit begins to be claimed in the year the property is placed in service and is spread ratably over 5 years, not the year in which the expenditures are made.

**Example**

**If you undertake a 2-year project beginning in 2020 and do not place the building in service until 2021, one-fifth of the credit is taken in 2021.**

Rehabilitation requires that you make substantial improvements to the building but leave a substantial portion of it intact. A *substantial portion* means that within any 2-year period you select, the rehabilitation expenditures exceed the adjusted basis of the building or $5,000, whichever is greater. The Secretary of the Interior must certify that the rehabilitation of certified historic structures will be in keeping with the building's historic status.

The credit is claimed on Form 3468, *Investment Credit*. For individuals and C corporations, it is part of the general business credit computed on Form 3800, *General Business Credit*. The credit may be limited by the passive loss rules explained in Chapter 4. The general business credit limitations are explained in Chapter 23.

### Demolition and Removal Expenses

As a general rule, the costs of demolishing a building are not deductible. Instead, they are added to the basis of the new building (that is, the building put up in the place of the demolished building). However, the costs of demolishing only a part of a building may be currently deductible. According to the IRS, if 75% or more of the existing external walls and 75% or more of the existing internal framework are both retained, the costs of demolition need not be capitalized (added to basis) but instead can be currently deducted.

Removal costs for tangible personal property (not realty) being disposed of are currently deductible if you do not realize gain or loss on the disposition.

## Qualified Improvement Property

Usually, the cost of capital improvements must be recovered through depreciation, as explained earlier in this chapter. There are some safe harbors that can be used to immediately deduct certain costs that would normally be capitalized and recovered through depreciation, explained later in this chapter. But special rules apply to **qualified improvement property.**

***Qualified improvement property*** **Any improvement to the interior of a portion of a commercial building, other than these excludable improvements: elevators and escalators, building enlargements, and changes to the internal structural framework of a building.**

- ***First-year expensing (Section 179 deduction).*** In 2021, you can elect to expense costs up to $1,050,000.
- ***Bonus depreciation.*** In 2021, you may deduct 100% of the costs, without any dollar limit, unless you choose not to do this and instead apply depreciation.
- ***Depreciation.*** You can write off costs ratably over 15 years.

**Example**

**In 2021, you spend $48,000 on improvements to your restaurant, such as installing plastic barriers between booths and other COVID-19 related permanent improvements, as well as other internal improvements that are qualified improvement property. Because qualified improvement property is eligible for bonus depreciation, you may deduct $48,000 in 2021.**

***Qualified real property.*** For purposes of the Section 179 deduction, qualified real property includes qualified improvement property as well as the following types of improvements to nonresidential real property:

- Roofs
- Heating, ventilation, and air-conditioning property
- Fire protection and alarm systems
- Security systems

## Small Business Safe Harbors

Under the repair regulations, there are some safe harbors specifically for small businesses. These safe harbors allow for immediate write-offs for capital improvements in special situations. They are intended to alleviate recordkeeping, but this does not mean you can forego recordkeeping entirely; you still need records.

### *Small Building Safe Harbor*

Usually, building improvements must be capitalized and their cost recovered through depreciation. However, small taxpayers can write-off certain costs.

To be eligible for this safe harbor:

- You must be a "small taxpayer." This means having average annual gross receipts in the 3 prior years of no more than $10 million. There is no aggregation rule here, so if you own multiple businesses, you don't have to aggregate your gross receipts; each business stands on its own.
- The unadjusted basis of the building is no greater than $1 million. Unadjusted basis usually is the original cost of the building, exclusive of the land.

The safe harbor applies only if your repairs, maintenance, and improvements for the year do not exceed the *lesser* of $10,000 or 2% of the unadjusted basis of the building. The IRS has the authority to adjust the $10,000, 2%, and $1 million amounts in the future.

The safe harbor applies separately to each such building owned by a small taxpayer. Thus, if you are a small taxpayer, you may qualify to use the safe harbor on one building but not for another, depending on the extent of your costs for the year.

The election to use this safe harbor must be made on an annual basis by attaching a statement to the income tax return indicating that it is a small taxpayer safe harbor election. Details about the election statement are at the end of this chapter. There is no special IRS form for this election. The election must be made on a timely filed original return (not an amended return) for the year of the election. For pass-through entities, the election is made by the entities and not by the owners on their personal returns.

### *Routine Maintenance Safe Harbor*

Even though certain maintenance costs should be treated as capital improvements, you can immediately deduct the cost if you qualify under this safe harbor. The write-off applies only to routine maintenance costs, which are recurring activities to keep a building or each system in the building in ordinarily efficient operating condition. Recurring work means activities reasonably expected to be performed more than once every 10 years. Activities that are routine maintenance are:

- Inspection, cleaning, and testing the building's structure or a system within the building
- Replacement of damaged or worn parts with comparable and commercially available replacement parts

**Example**

**You own an office building. Each year you test the HVAC system. During the course of an annual inspection, you replace a worn part. The cost of the inspection and the replacement part are currently deductible under this safe harbor.**

This election is treated as a change of accounting method. It is not made by filing an annual election statement. Usually you need to file Form 3115. See Chapter 2 for more details about changes in accounting methods and simplified procedures for certain changes.

## Rotable Spare Parts

Rotable spare parts are materials and supplies acquired for installation on a unit of property that are removable from the unit of property and then repaired or improved and either reinstalled on the same unit or stored for later installation. There are 3 ways to handle rotable spare parts for tax purposes:

1. Deduct the cost in the year the parts are disposed of
2. Elect to capitalize the cost of the parts and recover the cost over the applicable recovery period (see Chapter 14)
3. Use the optional method, a description of which follows

There are a lot of moving parts, as it were, to the optional method. Under the optional method for rotable spare parts, you deduct the cost to produce or acquire them upon initial installation and recognize as income the fair market value of the part (plus the cost to remove it) when removed from the unit. You add to the basis of the part any amount paid to repair, maintain, or improve it. You deduct the cost of reinstallation and any basis not previously deducted in the year in which the part is reinstalled. Finally, you deduct any remaining amount in the year in which the part is finally disposed of.

**Example**

**C operates a fleet of specialized vehicles that it uses in its service business; each vehicle is a unit of property. At the time that it acquires a new type of vehicle, C also acquires a substantial number of rotable spare parts that it will keep on hand to replace similar parts in the vehicles as those parts break down or wear out. These rotable parts are removable from the vehicles and are repaired so that they can be reinstalled on the same or similar vehicles. In Year 1, C acquires several vehicles and a number of rotable spare parts (the "Year 1 rotable parts") to be used as replacement parts in these vehicles. In Year 2, C repairs several vehicles and uses the Year 1 rotable parts to replace worn or damaged parts. In Year 3, C pays amounts to remove these Year 1 rotable parts from its vehicles. In Year 4, C pays amounts to maintain, repair, or improve the Year 1 rotable parts. In Year 5, C pays amounts to reinstall the Year 1 rotable parts on other similar vehicles. In Year 8, C removes the Year 1 rotable parts from these vehicles and stores these parts for possible later use. In Year 9, C disposes of the Year 1 rotable parts. Under paragraph (e) of this section, C must deduct the amounts paid to acquire and install the Year 1 rotable parts in Year 2, the taxable year in which the rotable parts are first installed by C in C's vehicles. In Year 3, when C removes the Year 1 rotable parts from its vehicles, C includes in its gross income the fair market value of each part. Also in Year 3, C includes in the basis of each Year 1 rotable part the fair market value of the rotable part and the amount paid to remove the rotable part from the vehicle. In Year 4, C includes in the basis of each Year 1 rotable part the amount paid to maintain, repair, or improve each. In Year 5, the year that C reinstalls the Year 1 rotable parts (as repaired**

**or improved) in other vehicles, C deducts the reinstallation costs and the amount previously included in the basis of each part. In Year 8, the year that C removes the Year 1 rotable parts from the vehicles, C includes in income the fair market value of each rotable part removed. In addition, in Year 8, C includes in the basis of each part, the fair market value of that part, and the amount paid to remove each rotable part from the vehicle. In Year 9, the year that C disposes of the Year 1 rotable parts, C can deduct the amount remaining in the basis of each rotable part.**

Different rules apply to temporary spare parts and standby emergency spare parts. Temporary spare parts are parts used temporarily until new or repaired parts can be installed. Temporary spare parts are then stored for use at a later time. Temporary spare parts can be written off under any of the three methods applicable to rotable spare parts.

Standby emergency spare parts have a rather lengthy definition; all 10 conditions must be satisfied. An emergency spare part is an item:

1. Acquired when particular machinery or equipment is acquired (or later acquired and set aside for use in particular machinery or equipment);
2. Set aside for use as replacements to avoid substantial operational time loss caused by emergencies due to particular machinery or equipment failure;
3. Located at or near the site of the installed related machinery or equipment so as to be readily available when needed;
4. Directly related to the particular machinery or piece of equipment they serve;
5. Normally expensive;
6. Only available on special order and not readily available from a vendor or manufacturer;
7. Not subject to normal periodic replacement;
8. Not interchangeable in other machines or equipment;
9. Not acquired in quantity (generally only one is on hand for each piece of machinery or equipment); and
10. Not repaired and reused.

Standby spare parts can be deducted using either of the first two methods applicable to rotable spare parts. The optional method cannot be used for standby spare parts.

## Change in Accounting Method

Switching from one method of handling the cost of rotable, temporary, or emergency spare parts may be a change in accounting method. For example, switching to the optional method for rotable spare parts is a change in accounting method. For more information about making a change in accounting method, see Chapter 2.

## Special Rules for Improvements for the Elderly and People with Disabilities

The Americans with Disabilities Act (ADA), which is now 30 years old, requires you to make certain modifications to your office, store, or factory if you have not done so already. You have to install ramps, widen doorways and lavatories to accommodate wheelchairs, add elevators, or make other similar changes to your facilities to render them more accessible to the elderly and people with disabilities.

These modifications may be more in the nature of capital improvements than repairs. Still, the law provides two special tax incentives to which you may be entitled. One is a tax credit; the other is a special deduction. These incentives allow for a current benefit rather than requiring capitalization of expenditures that will be recovered over long periods of time.

**NOTE**

**Work to make your website accessible to employees, customers, and others with disabilities. Learn more from W3C at https://www.w3.org/standards/webdesign/accessibility. This is important even though any costs associated with this do not qualify for the disabled access credit.**

### *Disabled Access Credit*

**Small business** owners can claim a tax credit for expenditures to remove barriers on business property that impede the access of individuals with disabilities and to supply special materials or assistance to visually or hearing-impaired persons.

***Small business*** **Businesses with gross receipts of no more than $1 million (after returns and allowances) or no more than 30 full-time employees for the tax year before the year of the credit. Full-time employees are those who work more than 30 hours per week for 20 or more calendar weeks in the year.**

The credit cannot exceed 50% of expenditures between $250 and $10,250. The maximum credit is $5,000.

**Example**

**You, as a small business owner, spend $4,000 to install ramps in your mall. You may take a tax credit of $1,875 ($4,000 – $250 = $3,750 × .50).**

The dollar limit applies at both the partner and partnership levels. The same rule applies to shareholders and S corporations, as well as to members and LLCs.

### *Qualifying Expenditures*

*Qualifying expenditures* are designed to meet the requirements of the ADA. For example, the cost of putting in handicapped parking spaces as required by federal law is a qualified expenditure. Many of these requirements are set forth in connection with the expense deduction for the removal of architectural and transportation barriers. However, eligible expenditures do not include those in connection with new construction. Thus, if you are in the process of building an office complex and you install special bathroom facilities to accommodate a wheelchair, you cannot claim the credit because this is new construction. If you claim the credit, you cannot also claim a deduction for the same expenditures. Businesses already in compliance with the ADA cannot claim the credit for equipment that may add some benefit for customers with disabilities. Also, the IRS has ruled that web-based businesses using software to enable customers with disabilities to shop cannot claim the credit; it is

**NOTE**

**In the past, there were a number of businesses claiming this credit even though they were not entitled to it. The IRS continues to be on the lookout for bogus claims, so make sure that you qualify before claiming this credit.**

limited to bricks-and-mortar businesses. However, a company with a physical place of business that uses a software service to communicate on-site with hearing-impaired customers qualifies for the credit.

### *Deduction for Removal of Architectural or Transportation Barriers*

As you have seen throughout this chapter, expenditures that improve or prolong the life of property generally must be capitalized and the cost recovered through depreciation. You have already seen two special credits that can be claimed for expenditures that would otherwise have to be capitalized. There is one more important exception to this capitalization rule: You can elect to deduct the expenses of removing architectural or transportation barriers to the elderly and people with disabilities. The election is made simply by claiming the deduction on a timely filed tax return.

The maximum deduction in any one year is $15,000. If your expenditures for a removal project exceed this limit, you can deduct the first $15,000 of costs and capitalize (and then depreciate) the balance.

The dollar limit applies at both the partner and partnership levels. A partner must combine his or her distributive share of these expenditures from one partnership with any distributive share of such expenditures from any other partnership. The partner may allocate the $15,000 limit among his or her own expenditures and the partner's distributive share of partnership expenditures in any manner. If the allocation results in all or a portion of the partner's distributive share of a partnership's expenditures not being an allocable deduction, then the partnership can capitalize the unallowable portion.

While the regulations on applying the dollar limits at both the partner and partnership levels do not specify other pass-through entities, presumably the same rules that apply to partners and partnerships apply as well to shareholders and S corporations.

If the election is made to expense these expenditures, then no disabled access credit can be claimed for the same expenses.

**Example**

**A partner's distributive share of partnership expenditures (after application of the $15,000 limit at the partnership level) is $7,500. The partner also has a sole proprietorship that made $10,000 of expenditures. The partner can choose to allocate the $15,000 limitation as follows: $5,000 to his or her distributive share of the partnership's expenditures and $10,000 to individual expenditures. If the partner provides written proof of this allocation to the partnership, the partnership can then capitalize $2,500, the unused portion of the partner's distributive share of expenditures ($7,500 distributive share minus $5,000 allocated as a deduction).**

### *Qualifying Expenditures*

These are expenses that conform a facility or public transportation vehicle to certain standards that make them accessible to persons over the age of 65 or those with physical or mental disability or impairment (see Table 10.2). It does not include any expense for the construction or comprehensive renovation of a facility or public transportation vehicle or the normal replacement of depreciable property.

**TABLE 10.2** Guidance on Standards for the Elderly and People with Disabilities

| Type of Expense | Requirements |
|---|---|
| Grading | The ground should be graded to attain a level with a normal entrance to make the facility accessible to individuals with physical disabilities. |
| Walks | A public walk should be at least 48″ wide and have a gradient of no more than 5%.<br>A walkway should have a continuing common surface (not interrupted by steps or abrupt changes in level).<br>A walkway or driveway should have a nonslip surface. |
| Parking lots | At least 1 space that is accessible and proximate to the facility must be set aside and designated for the handicapped.<br>The space must be open to 1 side to allow wheelchair access.<br>For head-on parking, the space must be at least 12′ wide. |
| Ramps | A ramp should not have a slope greater than a 1″ rise in 12″.<br>There must be a handrail 32″ in height.<br>A ramp should have a nonslip surface.<br>A ramp should have a level surface at the top and bottom (if a door swings into the platform, the platform should be at least 5′ by 5′).<br>A ramp should have level platforms at least every 30′.<br>A curb ramp should be provided at every intersection (the ramp should be 4′ wide, with transition between 2 surfaces and a nonslip surface). |
| Entrances | A building should have at least 1 primary entrance wheelchair accessible and on a level accessible to an elevator. |
| Doors and doorways | A door should have an opening of at least 32″.<br>The floor inside and outside the doorway should be level for at least 51″.<br>The threshold should be level with the floor.<br>The door closer should not impair the use of the door by someone who is handicapped. |
| Stairs | Stairs should have handrails at least 32″ from the tread at the face of the riser.<br>Steps should not have risers exceeding 7″. |
| Floors | Floors should have a nonslip surface. |
| Toilet rooms | The rooms should provide wheelchair access. At least 1 stall should be 66″ wide by 60″ deep, with 32″ door space and handrails. |
| Water fountains | A water fountain or cooler should have up-front spouts and hand and foot controls.<br>A water fountain should not be in an alcove unless there is 36″ of space. |
| Public telephones | Each phone should be placed so the dial and headset can be reached by someone in a wheelchair.<br>Coin slots should not be more than 48″ from the floor.<br>Public phones should be equipped for those with hearing impairments. |
| Elevators | An elevator should be on entry levels of buildings and in all areas normally used.<br>Cab size should allow a wheelchair to turn.<br>The door opening should be at least 32″. |

**TABLE 10.2** *(Continued)*

| Type of Expense | Requirements |
|---|---|
| Controls | Switches and controls for all essential uses (light, heat, ventilation, windows, draperies, and fire alarms) should be within reach of a person in a wheelchair (no higher than 48″ from the floor). |
| Identification | Raised letters or numbers should be used to identify rooms (letters or numbers placed on the left or right of the door at a height of 54″ to 66″). |
| Warning signals | A visual beaming signal should be accompanied by an audible sound for the benefit of the blind. |
| Hazards | Hanging signs, ceiling lights, and similar objects and fixtures should be placed at a minimum height of 7′ (measured from the floor). |
| International | Wheelchair-accessible entrances should be identified with the accessibility symbol. |

### *Recordkeeping*

If you elect to deduct these expenditures, you must maintain records and documentation, including architectural plans and blueprints, contracts, and building permits to support your claims. How long these records should be kept is discussed in Chapter 3.

## Lists of Deductible Repairs and Capital Improvements

Over the years, various expenditures have come under review by the IRS and the courts. The following lists, one of deductible repairs and the other of improvements that must be capitalized, are based on actual cases and rulings. However, some previously classified improvements listed below may be currently deductible under safe harbor rules described earlier in this chapter.

**DEDUCTIBLE REPAIRS**

- Altering building for street-widening program
- Caulking seams
- Replacing compressor for air conditioner
- Replacing copper sheeting for cornice (blown off by wind)
- Relining basement walls and floors with cement
- Cleaning a restaurant canopy
- Cutting and filling cracks in storage tanks
- Tuck pointing and cleaning exterior brick walls
- Adding timbers to support walkway over basement
- Mending plaster walls and ceilings
- Painting walls and ceiling over basement
- Papering walls
- Patching a leaking roof
- Relocating steam pipes and radiators
- Resurfacing floors
- Repairing sidewalks

- Shoring up building foundation
- Replacing retaining walls
- Repairing gutters

**CAPITAL IMPROVEMENTS**

- Installing new doors
- Installing new windows
- Replacing a coal burner with an oil burner heating system
- Installing skylights
- Installing fire escapes
- Replacing a roof
- Adding new floor supports
- Replacing iron piping with brass piping in hot water system
- Raising, lowering, or building new floors
- Erecting permanent partitions
- Installing fire sprinklers
- Bricking up windows
- Installing an air-conditioning system
- Installing a ventilation system
- Rewiring or upgrading electrical service
- Replacing windows and doors
- Expanding a building (building an addition)
- Installing a burglar alarm system
- Blacktopping a driveway
- Improving a storefront
- Adding new plumbing fixtures
- Constructing a drainage system

## Energy Improvements

Usually, capital improvements to a building must be recovered through depreciation, as explained earlier in this chapter. However, certain energy improvements to commercial realty can be immediately deducted. For example, some of the cost of adding insulation to the walls and attic of a commercial building may be deductible.

### *Commercial Buildings*

The deduction applies to property installed in a building as part of the interior lighting system; heating, cooling, ventilation, and hot water systems; or the building envelope as part of a plan to reduce annual energy and power costs by 50% or more in comparison with a reference building meeting standards of the American Society of Heating, Refrigerating, and Air Conditioning Engineers and the Illuminating Engineering Society of North America in effect 2 years prior to construction.

The deduction is $1.80 per square foot for a 50% energy savings target or 60¢ per square foot for a 16⅔% energy savings target. The dollar amounts may be adjusted annually for inflation. A reduced deduction can be claimed in certain situations. The basis of the building must be reduced by the amount of any such deduction.

To claim the deduction, you must obtain certification for your improvements from a field inspection conducted by a licensed engineer or contractor.

### *Alternative Fuel Vehicle Refueling Property Credit*

If you install certain refueling property for your business, you may claim a credit of up to $30,000. Refueling property is property for the storage or dispensing of a clean-burning fuel or electricity into the fuel tank or battery of a motor vehicle propelled by such fuel or electricity. The original use of the property must begin with you.

Clean-burning fuel is any fuel with at least 85% of the volume consisting of ethanol, natural gas, compressed natural gas, liquefied natural gas, liquefied petroleum gas, or hydrogen. In addition, any mixture of biodiesel and diesel fuel, determined without regard to any use of kerosene and containing at least 20% biodiesel, qualifies as a clean fuel.

The credit is part of the general business credit (see Chapter 23). If you use the credit, you must reduce the basis of the property by the amount of the credit (i.e., you figure depreciation on the adjusted basis). You cannot claim the credit if you elect the Section 179 deduction or if the property is used outside the United States.

**Looking Ahead**

**The credit for alternative fuel vehicle refueling property expires at the end of 2021, but could be extended by.**

### *Other Business Energy Improvements*

There is an energy tax credit for a specified percentage of the basis of each qualified energy property placed in service. Qualified energy property includes solar property, geothermal property, qualified fuel cell property or stationary microturbine property, combined health and power system property, qualified small wind energy property, and geothermal heat pumps. For example, the credit is 26% of the basis (generally cost) of qualified small wind energy property used to generate electricity.

The basis of the property for purposes of depreciation must be reduced by the credit. The basis of the property is *not* reduced for energy property financed by subsidized energy financing or industrial development bonds.

## Where to Take Deductions

### *Self-Employed*

Repair costs are deductible on Schedule C. This schedule contains a line specifically for repairs and maintenance. Farmers who are self-employed deduct repair costs on Schedule F.

### Partnerships and LLCs

Repair costs are trade or business expenses that are taken into account in determining the profit (or loss) of the partnership or LLC on Form 1065. There is a specific line for deducting repair and maintenance costs. They are not separately stated items passed through to partners and members. Therefore, partners and members in LLCs report their net income or loss from the business on Schedule E; they do not deduct repair costs on their individual tax returns.

An exception applies to expenditures for the removal of architectural and transportation barriers to the elderly and individuals with disabilities that are elected to be expensed. These items must be separately stated, since dollar limits apply at both the owner and entity levels.

### S Corporations

Repair costs are trade or business expenses that are taken into account in determining the profit (or loss) of the S corporation on Form 1120-S. There is a specific line for deducting repair and maintenance costs. They are not separately stated items passed through to shareholders. Therefore, shareholders report their net income or loss from the business on Schedule E; they do not deduct repair costs on their individual tax returns.

An exception applies to expenditures for the removal of architectural and transportation barriers to the elderly and individuals with disabilities that are elected to be expensed. These items must be separately stated, since dollar limits apply at both the owner and entity levels.

### C Corporations

Repair costs are trade or business expenses that are taken into account in determining the profit (or loss) of the C corporation on Form 1120. This form contains a separate line for deducting repairs and maintenance costs. Shareholders do not report any income (or loss) from the corporation.

### Rehabilitation Credit for All Taxpayers

This credit is computed on Form 3468, *Investment Tax Credit*. It is part of the general business credit and is subject to the limitations on the general business credit (explained in Chapter 23), which is computed on Form 3800, *General Business Credit*, filed with Form 1040 or 1040-SR and Form 1120. (Partners and S corporation shareholders figure the general business credit limitation on their individual returns.)

### Disabled Access Tax Credit for All Taxpayers

This credit is computed on Form 8826, *Disabled Access Credit*. It is part of the general business credit and is subject to the limitations on the general business credit, which is computed on Form 3800, *General Business Credit*, filed with Forms 1040 or 1040-SR and 1120. (Partners and S corporation shareholders figure the general business credit limitation on their individual returns.)

### Energy Credit for All Taxpayers

The energy credit, which is part of the investment credit, is claimed in Part II of Form 3468, *Investment Credit*. It is part of the general business credit, which is computed on Form 3800, *General Business Credit*, filed with Forms 1040 or 1040-SR and 1120. (Partner and S corporation shareholders figure the general business credit limitation on their individual returns.)

### *Small Building Safe Harbor Election for All Taxpayers*

If you are eligible for this safe harbor and want to elect it, you must attach your own statement to your return each year you want the election to apply. The statement must include:

- Your name
- Your address
- Your EIN
- A description of the property and its unadjusted basis
- A description of the costs for the year
- A statement that you qualify for the safe harbor. Make reference to Reg. §1.263(a)-3(h)(1).

CHAPTER 11

# Bad Debts


| | | | |
|---|---|---|---|
| Bad Debts in General | 225 | Guarantees That Result in Bad Debts | 231 |
| Collection of Bad Debts | 228 | Special Rules for Accrual Taxpayers | 232 |
| Business versus Nonbusiness Bad Debts | 228 | Reporting Bad Debts on the Tax Return | 232 |
| Loans by Shareholder-Employees | 229 | Collection Strategies | 233 |


No one thinks that the loans they make to others will go unpaid; otherwise, such loans would not be made in the first place. You never expect that the check you've accepted as payment for the goods or services you've provided will bounce or that you'll have a chargeback for a credit card payment, but unfortunately, these are common occurrences in business. No matter how careful you are, you may get stiffed! This may be especially true as a result of the economic impact of COVID-19. If, in the course of your business, you lend money or extend credit for your goods and services but fail to receive payment, you can take some comfort in the tax treatment for these transactions gone sour. You may be able to deduct your loss as a bad debt.

For further information about deducting bad debts, see IRS Publication 535, *Business Expenses*.

## Bad Debts in General

If you cannot collect money that is owed to you in your business, your loss may be deductible. You must prove 3 factors to establish a bad debt:

1. The debtor-creditor relationship
2. Worthlessness
3. Loss

### The Debtor-Creditor Relationship

You must prove that there is a *debtor-creditor relationship*. This means that there is a legal obligation on the part of the debtor to pay to the creditor (you) a fixed or determinable sum of money. The legal obligation can arise from making a loan or selling goods or services.

If you lend money to a friend or relative, the relationship between you and the borrower is not always clear. You may, for example, lend the money with the expectation of receiving repayment but later forgive some or all of the payments. This forgiveness with a friend or relative transforms what might have been a bad debt into a gift. The law does not bar loans between relatives or friends, but be aware that the IRS gives special scrutiny to loans involving related parties.

The simplest way to prove a debtor-creditor relationship is to have a written note evidencing the loan. The note should state the following terms:

- The amount of the loan
- A stated rate of interest
- A fixed maturity date
- A repayment schedule

If you advance wages to your employee, you are effectively making a loan. While it's not usual to put anything in writing, what if the employee fails to work the required amount to earn the advance? In such a case, you have a bad debt.

**Example**

**You advance $1,000 to an employee who quits two days later, having only worked enough to earn $320 and you cannot collect the balance (e.g., the employee's whereabouts are unknown). Your bad debt is $680.**

In making advances to an employee, make sure any repayment schedule does not run afoul of minimum wage rules (check with your state labor department). Also, take employment taxes into account when the work is performed, not when the advances are made.

If you have a corporation to which you lend money, establishing the debtor-creditor relationship is crucial. Unless you can show that an advance to the corporation is intended to be a loan, it will be treated as a contribution to the capital of the corporation (which is not deductible).

Over the years, the courts have developed a number of factors used to determine whether the funds given by a shareholder to a corporation are a loan or a contribution to capital:

1. The names given to the documents that would be evidence of the purported loans;
2. The presence or absence of a fixed maturity date;
3. The likely source of repayment;
4. The right to enforce payments;
5. Participation in management as a result of the advances;
6. Subordination of the purported loans to the loans of the corporation's creditors;
7. The intent of the parties;
8. Identity of interest between creditor and stockholder;

9. The ability of the corporation to obtain financing from outside sources;
10. Thinness of capital structure in relation to debt;
11. Use to which the funds were put;
12. The failure of the corporation to repay; and
13. The risk involved in making the transfers.

**Example**

**A shareholder advanced funds to his corporation, which he claimed were loans. The corporation made payments to him when it was operating at a loss. This factor strongly supported a debtor-creditor relationship, said the Tax Court.**

If your corporation lends money to others, it is advisable to include this arrangement in the corporate minutes (e.g., a corporate resolution authorizing the loan and spelling out the loan terms) as well as to carry the loan on the corporation's books.

### *Worthlessness*

You must also show that the debt has become *worthless* and will remain that way. You must be able to show that you took reasonable steps to collect the debt. It is not necessary that you actually go to court to collect the debt if you can show that a judgment would remain uncollectible. If the borrower is in bankruptcy, this is a very good indication that the debt is worthless, at least in part.

For business bad debts, the IRS Chief Counsel has said that amounts must be charged off the company's books to show that the business has abandoned hopes of a recovery. Merely reducing a reserve account is not sufficient for this purpose.

Generally, the debt is considered to be worthless as of the settlement date of the bankruptcy action, but facts can show that it was worthless before this time. If you use a collection agency to attempt collection of outstanding accounts receivable or other amounts owed to you and you agree to pay the agency a percentage of what is collected, you can immediately deduct that percentage of the outstanding amount as a bad debt; your agreement establishes that percentage will never be collected by you.

**Example**

**You have an open accounts receivable of $1,000. After 120 days, you turn it over to a collection agency that charges 30% of what it collects. At the point of your agreement with the agency, you are certain you will never recoup at least $300 of the outstanding amount (the fee that would be paid to the agency if it collects 100% of the debt) and can now deduct that amount.**

**You may, in fact, deduct more if the agency collects less than the full amount of the debt. For example, if it collects $500 of the $1,000 outstanding, it is entitled to a $150 fee, so you recoup only $350 of the $1,000. Result: You deduct a total of $650 ($300 of which you deducted when the agreement with the agency was made).**

Whether a loan is fully or only partially worthless affects whether you can claim a deduction for the loss. Business bad debts are deductible whether they are fully or partially worthless. If the loss is a nonbusiness bad debt, it is deductible only if the debt is fully worthless. No partial deduction is allowed for nonbusiness bad debts. The distinction between business and nonbusiness bad debts is explained later in this chapter.

### *Loss*

You must show that you sustained a *loss* because of the debt. A loss results when an amount has been included in income but the income is never received. This might happen, for example, where an accrual method taxpayer accrues income but later fails to collect it. If you sell goods on credit and fail to receive payment, you sustain an economic loss whether you are on the accrual method or the cash method of accounting.

If you are on the cash basis and extend services but fail to collect, you *cannot* claim a bad debt deduction. You are not considered to have an economic loss even though you might argue that you put in your time and effort and were not justly compensated.

**Example**

**A cash basis accountant prepares an individual's tax return. The bill comes to $400. The accountant never receives payment. She cannot deduct the $400. The accountant never reported the $400 as income, so she is not considered to have suffered an economic loss, even though she extended services and invested her time and energy.**

If you make payments to a supplier for future shipments and the supplier fails to deliver because of insolvency, you have a business bad debt, regardless of your method of accounting. Again, you have an economic loss (the money you advanced to the supplier) that gives rise to the bad debt deduction.

## Collection of Bad Debts

Suppose you fully investigated a debt, made every effort to collect it, and finally concluded it was worthless. You claim a deduction; then, lo and behold, the debtor repays you a year or two later. You need not go back and amend your return to remove the bad debt deduction. Instead, include the recovery of the bad debt in income in the year you receive payment.

## Business versus Nonbusiness Bad Debts

*Business bad debts,* as the term implies, arise in connection with a business. *Nonbusiness bad debts* are all other debts; they can arise in either a personal or investment context.

Business bad debts are deductible as ordinary losses. A C corporation's debts are always business bad debts. Nonbusiness bad debts are deductible by an individual only as short-term capital losses. As such, they are deductible only to offset your capital gains, and then up to $3,000 of ordinary income.

Business bad debts are deductible if partially or wholly worthless. Nonbusiness bad debts must be wholly worthless to be deductible.

### *Business Bad Debts*

Business bad debts are treated as ordinary losses that offset ordinary business income. To be treated as a business bad debt, the debt must be closely related to the activity of the business. There must have been a business reason for entering into the debtor-creditor relationship.

Business bad debts typically arise from credit sales to customers. They can also be the result of loans to suppliers, customers, employees, or distributors. Credit sales are generally reported on the books of the business as accounts receivable. Loans to suppliers, customers, employees, or distributors generally are reported on the books of the business as notes receivable. When accounts receivable or notes receivable become uncollectible, this results in a business bad debt.

### *Valuing a Bad Debt*

Accounts receivable and notes receivable generally are carried on the books at fair market value (FMV). Thus, when they go bad, they are deductible at FMV. This is so even where that value is less than the face value of the obligations.

### *Impact of Loans with Your Business or Associates*

If you lend money to your corporation and the corporation later defaults, you cannot claim a bad debt deduction unless it was a true loan. If, as explained earlier, the advance to the corporation was in fact a contribution to its capital, then you cannot claim a bad debt deduction.

If you have a partnership that breaks up and there is money owing from the partnership, you may be forced to make payments if your partner or partners do not. This payment may be more than your share of the partnership's debts. In this case, you can claim a bad debt deduction if your partner or partners were insolvent and you were required to pay their share.

If you go out of business but still try to collect outstanding amounts owed to you, potential bad debt deductions are not lost. You can still claim them as business bad debts if the debts become worthless after you go out of business.

**Example**

**An attorney lent money to a friend and is later unable to collect despite a number of attempts. Since the loan had nothing to do with the attorney's business, the failure to collect results in a nonbusiness bad debt; this assumes the debt is wholly worthless.**

### *Nonbusiness Bad Debts*

Loans made to protect investments or for personal reasons give rise to nonbusiness bad debts when they go bad.

## Loans by Shareholder-Employees

When a shareholder who is also an employee of a corporation lends the corporation money but fails to receive repayment, or guarantees corporate debt and is called upon to make good on the guarantee, it is not always clear whether the resulting debt is a business bad debt or a nonbusiness bad debt.

A business bad debt must arise in the context of a business. A shareholder who lends money to the corporation is doing so to protect his or her investment. An employee who lends money to his or her corporation is doing so to protect his or her business of being an employee. In this instance, employment is treated as a business. When an individual is both a shareholder and an employee, which status governs?

According to the U.S. Supreme Court, the *dominant motive* for making the loan to the corporation is what makes a debt a business or nonbusiness bad debt. Where the dominant motive is to protect one's investment, then the bad debt is treated as a nonbusiness bad debt. Where the dominant motive is to protect one's employment status to ensure continued receipt of salary, then the bad debt is treated as a business bad debt. In making this assessment, several factors are taken into account:

- *The size of your investment in the corporation*. If your investment is substantial, it indicates that a bad debt might be the result of a desire to protect this investment.
- *The size of your after-tax salary from the corporation*. If your salary is minimal, this indicates that your real interest may be protecting your investment rather than your salary.
- *Other sources of income available to you*. If the salary is an important source of income to you, then the debt may have been incurred to protect the income. Where the investment is large compared to the salary received and there are other sources of income available, this tends to support the view that the dominant motive was the protection of investment. On the other hand, where the investment is small compared with the salary received and there are no or only insubstantial other sources of income, then the dominant motive may be viewed as protection of salary.

A person's subjective intention in making a loan or guarantee is a factor to be considered, but it is not controlling. Rather, motive is deduced from all the facts and circumstances surrounding the making of the loan or guarantee.

**Example**

**A retired engineer formed a company of which he was the principal shareholder and chief executive officer (CEO). When the company experienced cash flow problems, he lent it money and gave personal guarantees for third-party loans to the company. When the company went under, he lost $450,000 (in addition to his investment in the company). This $450,000 comprised the loans to the company and the guarantees he had to make good on when the company could not. He claimed a business bad debt deduction, which an appellate court allowed. He was a retiree who wanted to continue to work. In view of his age and background, forming his own company was the way to optimal employment. His guarantees in this case far exceeded his initial investment, which was minimal. Therefore his dominant motive in making the loans and guarantees was to protect his employment.**

**Example**

**After being terminated from her job as president of a company and spending a year looking for another job, she formed her own company. She did not take salary for the first year; her salary thereafter was between $30,000 and $50,000. Her outside income was substantially more (over $1 million in the year she drew no salary). She guaranteed more than $1 million of loans to the company, which she was called on to repay. But here her bad debt was treated as a nonbusiness bad debt. Her dominant motive was protection of her investment. She could not prove that her dominant motive was protection of salary, since it is not reasonable to believe someone would guarantee over $1 million in loans to protect a salary of $30,000.**

**WHICH IS BETTER?**

Which position should an owner-employee argue in favor of? Given the tax rules in effect for 2018 through 2025, it's better to try for a nonbusiness bad debt. The reason: Nonbusiness bad debts are treated as short-term capital losses, a deduction for which may be limited in the current year, but unused amounts can be carried forward indefinitely. In contrast, business bad debts of an owner-employee are treated as a business deduction, which for a shareholder-employee means a business deduction that is treated as a miscellaneous itemized deduction, which can't be claimed in 2018 through 2025.

## Guarantees That Result in Bad Debts

Banks and other lending institutions are well aware of the limitation on personal liability of owners in corporations. If corporations are in their infancy and do not have significant assets to use as collateral for loans, shareholders are usually asked to extend their personal guarantees to induce the banks or other lending institutions to advance funds to the corporations. An owner with a 20% or greater ownership interest in the business usually must give a personal guarantee when obtaining an SBA loan (which is a loan guaranteed by the Small Business Administration).

If you guarantee, endorse, or indemnify someone else's loan made to your business and are then called on to make good on your guarantee, endorsement, or indemnity, how do you treat this payment? It depends on your motivation for making the guarantee.

If the dominant motive for making the guarantee was proximately related to your business (e.g., you guaranteed a loan to the corporation for which you work), then you claim a business bad debt. If the dominant motive for making the guarantee was to protect an investment, you claim a nonbusiness bad debt.

If the guarantee was made for a friend or relative without the receipt of consideration, no bad debt deduction can be claimed. The reason: You did not enter into the arrangement for profit or to protect an investment.

If there is more than one guarantor but only one co-guarantor pays the debt, the co-guarantor who pays the debt can claim only his or her proportional share of the obligation unless it can be proved that the other guarantors were unable to pay.

**Example**

**Three equal shareholders of Corporation X guarantee a bank loan made to the corporation. X defaults, and one of the shareholders pays off the entire loan. That shareholder can deduct only one-third of the debt unless he can prove that the other two shareholders were unable to make any payment.**

If you, as guarantor, give your own note to substitute or replace the note of the party for whom you became the guarantor, you cannot claim a bad debt deduction at that time. The deduction arises only when and to the extent you make payments on the notes.

When personally guaranteeing a business debt, take into account the impact on your personal credit score. Merely making the guarantee likely will not impact your score. However, if you're called upon to make good on your guarantee and you do not make the required payments, your personal credit score will suffer.

### *When to Claim the Deduction*

In general, a bad debt deduction in the case of a guarantee is claimed for the year in which payment is made by the guarantor. Suppose you guarantee a debt but have the right of subrogation or other right against the debtor to recoup your outlays. In this case, you claim your bad debt deduction only when the right against the debtor becomes worthless.

## Special Rules for Accrual Taxpayers

All taxpayers (other than certain financial institutions) use the *specific charge-off method* to account for bad debts. Under this method, business bad debts are deducted when and to the extent that they arise.

### *Nonaccrual-Experience Method*

Taxpayers on the accrual basis have an alternative way to account for bad debts: the nonaccrual-experience (NAE) method. Income that is not expected to be collected need not be accrued. If, based on prior experience, it is determined that certain receivables will not be collected, then they need not be included in gross income for the year. Since income is not taken into account, there is no need to then claim a bad debt deduction.

The nonaccrual-experience method applies only to accounts receivable for performing services if in the fields of health, law, engineering, architecture, accounting, actuarial science, performing arts, or consulting or whose business's average annual gross receipts for the 3 prior years is not more than $5 million. It cannot be used for amounts owed from activities such as lending money, selling goods, or acquiring receivables or the right to receive payments. Nor can this method be used if interest or penalties are charged on late payments. However, merely offering a discount for early payment is not treated as charging interest or a late penalty if the full amount is accrued as gross income at the time the services are provided and the discount for early payment is treated as an adjustment to gross income in the year of payment.

Under an IRS-created safe harbor restricted to businesses with an applicable financial statement (e.g., an audited financial statement), you can figure the uncollectible amount by multiplying the portion of the year-end allowance for doubtful accounts by 95%. This is the amount that you do not have to accrue as income for the year. Because most small businesses don't have an applicable financial statement, they cannot use this safe harbor.

This method can be used under either a separate receivable system or a periodic system. The separate receivable system applies the nonaccrual-experience method separately to each account receivable; the periodic system applies it to the total of the qualified accounts receivable at the end of the year. This is a highly technical accounting rule that should be discussed with an experienced accountant. The nonaccrual-experience method is explained more fully in IRS Publication 535, *Business Expenses*.

## Reporting Bad Debts on the Tax Return

If you want to claim a bad debt deduction on your return, you must do more than simply enter your loss. You also must attach a statement to your return explaining each element of the bad debt. (There is no special IRS form required for making this statement.) These elements include:

- A description of the debt
- The name of the debtor
- Your family or business relationship to the debtor

- The due date of the loan
- Your efforts to collect the debt
- How you decided the debt became worthless

This reporting requirement applies only to individuals who claim bad debts on Schedule C, E, or F. Partnerships, LLCs, S corporations, and C corporations need not attach a statement to their returns explaining their bad debt deductions.

The loss is claimed on the return for the year in which the debt becomes worthless (or partially worthless, where applicable). This is often not known by the end of that particular year. Fortunately, there is a 7-year period in which to amend an old return to claim a bad debt.

**Example**

**In 2016, Corporation X (a C corporation on the accrual basis) provided goods and services to Corporation Y. Partial payment was made in 2016, but the balance due in 2017 was never paid. Due to poor bookkeeping, X failed to claim a bad debt deduction for this nonpayment. X has until March 15, 2024, 7 years from the due date of its 2016 return, to file an amended return and claim the bad debt deduction.**

## Collection Strategies

Although the tax law may provide some help in alleviating the financial loss of bad debts, a better approach is to avoid or limit the loss by taking action.

### *Review Credit Policies*

To avoid bad debts, consider whether to eliminate or modify your credit policy. The SBA has a Toolkit covering the benefits of using electronic payments such as Automated Clearing House (ACH) credits and debits, wire transfers, and credit and debit cards at https://fedpaymentsimprovement.org/wp-content/uploads/small-business-toolkit.pdf?utm_medium=email&utm_source=govdelivery. For example, instead of billing customers when work is completed or goods are shipped, have customers charge the payments to a credit card that you accept.

If, because of industry policy or personal preference, you want to continue to extend credit to customers, consider:

- *Doing credit checks on customers*. When extending credit for B2C, check a consumer's credit through one of the 3 major credit bureaus: Equifax (www.equifax.com), Experian (www.experian.com), and TransUnion (www.transunion.com). You need the permission of the consumer to do this. For B2B, check a business's credit at D&B (https://www.dnb.com/) and Experian (https://www.experian.com/small-business/). You do not need the permission of the business customer do to this.
- *Limiting credit to customers*. You do not have to extend the same terms to all customers.
- *Billing wisely*. Instead of billing at the completion of a job, bill at completion points along the way. Bill promptly (don't wait until the end of the month to send invoices). Send bills electronically to make sure they arrive promptly.

### Review Collections Policies

The longer an account receivable goes unpaid, the less likely it becomes that you will receive full, or even *any,* payment. Make sure to stay on top of collections by monitoring receivables on a regular basis. Contact delinquent accounts to press for collections (work out payment terms where applicable). Observe debt collection practice rules under the Fair Debt Collection Practices Act (go to https://www.ftc.gov for more information).

If you are having difficulty collecting what is owed to you, consider:

- *Working with a collection agency*. The agency receives a fee, usually equal to a percentage of what is collected; you receive the balance. You can deduct the fee you pay to the agency.
- *Engaging an attorney*. The attorney can seek to collect on your behalf. Determine in advance what payment the attorney will receive (hourly, a percentage of collection, etc.). You can deduct the attorney's fee.
- *Taking customers to small claims court*. Determine your legal rights and whether you can bring your claim to small claims court. You can deduct any court costs you pay; you cannot deduct any amount for your time and effort.

### Strategies When Customers Go Bankrupt

If a customer files for bankruptcy, understand your options. Bankruptcy means you can't continue collection activities. Depending on the amount of money owed to you, you may want to file a proof of claim with the bankruptcy court (you'll get the details when you receive a bankruptcy notice) and pursue collection. Expect in most cases to collect only pennies on the dollars you're owed.

## Where to Deduct Bad Debts

### Employees

Nonbusiness bad debts are deducted on Form 8949, *Sales and Other Dispositions of Capital Assets*, and then on Schedule D of Form 1040 or 1040-SR as a short-term capital loss. On this schedule, enter the amount of the bad debt and Statement Attached. Then include on an accompanying statement more information about the bad debt, as explained earlier.

Nonbusiness bad debts are deductible only to the extent of an individual's capital gains, plus up to $3,000 of ordinary income. These capital loss limits are taken into account when completing Schedule D. Remember that unused capital losses can be carried forward indefinitely and used against future capital gains and up to $3,000 of ordinary income each year.

Employees, including corporate shareholder-employees, cannot deduct business bad debts in 2018 through 2025 because of the suspension of miscellaneous itemized deductions subject to the 2%-of-AGI floor on Schedule A of Form 1040 or 1040-SR.

### Self-Employed

Business bad debts are deducted from business income on Schedule C as "Other Expenses" (or Schedule F in the case of farming operations). Schedule C does not contain a specific line for claiming bad debts from sales or services. Be sure to attach a statement to the return explaining the bad debts.

Nonbusiness bad debts are reported as short-term capital losses on Form 8949 and Schedule D. Self-employed persons report nonbusiness bad debts in the same way as employees.

### Partnerships and LLCs

Partnerships and LLCs can deduct business bad debts on their return. Form 1065 contains a specific line for claiming bad debts. These bad debts reduce the partnerships' or LLCs' trade or business income. They are not passed through as separate items to partners or LLC members. Partnerships and LLCs need not attach a statement to the return explaining the bad debts.

To date there have been no cases or rulings in which bad debts of partnerships or LLCs have been treated as nonbusiness bad debts. However, should such debts occur, see the treatment of nonbusiness bad debts for S corporations in the section that follows.

### S Corporations

Bad debts are usually business bad debts. Business bad debts are not separately stated items passed through separately to shareholders. Instead, they serve to reduce the amount of business income or loss that passes through to shareholders. They are entered on Form 1120-S on the line specifically for bad debts. S corporations need not attach a statement to the return explaining the bad debts.

It should be noted that where the loss is considered a nonbusiness bad debt, it must be separately stated on Schedule K-1 and passed through to shareholders. In this way, the short-term capital loss for the shareholder is subject to that shareholder's capital loss limits.

### C Corporations

Bad debts are always business bad debts in the case of C corporations. They are reported on Form 1120 on the specific line provided for bad debts. Corporations need not attach a statement to the return explaining the bad debts.

CHAPTER 12

# Rents


| | |
|---|---|
| Deducting Rent Payments in General | 236 |
| Rent for Employee Parking | 239 |
| The Cost of Acquiring, Modifying, or Canceling a Lease | 240 |
| Improvements You Make to Leased Property | 241 |
| Rental of a Portion of Your Home for Business | 242 |
| Leasing a Car | 242 |
| Leveraged Leases | 243 |


Renting or leasing realty or equipment gives you the use of the property without owning it. From a financial standpoint, it might make more sense to rent than to buy property and equipment because renting may require a smaller cash outlay than buying. Also, the business may not as yet have established sufficient credit to make large purchases but can still gain the use of the property or equipment through renting. If you pay rent to use office space, a store, or other property for your business, or you pay to lease business equipment, you generally can deduct your outlays.

Sale-leasebacks are discussed in Chapter 6.

## Deducting Rent Payments in General

If you pay to use property for business that you do not own, the payments are *rent*. Leases may take various forms. For example, with a net lease, the tenant pays for the use of the space as well as costs associated with operating the property, such as taxes, property insurance, utilities, sewer and water, and trash collection. Regardless of the form of the lease, the payments are all considered rents (even if they may cover taxes). They may also be called *lease payments*. Rents paid for property used in a business are deductible business expenses. These include obligations you pay on behalf of your landlord. For example, if you are required by the terms of your lease to pay real estate taxes on the property, you can deduct these taxes as part of your rent payments. The rent payments are deductible even if made with funds from a PPP loan that's been forgiven.

The rents must be reasonable in amount. The issue of reasonableness generally does not arise where you and the landlord are at arm's length. However, the issue does come up when you and the landlord are related parties, such as family members or related companies. Rent paid to a related party is treated as reasonable if it is the same rent that would be paid to an unrelated party. A percentage rental is also considered reasonable if the rent paid is reasonable.

If the rent payments entitle you to receive equity in or title to the property at the end of some term, the payments are not rent. They may, however, be deductible in part as depreciation (see Chapter 14).

## Rent to Your Corporation

If you rent property to your corporation, the corporation can claim a rental expense deduction, assuming the rents are reasonable. However, you cannot treat the rents as passive income that you could use to offset your losses from other passive activities. A self-rental rule under the passive activity loss rules specifically prohibits you from arranging this type of rental for tax benefit. More specifically, if the self-rental rule applies, then the rental income that would otherwise be treated as passive income is recharacterized as non-passive income.

If you rent a portion of your home to your employer, see Chapter 18.

## Rent with an Option to Buy

Sometimes it is not clear whether payments are made to lease or purchase property. There are a number of factors used to make such a determination.

### NATURE OF THE DOCUMENT

If you have a lease, payments made pursuant to the lease generally are treated as rents. If you have a conditional sales contract, payments made pursuant to the lease are nondeductible purchase payments. A document is treated as a conditional sales contract if it provides that you will acquire title to or equity in the property upon completing a certain number or amount of payments.

### INTENT OF THE PARTIES

How the parties view the transaction affects whether it is a lease or a conditional sales contract. *Intent* can be inferred from certain objective factors. A conditional sales contract exists if any of the following are found:

- The agreement applies part of each payment toward an equity interest.
- The agreement provides for the transfer of title after payment of a stated amount.
- The amount of the payment to use the property for a short time is a large part of the amount paid to get title to the property.
- The payments exceed the current fair rental value of the property (based on comparisons with other similar properties).
- There is an option to buy the property at a nominal price as compared with the property's value at the time the option can be exercised.
- There is an option to buy the property at a nominal price as compared with the total amount required to be paid under the agreement.
- The agreement designates a part of the payments as interest or in some way makes part of the payments easily recognizable as interest.

**Example**

**You lease an office building for a period of 2 years. The lease agreement provides that at the end of that term you have the option of buying the property and all of the payments made to date will be applied toward the purchase price. In this case, your payments probably would be viewed as payments to purchase rather than payments to lease the property.**

### *Advance Rents*

Generally, rents are deductible in the year in which they are paid or accrued. What happens if you pay rent in advance? The answer depends on your method of accounting. If you are on the accrual basis, prepaid rent must be capitalized (it cannot be deducted at the time of payment).

**Example**

**X Corporation, an accrual basis taxpayer, leases office space from Y Corporation at a monthly rental rate of $2,000. On August 1, 2021, X prepays its office rent expense for the first 6 months of 2022 in the amount of $12,000. Because economic performance with respect to X's prepayment of rent does not occur until 2022, X's prepaid rent is not incurred in 2021 and therefore is not properly taken into account in 2021.**

If you are on the cash basis, prepaid rent can be immediately deducted provided that prepayments do not extend beyond 12 months.

**Example**

**X Corporation uses the cash method of accounting and pays Y Corporation $12,000 on August 1, 2021, to cover rent for the first 6 months of 2022. With the 12-month rule, the $12,000 payment is deductible in 2021 because the rights or benefits attributable to X's prepayment of its rent do not extend beyond December 31, 2022.**

Security deposits generally are not deductible when paid because the landlord is usually obligated to refund them if the terms of the lease are met. However, if the landlord keeps some or all of the deposit (e.g., because you failed to live up to the terms of the lease), you can then deduct such amount as rent.

### *Gift-Leasebacks*

If you own property that you have already depreciated, you may want to create a tax deduction for your business by entering into a *gift-leaseback* transaction. (Sale-leasebacks are discussed in Chapter 6.) Typically, the property is gifted to your spouse or children, to whom you then pay rent. In the past, this type of arrangement was more popular, but the passive loss rules put a damper on deducting losses created by these arrangements. If you still want to shift income to your children when the "kiddie tax" is not an issue (who presumably are in a lower tax bracket than you) while getting a tax deduction for your business, be sure that you meet these 3 requirements:

1. You do not retain control over the property after the gift is given.
2. The leaseback is in writing, and the rent charged is reasonable.
3. There must be a business purpose for the leaseback. (For example, where a doctor transferred the property in which his practice was located to his children in fear of malpractice suits, this was a valid business reason for leasing rather than owning the property.)

There are other factors to consider before entering into a gift-leaseback. Consider the impact of the kiddie tax if your children are subject to it. It is strongly suggested that you consult with a tax adviser before giving business property to your children and then leasing it back for use in your business.

### *Miscellaneous Rentals*

Some payments for the use of property that you may not otherwise think of as rentals but that may be required by your business include safety deposit box rental fees and post office box rental fees.

## Rent for Employee Parking

If, as part of your rent, you pay for employee parking spots, you cannot deduct the portion of your monthly payments allocable to this expense. Regulations provide a general rule plus 3 simplified methods for figuring what part of rent is or is not deductible. Costs related to providing parking for the general public are deductible (even if employees use them).

The general rule is a 4-step process for determining the disallowed amount for employee parking and if you use it, then it is considered to be reasonable. The steps vary depending on whether the spots are reserved for employees because no deduction can be claimed with respect to any reserved employee spaces.

- Step 1: Calculate the disallowance for reserved employee spots during peak demand
- Step 2: Determine the primary use of remaining spots (the "primary use test")
- Step 3: Calculate the allowance for reserved nonemployee spots (including spaces reserved for drivers with disabilities, whether or not employees)
- Step 4: Determine remaining use and allocable expenses if there is any remaining parking expense

**Example 1**

**An accounting firm leases a parking lot adjacent to its office building and incurs $10,000 in total parking expenses related to the lease payments. The lot has 100 spots used by employees and clients. Parking is not provided to the general public. About 60 employees use non-reserved spots during normal business hours.**

**Step 1: Because there are no reserved spots, there is no amount allocated to reserved employee spots.**

**Step 2: 60% of the lot is used by employees (60/100 = 60%).**

**Step 3: Because none of the spots are reserved for nonemployees, there is no amount allocated to nonemployee spots.**

**Step 4: The firm must reasonably determine the expenses allocable to employee parking. Because 60% of the parking spots are used by employees, a reasonable allocation would be that $6,000 of the total $10,000 cost is nondeductible.**

**Example 2**

**Same as Example 1 except that one part of the lot is restricted for employee parking ("reserved parking").**

**Step 1: Because there are 60 reserved spots out of the total 100 spots, $6,000 (60/100 spots x $10,000 = $6,000).**

**Step 2: The primary use of remaining spots is for public parking so there is no disallowance for the remaining $4,000**

**Step 3: There is nothing to figure here**

**Step 4: There is nothing to figure here**

In addition to this general rule, there are 3 simplified methods:

- *Qualified parking limit methodology*. Figure the disallowance of the deduction for employee free parking by multiplying the total number of spaces used by employees during peak hours or the total number of employees' monthly exclusion.
- *Primary use methodology*. This follows a 4-step method that differs slightly from the general method above.
- *Cost per space methodology*. Figure the disallowance by multiplying the cost per square space by the total number of available parking spaces used by employees during peak demand period.

## The Cost of Acquiring, Modifying, or Canceling a Lease

### *The Cost of Acquiring a Lease*

When you pay a premium to obtain immediate possession under a lease that does not extend beyond the tax year, the premium is deductible in full for the current year. Where the premium relates to a long-term lease, the cost of the premium is deductible over the term of the lease. The same amortization rule applies to commissions, bonuses, and other fees paid to obtain a lease on property you use in your business.

What is the term of the lease for purposes of deducting lease acquisition premiums when the lease contains renewal options? The tax law provides a complicated method for making this determination. The term of the lease for amortization purposes includes all renewal option periods if less than 75% of the cost is attributable to the term of the lease remaining on the purchase date. Do not include any period for which the lease may be renewed, extended, or continued under an option exercisable by you, the lessee, in determining the term of the lease remaining on the purchase date.

**Example**

**You pay $10,000 to acquire a lease with 20 years remaining on it. The lease has 2 options to renew, for 5 years each. Of the $10,000, $7,000 is paid for the original lease and $3,000 for the renewal options. Since $7,000 is less than 75% of the total cost, you must amortize $10,000 over 30 years (the lease term plus the 2 renewal option periods).**

**Example**

**The circumstances are the same as in the previous example, except that $8,000 is allocable to the original lease. Since this is not less than 75% of the total cost, the entire $10,000 can be amortized over the original lease term of 20 years.**

### *The Cost of Modifying a Lease*

If you pay an additional rent to change a lease provision, you amortize this additional payment over the remaining term of the lease.

### *The Cost of Canceling a Lease*

If you pay to get out of your lease before the end of its term, the cost generally is deductible in full in the year of payment. However, where a new lease is obtained, the cost of canceling the lease must be capitalized if the cancellation and new lease are viewed as part of the same transaction.

**Example**

**A company leased a computer system for 5 years. To upgrade its system, the company canceled the original lease and entered into a new one with the same lessor. Because the termination of the old lease was conditioned on obtaining a new lease, the cost of termination had to be capitalized (i.e., added to the cost of the new lease and deducted ratably over the term of the new lease).**

## Improvements You Make to Leased Property

If you put up a building on leased property or make other permanent improvements to leased property, you can depreciate the cost of the improvements using Modified Accelerated Cost Recovery System (MACRS) depreciation. (For a further discussion of depreciation, see Chapter 14.) Generally, the improvements are depreciated over their recovery period, a time fixed by law. They are not depreciated over the remaining term of the lease. However, special rules may allow for much faster write-offs (mentioned later in this chapter and discussed in Chapter 10).

**Example**

**You construct a building on land you lease. The recovery period of the building is 39 years. When the building construction is completed, there are 35 years remaining on the lease. You depreciate the building over its recovery period of 39 years, not over the 35 years remaining on the lease.**

If you acquire a lease through an assignment and the lessee has made improvements to the property, the amount you pay for the assignment is a capital investment. Where the rental value of the leased land has increased since the beginning of the lease, part of the capital investment is for the increase in that value; the balance is for your investment in the permanent improvements. You amortize the part of the increased rental value of the leased land; you depreciate the part of the investment related to the improvements.

### *Special Rules for Qualified Improvements*

If you make improvements to leased property that meet the definition of **qualified improvement property**, special tax rules apply. They are explained in greater detail in Chapters 10 and 14.

***Qualified improvement property*** **Any improvement to the interior of a portion of a commercial building, other than these excludable improvements: elevators and escalators, building enlargements, and changes to the internal structural framework of a building.**

Prior to 2018, special rules applied to qualified leasehold, qualified retail improvement property, and qualified restaurant property. Improvements made before 2018 continue to be written off using former rules.

## Rental of a Portion of Your Home for Business

If you rent your home and use part of it for business, you may be able to deduct part of your rent as a business expense if you are self-employed. This part of the rent is treated as a home office deduction if you meet certain requirements. See Chapter 18 for details on the home office deduction.

## Leasing a Car

If you lease a car for business use, the treatment of the rental costs depends upon the term of the lease. If the term is less than 30 days, the entire cost of the rental is deductible. Thus, if you go out of town on business and rent a car for a week, your rental costs are deductible.

If the lease term exceeds 30 days, the lease payments are still deductible if you use the car entirely for business. If you use it for both business and personal purposes, you must allocate the lease payments and deduct only the business portion of the costs. However, depending on the value of the car at the time it is leased, you may be required to include an amount in gross income called an inclusion amount (explained later).

If you make advance payments, you must spread these payments over the entire lease period and deduct them accordingly. You cannot depreciate a car you lease, because depreciation applies only to property that is owned.

### *Lease with an Option to Buy*

When you have this arrangement, are you leasing or buying the car? The answer depends on a number of factors:

1. Intent of the parties to the transaction.
2. Whether any equity results from the arrangement.
3. Whether any interest is paid.
4. Whether the fair market value (FMV) of the car is less than the lease payment or option payment when the option to buy is exercised.

If the factors support a finding that the arrangement is a lease, the payments are deductible. If, however, the factors support a finding that the arrangement is a purchase agreement, the payments are not deductible.

### *Inclusion Amount*

If the car, truck, or van price exceeds a certain amount (which is adjusted periodically for inflation) and you do not use the standard mileage rate to account for expenses, you may have to include in income an amount called an *inclusion amount*. The law seeks to equate buying with leasing. Since there is a dollar limit on the amount of depreciation that can be claimed on a luxury vehicle that is owned, the law requires an amount to be included in income as an offset to high lease payments on a vehicle that is leased. In essence, the inclusion amount seeks to limit your deduction for lease payments to what it would be if you owned the vehicle and claimed depreciation.

The inclusion amounts are taken from IRS tables. See Chapter 9 for inclusion amounts.

Remember that if you use your car for commuting or other nonbusiness purposes, you cannot deduct that allocable part of the lease.

Car leasing, including the advisability of leasing versus buying a business car, is discussed more fully in Chapter 9.

## Leveraged Leases

If you are the lessee in a transaction referred to as a **leveraged lease**, you generally can deduct your lease payments.

---

***Leveraged lease*** **A 3-party transaction in which the landlord (lessor) obtains financing from a third party and in which lease payments are sufficient to cover the cost of repaying the financing. Also, the lease term generally covers the useful life of the property.**

---

It is important that the lessor, and not the lessee, be treated as the owner of the property if lease payments are to be deductible. The lessor is treated as the owner if he or she has a minimum amount at risk (at least 20%) during the entire term of the lease and the lessee does not have a contractual right to buy the property at its FMV at the end of the lease term. Other factors that are necessary to show that the lessor and not the lessee is the owner of the property are that the lessor has a profit motive (apart from tax benefits), the lessee does not lend money to the lessor, and the lessee does not invest in the property.

If you are about to become the lessee of a leveraged lease and want to be sure that you will not be treated as the owner (which means your rental expenses would not be deductible), you can ask the IRS for an advance ruling on the issue. (However, the IRS will not issue an advance ruling on leveraged leases of so-called **limited use property**.) There is a user fee for this service. It may be advisable to seek the assistance of a tax professional in obtaining the ruling.

***Limited use property*** **Property not expected to be either useful to or usable by a lessor at the end of the lease term except for continued leasing or transfer to the lessee or a member of a lessee group.**

## Where to Deduct Rent Payments

### *Employees*

Employees cannot deduct rent payments in 2018 through 2025. Employees listed on pages 184 and 185 may be able to deduct rent payments.

### *Self-Employed*

Rents are deductible on Schedule C. This schedule provides two separate lines for reporting rents and leases so that rents and leases for vehicles, machinery, and equipment are reported separately from those of other business property. If you lease a car for more than 30 days, you must complete Part IV of Schedule C if you are not otherwise required to file Form 4562, *Depreciation and Amortization*, or directly on this form if you placed in service any property in 2020 that is subject to depreciation or amortization. Farmers who are self-employed deduct rents on Schedule F. Information about leased cars must be entered on Form 4562, *Depreciation and Amortization*.

If you rent your home and use part of it for business and file Schedule C, you can claim a home office deduction for that part of the rent. Home office expenses, including rent, are computed on Form 8829, *Expenses for Business Use of Your Home*, if you use the actual expense method (or on a worksheet in the instructions to Schedule C of Form 1040 or 1040-SR if you use the optional method). The deductible portion is entered on Schedule C. If you are a farmer who files Schedule F, figure your home office deduction on the worksheet found in IRS Publication 587. Then enter the deductible portion on Schedule F.

### *Partnerships and LLCs*

Rent and lease payments are deducted by partnerships and LLCs on their returns as part of the entity's ordinary trade or business income, on Form 1065. The return contains a separate line for reporting rents. Rent and lease payments are not passed through to partners or LLC members as separate items.

If you rent your home and use part of it for the business of the partnership, you can claim a home office deduction for that part of the rent. There is no special form that a partner must use for calculating his or her home office deduction. However, you may figure the deduction on a special worksheet for this purpose in IRS Publication 587. The deductible portion of your rent (along with other home office expenses) is entered on Schedule E as part of your share of partnership income and expenses.

### *S Corporations*

Rents and lease payments are deducted by the S corporation as part of its ordinary trade or business income on Form 1120-S. The return contains a separate line for reporting rents. Rents and lease payments are not passed through to shareholders as separately stated items.

### *C Corporations*

C corporations deduct rent and lease payments on Form 1120. The return contains a separate line for reporting rents.

CHAPTER 13

# Taxes and Interest


| | | | |
|---|---|---|---|
| Deductible Taxes | 246 | Nondeductible Interest and Other Limitations on Deductibility | 258 |
| Nondeductible Taxes | 252 | | |
| Deductible Interest | 253 | | |


Taxes and interest are two types of expenses that are hard to avoid. In the course of your business activities, you may pay various taxes and interest charges. Most taxes and interest payments are deductible; some are not.

For further information about deducting taxes and interest, see IRS Publication 535, *Business Expenses*.

## Deductible Taxes

### *General Rules*

In order to deduct taxes, they must be imposed on you. The tax must be owed by the party who pays it. If your corporation owns an office building, it is the party that owes the real property taxes. If, as part of your lease, you are obligated to pay your landlord's taxes, you can deduct your payment as an additional part of your rent; you do not claim a deduction for taxes, since you are not the owner of the property.

Taxes must be paid during the year if you are on a cash basis. If you pay taxes at year end by means of a check or even a credit card charge, the tax is deductible in the year the check is sent or delivered or the credit card charge is made. This is so even though the check is not cashed until the following year or you do not pay the credit card bill until the following year. If you pay any tax by phone or through your computer, the tax is deductible on the date of payment reported on the statement issued by the financial institution through which the payment is made. If you contest a liability and do not pay it until the issue is settled, you cannot deduct the tax until it is actually paid. It may be advisable to settle a disputed liability in order to fix the amount and claim a deduction. If you pay tax after the end of the year for a liability that relates to the prior year, you deduct the tax in the year of payment.

If you receive a state or local location tax incentive in the form of an abatement, a credit, a deduction, a rate reduction, or an exemption in order to attract your company to a particular area, the incentive is not deductible. Only the amount of tax you are liable for, after reduction by any location tax incentive(s), is deductible.

**Example**

**An S corporation on a calendar year, using the cash basis method, pays its state franchise fee for 2021 in March 2022. The payment is deductible on the S corporation's 2022 income tax return, not on its 2021 return.**

If you receive state tax credits that exceed your state tax liability and have the option of receiving the excess as cash, according to some courts the receipt of this cash is taxable income to you.

### *Real Estate Taxes*

In general, real property taxes are deductible. Assessments made to real property for the repair or maintenance of some local benefit (such as streets, sidewalks, or sewers) are treated as deductible taxes.

If you acquire real property for resale to customers, you may be required under uniform capitalization rules to capitalize these taxes. The uniform capitalization rules are discussed in Chapter 2.

Special rules apply when real estate is sold during the year. Real property taxes must be allocated between the buyer and seller according to the number of days in the real property tax year. The seller can deduct the taxes up to, but not including, the date of sale. The buyer can deduct the taxes from the date of sale onward.

Accrual basis taxpayers can deduct only taxes accruing on the date of sale. An accrual basis taxpayer can elect to accrue ratably real property taxes related to a definite period of time over that period of time.

**Example**

**X Corporation, a calendar-year taxpayer on the accrual basis, owns an office building on which annual taxes are $1,200 for the fiscal year beginning July 1, 2021, through June 30, 2022. If X elects to ratably accrue taxes, $600 of the taxes is deductible in 2021, the balance in 2022.**

The election to accrue taxes ratably applies for each separate business. If one business owns two properties, an election covers both properties. The election is binding and can be revoked only with the consent of the IRS. You make the election by attaching a statement to your return for the first year that real property taxes are due on property that includes the businesses for which the election is being made, the period of time to which the taxes relate, and a computation of the real property tax deduction for the first year of the election. The election must be filed on time with your income tax return (including extensions).

If you have already owned property for some time but want to switch to the ratable accrual method, you must obtain the consent of the IRS. To do so, file Form 3115, *Change in Accounting Method*, within the year for which the change is to be effective.

### *State and Local Income Taxes*

A corporation that pays state and local income taxes can deduct the taxes on its return. Taxes may include state corporate income taxes and any franchise tax (which is a tax for operating as a corporation and has nothing to do with being a franchise business).

A self-employed individual who pays state and local taxes with respect to business income reported on Schedule C or E can deduct them only as an itemized deduction on Schedule A, subject to the overall $10,000 limit on state and local taxes (SALT). However, the IRS said that state and local income taxes imposed on and paid by a partnership or S corporation are not subject to the SALT cap and are allowed in computing non-separately stated income or loss for the entity (and passed through to the owner). Also, New York City's Unincorporated Business Tax (UBT) may be deducted as a business tax (i.e., on Schedule C or Form 1065) by sole proprietorships, partnerships, and limited liability companies. Similarly, an employee who pays state and local taxes with respect to compensation from employment usually deducts these taxes on Schedule A, subject to the overall $10,000 limit on SALT.

Some states enacted work-arounds to the SALT limit using charitable deductions, but the IRS essentially nixed most work-arounds (see Chapter 22).

### *Self-Employment Tax*

Businesses do not pay self-employment tax; individuals do. Sole proprietors, general partners (whether active or inactive), and certain LLC members pay self-employment tax on their net earnings from self-employment (amounts reported on Schedule C or as self-employment income on Schedule K-1). Limited partners do not pay self-employment tax on their share of income from the business. However, limited partners are subject to self-employment tax if they perform any services for the business or receive any guaranteed payments. LLC members who are like general partners pay self-employment tax; those who are like limited partners do not. The IRS had been precluded from issuing regulations defining a limited liability member before July 1,1998. To date, the IRS still has not issued any regulations even though it has been on the IRS Priority Guidance List for a number of years.

The tax rate for the Social Security portion of self-employment tax is 12.4% and, in 2021, applies to net earnings from self-employment up to $142,800. The Medicare tax rate is 2.9%, and it applies to *all* net earnings from self-employment (there is no limit for the Medicare portion of self-employment tax).

**NOTE**

**If you elected to defer one-half of the Social Security portion of self-employment tax in 2020, you must pay 50% of the deferred amount by the end of 2021. The other 50% is due by the end of 2022.**

Those who pay self-employment tax are entitled to deduct one half of the self-employment tax as an adjustment to gross income on their personal income tax returns. The deduction on Schedule 1 of Form 1040 or 1040-SR reduces your gross income.

In figuring self-employment tax, net earnings from self-employment cannot be reduced by any net operating loss (NOL) carryback or carryover.

While S corporations are pass-through entities similar to partnerships and LLCs, owners of S corporations who work for their businesses are not treated the same as partners and LLC members for purposes of self-employment tax. Owners of S corporations who are also employees of their businesses do not pay self-employment tax on their compensation—they are employees of the corporation for purposes of employment tax. They also don't pay self-employment tax on their share of business income passed through to them. Their compensation is subject to FICA, not to self-employment tax. Individuals who are both self-employed and have an interest in an S corporation cannot use losses from the S corporation to reduce net earnings from self-employment.

For more on self-employment tax, see Chapter 30.

### Additional Medicare Taxes

The additional 0.9% Medicare tax on earnings (wages, other taxable compensation, and self-employment income) over a threshold amount and the 3.8% tax on net investment income (which includes, for example, income from a partnership or an S corporation in which you do not materially participate and gains from the sale of an interest in a partnership or S corporation in which you do not materially participate) are *not* deductible. They are viewed as personal taxes even though they relate to business income.

### Personal Property Tax

Personal property tax on any property used in a business is deductible. Personal property tax is an *ad valorem tax*—a tax on the value of personal property. For example, a *floor tax* is a property tax levied on inventory that is sitting on the floor (or shelves) of your business. Registration fees for the right to use property within the state in your trade or business are deductible. If the fees are based on the value of the property, they are considered a personal property tax.

### Sales and Use Taxes

Sales tax to acquire a depreciable asset used in a trade or business is added to the basis of the asset and is recovered through depreciation. If sales tax is paid to acquire a nondepreciable asset, it is still treated as part of the cost of the asset and is deducted as part of the asset's expense. For example, sales tax on business stationery is part of the cost of the stationery and is deducted as part of that cost (not as a separate sales tax deduction). Sales tax paid on property acquired for resale is also treated as part of the cost of that property. (There may be an exemption from sales tax on items acquired for resale.)

Sales tax you collect as a merchant or other business owner and turn over to the state is deductible only if you include it in your gross receipts. If the sales tax is not included, it is not deductible.

When sales tax is imposed on the seller or retailer and the seller or retailer can separately state the tax or pass it on to the consumer, then the consumer, rather than the seller or retailer, gets to deduct the tax. When the consumer is in business, the tax is treated differently depending on how the asset is acquired. (See the aforementioned details for depreciable property, nondepreciable property, and property held for sale or resale.)

A compensating use tax is treated as a sales tax. This type of tax is imposed on the use, storage, or consumption of an item brought in from another taxing jurisdiction. Typically, it is imposed at the same percentage as a sales tax.

To learn about obtaining a resale number or certificate needed for the collection of sales taxes and your sales tax obligations, contact your state tax department. You can find it through a link to your state's government from the IRS at https://www.irs.gov/Businesses/Small-Businesses-&-Self-Employed/State-Links-1. You may also have to collect sales tax on sales to customers in other states (see Chapter 30).

### Luxury Tax

Like sales tax, a luxury tax that is paid to acquire a depreciable asset is added to the basis of the asset; it is not separately deductible. At present, there are no luxury taxes at the federal level.

Some states impose luxury taxes on certain items. For example, Arizona has a luxury tax on liquor wholesalers. This is a deductible tax in the nature of a sales tax.

### *Employment Taxes*

Employment taxes, also called payroll taxes, are a conglomerate of a number of different taxes:

- The employer share of Federal Insurance Contribution Act (FICA) tax covering Social Security and Medicare taxes
- Federal Unemployment Tax Act (FUTA) tax
- State unemployment tax

Employment taxes are fully deductible by an employer. This is so even if an employer claims certain tax credits with employment tax offsets, such as those related to COVID-19 (see Chapters 7, 23, and 30). The employer portion of the Social Security tax is 6.2%. This tax is applied to a current wage base of up to $142,800 in 2021, which is adjusted annually for inflation. The employer portion of the Medicare tax is 1.45%. This is applied to all wages paid to an employee; there is no wage base limit. If you, as an employer, pay both the employer and employee portion of the tax, you may claim a deduction for your full payments. Your payment of the employee's share of FICA is additional compensation to the employee but does not trigger additional FICA for you or the employee.

If you are in a dispute over employment taxes with the IRS and you lose, requiring you to pay back taxes and you pay the employee share to avoid adverse employee reaction, you may deduct the employee share as well. The IRS views your payment in this instance as having a valid business reason even though you are not legally obligated to pay the employee share of FICA.

You may also be liable for federal unemployment tax (FUTA) for your employees. The FUTA tax is fully deductible. The gross federal unemployment tax rate for FUTA is 6%. This is applied to employee wages up to $7,000, for a maximum FUTA tax of $434 per employee. However, you may claim a credit of up to 5.4% for state unemployment tax that you pay, bringing the maximum FUTA tax to $42 per employee. If your state unemployment tax rate is 5.4% or more, then the net FUTA rate is 0.6%. Even if your state unemployment rate is less than 5.4%, you are permitted to claim a full reduction of 5.4%.

However, if your state has failed to repay funds borrowed from the federal government to cover state unemployment tax benefits, the federal credit for FUTA is reduced.

There were no credit reduction states in 2020. The credit reduction states for 2021 FUTA are set to be announced by the Department of Labor in November 2021. Due to high unemployment related to COVID-19, there may be some such states for 2021. A final list of credit reduction states, if any, will be in the Supplement to this book and on Schedule A of the 2021 Form 940.

These tax payments are deductible by you as an employer. A complete discussion of employment taxes can be found in Chapter 30.

### *State Benefit Funds*

An employer who pays into a state disability, unemployment insurance or other fund may deduct the payments as taxes. An employee who must contribute to the following state benefit funds for disability, unemployment, or family leave benefits can deduct the payments as state and local income taxes (SALT) on Schedule A (subject to the overall $10,000 limit on state and local taxes in 2018 through 2025):

- *Alaska*—State Unemployment Fund
- *California*—Nonoccupational Disability Benefit Fund, Paid Family Leave program and the State Unemployment Fund
- *New Jersey*—Nonoccupational Disability Benefit Fund, the State Unemployment Fund, and Family Leave Insurance program
- *New York*—Nonoccupational Disability Benefit Fund
- *Pennsylvania*—State Unemployment Fund
- *Rhode Island*—Temporary Disability Benefit Fund
- *Washington*—Supplemental Workers' Compensation Trust Fund

Hawaii requires employers to maintain temporary disability insurance. Employers are permitted to pass on up to 50% of premium costs to employees, but employees cannot deduct their withholding; their payments are not a tax.

Massachusetts has a payroll tax on the employer to cover paid family and medical leave (PFML) unless this benefit is provided privately. Businesses with 25 or fewer employees may deduct the entire payroll tax for PFML from employees' wages (there's a limit on larger employers).

### Franchise Taxes

Corporate franchise taxes (which is another term that may be used for state corporate income taxes and has nothing to do with whether the corporation is a franchise) are a deductible business expense. Your state may or may not impose franchise taxes on S corporations, so check with your state corporate tax department.

### Excise Taxes

Excise taxes paid or incurred in a trade or business are deductible as operating expenses. For example, indoor tanning salons can deduct the 10% excise tax that they pay on their services. A credit for federal excise tax on certain fuels may be claimed as explained in the following section.

### Fuel Taxes

Taxes on gas, diesel fuel, and other motor fuels used in your business are deductible. As a practical matter, they are included in the cost of the fuel and are not separately stated. Thus, they are deducted as a fuel cost rather than as a tax.

However, in certain instances, you may be eligible for a credit for the federal excise tax on certain fuels. The credit applies to fuel used in machinery and off-highway vehicles (such as tractors), and kerosene used for heating, lighting, and cooking on a farm.

You have a choice: Claim a tax credit for the federal excise tax or claim a refund of this tax. You can claim a quarterly refund for the first 3 quarters of the year if the refund is $750 or more. If you do not exceed $750 in a quarter, then you can carry over this refund amount to the following quarter and add it to the refund due at that time. But if, after carrying the refund forward to the fourth quarter you do not exceed $750, then you must recoup the excise tax through a tax credit.

Alternatively, if you have pesticides or fertilizers applied aerially, you may waive your right to the credit or refund, allowing the applicator to claim it (something that would reduce your application charges). If you want to waive the credit or refund, you must sign an irrevocable waiver and give a copy of it to the applicator. For further information on this credit, see Chapter 30 and IRS Publication 510, *Excise Taxes*.

### Foreign Taxes

Income taxes paid to a foreign country or U.S. possession may be claimed as a deduction or a tax credit. To claim foreign income taxes as a tax credit, you must file Form 1116, *Foreign Tax Credit* (unless as an individual you have foreign tax of $300 or less, or $600 or less on a joint return).

Corporations claim the foreign tax credit on Form 1118. However, because the rules on taxing corporations on foreign income have changed as a result of the Tax Cuts and Jobs Act, the credit computations are more complex. For example, a U.S. shareholder (typically a C corporation) must include global intangible low-taxed income (GILTI) tax in gross income, but can essentially claim only an 80% credit, with no carryforwards. Because the foreign tax rules generally apply to multinational corporations even though the way the law is written small businesses could be impacted, they are not discussed further in this book.

The same rules apply for foreign real property taxes paid with respect to real property owned in a foreign country or U.S. possession.

### Built-In Gains Tax

If an S corporation pays a built-in gains tax on the sale of certain property (see Chapter 4), the tax it pays is deductible. If the tax is attributable to ordinary gain, then it is deductible as a tax (on page 1 of Form 1120-S). If it is attributable to short-term or long-term capital gain, then it is claimed as a short-term or long-term capital loss on Schedule D of Form 1120-S.

### Other Rules

If a corporation pays a tax imposed on a shareholder and the shareholder does not reimburse the corporation, then the corporation, and not the shareholder, is entitled to claim the deduction for the payment of the tax.

## Nondeductible Taxes

You may not deduct federal income taxes, even the amount paid with respect to your business income. These are nondeductible taxes.

Other nondeductible taxes include:

- Additional 0.9% Medicare tax on earned income and 3.8% net investment income tax (see Chapter 30).
- Assessments on real property for local benefits that tend to add to the value of the property. Such assessments may be made, for example, to build sidewalks, streets, sewers, or parks. These assessments are added to the basis of the property. But assessments for maintenance purposes (such as for repairs to sidewalks, streets, and sewers) are deductible. Water bills, sewage, and other service charges are not treated as taxes. They are, however, deductible as business expenses.
- Employee portion of FICA and railroad retirement taxes covering Social Security and Medicare contributions.
- Employee contributions to private or voluntary disability plans.

- Employee state and local taxes (including mandatory contributions to various benefit funds) in excess of a total of $10,000 ($5,000 if married filing separately) in 2018 through 2025.
- Fines imposed by a governmental authority. These are not deductible as a tax even if incurred in a trade or business. For example, if while traveling away from home on business you receive a fine for a speeding ticket, the fine is not deductible.
- Penalties imposed by the federal government on taxes or for failing to file returns. These are not deductible even though they may be computed with regard to the length of time the taxpayer has failed to comply with a tax law requirement.
- Occupational taxes.

## Deductible Interest

### *General Rules*

Interest paid or incurred on debts related to your business usually is fully deductible as business interest. But what is business interest? Interest expense is characterized by how and for what the proceeds of the loan that generated the interest are used.

*Business interest* usually is fully deductible for small businesses or electing farming and real property businesses (explained later). For all other businesses, there is an interest expense limitation, referred to by tax professionals as the Section 163(j) limitation. The tax form used to apply the limitation is explained at the end of this chapter. In some cases, interest may not be currently deductible by any business. For example, construction period interest and taxes must be capitalized, as explained earlier in this chapter.

All interest paid by a C corporation is treated as business interest for purposes of the interest expense limitation. Interest of noncorporate taxpayers with a C corporation owner (e.g., a partnership with a C corporation that is a partner) is characterized as business interest to such C corporation.

*Personal interest* is nondeductible (except to the extent of qualified home mortgage interest and a limited amount of student loan interest).

*Investment interest* is deductible only to the extent of net investment income.

*Passive activity interest*. Interest characterized as incurred in a passive activity is subject to the passive loss rules.

**NOTE**

**A current deduction for self-charged interest (interest you effectively charge yourself through multiple business activities) is limited under the passive activity loss rules (see Chapter 4).**

The characterization of interest is not dependent on what type of property—business or personal—is used as collateral for the loan; it hinges on how you use the proceeds. For example, if you borrow against your personal life insurance policy and use the proceeds to buy equipment for your business, treat the interest as business interest. On the other hand, if you take a bank loan using your partnership interest as collateral and use the proceeds to invest in the stock market, the interest is characterized as investment interest.

Interest on a tax deficiency relating to Schedules C, E, or F is nondeductible personal interest. While the Tax Court had allowed a deduction for this interest, several appellate courts have sided with the IRS in denying a deduction for this interest.

If the proceeds are used for more than one purpose, you must make an allocation based on the use of the loan's proceeds. When you repay a part of the loan, the repayments are treated as repaying the loan in this order:

- Amounts allocated to personal use
- Amounts allocated to investments and passive activities

- Amounts allocated to passive activities in connection with rental real estate in which you actively participate
- Amounts allocated to business use

The interest obligation must be yours in order for you to claim an interest deduction. If you pay off someone else's loan, you cannot deduct the interest you pay. If you are contractually obligated to make the payment, you may be able to deduct your payment as some other expense item, but not as interest.

### BUSINESS EXPENSE LIMITATION

For 2021, the interest expense deduction is limited to the sum of business interest income, floor plan financing (used by dealerships of cars and other vehicles), and 30% **adjusted taxable income (ATI)**.

---

***Adjusted taxable income (ATI)*** **Regular taxable income determined without regard to any item of income, gain, deduction, or loss not allocable to a trade or business; business interest or interest income; 20% qualified small business income deduction; and depreciation, amortization, or depletion. Effectively, it means earnings before interest, taxes, depreciation, and amortization (EBITA). After 2021, depreciation, amortization, or depletion is part of adjusted taxable income; effectively this means earnings before interest and taxes (EBIT). Wages of an employee (e.g., an owner-employee of an S corporation) are not treated as trade or business income.**

---

Special limitation rules apply to partnerships and S corporations:

***For partnerships***. The amount of deductible business interest expense in a taxable year cannot exceed the sum of the partnership's business interest income, 30% of the partnership's ATI, and the partnership's floor plan financing interest expense. Business interest expense that may be deducted after applying the limitation is taken into account in determining the non-separately stated taxable income or loss of the partnership (i.e., ordinary business income or loss from line 22 of Form 1065).

Any business interest expense of the partnership that is disallowed after applying the limitation is allocated to each partner in the same manner as the non-separately stated taxable income or loss of the partnership. This amount is called excess business interest expense.

Each partner carries forward his or her share of excess business interest expense. In a succeeding taxable year, a partner may treat the excess business interest expense as business interest expense paid or accrued by the partner to the extent the partner is allocated excess taxable income or excess business interest income from the same partnership.

To the extent that interest expense of a partnership allocable to ***per se non-passive activities*** is then allocated to partners that do not materially participate (explained in Chapter 4), such interest expense is not considered business interest expense for purposes of the interest expense limitation.

---

***Per se non-passive activity*** **An activity that is not treated as a passive activity for purposes of passive activity loss rules (see Chapter 4) regardless of whether the owners of the activity materially participate in the activity.**

---

Excess taxable income is the amount of ATI of the partnership that was in excess of what it needed to deduct its business interest expense, and excess business interest income is the amount by which business interest income exceeded business interest expense at the partnership level. Excess taxable income is allocated to each partner in the same manner as the non-separately stated taxable income or loss of the partnership. An allocation of excess taxable income to a partner increases the partner's ATI. Similarly, an allocation of excess business interest income to a partner increases the partner's business interest income. Once excess business interest expense is treated as business interest expense paid or accrued by the partner, such business interest expense is subject to the limitation at the partner level.

Special rules apply to self-charged lending transactions between partnerships and partners. These rules are covered extensively in final regulations issued in January 2021 (see T.D. 9943).

***For S corporations.*** Any business interest expense of the S corporation that is disallowed upon application of the interest expense limitation is not allocated to its shareholders, but is instead carried over at the S corporation level to its succeeding taxable years. An S corporation allocates any excess taxable income and excess business interest income to its shareholders on a pro-rata basis.

Disallowed business interest expense may be carried forward indefinitely. As explained previously, for partnerships and S corporations, the interest limitation applies at the entity level unless disallowed interest of the entity is allocated to each owner as excess business interest.

#### SMALL BUSINESS EXCEPTION

Small businesses are automatically exempt from the interest expense limitation. They may deduct all of their business interest expense unless some other rule (e.g., capitalization, self-charged interest rule) applies. In 2021, small businesses mean those with average annual gross receipts in the 3 prior years not exceeding $26 million. This is referred to as the gross receipts test.

#### ELECTING OUT OF INTEREST EXPENSE LIMITATION

Even if the gross receipts test is not met, certain businesses may elect to be excluded from the business interest limitation:

- A real property trade or business (a business involved in real estate development, redevelopment, construction, reconstruction, acquisition, conversion, rental, operation, management, leasing, or brokerage trade or business).
- Farming business (a business involved in the cultivation of land or the raising or harvesting of any agricultural or horticultural commodity, the operations of a nursery or sod farm, or the raising or harvesting of trees bearing fruit, nuts, or other crops, or ornamental trees).

If an election is made by a real property trade or business or a farming business, the alternative depreciation system (ADS) must be used for both existing and newly acquired property (see Chapter 14). The IRS has said that businesses making the election do not have to file for a change in accounting method.

### Debt Incurred to Buy an Interest in a Business

If you use loan proceeds to buy an interest in a partnership, LLC, or S corporation or to make a contribution to capital, this is treated as a *debt-financed acquisition*. In this case, you must allocate the interest on the loan based on the assets of the pass-through business. The allocation can be based on book value, market value, or the adjusted bases of the assets.

**Example**

**You borrow $25,000 to buy an interest in an S corporation. The S corporation owns $90,000 of equipment and $10,000 of stocks (based on fair market value (FMV)). In this case, 9/10 of the interest on the loan is treated as business interest ($90,000 ÷ $100,000); 1/10 of the interest is treated as investment interest ($10,000 ÷ $100,000).**

If you, as an S corporation shareholder, LLC member, or partner, receive proceeds from a debt, you must also allocate the debt proceeds. These are called *debt-financed distributions*. Under a general allocation rule, debt proceeds distributed to an owner of a pass-through entity are allocated to the owner's use of the proceeds. Thus, if the owner uses the proceeds for personal purposes, the pass-through entity must treat the interest as nondeductible personal interest. Under an optional allocation rule, the pass-through entity may allocate the proceeds (and related interest) to one or more of the entity's expenditures other than distributions. The expenditures to which the debt is allocated are those made in the same year as the allocation is made (see IRS Notice 89-35 for allocations in pass-through entities).

If you borrow money to buy stock in a closely held C corporation, the Tax Court considers the interest to be investment interest. The reason: C corporation stock, like any publicly traded stock, is held for investment. This is so even if the corporation never pays out investment income *(dividends)* or the purchase of the stock is made to protect one's employment with the corporation.

### *Loans between Shareholders and Their Corporations*

Special care must be taken when shareholders lend money to their corporation, and vice versa, or when shareholders guarantee third-party loans made to their corporation.

#### CORPORATION'S INDEBTEDNESS TO SHAREHOLDERS

If a corporation borrows from its shareholders, the corporation can deduct the interest it pays on the loan. The issue sometimes raised by the IRS in these types of loans is whether there is any real indebtedness. Sometimes loans are used in place of dividends to transform nondeductible dividend payments into deductible interest. In order for a loan to withstand IRS scrutiny, be prepared to show a written instrument bearing a fixed maturity date for the repayment of the loan. The instrument should also state a fixed rate of interest. There should be a valid business reason for this borrowing arrangement (such as evidence that the corporation could not borrow from a commercial source at a reasonable rate of interest). The loan should be included in the liabilities section of the corporation's balance sheet. If the loan is subordinated to the claims of corporate creditors, this tends to show that it is not a true debt, but other factors may prove otherwise. Also, when a corporation is heavily indebted to shareholders, the debt-to-equity ratio may indicate that the loans are not true loans but are merely disguised equity.

When a corporation fails to repay a loan to a shareholder, this may give rise to a bad debt deduction for the shareholder. Bad debts are discussed in Chapter 11.

#### SHAREHOLDER GUARANTEES OF CORPORATE DEBT

For small businesses, banks or other lenders usually require personal guarantees by the corporation's principal shareholders as a condition for making loans to the corporation. This arrangement raises one of the basic rules for deducting interest discussed earlier: The obligation must be yours in order for you to deduct the interest. (The impact of a guarantee by an S corporation shareholder on his or her basis in debt is discussed in Chapter 5.)

**Example**

**A sole shareholder paid interest on a loan made by a third party to his corporation. He agreed that he would pay any outstanding debt if the corporation failed to do so. He was not entitled to claim an interest deduction because it was the corporation, not he, who was primarily liable on the obligation. The shareholder was only a guarantor.**

## *Below-Market and Above-Market Loans*

When shareholders and their corporations arrange loans between themselves, they may set interest rates at less than or more than the going market rate of interest. This may be done for a number of reasons, including to ease the financial burden on a party to the loan or to create a tax advantage. Whatever the reason, it is important to understand the consequences of the arrangement.

### BELOW-MARKET LOANS

If you receive an interest-free or below-market-interest loan, you may still be able to claim an interest deduction. You can claim an interest deduction equal to the sum of the interest you actually pay, plus the amount of interest that the lender is required to report as income under the below-market loan rules. The amount that the lender is required to report as income is fixed according to interest rates set monthly by the IRS. Different rates apply according to the term of the loan.

- *Short-term* loans run 3 years or less.
- *Mid-term* loans run more than 3 but less than 9 years.
- *Long-term* loans run more than 9 years.

Rates required to be charged in order to avoid imputed interest are called the *applicable federal rates* (AFRs). You can find an index of AFRs by entering "applicable federal rates" in the search box at www.irs.gov. If a loan is payable on demand, the short-term rate applies. However, if the loan is outstanding for an entire year, you can use a blended annual rate (0.13% for 2021) provided by the IRS to simplify the computation of the taxable imputed interest.

**Example**

**On January 1, 2021, you borrowed $40,000 from your corporation for investments. You were not charged any interest by your corporation, and the loan was payable on demand. The AFR for determining interest that the lender must report and the borrower can potentially deduct for 2021 is the blended rate of 0.13% for demand loans outstanding for the entire year. Thus, your interest deduction is $52 (subject to the limitation on deducting investment interest).**

Whether you are required to report this amount as income (which would, in effect, offset the interest deduction) depends on the amount of the loan and the context in which it was made. If it was treated as compensation or a dividend, you have to include it in income. If it was considered a gift loan, you do not have additional income. Gift loans are loans up to $10,000 (as long as the loan is not made for tax avoidance purposes). The corporation (lender) must report the interest as income. If the loan is to an employee, an offsetting deduction can be taken for compensation. But if the loan is to a nonemployee, such as a shareholder who does not work for the corporation, no offsetting deduction can be taken.

#### ABOVE-MARKET LOANS

Instead of borrowing from a bank, your corporation may be able to borrow from a relative of yours, such as your child or parent, to whom you want to make gifts. You can turn the arrangement into a profitable one for both your corporation and your relative (the lender). Set the interest rate at more than what would be charged by the bank. Provided that the interest is still considered "reasonable" and the loan is an arm's-length transaction, your corporation deducts the interest, and the lender receives it. If an unreasonably high rate of interest is charged and the arrangement is not at arm's length, however, the IRS will attack the arrangement and may disallow the interest as being a disguised dividend payment to you.

### *Home Mortgage Interest and Home Offices*

If you are self-employed, use a portion of your home for business, and claim a home office deduction under the actual expense method (explained in Chapter 18), you must allocate the home mortgage interest. The portion of the interest on the mortgage allocated to the business use is deducted on Form 8829, *Expenses for Business Use of Your Home*. The balance is treated as personal mortgage interest deductible as an itemized expense on Schedule A.

## Nondeductible Interest and Other Limitations on Deductibility

If you borrow additional funds from the same lender to pay off a first loan for business, you cannot claim an interest deduction. Once you begin paying off the new loan, you can deduct interest on both the old and new loans. Payments are treated as being applied to the old loan first and then to the new loan. All interest payments are then deductible.

As in the case of taxes, if interest is paid to acquire a capital asset for resale, you must capitalize the interest expense. The interest is recovered when the asset is sold.

### *Commitment Fees*

Fees paid to have business funds available for drawing on a standby basis are not treated as deductible interest payments. They may, however, be deductible as business expenses. Fees paid to obtain a loan may be treated as deductible interest. However, the fees are not immediately deductible; rather, they are deductible only over the term of the loan. If the loan falls through, the fees can be deducted as a loss.

Similarly, points paid to acquire a loan on business property are treated as prepaid interest. They are not currently deductible as such. Instead, they are deductible over the term of the loan.

**Example**

**Your business pays a $200 commitment fee for a $10,000 loan with a 10-year term. Each year the business may deduct $20 ($200 divided by 10 years).**

If you pay off the loan before the end of the term (before you have fully deducted the prepaid interest), you can deduct the remaining balance of prepaid interest in the final year of payment.

### Interest Paid on Income Tax Deficiencies

If you pay interest on a tax deficiency arising from business income from your sole proprietorship, S corporation, partnership, or LLC, you cannot deduct the interest on your individual return. This interest is treated as nondeductible personal interest even though business income generated the deficiency.

A C corporation can deduct interest it pays on any tax deficiency, but it cannot deduct tax penalties. This rule applies to both civil and criminal penalties.

For both individuals and corporations, amounts assessed for the delay of filing a return are considered penalties. Thus, estimated tax penalties, which are imposed because of a delay in payment, are not deductible even though they are calculated by application of an interest rate. Similarly, amounts owed because of the failure to deposit employment taxes are treated as penalties. Additions to tax contained in Sections 6651 through 6658 of the Internal Revenue Code are considered penalties. The shared responsibility payments for employers under the Affordable Care Act are nondeductible tax penalties.

### Interest Related to Tax-Exempt Income

No deduction is allowed for interest paid or incurred to buy or carry tax-exempt securities.

## Where to Deduct Taxes and Interest

### Employees

State and local taxes are deductible as itemized deductions on Schedule A of Form 1040 or 1040-SR only up to a total of $10,000 ($5,000 for married persons filing separately) in 2018 through 2025. No deduction is allowed during these years for business-related interest of employees. However, employees can elect to claim an itemized deduction or a credit for foreign taxes.

### Self-Employed

Taxes and interest are deducted on Schedule C (or Schedule F, in the case of farming operations). This form provides a separate space for claiming deductions for mortgage interest and for other interest. It also provides a specific line for claiming a deduction for taxes and licenses.

Instead of deducting foreign taxes on Schedule C (or Schedule F), a sole proprietor may choose to claim a foreign tax credit. If foreign taxes are $300 or less (or $600 or less if the self-employed person files a joint return) and result from passive income, an election can be made to claim the credit directly on Schedule 3 of Form 1040 or 1040-SR. Otherwise, the credit must be figured on Form 1116, *Foreign Tax Credit.*

### Partnerships and LLCs

In general, partnerships and LLCs deduct taxes and interest on Form 1065. Separate lines are provided for deducting interest, taxes, and licenses. These items are part of the business's operating expenses and figure into its income or loss passed through to partners or LLC members on Schedule K-1 and then reported on the owner's Schedule E. These items are not separately reported to partners or LLC members on Schedule K-1 for special treatment on an owner's individual income tax return.

However, interest that may be classified as investment interest is separately stated in Schedule K-1, since it is subject to an investment interest limitation on the partner's or member's individual income tax return.

Also, foreign taxes are separately stated items on Schedule K-1 to allow the owner to take a credit on his or her individual return. Partners and LLC members treat foreign taxes in the same manner as self-employed individuals.

### S Corporations

In general, the S corporation deducts taxes and interest on Form 1120-S. Separate lines are provided for deducting interest, taxes, and licenses. These items are part of the business's operating expenses and figure into its income or loss passed through to shareholders on Schedule K-1 and then reported on the owner's Schedule E. These items are not separately reported to shareholders on Schedule K-1 for special treatment on an owner's individual income tax return.

However, interest that may be classified as investment interest is separately stated in Schedule K-1, since it is subject to an investment interest limitation on the shareholder's individual income tax return.

Also, foreign taxes are separately stated items on Schedule K-1 to allow the shareholder to take a credit on his or her individual return. S corporation shareholders treat foreign taxes in the same manner as self-employed individuals.

### C Corporations

C corporations deduct taxes and interest on Form 1120. Separate lines are provided for deducting interest, taxes, and licenses.

If the corporation chooses to take a credit for foreign taxes instead of deducting them, the foreign tax credit is figured on Form 1118, *Foreign Tax Credit—Corporations*.

### Business Interest Expense Limitation for All Taxpayers

The business interest expense limitation, including a determination of adjusted taxable income (ATI), the partnership and S corporation pass-through items, and the carryforward of the disallowed business interest expense, are figured on Form 8990, *Limitation on Business Interest Expense Under Section 163(j)*.

CHAPTER 14

# First-Year Expensing, Depreciation, Amortization, and Depletion


| | | | |
|---|---|---|---|
| Section 179 Expensing | 262 | Limitations on Listed Property | 280 |
| Other Expensing Opportunities | 266 | De Minimis Safe Harbor Rule | 281 |
| Bonus Depreciation | 267 | Putting Personal Property to Business Use | 281 |
| General Rules for Depreciation | 268 | Amortization | 282 |
| Modified Accelerated Cost Recovery System | 271 | Depletion | 287 |
| Depreciation Methods | 276 | | |


There are a number of ways in which you can write off the cost of machinery and equipment. The method you use depends on your situation. And there are special write-off rules for realty and intangible property, and other types of property.

*First-year expensing*, which is also called the Section 179 deduction after the section in the Tax Code that created it, is a write-off allowed for the purchase of equipment used in your business. This deduction takes the place of depreciation—the amount expensed is not depreciated. For example, if you buy a desk for your business for $1,000, you can opt to deduct its cost in full in the year you place the desk into service. If you don't make this election and no other write-off option applies, you must write off the cost using depreciation over a number of years fixed by law or use bonus depreciation, described next.

*Bonus depreciation*, which is also called the special depreciation allowance, is another first-year allowance that is claimed unless you elect not to use it. Bonus depreciation applies to a variety of property (explained in Chapter 10).

*Depreciation* is an allowance for a portion of the cost of equipment or other property owned by you and used in your business. Depreciation is claimed over the life of the property, although it may be accelerated, with a greater amount claimed in the early years of ownership. The thinking behind depreciation is that equipment wears out. In theory, if you were to put into a separate fund the amount you claim each year as a depreciation allowance, when your equipment reaches the end of its usefulness, you will have sufficient funds to buy a replacement (of course, the replacement may not cost the same as the old equipment). To claim a depreciation deduction,

**NOTE**
**The rules covered in this chapter are exclusively federal income tax rules. States may have very different rules for Section 179 expensing, bonus depreciation, depreciation, amortization, and depletion, so check with the applicable state tax department for state income tax rules.**

you do not necessarily have to spend any money. If you have already bought the property, future depreciation deductions do not require any additional out-of-pocket expenditures. Depreciation also applies to buildings and certain other improvements to land, but not to the land itself.

*De minimis safe harbor rule* is an alternative to the other write-offs in this chapter. These other write-offs require you to capitalize the cost of the purchase, which means you add the item to your books and carry it on your balance sheet. This IRS-created de minimis safe harbor rule allows you to elect to effectively treat a purchase of tangible personal property as material and supplies, which are not part of your balance sheet.

*Amortization* is conceptually similar to depreciation. It is an allowance for the cost of certain capital expenditures, such as goodwill and trademarks, acquired in the purchase of a business. Amortization can be claimed only if it is specifically allowed by the tax law. It is always deducted ratably over the life of the property. As you will see, amortization is also allowed as an election for some types of expenditures that would otherwise not be deductible.

*Depletion* is a deduction allowed for certain natural resources. The tax law carefully controls the limits of this deduction.

For a further discussion of depreciation, amortization, and depletion, see IRS Publication 946, *How to Depreciate Property*.

## Section 179 Expensing

Instead of depreciating the cost of tangible personal property over a number of years, you may be able to write off the entire cost in the first year. This is *first-year expensing* or a *Section 179 deduction* (named after the section in the Internal Revenue Code that governs the deduction). A Section 179 expense deduction may be claimed whether you pay for the item with cash or credit. If you buy the item on credit, the Section 179 expense deduction can be used to enhance your cash flow position (you claim an immediate tax deduction but pay for the item over time).

You can elect to deduct up to a set dollar amount of the cost of tangible personal property used in your business. In 2021, you may deduct up to $1,050,000.

### *Property Eligible for Section 179 Expensing*

The Section 179 deduction is commonly referred to as a write-off for equipment and machinery, also known as tangible personal property. However, other types of property may qualify, including:

- Certain improvements to nonresidential real property placed in service after the date that the underlying property was first placed in service: roofs; heating, ventilation, and air-conditioning property; fire protection and alarm systems; and security systems
- Certain property used predominantly to furnish lodging or in connection with the furnishing of lodging
- Livestock, including horses, cattle, hogs, sheep, goats, and mink and other furbearing animals
- Off-the-shelf software

- Qualified improvement property (an improvement to the interior portion of a building other than an enlargement to the building, an elevator or escalator, or the internal structure of the building)
- Single purpose agricultural (livestock) or horticultural structures

The property must be acquired by purchase. If you inherit property, for example, and use it in your business, you cannot claim a Section 179 deduction.

A Section 179 deduction may be claimed for property that has been pre-owned (i.e., used property), as long as the property is new to you and you acquire it by purchase.

If you buy property on credit, you can still use the Section 179 deduction even though you are not yet out of pocket for the purchase price. A purchase on credit that entitles you to a Section 179 deduction is a strategy for aiding your cash flow (i.e., you gain a tax deduction even though you have not expended the cash).

The property must have been acquired for business. If you buy property for personal purposes and later convert it to business use, you cannot claim a Section 179 deduction.

Generally, the Section 179 deduction does not apply to property you buy and then lease to others. (There is no restriction on leased property by corporations.) However, a Section 179 deduction is allowed for leased property you manufactured and leased if the term of the lease is less than half of the property's class life and, for the first 12 months, the property is transferred to the lessee, and the total business deductions for the property are more than 15% of the rental income for the property.

### *Limits on Section 179 Expensing*

Three limits apply for the Section 179 expensing: a *dollar limit*, an *investment limit*, and a *taxable income limit*.

#### DOLLAR LIMIT

You cannot deduct more than the applicable dollar amount in any one year. The dollar limit for 2021 is $1,050,000.

If an individual owns more than one business, he or she must aggregate Section 179 deductions from all businesses and deduct no more than a total of $1,050,000. Married persons are treated as one taxpayer and are allowed a single dollar limit. However, if they file separate returns, each can claim only one-half of the dollar limit (i.e., $525,000 in 2021).

**NOTE**

**A special dollar limit for cars used in business supersedes the first-year expense deduction limit. (See Chapters 7 and 9 for more details on deducting the costs of business cars.) No first-year expense deduction can be claimed for listed property unless it is used more than 50% for business.**

#### INVESTMENT LIMIT

The Section 179 deduction is really designed for small businesses. This is because every dollar of investments in equipment over $2.62 million in 2021 reduces the dollar limit.

**Example**

**In 2021, you buy equipment costing $3 million. Your Section 179 deduction is limited to $670,000 ($1.05 million – [$3 million – $2.26 million]).**

If a business buys equipment costing $3.67 million, the deduction limit is fully phased out, so no Section 179 deduction is allowed.

#### TAXABLE INCOME LIMIT

The total Section 179 deduction cannot exceed taxable income from the active conduct of a business. You are treated as actively conducting a business if you participate in a meaningful way in the management or operations of a business.

Taxable income for purposes of this limit has a special meaning. Start with your net income (or loss) from all businesses that you actively conduct. If you are married and file jointly, add your spouse's net income (or loss). This includes certain gains and losses, called Section 1231 gains and losses (see Chapter 6), and interest from working capital in your business. It also includes salary, wages, and other compensation earned as an employee, so even though a moonlighting business that bought the equipment has little or no income, you may still be eligible for a full Section 179 deduction if your salary from your day job is sufficient. Figure taxable income without regard to the Section 179 deduction, the deduction for the employer portion of self-employment tax, and any net operating loss carryback or carryforward for any type of business. This, then, is your taxable income for purposes of the taxable income limitation (it does not reflect the qualified business income deduction, which isn't taken into account for this purpose). If your taxable income limits your deduction, any unused deduction can be carried forward and used in a future year.

**Example**

**Your taxable income for purposes of the limit in 2021 (without regard to a Section 179 deduction and other deductions not taken into account in figuring taxable income for this purpose) is $68,000. You place in service in 2021 a machine costing $75,000. Your first-year expense deduction is limited to $68,000. You can carry forward the additional $7,000 to 2021.**

Carryforwards of unused Section 179 deductions can be used if there is sufficient taxable income in the next year. You can choose the properties for which the costs will be carried forward. You can allocate the portion of the costs to these properties as long as the allocation is reflected on your books and records.

### *Special Rules for Pass-Through Entities*

The dollar limit, investment limit, and taxable income limit apply at both the entity and owner levels. This means that partnerships, as well as their partners, and S corporations, as well as their shareholders, must apply all the limits. The same is true for LLCs and members.

While the dollar limit and the investment limits are unlikely to be exceeded for small business owners, the taxable income limit could easily cap a deduction for the year.

For fiscal-year entities, the dollar limit in effect at the start of their fiscal year applies. For owners of fiscal-year pass-through entities, the dollar limit at the owner level applies at the start of the owner's tax year.

### *Should the Section 179 Deduction Be Elected?*

You don't automatically claim this deduction; you must elect it on Form 4562. While the Section 179 deduction provides a great opportunity for matching your tax write-off with your cash outlay, it is not always advisable to take advantage of this opportunity. Consider forgoing the election in the following situations:

- You use bonus depreciation for eligible property (described later).
- You receive the write-off through a pass-through entity but your taxable income is not enough to permit you to claim it for purchases made through your sole proprietorship.
- You are in a low tax bracket this year but expect to be more profitable in the coming years so that depreciation deductions in those years will be more valuable.
- You want to report income to obtain credits for Social Security benefits.
- You are not profitable this year. The Section 179 deduction cannot be used to create or increase a net operating loss.

**NOTE**

**The Section 179 deduction election on a federal income tax return does not automatically provide the same tax break for state income tax purposes. Some states restrict this deduction.**

Keep in mind the impact of the Section 179 deduction the QBI deduction. It may be useful to reduce taxable income below the threshold amount for the QBI deduction.

**Example**

**A dentist is married and has taxable income in 2021 of $490,000 ($400,000 of which is from his dental practice). Because his taxable income is above the $429,800 limit for claiming any QBI deduction by someone performing services in a specified service trade or business (a dentist), he is barred from any QBI deduction. However, if he were to purchase and place in service equipment for his practice of $150,000 and elect to use the Section 179 deduction, he would reduce the income from his practice and his taxable income by $150,000. The effect of the investment in new equipment produces the following positive results:**

- **Better business activity**
- **A partial QBI deduction**
- **Overall savings on federal income taxes**

### *Making or Revoking a Section 179 Expensing Election*

Usually, a Section 179 expensing election must be made on an original tax return for the year to which the election applies. However, you can make or revoke an election to use Section 179 expensing without obtaining IRS permission. The change is made on an amended return that must specify the item and portion of its cost for which an election is being made or revoked. You have until the time limit for filing an amended return (e.g., April 15, 2025, for a 2021 return filed on April 18, 2022).

### *Dispositions of Section 179 Expense Property*

If you sell or otherwise dispose of property for which a Section 179 deduction was claimed, or cease using the property for business, there may be recapture of your deduction. This means that you must include in your income a portion of the deduction you previously claimed. The amount you must recapture depends on when you dispose of the property. The longer you hold it, the less recapture you have. If you sell property at a gain, recapture is not additional income; it is merely a reclassification of income. If you realize gain on the sale of Section 179 property, instead of treating the gain as capital gain, the recapture amount is characterized as ordinary income.

Recapture is calculated by comparing your Section 179 deduction with the deduction you would have claimed had you instead taken ordinary depreciation.

**Example**

**In 2018, you placed in service office furniture (7-year property) costing $10,000, which you fully expensed. In 2021, you used the property only 40% for business (and 60% for personal purposes). You calculate your recapture as shown in Table 14.1.**

If you transfer Section 179 property in a transaction that does not require recognition of gain or loss (e.g., if you make a tax-free exchange or contribute the property to a corporation in a tax-free incorporation), an adjustment is made in the basis of the property. The adjusted basis of the property is increased before the disposition by the amount of the first-year expense deduction that is disallowed. The new owner cannot claim a first-year expense deduction with respect to this disallowed portion.

## Other Expensing Opportunities

In addition to Section 179 expensing, the tax law is peppered with provisions that let businesses expense certain types of expenditures instead of amortizing them or treating them simply as a capital cost. Some of these provisions have broad application, while many of them are limited to specific industries.

- Acquired intangibles (later in this chapter)
- Business start-up costs (later in this chapter)
- Corporate organizational expenses (later in this chapter)
- EPA sulfur regulation costs (Chapter 10)
- Expenditures to remove architectural barriers to the elderly and the handicapped (Chapter 10)

**TABLE 14.1 Calculating Recapture**

| | | |
|---|---|---|
| **Section 179 Deduction** | | **$10,000** |
| **Allowable Depreciation** | | |
| **$10,000 × 14.29%*** | **$1,429** | |
| **10,000 × 24.49** | **2,449** | |
| **10,000 × 17.49** | **1,749** | |
| **10,000 × 12.49 × 40%** | **500** | **$6,127** |
| **Recapture amount** | | **$3,873** |

*MACRS percentages from Table 14.2.

- Fertilizer used by farmers (Chapter 20)
- Partnership organizational expenses (later in this chapter)
- Qualified disaster costs (later in this chapter)
- Reforestation expenses (Chapter 20)

## Bonus Depreciation

There is a special first-year depreciation allowance that can be claimed for eligible property placed in service in 2021. The deduction is sometimes referred to as a first-year expense deduction. The allowance does not change the amount of depreciation over the property's life; it merely accelerates it so you get the benefit up front.

The bonus depreciation allowance in 2021 is 100% of the adjusted basis of the property.

**Looking Ahead**

**Bonus depreciation is scheduled to decrease to 80% in 2023, 60% in 2024, 40% in 2025, and 20% in 2026. No bonus depreciation will be permissible after 2026 unless Congress changes the law.**

While bonus depreciation is automatic (you don't have to elect it), you can choose *not* to use it. Instead, you can waive it for any or all classes of assets (for example, you can waive it for all 5-year property). However, you cannot use it for some assets within the class but not for others within the same class. Also, state income tax rules on bonus depreciation vary. Even if you claim it for federal income tax purposes, you may not enjoy a similar break at the state income tax level.

### *Eligible Property*

Generally, eligible property for bonus depreciation means tangible personal property with a recovery period of 20 years or less.

Computer software acquired separately from hardware also qualifies for bonus depreciation.

Property used by certain motor vehicle, boat, and farm machinery businesses that uses floor financing indebtedness (debt secured by motor vehicles, boats, and farm machinery held for sale or lease) is qualified property for bonus depreciation in some situations. It doesn't qualify if the business is subject to the interest deduction limit and deducts interest (it appears that if it is subject to the limit but doesn't deduct any interest, it can use bonus depreciation). However, for small businesses (for 2021, this means having average annual gross receipts in the 3 prior years not exceeding $26 million) that are not subject to the limit on the interest deduction, the property qualifies for bonus depreciation.

The costs of certain television, film productions, and live theatrical productions qualify for bonus depreciation.

Certain limitations apply for claiming bonus depreciation for production costs:

- 75% of the costs must be incurred in the U.S.
- For TV production costs, only costs for the first 44 episodes qualify.
- No bonus depreciation can be claimed for productions or programs that depict sexually explicit conduct.

The deduction is claimed when the property is placed in service (not when the costs are paid or incurred) and "placed in service" occurs at the time of the initial broadcast, release, or live staged performance.

Certain specified plants bearing fruits and nuts are eligible property. These include any tree or vine that bears fruit or nuts, and any other plant that will have more than one yield of fruit or nuts and generally has a pre-productive period of more than 2 years from planting or grafting to the time it begins bearing.

## General Rules for Depreciation

### *Depreciable Property*

Depreciation is a deduction allowed for certain property used in your business. The importance of depreciation is lessened in view of first-year write-off opportunities (Section 179 deduction and bonus depreciation) for a wide range of properties. However, depreciation still comes into play in some situations. It is a write-off option that is designed to offset the cost of acquiring it, so you cannot depreciate leased property. To be depreciable, the property must be the kind that wears out, decays, gets used up, becomes obsolete, or loses value from natural causes. The property must have a determinable useful life that is longer than one year.

As a practical matter, computations for depreciation are made by computer once the necessary information, such as **basis**, date of acquisition, and the applicability of any special depreciation rules, are entered in the tax preparation program. However, because depreciation is deduction that extends beyond the current tax year, it is necessary to keep track of depreciation deductions each year (again, something that is done automatically by tax preparation programs).

***Basis*** **Generally, basis is the amount you pay for property. It does not matter whether you finance your purchase or pay cash. You add to basis sales taxes and other related expenses (such as nondeductible closing costs if you get a mortgage, or attorney's fees). But you cannot include the value of trade-ins in your basis. You need records to prove basis and cannot merely estimate it.**

If you convert personal property to business use (explained later in this chapter), the basis for purposes of depreciation is the lower of its adjusted basis (generally cost) or fair market value at the time of the conversion to business use.

If you acquire replacement property in a like-kind exchange or an involuntary conversion, special rules govern basis for purposes of depreciation (see IRS Publication 946, *How to Depreciate Property*).

**Example**

**In 2021, you begin to use a personal computer for a business you have just started up. You paid $2,500 for it in 2020, and it is now worth $1,200. Your basis for depreciation is $1,200. At the same time, you begin to use one room in your home as a home office. You bought your home in 2012 for $200,000, and it is now worth $300,000 (exclusive of land). Assuming that the home office allocation is 12.5% of the home, your basis for depreciation (if you use the actual expense method to figure the home office deduction) is $25,000 (12.5% of $200,000, which is lower than 12.5% of $300,000, or $37,500).**

Property that can be expected to last for one year or less is simply deducted in full as some other type of deduction. For example, if you buy stationery that will be used up within the year, you simply deduct the cost of the stationery as supplies. In order to claim depreciation, you must be the owner of the property. If you lease property, like an office, you cannot depreciate it; only the owner can, since it is the owner who suffers the wear and tear on his or her investment.

Depreciable property may be tangible or intangible. *Tangible property* is property you can touch—office furniture, a machine, or a telephone. Tangible property may be personal property (a machine) or real property (a factory). *Intangible property* is property you cannot touch, such as copyrights, patents, and franchises. *Personal property* does not mean you use the property for personal purposes; it is a legal term for tangible property that is not real property.

If you use property for both business and personal purposes, you must make an allocation. You can claim depreciation only on the business portion of the property. For example, if you use your car 75% for business and 25% for personal purposes (including commuting), you can claim depreciation on only 75% of the property. However, special rules apply to a building that is used partly for residential rental and partly for commercial purposes (see later in this chapter).

### Certain Property Can Never Be Depreciated

- *Antiques* generally cannot be depreciated because they do not have a determinable useful life; they can be expected to last indefinitely. The same is true for goodwill you build up in your business (though if you buy a business and pay for its goodwill, you may be able to amortize the cost, as explained later in this chapter).
- *Inventory* is property held primarily for sale to customers in the ordinary course of your business. Sometimes, you may question whether an asset is really part of your inventory or if it is a separate asset that can be depreciated. For example, containers generally are treated as part of the cost of your inventory and cannot be separately depreciated. However, containers used to ship products can be depreciated if your invoice treats them as separate items, whether your sales contract shows that you retain title to the containers and whether your records properly state your basis in the containers.
- *Land* is not depreciable because it, too, can be expected to last indefinitely. Land includes not only the cost of the acreage but also the cost of clearing, grading, planting, and landscaping. However, some land preparation costs can be depreciated if they are closely associated with a building on the land rather than the land itself. For example, shrubs around the entry to a building may be depreciated; trees planted on the perimeter of the property are nondepreciable land costs. Also, the cost of the minerals on the land may not be depreciated but may be subject to depletion.

  When you own a building, you must allocate the basis of the property between the building and the land, since only the building portion is depreciable.

  There is no special rule for making an allocation of basis. Obviously, you would prefer to allocate as much as possible to the building and as little as possible to the land. However, the allocation must have some logical basis. It should be based on the relative value of each portion. What is the land worth? What is the building worth? You may want to use the services of an appraiser to help you derive a fair yet favorable allocation that will withstand IRS scrutiny.

### When to Claim Depreciation

You claim depreciation beginning with the year in which the property is **placed in service**.

***Placed in service*** **When an item is ready and available for a specific use, whether or not the item is actually used.**

**Example**

**You buy a machine in December, which is delivered to you before the end of the year. However, it's not installed or operational until January. It is not placed in service in December.**

When you convert personal items to business use (e.g., you open a business from home and begin to use your desk for business), the desk is treated as having been placed in service on the date of the change (the conversion to business use).

You continue to claim depreciation throughout the life of the asset. The life of the asset is also called its *recovery period*. Different types of assets have different recovery periods fixed by law. The length of the recovery period has nothing to do with how durable a particular item may be. You simply check the classifications of property to find the recovery period for a particular item.

You stop claiming depreciation on the item when the property's cost has been fully depreciated or when the property is retired from service. Property is retired from service when it is permanently withdrawn from use by disposing of it (selling or exchanging it, abandoning it, or destroying it). It's also treated has having been disposed of when converted to personal use (no longer used for business).

**Example**

**A machine with a 5-year recovery period is no longer needed after 3 years for the task for which it was purchased. The machine is sold to another company that still has a use for it. Once the machine is sold, it has been permanently removed from your service. You cannot claim depreciation after this occurs.**

When you replace a roof or other building component, you have a choice of how to treat the undepreciated basis of the replaced component. This is explained in Chapter 10.

The amount of depreciation you can claim in the year in which property is placed in service or retired from service is limited and is discussed later in this chapter.

Even if you do not actually claim depreciation, you are treated as having done so for purposes of figuring the basis of property when you dispose of it.

If you failed to claim depreciation in the past, file an amended return to fix the error if the tax year is still open (the statute of limitations on amending the return has not expired). Alternatively, you can correct the underdepreciation (even for a closed tax year) by filing for a change in accounting method on Form 3115 (follow filing instructions to Form 3115). Under a special IRS procedure, you simply adjust your income in the current year.

**Example**

**You place a piece of machinery in service in 2020 and claim a depreciation deduction on your 2020 return. In 2021, your revenues are low, and you forget to report your depreciation deduction on your 2021 return. In 2022, you sell the machine. In calculating gain or loss on the sale, you must adjust basis for the depreciation you actually claimed in 2020 and the depreciation you should have claimed in 2021.**

If you abandon property before it has been fully depreciated, you can deduct the balance of your depreciation deductions in the year of abandonment. For instance, if you have a machine with a 7-year recovery period that you abandon in the fifth year because it is obsolete, you can claim the depreciation that you would have claimed in the sixth, seventh, and eighth years in the fifth year along with depreciation allowable for that year.

## Modified Accelerated Cost Recovery System

Modified Accelerated Cost Recovery System (MACRS) is the current depreciation system. It is composed of 2 systems: a basic system, called the *General Depreciation System* (GDS), and an alternate system, called the *Alternative Depreciation System* (ADS). The difference between the 2 systems is the recovery period over which you claim depreciation and the method for calculating depreciation. You use the basic system unless the alternative system is required or you make a special election to use the alternative system. You cannot use either system for certain property: Intangible property (patents, copyrights, etc.), motion picture films or videotapes, sound recordings, and property you elect to exclude from MACRS so that you can use a depreciation method based on some other measuring rod than a term of years (these other methods are not discussed in this book).

### *Basic System*

You can use the basic General Depreciation System (GDS) to depreciate any tangible property unless you are required to use the Alternative Depreciation System (ADS), elect to use the ADS, or are required to use some other depreciation method. To calculate your depreciation deduction, you need to know:

- *The property's basis*. If you purchase property, basis is your cost. If you acquire property in some other way (get it by gift, inheritance, or in a tax-free exchange), basis is figured in another way. For example, if your corporation acquires property from you upon its formation in a tax-free incorporation, then the corporation steps into your shoes for purposes of basis.

**Example**

**You form a corporation (C or S) and contribute cash and a computer. In exchange, you receive all of the stock of the corporation. Your basis for the computer was $4,000. The corporation assumes your basis—$4,000.**

A similar rule applies to property you contribute to a partnership or LLC upon its formation. If you are a sole proprietor or an employee and convert property from personal use to business use, your basis for depreciation is the lesser of the fair market value (FMV) on the date of conversion to business use or the adjusted basis of the property on that date.

The cost of property includes sales taxes. If you hire an architect to design a building, the fees are added to the basis of the property and recovered through depreciation.

In the case of realty, basis is restricted to the building and certain other improvements to the land; the land is not depreciable. For basis purposes, you must make an allocation between the building and the land. This allocation can be based on an assessor's office assessment of improvements (the building) or a good appraisal.

The following are more items to consider when calculating your depreciation deduction.

- *The property's **recovery period***. Recovery periods are fixed according to the claim in which a property falls. In the past, recovery period was referred to as the useful life of the property, and you may occasionally see this old phrase still in use.
- *The date the property is placed in service*. Remember, this is the date the property is ready and available for its specific use.
- *The applicable convention*. These are special rules that govern the timing of deductions (explained later in this chapter).
- *The depreciation method*. MACRS has 5 different depreciation methods.

***Recovery period*** **The period over which an asset may be depreciated.**

### *Recovery Periods*

The ***class life*** assigned to a property is designed to match the period over which the basis of property is recovered (e.g., cost is deducted). Five-year property allows the cost of certain equipment to be deducted over 5 years (subject to adjustment for conventions, discussed later, actually means deductions over 6 years).

***Class life*** **The useful life of a type of property set under the General Depreciation System or the Alternative Depreciation System.**

The actual recovery periods are listed in Table 14.2.

**TABLE 14.2 Property Class Life under GDS versus Actual Recovery Period**

| Property Class Life under GDS | Actual Recovery Period |
|---|---|
| 3-year | 4 years |
| 5-year | 6 years |
| 7-year | 8 years |
| 10-year | 11 years |
| 15-year | 16 years |

### 3-YEAR PROPERTY

This property includes taxis, tractor units for use over the road, racehorses 2 years and younger (but only for 2021 unless Congress extends this rule), any other horse over 12 years old when placed in service, breeding hogs, certain handling devices for manufacturing food and beverages, and special tools for manufacturing rubber products. Special rules for computer software specially created for your business are discussed under "Amortization" later in this chapter.

### 5-YEAR PROPERTY

This property includes cars, buses, trucks, airplanes, trailers and trailer containers, computers and peripheral equipment, some office machinery (calculators, copiers, typewriters), assets used in construction, logging equipment, assets used to manufacture organic and inorganic chemicals, and property used in research and experimentation. It also includes breeding and dairy cattle and breeding and dairy goats. It also includes machinery used in a farming business that previously was treated as 7-year property.

### 7-YEAR PROPERTY

This property includes office fixtures and furniture (chairs, desks, files, safes); communications equipment (fax machines); breeding and workhorses; assets used in printing; recreational assets (miniature golf courses, billiard establishments, concert halls); assets used to produce jewelry; musical instruments; toys; sporting goods; motorsports entertainment complexes (through 2025); and motion picture and television films and tapes. This class is also the catchall for other property. It includes any property not assigned to another class.

### 10-YEAR PROPERTY

This property includes barges, tugs, vessels, and similar water transportation equipment; single-purpose agricultural or horticultural structures placed in service after 1988; and trees or vines bearing fruits or nuts.

### 15-YEAR PROPERTY

This property includes certain depreciable improvements made to land (bridges, fences, roads, shrubbery). It also includes qualified improvement property.

### 20-YEAR PROPERTY

This property includes farm buildings (other than single-purpose agricultural or horticultural structures) and any municipal sewers.

### RESIDENTIAL RENTAL REALTY

Rental buildings qualify if 80% or more of the gross rental is from dwelling units. The recovery period is 27.5 years.

Some buildings are used partly for residential rentals and partly for commercial activities, such as retail stores. The IRS has ruled privately that if at least 80% of the gross rental income from a mixed-use building is from residential rentals, then the entire building is treated as residential realty depreciated over 27.5 years. The residential rental space includes income from a parking garage. The IRS ruled privately that a house used to operate an adult home care business is treated as residential realty, depreciable over 27.5 years.

#### NONRESIDENTIAL REALTY

This class applies to factories, office buildings, and any other realty other than residential rental realty. The recovery period is 39 years (31.5 years for property placed in service before May 13, 1993). If you begin to use a portion of your home for business (e.g., a home office), use the recovery period applicable on the date of conversion. For example, if you begin to use a home office in your single-family house in 2021 (and use the actual expense method to figure the home office deduction), depreciate that portion of your home using a 39-year recovery period, even if you bought your home in 1992.

#### COMPONENTS OF REALTY

Structural components of a building are part and parcel of the realty and generally must be depreciated as such (e.g., over 39 years). However, certain components, such as electrical systems and wiring, carpeting, floor covering, plumbing connections, exhaust systems, handrails, room partitions, tile ceilings, and steam boilers, may be treated as tangible personal property instead of realty in certain situations (see Cost Segregation below). As such, they can be depreciated over shorter recovery periods rather than being treated as part of realty subject to longer recovery periods.

#### IMPROVEMENTS OR ADDITIONS

In general, improvements or additions to property are treated as separate property and are depreciated separately from the property itself. The recovery period for improvements begins on the later of the date the improvements are placed in service or the date the property to which the improvements are made is placed in service. Use the same recovery period for the improvements that you would for the underlying property (unless an improvement is a component of realty that can be depreciated according to its own recovery period).

#### COST SEGREGATION

Obtain a cost segregation (or component of cost) study when buying, building, or improving realty, or making a partial disposition of a building component. This analysis can be the basis for allocating costs to components that will be separately depreciated over shorter recovery periods for greater upfront deductions. Cost segregation does not apply to components that are part of the operation and maintenance of the building. The analysis should be performed by an engineer, architect, or realty appraiser and not by you or your accountant (unless skilled in cost segregation).

The IRS has created a cost segregation audit technique guide at https://www.irs.gov/businesses/cost-segregation-audit-techniques-guide-table-of-contents, which details the requirements for an acceptable study.

#### PROPERTY ACQUIRED IN A LIKE-KIND EXCHANGE

The property acquired in a like-kind exchange is depreciated over the remaining recovery period of the *old* property. Thus, the new property, which has the basis of the old property, also has the old property's remaining recovery period. This enables you to write off the newly acquired asset more rapidly than if the recovery period of the new asset were used.

### *Conventions*

There are 3 conventions (special rules) that affect the timing of depreciation deductions. Two apply to property other than residential or nonresidential real property (essentially personal property such as equipment); the other applies to residential or nonresidential real property (rental units, offices, and factories).

### HALF-YEAR CONVENTION

The *half-year convention* applies to all property (other than residential or nonresidential real property) unless superseded by the mid-quarter convention (explained next). Under the half-year convention, property is treated as if you placed it in service in the middle of the year. You are allowed to deduct only one-half of the depreciation allowance for the first year. This is so even if you place the property in service on the first day of the year. Under this convention, property is treated as disposed of in the middle of the year, regardless of the actual date of disposition.

The half-year convention means that property held for its entire recovery period will have an additional year for claiming depreciation deductions. Only one-half of the first year's depreciation deduction is claimed in the first year; the balance of depreciation is claimed in the year following the last year of the recovery period.

**Example**

**A desk (7-year property) is placed in service on January 1, 2021, and neither first-year expensing or bonus depreciation is used. One-half of the depreciation deduction that would otherwise be claimed in the first year is allowed. Normal depreciation is claimed in years 2 through 7. The remaining depreciation is claimed in the eighth year.**

### MID-QUARTER CONVENTION

Under the *mid-quarter convention*, all property placed in service during the year (or disposed of during the year) is treated as placed in service (or disposed of) in the middle of the applicable quarter. The mid-quarter convention applies (and the half-year convention does not) if the total bases of all property placed in service during the last 3 months of the year (the final quarter) exceed 40% of the total bases of property placed in service during the entire year. In making this determination, do not take into consideration residential or nonresidential real property or property placed in service and then disposed of in the same year.

**Example**

**You are on a calendar year. In January 2021, you place in service machine A, costing $3,000. In November 2021, you place in service another machine, machine B, costing $10,000. (Assume neither machine qualifies for bonus depreciation.) You must use the mid-quarter convention to calculate depreciation for both machines. This is because more than 40% of all property placed in service during the year ($13,000) was placed in service in the final quarter of the year ($10,000). (Actually, 77% of all property placed in service in the year was placed in service in the final quarter of the year.)**

**Example**

**Continue with the same machine situation, except that machine B is placed in service in January and machine A is placed in service in November. In this instance, the mid-quarter convention does not apply because only 23% of all property placed in service in 2021 was placed in service in the final quarter of the year.**

#### MID-MONTH CONVENTION

This convention applies to real property. You must treat all real property as if it were placed in service or disposed of in the middle of the month. The mid-month convention is taken into account in the depreciation tables from which you can take your deduction. Simply look at the table for the type of realty (residential or nonresidential) you own, and then look in the table for the month in which the property is placed in service.

## Depreciation Methods

There are 5 ways to depreciate property: the 200% declining balance rate, the 150% declining balance rate, the straight-line election, the 150% election, and the ADS method. Both 200% and 150% declining balance rates are referred to as accelerated rates.

You may use the 200% rate for 3-, 5-, 7-, and 10-year property over the GDS actual recovery period. The half-year or mid-quarter convention must be applied. The 200% declining balance method is calculated by dividing 100 by the recovery period and then doubling it. However, as a practical matter, you do not have to compute the rates. They are provided for you in Tables 14.3 and 14.4, which take into account the half-year or mid-quarter conventions.

If the 200% declining balance rate is used, you can switch to the straight line in the year when it provides a deduction of value equal to or greater than the accelerated rate. Of course, total depreciation can never be more than 100% of the property's basis. The switch to straight line merely accelerates the timing of depreciation. Table 14.5 shows you when it becomes advantageous to switch to the straight-line rate.

You use the 150% rate for 15- and 20-year property over the GDS recovery period. Again, you must also apply the half-year or mid-quarter convention. You change over to the straight-line method when it provides a greater deduction. Tables for this rate may be found in IRS Publication 946, *How to Depreciate Property*.

Residential and nonresidential realty must use the straight-line rate (see Tables 14.6 to 14.8). *Straight line* is simply the cost of the property (exclusive of the land) divided by the life of the property. However, you begin depreciation with the month in which the property is placed in service. This makes the rate vary slightly over the years. The tables can be used to calculate depreciation for residential and nonresidential real property using basic depreciation (GDS). If

**TABLE 14.3 MACRS Rates—Half-Year Convention**

| Year | 3-Year Property | 5-Year Property | 7-Year Property |
|---|---|---|---|
| 1 | 33.33% | 20.00% | 14.29% |
| 2 | 44.45 | 32.00 | 24.49 |
| 3 | 14.81 | 19.20 | 17.49 |
| 4 | 7.81 | 11.52 | 12.49 |
| 5 | | 11.52 | 8.93 |
| 6 | | 5.76 | 8.92 |
| 7 | | | 8.93 |
| 8 | | | 4.46 |

**TABLE 14.4 MACRS Rates—Mid-Quarter Convention (200% Rate)**

| Year | First Quarter | Second Quarter | Third Quarter | Fourth Quarter |
|---|---|---|---|---|
| | | 3-Year Property | | |
| 1 | 58.33% | 41.67% | 25.00% | 8.33% |
| 2 | 27.78 | 38.89 | 50.00 | 61.11 |
| 3 | 12.35 | 14.14 | 16.677 | 20.37 |
| 4 | 1.54 | 5.30 | 8.33 | 10.19 |
| | | 5-Year Property | | |
| 1 | 35.00 | 25.00 | 15.00 | 5.00 |
| 2 | 26.00 | 30.00 | 34.00 | 38.00 |
| 3 | 15.60 | 18.00 | 20.40 | 22.80 |
| 4 | 11.01 | 11.37 | 12.24 | 13.68 |
| 5 | 11.01 | 11.37 | 11.30 | 10.94 |
| 6 | 1.38 | 4.26 | 7.06 | 9.58 |
| | | 7-Year Property | | |
| 1 | 25.00 | 17.85 | 10.71 | 3.57 |
| 2 | 21.43 | 23.47 | 25.51 | 27.55 |
| 3 | 15.31 | 16.76 | 18.22 | 19.68 |
| 4 | 10.93 | 11.97 | 13.02 | 14.06 |
| 5 | 8.75 | 8.87 | 9.30 | 10.04 |
| 6 | 8.74 | 8.87 | 8.85 | 8.73 |
| 7 | 8.75 | 8.87 | 8.86 | 8.73 |
| 8 | 1.09 | 3.33 | 5.53 | 7.64 |

**TABLE 14.5 When to Change to Straight-Line Method**

| Class | Changeover Year |
|---|---|
| 3-year property | 3rd |
| 5-year property | 4th |
| 7-year property | 5th |
| 10-year property | 7th |
| 15-year property | 7th |
| 20-year property | 9th |

you place nonresidential realty in service in 2021, be sure to use the 39-year table. For all tables, find your annual depreciation rate by looking in the column for the month in which the property was placed in service (for example, for calendar-year businesses, March is 3; August is 8). Then look at the year of ownership you are in (e.g., the year in which you place property in service, look at year number 1).

**TABLE 14.6** Rates for Residential Realty Years (27 Years), Straight-Line, Mid-Month Convention

| | Month in the First Recovery Year the Property Is Placed in Service | | | | | |
|---|---|---|---|---|---|---|
| Year | 1 | 2 | 3 | 4 | 5 | 6 |
| 1 | 3.485% | 3.182% | 2.879% | 2.576% | 2.273% | 1.970% |
| 2–9 | 3.636 | 3.636 | 3.636 | 3.636 | 3.636 | 3.636 |
| Year | 7 | 8 | 9 | 10 | 11 | 12 |
| 1 | 1.677% | 1.364% | 1.061% | 0.758% | 0.455% | 0.152% |
| 2–9 | 3.636 | 3.636 | 3.636 | 3.636 | 3.636 | 3.636 |

**TABLE 14.7** Rates for Nonresidential Realty Years (31.5 Years), Straight-Line, Mid-Month Convention

| | Month in the First Recovery Year the Property Is Placed in Service* | | | | | |
|---|---|---|---|---|---|---|
| Year | 1 | 2 | 3 | 4 | 5 | 6 |
| 1 | 3.042% | 2.778% | 2.513% | 2.249% | 1.984% | 1.720% |
| 2–7 | 3.175 | 3.175 | 3.175 | 3.175 | 3.175 | 3.175 |
| 8 | 3.175 | 3.174 | 3.175 | 3.174 | 3.175 | 3.174 |
| 9 | 3.174 | 3.175 | 3.174 | 3.175 | 3.174 | 3.175 |
| Year | 7 | 8 | 9 | 10 | 11 | 12 |
| 1 | 1.455% | 1.190% | 0.926% | 0.661% | 0.397% | 0.132% |
| 2–7 | 3.175 | 3.175 | 3.175 | 3.175 | 3.175 | 3.175 |
| 8 | 3.175 | 3.175 | 3.175 | 3.175 | 3.175 | 3.175 |
| 9 | 3.174 | 3.175 | 3.174 | 3.175 | 3.174 | 3.175 |

*Property placed in service before May 13, 1993.

**TABLE 14.8** Rates for Nonresidential Realty Years (39 Years), Straight-Line, Mid-Month Convention

| | Month in the First Recovery Year the Property Is Placed in Service | | | | | |
|---|---|---|---|---|---|---|
| Year | 1 | 2 | 3 | 4 | 5 | 6 |
| 1 | 2.461% | 2.247% | 2.033% | 1.819% | 1.605% | 1.391% |
| 2–39 | 2.564 | 2.564 | 2.564 | 2.564 | 2.564 | 2.564 |
| Year | 7 | 8 | 9 | 10 | 11 | 12 |
| 1 | 1.177% | 0.963% | 0.749% | 0.535% | 0.321% | 0.107% |
| 2–39 | 2.564 | 2.564 | 2.564 | 2.564 | 2.564 | 2.564 |

**Example**

**You are on a calendar year and placed in service a factory in April 2018. In 2021, your depreciation rate is 2.564%. You find this rate by looking at the table for 39-year nonresidential property under month 4, year 4.**

Usually, when the actual expense method is used for the home office deduction, a home office is depreciated over 39 years. The 27.5-year recovery period can be used only for a home office in a multifamily residence where more than 80% of the space is leased to third parties.

Tables for depreciation of residential and nonresidential real property using ADS nonresidential realty may be found in Appendix A of IRS Publication 946, *How to Depreciate Property*.

You can elect to use the 150% rate for properties eligible for the 200% rate. If the election is made, the 150% rate is used over the ADS recovery period. Again, a half-year or mid-quarter convention is applied, and there is a changeover to the straight-line method when it provides a greater deduction. The election may be advisable if you do not think you will have sufficient income to offset larger depreciation deductions. It may also be advisable to lessen or avoid the alternative minimum tax for your personal return.

**NOTE**

**Once you make the election to use the 150% rate over the ADS recovery period, you cannot change your mind.**

### *Alternative Depreciation System*

You must use the alternative system (ADS) (and not the basic system, GDS) for an electing real property trade or business or farming business. This is a business that elects out of the interest deduction limitations that essentially cap a deduction in 2020 for net interest expenses at 50% of a business's adjusted taxable income (see Chapter 13). A real property trade or business and a farming business are explained further in Chapter 13.

Also, you must use ADS for the following property (see Table 14.9):

- Listed property not used more than 50% for business. Listed property includes cars and other transportation vehicles.
- Tangible property used predominantly outside the United States.
- Tax-exempt use property.
- Tax-exempt bond-financed property.
- Imported property covered by an executive order of the president of the United States.
- Property used predominantly in farming and placed in service during any year in which you elect not to apply the uniform capitalization rules to certain farming costs.

**TABLE 14.9 Recovery Periods under Alternative Depreciation System (ADS)**

| Property | Years |
|---|---|
| Cars, computers, light-duty trucks | 5 |
| Furniture and fixtures | 10 |
| Personal property with no class life | 12 |
| Nonresidential/residential real estate* | 30 |

*For residential rental property placed in service before January 1, 2018, the ADS recovery period is 40 years.

The ADS requires depreciation to be calculated using the straight-line method. This is done by dividing the cost of the property by the alternative recovery period. In some cases, the recovery period is the same as for the basic system; in others, it is longer. Note that the ADS recovery period for residential rental property placed in service after December 31, 2017, is 30 years (it was 40 years for pre-January 1, 2018, property).

You can elect to use ADS for other property in order to claim more gradual depreciation. The election applies to all property within the same class placed in service during the year (other than real estate). For residential rental and nonresidential real property, you can make the election to use ADS on a property-by-property basis.

An election to use ADS may be helpful, for example, if you are first starting out and do not have sufficient income to offset large depreciation deductions. Use of ADS can help to avoid alternative minimum tax and the special depreciation computations required for alternative minimum tax.

You can calculate depreciation for regular tax purposes using the same recovery periods as required for alternative minimum tax (AMT) purposes. This eliminates the need to make any adjustments for alternative minimum tax and to keep separate records of depreciation taken for regular and alternative minimum tax purposes. Because C corporations are not subject to the AMT, this is not a consideration.

### Recapture of Depreciation

If you sell or otherwise dispose of depreciable or amortizable property at a gain, you may have to report all or some of your gain as ordinary income. The treatment of what would otherwise have been capital gain as ordinary income is called *recapture*. In effect, some of the tax benefit you enjoy from depreciation deductions may be offset later on by recapture.

Also, if you sell or otherwise dispose of real property (e.g., residence containing a home office) on which straight-line depreciation was claimed after May 6, 1997, all such depreciation is taxed as capital gain up to 25%. This taxable portion is referred to as *unrecaptured depreciation*. The treatment of income from depreciation recapture is explained in Chapter 6.

### Recordkeeping for Depreciation

Since depreciation deductions go on for a number of years, it is important to keep good records of prior deductions. It is also necessary to maintain records since depreciation deductions may differ for regular income tax purposes and the alternative minimum tax. Recordkeeping is explained in Chapter 3.

## Limitations on Listed Property

Certain property is called *listed property* and is subject to special depreciation limits. Listed property includes:

- Cars
- Other transportation vehicles (including boats)
- Property generally used for entertainment, recreation, or amusement

These are the only items considered listed property because they have been specified as such in the tax law.

Keep a log or other record for the use of listed property. This will help you show that business use is more than 50%.

If business use of listed property is not more than 50% during the year, the basic depreciation system cannot be used. In this case, you must use the ADS. Under this system, depreciation can be calculated only with the straight-line method. Divide the cost of the property by the alternative recovery period. For cars and other listed property, the alternative recovery period happens to be the same as the basic recovery period—6 years.

Use of the ADS means that instead of accelerating depreciation deductions to the earlier years of ownership, depreciation deductions will be spread evenly over the recovery period of the property.

## De Minimis Safe Harbor Rule

Instead of treating items you purchase as assets on your books and then taking first-year expensing, bonus depreciation, and/or regular depreciation, you can use what is known as the de minimis safe harbor for tangible personal property. While the word "personal" is used, it doesn't mean items for your personal use. It refers to items you can touch as opposed to realty or intangible items. Under this safe harbor, you can elect to treat them as nonincidental materials and supplies. Making this election allows you to currently deduct the cost. In 2021, the limit per item or invoice for businesses without an applicable financial statement, such as an audited financial statement or SEC filing (i.e., almost all small businesses) is $2,500.

**Example**

**You own a small motel with 24 rooms. You buy new irons for each of them at a cost of $28 each. Instead of capitalizing the cost of $672 ($28 x 24), you can elect to treat the purchase as nonincidental materials and supplies.**

Nonincidental materials and supplies are items for which there is a record of use (e.g., a physical count of the items on hand). As such, these items are deductible when used or consumed.

An election to use this de minimis rule must be made on a timely filed original tax return each year you want to use it by attaching your own statement to the return. The statement must include certain information specified at the end of this chapter.

## Putting Personal Property to Business Use

You may already own some items that can be useful to your business, such as a home computer, office furniture, and a cell phone. You don't have to go out and buy new items for the business; you can convert what you already own from personal to business use.

For depreciation purposes, the basis of each item is the lower of its adjusted basis (usually its cost) or its value at the time of conversion. For most items that decline in value over time, this means that depreciation is usually based on value. But for other property, such as realty that typically increases in value, depreciation is usually based on adjusted basis.

**Example**

**In 2020, you purchased some office furniture for home use at a cost of $3,000. In 2021, you start a business and begin to use the furniture for business activities. Its value in 2021 is $1,000. For depreciation purposes, you are limited to $1,000; in this case the computer's value is lower than its adjusted basis.**

**Example**

**In 2018, you bought your home for $200,000. In 2021, you start a business from home and use 10% of the space exclusively for this purpose. The house is now worth $240,000. For depreciation purposes, you are limited to $20,000 (10% of $200,000); in this case the adjusted basis is lower than the home's current value.**

You cannot use the Section 179 deduction for property you convert from personal to business use in a year that is after the year you acquired the property. The law limits this deduction to the year in which property is initially placed in service.

## Amortization

Certain capital expenditures can be deducted over a term of years. This is called *amortization*. This deduction is taken evenly over a prescribed period of time. Amortization generally applies to the following expenditures:

- Intangibles acquired on the purchase of a business
- Business start-up costs and organizational expenses
- Construction period interest and taxes
- Research and experimentation costs
- Bond premiums
- Reforestation costs
- Costs of acquiring a lease

Amortization for pollution control facilities, which are typically set up only by large corporations, is not discussed in this book.

### *Intangibles Acquired on the Purchase of a Business*

If you buy a business, a portion of your cost may be allocated to certain intangible items:

- Goodwill
- Going concern value
- Workforce in place
- Patents, copyrights, formulas, processes, designs, patterns, and know-how

- Customer-based intangibles
- Supplier-based intangibles
- Licenses, permits, and other rights granted by a governmental unit or agency
- Covenants not to compete
- Trademarks or trade names
- Franchises (including sports franchises) (but ongoing franchise fees are currently deductible)

These items are called *Section 197 intangibles*, named after a section in the Internal Revenue Code. You may deduct the portion of the cost allocated to these items ratably over a period of 15 years.

**Example**

**You buy out the accounting practice of someone else. As part of the sale, the other accountant signs a covenant not to compete with you for 2 years within your same location. You may amortize the portion of the cost of the practice relating to the covenant over 15 years.**

Section 197 intangibles do not include interests in a corporation, partnership, trust or estate, interests in land, certain computer software, and certain other excluded items. Also, you cannot amortize the cost of self-created items. Thus, if you generate your own customer list, you cannot claim an amortization deduction.

There is a special rule for domain names that you buy in the secondary market. How you treat the cost to acquire a domain name depends on whether the name is generic (describes a product or service in terms that people associate with the topic) or nongeneric (usually a company name or product which is or functions like a trademark to identify goods or services and to distinguish them from those provided by others). More specifically, if the domain name is similar to a Section 197 intangible, it may be treated as such, with costs amortized over 15 years (see Chief Counsel Memorandum 201543014 for more details).

If a domain name is not a Section 197 intangible, the 15-year amortization rule for Section 197 intangibles doesn't apply and the domain name's cost can be amortized only if you can show there is a limited useful life to it. If not (as will usually be the case), it's just an asset carried on your books with no tax write-off.

#### ANTICHURNING RULES

If you already own a business with goodwill and other intangibles, you cannot convert these into Section 197 intangibles, for which an amortization deduction would be allowed, by engaging in a transaction solely for this purpose. Special antichurning rules prevent amortization for intangibles acquired in transactions designed to create an acquisition date after August 10, 1993 (the date on which Section 197 intangibles came into being), for assets that were previously owned as of that date.

#### DISPOSITIONS

If you sell a Section 197 asset that you held for more than one year, gain is ordinary income up to the amount of amortization allowed; the balance, if any, is Section 1231 gain (this gain is explained in Chapter 6). If the asset was held for only one year or less, all of the gain is ordinary income.

If you sell multiple Section 197 assets in a single transaction or a series of related transactions, ordinary recapture is figured as if all such intangibles were a single asset.

If a Section 197 intangible is sold at a loss but other such intangibles are still owned, no loss can be taken on the sale. Instead, the bases of the remaining Section 197 intangibles are reduced by the unclaimed loss. The same rule applies if a Section 197 intangible becomes worthless or is abandoned. No loss is recognized on the worthlessness or abandonment. Instead, the bases of remaining Section 197 intangibles are increased by the unrecognized loss.

### *Self-Created Intangibles*

If you create an intangible, such as a trademark, you cannot amortize the costs you incur (e.g., registration fees to the U.S. Patent and Trademark Office and attorney's fees). These costs are capitalized (carried on the company's books as an asset).

### *Business Start-Up Costs and Organizational Expenses*

When you start up a business, you may incur a variety of expenses. Ordinarily, these are capital expenditures that are not currently deductible. They are expenses incurred to acquire a capital asset, namely, your business. However, the tax law allows you to write off start-up costs. The timing of your deduction depends on when you started your business.

- For start-up costs paid or incurred after October 22, 2004, and before January 1, 2010, and after December 31, 2010—you can elect to deduct $5,000 in the first year, with the balance of start-up costs amortized over 180 months. However, if costs exceed $50,000, the $5,000 immediate deduction is reduced dollar-for-dollar, so that no immediate deduction can be claimed when start-up costs exceed $55,000. In this case, *all* start-up costs must be amortized over 180 months.
- For start-up costs paid or incurred in 2010 only—you were able to elect to deduct $10,000 in the first year, with the balance of start-up costs amortized over 180 months. However, if costs exceeded $60,000, the $10,000 immediate deduction was reduced dollar-for-dollar, so that no immediate deduction could have been claimed when start-up costs exceeded $70,000. In this case, *all* start-up costs must be amortized over 180 months.

If you sell your business before the end of the amortization period or the business folds before that time, you can deduct the unamortized amount in your final year.

#### BUSINESS START-UP COSTS

Generally, you think of start-up costs as expenses you pay during the first few years of your business. But for tax purposes, the term "start-up costs" has a very specific meaning. These include amounts paid to investigate *whether* to start or purchase a business and *which* business to start or purchase (this is called the *whether and which* test for determining amortization of start-up costs). Expenses related to these activities are treated as start-up expenses. Examples of start-up costs include:

- A survey of potential markets
- An analysis of available facilities, labor, supplies, and transportation facilities
- Advertisements for the opening of the business

- Travel and other expenses incurred to get prospective distributors, suppliers, or customers
- Salaries and wages for employees who are being trained and their instructors
- Salaries and fees for consultants and executives, and fees for professional services

Other similar expenses are amortizable if they would have been deductible if paid or incurred to operate a going business and were actually paid or incurred prior to the commencement of business operations. Otherwise, such expenses must be treated as part of the cost of acquiring a capital asset—the business. For example, legal fees to prepare contracts for the purchase of a business are no longer start-up fees but, rather, are expenses that must be added to the cost of the business. You cannot deduct the value of your time spent in exploring a prospective business.

Once you have passed the start-up phase and identified a target business you want to acquire, you can no longer amortize related expenses under this rule.

**Example**

**You are looking for a business to buy and have your accountant review the financial data from several prospects. You then zero in on a business and examine its financial data in detail. The accountant's fee related to the general search is amortizable, but the fee related to the detailed examination of the target business is not.**

### ORGANIZATIONAL COSTS FOR A CORPORATION

If you set up a corporation (C or S), certain expenses unique to this form of business can be written off under the same rules that apply to business start-up costs. These expenses include the cost of:

- Temporary directors
- Organizational meetings
- State incorporation fees
- Accounting services for setting up the corporate books
- Legal services to draft the charter, bylaws, terms of the original stock certificates, and minutes of organizational meetings

You can deduct any other organizational costs if they are incidental to the creation of a corporation, they are chargeable to the capital account, and the cost could have been amortized over the life of the corporation if the corporation had a fixed life.

You cannot amortize expenses related to selling stock, such as commissions, professional fees, and printing costs.

### ORGANIZATIONAL COSTS OF A PARTNERSHIP

If you set up a partnership, certain expenses unique to this form of business can be written off under the same rules that apply to business start-up costs. As in the case of corporate organizational costs, partnership organizational costs include those that are incidental to the creation of a partnership, are chargeable to the capital account, and would have been amortizable over the life of the partnership if the partnership had a fixed life.

Syndication costs to sell partnership interests are not treated as amortizable organizational costs. These nonamortizable costs include commissions, professional fees, and printing costs related to the issuing and marketing of partnership interests.

### *Computer Software*

There are several different rules for treating the cost of software:

- If it is purchased separately from the purchase of a computer (i.e., it is not bundled with the hardware), the cost can be expensed. Alternatively, if the Section 179 deduction is not elected, the cost can be amortized over 36 months. However, if the useful life of the software is less than 36 months, amortize it over its useful life. If it has a useful life of less than one year (e.g., an annual tax preparation program), deduct it in full in the year of purchase (in effect, the same write-off as expensing, but there is no taxable income limitation in this instance as there is for expensing).
- If it is bundled with hardware, depreciate as part of the hardware (generally over 5 years as explained earlier in this chapter).
- If it is purchased as part of the acquisition of a business, it is amortized as a Section 197 asset over 15 years.
- If it is developed by you for use in your business, treat it as a research and development cost (explained later).
- If it is leased, deduct the lease payments over the term of the lease as you would any other rental expense.

### *Research and Experimentation Costs*

If you have research and experimentation costs (usually referred to as R&D costs), you have a choice of ways to deduct them. You can claim a current deduction for amounts paid or incurred in the year.

Alternatively, you can elect to amortize them over a period of not less than 60 months. Where you do not have current income to offset the deduction, it may be advisable to elect amortization. And there is a 10-year amortization option that avoids any AMT adjustment for owners of pass-through entities.

**Looking Ahead**

**For tax years beginning after December 31, 2021, research and experimentation costs must be capitalized and amortized over 60 months; there will be no choice to expense the cost.**

You may be able to claim a tax credit for increasing your research and experimentation program. For further information on this credit, see instructions for Form 6765, *Credit for Increasing Research Activities*. The research credit is further explained in Chapter 23.

### *Bond Premiums*

If you pay a premium to buy bonds (a cost above the face amount of the bonds), you may be required to—or can elect to—amortize the premium. For taxable bonds, there is an election.

You can amortize the bond premium or instead treat the unamortized premium as part of the basis of the bond. The bond premium is calculated with the amount that the bond issuer will pay at maturity or the earlier call date if it results in a smaller amortizable bond premium attributable to the period ending on the call date. Do not take into account any premium paid for a conversion feature. (Dealers in taxable bonds cannot deduct the amortizable bond premium.)

For tax-exempt bonds you must amortize the premium. However, you do not deduct the amortizable premium in calculating taxable income.

If you are required or elect to amortize the bond premium, decrease the basis of the bond by the amortizable premium.

### *Reforestation Costs*

If you spend money on forestation or reforestation—planting and seeding, site preparation, and the costs of seeds, tools, and labor—you can elect to deduct up to $10,000 ($5,000 for married persons filing separate returns) in the year paid or incurred.

Costs in excess of the amount deducted are amortized over 84 months. The 84-month period begins on the first day of the first month of the second half of the tax year in which the amortizable basis is acquired. Because the half-year convention applies to amortizing reforestation expenses, 1/14th is deducted in the first year, 1/7th in years 2 through 7, and 1/14th in year 8.

**Example**

**On January 1, 2021, you incur reforestation expenses of $20,000. You can deduct $10,000 on your 2021 return and charge the remaining $10,000 to the capital account, amortizing the expenses over 84 months. The monthly amortization is $119.50 ($10,000 ÷ 84). The amortization deduction on your 2022 return is $717 ($119.50 × 6 months). The amortization deduction in 2022 is $1,434 ($119.50 × 12 months).**

### *Costs of Acquiring a Lease*

If you pay a fee to obtain a lease, you can amortize the cost over the term of the lease. The lease term includes all renewal options if less than 75% of the cost is attributable to the term of the lease remaining on the acquisition date. The remaining term of the lease on the acquisition date does not include any period for which the lease may be subsequently renewed, extended, or continued under an option exercisable by the lessee.

## Depletion

*Depletion* is a deduction allowed for certain mineral properties or timber to compensate the owner for the use of these resources. *Mineral properties* include oil and gas wells, mines, other natural deposits, and standing timber. In order to claim depletion, you must be an owner or operator with an economic interest in the mineral deposits or standing timber. This means that you are adversely affected economically when mineral properties or standing timber is mined or cut. Depletion is claimed separately for each mineral property, which is each mineral deposit in each separate tract or parcel of land. Timber property is each tract or block representing a separate timber account.

**NOTE**

**Claiming depletion may result in alternative minimum tax (AMT) for individuals.**

## Methods of Depletion

There are 2 ways to calculate depletion: *cost depletion* and *percentage depletion*.

### COST DEPLETION

Cost depletion is determined by dividing the adjusted basis of the mineral property by the total number of recoverable units in the property's natural deposit (as determined by engineering reports). This figure is multiplied by the number of units sold if you use the accrual method of accounting, or the number of units sold and paid for if you use the cash method. Cost depletion is the only method allowed for standing timber. The depletion deduction is calculated when the quantity of cut timber is first accurately measured in the process of exploitation. Special rules are used to determine depletion for timber, and the deduction is taken when standing timber is cut.

### PERCENTAGE DEPLETION

Percentage depletion is determined by applying a percentage, fixed by tax law according to each type of mineral, to your gross income from the property during the tax year (see Table 14.10).

The deduction for percentage depletion is limited to no more than 50% (100% for oil and gas properties allowed to use percentage depletion) of taxable income from the property calculated without the depletion deduction and certain other adjustments. However, percentage depletion on the marginal production of oil or natural gas by independent producers and royalty owners is *not* limited to taxable income from the property (figured without the depletion deduction).

Only small producers are allowed to use percentage depletion for oil and gas properties. If you use percentage depletion for mineral properties but it is less than cost depletion for the year, you must use cost depletion.

## Partnership Oil and Gas Properties

The depletion allowance, whether cost depletion or percentage depletion, must be calculated separately for each partner and not by the partnership. Each partner can decide on the depletion method. The partnership simply allocates to the partner his or her proportionate share of the adjusted basis of each oil and gas property. Each partner must keep this information separately.

In separate records, the partner must reduce the share of the adjusted basis of each property by the depletion taken on the property each year by that partner. The partner will use this

**TABLE 14.10 Percentage for Mineral Properties**

| Type of Property | Percentage |
|---|---|
| Oil and gas—small producers | 15.0% |
| Sulfur, uranium, and U.S. asbestos, lead, zinc, nickel, mica, and certain other ores and minerals | 22.0 |
| Gold, silver, copper, and iron ore, and certain U.S. oil shale | 15.0 |
| Coal, lignite, sodium chloride | 10.0 |
| Clay and shale used for sewer pipe | 7.5 |
| Clay used for flowerpots and so on, gravel, sand, stone | 5.0 |
| Most other minerals and metallic ores | 14.0 |

reduced adjusted basis to figure gain or loss if the partnership later disposes of the property. (This partnership rule also applies to members in LLCs filing partnership returns.)

### S Corporation Oil and Gas Properties

The depletion allowance, whether by cost or by percentage, must be computed separately by each shareholder and not by the S corporation. The same rules apply to S corporations that apply to partnerships, with some modifications. To enable a shareholder to calculate cost depletion, the S corporation must allocate to each shareholder his or her adjusted basis of each oil and gas property held by the S corporation. This allocation is made on the date the corporation acquires the property. The shareholder's share of the adjusted basis of each oil and gas property is adjusted by the S corporation for any capital expenditures made for each property. Again, each shareholder must separately keep records of his or her pro rata share of the adjusted basis of each property and must reduce that share by depletion taken on the property. The reduced adjusted basis is used by the shareholder to determine gain or loss on the disposition of the property by the S corporation.

## Where to Claim Depreciation, Amortization, and Depletion

### All Taxpayers

In general, depreciation, including any first-year expense deduction, is computed on Form 4562, *Depreciation and Amortization*, regardless of your form of business organization. If you qualify for a higher dollar limit, simply cross out the preprinted dollar limit on Form 4562 and write your applicable dollar limit in the margin. However, special rules apply to different entities.

If an election is made to use the 150% rate for property that could have used the 200% rate, you make the election by entering "150DB" in column (f) of Part III of Form 4562.

An election to use ADS is made by completing line 20a, b, or c of Part III of Form 4562.

If depletion is taken for timber, you must attach Form T to your return.

In general, recapture of the depreciation and the first-year expense deduction is computed on Form 4797, *Sales of Business Property*, regardless of your form of business organization (explained in Chapter 6).

See Table 14.11 for a worksheet such as one that might be generated on Excel to show depreciation for a business that placed equipment in service in the current year. Form 4562 is shown in Figure 14.1.

### Self-Employed

You complete Form 4562 only if you place depreciable property in service in the current year or have amortization costs that begin in the current year. Your deductions are then entered on Part II of Schedule C (or Schedule F for farmers). Depreciation and first-year expensing not included in Part II of Schedule C (for cost of goods sold) are entered on a specific line in Part I of Schedule C. You do not have to file Form 4562 if you only need to provide information on vehicle use. You can enter this information on Schedule C (Part IV).

### Partnerships and LLCs

You complete Form 4562 only if you place depreciable property in service in the current year, are claiming depreciation on a car (regardless of when it was placed in service), or have amortization costs that begin in the current year. The partnership or LLC decides on the depreciation method

**TABLE 14.11** Depreciation Worksheet

| Description of Property | Date Placed in Service | Cost or Other Basis | Business/ Investment/ Use % | Section 179 Deduction | Depreciation Prior Years | Basis for Depreciation | Method/ Convention | Recovery Period | Rate or Table % | Depreciation Deduction |
|---|---|---|---|---|---|---|---|---|---|---|
| Building | 2-2-19 | $65,000 | 100% | | $4,793.75 | $65,000 | SL/MM | GDS 39 | 2.564% | $1,666.60 |
| Desk and chair | 2-2-19 | 600 | 100% | $ 600 | –0– | –0– | | | | –0– |
| Refrigeration equipment | 2-2-19 | 4,500 | 100% | | 3,204.00 | 4,500 | 200DB/HY | GDS/5 | 11.52% | 518.40 |
| Work tables | 2-2-19 | 1,200 | 100% | | 854.40 | 1,200 | 200DB/HY | GDS/5 | 11.52% | 138.24 |
| Cash register | 2-2-19 | 270 | 100% | | 192.24 | 270 | 200DB/HY | GDS/5 | 11.52% | 31.10 |
| Subtotal—2019 Property | | | | | | | | | | 2,354.34 |
| Delivery truck* | 4-16-20 | 31,500 | 100% | 31,500 | –0– | –0– | | | | –0– |
| Scanner machine | 7-3-20 | 300 | 100% | | 103.14 | 300 | 150BD/HY | ADS/6 | 16.41% | 49.23 |
| Subtotal—2020 Property | | | | | | | | | | 49.23 |
| Computer | 6-21-21 | 3,000 | 100% | 3,000 | –0– | –0– | | | | –0– |
| File cabinets | 9-9-21 | 475 | 100% | 475 | –0– | –0– | | | | –0– |
| Store counters | 11-1-21 | 1,870 | 100% | 1,870 | –0– | –0– | | | | –0– |
| Van* | 11-16-21 | 32,500 | 100% | 32,500 | –0– | –0– | | | | –0– |
| Subtotal—2021 Property | | | | 37,845 | | | | | | –0– |
| Grand Total—2021 | | | | $37,845 | | | | | | $2,354.34 |

*Nonpersonal vehicles.

Form **4562** — Department of the Treasury, Internal Revenue Service (99)

# Depreciation and Amortization

**(Including Information on Listed Property)**

▶ Attach to your tax return.

▶ Go to *www.irs.gov/Form4562* for instructions and the latest information.

OMB No. 1545-0172 — **2021** — Attachment Sequence No. **179**

| Name(s) shown on return | Business or activity to which this form relates | **Identifying number** |
|---|---|---|
| | | |

**Part I — Election To Expense Certain Property Under Section 179**

**Note:** If you have any listed property, complete Part V before you complete Part I.

| | | | |
|---|---|---|---|
| 1 | Maximum amount (see instructions) | 1 | |
| 2 | Total cost of section 179 property placed in service (see instructions) | 2 | |
| 3 | Threshold cost of section 179 property before reduction in limitation (see instructions) | 3 | |
| 4 | Reduction in limitation. Subtract line 3 from line 2. If zero or less, enter -0- | 4 | |
| 5 | Dollar limitation for tax year. Subtract line 4 from line 1. If zero or less, enter -0-. If married filing separately, see instructions | 5 | |

| 6 (a) Description of property | (b) Cost (business use only) | (c) Elected cost |
|---|---|---|
| | | |
| | | |
| 7 Listed property. Enter the amount from line 29 | 7 | |

| | | | |
|---|---|---|---|
| 8 | Total elected cost of section 179 property. Add amounts in column (c), lines 6 and 7 | 8 | |
| 9 | Tentative deduction. Enter the **smaller** of line 5 or line 8 | 9 | |
| 10 | Carryover of disallowed deduction from line 13 of your 2020 Form 4562 | 10 | |
| 11 | Business income limitation. Enter the smaller of business income (not less than zero) or line 5. See instructions | 11 | |
| 12 | Section 179 expense deduction. Add lines 9 and 10, but don't enter more than line 11 | 12 | |
| 13 | Carryover of disallowed deduction to 2022. Add lines 9 and 10, less line 12 ▶ 13 | | |

**Note:** Don't use Part II or Part III below for listed property. Instead, use Part V.

**Part II — Special Depreciation Allowance and Other Depreciation (Don't** include listed property. See instructions.)

| | | | |
|---|---|---|---|
| 14 | Special depreciation allowance for qualified property (other than listed property) placed in service during the tax year. See instructions | 14 | |
| 15 | Property subject to section 168(f)(1) election | 15 | |
| 16 | Other depreciation (including ACRS) | 16 | |

**Part III — MACRS Depreciation (Don't** include listed property. See instructions.)

**Section A**

| | | | |
|---|---|---|---|
| 17 | MACRS deductions for assets placed in service in tax years beginning before 2021 | 17 | |
| 18 | If you are electing to group any assets placed in service during the tax year into one or more general asset accounts, check here ▶ ☐ | | |

**Section B—Assets Placed in Service During 2021 Tax Year Using the General Depreciation System**

| (a) Classification of property | (b) Month and year placed in service | (c) Basis for depreciation (business/investment use only—see instructions) | (d) Recovery period | (e) Convention | (f) Method | (g) Depreciation deduction |
|---|---|---|---|---|---|---|
| 19a 3-year property | | | | | | |
| b 5-year property | | | | | | |
| c 7-year property | | | | | | |
| d 10-year property | | | | | | |
| e 15-year property | | | | | | |
| f 20-year property | | | | | | |
| g 25-year property | | | 25 yrs. | | S/L | |
| h Residential rental | | | 27.5 yrs. | MM | S/L | |
| property | | | 27.5 yrs. | MM | S/L | |
| i Nonresidential real | | | 39 yrs. | MM | S/L | |
| property | | | | MM | S/L | |

**Section C—Assets Placed in Service During 2021 Tax Year Using the Alternative Depreciation System**

| (a) Classification of property | (b) | (c) | (d) | (e) | (f) | (g) |
|---|---|---|---|---|---|---|
| 20a Class life | | | | | S/L | |
| b 12-year | | | 12 yrs. | | S/L | |
| c 30-year | | | 30 yrs. | MM | S/L | |
| d 40-year | | | 40 yrs. | MM | S/L | |

**Part IV — Summary** (See instructions.)

| | | | |
|---|---|---|---|
| 21 | Listed property. Enter amount from line 28 | 21 | |
| 22 | **Total.** Add amounts from line 12, lines 14 through 17, lines 19 and 20 in column (g), and line 21. Enter here and on the appropriate lines of your return. Partnerships and S corporations—see instructions | 22 | |
| 23 | For assets shown above and placed in service during the current year, enter the portion of the basis attributable to section 263A costs | 23 | |

**For Paperwork Reduction Act Notice, see separate instructions.** Cat. No. 12906N Form **4562** (2021)

**FIGURE 14.1** Form 4562, Depreciation and Amortization

Form 4562 (2021) Page 2

**Part V Listed Property** (Include automobiles, certain other vehicles, certain aircraft, and property used for entertainment, recreation, or amusement.)

**Note:** For any vehicle for which you are using the standard mileage rate or deducting lease expense, complete **only** 24a, 24b, columns (a) through (c) of Section A, all of Section B, and Section C if applicable.

**Section A—Depreciation and Other Information (Caution:** See the instructions for limits for passenger automobiles.)

**24a** Do you have evidence to support the business/investment use claimed? ☐ **Yes** ☐ **No** | **24b** If "Yes," is the evidence written? ☐ **Yes** ☐ **No**

| (a) Type of property (list vehicles first) | (b) Date placed in service | (c) Business/ investment use percentage | (d) Cost or other basis | (e) Basis for depreciation (business/investment use only) | (f) Recovery period | (g) Method/ Convention | (h) Depreciation deduction | (i) Elected section 179 cost |
|---|---|---|---|---|---|---|---|---|
| **25** Special depreciation allowance for qualified listed property placed in service during the tax year and used more than 50% in a qualified business use. See instructions . | | | | | | 25 | | |
| **26** Property used more than 50% in a qualified business use: | | | | | | | | |
| | | % | | | | | | |
| | | % | | | | | | |
| | | % | | | | | | |
| **27** Property used 50% or less in a qualified business use: | | | | | | | | |
| | | % | | | | S/L – | | |
| | | % | | | | S/L – | | |
| | | % | | | | S/L – | | |
| **28** Add amounts in column (h), lines 25 through 27. Enter here and on line 21, page 1 . | | | | | | 28 | | |
| **29** Add amounts in column (i), line 26. Enter here and on line 7, page 1 . . . . . . . . . . . . . . | | | | | | | 29 | |

**Section B—Information on Use of Vehicles**

Complete this section for vehicles used by a sole proprietor, partner, or other "more than 5% owner," or related person. If you provided vehicles to your employees, first answer the questions in Section C to see if you meet an exception to completing this section for those vehicles.

| | (a) Vehicle 1 | | (b) Vehicle 2 | | (c) Vehicle 3 | | (d) Vehicle 4 | | (e) Vehicle 5 | | (f) Vehicle 6 | |
|---|---|---|---|---|---|---|---|---|---|---|---|---|
| **30** Total business/investment miles driven during the year (**don't** include commuting miles) . | | | | | | | | | | | | |
| **31** Total commuting miles driven during the year | | | | | | | | | | | | |
| **32** Total other personal (noncommuting) miles driven . . . . . . . . . | | | | | | | | | | | | |
| **33** Total miles driven during the year. Add lines 30 through 32 . . . . . . . | | | | | | | | | | | | |
| | **Yes** | **No** | **Yes** | **No** | **Yes** | **No** | **Yes** | **No** | **Yes** | **No** | **Yes** | **No** |
| **34** Was the vehicle available for personal use during off-duty hours? . . . . . | | | | | | | | | | | | |
| **35** Was the vehicle used primarily by a more than 5% owner or related person? . . . | | | | | | | | | | | | |
| **36** Is another vehicle available for personal use? | | | | | | | | | | | | |

**Section C—Questions for Employers Who Provide Vehicles for Use by Their Employees**

Answer these questions to determine if you meet an exception to completing Section B for vehicles used by employees who **aren't** more than 5% owners or related persons. See instructions.

| | **Yes** | **No** |
|---|---|---|
| **37** Do you maintain a written policy statement that prohibits all personal use of vehicles, including commuting, by your employees? . . . . . . . . . . . . . . . . . . . . . . . . . . . . . . | | |
| **38** Do you maintain a written policy statement that prohibits personal use of vehicles, except commuting, by your employees? See the instructions for vehicles used by corporate officers, directors, or 1% or more owners . . | | |
| **39** Do you treat all use of vehicles by employees as personal use? . . . . . . . . . . . . . . . . | | |
| **40** Do you provide more than five vehicles to your employees, obtain information from your employees about the use of the vehicles, and retain the information received? . . . . . . . . . . . . . . . . . . . . . | | |
| **41** Do you meet the requirements concerning qualified automobile demonstration use? See instructions. . . . . . | | |
| **Note:** If your answer to 37, 38, 39, 40, or 41 is "Yes," don't complete Section B for the covered vehicles. | | |

**Part VI Amortization**

| (a) Description of costs | (b) Date amortization begins | (c) Amortizable amount | (d) Code section | (e) Amortization period or percentage | (f) Amortization for this year |
|---|---|---|---|---|---|
| **42** Amortization of costs that begins during your 2021 tax year (see instructions): | | | | | |
| | | | | | |
| | | | | | |
| **43** Amortization of costs that began before your 2021 tax year . . . . . . . . . . . . . . . . | | | | 43 | |
| **44** **Total.** Add amounts in column (f). See the instructions for where to report . . . . . . . . . | | | | 44 | |

Form **4562** (2021)

**FIGURE 14.1** ***(Continued)***

and whether to claim a Section 179 deduction. Ordinary depreciation is then entered on Form 1065 and is taken into account in calculating a partnership's or LLC's ordinary income or loss. Depreciation is reported on a specific line on Form 1065 and is reduced by depreciation included in the cost of goods sold. Similarly, depletion (other than on oil and gas properties) is part of a partnership's or LLC's ordinary income or loss and is reported on the specific line provided for depletion.

Amortization items, such as a deduction for organizational expenses, are part of other deductions. An explanation for these items is included in a separate statement attached to the return.

The Section 179 deduction is a separately stated item reported on Schedule K, and the allocable portion is passed through separately to partners or members on Schedule K-1.

Depletion of oil and gas properties is also a separately stated item reported on Schedule K. The allocable portion is passed through separately to partners and/or members on Schedule K-1.

### S Corporations

You complete Form 4562 only if the corporation placed depreciable property in service in the current year, is claiming depreciation on a car (regardless of when it was placed in service), or has amortization costs that begin in the current year. The S corporation decides on the depreciation method and whether to claim a Section 179 deduction. Ordinary depreciation is then entered on Form 1120-S and is taken into account in calculating an S corporation's ordinary income or loss. Depreciation is reported on a specific line on Form 1120-S and is reduced by depreciation included in the cost of goods sold. Similarly, depletion (other than of oil and gas properties) is part of an S corporation's ordinary income or loss and is reported on the specific line provided for depletion.

Amortization items, such as a deduction for organizational expenses, are part of other deductions. An explanation for these items is included in a separate statement attached to the return.

The Section 179 deduction is a separately stated item reported on Schedule K, and the allocable portion is passed through separately to shareholders on Schedule K-1.

Depletion of oil and gas properties is also a separately stated item reported on Schedule K. The allocable portion is passed through separately to shareholders on Schedule K-1.

### C Corporations

Form 4562 must be completed if any depreciation is claimed (regardless of the year in which the property is placed in service) or if amortization of costs begins in the current year. The depreciation deduction is then entered on Form 1120 on the specific line provided for depreciation. This deduction must be reduced by depreciation claimed in the cost of goods sold or elsewhere on the return. Depletion is entered on the specific line provided for depletion. Amortization is part of other deductions, an explanation of which must be attached to the return.

### All businesses

If you use the de minimis safe harbor election discussed earlier in this chapter, you must attach your own statement to your return each year you want the election to apply. The statement must include:

- Your name
- Your address
- Your EIN
- A statement that you are hereby making the de minimis safe harbor election under Reg. Sec. 1.263(a)-1(f)).

CHAPTER 15

# Advertising Expenses


| | | | |
|---|---|---|---|
| Ordinary Advertising Expenses | 294 | Help-Wanted Ads | 297 |
| Promotion of Goodwill | 295 | Websites and Apps | 297 |
| Prizes, Contests, and Other Promotional Activities | 297 | Social Media | 298 |


You may run advertisements on websites, in newspapers, on the radio or television, or in magazines or trade journals to sell your products or services. You can deduct these costs, as well as the costs of other promotional activities. At the same time, you will discover that some costs cannot be deducted or that certain costs need to be deducted as another type of business expense.

For further information about deducting advertising costs, see IRS Publication 535, *Business Expenses*.

## Ordinary Advertising Expenses

Like all other business expenses, advertising costs must be ordinary and necessary business expenses in order to be deductible. They must have a reasonable relationship to your business activities, and they must be reasonable in amount. However, there are no guidelines on what is "reasonable" in amount.

Deductible advertising expenses include the costs of:

- Business cards
- Ads in print or the media (such as newspaper or magazine advertisements, charitable organization publications, radio or television spots, or online and mobile messages)
- Ads in printed or online telephone directories (such as YP listings)
- Package design costs that are part of an advertising campaign
- Billboards (rental fees are an advertising expense)
- Signs with a useful life of not more than one year. (Signs expected to last longer than a year can be depreciated, as explained in Chapter 14.)

In the case of signs placed on the sides of cars or trucks, only the cost of the sign is deductible as advertising. The cost of the driving is not an advertising expense (although business use of the car may be otherwise deductible as explained in Chapter 9).

**Example**

**The cost of metal or plastic signs with a life of more than 1 year has to be capitalized and deducted using first-year expensing, bonus depreciation, or regular depreciation. The cost of restaurant menu folders is currently deductible, since the folders have a life of not more than 1 year.**

The cost of public relations can be deducted as an ordinary advertising cost. PR expenses can include fees to PR professionals and agencies, costs associated with PR events (e.g., press conferences), and costs for developing, printing, and distributing press kits.

Some businesses treat the cost of maintaining their websites as an advertising expense. The IRS has not yet ruled on whether this treatment is correct (see "Websites and Apps" later in this chapter). However, if a business uses the site only for advertising (e.g., a law firm that posts its areas of specialty and personnel) and not for selling (e.g, a bricks-and-mortar store that posts its online catalog and accepts purchases through the Internet), it seems reasonable to handle the cost in this manner.

## Promotion of Goodwill

Expenses designed to create goodwill in the public's eye rather than to obtain immediate sales are also deductible. For example, the IRS says that the cost of advertising that encourages people to contribute to the American Red Cross, to buy U.S. Savings Bonds, or to participate in similar causes is usually deductible. In fact, the advertising program can be of a long-term nature and still result in an immediate deduction. The IRS has ruled that the ordinary costs of advertising are currently deductible despite the fact that they produce a long-term benefit.

In some instances, design costs may be considered deductible advertising expenses. In one case, the Tax Court said that graphic design costs could be currently deductible as advertising expenses even though they may produce future patronage or goodwill. The IRS has announced its disagreement with this decision, so if you claim a deduction for package design costs, you may face an IRS challenge.

**Example**

**The costs of installing window treatments in model homes as part of an advertising campaign are currently deductible. The costs are incurred to promote the name of the business.**

The cost of distributing a company's samples can be deducted as an advertising expense when the distribution is designed to engender goodwill.

Another type of advertising involves sponsorships of teams. Your business may, for example, sponsor a bowling team or a Little League team. In return for the sponsorship, your company's name is displayed on the team uniform and may also be a part of the team's name. These costs of sponsorship are deductible as advertising expenses.

Free services provided to generate goodwill cannot be deducted as an advertising expense. For example, in one case, a doctor provided free medical services and deducted the value of his uncompensated services as an advertising expense. The Tax Court disallowed the deduction because the doctor's labor was not an expense (it was not an amount paid or incurred).

### *Personal versus Business Expenses*

Expenses that smack of a personal nature may still constitute deductible advertising costs when it can be shown that the expenses were incurred *primarily* for business purposes. The following examples demonstrate when expenses may be considered primarily for business and when they may not—the distinction is not always clear.

**Example**

**A restaurant chain owner who maintained show horses for the purpose of advertising the company's name was allowed a current deduction. But an owner who bought a horse, named it after himself, and entered it in shows was not allowed a deduction when he failed to show there was any connection between the horse and his business.**

**Example**

**A business owner who invited customers to his child's wedding reception could not deduct the cost for these guests as advertising. The nature of the expense was just too personal and the business aspect of the expense just too attenuated to make the cost a deductible advertising expense.**

**Example**

**An attorney was not allowed to deduct the cost of new suits as an advertising expense. He claimed he needed to look good to attract new clients. Again, the expense was personal in nature and so was not deductible.**

**Example**

**Costs of car racing by an officer of a computer research and design corporation were not deductible. Again, the expenses were personal in nature. In comparison, a meat processor that sponsored a race car could deduct expenses. The sponsorship allowed the company to display its logo on the car, and track announcers mentioned the car's sponsor during the race. Deductibility turns on the facts and circumstances of a particular situation.**

### *Lobbying Expenses*

In general, the costs of advertising to influence legislation at the federal, state, or even local level are not deductible. Nondeductible expenses include:

- The costs of participating or intervening in any political campaign for or against any candidate in public office.

- The costs of attempting to influence the general public or segments of the public about elections, legislative matters, or referendums.
- The costs of communicating directly with certain executive branch officials in any attempt to influence the official actions or positions of such officials. These executives include the president, vice president, any officer or employee of the Executive Office of the President and the 2 most senior officers of each of the other agencies in the Executive Office, and certain other individuals.
- The costs of research, preparation, planning, or coordinating any of the activities already mentioned.

Not all lobbying expenses are nondeductible. For example, professional lobbyists are entitled to deduct their own business expenses even though payments to them are not deductible.

## Prizes, Contests, and Other Promotional Activities

Amounts paid for prizes, contests, and other promotional activities that your business gives away may be deducted as advertising expenses if you can show that the expenses have a relationship to your business. The amounts expended must be reasonable; they must not be out of proportion to the amount of business expected to be obtained as a result of the prize, contest, or other promotional activity.

**Example**

**A restaurant owner gave away a car to the holder of a lucky-number ticket. These tickets had been distributed to patrons. The cost of the car was a deductible business expense.**

Sponsorships of teams and other events can be deducted as advertising expenses (e.g., sponsorship of a tennis match or golf tournament).

Prizes and other awards given to employees are not treated as advertising costs. They are part of compensation (see Chapter 7).

## Help-Wanted Ads

Most advertising is designed to sell products or services. However, you may also advertise when trying to fill a position in your company. The cost of running help-wanted ads in newspapers, trade magazines, and online (such as paid postings through Indeed.com, LinkedIn, Monster.com, and Glassdoor.com) is deductible as an ordinary and necessary business expense. It is not an advertising cost.

## Websites and Apps

Today, websites are an integral part of advertising and promoting a business. Some companies use websites to transact business online; others use their sites as online brochures to highlight the features of their businesses and establish credibility. Mobile versions of websites are also a growing part of advertising and promotion, enabling businesses to offer coupons or direct readers to their websites. So too are apps that can be viewed on mobile devices. The cost of acquiring a domain name in the secondary market is covered in Chapter 14.

### *Costs of Creation*

Creating a website and, perhaps, a mobile version of it, is an important way to brand your business and keep your name before the public because 97% of consumers search for products and services online. Website creation includes domain registration fees, site design, and, in some cases, professional copy, photography, and artwork used to populate the site. While there have not yet been any cases or rulings on the extent to which website-related expenses are deductible, it can certainly be argued that these expenses relate to the promotion of goodwill for the company using a site for promotional purposes and should be treated as fully deductible ordinary advertising costs. For those using their sites for transacting business (e.g., online stores), the IRS may argue that costs should be amortized rather than immediately deductible (see Chapter 14).

The cost of adapting a website for mobile viewing may be treated similarly to website creation costs. They may qualify as fully deductible ordinary advertising costs under the right circumstances.

Not all small businesses as yet have a mobile app of their own, even though there are compelling business reasons to have one (e.g., personalized customer engagement). If your business gets one in 2021, how you go about it determines the tax treatment of the costs involved. If you use in-house resources to develop and maintain apps, it would not trigger separate deductions (deductions for employee wages are explained in Chapter 7). However, if you use an outside firm to develop and maintain an app for your business, the costs likely are deductible. The annual Apple App developer membership fee that you pay to have your app in the Apple Store (even though free to customers) is deductible. As with costs for websites, the IRS has yet to rule on deductibility.

### *Maintenance Costs*

Web hosting is an ongoing cost for maintaining a website. So, too, is the cost of keeping your website up to date, which can entail fees to outside webmasters. These maintenance fees are fully deductible, as is the cost of search engine optimization (SEO) services.

Various subscription services to maintain the security of your website, such as Norton, Securi, and Cloudflare, are treated as other subscription costs. Monthly charges are fully deductible. If you pay for a subscription covering more than 12 months, your deduction for the year may be limited (see Dues and Subscriptions in Chapter 22).

**NOTE**

**Deducting the cost of software related to social media, such as offline blogging software, may not necessarily be fully deductible in the year you buy it. How to deduct the cost of software is discussed in Chapter 14.**

## Social Media

Increasingly, small businesses are relying on social media, such as LinkedIn, Facebook, Pinterest, and Twitter, to market their products and services. Many are using blogs and e-newsletters to reach customers and prospects. Much of social media is free (other than the cost of your own or your staff's time spent working on these sites). However, some social media-related services can cost money, and they are fully tax deductible. **Examples:**

- E-mail distribution costs (such as Constant Contact)
- Google Ads or Facebook Ads
- LinkedIn Premium, which is a paid upgrade
- Paid blogging platforms (such as Ghost and Squarespace)
- Surveys (using sites such as Survey Monkey or Constant Contact)
- Twitter ads

## Where to Deduct Expenses

### *Self-Employed*

Advertising costs are deductible on Schedule C. There is a specific line for this type of expense.

### *Partnerships and LLCs*

Advertising costs are trade or business expenses that are taken into account in determining the profit or loss of the partnership or LLC on Form 1065. They are entered in the category of Other Deductions on Form 1065. A schedule is attached to the return explaining the deductions claimed in this category. They are not separately stated items passed through to partners and members. Therefore, partners and members in LLCs report their net income or loss from the business on Schedule E; they do not deduct advertising costs on their individual tax returns.

### *S Corporations*

Advertising costs are trade or business expenses that are taken into account in determining the profit or loss of the S corporation. They are reported on the specific line provided for advertising on Form 1120-S. They are not separately stated items passed through to shareholders. Therefore, shareholders report their net income or loss from the business on Schedule E; they do not deduct advertising costs on their individual tax returns.

### *C Corporations*

Advertising costs are trade or business expenses that are taken into account in determining the profit or loss of the C corporation. They are reported on the specific line provided for advertising on Form 1120. The corporation then pays tax on its net profit or loss. Shareholders do not report any income (or loss) from the corporation.

CHAPTER 16

# Retirement Plans


| | |
|---|---|
| Qualified Retirement Plans | 301 |
| Added Costs for Retirement Plans | 308 |
| Credit for Plan Start-Up Costs | 309 |
| Retirement Plans for Self-Employed Individuals | 310 |
| Regular 401(k)s and Designated Roth Accounts | 316 |
| Pooled Employer Plans (PEPs) | 318 |
| Individual Retirement Accounts | 318 |
| COVID-19-Related Rules | 322 |
| Disaster-Related Rules | 322 |
| State-Sponsored Plans for the Private Sector | 323 |
| When to Take Action | 323 |
| Plan Problems and Corrections | 325 |
| Comparison of Qualified Retirement Plans | 326 |
| ESOPs | 328 |
| Retirement Plans Owning Your Business | 330 |
| Terminating Plans | 330 |
| Nonqualified Retirement Plans | 331 |
| Glossary of Terms for Retirement Plans | 332 |


Retirement plans are a vital way for you, and your employees if you have any, to save for the future on a tax-advantaged basis.

The Social Security benefits you may expect to receive will make up only a portion of your retirement income. And income from your business—through a sale, consulting agreement, or otherwise—may not be as much as you expected.

Having a retirement plan fosters employee goodwill and may aid in recruiting for new employees and retaining valued talent. In order to help you save for your own retirement and to encourage employers to provide retirement benefits to employees, the tax law contains special incentives for retirement savings. Broadly speaking, if a retirement plan conforms to special requirements, then contributions are deductible while earnings are not currently taxable and forever escape employment taxes that would apply if wages had been paid instead of contributions. What's more, employees covered by such plans are not immediately charged with income on account of employer contributions and, if they contribute from their salaries, their contributions aren't currently taxed. For owners, having a retirement plan can be a handy source of funding (see Chapter 26). Funds in retirement plans can provide a secure financial future (see Chapter 32).

At the end of December 2019, Congress enacted the Setting Every Community Up for Retirement Enhancement (SECURE) Act, which makes many dramatic changes in retirement plans. Most of the changes were effective in 2020, although some become effective after 2020.

Also, the Coronavirus Aid, Relief and Economic Security (CARES) Act created a number of special rules for qualified retirement plans and IRAs for 2020, but they continue to impact taxes for 2021. These special rules are discussed later in this chapter.

A number of states have some mandates (see "State-Sponsored Plans for the Private Sector" later in this chapter) as a way to increase retirement savings. The type of plan you set up governs both the amount you can deduct and the time when you claim the deduction. Certain plans offer special tax incentives designed to encourage employers to help with employee retirement benefits. Even though you may be an employer, if you are self-employed (a sole proprietor, partner, or LLC member), you are treated as an employee for purposes of participating in these plans.

From time to time, Congress makes changes to qualified retirement plans. For example, in 2006, it created a DbK, which was a hybrid of a 401(k) plan and a defined benefit (pension) plan for small employers. Use of this type of plan never took hold (although it is still in the law). And at the time of publication, Congress was considering mandating businesses to offer retirement plans; see the Supplement for any update.

For further information about retirement plans, see IRS Publication 560, *Retirement Plans for Small Business*, IRS Publication 598, *Tax on Unrelated Business Income of Exempt Organizations*, IRS Publication 590-A, *Contributions to Individual Retirement Accounts (IRAs)*, IRS Publication 590-B, *Distributions from Individual Retirement Accounts*, and IRS Publication 3998, *Choosing a Retirement Solution for Your Small Business*.

## Qualified Retirement Plans

*Qualified retirement plans* provide retirement benefits and meet stringent requirements under federal law. (The Employee Retirement Income Security Act, or ERISA, is the controlling legislation.) Some of these laws fall under the jurisdiction of the Treasury Department and the IRS; others fall under the Department of Labor. Qualified plans allow employees to defer reporting income from benefits until retirement or even to earn tax-free income while at the same time allowing employers to claim a current deduction for contributions to the plans.

Income earned by the plan is not currently taxed. Eventually, it is taxed to employees when distributed to them as part of their benefits or, in the case of a designated Roth account, becomes tax free.

### *Types of Retirement Plans*

There are 2 main categories of plans: *defined benefit plans* and *defined contribution plans*.

#### DEFINED BENEFIT PLANS

Defined benefit plans, which are pension plans, predict what an employee will receive in benefits upon retirement. This prediction is based on the employee's compensation, age, and anticipated age of retirement. It is also based on an estimation of what the plan can earn over the years. Then an actuary determines the amount that an employer must contribute each year in order to be sure that funds will be there when the employee retires. The employer takes a deduction for the actuarially determined contribution.

There are, however, variations of defined benefit plans. For example, in a cash balance defined benefit plan, benefits payable upon retirement depend in part on plan performance.

### DEFINED CONTRIBUTION PLANS

Defined contribution plans are more like savings accounts. The employer contributes to an account for each employee. The contribution is based on a defined formula, such as a percentage of the employee's compensation. The account may not really be a separate account. In corporate plans, it is a bookkeeping notation of the benefits that belong to each employee. The benefits that are ultimately paid to an employee are based on what the contributions actually earn over the years.

There are a variety of plans under the umbrella of defined contribution plans. The most common is the *profit-sharing plan*. Under this plan, the employer agrees to contribute a percentage of employee compensation to the plan. The allocation is usually based purely on an employee's relative compensation (other factors, such as age, can be taken into account). Another common plan is a *money purchase plan*. Under this plan, the employer also agrees to contribute a fixed percentage of compensation each year.

The most popular type of defined contribution plan today is the *401(k) plan* (also called a cash and deferred compensation arrangement). The reason for its popularity: Contributions are made by employees through salary reduction arrangements that let them fund their retirement plan with pretax dollars. These employee contributions are called *elective deferrals*. Employers often match to some extent employee elective deferrals as a way of encouraging participation or because they are required to do so under the type of plan they use.

Regardless of the plan selected, all plans have the same requirements designed to ensure that they do not benefit only owners and top executives but also ordinary workers. Many of these requirements are highly technical. They are explained here so that you will recognize how complicated the use of qualified plans can become. It may be helpful to discuss your retirement plans or anticipated plans with a retirement plan expert.

Businesses that do not want to become involved with the complexities of qualified plans can use simplified employee pensions (SEPs) or savings incentive match plans for employees (SIMPLEs), discussed later in this chapter in connection with plans for self-employed persons.

#### *Covering Employees*

A plan will be treated as qualified only if it allows employees who meet certain requirements to participate and receive benefits under it. In general, the plan must satisfy one of 3 coverage tests. The first test stipulates that the plan must cover at least 70% of all **nonhighly compensated employees**. This is called the *percentage test*.

---

***Nonhighly compensated employees*** **All employees who are not treated as highly compensated employees and do not have an ownership interest in the business. These are essentially rank-and-file employees.**

---

Alternatively, the plan must cover a percentage of nonhighly compensated employees that is at least 70% of the percentage of **highly compensated employees**. This second test is called the *ratio test*. The third alternative is called the *average benefit percentage test* (ABP test). This test also looks at the percentage of nonhighly compensated employees to be sure that there is no discrimination against them.

***Highly compensated employees (HCEs)*** **These include owners and highly paid employees earning specified amounts ($130,000 in 2021). These amounts are adjusted annually for inflation. Thus, the coverage test needs to be checked annually.**

### *Participation*

Participation is the right of an employee to be covered by a plan after meeting certain participation requirements. In order to be qualified, the plan must not only meet a coverage test but also meet a participation test. The plan must benefit the lesser of 50 employees or 40% or more of all employees. If an employer maintains more than one plan, participation must be satisfied by each plan individually. The plans cannot be grouped together (aggregated) for this purpose.

There are also age and service requirements. The plan can defer participation until the latter of the employee attaining the age of 21 or completing one year of service. A 2-year service requirement can be used if there is immediate and full vesting (vesting is discussed later in the chapter). A year of service usually means 1,000 hours of work. Employers must begin to count hours for part-timers as of January 1, 2021, so they're included in 401(k) plans as of 2024 if they have at least 500 hours of work in the prior 3 years.

### *Automatic Enrollment*

Employers can adopt an automatic enrollment feature for 401(k)s to increase employee participation and eliminate the need for testing whether the plan is nondiscriminatory. Employers that adopt an automatic enrollment plan or change an existing plan to automatic enrollment may be eligible for a new tax credit explained later in this chapter. Employers must choose an investment for employees' automatically deducted salary deferral contributions. You can limit your liability for plan investment losses by choosing default investments for deferrals that meet certain criteria for transferability and safety, such as a life-cycle fund or balanced funds. Your employees must be given an opportunity to change the investment choice.

There are 3 types of automatic enrollment:

1. *Basic automatic contribution arrangement*. This automatic enrollment option, also called an Automatic Contribution Arrangement (ACA), requires you to automatically enroll eligible employees in the plan unless they elect otherwise. Your plan document must specify the percentage of wages that will be automatically deducted. Employees can elect not to contribute or to contribute a different percentage of pay (within the limit allowed by law).
2. *Eligible automatic contribution arrangement*. This automatic enrollment option, called an EACA, uniformly applies the plan's default deferral percentage to all employees after giving them the required notice. There are no specified automatic salary deferral contribution levels or any required escalation in contributions (see QACA below).

   The plan may allow employees to withdraw automatic contributions ("a withdrawal election"), including earnings, no earlier than 30 days or later than 90 days of the date of the first automatic contribution is withheld from an employee's wages. There is no 10% penalty on these withdrawals.

   There are no required employer matching or non-elective contributions for participating employees.

3. *Qualified automatic contribution arrangement*. This automatic enrollment option, called a QACA, also uniformly applies the plan's default deferral percentage to all employees after giving them the required notice. However, this option has additional safe harbor provisions that exempt the plan from annual actual deferral percentage and actual contribution percentage nondiscrimination testing requirements explained earlier in this chapter.

   The default deferral percentage must be at least 3% for the initial period, with a cap on the percentage thereafter up to 15% (but no more than 10% in the first year). Elective deferrals (employees' pre-tax contributions) gradually increase by one percentage point to 6% with each year that an employee participates. Thus, if the percentage for the initial period is 3%, then the contribution rate for year 2 is 4%; it is 5% in year 3, and usually 6% in year 4 and thereafter.

**Example**

**An employee is hired on June 1, 2021, and begins participation on July 1, 2021. He's automatically enrolled in a QACA at 3% on that date; this rate continues through December 31, 2021 (the end of the initial period). On January 1, 2022, his contribution rate becomes 4%; it's 5% in year 2023, and 6% in year 2024 and thereafter.**

There is a choice of formulas used to figure required employer contributions. You must use the same choice for all participants. Pick either:

- Nonelective contribution: At least 3% of compensation for all participants, including those who choose not to make any elective deferrals ("Alternative 1" in Table 16.1). This may be 10% the first year, with a maximum of 15% in a subsequent year.
- Matching contribution: 100% match for elective deferrals that do not exceed 1% of compensation, plus 50% match for elective deferrals between 1% and 6% of compensation ("Alternative 2" in Table 16.1 assuming a 6% match rate).

**Example**

**You have a 401(k) plan in which you and your 8 employees participate. Table 16.1 shows what you have to contribute if you use automatic contributions by employees.**

Employees must be 100% vested in the employer's nonelective or matching contributions after no more than 2 years of service. A plan may not distribute any of the required employer contributions (below) due to an employee's financial hardship.

Distressed employers operating at an economic loss—something common during the pandemic—can opt to reduce or suspend their safe harbor nonelective contributions to their 401(k) retirement plans midyear. No IRS request for relief in this case is necessary, but you must give notice to employees about the reduction or suspension in employer contributions and allow employees to change their salary deferral amounts. More details about suspending

**TABLE 16.1** Safe Harbor Contributions by Employer (You) for Employees in 401(k) Plan

| Employee | Compensation | Elective Deferral | Alternative 1 | Alternative 2 |
|---|---|---|---|---|
| You | $90,000 | $19,500 | $2,700 | $5,400 |
| #1 | 75,000 | 19,500 | 2,250 | 4,500 |
| #2 | 60,000 | 0 | 1,800 | 0 |
| #3 | 50,000 | 1,000 | 1,500 | 2,000 |
| #4 | 40,000 | 0 | 1,200 | 0 |
| #5 | 30,000 | 3,000 | 900 | 1,200 |
| #6 | 25,000 | 2,500 | 750 | 1,000 |
| #7 | 20,000 | 1,000 | 600 | 1,000 |
| #8 | 20,000 | 0 | 600 | 0 |
| | | | $12,300 | $15,100 |

plan contributions midyear can be found in Notice 2020-52. The distinction between suspending contributions and partial plan terminations are discussed later in this chapter.

Employers gain fiduciary protection (employees can't object to investment performance) if they use qualified default investment alternatives (QDIAs). The Department of Labor has specified only 3 types of investments that are QDIAs:

1. A product with a mix of investments that takes into account the individual's age or retirement date (for example, a life cycle or targeted retirement date fund).
2. An investment service that allocates contributions among existing plan options to provide an asset mix that takes into account the individual's age or retirement date (for example, a professionally managed account).
3. A product with a mix of investments that takes into account the characteristics of the group of employees as a whole, rather than each individual (for example, a balanced fund).

A capital preservation product is permissible for only the first 120 days of participation (for example, a money market fund). This option enables plan sponsors to simplify administration if workers opt out of participation before incurring an additional tax. After 120 days of participation, the funds must be transferred to one of the options above.

### *Vesting*

While the plan must permit certain employees to participate and have contributions made on their behalf, employers can, if they choose, require a certain number of years in the plan before benefits will belong absolutely to the participants. This delay in absolute ownership of benefits is called *vesting*. In order for plans to be qualified, employers cannot defer vesting beyond set limits.

For employer contributions, a plan can provide for *cliff vesting*. Under this type of vesting, there is no ownership of benefits before the completion of 3 years in the plan. At the end of 3 years, all benefits are fully owned by the employee.

The other vesting schedule is called *6-year graded vesting*. This permits vesting of 20% of benefits each year after the first year of service. Under this vesting schedule, there is full vesting after 6 years of participation in the plan.

### Permitted Disparity

An employer can reduce the cost of covering employees by integrating the plan with Social Security. This means that the employer can take into account the employer contribution to Social Security for each participant. In effect, the employer's contribution to Social Security is treated as the plan contribution so the employer saves the cost of having to make this contribution a second time to a qualified plan. The employer payment of Social Security tax for each participant is deducted as taxes, not as a pension plan contribution.

Ordinarily, the disparity in contributions to employees is viewed as discriminatory. But integrating Social Security contributions with plan contributions is viewed as permitted disparity (i.e., is not discriminatory). The rules for permitted disparity are highly complex, and different rules apply to defined benefit plans and defined contribution plans.

### Obtaining and Maintaining Plan Approval

Your plan must be qualified, and only the IRS can tell you if your plan falls within this category. You can use a master or prototype plan for setting up your retirement plan. These are boilerplate plans offered to you by the financial institution where you set up the plan. Plans following these prototypes generally meet IRS requirements, although they are not deemed to have automatic IRS approval. If you design your own plan (or have a professional design one for you), in order to be qualified, the plan must obtain IRS approval. This approval is granted on the basis of how the plan is written and how it will operate. There is no requirement that you obtain approval prior to operating a plan, but it is a good idea to get it. The process is complicated, and the use of a tax or pension professional is advisable.

After initial qualification, your plan may be amended from time to time. For example, you may wish to make changes in how the plan operates—for example, increasing the percentage of compensation upon which your contributions are based. You must amend your plan to reflect law changes that are continually being made.

### Compensation Limit

Benefits and contributions are based on a participant's taxable compensation reported on an employee's W-2 form. It does not include tax-free fringe benefits or other excludable wages.

The law limits the amount of compensation that can be taken into account. For 2021, there is a $290,000 limit. If an employee earns $300,000, only the first $290,000 is used to compute benefits and contributions.

**Looking Ahead**

**The compensation limit may be adjusted for inflation annually in increments of $5,000.**

When both spouses work for the same employer, each can receive a contribution based on his or her respective compensation (up to the compensation limit). In the past, spouses working for the same employer were treated as one unit.

### Contribution Limit

The contribution limit depends on the type of plan involved. For defined contribution plans, the 2021 limit is the lesser of 25% of compensation or $58,000. This percentage is the top limit. Plans can adopt lesser percentages for contributions.

For defined benefit plans, there is no specific limit on contributions. Rather, the limit is placed on the benefits that can be provided under the plan. Contributions are then actuarially determined to provide these benefits. For 2021, the plan cannot provide benefits exceeding $230,000 per year, adjusted annually for inflation.

**Looking Ahead**

**The benefits limit may be adjusted annually for inflation in increments of $5,000.**

### Borrowing from the Plan

Owners may be able to borrow from the plan without adverse tax consequences. (Special coronavirus-related loan rules and disaster-related loan rules are discussed later in this chapter.) The plan may permit loans, but they're limited to the lesser of:

- $50,000, or
- The greater of ½ your accrued benefit or $10,000.

**NOTE**

**Plan loans are not dependent on having a financial hardship. Hardship withdrawals are taxable distributions.**

**Example**

**A participant's vested account balance is $80,000. She can take a loan up to $40,000, which is the lesser of 50% of the vested account balance and $50,000.**

**Example**

**A participant's vested account balance is $120,000. He can take a loan up to $50,000, which is the lesser of 50% of his account balance ($60,000) or $50,000.**

The loan must be amortized over a period of no more than 5 years (except for loans that are used to buy personal residences) and charge a reasonable rate of interest. As an owner, you cannot deduct interest on the loan.

The plan must also allow rank-and-file employees the opportunity to borrow from the plan on the same basis as owners and top executives. The plan must set the rules for repayment when a participant leaves the company. The plan fixes the repayment period, such as 60 days. If the loan is not repaid in this period, it becomes a taxable distribution. The plan may suspend loan repayments for employees performing military service. The plan may also suspend loan repayments during a leave of absence of up to one year. In this situation, however, the returning employee must make up the missed payments so that the term of the loan does not exceed the 5-year limit.

## Added Costs for Retirement Plans

In addition to the contributions you make to the plan, there may be other costs to consider. The type of plan you have affects the nature and amount of these added costs.

Whether you have a defined contribution or a defined benefit plan, you may be required to maintain a bond for yourself or someone else who acts as a fiduciary in your plan. You must also update your plan documents so they reflect the latest law changes.

If you are approaching retirement age and want to obtain the maximum retirement benefits for your contributions (the biggest bang for your buck), you may want to adopt a defined benefit plan. Before doing so, it is important to recognize that these types of plans entail additional costs not associated with defined contribution plans.

### *Cost of Plan Maintenance*

You may set up your plan at a brokerage firm, mutual fund, or other financial institution. There typically are fees for setting up and maintaining the plan. Fees billed to the company are deductible as an ordinary and necessary business expense.

**Looking Ahead**

**Plans must begin to provide a statement to each participant in a defined contribution plan, such as a 401(k) plan, illustrating how much an account balance could produce on a monthly basis if converted to a single life annuity (a qualified joint and survivor annuity for a married participant). If a plan issues quarterly statements, then the first illustration is due for statements for the second quarter of 2022. The requirement to provide illustrations likely will increase administrative costs.**

### *Investment Advice*

Employers can, but are not required to, provide investment advice to participants and beneficiaries. In the past, doing this was a prohibited transaction that was penalized. Now, it is a way to help staff increase their retirement savings.

### *Bonding Requirement*

To ensure that you will not run off with the funds in your company retirement plan, leaving participants high and dry, you are required to be bonded if you have any control over the plan or its assets. This includes, for example, authority to transfer funds or make disbursements from the plan. The bond must be at least 10% of the amount over which you have control ("currently handled assets"). The bond cannot be less than $1,000, but it need not exceed $1 million.

No bond is required if the plan covers only you as the owner (a self-employed person or a single shareholder-employee) or only partners and their spouses.

**NOTE**

**You frequently have an extended period of time to amend your plan documents to reflect law changes. But you must operate your plan in accordance with new laws as soon as they become effective.**

### *Plan Amendments*

You are required to keep your plan up to date and operate it in accordance with law changes that are enacted from time to time. Amendments reflecting changes made by the SECURE Act and other law changes must be made by the end of the plan year beginning on or after January 1, 2022, unless the IRS grants more time for this action. A list of required amendments through 2020 is in IRS Notice 2020–83. If you have a prototype plan provided by a bank, brokerage firm, mutual fund, or insurance company, amendments will be made for you; retain copies of plan amendments. If you have your own uniquely designed plan, it's your responsibility to make amendments and you'll incur professional fees for this action.

If you discover errors in your plan (either in how it is written or how it is being operated), you can correct the errors and avoid or minimize penalties. If you do not take the initiative and the IRS discovers the problems, you can be subject to greater penalties, interest, and even plan disqualification. More information is contained later in this chapter under "Correcting Plan Defects."

### *Actuarial Costs for Defined Benefit Plans*

If you have a defined benefit plan, you must use the services of an enrolled actuary to determine your annual contributions. You must expect to pay for this service year after year.

### *Pension Benefit Guaranty Corporation Premiums for Defined Benefit Plans*

The Pension Benefit Guaranty Corporation (PBGC) is a quasi-federal agency designed to protect employee pension plans in the event that the employer goes under. In order to provide this protection, the PBGC charges annual premiums for each participant in the plan. First, there is a flat-rate premium, which, for 2021, is $86 per participant (a different rate applies to multiemployer plans).

Then, for underfunded plans of a single employer (other than "small employers"), there is an additional variable-rate premium (interest rates change monthly) applied to the plan's underfunding. (*Underfunding* means that the employer has not contributed sufficient amounts to pay all anticipated pensions that have already vested.) In 2021, the variable-rate premium per participant is $45 per $1,000 of unfunded vested benefits, with a cap of $582 per participant. Small employers (those with 25 or fewer employees) have their variable rate premium capped at $5 multiplied by the number of plan participants.

You can find instructions for submitting your 2021 premiums to the PBGC at https://www.pbgc.gov/prac/prem/premium-payment-instructions-and-addresses.html. Any changes for premiums will be noted in the Supplement to this book.

There is a termination premium payable when a company transfers its underfunded pension plan to the PBGC. The premium is $1,250 per participant per year, payable for each of the 3 years after plan termination.

There is an online system, called My Plan Administration Account (PAA), for paying premiums and filing returns. For information, go to https://www.pbgc.gov/prac/prem/premium-filing-payment-and-instructions.

## Credit for Plan Start-Up Costs

If you set up a plan, you may be eligible for special tax credits designed to encourage small business owners to start retirement plans and use automatic enrollment.

### *Start-Up Credit*

A small employer eligible for the credit is one with no more than 100 employees who received at least $5,000 of compensation from the company in the preceding year. However, the plan must cover at least one employee who is not a highly compensated employee. Thus, a self-employed individual with no employees who sets up a profit-sharing plan cannot claim a tax credit for any of the start-up costs.

In addition to the employee requirement, to qualify for the credit you must not have had a qualified plan in any of the 3 preceding years.

The credit is 50% of costs up to the greater of $500 or the lesser of (a) $250 for each employee not highly compensated who's eligible to participate or (b) $5,000. The credit can be claimed for 3 years starting with the year in which the plan is effective. However, you can opt to first claim the credit in the year immediately preceding the start-up year based on costs incurred in the preceding year.

**Example**

**Your corporation sets up a 401(k) plan that begins on January 1, 2022, and the business qualifies as a small employer. The corporation can opt to take a credit for start-up expenses incurred in 2021 on its 2021 return.**

The credit applies only to qualified start-up costs. These include ordinary and necessary expenses to set up the plan, run it, and educate employees about the plan and participation in it. Qualified expenses in excess of the amount taken into account in figuring the maximum credit can be deducted as ordinary and necessary business expenses.

The credit is part of the general business credit (see Chapter 23).

### *Automatic Enrollment Credit*

There is a credit for creating or adopting an automatic enrollment feature for a qualified retirement plan. The same eligibility rules for the start-up credit apply to the automatic enrollment credit. The credit is $500 for each year, up to 3 years. The credit is in addition to the start-up credit above and is also subject to the general business credit limit (Chapter 23).

## Retirement Plans for Self-Employed Individuals

Self-employed individuals have 3 main options in retirement plans. First, they can set up qualified retirement plans, which used to be called Keogh plans, named after Rep. Eugene Keogh, who crafted them, or H.R.10 plans, reflecting the number of the bill in Congress under which qualified plans for self-employed individuals were created in 1962. These terms are no longer used. Instead, retirement plans for self-employed individuals are given names by a bank, brokerage firm, insurance company, or other financial institution offering pension plans or profit-sharing plans for the self-employed. A second option in retirement plans for self-employed individuals is a simplified employee pension plan (SEP). A third option in retirement plans is a savings incentive match plan for employees (SIMPLE). There is a single reference on the tax return to these plans: Self-employed SEP, SIMPLE, and qualified plans.

### *Self-Employed Qualified Plans in General*

Qualified plans for self-employed individuals are subject to the same requirements as qualified plans for corporations. (Banks, brokerage firms, mutual funds, and insurance companies offering plans for self-employed individuals may generally denominate them as basic plans or simply by the type of plan established, such as a profit-sharing plan.) Like corporate qualified plans, self-employed qualified plans must cover employees of a self-employed person on a nondiscriminatory basis. Also like corporate plans, they are limited in the amount that can be contributed and deducted.

There is an important distinction between self-employed qualified plans and corporate qualified plans: the way in which contributions are calculated on behalf of owner-employees.

### *Contributions to Self-Employed Qualified Plans*

Contributions to all retirement plans are based on compensation. For qualified plans covering employees, this is simply W-2 taxable wages. For self-employed individuals under self-employed qualified plans, the basis for contributions is a little more complicated. Essentially, the basis for contributions on behalf of owner-employees is net earnings from self-employment. But this is not merely the net profit from your business on which self-employment tax is paid. Net earnings from self-employment must be further reduced by the deduction for the employer portion of the self-employment tax.

To calculate compensation of the owner-employee, start with the profit from Schedule C (or Schedule F, in the case of farming) or the net earnings from self-employment on Schedule K-1 of Form 1065. For partners, this is essentially your distributive share of partnership income plus any guaranteed payments. Net earnings from self-employment from various activities are totaled on Schedule SE, *Self-Employment Tax*. After you have your compensation amount, subtract from this amount the employer portion of the self-employment tax computed on Schedule SE. This net amount is the figure upon which contributions to qualified retirement plans are based.

In order to make contributions on your own behalf, you must have net earnings from self-employment derived from your personal services. If you merely invest capital in a partnership while your personal services are not a material income-producing factor, you cannot make a plan contribution. If you are a limited partner, you cannot base a plan contribution on your distributive share of partnership income. Similar rules apply to members in LLCs. Income received from property, such as rents, interest, or dividends, is not treated as net earnings from self-employment.

***Special rules for partnerships***. Each partner in a partnership cannot maintain a separate SEP or other retirement plan. Only an employer can maintain and contribute to a plan for its employees, and for retirement plan purposes only, each partner or member of an LLC taxed as a partnership in an employee of the partnership.

But payments for partners and LLC members to a SEP or other retirement plan are not deducted by the partnership. These amounts are reported to the partner on his or her Schedule K-1 (box 13, code R). The partners then deduct these contributions on their individual returns as explained later.

#### CALCULATING YOUR CONTRIBUTION RATE

For self-employed individuals, the contribution rate must be adjusted for the employer deduction on behalf of yourself. This is a roundabout way of saying that the base percentage rate you use to determine contributions on behalf of employees, if any, must be adjusted for determining contributions on your own behalf. To arrive at this reduced percentage rate, divide the contribution rate, expressed as a decimal number, by one plus the contribution rate.

**Example**

**The contribution rate for your profit-sharing plan is 25%. You divide 0.25 by 1.25 to arrive at the contribution rate on your behalf: 20%.**

Remember, the maximum deduction for 2021 contributions cannot exceed the lesser of $58,000 or $290,000 times your contribution rate.

**Example**

**You maintain a 25% profit-sharing plan for your sole proprietorship, for which you are the only worker. In 2021, your net profit reported on Schedule C is $325,000. Your net earnings from self-employment for purposes of calculating plan contributions are $311,794 ($325,000 – $13,206 [employer portion of the self-employment tax]). Your contribution is limited to $58,000 (20% of $290,000). You cannot base your contribution on your full net earnings from self-employment because of the $290,000 compensation limit and $58,000 deduction limit.**

### *Simplified Employee Pensions in General*

Simplified employee pensions, or SEPs, are another type of retirement plan that self-employed individuals can use to save for retirement on a tax-advantaged basis. (Corporations can use SEPs as well.) The name is a misnomer because the plan does not provide a pension; it merely allows funds to accumulate and be used in retirement. But, as the name implies, these plans do not entail all the administrative costs and complications associated with other qualified retirement plans. There are no annual reporting requirements, as is the case for qualified plans and qualified corporate retirement plans.

*Simplified employee pensions* are individual retirement accounts set up by employees to which an employer makes contributions, then deducts them. The contributions are a fixed percentage of each employee's compensation. To set up a SEP, an employer need only sign a form establishing the percentage rate for making contributions and for setting eligibility requirements. This is a one-page form, Form 5305-SEP, *Simplified Employee Pension-IRA Contribution Agreement* (Figure 16.1).

The form is not filed with the IRS. Instead, it serves merely as an agreement under which the employer makes contributions. The employer then instructs employees where to set up SEP-IRAs to receive employer contributions. Banks, brokerage firms, and insurance companies generally have prototype plans designed for this purpose.

The maximum deduction for a contribution under a SEP is essentially the same as for a deferred contribution plan: 25% of compensation or $57,000, whichever is less. For contributions made on behalf of self-employed individuals (called owner-employees), this percentage works out to 20%. As with other qualified plans, no more than $290,000 of compensation in 2021 can be taken into account in computing contributions.

***Covering employees in SEPs.*** You must cover all employees who meet an age and service test. The SEP must cover employees who are 21 or older, earn over $650 in 2021, and have worked for you at any time in at least 3 out of 5 years. You can provide for more favorable coverage (for example, you can cover employees at age 18). The compensation requirement of $650 is adjusted annually for inflation in $50 increments.

There is no age limit on employees participating in a SEP and receiving employer contributions. Similarly, self-employed individuals over this age can continue to make contributions to their SEPs. However, required minimum distributions must also be made to participants age 70½ if they attained this age before 2020 and age 72 for those whose 70th birthday is July 1, 2019, or later.

***Salary reduction arrangements for SEPs.*** Before 1997, a SEP of a small business (with no more than 25 employees who were eligible to participate in the SEP at any time during the prior year) could be designed so that employees funded all or part of their own retirement plans. Employees agreed to reduce their compensation by a set amount. That amount, called an *elective deferral*, was then contributed to the SEP. Employees were treated as not having received the

| Form **5305-SEP** (Rev. December 2004) Department of the Treasury Internal Revenue Service | **Simplified Employee Pension—Individual Retirement Accounts Contribution Agreement** **(Under section 408(k) of the Internal Revenue Code)** | OMB No. 1545-0499 **Do not** file with the Internal Revenue Service |
|---|---|---|

______________________ (Name of employer) makes the following agreement under section 408(k) of the Internal Revenue Code and the instructions to this form.

**Article I—Eligibility Requirements** (check applicable boxes—see instructions)

The employer agrees to provide discretionary contributions in each calendar year to the individual retirement account or individual retirement annuity (IRA) of all employees who are at least ________ years old (not to exceed 21 years old) and have performed services for the employer in at least ________ years (not to exceed 3 years) of the immediately preceding 5 years. This simplified employee pension (SEP) ☐ includes ☐ **does not** include employees covered under a collective bargaining agreement, ☐ includes ☐ **does not** include certain nonresident aliens, and ☐ includes ☐ **does not** include employees whose total compensation during the year is less than $450*.

**Article II—SEP Requirements** (see instructions)

The employer agrees that contributions made on behalf of each eligible employee will be:

**A.** Based only on the first $205,000* of compensation.
**B.** The same percentage of compensation for every employee.
**C.** Limited annually to the smaller of $41,000* or 25% of compensation.
**D.** Paid to the employee's IRA trustee, custodian, or insurance company (for an annuity contract).

______________________ Employer's signature and date ______________________ Name and title

**FIGURE 16.1** Form 5305-SEP, Simplified Employee Pension

amount by which their salary was reduced so that they did not pay income taxes on that amount. Salary reduction arrangements in SEPs (SARSEPs), were repealed for 1997 and later years. However, employers that had SARSEPs before 1997 can continue these plans, and employees hired after 1996 may participate in these plans. So, for example, if you had a SARSEP plan in 1996, you can continue to fund it with salary reduction amounts in 2021.

## *Savings Incentive Match Plans for Employees*

Self-employed individuals as well as other small employers have another retirement plan alternative: Savings Incentive Match Plans for Employees (SIMPLE). These plans are open to **small employers** who want to avoid complicated nondiscrimination rules and reporting requirements. These SIMPLE plans can be used by corporations as well as by self-employed business owners.

***Small employers*** **For purposes of SIMPLE plans, those employers with 100 or fewer employees who received at least $5,000 in compensation in the preceding year.**

Savings Incentive Match Plans for Employees may be set up as either IRAs or 401(k) plans. The rules for both types of SIMPLE plans are similar but not identical. Employees can contribute to the plans on a salary reduction basis up to $13,500 in 2021 (plus an additional $3,000 if age 50 or older by the end of the year). Self-employed individuals can make similar contributions based on earned income.

Employers satisfy nondiscrimination rules simply by making required contributions. Employers have a choice of contribution formulas:

- Matching contributions (dollar-for-dollar) up to 3% of an employee's compensation for the year. For example, in 2021, if an employee under age 50 earning $35,000 makes the maximum salary reduction contribution of $13,500, the employer must contribute $1,050 (3% of

Form **5304-SIMPLE**
(Rev. March 2012)
Department of the Treasury
Internal Revenue Service

# Savings Incentive Match Plan for Employees of Small Employers (SIMPLE)—Not for Use With a Designated Financial Institution

OMB No. 1545-1502
**Do not** file with the Internal Revenue Service

_______________________________________________ establishes the following SIMPLE
Name of Employer
IRA plan under section 408(p) of the Internal Revenue Code and pursuant to the instructions contained in this form.

## Article I—Employee Eligibility Requirements *(complete applicable box(es) and blanks—see instructions)*

1 **General Eligibility Requirements.** The Employer agrees to permit salary reduction contributions to be made in each calendar year to the SIMPLE IRA established by each employee who meets the following requirements (select either 1a or 1b):

a ☐ **Full Eligibility.** All employees are eligible.

b ☐ **Limited Eligibility.** Eligibility is limited to employees who are described in both (i) and (ii) below:

(i) **Current compensation.** Employees who are reasonably expected to receive at least $ ____________ in compensation (not to exceed $5,000) for the calendar year.

(ii) **Prior compensation.** Employees who have received at least $ ____________ in compensation (not to exceed $5,000) during any ________ calendar year(s) (insert 0, 1, or 2) preceding the calendar year.

2 **Excludable Employees.**
☐ The Employer elects to exclude employees covered under a collective bargaining agreement for which retirement benefits were the subject of good faith bargaining. **Note:** *This box is deemed checked if the Employer maintains a qualified plan covering only such employees.*

## Article II—Salary Reduction Agreements *(complete the box and blank, if applicable—see instructions)*

1 **Salary Reduction Election.** An eligible employee may make an election to have his or her compensation for each pay period reduced. The total amount of the reduction in the employee's compensation for a calendar year cannot exceed the applicable amount for that year.

2 **Timing of Salary Reduction Elections**

a For a calendar year, an eligible employee may make or modify a salary reduction election during the 60-day period immediately preceding January 1 of that year. However, for the year in which the employee becomes eligible to make salary reduction contributions, the period during which the employee may make or modify the election is a 60-day period that includes either the date the employee becomes eligible or the day before.

b In addition to the election periods in 2a, eligible employees may make salary reduction elections or modify prior elections ____________, ________________________________________. If the Employer chooses this option, insert a period or periods (for example, semi-annually, quarterly, monthly, or daily) that will apply uniformly to all eligible employees.

c No salary reduction election may apply to compensation that an employee received, or had a right to immediately receive, before execution of the salary reduction election.

d An employee may terminate a salary reduction election at any time during the calendar year. ☐ If this box is checked, an employee who terminates a salary reduction election not in accordance with 2b may not resume salary reduction contributions during the calendar year.

## Article III—Contributions *(complete the blank, if applicable—see instructions)*

1 **Salary Reduction Contributions.** The amount by which the employee agrees to reduce his or her compensation will be contributed by the Employer to the employee's SIMPLE IRA.

2a **Matching Contributions**

(i) For each calendar year, the Employer will contribute a matching contribution to each eligible employee's SIMPLE IRA equal to the employee's salary reduction contributions up to a limit of 3% of the employee's compensation for the calendar year.

(ii) The Employer may reduce the 3% limit for the calendar year in (i) only if:

**(1)** The limit is not reduced below 1%; **(2)** The limit is not reduced for more than 2 calendar years during the 5-year period ending with the calendar year the reduction is effective; and **(3)** Each employee is notified of the reduced limit within a reasonable period of time before the employees' 60-day election period for the calendar year (described in Article II, item 2a).

b **Nonelective Contributions**

(i) For any calendar year, instead of making matching contributions, the Employer may make nonelective contributions equal to 2% of compensation for the calendar year to the SIMPLE IRA of each eligible employee who has at least $ ____________, (not more than $5,000) in compensation for the calendar year. No more than $250,000* in compensation can be taken into account in determining the nonelective contribution for each eligible employee.

(ii) For any calendar year, the Employer may make 2% nonelective contributions instead of matching contributions only if:
**(1)** Each eligible employee is notified that a 2% nonelective contribution will be made instead of a matching contribution; and
**(2)** This notification is provided within a reasonable period of time before the employees' 60-day election period for the calendar year (described in Article II, item 2a).

3 **Time and Manner of Contributions**

a The Employer will make the salary reduction contributions (described in 1 above) for each eligible employee to the SIMPLE IRA established at the financial institution selected by that employee no later than 30 days after the end of the month in which the money is withheld from the employee's pay. See instructions.

b The Employer will make the matching or nonelective contributions (described in 2a and 2b above) for each eligible employee to the SIMPLE IRA established at the financial institution selected by that employee no later than the due date for filing the Employer's tax return, including extensions, for the taxable year that includes the last day of the calendar year for which the contributions are made.

* *This is the amount for 2012. For later years, the limit may be increased for cost-of-living adjustments. The IRS announces the increase, if any, in a news release, in the Internal Revenue Bulletin, and on the IRS's internet website at* ***IRS.gov.***

**For Paperwork Reduction Act Notice, see the instructions.** Cat. No. 23377W Form **5304-SIMPLE** (Rev. 3-2012)

**FIGURE 16.2** Form 5304-SIMPLE, Savings Incentive Match Plan for Employees of Small Employers

$35,000). The maximum matching contribution per employee in 2021 to a SIMPLE 401(k) is $8,550 (100% of the matching employee contribution, which is up to 3% of $290,000). However, there is no limit on compensation taken into account for employer matching contributions to a SIMPLE-IRA.

**Looking Ahead**

**The elective deferral of $13,500 may be adjusted annually for inflation in increments of $500. The catch-up contribution of $3,000 for those age 50 or older by year-end may also be adjusted annually for inflation in increments of $500.**

- Nonelective contributions of 2% of compensation (regardless of whether the employee makes any contributions) for any employee earning at least $5,000. For example, in 2021, if an employee's compensation is $25,000, the employer's contribution is $500 (2% of $25,000). The maximum contribution per employee in 2021 is $5,800 (2% of $290,000, the maximum compensation that can be used to determine contributions).

***Contribution reduction for distressed companies.*** The 3% matching contribution can be reduced at the employer's election, but not below 1%. The reduction cannot be made for more than 2 years of the 5-year period that ends with the year of the election, and you must give notice of the reduced limit to your employees within a reasonable time *before* the 60-day election period in which employees make their salary reduction agreements.

Self-employed persons can make employer contributions to SIMPLE-IRAs on their own behalf as well as make their own contributions. In effect, they are treated as both employer and employee.

Employee and employer contributions vest immediately. This means that employees can withdraw contributions at any time (although withdrawals prior to age 59½ are subject to a 25% penalty if taken within the first 2 years of beginning participation, and 10% if taken after that period).

Employers who want to let employees choose their own financial institutions can adopt SIMPLE plans merely by completing Form 5304-SIMPLE (Figure 16.2). Employers who want to choose the financial institutions for their employees use Form 5305-SIMPLE. Whichever option is chosen, the form is not filed with the IRS but is kept with the employer's records. This form gives the necessary notification to eligible employees and a model salary reduction agreement that can be used by employees to specify their salary reduction contributions. Employers who use SIMPLE plans cannot maintain any other type of qualified retirement plan.

### *Individual Retirement Accounts as a Plan Alternative*

If the cost of covering employees is prohibitive for a self-employed individual, neither a qualified plan, a SEP, nor a SIMPLE plan may be the answer. Instead, the self-employed individual may want to use an IRA. In this case, the maximum that can be deducted is $6,000 (plus $1,000 if the person is age 50 or older by year-end). However, if a self-employed's spouse is a participant in a qualified plan, the self-employed person may deduct $6,000 (or $7,000) only if the couple's combined adjusted gross income in 2021 does not exceed $198,000. The $6,000 deduction phases out as the couple's adjusted gross income (AGI) reaches a threshold amount explained later. If a self-employed individual contributes $6,000 (or $7,000) to a Roth IRA, he or she cannot make deductible contributions to an IRA. Individual retirement accounts are discussed later in this chapter.

## Regular 401(k)s and Designated Roth Accounts

A 401(k) plan is a qualified retirement plan that is funded primarily through employee contributions via salary reductions (self-employed individuals can make so-called employee contributions). Companies can or must make certain matching contributions, depending on the circumstances. Company (employer) contributions vest for participants in the same manner as contributions to other defined contribution plans explained earlier in this chapter. They were legislatively created in 1978, and by 1981, half of all large corporations had adopted them. Today, use of 401(k)s is not exclusive to large corporations; even a sole proprietor with no employees can use a 401(k).

These 401(k) plans allow employers to offer retirement benefits to employees that are largely funded by the employees themselves. To encourage employees to participate in the plans (employers cannot force employees to make contributions), employers may offer matching contributions. For example, an employer may match each dollar of employee deferral with a dollar of employer contributions or some other ratio. Employers who offer 401(k) plans must be careful that stringent nondiscrimination rules are satisfied.

Essentially, these rules require that a sufficient number of rank-and-file employees participate in the plan and make contributions. If the nondiscrimination rules are not satisfied, the plan will not be treated as a qualified plan, and tax benefits will not be available. Explaining the advantages of participating to rank-and-file employees and offering matching contributions are 2 ways to attract the necessary participation; adopting automatic enrollment (as explained earlier in this chapter in connection with participation) is yet another way.

Employees who take advantage of elective deferral options cannot deduct their contributions to the 401(k) plan. They have already received a tax benefit by virtue of the fact that deferrals are excluded from taxable income for income tax purposes. They are still treated as part of compensation for purposes of FICA and FUTA.

From an employer perspective, using 401(k) plans can shift the investment responsibility to employees. Instead of making all of the investment decisions, the employer simply has to offer a menu of investment options to employees. Then the employees decide how they want their funds invested. Employees can be as conservative or as aggressive as they choose. Treasury and Department of Labor regulations detail the number and types of investment options that must be offered and what must be communicated to employees about these investment options.

There is a dollar limit on the elective deferral. In 2021, the elective deferral cannot exceed $19,500. The catch-up (additional) elective deferral limit for those who attain age 50 by December 31, 2021, is $6,500. Thus, the top elective deferral for a participant age 50 or older in 2021 is $26,000.

Those who work for certain tax-exempt organizations—schools, hospitals, and religious organizations—may be able to make elective deferrals used to buy tax-deferred annuities, called 403(b) annuities. The same elective deferral limit applies here.

**Looking Ahead**

**The limits on the basic elective deferral limit as well as the catch-up amount can be adjusted annually for inflation.**

### One-Person 401(k) Plans

If you work alone, with no employees, can you have a 401(k) plan? The answer is yes, even if you are self-employed. This type of plan may enable you to maximize contributions because you can make both employee salary reduction contributions (elective deferrals) and employer contributions.

**Example**

**You are self-employed, age 45, and have net earnings from self-employment of $140,000. If you have a profit-sharing plan, your contribution is limited to $26,022 (20% of $130,109 [$140,000, after a reduction of $9,891, which is one-half of the self-employment tax]). But with a one-person 401(k) plan, the maximum contribution of $58,000 can be attained with these earnings (salary reduction contribution of $19,500, plus employer contribution of $38,500). For those with an incorporated business who are under age 50, the maximum contribution is attained with salary of $150,000.**

### Designated Roth Accounts

Now, 401(k) plans can offer an option that's like a Roth IRA called a designated Roth account. Contributions to designated Roth accounts are made with after-tax dollars (rather than salary reduction amounts). Thus, there is no tax advantage when the money goes into the plan. However, the benefit to this alternative is that all withdrawals (not merely contributions) can be withdrawn tax free after age 59½ (or on account of disability or death or up to $10,000 for first-time homebuying expenses) as long as they have been in the plan for at least 5 years. The 5-year period starts on January 1 of the year in which designated Roth contributions are first made.

Contribution limits to these accounts are the same as for regular 401(k)s. Contributions can be split between regular and Roth 401(k)s as long as the total does not exceed the annual limit. Plans can permit in-plan rollovers from traditional 401(k)s to designated Roth accounts. There is no 20% mandatory withholding, but those making such a rollover must report the amount as taxable income (it is a conversion from a tax-deferred to a tax-free account). There is no 10% early distribution penalty even if the person making the conversion is under age 59½.

Funds from a designated Roth account can be rolled over tax free to another designated Roth account or to a Roth IRA.

How do designated Roth accounts compare with Roth IRAs? Unlike Roth IRAs, designated Roth accounts cannot be undone once the conversion (called an in-plan Roth rollover) is made. Also, there are lifetime withdrawal requirements on designated Roth accounts that do not apply to Roth IRAs (although this can be avoided by rolling over the designated Roth account into a Roth IRA). But there are no income limits for making contributions to designated Roth accounts as there are for contributing to Roth IRAs.

### Loans from 401(k) Plans

The rules governing loans from 401(k) plans were discussed earlier in this chapter; special rules related to the coronavirus and disasters are discussed later. It should be noted that all participants, not just owners, are prohibited from deducting interest on plan loans. But the interest is really being paid to the participant's own account, so the loss of a deduction is not so important.

### Selecting Plan Investments

Generally, a 401(k) plan must offer a menu of investment options to participants. Usually, this is done by opting to have the plan with a family of mutual funds, such as Fidelity or Vanguard. In choosing the mutual fund or other company with which to place the plan, consider:

- ***Investment choices.*** The Department of Labor has regulations governing the minimum number and type of investment choices that must be offered by the plan.
- ***Fees.*** The Departments of Labor and the Treasury have rules regarding fees and their disclosure. Check on administrative fees (the amount charged for maintaining the plan), asset-based fees (amounts paid for specific types of investments), and service fees (amounts paid for optional services).

## Pooled Employer Plans (PEPs)

While most large employers offer their employees retirement plans, many small employers have been reluctant to do so for several reasons: cost of contributions, administrative costs, and the burden of fiduciary responsibility. The cost of contributions can be easily addressed by adopting plans funded entirely or mainly by employees, but the other issues remain. As a result of the SECURE Act, these issues may be alleviated by the introduction of Pooled Employee Plans (PEPs). PEPs are open Multiple Employer Plans (MEPs) in which 2 or more unrelated employers join together to enable their employees to participate in a 401(k) plan. PEPs were scheduled to begin registration with the Department of Labor after November 25, 2020, but a final rule for this is under review (i.e., registrations are on hold). Check the Supplement for any update.

### Overview

PEPs are open to businesses of any size. But as a practical matter, it's likely they will be used by small employers. Because of economies of scale with PEPs, the administrative costs for employers joining the plan are greatly reduced as compared with costs for setting up and running an individual plan for the company.

Also, it is expected that the plan can offer participants a greater range of investment options that you could in an individual plan for your business.

### Fiduciary Responsibilities

Most of the fiduciary responsibilities for the plan are those of the pooled plan provider (PPP). This is an institution that meets certain government-set requirements. The PPP is the primary fiduciary. The plan assets are held by a bank or trust company, with various safeguards in place to protect participants' accounts.

However, as an employer, you retain responsibility for timely depositing employee elective deferrals into the plan.

## Individual Retirement Accounts

Another retirement plan option to consider is an IRA. There are now 3 types of personal IRAs to consider for retirement savings: traditional deductible IRAs, traditional nondeductible IRAs, and Roth IRAs. The maximum amount that can be contributed in 2021 is $6,000 (or taxable earned income if less than $6,000). If you have a nonworking spouse, the contribution limit is $6,000 for each spouse (as long as you have earned income of at least $12,000). (The account for a nonworking spouse is called a Kay Bailey Hutchison IRA.) Therefore, the limit is considerably lower than the limit for other retirement plans.

In addition to the basic contribution limit, those who attain age 50 by year-end can make additional catch-up contributions. The limit on catch-up contributions to IRAs in 2021 is $1,000.

If you are self-employed and have more than one business, you must aggregate your business income to determine compensation for purposes of calculating contributions. You cannot base an IRA contribution on a pension or annuity income or income received from property, such as rents, interest, or dividends. (A special rule allows alimony and military combat pay to be treated as compensation for purposes of IRA contributions.)

However, if you are in business and set up an IRA for yourself, you need not cover your employees. For some, this factor alone may dictate in favor of an IRA.

In the past, there was an age limit on contributing to an IRA or Roth IRA of 70½. This limit does not apply after 2019, so those above this age threshold in 2021 can make a contribution if otherwise eligible to do so.

### *Individual Retirement Accounts and Other Retirement Plans*

Whether you can make deductible contributions to both an IRA and another retirement plan depends on your overall income. Individuals who are considered active participants in qualified retirement plans cannot deduct contributions to an IRA if adjusted gross income exceeds a certain amount. More specifically, in 2021 no deduction can be claimed by an active participant when modified adjusted gross income (MAGI) exceeds a certain amount. Table 16.2 shows the starting MAGI amounts for the phase-out and the MAGI amounts at which the phase-out is complete so that no deduction is allowed.

You are considered an *active participant* if, at any time during the year, either you or your spouse is covered by an employer retirement plan. An employer retirement plan includes all of the following plans:

- Qualified pension, profit-sharing, or stock bonus plan
- SEP plan
- SIMPLE plan
- Qualified annuity plan
- Tax-sheltered annuity
- A plan established by the federal, state, or political subdivision for its employees (other than a state Section 457 plan)

If you are an active participant (or your spouse is an active participant) and your AGI is over the limit for your filing status, you can make a traditional non-deductible IRA contribution. There is no AGI limit on making this type of IRA contribution.

Alternatively, you may want to make contributions to a Roth IRA. Contributions must be based on compensation (just as they are for traditional IRAs), but there are some important differences between the Roth and a traditional IRA. There are no required lifetime minimum distributions, as there are for owners of traditional IRAs commencing at age 70½ (different rules apply to inherited

**TABLE 16.2** Active Participants' MAGI Phase-Outs for Deducting IRA Contributions in 2021

| Filing Status | MAGI Phase-Out Begins | MAGI Phase-Out Range | No Deduction if MAGI is |
|---|---|---|---|
| Married filing jointly and both spouses are active participants/ surviving spouse | $105,000 | Over $105,000 but under $125,000 | $125,000 or more |
| Married filing jointly/surviving spouse one spouse is an active participant | $105,000 for participant spouse and $198,000 for nonparticipant spouse | Over $195,000 for participant spouse/$198,000 for nonparticipant spouse but under $125,000 for participant spouse/$208,000 for nonparticipant spouse | $125,000 or more for participant spouse/$208,000 for nonparticipant spouse |
| Single/head of household | $66,000 | Over $66,000 but under $76,000 | $76,000 or more |
| Married filing separately and lived with spouse at any time during the year | $0 | Over $0 but under $10,000 | $10,000 or more |
| Married filing separately and lived apart the entire year | $66,000 for participant spouse/no phase-out for nonparticipant spouse | Over $66,000 but under $76,000 for participant spouse/no phase-out for nonparticipant spouse | $76,000 or more for participant spouse/no phase-out for nonparticipant spouse |

Roth IRAs). Contributions can be made regardless of whether you (or your spouse) are an active participant in a qualified retirement plan. If funds remain in the Roth IRA for at least 5 years, withdrawals after age 59½, or because of disability, or to pay first-time home-buying expenses (up to $10,000 in a lifetime) are completely free from income tax.

The 5-year period starts on the first day of the year in which contributions are made (or to which they relate). So, for example, if you make a 2021 contribution to a Roth IRA on April 18, 2022 (the due date of your 2021 return), the 5-year holding period commences on January 1, 2021, the year to which the first contribution relates. However, you can make full Roth IRA contributions only if your MAGI is no more than an amount listed in Table 16.3.

***Spousal IRAs.*** Called Kay Bailey Hutchinson IRAs, these accounts can be opened for a non-working spouse to enable a couple to double the annual contributions to IRAs and Roth IRAs. If one spouse is age 50 or older, add $1,000 to the contribution limit; if both are age 50 or older, add $2,000 to the contribution limit.

**TABLE 16.3** MAGI Phase-Outs for Making Roth IRA Contributions in 2021

| Filing Status | MAGI Phase-Out Begins | MAGI Phase-Out Range | No Roth IRA Contributions if MAGI is |
|---|---|---|---|
| Single/head of household | $125,000 | Over $125,000 but under $140,000 | $140,000 |
| Married filing jointly/surviving spouse | $198,000 | Over $198,000 but under $208,000 | $208,000 |
| Married filing separately | $0 | $0 | $0 |

**Example**

In 2021, you are self-employed (and you don't work for anyone else with a retirement plan), while your spouse does not work outside the home and does not perform services for your business. Assuming you are both under age 50, you can contribute up to $12,000 ($6,000 for your IRA and $6,000 for your spouse's IRA). If your contributions are to a traditional IRA, then you can deduct $12,000 on your joint return as long as your net earnings from self-employment are at least $12,000. (If one spouse was age 50 or older, the deduction would be $13,000; if both were age 50 or older, the deduction would be $14,000. If your contributions are to a Roth IRA, no deduction is allowed, but you still must file jointly to make the Roth IRA contributions for your nonworking spouse.

***Converting to a Roth IRA.*** In planning to maximize your retirement funds, you may want to convert your traditional IRAs to a Roth IRA if you did not do so already. This will allow you to build up a tax-free retirement nest egg (provided the funds remain in the Roth IRA at least 5 years and are not withdrawn unless you meet a withdrawal condition). The price of conversion is that you must report all the income that would have resulted had you simply taken a distribution from your IRAs. Conversions are permanent and cannot be recharacterized or undone, as was possible in prior years.

There is no 10% penalty on conversion income even if you are under age 59½, as long as the funds remain in the Roth IRA for at least 5 years. This 5-year period is measured from January 1 of the year in which the conversion is made.

In deciding to use a traditional IRA, be aware of certain restrictions designed to encourage savings and prevent dissipation of the account prior to retirement. First, you generally cannot withdraw IRA contributions, or earnings on those contributions, before age 59½. Doing so may result in a 10% early distribution penalty. There are a number of exceptions to the early distribution penalty:

- Disability
- Withdrawals taken in substantially equal periodic payments

- Distributions to pay medical expenses in excess of the applicable percentage of AGI
- Distributions to pay health insurance premiums by those who are unemployed (self-employed can be treated as unemployed for this purpose)
- Distributions to pay qualified higher education costs
- Distributions for first-time home-buying expenses (up to $10,000 in a lifetime)
- Involuntary distributions resulting from IRS levies upon IRAs to satisfy back taxes
- Distributions by reservists called to active duty

However, there is no exception to the 10% penalty for economic or financial hardship.

Second, you must begin withdrawals from traditional IRAs no later than April 1 of the year following the year of attaining the starting age for required minimum distributions. The failure to take certain minimum distributions designed to exhaust the account over your life expectancy results in a 50% penalty tax. The minimum distribution requirement applies as well to qualified retirement plans, SEP-IRAs, and SIMPLE plans.

## COVID-19-Related Rules

Due to the pandemic, Congress added special breaks in the CARES Act for qualified retirement plans and IRAs for 2020. These rules continue to impact 2021 and later years.

- Coronavirus-related distributions up to $100,000 between March 27, 2020, and December 31, 2020, were permissible if the plan allowed it. The income was spread over 3 years unless the taxpayer opted to report it all in 2020. The distribution can be recontributed within 3 years, so plans may receive recontributions in 2021 and need to report them on Form 1099-R.
- Coronavirus-related loans up to $100,000 (up to 100% of the account balance) between March 27, 2020, and December 31, 2020, could have been taken if the plan allowed it. Loans were not restricted to financial needs. Payments on current loans outstanding in 2020 were delayed for one year, although interest continued to accrue. Starting with the first payment due in 2021, the plan, including accrued interest, must be re-amortized from January 1, 2021, through the date that is one year after the original loan repayment date.
- Required minimum distributions (RMDs) from all defined contribution plans and IRAs were waived for 2020. But defined benefit (pension) plans had to continue to make payouts. RMDs must commence for 2021.
- Plans were allowed to operate in accordance with the special rules, but have time to make amendments as explained earlier in this chapter.

## Disaster-Related Rules

For federal disasters (other than COVID-19) declared during the period from January 1, 2020, through February 25, 2021, rules for distributions and loans mirror those related to COVID-19 explained earlier in this chpater. This means participants impacted by the disaster may take distributions from qualified retirement plans and IRAs up to $100,000 without incurring the 10% early distribution penalty. This is limited to distributions and loans taken from December 27, 2020, through June 25, 2021. Check the Supplement for any additional disasters for which Congress may provide relief.

Amounts withdrawn are included ratably in gross income over 3 years unless the participant chooses to report the distribution in full in the year received. The withdrawn funds may be recontributed to the same or other qualified retirement plan or IRA within 3 years. The plans were not required to offer these options, but need to be amended accordingly if they did.

## State-Sponsored Plans for the Private Sector

At present, there is no federal mandate requiring employers to offer qualified retirement plans. However, some states mandate retirement plan coverage for employees. As of May 2021, this is true in California, Connecticut, Illinois, Maryland, Massachusetts, New Jersey, Oregon, Vermont, and Washington, (check the Supplement for any update) where programs are either active or being implemented now. In these states, employers of a certain size that do not have a qualified retirement plan must enroll eligible employees into the state-run plan. Employers in these states do not have to use the state program if they have their own qualified retirement plans for employees. Some other states have such programs under consideration. The state-run programs are not operational in all of these states.

> **NOTE**
> **None of these state-sponsored plans permit any employer contributions and are viewed as non-ERISA plans.**

## When to Take Action

Using a retirement plan for your business means setting one up within set time limits, making timely contributions, and taking other action when required.

### *Setting Up a Plan*

Qualified retirement plans can be set up as late as the extended due date of the return. For example, a self-employed individual can set up a SEP for 2021 as late as October 17, 2022, if this person obtained a filing extension for the 2021 return. Despite the ability to use the extended due date as the deadline for setting up plans, certain plans must be set up earlier than this in order to comply with notice requirements to participants. So SIMPLE-IRAs and 401(k) plans usually must be set up by November 2 to give employees the required 60 days notice for participation. If plans are not set up early enough to provide the notice for participants to elect their salary reduction contributions before the start of the plan year, then only employer contributions are permitted for that year.

For IRAs, the deadline is the due date of the return, regardless of extensions. Thus, the deadline for setting up an IRA for 2021 is April 18, 2022, even if a filing extension is obtained.

### *Making Contributions*

Contributions to defined benefit plans must be made on a quarterly basis. In order to avoid a special interest charge, contributions made in quarterly installments must be at least 90% of contributions for the current year or 100% of contributions for the prior year. If contributions are based on the current year, the balance of the contributions may be made as late as the due date for the employer's return, including extensions.

Contributions for defined contribution plans and SEPs can be made at any time up to the due date of the employer's return, including extensions. In fact, contributions can be made even after the employer's tax return is filed as long as they do not exceed the return's due date. In effect, contributions can be funded through a tax refund.

> **NOTE**
> **Under a safe harbor rule for small employers (those with fewer than 100 employees), employees' contributions to the plan are deemed timely if made within 7 business days following receipt or withholding by the employer.**

**Example**

**A calendar-year employer (C corporation) in Utah, whose 2021 return is due on April 18, 2022, obtains a filing extension to October 17, 2022. The return is filed on June 1, 2022, and a refund is received on August 15, 2022. The employer has until October 17, 2022, to complete contributions to its profit-sharing plan, a deduction for which was reported on the return. The employer can use the refund for this purpose. However, the refund cannot be directly deposited into the profit-sharing plan as is the case with a direct deposit of a refund in an IRA.**

The only way to extend the deadline for making contributions is to obtain a valid filing extension. For example, an owner of a professional corporation on a calendar year who wants to extend the time for making contributions must obtain an extension of time to file Form 1120, the return for that corporation. To do this, Form 7004, *Application for Automatic Extension of Time to File Corporation Income Tax Return*, must be filed no later than April 18, the due date for Form 1120 for calendar-year corporations.

Filing Form 7004 gives the calendar-year corporation an automatic 6-month filing extension, to October 15. The corporation then has until October 15 to make its contributions to the plan.

Contributions must generally be made in cash. When cash flow is insufficient to meet contribution requirements (and there are no refunds available for this purpose, as explained earlier), employers may be forced to borrow to make contributions on time. In some instances, contributions can be made by using employer stock.

Watch the timing of making contributions to a SIMPLE plan. While employer contributions can be made up to the extended due date of the employer's return, contributions through elective deferrals must be made no later than 30 days after the end of the month for which the contributions are to be made (e.g., January 30, 2022, for a 2021 plan).

**Example**

**Sally, age 45, has a SIMPLE IRA plan for her consulting business in which she nets $90,000. For 2021, her elective deferral contribution is $13,500, and the business makes a $2,700 contribution (3% of $90,000). The $13,500 must actually be contributed by January 30, 2022. If Sally obtains an automatic filing extension, she has until October 17, 2022, to make the $2,700 contribution.**

Contributions for 2021 to IRAs and Roth IRAs must be completed no later than April 18, 2022, even if you obtain a filing extension. Contributions to an IRA or a Roth IRA can be made directly or through direct deposit of a tax refund. The deposit is made by providing account information directly on the return or, if directing the refund to 2 or 3 different accounts, on Form 8888, *Allocation of Refund (Including Savings Bond Purchases)*. If you are using a direct deposit to make a 2021 contribution, be sure that the return is filed early enough in 2022 to allow for processing and fund transfer to the IRA before April 18, 2022 (the deadline for 2021 IRA contributions).

### *Filing Information Returns*

Qualified retirement plans (other than some small plans as well as SEPs and SIMPLE IRAs of any size) are required to report their activities annually to the Department of Labor's Employee Benefits Security Administration. For details, see Appendix A.

### *Monitoring Plan Investments*

Check the plan's investment options each year to make sure you are offering those with the lowest fees and charges.

## Plan Problems and Corrections

While qualified retirement plans offer the opportunity for building wealth on a tax-advantaged basis, they are fraught with potential penalties for missteps. Some errors can be easily corrected, as explained later in this chapter. Others can be fatal to the plan, and cost owners and other participants dearly. Here are some actions that should *not* be taken.

### *Excess Contributions*

If you contribute more than the dollar amount permissible, you have made an excess contribution. The excess contribution is subject to an excise tax (essentially a penalty) of 6% per year, each year, for as long as the excess amount remains in the plan.

You can avoid or limit the tax by withdrawing the funds or applying them to future contributions. No penalty applies if the excess contributions are withdrawn by the due date of the return (including extensions) for the year to which the excess contributions relate.

### *Plan Errors*

Because retirement plan rules are complicated, it's easy to make mistakes. The IRS has this list of common errors:

- Not covering the proper employees
- Not giving employees required information
- Not depositing employee deferrals timely
- Not depositing employer contributions timely
- Not following the terms of the plan document
- Not limiting employee deferrals and employer contributions to the proper maximum limits

You can correct mistakes using the IRS's Employee Plans Compliance Resolution System (EPCRS) at https://www.irs.gov/retirement-plans/epcrs-overview. Some mistakes can be self-corrected without penalty; others require IRS approval and entail a penalty. Always consult a benefits expert if you have questions about your plan and possible errors that may exist.

### *Prohibited Transactions*

The tax law has strict rules about what you can and cannot do when it comes to your qualified retirement plans and IRAs. The funds are designed for retirement savings; the rules prevent you from self-dealing and certain other actions that are thought to run counter to the purpose of these plans.

Paraphrasing the Senate Report from 1974, the purpose of prohibited transactions is to prevent taxpayers from using their qualified retirement plans to engage in transactions that could place plan assets and income at risk of loss before retirement. Prohibited transactions are listed in Section 4975 of the Internal Revenue Code. They include any direct or indirect:

1. Sale, exchange, or leasing of any property between a plan and a disqualified person.
2. Lending of money or other extension of credit between a plan and a disqualified person.

3. Furnishing of goods, services, or facilities between a plan and a disqualified person.
4. Transfer to, or use by or for the benefit of, a disqualified person of the income or assets of a plan.
5. Action by a disqualified person who is a fiduciary whereby he deals with the income or assets of a plan in his own interests or for his own account.
6. Receipt of any consideration for his own personal account by any disqualified person who is a fiduciary from any party dealing with the plan in connection with a transaction involving the income or assets of the plan.

The fact that a transaction would qualify as a prudent investment under the highest fiduciary standards does not change the character of the transaction.

Prohibited transactions are subject to excise taxes:

- 15% excise tax. For example, failing to deposit employee contributions into 401(k) plans on time is a prohibited transaction subject to a 15% excise tax. It's a prohibited transaction because the company is holding on to the funds (i.e., a disqualified entity is using funds for its own purposes).
- 100% excise tax if the prohibited transaction is not corrected in time.

In some situations, the prohibited transaction results in the loss of tax-deferred status for the plan or account as of the first day of the year in which the prohibited transaction occurs. This means that all of the funds in the account become immediately taxable to the account owner. And, if the account owner is under age 59½ at the time, there is a 10% early distribution penalty as well.

The best way to avoid problems is to talk with a knowledgeable tax adviser before making any moves with a qualified plan or IRA that could raise questions about self-dealing.

***Abuse of Roth IRAs.*** There are many schemes being promoted to business owners that involve Roth IRAs. The IRS has identified transactions that improperly avoid the limitations on Roth IRAs as an abusive transaction that can result in severe penalties and tax costs to owners that use them.

Typically these abusive Roth IRAs involved 3 parties: an individual with an existing business, a Roth IRA maintained for this individual, and a corporation or limited liability company owned by the Roth IRA ("Roth IRA corporation") that is a wholly owned subsidiary of the individual's Roth IRA. Then the Roth IRA corporation acquires assets (e.g., accounts receivable) from the individual's business for less than fair market value, or contributions of property are made by a person other than the Roth IRA to the Roth IRA corporation without the receipt of stock ownership equal to the value of the property.

## Comparison of Qualified Retirement Plans

The different choices of qualified retirement plans have been discussed at length. But how do you know which plan is best for you? There are several factors to consider:

- *How much money do you have to set aside in a retirement plan?* If your business is continually profitable, you may want to commit to a type of plan that requires contributions without regard to profits. If your business is good in some years but bad in others, you may want to use a profit-sharing-type plan that does not require contributions in poor years.

- *How much will it cost to cover employees?* When there are few or no employees, then the choice of plan is largely a question of what will be the most beneficial to you. When a great number of employees will have to be covered, the cost may be too prohibitive to provide substantial retirement benefits. However, if your competitors offer plans to their employees, you may be forced to offer similar benefits as a means of attracting or retaining employees.
- *How soon do you expect to retire?* The closer you are to retirement, the more inclined you may be to use a defined benefit plan to sock away as much as possible.
- Also consider the costs of administration, the amount of entanglement with the IRS, and your financial sophistication and comfort level with more exotic arrangements.

Table 16.4 offers a comparison of the retirement plans.

### Defined Benefit Plans versus Defined Contribution Plans

Defined benefit plans offer owners the opportunity to slant more contributions to their own benefit, especially if they are older than their employees. However, most small business employers are moving away from defined benefit plans because of the complexities and costs of administration. Defined benefit plans are by far more costly to administer than defined contribution plans. First, there are the costs of plan design. Defined benefit plans may be specially tailored to each employer, whereas defined contribution plans generally use prototypes readily available. Second, there is the cost of the actuary to determine contributions necessary to fund the promised benefits. Third, there are annual premiums paid to the Pension Benefit Guaranty Corporation (PBGC), a federal agency designed to provide some measure of protection for employees (somewhat akin

**TABLE 16.4 Comparison of Retirement Plans in 2021**

| Type of Plan | Maximum Contribution | Last Date for Contribution |
|---|---|---|
| IRA | $6,000 or taxable compensation, whichever is smaller ($7,000 for those 50 or older) | Due date of your return (without extensions) |
| SIMPLE plan | $13,500 (not to exceed taxable compensation), plus catch-up contributions, plus employer contributions | Due date of employer's return for employer contributions (including extensions); 30 days after end of month for salary reduction contributions |
| SEP-IRA | $58,000 or 20% of participant's taxable compensation, whichever is smaller | Due date of employer's return (including extensions) |
| Qualified plan | Defined contribution plan—smaller of $58,000 or 25% of compensation (20% of self-employed's income) | Generally, the due date of employer's return (including extensions). |
| | Defined benefit plan—amount needed to provide retirement benefit no larger than the lesser of $230,000 or 100% of the participant's average taxable compensation for highest 3 consecutive years | Due date of employer's return (including extensions) but not later than the minimum funding deadline. Note: Plan must be set up by the due date of the employer's return (including extensions). |

to FDIC insurance for bank accounts). These premiums are calculated on a per-participant basis, with an additional premium for underfunded plans (as discussed earlier in this chapter).

Another factor to consider when deciding between defined benefit and defined contribution plans is the timing of making contributions. Contributions to defined contribution plans can be made at any time during the year to which they relate but can also be made as late as the due date for the employer's return, including extensions. In the case of defined benefit plans, contributions must be made more rapidly than those to defined contribution plans. Defined benefit plans have quarterly contribution requirements, and the failure to make sufficient contributions quarterly can result in penalties.

**NOTE**

**Those who were born before 1936 can continue to use 10-year averaging to report distributions from qualified plans, an option not open to distributions from SEPs, regardless of the participant's age.**

### *Qualified Plan versus Simplified Employee Pension*

If you use a profit-sharing plan, the contribution limit is the same for both self-employed qualified plans and SEPs. However, there is one advantage to a SEP versus a self-employed retirement plan: There is less paperwork involved in a SEP than in a qualified plan. While qualified plans must file information returns with the IRS annually, SEPs have no similar annual reporting requirements.

### *SIMPLE-IRA versus Self-Employed Qualified Plan or SEP*

Business owners with modest earnings may be able to put more into a SIMPLE-IRA than a qualified plan. The reason: The employee contribution (which a self-employed individual can also make) to a SIMPLE-IRA is not based on a percentage of income but rather a dollar amount up to $13,500 in 2021 ($16,500 for those age 50 or older). (The 25% annual compensation limit applies to employee contributions to SIMPLE-401(k)s.)

**Example**

**Assume a 40-year-old self-employed individual's net earnings from self-employment are $25,000. The top contribution to a SIMPLE-IRA is $14,250 ($13,500 salary reduction contribution, plus $750 employer matching contribution). In contrast, the contribution limit to a profit-sharing plan or SEP in this instance is only $5,000, considerably less than that allowed for a SIMPLE-IRA.**

The bottom line is that business owners who want to maximize their retirement plan contributions need to run the numbers to determine which plan is preferable.

## ESOPs

An employee stock ownership plan (ESOP) is a type of employee benefit plan that effectively gives workers an ownership interest in your business. Since it is a stock-based plan, it can be used only for corporations (both C and S), although it cannot be used for most professional corporations.

### *How an ESOP Works*

The corporation sets up a trust into which it contributes either shares of its stock or cash to buy shares. Or the corporation can borrow money to buy shares and contribute cash to the trust to repay the loan. Shares are then allocated to plan participants (employees) in a manner similar to a profit-sharing plan; vesting rules apply.

Typically, professional fees and other costs for setting up an ESOP are substantial ($25,000 to $50,000 for even small companies). Thus, such plans are not used for very small companies (e.g., fewer than 50 employees).

### *Tax Breaks*

For the corporation:

- Contributions of cash to buy shares or to repay a loan, or to buy shares of stock are tax deductible. Contribution limits are lower for S corporations than for C corporations.
- In C corporations, once the ESOP owns 30% of all the shares in the company, the seller can reinvest the proceeds of the sale in other securities and defer any tax on the gain.
- In S corporations, the percentage of ownership held by the ESOP is not subject to income tax at the federal level (and usually not the state level, either). This means earnings of the S corporation escape federal income tax; they are not taxed to the corporation because it is an S corporation, and they are not taxed to the ESOP because it is an exempt trust. For example, there is no income tax on 40% of the profits of an S corporation that has an ESOP holding 40% of the stock, and no income tax on the profits of an S corporation wholly owned by its ESOP. However, the ESOP must still get a pro-rata share of any distributions the company makes to owners.
- Dividends used to repay an ESOP loan, passed through to employees, or reinvested by employees in company stock are tax-deductible.

For employees:

- Employees are not taxed on contributions made to the plan on their behalf.
- For stock in C corporations, departing employees can roll over the shares to an IRA or other qualified retirement plan. If they opt to report the income, then any future appreciation on the shares will be taxed at capital gains rates when the shares are eventually sold. No rollover of S corporation stock is allowed.

### *Uses for ESOPs*

ESOPs are a way to shift ownership to employees. This is viewed as an important employee benefit.

ESOPs can also be used to buy out the interest of a departing owner. For example, say an owner wants to retire but has no obvious person, such as a son or daughter, to be the successor-owner; the employees become the owners through the ESOP. From the owner's perspective, a sale of 30% or more of an interest in a closely held business enables the owner to defer tax on the gain from the sale by buying so-called replacement securities; gain is recognized when and to the extent that replacement securities are sold.

ESOPs can borrow money and effectively convert repayments of *both* interest and principal into tax-deductible amounts. The borrowed funds are used to buy company shares or shares from existing owners. The corporation then makes tax-deductible contributions to the ESOP to repay the loan.

## Retirement Plans Owning Your Business

When some business owners cannot find funding through traditional sources, such as bank loans or family and friends, they may turn to their retirement plans as a ready source of cash. For example, they may use 401(k) funds they built up when working for another company to start their own businesses. Here's how it works: An entrepreneur starts a business and incorporates, and then the business sets up a retirement plan. Then the owner rolls over his or her 401(k) money to the retirement plan of the new business and the plan acquires the stock of the new business, infusing it with the 401(k) cash. So the owner owns the plan and the plan owns the business. These funding arrangements are known as rollovers as business start-ups (ROBS).

Technically, a qualified retirement plan and IRA can own the business of the account owner. Using retirement plans for this purpose may be useful in some situations, but the arrangements are fraught with perils:

- The IRS has said ROBS are potentially *abusive transactions*.
- The arrangement doesn't avoid income tax on the business earnings even though they are held in a tax-exempt retirement account. The retirement plan pays income tax on business profits using tax rates applicable to trusts; these rates are highly unfavorable. For 2021, unrelated business taxable income (UBTI) of the plan (i.e., business profits) is taxed at a flat 37% rate for taxable income over $13,050. Find more information about UBTI in IRS Publication 595.
- Interaction between the entrepreneur and the plan can trigger prohibited transaction penalties (discussed earlier in this chapter).
- It is very costly to get ownership of the business out of the plan. Doing so triggers a taxable distribution to the owner as ordinary income. Thus, it usually happens that ownership goes into the plan but never comes out.
- If the business fails, owners lose their companies *and* their retirement savings.

Despite what promotors say about ROBS, be sure to get an outside tax opinion and guidance from a knowledgeable CPA or other tax professional.

## Terminating Plans

A business may want or need to terminate its qualified retirement plan. Doing so has certain consequences. If handled correctly, participants aren't taxed on their benefits and employers aren't subject to penalty. Follow these steps:

- Amend the plan to set a termination date (e.g., last day of the plan year), cease plan contributions, provide full vesting of benefits to all participants regardless of the usual vesting schedule (employee contributions are always fully vested but full vesting here means employer contributions), and authorize the plan to distribute all benefits as soon as it's administratively feasible (generally within 12 months after the plan's termination).

- Notify participants and beneficiaries of the plan's termination and the rollover option so they aren't taxed on the distribution of benefits. For example, participants may transfer their benefits directly to their IRAs.
- Complete the distributions and/or rollovers.
- File a final return in the Form 5500 series. For self-employed individuals filing Form 5500-EZ, the return is required even though plan assets are less than $250,000.

***Missing participants.*** When a plan ends, it must make efforts to find those entitled to benefits. The DOL has some best practices at https://www.dol.gov/agencies/ebsa/employers-and-advisers/plan-administration-and-compliance/retirement/missing-participants-guidance/best-practices-for-pension-plans on how to maintain complete and accurate information on participants and beneficiaries so that there aren't any entitled to benefits who will fail to respond to correspondence about termination or other matters.

Despite following best practices, if there are missing participants, the plan must make arrangements with another entity to provide benefits for them. You can use PBGC's Missing Participant Program at https://www.pbgc.gov/prac/missing-participants-program or a private financial institution.

### Partial Terminations

A partial termination occurs with a significant event, such as the closing of one of a business's multiple locations or the result of significant employee turnover or termination due to adverse economic conditions or other reasons not within an employer's control (usually 20% or more). Employees who terminate voluntarily aren't counted for determining whether there's been a partial termination. The pandemic caused many companies to furlough or lay off employees, and such action may or may not have triggered a partial termination. The IRS said that if a worker is rehired before the end of the year, they aren't counted as part of an employer-initiated severance. What's more, the 20% turnover rate is only a rebuttable presumption that there's been a partial termination.

When a partial termination occurs, all "affected employees" (including those who terminated voluntarily) become fully vested in their account balance. An affected employee in a partial termination generally is anyone who left employment for any reason during the plan year in which the partial termination occurred and who still has an account balance under the plan.

Because of the consequences of partial or full termination, small businesses should consult with their CPA or other expert to assess the situation and follow the right steps for handling it.

## Nonqualified Retirement Plans

If you have a business and want to provide retirement benefits without the limitations and requirements imposed on qualified plans, you can use nonqualified plans. Nonqualified plans are simply plans you design yourself to provide you and/or your employees with whatever benefits you desire. Benefits under the plan are not taxed to the employees until they receive them and include them in their income. But the plan must restrict distributions to fixed events (e.g., separation from service, a fixed date, a change in company ownership, or an unfortunate emergency), or participants become subject to interest and penalties.

There are no nondiscrimination rules to comply with. You can cover only those employees you want to give additional retirement benefits to, and this can be limited to owners or key executives. There are no minimum or maximum contributions to make to the plan. However, because nonqualified plans give you all the flexibility you need to tailor benefits as you see fit, the law prevents you, as the employer, from enjoying certain tax benefits. You cannot deduct amounts now that you will pay in the future to employees under the plan. Your deduction usually cannot be claimed until benefits are actually paid to employees. However, there is a circumstance under which you can deduct these amounts: If you segregate the amounts from the general assets of your business so that they are not available to meet the claims of your general creditors, the amounts become immediately taxable to the employees and thus deductible by you.

### *How a Nonqualified Plan Works*

Suppose you want to allow your key employees the opportunity to defer bonuses or a portion of their compensation until retirement. To do this, you set up a nonqualified plan. These employees can defer specified amounts until termination, retirement, or some other time or event.

The employees in the plan must agree to defer the compensation before it is earned. They generally have no guarantee that the funds they agree to defer will, in fact, be there for them upon retirement. If your business goes under, they must stand in line along with all your other creditors. Employees should be made to understand the risk of a deferred compensation arrangement.

Once you set up the terms of the plan, you simply set up a bookkeeping entry to record the amount of deferred compensation. You may also want to credit each employee's deferred compensation account with an amount representing interest. In the past, there had been some controversy on the tax treatment of this interest. One court allowed a current deduction for the interest. The IRS, on the other hand, had maintained that no deduction for the interest could be claimed until it, along with the compensation, was paid out to employees and included in their income. However, that court changed its view and now agrees with the IRS. As long as receipt of the interest is deferred, so, too, is your deduction for the interest.

**NOTE**

**Nonqualified deferred compensation plans may permit a participant to take a distribution for an "unforeseen emergency." The IRS has not said whether COVID-19 amounts to such an event, so caution should be exercised in taking a distribution prior to a date or event specified in the plan.**

### *Rabbi Trusts*

This is a special kind of nonqualified deferred compensation that got its name from the original employees covered by the plan—rabbis. The plans provide a measure of security for employees without triggering current taxation on contributions under the plan. Employers are prevented from claiming a current deduction. These plans have now been standardized, and the IRS even provides model rabbi trust forms to be used in setting them up.

### *Deferred Compensation Plans*

These are explained in Chapter 7.

## Glossary of Terms for Retirement Plans

The following terms have been used throughout this chapter in connection with retirement plans.

**Association Retirement Plans (ARPs)** Defined contribution plans offered to members of trade associations or chambers of commerce; "open multiple employer plans."

**Catch-up contributions** Additional employee contributions that can be made only by those who attain age 50 by the end of the year.

**Compensation** The amount upon which contributions and benefits are calculated. Compensation for employees is taxable wages reported on Form W-2. Compensation for self-employed individuals is net profit from a sole proprietorship or net self-employment income reported to a partner or limited liability member on Schedule K-1.

**Coronavirus-related distributions and loans** These are made after March 27, 2020, through December 31, 2020, on account of being related to COVID-19.

**Coverage** Qualified plans must include a certain percentage of rank-and-file employees.

**Defined benefit plans** Pension plans in which benefits are fixed according to the employee's compensation, years of participation in the plan, and age upon retirement. Contributions are actuarially determined to provide sufficient funds to cover promised pension amounts.

**Defined contribution plans** Retirement plans in which benefits are determined by annual contributions on behalf of each participant, the amount these contributions can earn, and the length of time the participant is in the plan.

**Designated Roth accounts** An option for 401(k) plans to permit after-tax contributions that grow tax free.

**Disaster-related distributions and loans** These are made on or after January 1, 2020, and through February 25, 2021.

**Elective deferrals** A portion of the employee's salary that is contributed to a retirement plan on a pretax basis. Elective deferrals apply in the case of 401(k) plans, 403(b) annuities, SARSEPs (established before 1997), and SIMPLE plans.

**Eligible automatic contribution arrangements (EACAs)** A type of automatic enrollment plan for 401(k)s.

**Employee plans corrections resolution system (EPCRS)** An IRS program that can be used to correct defects and problems in qualified retirement plans with little or no penalty.

**Employee stock ownership plans (ESOPs)** An employee benefit plan giving ownership interests in a corporation to employees.

**Excess contribution penalty** A 6% cumulative penalty imposed on an employer for making contributions in excess of contribution limits.

**Funding** In the case of defined benefit plans, the amount of assets required to be in the plan in order to meet plan liabilities (current and future pension obligations).

**Highly compensated employees** Owners and employees earning compensation over certain limits that are adjusted annually for inflation.

**Keogh plans** A term that had been used to designate qualified retirement plans for self-employed individuals (also called H.R.10 plans). This term is no longer in use.

**Master and prototype plans** Plans typically designed by banks and other institutions to be used for qualified retirement plans.

**Money purchase plans** Defined contribution plans in which the annual contribution percentage is fixed without regard to whether the business has profits.

**Multiple Employer Plan (MEP)** A plan in which two or more unrelated employers join together to offer a retirement plan option to their employees. Also referred to as a pooled employer plan (PEP).

**Nondiscrimination** Requirements to provide benefits for rank-and-file employees and not simply to favor owners and highly paid employees.

**Participation** The right of an employee to be a member of the retirement plan and have benefits and contributions made on his or her behalf.

**Pension Benefit Guaranty Corporation (PBGC)** A federal agency that will pay a minimum pension to participants of defined benefit plans in companies that have not made sufficient contributions to fund their pension liabilities.

**Pooled employer plan (PEP)** A plan in which two or more employees join together to offer 401(k)s to their employees (see MEP).

**Pooled plan provider** The fiduciary responsible for a PEP.

**Premature distribution penalty** A 10% penalty imposed on a participant for receiving benefits before age 59 ½ or some other qualifying event.

**Profit-sharing plan** A defined contribution plan with contributions based on a fixed percentage of compensation.

**Prohibited transactions** Dealings between employers and the plan, such as certain loans, sales, and other transactions between these parties. Prohibited transactions result in penalties and can even result in plan disqualification.

**Qualified automatic contribution arrangements (QACAs)** A type of automatic enrollment option for 401(k)s providing for specified elective deferrals by employees.

**Qualified default investment alternative (QDIA)** Permissible 401(k) investments by a plan with automatic enrollment.

**Required distributions** Plans must begin to distribute benefits to employees at a certain time. Generally, benefits must begin to be paid out no later than April 1 following the year in which a participant attains age 70 ½ for those attaining this age before January 1, 2020, and 72 for those attaining age 70 ½ after December 31, 2019. Failure to receive required minimum distributions results in a 50% penalty on the participant.

**ROBS** Rollovers as business start-ups are financing arrangements using a qualified retirement plan.

**Roth 401(k)s** See Designated Roth accounts.

**Roth IRAs** Nondeductible IRAs that permit tax-free withdrawals if certain holding period requirements are met.

**Salary reduction arrangements** Arrangements to make contributions to qualified plans from an employee's compensation on a pretax basis. In general, salary reduction arrangements relate to 401(k) plans, 403(b) annuities, SARSEPs in existence before 1997, and SIMPLE plans.

**Savings incentive match plans of employees (SIMPLEs)** IRA- or 401(k)-type plans that permit modest employee contributions via salary reduction and require modest employer contributions. SIMPLE plans are easy to set up and administer.

**Simplified employee pensions (SEPs)** IRAs set up by employees to which an employer makes contributions based on a percentage of income.

**Stock bonus plans** Defined contribution plans that give participants shares of stock in the employer rather than cash.

**Top-heavy plans** Qualified retirement plans that provide more than a certain amount of benefits or contributions to owners and/or highly paid employees. Top-heavy plans have special vesting schedules.

**Vesting** The right of an employee to own his or her pension benefits. Vesting schedules are set by law, although employers can provide for faster vesting.

## Where to Claim Deductions for Retirement Plans

### *Employees*

If you contribute to an IRA and are entitled to a deduction, you claim it on Schedule 1 of Form 1040 or 1040-SR. If you contribute to a salary reduction plan (such as a SIMPLE or a 401(k) plan), you cannot deduct your contribution. You do not report it on the return.

### *Self-Employed*

Contributions you make to self-employed qualified retirement plans, SEPs, or SIMPLEs on behalf of your employees are entered on Schedule C (or Schedule F, for farming operations) on the specific line provided on the form, called pension and profit-sharing plans. Contributions you make on your own behalf are claimed in the adjustments to income section on Schedule 1 of Form 1040 or 1040-SR. Contributions you make to an IRA are also claimed on Schedule 1 of Form 1040 or 1040-SR as an adjustment to gross income.

### *Partnerships and LLCs*

Deductions for contributions to qualified plans on behalf of employees are part of the partnership's or LLC's ordinary trade or business income on Form 1065. The deductions are entered on the line provided for retirement plans.

The entity does not make contributions on behalf of partners or members. Partners and members can set up their own retirement plans based on their self-employment income. Thus, if partners and members set up qualified retirement plans, they claim deductions for their contributions on Schedule 1 of Form 1040 or 1040-SR.

As a practical matter, small partnerships and LLCs generally do not establish qualified plans for employees, since the partners and members do not get any direct benefit.

### *S Corporations*

Deductions for contributions to qualified plans are taken by the corporation as part of its ordinary trade or business income on Form 1120-S. Enter the deduction on the line provided for pension plans, profit-sharing plans, and so on. This line includes contributions to nonqualified plans if the corporation is entitled to claim a current deduction for such contributions.

### *C Corporations*

C corporations deduct contributions to retirement plans on Form 1120. The deduction is entered on the line provided for pension plans, profit-sharing plans, and so on. This line includes contributions to nonqualified plans if the corporation is entitled to claim a current deduction for such contributions.

### All Employers

To claim the credit for plan start-up costs of small employers and/or for automatic enrollment, file Form 8881, *Credit for Small Employer Pension Plan Startup Costs and Auto-Enrollment*. The credit is part of the general business credit and so must be entered on Form 3800, *General Business Credit*, if you have another credit that is part of the general business credit.

### Other Reporting Requirements for All Taxpayers

Qualified plans entail annual reporting requirements. If you maintain a qualified plan, you must file certain information returns each year to report on the amount of plan assets, contributions, number of employees, and such (unless you are exempt from reporting). (There is no annual reporting for SEPs, regardless of assets or the number of employees.) Information returns in the 5500 series are *not* filed with the IRS. Instead, these rules are filed with the Department of Labor's Pension and Welfare Benefits Administration (PWBA) at www.efast.dol.gov. These returns must be filed electronically in most cases. There are penalties for failure to file these returns on time and for overstating the pension plan deduction.

Plans other than one-person plans must file Form 5500, *Annual Return/Report of Employee Benefit Plan*, each year. The return is due by the last day of the seventh month following the close of the plan year (July 31 of a calendar-year plan). For 2021 calendar year plans, the due date is August 1, 2022 (July 31, 2022, is Sunday).

One-participant plans are automatically exempt from annual reporting if the plan assets at the end of the year are $250,000 or less. (This exemption does not apply to the final plan year.) For plans with fewer than 25 participants, there is voluntary reporting. Details of eligibility for voluntary reporting and what to report are in the instructions to Form 5500.

For businesses that have defined benefit plans for which premiums must be paid to the Pension Benefit Guaranty Corporation, the deadline for premium payments is October 15 of the year following the end of the year for calendar-year plans of small employers (fewer than 500 participants) (e.g., October 17, 2022, for the 2021 year of a defined benefit plan on a calendar-year basis). Payment is accompanied by PBGC Form 1 or PBGC Form 1-EZ; for details about which form to use, where to file, and more, see https://www.pbgc.gov.

**NOTE**

**There are no special annual reporting requirements for IRA plans, SEPs, or SIMPLE-IRAs.**

As mentioned earlier, the return is due by the last day of the seventh month following the close of the plan year. Thus, if the plan is on a calendar year, the return is due no later than July 31 of the following year. Obtaining an extension to file an income tax return generally does *not* extend the time for filing these returns. However, if you are self-employed and obtain a filing extension for your individual return to October 17, you have until the extended due date to file Form 5500-EZ (Figure 16.3 is the 2020 form because the 2021 version was not yet available). If you do not have a filing extension for your personal return, you can request an extension of time to file Form 5500-EZ by filing Form 5558, *Application for Extension of Time to File Certain Employee Plan Returns*, to obtain an automatic 2½ month extension (to October 15) for the 2021 return.

Form **5500-EZ**

Department of the Treasury
Internal Revenue Service

**Annual Return of A One-Participant (Owners/Partners and Their Spouses) Retirement Plan or A Foreign Plan**

This form is required to be filed under section 6058(a) of the Internal Revenue Code.
*Certain foreign retirement plans are also required to file this form (see instructions).*
▶ **Complete all entries in accordance with the instructions to the Form 5500-EZ.**
▶ **Go to *www.irs.gov/Form5500EZ* for instructions and the latest information.**

OMB No. 1545-1610

**2020**

**This Form is Open to Public Inspection.**

**Part I Annual Return Identification Information**

**For the calendar plan year 2020 or fiscal plan year beginning (MM/DD/YYYY)** **and ending**

A This return is: (1) ☐ the first return filed for the plan (3) ☐ the final return filed for the plan
(2) ☐ an amended return (4) ☐ a short plan year return (less than 12 months)

B If filing under an extension of time, check this box (see instructions) . . . ▶ ☐

C If this return is for a foreign plan, check this box (see instructions) . . . ▶ ☐

D If this return is for the IRS Late Filer Penalty Relief Program, check this box (see instructions) . . . ▶ ☐

**Part II Basic Plan Information** — enter all requested information.

| | |
|---|---|
| **1a** Name of plan | **1b** Three-digit plan number (PN) ▶ |
| | **1c** Date plan first became effective (MM/DD/YYYY) |
| **2a** Employer's name | **2b** Employer Identification Number (EIN) (Do not enter your Social Security Number) |
| Trade name of business (if different from name of employer) | |
| In care of name | **2c** Employer's telephone number |
| Mailing address (room, apt., suite no. and street, or P.O. box) | **2d** Business code (see instructions) |
| City or town, state or province, country, and ZIP or foreign postal code (if foreign, see instructions) | |
| **3a** Plan administrator's name (if same as employer, enter "Same") | **3b** Administrator's EIN |
| In care of name | **3c** Administrator's telephone number |
| Mailing address (room, apt., suite no. and street, or P.O. box) | |
| City or town, state or province, country, and ZIP or foreign postal code (if foreign, see instructions) | |

**4** If the employer's name, the employer's EIN, and/or the plan name has changed since the last return filed for this plan, enter the employer's name and EIN, the plan name, and the plan number for the last return in the appropriate space provided

| | |
|---|---|
| **a** Employer's name | **4b** EIN |
| **4c** Plan name | **4d** PN |

| | | |
|---|---|---|
| **5a(1)** Total number of participants at the beginning of the plan year . . . | **5a(1)** | |
| **a(2)** Total number of active participants at the beginning of the plan year . . . | **5a(2)** | |
| **b(1)** Total number of participants at the end of the plan year . . . | **5b(1)** | |
| **b(2)** Total number of active participants at the end of the plan year . . . | **5b(2)** | |
| **c** Number of participants who terminated employment during the plan year with accrued benefits that were less than 100% vested . . . | **5c** | |

**Part III Financial Information**

| | | (1) Beginning of year | (2) End of year |
|---|---|---|---|
| **6a** Total plan assets . . . | **6a** | | |
| **b** Total plan liabilities . . . | **6b** | | |
| **c** Net plan assets (subtract line **6b** from **6a**) . . . | **6c** | | |

**For Privacy Act and Paperwork Reduction Act Notice, see the Instructions for Form 5500-EZ.** Cat. No. 63263R Form **5500-EZ** (2020)

Note: This form is the 2020 version.

**FIGURE 16.3** **Form 5500-EZ, Annual Return of One-Participant Retirement Plan**

Form 5500-EZ (2020) Page 2

**Part III Financial Information** *(continued)*

| | | | Amount |
|---|---|---|---|
| 7 | Contributions received or receivable from: | | |
| a | Employers | 7a | |
| b | Participants | 7b | |
| c | Others (including rollovers) | 7c | |

**Part IV Plan Characteristics**

8 Enter the applicable two-character feature codes from the List of Plan Characteristics Codes in the instructions.

**Part V Compliance and Funding Questions**

| | | | Yes | No | Amount |
|---|---|---|---|---|---|
| 9 | During the plan year, did the plan have any participant loans? If "Yes," enter amount as of year end | 9 | | | |
| 10 | Is this a defined benefit plan that is subject to minimum funding requirements? If "Yes," complete Schedule SB (Form 5500) and line 10a below (see instructions) | 10 | | | |
| a | Enter the unpaid minimum required contributions for all years from Schedule SB (Form 5500), line 40 | | | 10a | |
| 11 | Is this a defined contribution plan subject to the minimum funding requirements of section 412 of the Code? | 11 | | | |
| | If "Yes," complete lines 11a or 11b, 11c, 11d, and 11e below, as applicable. | | | | |
| a | If a waiver of the minimum funding standard for a prior year is being amortized in this plan year, enter the month, day, and year (MM/DD/YYYY) of the letter ruling granting the waiver (see instructions) | | | 11a | |
| b | Enter the minimum required contribution for this plan year | | | 11b | |
| c | Enter the amount contributed by the employer to the plan for this plan year | | | 11c | |
| d | Subtract the amount in line 11c from the amount in line 11b. Enter the result (enter a minus sign to the left of a negative amount) | | | 11d | |

| | | | Yes | No | N/A |
|---|---|---|---|---|---|
| e | Will the minimum funding amount reported on line 11d be met by the funding deadline? | 11e | | | |

**Caution: A penalty for the late or incomplete filing of this return will be assessed unless reasonable cause is established.**

Under penalties of perjury, I declare that I have examined this return including, if applicable, any related Schedule MB (Form 5500) or Schedule SB (Form 5500) signed by an enrolled actuary, and, to the best of my knowledge and belief, it is true, correct, and complete.

**Sign Here**

Signature of employer or plan administrator | Date | Type or print name of individual signing as employer or plan administrator

Form **5500-EZ** (2020)

Note: This form is the 2020 version.

**FIGURE 16.3** ***(Continued)***

CHAPTER 17

# Casualty and Theft Losses


Casualties and Thefts 339
Condemnations and Threats of Condemnation 345
Disaster Losses 347
Deducting Property Insurance and Other Casualty/Theft-Related Items 348
Disaster Assistance 349


Wildfires in the West, severe winter storms in the Midwest, tropical storms and hurricanes in the South, and Hurricane Ida in a dozen states—these are just some examples of the types of weather-related events that may have done severe damage to your business property in 2021. In addition, the Surfside building collapse in Florida is another example of a FEMA-designated disaster. Terrorist attacks and civil riots are other means of causing damage to business property as are accidents, such as oil spills. If you suffer casualty or theft losses to your business property, you can deduct the losses. You may also suffer a loss through condemnation or a sale under threat of condemnation. Again, the loss is deductible. Certain losses—those from events declared to be federal disasters—may even allow you to recover taxes you have already paid in an earlier year. But if you receive insurance proceeds or other property in return, you may have a gain rather than a loss. The law allows you to postpone reporting of the gain if certain steps are taken.

For further information about deducting casualty and theft losses, see IRS Publication 547, *Casualties, Disasters, and Thefts (Business and Nonbusiness)* and IRS Publication 2194B, *Disaster Losses Kit for Businesses*.

## Casualties and Thefts

If you suffer a casualty or theft loss to business property, you can deduct the loss. Unlike individuals who can only deduct disaster losses and are subject to various limitations on these losses, there are no limitations on business casualty and theft losses. While losses from investment property may be deductible, the rules are not discussed here; only losses to business property are covered.

## Definition of Casualty

If your business property is damaged, destroyed, or lost because of a storm, earthquake, flood, or some other "sudden, unexpected or unusual event," you have experienced a *casualty*. For losses to nonbusiness property (such as your personal residence), the loss must fall squarely within the definition of a casualty loss. Losses to business property need not necessarily satisfy the same definition. The tax law details what is considered a "sudden, unexpected or unusual event." To be sudden, the event must be one that is swift, not one that is progressive or gradual. To be unexpected, the event must be unanticipated or unintentional on the part of the one who has suffered the loss. To be unusual, the event must be other than a day-to-day occurrence. It cannot be typical of the activity in which you are engaged.

**NOTE**

**Business losses are deductible without having to establish that the cause of the loss was a casualty. Thus, if your equipment rusts or corrodes over time, you can deduct your loss even though it does not fit into the definition of a casualty loss (assuming you can fix the time of the loss). The reason for understanding the definition of the term "casualty" is that it determines where the loss is reported. It also comes into play in connection with deferring tax on gains from casualties, as discussed later in this chapter.**

### EXAMPLES OF CASUALTIES

Certain events in nature automatically are considered a casualty: earthquake, hurricane, tornado, cyclone, flood, storm, and volcanic eruption. Other events have also come to be known as casualties: avalanches, sonic booms, mine cave-ins, mudslides, riots, shipwrecks, wildfires, and acts of vandalism. The IRS has also recognized as a casualty the destruction of crops due to a farmer's accidental poisoning of his fields. Fires are considered casualties if you are not the one who started them (or did not pay someone to start them). Car or truck accidents are casualties provided they were not caused by willful negligence or a willful act.

Progressive or gradual deterioration, such as rust or corrosion of property, is not considered a casualty.

### PROOF OF CASUALTIES

You must show that a specific casualty occurred and the time it occurred. You must also show that the casualty was the direct cause of the damage or destruction to your property. Finally, you must show that you were the owner of the property. If you leased property, you must show that you were contractually liable for damage so that you suffered a loss as a result of the casualty.

## Definition of Theft

The taking of property must constitute a theft under the law in your state. Generally, *theft* involves taking or removing property with the intent to deprive the owner of its use. Typically, this includes robbery, larceny, and embezzlement. Inventory shrinkage may also be the result of theft (discussed later in this chapter).

If you are forced to pay extortion money or blackmail in the course of your business (e.g., ransomware), the loss may be treated as a theft loss if your state law makes this type of taking illegal.

If you lose or misplace property, you cannot claim a theft loss unless you can show that the disappearance of the property was due to an accidental loss that was sudden, unexpected, or unusual. In other words, if you misplace property and cannot prove a theft loss occurred, you may be able to deduct a loss if you can establish a casualty was responsible for the loss.

#### PROOF OF THEFT

You must show when you discovered the property was missing. You must also show that a theft (as defined by your state's criminal law) took place. Finally, you must show that you were the owner of the property.

### *Determining a Casualty or Theft Loss*

To calculate your loss, you must know your **adjusted basis** in the property.

***Adjusted basis*** **This is generally your cost of the property, plus any improvements made to it, less any depreciation claimed. Basis is also reduced by any prior casualty losses claimed with respect to the property.**

You also need to know the fair market value (FMV) of the property. If the property was not completely destroyed, you must know the extent of the damage. This is the difference between the FMV of the property before and after the casualty.

**Example**

**Your business car is in an accident, and you do not have collision insurance. The car's FMV before the accident was $9,000. After the accident, the car is worth only $6,000. The decrease in the FMV is $3,000 ($9,000 value before the loss, less $6,000 value after the loss).**

How do you determine the decrease in FMV? This is not based simply on your subjective opinion. In most cases, the decrease in value is based on an appraisal by a competent appraiser. If your property is located near an area affected by a casualty that causes your property value to decline, you cannot take this general decline in value into account. Only a direct loss of value may be considered. Presumably, a competent appraiser will be able to distinguish between a general market decline and a direct decline as a result of a casualty. The IRS looks at a number of factors to determine whether an appraiser is competent and his or her appraisal can be relied upon to establish FMV. These factors include:

- Familiarity with your property both before and after the casualty
- Knowledge of sales of comparable property in your area
- Knowledge of conditions in the area of the casualty
- Method of appraisal

Remember that if the IRS questions the reliability of your appraiser, it may use its own appraiser to determine value. This may lead to legal wrangling and ultimately to litigation on the question of value. In order to avoid this problem and the costs entailed, it is advisable to use a reputable appraiser, even if this may seem costly to you.

Appraisals used to secure a loan or loan guarantee from the government under the Federal Emergency Management Agency (FEMA) are treated as proof of the amount of a disaster loss. Disaster losses are explained later in this chapter.

You may be able to establish value without the help of an appraiser in certain situations.

If your business car is damaged, you can use "blue book" value (the car's retail value, which is printed in a book used by car dealers). You can ask your local car dealer for your car's retail value reported in the blue book (or look it up at www.kbb.com). You can modify this value to reflect such things as mileage, options, and the car's condition before the casualty. Book values are not official, but the IRS has come to recognize that they are useful in fixing value. Of course, if your car is not listed in the blue book, you must find other means of establishing value. Value before the casualty can be established by a showing of comparable sales of similar cars in your area. According to the IRS, a dealer's offer for your car as a trade-in on a new car generally does not establish value.

Repairs may be useful in showing the decrease in value. To use repairs as a measure of loss, you must show that the repairs are needed to restore the property to its precasualty condition and apply only to the damage that resulted from the casualty. You must also show that the cost of repairs is not excessive and that the repairs will not restore your property to a value greater than it had prior to the casualty. Making repairs to property damaged in a casualty can result in double deductions: one for the cost of repairs and the other for the casualty loss.

**Example**

**Severe flooding destroys a business owner's property. He is not compensated by insurance. The IRS, in a memorandum to a district counsel, allows him to claim a casualty loss for the damage as well as deducting the cost of repairs to the property where such repairs merely restore it to its precasualty condition.**

The last piece of information necessary for determining a casualty or theft loss is the amount of insurance proceeds or other reimbursements, if any, you received or expect to receive as a result of the casualty or theft. While insurance proceeds are the most common reimbursement in the event of a casualty or theft, there are other types of reimbursements that are taken into account in the same way as insurance proceeds. These include:

- Court awards for damages as a result of suits based on casualty or theft. Your reimbursement is the net amount of the award—the award less attorney's fees to obtain the award.
- Payment from a bonding company for a theft loss.
- Forgiveness of a federal disaster loan under the Disaster Relief and Emergency Assistance Act. Typically, these are given under the auspices of the Small Business Administration (SBA) or the Farmers Home Administration (FHA). The part that you do not have to repay is the amount of the reimbursement. Services provided by relief agencies for repairs, restoration, or cleanup are considered reimbursements that must be taken into account.
- Repairs made to your property by your lessee, or repayments in lieu of repairs.

What happens if you have not received an insurance settlement by the time you must file your return? If there is a reasonable expectation that you will receive a settlement, you treat the anticipated settlement as if you had already received it. In other words, you take the expected insurance proceeds into account in calculating your loss. Should it later turn out that you received more or less than you anticipated, adjustments are required in the year you actually receive the insurance proceeds, as explained later in this chapter.

If the amount of insurance proceeds or other reimbursements is greater than the adjusted basis of your property, you do not have a loss. Instead, you have a gain as a result of your casualty or theft loss. How can this be, you might ask? Why should a loss of property turn out to be a gain for tax purposes? Remember that your adjusted basis for business property in many instances reflects deductions for depreciation. This brings your basis down. But your insurance may be based on the value of the property, not its basis to you. Therefore, if your basis has been adjusted downward for depreciation but the value of the property has remained constant or increased, your insurance proceeds may produce a gain for you. Gain and how to postpone it are discussed later in this chapter.

### CALCULATING LOSS WHEN PROPERTY IS COMPLETELY DESTROYED OR STOLEN

Reduce your adjusted basis by any insurance proceeds received or expected to be received and any salvage value to the property. The result is your casualty loss deduction. The FMV of the property does not enter into the computation.

If the casualty or theft involves more than one piece of property, you must determine the loss (or gain) for each item separately. If your reimbursement is paid in a lump sum and there is no allocation among the items, you must make an allocation. The allocation is based on the items' FMV before the casualty.

**Example**

**Your machine is completely destroyed by a flood. You have no flood insurance, and the destroyed machine has no salvage value. The adjusted basis of the machine is $6,000. Your casualty loss is $6,000 (adjusted basis of the property [$6,000], less insurance proceeds [zero]).**

### CALCULATING LOSS WHEN PROPERTY IS PARTIALLY DESTROYED

Calculate the difference between the FMV of the property before and after the casualty. Reduce this by any insurance proceeds. Compare this figure with your adjusted basis in the property, less any insurance proceeds. Your casualty loss is the smaller of these two figures.

**Example**

**Your machine is damaged as a result of a flood. You do not have flood insurance. The machine is valued at $8,000 before the flood and $3,000 after it. Your adjusted basis in the machine is $6,000. Your loss is $5,000, the difference between the FMV of the machine before and after the flood, which is smaller than your adjusted basis.**

If you lease property from someone else (e.g., if you lease a car used for business), your loss is limited to the difference between the insurance proceeds you receive, or expect to receive, and the amount you must pay to repair the property.

### Inventory and Crops

Typically, a casualty or theft of inventory is not treated as a separate loss. Inventory losses may be from shrinkage, which is the difference between what a business shows as the inventory count in its records versus an actual physical count of items on hand. Shrinkage can result from a natural disaster, employee or customer theft, or just mismanagement (a miscount). The 2020 National Retail Security Survey reported that shrinkage was $61.7 billion. Whatever the reason for a loss in inventory, there are 2 ways to report it on your return:

- *Factor shrinkage into COGS*. Reduce ending inventory by the amount of shrinkage, which increases the cost of goods sold (COGS). Because of larger COGS, the amount of gross revenue reported from inventory sales is reduced.
- *Deduct inventory shrinkage*. If this separate deduction is taken, then reduce beginning inventory by the amount of shrinkage to reduce COGS.

If you expect reimbursement for the loss under your insurance policy, reduce the amount of the loss handled under either of the ways above (and exclude the reimbursement from gross income).

In the case of crops, the cost of raising them has already been deducted, so no additional deduction is allowed if they are damaged or destroyed by a casualty.

### Recovered Property

What happens if you deduct a loss for stolen property and the property is later recovered? Do you have to go back and amend the earlier return on which the theft loss was taken? The answer is no. Instead, you report the recovered property as income in the year of recovery.

But what if the property is not recovered in good shape or is only partially recovered? In this instance, you must recalculate your loss. You use the smaller of the property's adjusted basis or the decrease in the FMV from the time it was stolen until you recovered it. This smaller amount is your recalculated loss. If your recalculated loss is less than the loss you deducted, you report the difference as income in the year of recovery. The amount of income that you must report is limited to the amount of loss that reduced your tax in the earlier year.

### Insurance Received (or Not Received) in a Later Year

If you had anticipated the receipt of insurance proceeds or other property and took that anticipated amount into account when calculating your loss but later receive more (or less) than you anticipated, you must account for this discrepancy. As with recovered stolen property, you do not go back to the year of loss and make an adjustment. Instead, you take the insurance proceeds into account in the year of actual receipt.

If you receive more than you had expected (by way of insurance or otherwise), you report the extra amount as income in the year of receipt. You do not have to recalculate your original loss deduction. The additional amount is reported as ordinary income to the extent that the deduction in the earlier year produced a tax reduction. If the additional insurance or other reimbursement, when combined with what has already been received, exceeds the adjusted basis of your property, you now have a gain as a result of the casualty or theft. The gain is reported in the year you receive the additional reimbursement. However, you may be able to postpone reporting the gain, as discussed later in this chapter.

If you receive less than you had anticipated, you have an additional loss. The additional loss is claimed in the year in which you receive the additional amount.

**Example**

In 2021, your business car was completely destroyed in an accident. Your adjusted basis in the car was $8,000. The car had a value of $10,000 before the accident and no value after the accident. You expected the driver responsible for the accident to pay for the damage. In fact, a jury awarded you the full extent of your loss. However, in 2022, you learn that the other driver will not pay the judgment and does not have any property against which you can enforce your judgment. In this instance, you have received less than you anticipated. You do not recalculate your 2021 taxes. Instead, you deduct your loss (limited to your adjusted basis of $8,000) in 2022.

### Basis

If your property is partially destroyed in a casualty, you must adjust the basis of the property:

- Decrease basis by insurance proceeds or other reimbursements and loss deductions claimed.
- Increase basis by improvements or repairs made to the property to rebuild or restore it.

### Year of the Loss

In general, the loss can be claimed only in the year in which the casualty or other event occurs. However, in the case of the theft, the loss is treated as having occurred in the year in which it is discovered.

### Coordination with Repairs

You cannot take both a casualty loss deduction and a deduction for repair costs. If you claim a casualty loss deduction, then no deduction can be taken for repair costs, even if the amount of the casualty loss relative to the repair expenditure is small.

## Condemnations and Threats of Condemnation

The government can take your property for public use if it compensates you for your loss. The process by which the government exercises its right of eminent domain to take your property for public use is called *condemnation*. In a sense, you are being forced to sell your property at a price essentially fixed by the government. You can usually negotiate a price; sometimes you are forced to seek a court action and have the court fix the price paid to you. Typically, an owner is paid cash or receives other property upon condemnation of property.

Sometimes, the probability of a condemnation becomes known through reports in a newspaper or other news medium or proposals at a town council meeting. For example, there may be talk of a new road or the widening of an existing road that will affect your property. If you do not voluntarily sell your property, the government will simply go through the process of condemnation.

Where there is a condemnation, you may also voluntarily sell other property. If the other property has an economic relationship to the condemned property, the voluntary sale can be treated as a condemnation.

Not every condemnation qualifies for special tax treatment. When property is condemned because it is unsafe, this is not a taking of property for public use. It is simply a limitation on the use of the property by you.

For tax purposes, a condemnation or threat of condemnation of your business property is treated as a sale or exchange. You may have a gain or you may have a loss, depending on the condemnation award or the proceeds you receive upon a forced sale. But there is something special in the tax law where condemnations are concerned. If you have a gain, you have an opportunity to avoid immediate tax on the gain. This postponement of reporting the gain is discussed in Chapter 6.

### *Condemnation Award*

The amount of money you receive or the value of property you receive for your condemned property is your *condemnation award*. Similarly, the amount you accept in exchange for your property in a sale motivated by the threat of condemnation is also treated as your condemnation award. The amount of the condemnation award determines your gain or loss for the event.

If you are in a dispute with the city, state, or federal government over the amount that you should be paid and you go to court, the government may deposit an amount with the court. You are not considered to have received the award until you have an unrestricted right to it. This is usually after the court action is resolved and you are permitted to withdraw the funds for your own use.

Your award includes moneys withheld to pay your debts. For example, if the court withholds an amount to pay a lien holder or mortgagee, your condemnation award is the gross amount awarded to you, not the net amount paid to you.

The condemnation award does not include **severance damages** and **special assessments**.

***Severance damages*** **Compensation paid to you if part of your property is condemned and the part not condemned suffers a reduction in value as a result of the condemnation. Severance damages may cover the loss in value of your remaining property or compensate you for certain improvements you must make to your remaining property (such as replacing fences, digging new wells or ditches, or planting trees or shrubs to restore the remaining property to its condition prior to the condemnation of your other property).**

***Special assessments*** **Charges against you for improvements that benefit the remaining property as a result of the condemnation of your other property (such as widening of the streets or installing sewers).**

#### TREATMENT OF SEVERANCE DAMAGES

Severance damages are not reported as income. Instead, they are used to reduce the basis of your remaining property. However, only net severance damages reduce basis. This means that you must first subtract from severance damages any expenses you incurred to obtain them. You also reduce severance damages by any special assessments levied against your remaining property if the special assessments were withheld from the award by the condemning authority. If the severance damages relate only to a specific portion of your remaining property, then you reduce the basis of that portion of the property.

If the net severance damages are greater than your basis in the remaining property, you have a gain. However, you can postpone reporting the gain, as discussed in Chapter 6.

Generally, you and the condemning authority will contractually agree on which portion of an award is for condemnation and which part, if any, is for severance damages or other awards. This allocation should be put in writing. You cannot simply go back after the transaction is completed and try to make an allocation. You may, however, be able to convince the IRS that the parties intended to make a certain allocation if the facts and circumstances support this argument. If there is no written allocation and you cannot convince the IRS otherwise, all of the amounts received will be treated as a condemnation award (and no part will be treated as severance damages).

#### TREATMENT OF SPECIAL ASSESSMENTS

Special assessments serve to reduce the condemnation award. They must actually be withheld from the award itself; they cannot be levied after the award is made, even if it is in the same year.

If a condemnation award includes severance damages, then the special assessments are first used to reduce the severance damages. Any excess special assessments are then used to reduce the condemnation award.

## Disaster Losses

In the past several years, the United States has experienced a large number of major disasters, including hurricanes, floods, fires, blizzards, earthquakes, terrorist attacks, and a volcanic eruption. When large areas suffer sizable losses, the President may declare the areas as disaster areas. A federally declared disaster is a disaster determined by the President to warrant assistance by the federal government under the Robert T. Stafford Disaster Relief and Emergency Assistance Act (Stafford Act). A federally declared disaster includes a major disaster declaration or an emergency declaration under the Stafford Act. There are 3 types of losses from federally-declared disasters, although only one is relevant to losses of business property (the others are listed here to differentiate them from disaster losses for business property):

- *Federal casualty losses.* A federal casualty loss is an individual's casualty or theft loss of personal-use property that is attributable to a federally declared disaster (i.e., a loss occurring in a state receiving a federal disaster declaration). This definition is not relevant to losses of business property.
- *Disaster losses.* A disaster loss is a loss that is attributable to a federally declared disaster and that occurs in an area eligible for assistance pursuant to the Presidential declaration. The disaster loss must occur in a county eligible for public or individual assistance (or both). Disaster losses may be claimed for business property by corporations, S corporations, partnerships, and sole proprietorships.
- *Qualified disaster losses.* A qualified disaster loss is an individual's casualty or theft loss of personal-use property that is attributable to a major disaster declared by the President under section 401 of the Stafford Act. It includes an individual's casualty and theft of personal-use property that is attributable to a major disaster (other than COVID-19) that was declared by the President as a major disaster during the period between January 1, 2020, and February 25, 2025. Because this definition relates to personal-use property, it is not relevant to business property.

With a disaster declaration comes disaster assistance the form of disaster relief loans, special grants (money that does not have to be repaid), special unemployment benefits, and other types of assistance. Still, despite all these efforts by the federal government, as well as state, local, and private agencies, you may experience serious disruption to your business and loss to your business property. The tax law provides a special rule for certain disaster losses that will give you up-front cash to help you get back on your feet.

Typically, you deduct your loss in the year in which the disaster occurred. However, you may elect to deduct your loss on a prior year's return, which can result in a tax refund that may provide you with needed cash flow.

**Example**

**In January 2021, you suffer an uninsured disaster loss of $25,000. You may, of course, deduct the loss on your 2021 return, which is filed in 2022 (assuming you are on a calendar-year basis). Alternatively, you may elect to deduct your loss on your 2021 return.**

If your loss occurs later in the year, after you have already filed your tax return for the prior year, you can still get a tax refund by filing an amended return for the prior year. For instance, if in the Example above, your loss occurred in December 2022 (after you filed your 2021 return), you can file an amended return for 2021 to claim the disaster loss.

You must make the election to claim the loss on the prior year's return by the date that is 6 months after the regular due date for filing your original return (without extensions) for the tax year in which the disaster actually occurred.

**Example**

**You are a sole proprietor who experienced a disaster loss in 2021 and determine it would be advantageous to claim it on your 2020 return. You have until October 17, 2022, to amend your 2020 tax return to claim a casualty loss that occurred during 2021.**

You can revoke an election, if you act in time. The revocation period ends 90 days after the date for making the election. Make the election by filing an amended return and include your own revocation statement that identifies the disaster.

Not all seeming disasters qualify for this special tax election. To be treated as a disaster, your loss must have resulted from a casualty in an area declared to be eligible for federal disaster assistance.

If you suffer a loss in your inventory due to a disaster, you need not account for your loss simply by a reduction in the cost of goods sold. Instead, you can claim a deduction for your loss. The loss can be claimed on the return for the year of the disaster or on a return (or amended return) for the preceding year. If you choose to deduct your inventory loss, then you must also reduce your opening inventory for the year of the loss so that the loss is not also reflected in the inventory; you cannot get a double benefit for the loss.

## Deducting Property Insurance and Other Casualty/Theft-Related Items

It is well and good that you can write off your business's casualty and theft losses. But as a practical matter, you should carry enough insurance to cover these situations so that you will not suffer any financial loss should these events befall your business. If you carry insurance to cover fire, theft, flood, or any other casualty related to your business, you can deduct your premiums (see Chapter 22).

If you maintain a home office, you must allocate the cost of your homeowner's policy and deduct only the portion allocated to the business use of your home as part of your home office deduction, assuming you use the actual expense method for figuring this deduction (as discussed in Chapter 18). Be sure to check your homeowner's policy to see that it covers your business use. You may have to obtain additional coverage if you use your home for certain types of business activities. For example, if clients or customers come to your home, it may be advisable to increase your liability coverage. The cost of additional coverage for business guests (which may be in the form of a rider to your policy) may be rather modest. Similarly, your homeowner's policy may not cover business equipment or other business property in your home office (e.g., computer, inventory). Again, a small rider may be necessary to protect you against equipment loss.

If you are a manufacturer that includes business insurance as part of the cost of goods sold, no separate deduction can be taken for these insurance premiums.

If you self-insure to cover casualty or theft by putting funds aside, you cannot deduct the amount of your reserves. In this case, only actual losses are deductible, as explained earlier in this chapter. Self-insurance may be advisable to cover certain casualties that may not be covered by your policy. For example, your policy may not cover damage from civil riots. Self-insurance is also a good idea where you have a high deductible (for example, a state-prescribed deductible for flood insurance in a coastal area). Be sure to carefully review your policy's exclusions (the types of events not covered by your insurance). Are you covered for damages resulting from riots or a terrorist attack?

### *Use and Occupancy Insurance*

If you carry insurance to cover profits that are lost during a time you are forced to close down due to fire or other cause, you may deduct the premiums. If you then do shut down and collect on the insurance, you report the proceeds as ordinary income.

### *Car Insurance*

The same rule that applies to business property insurance also applies to insurance for your car or other vehicles used in your business. This insurance covers liability, damages, and other losses in accidents involving your business car. However, if you use your car only partly for business, you must allocate your insurance premiums. Only the portion related to business use of your car is deductible. The portion related to personal use of your car is not deductible.

If you use the standard mileage allowance to deduct expenses for business use of a car, you cannot deduct any car insurance premiums. The standard mileage rate already takes into account an allowance for car insurance. Deductions for various types of insurance are discussed in greater detail in Chapter 22.

### *Appraisals*

If your property is damaged by a casualty and you pay a qualified appraiser to establish the FMV of the property in order to prove your damage and the extent of your loss, you claim a separate deduction for appraisal fees. You do not take the appraisal fees into account when calculating your casualty loss deduction.

## Disaster Assistance

Tax rules can certainly ameliorate losses resulting from disasters impacting your business. However, planning to avoid or mitigate a disaster and having monetary assistance, in the form of loans and grants, may be more helpful. Usually, disaster mitigation payments, grants, and other similar payments to businesses are taxable (an exclusion for qualified disaster mitigation payments apply only to individuals), but some are tax free due to special legislation.

### COVID-19-Related Relief

The pandemic triggered a number of measures to help businesses in various ways. The following is tax-free assistance:

- Loan forgiveness of first draw or second draw loans under the Paycheck Protection Program.
- $10,000 advance under the SBA's Economic Injury Disaster Loan (EIDL) program.
- Shuttered Venue Operators Grants (SVOGs) available through the SBA are tax free. These are payments to small live venue operators or promoters, theatrical producers, live performing arts organization operators, museum operators, motion picture theater operators, and talent representatives in operation as of February 29, 2020, who have not applied for a PPP loan. The maximum grant is 45% of gross earned income not exceeding $10 million.
- Restaurant Revitalization Program grants for restaurants. The maximum grant is up to $10 million (but no more than $5 million per physical location).

Special disaster-related rules for retirement plans are covered in Chapter 16. The employee retention credit and other COVID-19-related credits that are offsets to employment taxes are discussed in Chapter 7.

### Tax Relief for Other Disasters

When there is a federally-declared disaster, various tax rules come into play.

***Extensions for filing and other tax actions.*** You have more time for certain tax actions, such as filing returns and paying estimated taxes. There is an automatic 6-month extension to file income tax, employment tax, and excise tax returns and pay estimated taxes. The IRS has discretion to extend various tax deadlines for up to one year. But the postponement of time to file and pay does not apply to information returns (e.g., W-2s, 1099s) or to employment and excise tax deposits. However, penalties for late deposits may be abated.

#### FEDERAL DISASTERS BETWEEN JANUARY 1, 2020, AND FEBRUARY 25, 2020.

- *Employee retention credit.* A business operating in a qualified disaster zone and became inoperable due to a federal disaster may claim an income tax credit of 40% of qualified wages (up to $6,000 per employee). The credit may be claimed without regard to whether the employee performs any services in order to receive the wages. This credit is subject to the general business credit limitation and requires the employer to reduce the deduction for employee compensation by the amount of the credit (even if the general business credit limitation applies). The general business credit limitation is explained in Chapter 23. The reference on page 459 to "a prior employee retention credit" is, in fact, this employee retention credit, but for disasters occurring in a different period. Note: This employee retention credit is *not* the same as the employment tax-related employee retention credit for retaining employees related to COVID-19.
- *Distributions and loans.* Distributions from qualified retirement plans and IRAs are allowed up to $100,000 without incurring the 10% early distribution penalty. Amounts withdrawn are included ratably in gross income over 3 years. The withdrawn funds can be

recontributed to the same or other qualified retirement plan or IRA within 3 years. These breaks mirror the distribution provisions in the CARES Act for COVID-19-related purposes.

- *Charitable contributions.* Charitable contribution limits are increased to 100% of a C corporation's taxable income (similar to CARES Act relief for COVID-19).

### Other Relief

Some federal and state agencies offer special programs to help small businesses get through disasters, including:

- Farm Services Agency (FSA). The Agricultural Act of 2014 indefinitely extended the four disaster programs that were previously authorized by the Food, Conservation, and Energy Act of 2008. Find details at https://www.fsa.usda.gov/programs-and-services/disaster-assistance-program/index.
- FEMA. FEMA has a disaster relief fund, which consists of appropriations that it can direct to states for disaster assistance; it does not provide any direct relief for businesses, but does offer disaster planning continuity planning templates to help you plan for a disaster (go to https://www.fema.gov/planning-templates).
- SBA loans. Two low-interest loan programs—Disaster Loans and Economic Injury Loans—are available for small businesses impacted by a federal disaster. Find details at https://www.sba.gov.
- State government. Your state can help to plan and may provide disaster recovery assistance. Find links to your state from https://www.sba.gov/content/state-government-information.

Find links to many resources through DisasterAssistance.gov at https://www.disasterassistance.gov.

## Where to Deduct Casualty and Theft Losses and Related Items

### Employees

Casualty and theft losses to business property are calculated in Section B of Form 4684, *Casualty and Thefts*. Losses are then netted against gains and are entered on Form 4797, *Sales of Business Property*. Your losses are entered directly on Schedule 1 of Form 1040 or 1040-SR. They are not limited by the $100 per casualty or 10%-of-adjusted-gross-income limitation that applies to disaster losses to personal-use property (or the special limitations for net disaster losses for certain disasters occurring within a set period as explained in Chapter 16).

If the casualty or theft happened to property used for both business and personal purposes, you must make an allocation. Only the business portion of the loss is deductible even if the event is not a federally declared disaster and is free from the $100/10% limitations. For example, if you use a car 75% for business and 25% for personal purposes and the car is totaled in a federally declared disaster not covered by insurance, 75% of your loss (the business portion) is claimed without regard to the $100/10% limits; the other 25% of your loss (the personal portion) is deductible subject to the limits. If the event is not in a disaster area, then the personal portion is not deductible.

### Self-Employed

Casualty and theft losses to business property are calculated in Section B of Form 4684. Losses are then netted against gains and are entered on Form 4797. The net result is then entered on Schedule 1 of Form 1040 or 1040-SR; you do not enter the amount on Schedule C.

Losses from involuntary conversions are netted against gains and losses from Section 1231 property. This is essentially depreciable property, used in a trade or business and held for more than one year that is not held for inventory or for sale to customers in the ordinary course of business. (Certain livestock, crops, timber, coal, and domestic iron ore can also be Section 1231 property.) Thus, even if you have a casualty loss, you may not get the benefit of the loss if you have gains from the sale or exchange of Section 1231 property. However, losses to inventory are taken into account in the cost of goods sold.

### Partnerships and LLCs

The partnership or LLC reports income or loss from an involuntary conversion (casualty, theft, or condemnation) on Form 4797. The net gain or loss is taken into account when arriving at the total trade or business income or loss on Form 1065 on the specific line provided for net gain or loss from Form 4797.

Even if you are a silent partner in an activity that is treated as a passive activity, casualty and theft losses are not subject to the passive loss limitations. You may claim these losses as long as they are not a recurrent part of the business.

### S Corporations

If the S corporation has income or loss from an involuntary conversion (casualty, theft, or condemnation), it must file Form 4797. The net gain or loss is taken into account in arriving at the S corporation's total trade or business income or loss on Form 1120-S. Net gain or loss from Form 4797 is reported on the specific line provided on Form 1120-S for this purpose.

Even if you are a silent partner in an activity that is treated as a passive activity (a shareholder who does not materially participate in the business), casualty and theft losses are not subject to the passive loss limitations. You may claim these losses as long as they are not a recurrent part of the business.

### C Corporations

C corporations report net gains or losses from involuntary conversions on Form 4797 and then use the net amount to arrive at taxable income on Form 1120. Net gains or losses from Form 4797 are reported on the specific line provided on Form 1120 for this purpose.

CHAPTER 18

# Home Office Deductions


| | | | |
|---|---|---|---|
| Home Office Deductions in General | 354 | Mobile Offices | 366 |
| Actual Expense or Simplified Method | 358 | Ancillary Benefit of Claiming Home Office Deductions | 367 |
| Actual Expense Method | 358 | Impact of Home Office Deductions on Home Sales | 367 |
| Simplified Method | 362 | | |
| Special Business Uses of a Home | 364 | | |


Today millions of Americans work at home at least some of the time, and due to the pandemic, the number is growing. Computers, smartphones, online meeting options such as Zoom and GoToMeeting, and the internet make it easier and, in some cases, more profitable to operate a home office. The U.S. Small Business Administration reported that 60.1% of all small businesses with no paid employees and 23.3% of those with paid employees are home-based.

As a general rule, the cost of owning or renting your home is a personal one and, except for certain specific expenses (such as mortgage interest, real estate taxes, and casualty losses), you cannot deduct personal expenses. However, if you use a portion of your home for business and you are self-employed, you may be able to deduct a number of expenses, including rent or depreciation, mortgage and real estate taxes, maintenance, and utilities.

Schedule C filers in 2018 (the most recent year for statistics) claimed home office deductions totaling $1,242.4 billion. The pandemic normalized remote work arrangements. As a result, there may be even more Schedule C filers claiming this deduction for 2021.

The deduction may take the form of a write-off of your actual expenses or an allowance according to an IRS-set amount called the simplified method. Whichever type of write-off method you use, the result is a home office deduction.

The deduction is allowed for both self-employed individuals and employees who meet special requirements.

This chapter covers home *office* expenses; however, you need not use your home as an office to claim this deduction. Home office is simply a name assigned to a category of deductible business expenses. For example, you may use your garage to do mechanical repairs, or a greenhouse to grow plants for sale. The expenses related to these uses may be treated as home office expenses.

It has long been thought that claiming a home office deduction is an automatic red flag for an audit. However, there are no statistics to show that this is true. If you meet the tests for claiming a home office deduction as explained in this chapter and you have proof of your expenses, you should have nothing to fear, even if your return is questioned.

For 2018 through 2025, no home office deduction is allowed for an employee. This is so even if an employee works full time at home and is required to work there as a condition of employment. This is because the deduction for miscellaneous itemized deductions is suspended for this period. However, some home office costs (e.g., Internet access) of an employee can be reimbursed by an employer on a tax-free basis under an accountable plan (see Chapters 8 and 9).

For more information about home office deductions, see IRS Publication 587, *Business Use of Your Home*.

## Home Office Deductions in General

Whether you own your home or rent it, you may be able to deduct a portion of the costs of your home if you use it for business. This is so for both employees and self-employed individuals. However, the law is very strict on what constitutes business use of a home. First, you must use the portion of your home exclusively and regularly for business. The home office must be one of the following:

1. Your principal place of business,
2. A place to meet or deal with patients, clients, or customers in the normal course of your business, or
3. A separate structure (not attached to your house or residence) that is used in connection with your business.

**NOTE**

**Because the IRS may question your home office deduction (an IRS agent can even come into your home to view your claimed home office), it is a good idea to photograph your home office and keep it with the copy of your return as proof that you used it exclusively for business. This is especially important if you have stopped using a home office (e.g., moved into outside business space) by the time the IRS examines your return.**

### *Exclusively and Regularly*

*Exclusive use* of a home office means that it is used solely for your business activities and not for personal purposes, including investment activities. If you have a spare bedroom or a den that you have equipped with a computer, telephone, and a file cabinet, you cannot meet the exclusive use test for a home office if you also use that room as a guest room or family den. A kitchen will never qualify even though it is used for a legitimate business purpose because it is also used for personal reasons (although a portion may be used solely for business in some cases).

The exclusive use test does not require you to set aside an entire room for business purposes. You can meet this test if you clearly delineate a portion of a room for business. It must be a separately identifiable space. However, you need not mark off this separate area by a permanent partition to satisfy the separately identifiable space requirement.

The fact that you have some personal papers in your home office, however, won't disqualify you from meeting the exclusive use test.

There have been several cases that help to define *exclusive use*. It appears that if a taxpayer or family member merely walks through a room used as a home office, this nominal use does not prevent the taxpayer from meeting the exclusive use test. However, even occasional use of a space by family, relatives, or other guests prevents a taxpayer from meeting the exclusive use test.

There are 2 important exceptions to the exclusive use requirement: day-care facilities and certain storage space. Each of these exceptions is discussed later in this chapter.

The home office must also be used on a regular basis for your business activity. This determination is based on all the facts and circumstances. There is no minimum number of hours to meet. Occasional or incidental use of a home office will not satisfy this requirement, even if such space is used exclusively for business purposes.

### *Principal Place of Business*

Your home office is treated as your principal place of business if it is the place where you conduct your business. It may be your prime activity or a sideline business. As long as it is the main location for the particular activity, it is your principal place of business. Generally, this means the location where you earn your money. However, one court has recognized that a musician who spends considerably more time using one room in a home for practice so that she can perform with symphonies and make recordings can treat that room as the principal place of business. It remains to be seen whether this reasoning will be extended to other types of professionals—for example, an attorney who prepares and rehearses his opening and closing arguments in a home office.

Business owners who normally work in an office, storefront, or other location may have been forced due to COVID-19 quarantine or stay-at-home orders to operate from home. Arguably, the home is the principal place of business for the portion of the year that there is no other business location that can be used. If so, a home office deduction could be claimed for part of the year by an owner who is self-employed using a portion of the home exclusively for business (employees cannot claim a home office deduction). The IRS has not ruled on this matter.

Your home office is also considered to be your principal place of business if it is used for substantial managerial or administrative activities and there is no other fixed location for such activities.

**Example**

**You run an interior design business, seeing clients in their homes and offices. You use your home office to schedule appointments, keep your books and records, and order supplies. You can treat your home office as your principal place of business because you use it for substantial managerial or administrative activities and you do not have a store front or other office for such work.**

Examples of substantial administrative or management activities include:

- Billing customers, clients, and patients
- Estimating projects
- Forwarding orders
- Keeping books and records
- Ordering supplies
- Preparing presentations
- Reading professional or trade journals and papers
- Scheduling appointments
- Writing reports

Even if you perform administrative or management activities at places other than your home office, you can still take the home office deduction if you fall into one of the following categories:

- You do not conduct substantial administrative or management activities at a fixed location other than your home office, even if such activities are performed by other people at other locations. For example, another company handles your billing from its own place of business.
- You carry out administrative or management activities at sites that are not fixed locations of the business in addition to performing the activities at home. For example, you do these tasks in your car or in a motel room while on the road.
- You conduct insubstantial amounts of administrative and management activities at a fixed location other than the home office. For example, you do minimal paperwork at an office—not your home office—once in a while.
- You conduct substantial nonadministrative and nonmanagement business activities at a fixed location other than a home office. For example, you meet with or provide services to customers, clients, or patients at a fixed location other than your home office.
- You have suitable space to conduct administrative or management activities outside your home but instead choose to use your home office for doing these activities.

**Example**

**Same as the earlier example, but you schedule appointments for your interior design business from your car phone. Because your car is not considered a fixed location, you can still claim a home office deduction.**

#### MORE THAN ONE BUSINESS

If you are an employee and also conduct a sideline business from a home office, such as actively selling on eBay, Amazon, or Etsy, you may deduct your home office expenses for the sideline business. The business activity from the home office need not be your main activity; the home office simply must be the principal place of business for the sideline activity.

However, if you conduct more than one activity from a home office, be sure that each activity meets all home office requirements. Otherwise, you may lose out on deductions. For example, if you are an employee and also have a business that you run from your home, if you use the home office for your employment-related activities (and not for the convenience of your employer), then you fail the exclusive use test for the home-based business. You will not be able to deduct any home office expenses even though the home office is the principal place of business for the home-based activity.

**NOTE**

**If your principal place of business is in one state and your home office is in another, you may have to contend with two different state income tax rules. Check the states' tax/revenue/finance departments on this matter.**

### *Place to Meet or Deal with Patients, Clients, or Customers*

If you meet with patients, clients, or customers in a home office, you can deduct home office expenses. The home office need not be your principal place of business. You can conduct business at another location, and your home office can be a satellite office. However, if you use your home office only to make or receive phone calls with patients, clients, and customers occasionally, you do not meet this test. While making or receiving phone calls can arguably be viewed as dealing with patients, clients, or customers, it must be done on a regular basis, and not just occasionally.

This test generally allows professionals—attorneys, doctors, accountants, architects, and others—to deduct home office expenses. Even though they have another office, they can still use a home office and deduct related expenses. Of course, the meeting or dealing with clients and others must be more than occasional; it must be on a regular basis. However, the home office must be used exclusively for business. You cannot use it for personal activities during the time when it is not used for business.

**Example**

**An attorney with an office in the city has a den in her home in the suburbs that she uses to meet with clients on weekends and in the evenings. If the den is also used by her family for recreation, then it cannot be treated as a home office because it fails the exclusive use test. However, if it is used only for regularly meeting with her clients, home office expenses are deductible.**

### *Separate Structure*

If you have a separate freestanding structure on your property, you can treat it as a home office if you use it exclusively and regularly for your home office activity. A separate structure may be a garage, a studio, a greenhouse, or even a barn. It need not be an office in order for expenses to be deducted as home office expenses. Nor does the separate structure need be the principal place of your business activity. Further, it need not be a place to meet or deal with patients, clients, or customers in the normal course of your business. It simply must be used in connection with your business. Expenses related to a separate structure are deductible without regard to the gross income limit (explained later).

**Example**

**You own a flower shop in town. You have a greenhouse on your property in which you grow orchids. You can deduct the home office expenses of the greenhouse.**

What constitutes a separate structure? The answer is not always clear. An attached garage is not viewed as a separate structure, nor is a freestanding garage 12 feet from the house because of its close relationship to the home. If your local real estate law treats a separate structure as *appurtenant* to the house, then it is not a separate structure for purposes of the home office deduction rules.

Examples of separate structures that may qualify as home offices include an artist's studio, a florist's greenhouse, a mechanic's freestanding garage, and a carpenter's workshop.

You cannot claim a home office deduction if you rent a portion of your home to your employer and then perform services in it as an employee. If you do rent space to your employer, the rent is still taxable income to you.

## Actual Expense or Simplified Method

You can choose the way in which to figure your home office deduction. You can deduct the actual expenses for the business use of your home or rely on an amount under a simplified method. You can change your election from year to year.

***Why use the actual expense method?*** You probably can deduct a greater amount if you use the actual expense method, especially if your home office space is greater than 300 square feet or you have unusually high utility costs or other expenses related to the home office. It also makes sense to use the actual expense method if the home office deduction is greater than the gross income limit (explained later in this chapter). The unused home office deduction (the amount in excess of the gross income limit) can be carried forward indefinitely, to save you taxes in future years.

***Why use the simplified method?*** You can eliminate some time-consuming recordkeeping by relying on the IRS-set deduction amount for your home office. You do not have to track and retain records showing what you paid for electricity and other expenses that are part of the home office deduction. Also, tax preparation time is greatly reduced by using this easy method.

## Actual Expense Method

If you deduct the actual expenses related to your home office, some expenses are directly related to business use and are fully deductible. For example, if you paint your home office, the entire cost of the paint job is a business expense. Other expenses are indirectly related to business use of your home office; rather, they relate to your entire home. Indirect expenses include:

- Deductible mortgage interest
- Real estate taxes
- Depreciation
- Rent
- Utilities
- Insurance
- General repairs to the home (such as servicing the heating system)
- Security systems
- Snow removal
- Cleaning

Only the portion of indirect expenses related to the business use of your home is deductible. How do you make an allocation of expenses? If you have 5 rooms and use one for business, can you allocate one-fifth of expenses, or 20%, for business? The answer is yes if the rooms are more or less the same size. This is often not the case. If rooms are of unequal size, you allocate expenses based on the square footage of business use. Determine the size of your home; then determine the size of your home office. Divide the size of your home office by the size of your home to arrive at a percentage of business use.

**Example**

**Your home is 1,800 square feet. Your home office is 12 feet × 15 feet, or 180 square feet. Therefore, your home office use is 10% (180 divided by 1,800).**

Once you have determined your business percentage, you apply this percentage against each indirect expense. If you itemize deductions and your total state and local taxes are over the $10,000 SALT cap (the limit for 2018 through 2025 for personal state and local taxes), then see the special rule for figuring the allowable portion of these indirect expenses.

**Example**

**Your business percentage is 20%, and your total real estate taxes for the year are $5,000. You may treat $1,000 ($5,000 × 20%) as part of your home office deduction. The balance of your real estate taxes continues to be deductible as an itemized deduction on Schedule A (assuming you are not subject to the SALT cap).**

**Example**

**Your business percentage is 20%, and instead of owning your home you rent it. If your annual rent is $12,000, you may treat $2,400 ($12,000 × 20%) as part of your home office deduction. The balance of your rent is not deductible, since it is a personal expense.**

***Special rule for state and local taxes.*** Because of the cap of $10,000 ($5,000 for married persons filing separately) on the personal itemized deduction for state and local taxes (SALT), computation of the home office deduction based on actual expenses can get complicated and is best illustrated by the following examples.

**Example**

**You have real estate taxes of $2,500 of state income tax, and use 1/10 of your home for business. Because your SALT is less than the $10,000 cap and your total itemized deductions do not in total exceed your standard deduction, you opt to take the standard deduction. In computing your home office deduction, you can use 1/10 of real estate taxes, or $250. This is called "excess real estate taxes," which are subject to the gross income limit (explained later in this chapter) on the home office deduction.**

**Example**

**You have real estate taxes of $5,500 ($5,000 allocated to personal and $550 allocated to business) and state and local income taxes of $4,000. Your other itemized deductions are high enough to itemize but you don't exceed the SALT cap. So again, $550 for real estate taxes is part of your home office deduction but it is *not* excess real estate taxes subject to the gross income limit (explained later in this chapter) on the home office deduction.**

**Example**

**Same as above ($5,000 of real estate taxes allocable to personal; $550 to business) except your state and local income taxes are $8,000 so you do exceed the SALT cap. In this case, you still get to use the $550 in real estate taxes in computing the home office deduction, but here, the $550 is excess real estate taxes subject to the gross income limit (explained later in this chapter) on the home office deduction.**

For mortgage interest taken into account for the office deduction, rules similar to those applicable to real estate taxes apply. If you claim the standard deduction and don't itemize mortgage interest, then all of the interest is treated as excess mortgage interest and subject to the gross income limitation explained later in this chapter.

Like real estate taxes and mortgage interest, casualty losses may be indirect expenses or treated as excess casualty losses subject to the gross income limitation. Casualty losses are figured on Schedule A of Form 4684. The part of casualty losses for business use of your home not allowed because of the limits on deducting casualty losses as a personal expense, including any losses that are not the result of a federally declared disaster, are excess losses subject to the gross income limitation. See Chapter 17 for more information on deducting casualty losses.

If you rent your home, you can deduct the business portion of rent as an indirect expense. If you own your home, you cannot deduct the fair rental value of your home office. However, you can claim depreciation on your home office. Usually, depreciation is based on a 39-year recovery period, the period that applies for commercial property. However, when a landlord of a multi-unit apartment building uses one room within the unit he lives in as a home office, that room can be depreciated as residential realty using a 27.5 year recovery period; 80% or more of the gross rental income must be from rental income within the dwelling units within the building to qualify as residential property. In a Tax Court case, a couple who ran an adult home care service from their residence was allowed to use a 27.5-year recovery period. See Chapter 14 for more information on depreciation.

Generally, utility expenses—for electricity, gas, oil, trash removal, and cleaning services—are treated as indirect expenses. The business portion is part of your home office deduction; the nonbusiness portion is not deductible. However, in some instances, you may be able to deduct a greater portion of a utility expense. For example, if you can show that electrical use for your home office is greater than the allocable percentage of the whole bill, you can claim that additional amount as a direct expense.

The business portion of a homeowner's insurance policy is part of your home office deduction. It is an indirect expense. If you also pay additional coverage directly related to your home office, treat the additional coverage as a direct expense. You may, for example, carry special coverage for your home office equipment (computer, library, etc.). In fact, if you do not now maintain special coverage for home office equipment, you should check your homeowner's policy to see if damage or loss to your business equipment would be covered. You may think your computer is covered, but some homeowner policies may exclude business equipment or inventory. Also check whether your homeowner's policy covers personal liability for on-premises injury to patients, clients, and customers who visit your home office. Again, you may have to carry additional insurance for this type of liability.

Repairs may be direct or indirect expenses, depending on their nature. A repair to a furnace is an indirect expense; a repair to a window in the home office itself is a direct expense.

A home security system for your entire home can give rise to 2 types of write-offs. First, the business portion of your monthly monitoring fees is an indirect expense. Second, the business portion of the cost of the system itself may be depreciated. This depreciation also becomes part of your indirect expenses.

You cannot deduct expenses for any portion of the year during which there was no business use of the home. If you use your home office for only part of the year for business, you can take into account only expenses for the home related to that portion of the year.

### *Telephone Expenses*

Telephone expenses are not part of your home office deduction. They are separately deductible. However, if you maintain a home office, there is a special rule that limits a deduction for a telephone line: You may not deduct the basic monthly service charge for the first telephone line to your home as a business expense. You can, however, deduct business-related charges, such as long-distance calls for business or call answering, call waiting, and call forwarding. You can also deduct the entire phone bill of a second phone line used exclusively for business. You can deduct any additional lines used for business, such as a separate phone line to which you hook up your scanner/fax/copier machine. These restrictions likely do not apply to smart phones, although the IRS has not ruled on this point.

### *Nondeductible Expenses*

Not every home-related expense can be treated as a home office deduction. For example, the cost of landscaping cannot be treated as a home office expense because it is a capital expense.

### *Deduction Limits*

The home office deduction cannot exceed your gross income from the home office activity. For those who conduct their primary business from home, this gross income limit poses no problem. Income from the home office activity usually will more than exceed home office expenses. Thus, for example, if a dentist conducts his or her practice from a home office, there should be no problem in deducting all home office expenses. For those who use a home office for a sideline activity, however, the gross income limit may pose a problem.

### *What Is Gross Income?*

For purposes of limiting home office deductions, *gross income* is income from the business activity conducted in the home office.

**Example**

**A teacher who teaches full-time at school conducts a retail business from a home office. For purposes of limiting home office deductions, gross income includes only the income from the retail business.**

To calculate gross income, look to your profit reported on Schedule C if you are self-employed, or the portion of your salary earned in the home office if you are an employee. You can adjust your Schedule C profit for certain items. If you sold your home, the portion of the gain related to the home office increases your gross income for purposes of limiting home office deductions. If you suffer a loss on the home office portion, you reduce your gross income.

If your gross income from your home office business activity is less than your total business expenses, your home office deduction is limited. Your deduction for otherwise nondeductible expenses (such as utilities or depreciation) cannot exceed gross income from the business activity, reduced by the business portion of otherwise deductible expenses (such as home mortgage interest or real estate taxes) and business expenses not attributable to business use of the home (such as salaries or supplies). This sounds rather complicated, but Form 8829, *Expenses for Business Use of Your Home*, incorporates this limitation. This rule merely orders the categories of deductions.

If, after applying this ordering of deductions, you still have an unused home office deduction, you can carry forward the unused portion, provided you used the actual expense method; there is no carryforward under the safe harbor method. The carryforward can be deducted in a future year when there is gross income from the same home office activity to offset it. There is no time limit on the carryforward. You can claim it even though you no longer live in the home in which the deduction arose, as long as there is gross income from the same activity to offset the deduction. Be sure to keep adequate records to support your carryforward deduction.

## Simplified Method

Instead of deducting the actual costs of the home that relate to the home office, you can rely on an IRS-created simplified method. This method lets you deduct up to $5 per square foot for up to 300 square feet for a home office. Thus, the maximum deduction is $1,500 ($5/sq. ft. × 300 sq. ft.). If the space you use for a home office is smaller than 300 square feet, your deduction will be less than $1,500. Figure the deduction for the simplified method using an IRS worksheet (see Figure 18.1; it is the 2020 worksheet but the same computation applies for 2021). (The current worksheet is not available, but this older one can be used to figure the deduction under the simplified method.)

**Looking Ahead**

**The IRS may, from time to time, increase the $5 per square foot limit (although it hasn't been increased since it's inception in 2013). There is no automatic inflation adjustment scheduled.**

To use the simplified method, the space must still meet the basic home office deduction rules (e.g., you use the space regularly and exclusively for business and the home office is your principal place of business or meets another home office deduction rule). If two people in the same home, such as spouses, each have a home office, each can use the safe harbor method as long as each office is a different portion of the home.

If the home office is used for only a portion of the year (e.g., the business starts in August or the business is seasonal), then you must make an allocation to determine the average monthly allowable square footage; no more than 300 square feet may be taken into account for any one month. You are treated as having a qualified home office in a month only if the office is used as such for at least 15 days in that month.

If you had more than one home during the year that you used for business, you can use the simplified method for only one home. Use the actual expense method to claim expenses for business use of the other home.

**Simplified Method Worksheet**

*Keep for Your Records* 

| | | | |
|---|---|---|---|
| 1. | Enter the amount of the gross income limitation. See the Instructions for the Simplified Method Worksheet | 1. | |
| 2. | Allowable square footage for the qualified business use. Do not enter more than 300 square feet. See the Instructions for the Simplified Method Worksheet | 2. | |
| 3. | Simplified method amount | | |
| | a. Maximum allowable amount | 3a. | $5 |
| | b. For daycare facilities not used exclusively for business, enter the decimal amount from the Daycare Facility Worksheet; otherwise, enter 1.0 | 3b. | |
| | c. Multiply line 3a by line 3b and enter result to 2 decimal places | 3c. | |
| 4. | Multiply line 2 by line 3c | 4. | |
| 5. | **Allowable expenses using the simplified method.** Enter the smaller of line 1 or line 4 here and include that amount on Schedule C, line 30. If zero or less, enter -0- | 5. | |
| 6. | **Carryover of unallowed expenses from a prior year that are not allowed in 2020.** | | |
| | a. Operating expenses. Enter the amount from your last Form 8829, line 43 (line 42 if before 2018). See the Instructions for the Simplified Method Worksheet | 6a. | |
| | b. Excess casualty losses and depreciation. Enter the amount from your last Form 8829, line 44 (line 43 if before 2018). See the Instructions for the Simplified Method Worksheet | 6b. | |

**Instructions for the Simplified Method Worksheet**

Use this worksheet to figure the amount of expenses you may deduct for a qualified business use of a home if you are electing to use the simplified method for that home. If you are not electing to use the simplified method, use Form 8829.

**Line 1.** If all gross income from your trade or business is from this qualified business use of your home, figure your gross income limitation as follows.

| | | |
|---|---|---|
| A. | Enter the amount from Schedule C, line 29 | |
| B. | Enter any gain derived from the business use of your home and shown on Form 8949 (and included on Schedule D) or Form 4797 | |
| C. | Add lines A and B | |
| D. | Enter the total amount of any losses (as a positive number) shown on Form 8949 (and included on Schedule D) or Form 4797 that are allocable to the business, but not allocable to the business use of the home | |
| E. | Gross income limitation. Subtract line D from line C. Enter the result here and on line 1 | |

If some of the income is from a place of business other than your home, you must first determine the part of your gross income (Schedule C, line 7, and gains from Form 8949, Schedule D, and Form 4797) from the business use of your home. In making this determination, consider the amount of time you spent at each location as well as other facts. After determining the part of your gross income from the business use of your home, subtract from that amount the total expenses shown on Schedule C, line 28, plus any losses shown on Form 8949 (and included on Schedule D) or Form 4797 that are allocable to the business in which you use your home but that are not allocable to the business use of the home. Enter the result on line 1.

**Note:** If you had more than one home in which you conducted this business during the year, include only the income earned and the deductions attributable to that income during the period you owned the home for which you elected to use the simplified method.

**Line 2.** If you used the same area for the entire year, enter the smaller of the square feet you actually used or 300. If you and your spouse conducted the business as a qualified joint venture, split the square feet between you and your spouse in the same manner you split your other tax attributes. If you shared space with someone else, used the home for business for only part of the year, or the area you used changed during the year, see *Figuring your allowable expenses for business use of the home* before entering an amount on this line. Do not enter more than 300 square feet or, if applicable, the average monthly allowable square footage on this line. See *Part-year use or area changes (for simplified method only)*, later, for more information on how to figure your average monthly allowable square footage.

**Line 3b.** If your qualified business use is providing daycare, you may need to account for the time that you used the same part of your home for other purposes. If you used the part of your home exclusively and regularly for providing daycare, enter 1.0 on line 3b. If you did not use the part of your home exclusively for providing daycare, complete the Daycare Facility Worksheet to figure what number to enter on line 3b.

**Line 6.** Since you are using the simplified method this year, you cannot deduct the amounts you entered on lines 6a and 6b this year. If you file Form 8829 next year for your qualified business use of this home, you will be able to include these expenses when you figure your deduction.

**6a.** If you did not file a 2019 Form 8829, then your carryover of prior year operating expenses is the amount of operating expenses shown in Part IV of the last Form 8829, if any, that you filed to claim a deduction for business use of the home.

**6b.** If you did not file a 2019 Form 8829, then your carryover of prior year excess casualty losses and depreciation is the amount of excess casualty losses and depreciation shown in Part IV of the last Form 8829, if any, that you filed to claim a deduction for business use of the home.

Note: This form is the 2020 version.

**FIGURE 18.1 Simplified Method Worksheet for Home Office Deduction**

**Example**

**You begin using 400 square feet of your home for a qualified business use on July 20, and continue that use until the end of the taxable year. The office has an average monthly allowable square footage of 125 sq. ft. (300 sq. ft. for each month from August through December divided by the number of months in the taxable year [300 + 300 + 300 + 300 + 300]/12).**

The amount of the deduction cannot exceed the gross income limit (explained in connection with the actual expense method).

***Depreciation.*** If the simplified method is used for a home office in a residence owned by you, no depreciation allowance can be claimed; depreciation for the year is deemed to be zero, and no basis adjustment to the home is required. If you use the actual expense method in a subsequent year, figure the depreciation deduction allowable in the subsequent year using the appropriate optional depreciation table applicable for the property, regardless of whether you used an optional depreciation table for the property in its placed-in-service year. Figure the allowable depreciation deduction for a subsequent year by multiplying the remaining adjusted depreciable basis allocable to the home office by the annual depreciation rate for the applicable year specified in the appropriate optional depreciation table. The applicable year is the year that corresponds with the current taxable year based on the placed-in-service year of the property.

**Example**

**In January 2019, you started a business from home (assume you own your home) and claimed a home office deduction in 2019 and 2020 using the actual expense method. In 2022, you opt to use the safe harbor method. In 2022, you switch back to the actual expense method. In figuring depreciation in 2022, the applicable year is 3 even though you did not take any depreciation allowance in 2021.**

***Electing the simplified method.*** The election is made on a year-by-year basis. Making the election in 2021 does not bind you to using the safe harbor method in 2022. However, once you make the election, it is irrevocable for that year and can be changed only with IRS approval.

## Special Business Uses of a Home

There are 2 exceptions to the exclusive use requirement: day-care facilities and certain storage space. If either of these exceptions apply, you can deduct your home office expenses even though the space is also used for personal purposes.

### *Day-Care Facilities*

If you use all or part of your home on a regular basis as a facility to provide day-care services, you may claim home office deductions if you meet certain tests.

- You must provide day care for children, elderly persons (age 65 and older), or persons who are physically or mentally unable to care for themselves.

- You must have a license, certificate, registration, or other approval as a day-care center or family or group day-care home under your state law. You can claim home office expenses if you have applied for approval and are awaiting it. You cannot claim home office expenses if your application has been rejected or your approval revoked.

#### CALCULATING YOUR HOME OFFICE DEDUCTION FOR DAY-CARE SERVICES

If you use a portion of your home exclusively for day-care services (e.g., a basement playroom), you can deduct your expenses for any other type of business use of a home. If, however, you use a portion of your home for day-care services but also use it for personal purposes (e.g., your living room), you must follow special allocation rules to determine your home office deduction. You must compare the business use of the space with the total use of the space. There are 2 methods for making this comparison in 2021:

> **NOTE**
> **Special rules for meal costs of day-care providers are covered in Chapter 22.**

1. Compare the number of hours of business use in a week with the number of hours in a week (168 hours).
2. Compare the number of hours of business use in the tax year with the number of hours in a tax year (8,760 in a 365-day year).

Then this percentage is applied to the business percentage of total space.

**Example**

**An individual uses her basement to provide day-care services. The basement represents 50% of her house's total square footage. She uses her basement for 12 hours per day, 5 days per week, 50 weeks per year, for day-care services. Her family uses the basement during the times it is not being used for day-care services. She uses her home for a total of 3,000 hours per year for business, or 34.25% of the total hours in the year (3,000 ÷ 8,760). In calculating the amount of indirect expenses allocable to her business use, she can deduct 17.13% (34.25% × 50%).**

If meals are provided as part of the day-care services, the cost of the meals is not included in a home office deduction. It is a separate expense. In calculating the deductible portion of the meal costs, 100% of the costs to day-care recipients is deductible (a standard meal allowance used by day-care providers is explained in Chapter 22). If you also provide meals to employees, only 50% of the cost of meals for them is deductible. No percentage of the cost of meals consumed by you or your family is deductible. If you receive reimbursements under the Child and Adult Food Care Program under the U.S. Department of Agriculture, you must include in income any reimbursements in excess of your expenses for eligible care recipients.

### *Storage*

If space is used on a regular basis for the storage of your inventory or sample products, you can deduct home office expenses even though you also use the space for personal purposes and thus fail the exclusive use test. The storage space that is deductible is only the actual space used. For example, if a portion of a basement is used for storage, only the expenses related to that portion are deductible even if the rest of the basement is not used for other purposes.

Expenses of storage space are deductible even though the exclusive use test is not satisfied if:

- The home is the fixed location of the business activity (you run the business from home).
- The business activity is selling goods wholesale or retail.
- The space is used as a separately identifiable space suitable for storage.

**Example**

**An individual runs from home a gift basket business and uses her family room to store samples. She may deduct the portion of the family room used to store her samples even though the family room is also used for personal purposes.**

If you aren't in the wholesale or retail business and aren't storing inventory or samples, you can't qualify for this exception to the exclusive use test. Examples of business owners who were denied a home office deduction for storage:

- Attorney who stored client files
- Dentist who stored patient files
- Smog inspector who stored records required to be maintained by the state

### *Bed and Breakfasts*

Typically, owners of a bed and breakfast live at their inn, using a portion of the premises as their personal residence. There is no exception to the exclusive use rule for bed and breakfasts as there is for day care and storage. The Tax Court has determined that no deduction can be taken for the portion of the inn used for both personal and business purposes (e.g., lobby, kitchen, and laundry room). A deduction is limited only to areas used *exclusively* for business (e.g., guest rooms).

## Mobile Offices

Today, some small business owners use mobile offices to run their businesses. Instead of operating from a house or apartment, they operate from a recreational vehicle (RV). Here are some cases addressing the deductibility of mobile offices:

- An orthopedic surgeon who parked his mobile home in the hospital driveway to be on call could deduct some costs of the vehicle, but not the 100% he had claimed.
- A consultant who used his motor home for business could deduct interest on the loan to buy the home but not for travel in it; he lacked substantiation for business travel (see Chapter 8).
- An insurance agent who took his RV to recreational vehicle rallies could not take a home office deduction because he used the RV for personal purposes more than 14 days of the year. Any personal use, including watching TV in the RV, makes the entire day a personal day.

## Ancillary Benefit of Claiming Home Office Deductions

Claiming home office deductions means more, taxwise, than simply deducting the expenses related to that office. Having a home office means that travel to and from the office for business is fully deductible (there is no such thing as commuting from a home office). So travel from your home to a customer's location and back again is a fully deductible business expense. Business use of your car is explained in Chapter 9.

## Impact of Home Office Deductions on Home Sales

Claiming a home office deduction does *not* impact your ability to claim the home sale exclusion (up to $250,000 of gain; $500,000 on a joint return) if you otherwise qualify for it. Regulations make it clear that the exclusion can be applied to the home office portion as well as the portion used as a residence, as long as the office is within the dwelling unit.

However, any depreciation taken on a home office for a period after May 6, 1997, must be *recaptured* at the rate of 25% (for taxpayers in tax brackets over this amount). This means you must report your total depreciation deductions related to home office use after this date and must pay tax on the total amount at the rate of 25%. You cannot use the exclusion to offset this tax.

You cannot avoid this recapture by choosing not to report depreciation to which you are entitled when you use the actual expense method to figure the home office deduction. Recapture applies to depreciation both allowed (the amount you actually claimed) *and* allowable (what you were entitled to claim). If you want to avoid depreciation recapture, you must sidestep the home office deduction entirely by disqualifying your home office or use the safe harbor method for the home office deduction. You can do this easily by *not* using the space exclusively for business. By disqualifying your home office, you lose out on depreciation but can still claim many related costs, such as office maintenance and utility costs, as ordinary and necessary business expenses.

# Where to Deduct Home Office Expenses

### *Self-Employed*

Self-employed individuals compute home office deductions for the actual expense method on Form 8829, *Expenses for Business Use of Your Home* (Figure 18.2). This form allows you to calculate the portion of your home used for business. This portion, or percentage, is then used to allocate your home-related expenses. You also use the form to calculate any carryover of unused home office expenses.

If you first begin to use your home office this year and you own your home, you must also complete Form 4562, *Depreciation and Amortization*, to calculate the depreciation deduction entered on Form 8829.

Depreciation is explained in full in Chapter 14. Note that when you begin to use part of your home for business, it is usually depreciated as nonresidential realty over 39 years (31.5 years if you began home office use before May 13, 1993). You must determine the basis of your home office in order to calculate depreciation. Basis on the conversion of property from personal use to business use is the lesser of the FMV of the office on the date you begin business use or the adjusted basis of the property on that date. If you are not sure about the FMV of your home office, get an appraisal. Ask a local real estate agent to assist you in this task.

The home office deduction calculated on Form 8829 is entered on a specific line on Schedule C for expenses for business use of your home.

Form **8829**

Department of the Treasury
Internal Revenue Service (99)

# Expenses for Business Use of Your Home

▶ File only with Schedule C (Form 1040). Use a separate Form 8829 for each home you used for business during the year.

▶ Go to *www.irs.gov/Form8829* for instructions and the latest information.

OMB No. 1545-0074

2021

Attachment Sequence No. 176

Name(s) of proprietor(s) | Your social security number

**Part I — Part of Your Home Used for Business**

| | | | | | |
|---|---|---|---|---|---|
| 1 | Area used regularly and exclusively for business, regularly for daycare, or for storage of inventory or product samples (see instructions) | | | 1 | |
| 2 | Total area of home | | | 2 | |
| 3 | Divide line 1 by line 2. Enter the result as a percentage | | | 3 | % |
| | **For daycare facilities not used exclusively for business, go to line 4. All others, go to line 7.** | | | | |
| 4 | Multiply days used for daycare during year by hours used per day | 4 | hr. | | |
| 5 | If you started or stopped using your home for daycare during the year, see instructions; otherwise, enter 8,760 | 5 | hr. | | |
| 6 | Divide line 4 by line 5. Enter the result as a decimal amount | 6 | . | | |
| 7 | Business percentage. For daycare facilities not used exclusively for business, multiply line 6 by line 3 (enter the result as a percentage). All others, enter the amount from line 3 ▶ | | | 7 | % |

**Part II — Figure Your Allowable Deduction**

| | | | (a) Direct expenses | (b) Indirect expenses | | |
|---|---|---|---|---|---|---|
| 8 | Enter the amount from Schedule C, line 29, **plus** any gain derived from the business use of your home, **minus** any loss from the trade or business not derived from the business use of your home. See instructions. | | | | 8 | |
| | **See instructions for columns (a) and (b) before completing lines 9–22.** | | | | | |
| 9 | Casualty losses (see instructions) | 9 | | | | |
| 10 | Deductible mortgage interest (see instructions) | 10 | | | | |
| 11 | Real estate taxes (see instructions) | 11 | | | | |
| 12 | Add lines 9, 10, and 11 | 12 | | | | |
| 13 | Multiply line 12, column (b), by line 7 | | 13 | | | |
| 14 | Add line 12, column (a), and line 13 | | | | 14 | |
| 15 | Subtract line 14 from line 8. If zero or less, enter -0- | | | | 15 | |
| 16 | Excess mortgage interest (see instructions) | 16 | | | | |
| 17 | Excess real estate taxes (see instructions) | 17 | | | | |
| 18 | Insurance | 18 | | | | |
| 19 | Rent | 19 | | | | |
| 20 | Repairs and maintenance | 20 | | | | |
| 21 | Utilities | 21 | | | | |
| 22 | Other expenses (see instructions) | 22 | | | | |
| 23 | Add lines 16 through 22 | 23 | | | | |
| 24 | Multiply line 23, column (b), by line 7 | | 24 | | | |
| 25 | Carryover of prior year operating expenses (see instructions) | | 25 | | | |
| 26 | Add line 23, column (a), line 24, and line 25 | | | | 26 | |
| 27 | Allowable operating expenses. Enter the **smaller** of line 15 or line 26 | | | | 27 | |
| 28 | Limit on excess casualty losses and depreciation. Subtract line 27 from line 15 | | | | 28 | |
| 29 | Excess casualty losses (see instructions) | | 29 | | | |
| 30 | Depreciation of your home from line 42 below | | 30 | | | |
| 31 | Carryover of prior year excess casualty losses and depreciation (see instructions) | | 31 | | | |
| 32 | Add lines 29 through 31 | | | | 32 | |
| 33 | Allowable excess casualty losses and depreciation. Enter the **smaller** of line 28 or line 32 | | | | 33 | |
| 34 | Add lines 14, 27, and 33 | | | | 34 | |
| 35 | Casualty loss portion, if any, from lines 14 and 33. Carry amount to **Form 4684.** See instructions | | | | 35 | |
| 36 | **Allowable expenses for business use of your home.** Subtract line 35 from line 34. Enter here and on Schedule C, line 30. If your home was used for more than one business, see instructions. ▶ | | | | 36 | |

**Part III — Depreciation of Your Home**

| | | | |
|---|---|---|---|
| 37 | Enter the **smaller** of your home's adjusted basis or its fair market value. See instructions | 37 | |
| 38 | Value of land included on line 37 | 38 | |
| 39 | Basis of building. Subtract line 38 from line 37 | 39 | |
| 40 | Business basis of building. Multiply line 39 by line 7 | 40 | |
| 41 | Depreciation percentage (see instructions) | 41 | % |
| 42 | Depreciation allowable (see instructions). Multiply line 40 by line 41. Enter here and on line 30 above | 42 | |

**Part IV — Carryover of Unallowed Expenses to 2022**

| | | | |
|---|---|---|---|
| 43 | Operating expenses. Subtract line 27 from line 26. If less than zero, enter -0- | 43 | |
| 44 | Excess casualty losses and depreciation. Subtract line 33 from line 32. If less than zero, enter -0- | 44 | |

For Paperwork Reduction Act Notice, see your tax return instructions. Cat. No. 13232M Form **8829** (2021)

**FIGURE 18.2** Form 8829, Expenses for Business Use of Your Home

### Worksheet To Figure the Deduction for Business Use of Your Home

**PART 1—Part of Your Home Used for Business:**

1) Area of home used for business . . . 1) ______
2) Total area of home . . . 2) ______
3) Percentage of home used for business (divide line 1 by line 2 and show result as percentage) . . . 3) ______ %

**PART 2—Figure Your Allowable Deduction**

4) Gross income from business (see instructions) . . . 4) ______

| | (a) Direct Expenses | (b) Indirect Expenses |
|---|---|---|
| 5) Casualty losses | 5) ______ | ______ |
| 6) Deductible mortgage interest | 6) ______ | ______ |
| 7) Real estate taxes | 7) ______ | ______ |
| 8) Total of lines 5 through 7 | 8) ______ | ______ |

9) Multiply line 8, column (b), by line 3 . . . 9) ______
10) Add line 8, column (a), and line 9 . . . 10) ______
11) Business expenses not from business use of home (see instructions) . . . 11) ______
12) Add lines 10 and 11 . . . 12) ______
13) Deduction limit. Subtract line 12 from line 4. . . . 13) ______

| | (a) Direct Expenses | (b) Indirect Expenses |
|---|---|---|
| 14) Excess mortgage interest | 14) ______ | ______ |
| 15) Insurance | 15) ______ | ______ |
| 16) Repairs and maintenance | 16) ______ | ______ |
| 17) Utilities. | 17) ______ | ______ |
| 18) Other expenses | 18) ______ | ______ |
| 19) Add lines 14 through 18 | 19) ______ | ______ |

20) Multiply line 19, column (b) by line 3 . . . 20) ______
21) Carryover of operating expenses from prior year (see instructions) . . . 21) ______
22) Add line 19, column (a), line 20, and line 21 . . . 22) ______
23) Allowable operating expenses. Enter the **smaller** of line 13 or line 22 . . . 23) ______
24) Limit on excess casualty losses and depreciation. Subtract line 23 from line 13 . . . 24) ______
25) Excess casualty losses (see instructions) . . . 25) ______
26) Depreciation of your home from line 38 below . . . 26) ______
27) Carryover of excess casualty losses and depreciation from prior year (see instructions) 27) ______
28) Add lines 25 through 27 . . . 28) ______
29) Allowable excess casualty losses and depreciation. Enter the **smaller** of line 24 or line 28 . . . 29) ______
30) Add lines 10, 23, and 29 . . . 30) ______
31) Casualty losses included on lines 10 and 29 (see instructions) . . . 31) ______
32) Allowable expenses for business use of your home. (Subtract line 31 from line 30.) See instructions for where to enter on your return . . . 32) ______

**PART 3—Depreciation of Your Home**

33) Smaller of adjusted basis or fair market value of home (see instructions) . . . 33) ______
34) Basis of land . . . 34) ______
35) Basis of building (subtract line 34 from line 33) . . . 35) ______
36) Business basis of building (multiply line 35 by line 3) . . . 36) ______
37) Depreciation percentage (from applicable table or method) . . . 37) ______
38) Depreciation allowable (multiply line 36 by line 37) . . . 38) ______

**PART 4—Carryover of Unallowed Expenses to Next Year**

39) Operating expenses. Subtract line 23 from line 22. If less than zero, enter -0- . . . 39) ______
40) Excess casualty losses and depreciation. Subtract line 29 from line 28. If less than zero, enter -0- . . . 40) ______

**FIGURE 18.3** Worksheet to Figure the Deduction for Business Use of Your Home

## *Farmers*

Self-employed farmers who file Schedule F instead of Schedule C and want to deduct their actual expenses do not compute home office deductions on Form 8829. Instead, they should calculate these deductions on the worksheet (see Figure 18.3 on this page). Then the home office deduction is entered on Schedule F.

### Partners and LLC Members

If you use a home office for your business, you figure your deduction for the actual expense method in the same way as an employee. Use the worksheet in Figure 18.3 (do not use Form 8829 to figure your home office deduction).

### Simplified Method

Figure the home office deduction on the worksheet in Figure 18.1 on page 363.

CHAPTER 19

# Medical Coverage


Health Care Mandates 372
Deducting Medical Insurance for Covering Employees 374
Deducting Health Coverage for Self-Employed Persons and More-Than-2% S Corporation Shareholders 376
Using Reimbursement Plans 377
Tax Credit for Contributions to Employee Health Coverage 379
Shifting the Cost of Coverage to Employees 380
Health Savings Accounts (HSAs) 382
Archer Medical Savings Accounts (MSAs) 385
COBRA Coverage 386
Wellness Programs 387
Reporting Health Coverage on W-2s 387
Glossary of Terms for Health Coverage 387


The pandemic was still a fact of life in 2021, with individuals and businesses across the United States impacted directly or indirectly by COVID-19. Under federal law, health insurance plans and insurers must cover the cost of certain items and services related to diagnostic testing for COVID-19 furnished on or after March 18, 2020, and during the applicable emergency period, which has yet to end. This must be done without any cost-sharing (no co-payments or deductibles). But the pandemic is not the only medical issue faced by many people in 2021.

Medical coverage is an expensive personal expense for most people. So, for many, a job that provides medical coverage offers an important benefit. For the small business owner there is often a need to obtain personal coverage. It may also be good business practice to offer medical coverage as a fringe benefit to attract and keep good employees. A write-off of all or a portion of the cost of medical coverage is a significant cost-saving feature of providing such coverage.

While the individual mandate is nonexistent because of the repeal of the penalty for not having required coverage, the employer mandate continues to apply. If you have employees, familiarize yourself not only with the tax rules on health coverage, but also how health insurance coverage now works. For example, medical conditions have no impact on health insurance today. Your costs depend on the age of workers and where they live. (All you need for a quote are their date of birth and home zip code.) Work with a knowledgeable agent who can advise you on options that won't trigger unintended consequences.

A discussion of mandated paid sick leave related to COVID-19 by small employers is explained in Chapter 7.

For more information about deducting medical coverage, see IRS Publication 535, *Business Expenses,* and IRS Publication 969, *Health Savings Accounts and Other Tax-Favored Health Plans*.

## Health Care Mandates

The individual mandate, which had required individuals to carry minimum essential health coverage or pay a penalty, effectively ended in 2018 with the repeal of the penalty. The employer mandate is still in place. Three government agencies are part of the regulatory mix: the IRS, the U.S. Department of Labor, and the U.S. Department of Health and Human Services (HHS).

### *Self-Employed Individuals*

If you are self-employed and do not have health coverage through a spouse's employer, Medicare, Medicaid, or other insurance program providing coverage, you may obtain coverage yourself through a private insurer or through a government Marketplace for individuals (self-employed individuals cannot use the Small Business Health Insurance Options Program, or SHOPs). If you cannot afford the coverage, you may qualify for assistance in the form of a tax credit. The premium tax credit usually applies to those with household income between 100% and 400% of the poverty line (the 2020 poverty level listed at https://aspe.hhs.gov/poverty-guidelines is used for purposes of 2021 credit eligibility). For 2021 and 2022, those with household income above the 400% poverty line may claim the credit if it is necessary to keep the cost of coverage at no more than 8.5% of household income. The credit is payable on an advanced basis, so it can be used monthly to lower premium costs.

A self-employed individual who had been an employee but was dislocated by foreign trade and who qualifies for Trade Adjustment Assistance (TAA) may be eligible for the health coverage tax credit. This is a refundable tax credit of 72.5% of premiums for health coverage for the individual and qualifying members of his or her family. However, a self-employed individual who qualifies for both the premium tax credit and health insurance tax credit must choose between them; no double dipping is allowed.

### *Employer Mandate*

Small employers are not required by federal law to offer health coverage to employees. If they choose to do so, they can act at any time during the year; there is no open enrollment period for buying health coverage by a small employer. Small employers are not barred from dropping coverage to allow employees to obtain coverage (often subsidized by means of the premium tax credit). Small employers can compensate employees to help them pay for individual coverage, or they can reimburse employees for the cost of individually obtained coverage up to set limits (see the discussion on "Health Reimbursement Arrangements" later in this chapter).

The requirement to offer certain health coverage to full-time employees and their dependents or pay a penalty ("play or pay") applies only to "applicable large employers" (ALEs). The definition of an ALE is a company with more than 50 full-time and/or full-time equivalent employees. Determining whether you meet this threshold is not as simple as doing a body count. This is because part-timers can add up to full-time equivalent employees (FTEs). A combination of employees working 120 hours per month (around 30 hours per week) counts as one employee.

To determine your payroll size, first tally the number of full-time employees (those working 120 hours per month or more). Then figure full-time equivalent employees:

- Step 1: Figure the aggregate number of hours of service (but not more than 120 hours of service for any employee) for all employees who were not employed on average at least 30 hours of service per week for that month (part-timers).
- Step 2: Divide the total hours of service in Step 1 by 120. This is the number of FTEs for the calendar month.

In determining the number of FTEs for each calendar month, fractions are *not* taken into account.

**NOTE**

**The definition of and the way in which FTEs are figured for the employer mandate differ from the FTE rules for the small employer health insurance credit discussed later in this chapter.**

**Example**

**In a calendar month, your company has employees who were not employed on average at least 30 hours of service per week; they have a total of 1,260 hours of service. In this situation, there would be 10.5 FTEs for that month (1,260 ÷ 120). In addition, there are 12 full-time employees. The company is treated as having 22 FTEs; the fraction is disregarded.**

***Off-time counts.*** In figuring the hours worked, take into account paid leave for vacation, sick days, personal days, and maternity leave for your employees. Do not count unpaid days off.

***Seasonal businesses.*** You don't have to be in retail or agriculture to have a seasonal business. As long as you are seasonal, there's a special rule to follow: If your workforce exceeds 50 FTEs for 120 days or fewer during a calendar year, and the employees in excess of 50 who were employed during that period of no more than 120 days were seasonal workers, you are not a large employer subject to the employer mandate.

***Annual determination.*** The determination of payroll size is made year by year, and is based on payroll for the prior year, called the look-back period. For example, your 2020 payroll is used to determine whether you are subject to the mandate in 2021. You must average the number of employees over the months to find your payroll numbers for the employer mandate. The look-back period is usually the full 12 months.

***Controlled businesses.*** Can you avoid the employer mandate by splitting up your business into multiple companies so that each has no more than 50 FTEs? Unfortunately not. Controlled groups of corporations and unincorporated businesses with a certain level of common ownership are treated as a single business for purposes of the employer mandate. Interestingly, the definitions of controlled groups of corporations and businesses under common control are the same tax-law definition used for qualified retirement plans. In addition, affiliated groups in service organizations (e.g., accounting firms; third-party administrators) are also treated as a single entity when there is some common ownership (it seems to be a 10% threshold).

***Penalty.*** There are two potential penalties (called shared responsibility payments) for employers that fail to comply with the employer mandate:

- Penalty A: The penalty is for failing to offer 95% of all full-time employees coverage (whether or not affordable). The penalty applies if any full-time employee who is not offered minimum essential health coverage enrolls in a government Marketplace and is eligible for the premium tax credit (explained earlier in this chapter under *self-employed individuals*). For 2021, the penalty is $2,700 multiplied by the number of full-time employees (reduced by the first 30 such employees).

- Penalty B: The penalty is for failing to provide coverage that is affordable or meets minimum value. For 2021, the penalty is $4,060 for each full-time employee who is not offered minimum essential coverage, offered unaffordable coverage, or offered coverage that does not provide minimum value and obtains coverage through a government Marketplace with the premium tax credit. "Affordable coverage" for 2021 means that the employee cost of self-only coverage is no more than 9.83% of the employee's household income. Because an employer is unlikely to know an employee's household income, the IRS created 3 safe harbors that can be used to determine whether coverage is affordable: (1) the Form W-2 wages safe harbor, (2) the rate of pay safe harbor, and (3) the federal poverty line safe harbor. The employer penalty is not deductible.

**Alert**

**If your business may be or becomes subject to the employer mandate, tread carefully. For example, cutting employee hours only to be exempt from the mandate may violate federal law protecting employee benefits. Also, Congress may change the rules; check the Supplement for further details.**

***Information reporting.*** If you provide minimum essential health coverage to employees, whether or not subject to the employer mandate, you are subject to annual reporting requirements explained later in this chapter.

**NOTE**

**Certain notices were required to be provided about COBRA premium assistance. Sample notices were available from the DOL at https://www.dol.gov/sites/dolgov/files/ebsa/laws-and-regulations/laws/cobra/premium-subsidy/model-general-and-election-notice.pdf. The failure to have provided the required notices may result in penalties.**

### *Mandated Cobra Assistance*

Employers that are subject to COBRA under federal or state law (explained later in this chapter) have a limited mandate to pay for COBRA coverage for the assistance period of April 1, 2021, through September 30, 2021. This mandate applies to employees who have been involuntarily terminated (other than for gross misconduct) and those who have had their hours reduced (e.g., changing from full-time to part-time; being furloughed). This includes the spouse or dependent child of the employee who had the reduction in hours or involuntary termination of employment resulting in a loss of coverage. This coverage does not apply to anyone eligible for health coverage under another program (e.g., Medicare).

The premium assistance is paid by employers claiming a refundable employment tax credit, called the COBRA premium assistance credit (i.e., it is not an out-of-pocket cost for employers). Details on calculating the credit are in Notice 2021-31.

## Deducting Medical Insurance for Covering Employees

According to a study from the Kaiser Family Foundation released in October 2020, 48% of all small businesses with 3 to 9 employees offer this benefit to their employees. This compares to 99% of firms with 200 or more employees.

If you provide medical insurance, you can deduct the cost of their group hospitalization and medical insurance. Deductible medical coverage also includes premiums for **long-term care insurance**.

***Long-term care insurance*** **An insurance contract that provides coverage for long-term care services necessary for diagnostic, preventive, therapeutic, curing, treating, mitigating, and rehabilitative services, as well as maintenance or personal care services required by a chronically ill person and provided pursuant to a plan of care prescribed by a licensed health care practitioner.**

To be deductible, long-term care insurance must:

- Be guaranteed renewable.
- Not provide for a cash surrender value or other money that can be repaid, assigned, pledged, or borrowed.
- Provide that refunds of premiums, other than refunds on the death of the insured or complete surrender or cancellation of the contract, and dividends under the contract may be used to reduce future premiums or increase future benefits.
- Not pay or reimburse expenses incurred for services or items that would be reimbursed under Medicare, except where Medicare is a secondary payer or the contract makes per diem or other periodic payments without regard to expenses.

***Special concerns for employees age 65 and older.*** If you have medical coverage for your staff, you must offer the same coverage to all employees, even those age 65 and older who are eligible for Medicare and must carry Part B. What's worse, you'll pay more for their coverage because premiums are age-based. (Because of the age rating law, the price for 64-year-olds also applies to anyone age 65 and older.) And:

- For employers with 20 or more employees, Medicare is the secondary payor, picking up where your insurance leaves off.
- For employers with fewer than 20 employees, Medicare is the primary payor; your insurance pays only what Medicare does not. The insurance companies require employees who work for small companies to enroll in Medicare Part B. Employers cannot pay or incent employees to leave the company plan because they are eligible for Medicare.

Medical coverage provided to employees is treated as a tax-free fringe benefit. According to the IRS, medical coverage provided to a domestic partner is taxable to the employee because a domestic partner is not a spouse under state law. However, an employer providing such medical coverage can still deduct it (since the employee is taxed on the cost of coverage for a domestic partner as additional compensation).

The value of long-term care insurance provided through a cafeteria plan or other flexible spending arrangement is not excludable from the employees' income.

You deduct medical premiums according to your method of accounting. If you use the cash method, you generally deduct premiums in the year you pay them. If you are on the accrual method, you generally deduct premiums in the year you incur the liability for them (whether or not you actually pay the bill at that time). The IRS maintains that premiums covering a period of more than one year cannot be deducted except for the portion of the premium that relates to the current year.

You cannot deduct amounts you set aside or put into reserve funds for self-insuring medical costs (see medical reimbursement plans). However, your actual losses (when you pay for uninsured medical costs) are deductible.

### *Coverage for Retirees*

You are not required to continue providing medical coverage for employees who retire (beyond COBRA requirements discussed later in this chapter or any contractual obligation). If you choose to pay for such coverage, you may deduct it. You may terminate your obligation for this coverage as long as you retained the right to do so in any plan or agreement you made to provide the coverage (for example, in an employee's early retirement package).

### *Special Rules for Partnerships and S Corporations*

The business may provide coverage not only for rank-and-file employees but for owners as well. Partnerships and S corporations follow special rules for health insurance coverage provided to owners because owners cannot receive this benefit on a tax-free basis.

First, partnerships deduct accident and health insurance for their partners as guaranteed payments made to partners. Alternatively, partnerships can choose to treat the payment of premiums on behalf of their partners as a reduction in distributions. In this alternative, the partnership cannot claim a deduction.

S corporations deduct accident and health insurance for its shareholder-employees in the same way they do for other employees.

Payment of accident and health insurance for a shareholder means the premiums are not treated as wages for purposes of FICA (which includes Social Security and Medicare taxes) if the insurance is provided under a plan or system for employees and their dependents. Of course, even where the payment is not treated as wages for FICA, it is still taxable to the shareholder for income tax purposes and reported on the shareholder's Form W-2.

A partnership must report the medical insurance that it provides to owners on the owners' Schedule K-1. This is picked up by the partners as income (unless the partnership doese not claim a deduction). Owners may be entitled to deduct a percentage of health insurance, as explained in the next section.

## Deducting Health Coverage for Self-Employed Persons and More-Than-2% S Corporation Shareholders

Self-employed persons (sole proprietors, partners, and LLC members), as well as more-than-2% S corporation shareholders, may deduct the cost of health insurance (including long-term care coverage) they receive through their business, but not as a business expense. A self-employed person who buys coverage in his or her personal name can deduct the premiums above-the-line (assuming there is sufficient income from the business as explained later).

A more-than-2% S corporation shareholder can only claim an above-the-line deduction for a policy purchased by the corporation, or the corporation reimburses the shareholder for premiums, and includes this amount on the shareholder's Form W-2 (box 1 for wages, tips, other compensation). If the policy is purchased by the shareholder and there is no reimbursement, premiums must be treated as an itemized medical expense (subject to the adjusted gross income floor). This is so even if state law bars a one-person S corporation from purchasing a policy.

If the S corporation employs a relative of a more-than-2% owner, the relative is treated as if he or she were also a more-than-2% shareholder. (A relative includes a spouse, child, and certain other related persons under family attribution rules.) If the corporation pays for health coverage for a relative who is an employee and includes the amount in this employee's Form W-2, then the employee can deduct 100% of the premiums as an above-the-line deduction on Form 1040 or 1040-SR.

**Example**

**You own 100% of your S corporation, which employs your child. Your child is considered to be a more-than-2% shareholder. Your company provides health insurance to all employees, including you and your child. Report employee health coverage on W-2s (box 12, code DD) for employees other than you and your child. For you and your child, health coverage is reported on W-2 in box 1 as wages, tips, other compensation. You can deduct 100% of the premiums from gross income on your Form 1040 or 1040-SR. Your child can do so on his/her Form 1040.**

The deduction is taken from gross income on page 1 of Form 1040 or 1040-SR (other than for a one-person S corporation whose shareholder personally buys the policy). This means the deduction is allowed even if the self-employed person does not itemize deductions. The policy can be purchased individually (it need not be purchased by the business).

The deduction cannot exceed the net earnings from the business in which the medical insurance plan is established. You cannot aggregate profits from 2 or more businesses to establish the net earnings ceiling required for deducting health insurance premiums. For S corporation shareholders, the deduction cannot be more than wages from the corporation (if this was the business in which the insurance plan was established).

You cannot take the deduction for any month if you were eligible to participate in any employer-subsidized health plan (including your spouse's) at any time during the month. For example, suppose you are a single, self-employed individual and pay for your own health coverage. On July 1, 2021, you begin a job in which your employer provides you with health insurance. You can deduct the applicable percentage of your health insurance from January 1 through June 30, 2021 (the time you did not receive any subsidized health coverage).

You can include "above the line" your Medicare Part B and Part D premiums. You can add your spouse's Medicare premiums if your spouse is covered by Medicare. There has been no IRS guidance on whether COBRA payments by a self-employed person can be deducted as an adjustment to gross income, but it is unlikely the payments can be deductible in this way because the insurance plan is not maintained by the self-employed person (but by the former employer).

In calculating self-employment tax, do not reduce net earnings from self-employment by your allowable medical insurance deduction.

## Using Reimbursement Plans

Health reimbursement arrangements (HRAs) explained below are employer-established employee benefits plans that pay up to a set amount annually toward employee health costs. Self-employed individuals cannot use HRAs. The HRAs must be funded solely by the employer.

Under a final rule issued jointly by the U.S. Departments of Treasury (i.e., the IRS), Labor, and Health and Human Services, employers may offer certain HRAs without running afoul of ACA. Two types of HRAs are allowable: individual coverage HRAs and excepted benefit HRAs.

### Individual Coverage HRAs

Individual coverage HRAs (ICHRAs) allow employers, both large and small, to reimburse employees for the cost of their individually obtained health coverage purchased from an insurer or through a government Marketplace or Medicare, provided certain conditions are met. ICHRAs cannot be used by self-employed individuals; they are not employees.

An employer cannot use an ICHRA if it offers group health coverage to the same class of employees (you have to offer one or the other). A large employer can use an ICHRA to satisfy the employer mandate (assuming coverage is affordable).

If an employer offers an ICHRA, it must be offered on the same terms to all individuals within a class of employees. However, this rule does not prevent an employer from increasing the amounts offered for older workers or for workers with dependents. An employer can make distinctions among classes of employees:

- Full-time employees
- Part-time employees
- Employees working in the same geographic location (generally the same insurance rating area)
- Seasonal employees
- Employees covered by collective bargaining
- Employees who have not met a waiting period
- Non-resident aliens with no U.S.-based income
- Salaried employees
- Hourly workers
- Temporary workers employed by staffing firms
- Any group of employees formed by combining two or more of the above classes

An employer must give notice to employees about an offer of individual coverage HRA. There is a model notice form at https://www.irs.gov/pub/irs-utl/health_reimbursement_arrangements_faqs.pdf. And employees must certify to you that they have individual coverage (private or through the government Marketplace) or Medicare for each month of contributions for the individual coverage HRA. Again, there is a model attestation form at https://www.irs.gov/pub/irs-utl/health_reimbursement_arrangements_faqs.pdf.

### Excepted Benefit HRAs

Employers with traditional group health coverage can offer an excepted benefit HRA (EBHRA) up to a set dollar amount set by the federal government that's adjusted annually for inflation ($1,800 in 2021). This reimbursement plan allows employees to pay out-of-pocket costs (e.g., co-payments, deductibles), premiums for COBRA (premiums not covered by mandatory employer premium assistance between April 1, 2021, and September 30, 2021), limited dental or vision plans, and short-term insurance coverage. The reimbursement cannot be used by an employee to pay his or her share of the employer's group health coverage.

### *Special Reimbursements*

An employer may reimburse an employee for coverage he or she obtains through a spouse's employer's plan. The reimbursement, which is fully deductible by the employer, is tax free to the employee.

**Example**

Employer X reimburses employee A so A can obtain coverage through his spouse B, under B's employer's health plan (Y's plan). A declines coverage under X's plan. B pays for the coverage on an after-tax basis. The reimbursement to A is tax free; it does not matter which employer is furnishing the coverage. However, if B pays for the coverage on a pretax basis (e.g., through a cafeteria plan), then A is taxed on the reimbursement. Either way, the employer can deduct the reimbursement.

### *Qualified Small Employer Health Reimbursement Arrangements*

A small employer (50 or fewer full-time and full-time equivalent employees) may use a qualified small employer health reimbursement arrangement (QSEHRA) to reimburse employees for the cost of their individually obtained health coverage. A QSEHRA cannot reimburse employees for other medical-related costs. A QSEHRA is not treated as a group health plan.

Reimbursements in 2021 cannot exceed $5,300 for individual coverage or $10,700 for family coverage. The dollar amount can be adjusted annually for inflation. If an employee is not covered for a full year, the dollar amount applicable to the employee must be prorated.

Your employees receiving a reimbursement must provide proof of coverage that meets the minimum essential coverage standard.

You must offer reimbursements to all employees if you reimburse any employee (i.e., you can't discriminate in making reimbursements). However, you do not have to reimburse any employee who has not yet worked for you for at least 90 days, is under the age of 25, or is covered by a collective bargaining agreement. Also, you do not have to reimburse any employee who works part time or is seasonal.

In general, the reimbursement must be the same for all employees. However, this requirement is not violated because the cost of employees' coverage varies with age or family size.

You must give notice about reimbursements no later than 90 days before the start of the year. You should tell employees that receiving a reimbursement bars them from claiming the premium tax credit. More specifically, they must reduce any credit to which they would otherwise be entitled by the amount of the reimbursement received from you.

## Tax Credit for Contributions to Employee Health Coverage

There is a credit to encourage small employers to help pay for employee health coverage. The credit is *very* complicated; it varies with the number of employees, their average full-time wages, the amount of premiums paid, and the average premiums by state for the small group market.

When the credit was created, it had been projected to help 4 million small employers. According to statistics released by the IRS, 188,383 small employers claimed the credit in 2010. That number has declined annually; only 6,952 claimed it in 2016 (the most recent year for statistics). Nonetheless, check your eligibility for it.

The tax credit is up to 50% of the employer's contribution to pay for employee health insurance. This credit is limited to small employers; they are defined as having no more than the equivalent of 25 full-time employees (FTEs) with average annual wages in 2021 of less than $55,600. A full credit is available to those with 10 or fewer FTEs with average wages of less than $27,800.

The amount of the credit is based on a percentage of the lesser of: (1) the amount of nonelective contributions paid by an eligible small employer on behalf of employees, or (2) the amount of nonelective contributions the employer would have paid under the arrangement if each such employee were enrolled in a plan that had a premium equal to the average premium for the small group market in the state (or in an area in the state) in which the employer is offering health insurance coverage. The average premium amounts are fixed by the Department of Health and Human Services. These amounts can be found in instructions to Form 8941).

The credit applies only for a maximum of 2 consecutive years, so an employer claiming the credit in 2019 and 2020 cannot claim it in 2021.

The credit also applies only for small employers that purchase health coverage through the Small Business Health Options Program (SHOP) marketplace. You don't actually enroll and choose a plan through the Marketplace; you do so with an insurance company or a SHOP-registered agent or broker. And your premiums are paid to the insurance company, agent, or broker and not to HealthCare.gov.

SHOPs generally are restricted to employers with up to 50 employees. However, your state may allow you to use it for up to 100 employees. You can buy coverage through a SHOP using your own agent or broker, working with any SHOP-registered agent or broker, or DIY. You can offer a single health care plan or let employees choose their own coverage ("employee choice").

Some states have their own SHOPs. The majority of states, however, have not set up their own SHOPs, so small employers must use the federal SHOP. In some counties, there are no plans available through a SHOP. The IRS has provided relief to employers in these locations. They may qualify for the credit even though they did not buy coverage through a SHOP (see Notice 2018-27).

The credit is part of the general business credit. The credit can be used to offset alternative minimum tax liability for owners of pass-through entities.

## Shifting the Cost of Coverage to Employees

Health insurance is increasingly costly to employers. There are several ways in which business owners can reduce their costs without putting employees out in the cold.

### *Sharing the Cost of Premiums*

Instead of employers paying the entire cost of insurance, employers can shift a portion of the cost to employees. For example, employers may provide free coverage for employees but shift the cost of spousal coverage to employees.

Other options (discussed elsewhere in this chapter) for cost sharing include:

- Individual coverage health reimbursement arrangements (ICHRAs)
- Qualified small employer health reimbursement arrangements (QSEHRAs)
- Premium-only cafeteria plans

### *Flexible Spending Arrangements*

Businesses can set up flexible spending arrangements (FSAs) to allow employees to decide how much they want to pay for medical expenses. The maximum amount that employees can add to a health FSA in 2021 is $2,750.

**Looking Ahead**

**The maximum amount that employees may add to a health FSA in 2022 is in the Supplement to this book.**

Employees pay for qualified medical expenses (prescription drugs and insulin as well as over-the-counter medications and menstrual supplies) on a pretax basis. At the beginning of the year, they agree to a salary reduction amount that funds their FSA. Contributions to an FSA are not treated as taxable compensation (and are not subject to FICA). Employees then use the amount in their FSA to pay for most types of medical-related costs, such as medical premiums, orthodontia, or other expenses during the year that are not covered by medical insurance (including over-the-counter medications, such as pain relievers and cold remedies, not prescribed by a doctor and menstrual supplies). This plan cannot be used to pay for cosmetic surgery unless it is required for medical purposes (such as to correct a birth defect).

**NOTE**

**For 2021, FSAs may permit mid-year changes by employees to opt in, opt out, or change their contributions. Any mid-year election is prospective only.**

**Example**

**Your employee agrees to a monthly salary reduction amount of $100. This means that the employee has $1,200 during the year to spend on medical costs.**

The downside for employers is that employees can use all of their promised contributions for the year whenever they submit proof of medical expenses. This means that if employees leave employment after taking funds out of their FSA but before they have fully funded them, the employer winds up paying the difference. So, for example, if an employee who promises to contribute $100 per month submits a bill for dental expenses of $1,200 on January 15 and leaves employment shortly thereafter, the employee has contributed only $100; the employer must bear the cost of the additional $1,100 submission.

Of course, the flip side benefits the employer. If employees fail to use up their FSA contributions before the end of the year or the 2½ month grace period (referred to as the "use it or lose it" rule) or the limited carryover rule does not apply, the employer keeps the difference. Nothing is refunded to the employees.

### *Cafeteria Plans*

Employers can set up cafeteria plans to let employees choose from a menu of benefits. This makes sense for some employers, since cafeteria plans allow working couples to get the benefits they need without needless overlap. For example, if one spouse has health insurance coverage from his employer, the other spouse can select dependent care assistance or other benefits offered through

**NOTE**

**Health Savings Accounts (HSAs) cannot be part of cafeteria plans.**

a cafeteria plan. Cafeteria plans do not require employees to reduce salary or make contributions to pay for benefits. Benefits are paid by the employer.

### *Premium-Only Plans*

In these plans, employees choose between salary or their share of health insurance costs. If they select the health insurance, it is paid by means of salary reduction. In effect, employees are paying for their share of health coverage, but with pretax dollars. The employer deducts the compensation (whether the employee chooses the coverage or takes the salary). The only cost to the employer under this type of plan is the cost of administering it. (Many payroll service companies will administer the plan for a modest charge.) Bonus: Both the employer and employee save on FICA if the medical coverage is chosen.

## Health Savings Accounts (HSAs)

The high cost of health insurance is considered by many small business owners to be their number-one concern. Now there's a way to cut costs by 40% or more by combining a high-deductible (lower-cost) health policy with a special savings account called a Health Savings Account (HSA). With the liberalization of certain HSA rules, combined with an ever-growing range of investment options, these accounts should continue to gain in popularity. According to Devenir 2020 year-end report, there were more than 30 million HSAs with an estimated $82.2 billion in assets.

### *MSAs Alternative*

The congressional experiment of combining high-deductible health insurance with savings accounts continues in the form of Archer Medical Savings Accounts (MSAs). These accounts, which have largely been replaced by HSAs, are available only to self-employed individuals and small-business owners who had MSAs set up by December 31, 2007. There are many restrictions on eligibility. If eligible, you can use an MSA instead of an HSA. You can roll over amounts to an HSA. Archer MSAs are discussed later in this chapter.

### *Eligibility*

HSAs are open to anyone who, on the first day of the month, is covered by a high-deductible health insurance plan, is not covered by another type of health insurance plan (other than workers' compensation, long-term care, disability, and vision and eye care), and who is not signed up for Medicare. This means that self-employed individuals, small business owners, and those who work for small businesses and are not enrolled in Medicare can use HSAs to obtain necessary health coverage. Each spouse's eligibility is determined separately; the fact that one spouse cannot have an HSA does not taint the other spouse's eligibility.

#### HIGH-DEDUCTIBLE PLAN

This is defined as a plan with an annual deductible in 2021 of at least $1,400 for self-only coverage or $2,800 for family coverage, and the sum of the annual deductible and other annual out-of-pocket expenses in 2021 is no more than $7,000 for self-only or $14,000 for family coverage.

**Looking Ahead**

**The annual deductible for an HDHP in 2022 is not less than $1,400 for self-only coverage, or $2,800 for family coverage. The cap on out-of-pocket expenses in 2022 for self-only coverage is $7,050, and for family coverage is $14,100.**

Generally, an HDHP cannot provide services until the deductible under the policy is met. However, a health plan can still be an HDHP if it offers preventive services without a deductible (or a deductible below the minimum annual deductible). These services can include periodic health evaluations (e.g., annual physicals), routine prenatal and well-child care, immunizations, tobacco cessation programs, obesity weight loss programs, and screening services for cancer and other conditions and diseases. The IRS ruled that male sterilization and contraception services are not preventive services, and plans that offer them with no deductible fail to be an HDHP. However, because some state laws require these benefits to be provided without a deductible, the IRS had granted transition relief; it won't disqualify an HDHP for offering these services through 2020. Check the Supplement on any update for 2021.

Under the CARES Act, HDHPs could cover telehealth and other remote services without a deductible, or a deductible below the minimum annual deductible for 2020. Check the Supplement to see whether this temporary rule was extended for 2021.

### Benefits of HSAs

HSAs give you an affordable way to offer health coverage for yourself and your employees. This example from the National Small Business Association shows you how.

**Example**

**A company with 15 employees is currently paying $72,000 for traditional health insurance. It changes to a high-deductible health plan with a $2,500 deductible for participants. The annual cost of the new plan is $40,000. The company also contributes $1,000 to each participant's HSA, so its total cost is $55,000 ($40,000 insurance premiums + $15,000 HSA contributions). This is $17,000 less than the company was paying for low-deductible health coverage.**

Contributions to HSAs are *not* subject to payroll taxes, which makes HSAs a better option than paying additional compensation to employees as a way to cover unreimbursed medical expenses.

### Contributions

For 2021, contributions are limited to $3,600 for those with self-only coverage or $7,200 for family coverage (any plan other than self-only); these limits are adjusted annually for inflation. The full contribution limit applies even though eligibility starts sometime during the year. For example, if a business buys a high-deductible health plan starting on July 1, a contribution of $3,600 can be made for someone with self-only coverage.

For those age 55 or older by the end of the year, the contribution limit is increased by $1,000. If both spouses are age 55 and older, each can add $1,000 only if they each have a separate HSA account.

You are not required by law to make contributions for your employees. HSAs can be funded with:

- *Employee contributions made on an after-tax basis*. Employees covered by an HDHP open their own accounts and make their own contributions. They deduct them as an adjustment to gross income; no itemizing is required. However, employees cannot contribute to an HSA if they have a general purpose FSA (discussed earlier in this chapter). But having a limited purpose FSA (e.g., to cover dental and vision costs) is permissible while making an HSA contribution.
- *Employees fund contributions through payroll deferral*. A cafeteria plan (discussed earlier in this chapter) is used to allow employees to add salary to the plan on a pretax basis. The amount added to the cafeteria plan and then used to fund the HSA is not included in the employee's gross income; no deduction is allowed for the HSA contribution. From the employer's perspective, it is also exempt from payroll taxes.
- *Employer contributions*. The employee doesn't make any contributions to the HSA; the employer does.

If, as the employer, you choose to do so, it must be on a nondiscriminatory basis (you can't simply contribute for owners and not for rank-and-file employees).

Contributions are fully deductible by the party that makes them. If the employer contributes to employee HSAs, the employer claims the deduction. If individuals and self-employed individuals make their own contributions, they claim the deductions. Deductions by individuals are adjustments to gross income; no itemizing is required.

**Looking Ahead**

**The HSA contribution limits for 2022 are $3,650 for self-only coverage and $7,300 for family coverage, plus an additional $1,000 if age 55 or older by year-end.**

Like IRAs, contributions to HSAs can be made up to the due date of the return (e.g., April 18, 2022, for 2021 contributions by individuals). Contributions can be made via a direct deposit of a tax refund. For example, if a refund is due to a self-employed individual on a 2021 return, it can be deposited into an HSA. But the return should be filed early enough to allow the IRS time to process it and transfer the funds to the designated account if it is to be credited as a 2021 contribution.

### *Taxation of HSAs*

There is no current tax on earnings in HSAs (most, but not, all states also exempt HSAs from state income tax). Funds withdrawn from HSAs to pay qualified medical costs (prescription drugs and insulin as well as over-the-counter medications and menstrual supplies) are not subject to tax.

Money can be taken out for any purpose, but nonmedical withdrawals are taxable, and there is a 20% penalty (the penalty is waived for disability or attainment of age 65).

When taking withdrawals for medical purposes, you are not required to prove this to the financial institution acting as the account's trustee or custodian. If you maintain the accounts for your employees, they are not required to prove the purpose of their withdrawal to you (it is their responsibility). If you have an HSA, you should save receipts and other proof to show that the withdrawals should not be subject to a 20% penalty if you are under age 65.

NOTE

**Employees own their HSAs and can take them when they leave the company.**

### *Permissible Corrections for Mistaken Contributions*

Usually, once contributions have been made by an employee or employer to an HSA, they cannot be recouped. What happens if contributions shouldn't have been made? Mistaken contributions can be recouped in various situations. For example, if an employee was never eligible for an HSA, then the HSA never existed and the employer can correct the error by requesting that the financial institution where the HSA is held return the contribution. The IRS has outlined some other situations, but this list is not exclusive:

- An amount withheld and deposited in an employee's HSA for a pay period is greater than the amount shown on the employee's HSA salary reduction election.
- An unintended employer contribution to an employee's HSA is transmitted due to accessing an incorrect spreadsheet, or because employees with similar names are confused for each other.
- An amount that an employee receives as an HSA contribution is incorrectly entered by a payroll administrator (whether by the employer or a third party) causing the incorrect amount to be withheld and contributed.
- An employee receives a second HSA contribution due to duplicate payroll file transmissions.
- An employee receives an incorrect HSA contribution due to a change in employee payroll elections not being processed timely (so that amounts withheld and contributed are greater or less than what the employee elected).
- An employee receives an incorrect HSA contribution because the amount is calculated incorrectly, such as when an employee elects a total amount for the year that is allocated by a payroll system over an incorrect number of pay periods.
- An employee receives an incorrect HSA contribution because the decimal position is set incorrectly, resulting in a contribution greater than intended.

## Archer Medical Savings Accounts (MSAs)

Small employers and self-employed individuals can use MSAs in lieu of Health Savings Accounts to combine low-cost high-deductible health coverage with a savings-type account. The opportunity to set up new MSAs expired at the end of 2007. However, existing MSAs can continue to receive contributions.

### *Eligibility*

Archer MSAs are open only to small employers (those with 50 or fewer employees) and self-employed individuals with high-deductible plans. In 2021, they are health insurance plans with an annual deductible between $4,800 and $7,150 for family coverage, or $2,400 and $3,600 for single (self-only) coverage. The health insurance must have an annual limit on out-of-pocket expenses of $8,750 or less for families, or $4,800 or less for singles. Employees covered by an Archer MSA must not be on Medicare.

### *Contributions*

As in the case of HSAs, employer contributions to MSAs for employees are not taxable to employees. Contributions are limited to 75% of the annual deductible for family coverage or 65% of the annual deductible for self-only coverage.

If a high-deductible health plan is not in place for the entire year, the contribution is limited to the ratable portion of the annual deductible for the time the plan is in effect.

These same contribution limits apply to self-employed individuals and employees who make contributions on their own behalf. Personal contributions within these limits are deductible. Contributions must be made in cash (they cannot be made in the form of stock or other property). The contribution must be made no later than the due date of the return (without regard to extensions).

### *MSAs versus HSAs*

While the options are strikingly similar, MSAs did not achieve any significant success in the public eye. This is partly because the plans were temporary.

As discussed earlier, those with existing MSAs might want to continue funding them rather than changing plans, and the IRS continues to provide limits for computing annual deductions for contributions. However, there is the option to roll over funds in MSAs to HSAs (see above).

## COBRA Coverage

Employers who normally employ 20 or more employees and who provide coverage for employees must extend continuation coverage (referred to as COBRA—the initials for the law that created continuation coverage). COBRA entitles employees who are terminated (whether voluntarily or otherwise) to pay for continued coverage of what they received while employed. (Special mandatory COBRA for certain employees was discussed earlier in this chapter.) It also covers families of deceased employees and former spouses of divorced employees. COBRA coverage generally applies for 18 months (36 months in some cases).

Employers can charge for COBRA coverage, but only up to the cost of the coverage to the employer plus an administrative fee. This limit on the total cost to the individual for COBRA coverage is 102% of the cost of the insurance. Employers who fail to provide COBRA and/or to provide proper notice of COBRA can be subject to a substantial penalty.

**NOTE**

**Federal COBRA does not include the cost of long-term care insurance.**

Most states have their own COBRA rules, referred to as *mini-COBRA*. Mini-COBRA rules may require coverage from 3 months to 18 months (36 months in special situations) for firms with as few as 2 employees. Be sure to check any state law requirements on providing continuation health coverage to terminated employees.

### *Special mandatory COBRA coverage*

For employees who were involuntarily terminated (other than for gross misconduct) or had their hours reduced (e.g., from full-time to part-time), employers had to pay premiums from April 1, 2021, through September 30, 2021. Employers also had to provide notice of this benefit, allow employees to choose COBRA under an extended period, and reimburse premiums paid for this period. See a full explanation earlier in this chapter.

## Wellness Programs

As a way to reduce health care expenditures, some companies have offered programs designed to encourage good health. These include weight-loss and stop-smoking programs.

A company can pay for wellness programs and deduct the costs as long as the programs adhere to government regulations. Access to a company's program must be nondiscriminatory (i.e., not limited to owners or other key people). Group wellness programs fall into two categories: participatory wellness programs (programs that are not conditioned on a participant's health and do not provide a reward that is based on an individual's satisfying a standard that is related to a health factor) and health-contingent wellness programs (programs that require an individual to satisfy a requirement related to a health factor in order to obtain a reward); each has its own rules.

Incentives, rewards, or other benefits to employees under a wellness program may be taxable or tax free to employees, as listed here:

- A cash benefit (e.g., gift card) is taxable.
- A benefit that is treated as a de minimis fringe benefit, such as a T-shirt, is tax free.
- Benefits akin to medical coverage, such as screening and testing, are tax free.
- Reimbursement of an employee's pretax payment for the wellness program is taxable.

**CAUTION**

**Use extreme caution when offering any wellness plan that it doesn't violate the Genetic Information Nondiscrimination Act and the Americans with Disabilities Act. A proposed rule from EEOC at https://www.eeoc.gov/newsroom/eeoc-provides-proposed-wellness-rules-review contains guidelines to follow. For example, you can offer no more than a de minimis incentive to participate (e.g., a water bottle or gift card of modest value).**

## Reporting Health Coverage on W-2s

Employer-paid health coverage continues to be a tax-free fringe benefit (see Chapter 7). However, employers must include the value of this coverage on employees' W-2s. The amount reported is the amount paid by the employer, employee, or a combination of both.

## Glossary of Terms for Health Coverage

**Affordable Care Act (ACA)** The federal law that instituted the employer mandate, requiring companies with at least 50 or more full-time and full-time equivalent employees to provide affordable health coverage or pay a penalty.

**Applicable Large Employers (ALEs)** For purposes of ACA, these are employers with least 50 or more full-time and full-time equivalent employees. Such employers are subject to the employer mandate.

**Archer Medical Savings Accounts (Archer MSAs)** For accounts set up prior to 2008, annual funding is still permissible.

**Association Health Plans (AHPs)** Pursuant to a final rule issued by the U.S. Department of Labor (DOL), associations, such as trade groups and chambers of commerce, can offer health coverage to their members regardless of where they are located. However, a federal court ruled that AHPs violated ACA. DOL is appealing the decision and not pursuing violations against employers' good faith reliance on the DOL rule.

**Cafeteria plans** Menu of fringe benefit options from which employees choose what they want, including health coverage if included in the menu of options.

**COBRA (Consolidated Omnibus Budget Reconciliation Act)** The acronym from the Consolidated Budget Reconciliation Act, COBRA is the option to remain in an employer's group health plan when an employee leaves the company (voluntarily or involuntarily other than for gross misconduct). Under federal law, it must be offered only by an employer with at least 20 employees, but states may have "mini COBRA" requiring smaller employers to offer such coverage. Special rules apply to mandatory coverage for certain workers from April 1, 2021, through September 30, 2021.

**Excepted Benefit Health Reimbursement Accounts (Excepted Benefit HRAs)** Employers with traditional health coverage can reimburse employees up to $1,800 in 2021 to pay for co-pays, deductibles, and other non-covered items, such as dental and vision care.

**Flexible Spending Accounts (FSAs)** Funded with salary reduction contributions by employees up to set annual limits, these accounts can be used to pay out-of-pocket medical expenses.

**Health Savings Accounts (HSAs)** These are IRA-like accounts for those covered by an HDHP, which allow contributions up to set annual limits to go in tax deductible, earnings to accumulate tax deferred, and distributions for qualified medical expenses to be tax free.

**High-Deductible Health Plans (HDHPs)** These are group health plans, which are a prerequisite to HSAs, that require employees to pay the annual deductible before insurance coverage kicks in.

**Individual Coverage Health Reimbursement Accounts (ICHRAs)** Employers without a group health plan can opt to reimburse employees for their individually purchased health insurance (on or off a government Marketplace) or Medicare up to limits fixed by the employer.

**Long-term care insurance** Insurance providing coverage for maintenance and personal care required by a chronically ill person and provided pursuant to a plan of care prescribed by a licensed health care practitioner.

**Qualified Small Employer Health Reimbursement Accounts (QSEHRAs)** Small employers (non-ALEs) without a group health plan can reimburse employees for their personal health insurance premiums up to set annual limits.

**Self-employed health insurance deduction** Personal deduction on Form 1040 or 1040-SR for self-employed individuals and more-than-2% S corporation shareholders for their premiums.

**Telehealth** Telehealth and other remote care services could be offered in 2020 by an HSA without a deductible. Check the Supplement on whether this has been extended for 2021.

**Wellness programs** Employer-offered benefit designed to encourage and maintain good health.

## Where to Write Off Health Coverage Costs

### *Employees*

If you pay for your own health insurance, you can deduct premiums only as an itemized deduction on Schedule A. Premiums, along with other unreimbursed medical expenses, are deductible only to the extent that they exceed 7.5% of adjusted gross income.

Health Savings Account contributions are treated separately from other medical expenses. If you make contributions to HSAs or MSAs, they are deductible on Schedule 1 of Form 1040 or 1040-SR (regardless of whether you itemize your other deductions). You must complete Form 8889 to claim a deduction for HSA contributions or Form 8853 to claim a deduction for MSA contributions. The premium tax credit is claimed on Form 8962, *Premium Tax Credit*. The health coverage credit is claimed on Form 8885, Health Coverage Tax Credit.

### *Self-Employed*

Coverage provided to employees is fully deductible on Schedule C (or Schedule F for farming operations). The cost coverage for the self-employed person is deducted on Schedule 1 of Form 1040 or 1040-SR.

Contributions to a Health Savings Account or Archer MSA on your own behalf are also deductible on Schedule 1 of Form 1040 or 1040-SR. You must complete Form 8889 to claim a deduction for HSA contributions or Form 8853 to claim a deduction for MSA contributions. The premium tax credit is claimed on Form 8962, *Premium Tax Credit*.

### *Partnerships and LLCs*

Insurance paid by the partnership is deducted on Form 1065. Coverage for partners is included in guaranteed payments and reported to them on Schedule K-1. If the partnership chooses to treat the payment of insurance premiums for partners as a reduction in distributions, no deduction can be claimed.

The cost of coverage for partners is deducted on Schedule 1 of their individual returns (Form 1040 or 1040-SR). You must complete Form 8889 to claim a deduction for HSA contributions or Form 8853 to claim a deduction for MSA contributions.

### *S Corporations*

Insurance paid by the S corporation is deducted on Form 1120-S. Coverage for more-than-2% S corporation shareholders is reported to them on Schedule K-1 as well as on their W-2 forms (as wages).

The cost of coverage for more-than-2% S corporation shareholders is deducted on Schedule 1 of their individual returns (Form 1040 or 1040-SR). Complete Form 8889 to claim a deduction for HSA contributions or Form 8853 to claim a deduction for MSA contributions.

### *C Corporations*

Insurance paid by the corporation is deducted on Form 1120.

### *All Employers*

If you claim the credit for paying health insurance premiums, file Form 8941, *Credit for Small Employer Health Insurance Premiums*.

If you have a self-insured medical plan, you provide employees with Form 1095-B, *Health Coverage*, and transmit copies to the IRS with Form 1094-B, *Transmittal of Health Coverage Information Returns*. If you are an applicable large employer, you must provide employees with Form 1095-C, *Employer-Provided Health Insurance Offer and Coverage*, and transmit copies to the IRS with Form 1094-C, *Transmittal of Employer-Provided Health Insurance Offer and Coverage Information Return*. See instructions for filing deadlines and other rules; these do not accompany the income tax return.

# CHAPTER 20

# Deductions and Tax Credits for Farmers


| | | | |
|---|---|---|---|
| Farm Expenses | 391 | Farm-Related Tax Credits | 398 |
| Interest on Loans | 395 | Nondeductible Farm-Related Expenses | 399 |
| Qualified Business Income Deduction | 396 | | |
| Farm Losses | 397 | | |


The U.S. Department of Agriculture 2017 Census (the next census is in 2022) reports that there were more than 2.04 million farms in the U.S. Business owners engaged in farming activities may be entitled to special deductions not claimed by other businesses. These special deductions are in addition to the same types of deductions that other business owners enjoy. A *farm* includes stock, dairy, poultry, fish, fruit, and truck farms. Thus, it encompasses plantations, ranches, ranges, and orchards.

Farmers have been given these special rules in recognition of their unique business arrangements and to make their tax reporting easier. Some of these rules have been highlighted in other parts of this book. For example, there are some special income rules for farmers (Chapter 4) and farmers (other than farming syndicates) are generally allowed to use the cash method of accounting to report their income and expenses regardless of the amount of their gross receipts. They also have a special 2-year carryback for net operating losses (in Chapter 4). And if they are not "small businesses," they may still elect out of the interest expense limitation (Chapter 13).

For further information about deducting farming expenses, see IRS Publication 225, *Farmer's Tax Guide*.

## Farm Expenses

Ordinary and necessary business expenses related to farming are generally deductible. The timing of the deduction is determined by their method of accounting (cash or accrual). However, in addition to the types of expenses claimed by nonfarm businesses, farmers may be able to claim deductions for expenses unique to farming activities and in ways more favorable than general tax rules would allow.

Farms raising marijuana cannot deduct any business expenses other than the cost-of-goods sold. This is because there is a special tax rule (Code Sec. 280E), which bars deductions other than the cost of goods sold for trafficking in controlled substances, and even though marijuana is legal in many states, it's still a controlled substance under federal law. This was confirmed by a U.S. Supreme Court decision in June 2021. (There are proposals to change this, so check the Supplement for any update.) However, hemp containing no more than 0.3% of THC is legal, so business expenses related to growing it are deductible.

### *Prepaid Farm Supplies*

If you are on the cash method of accounting, expenses are generally deductible when paid. However, if you prepay farm supplies, they must be deducted ratably over the period during which they will be used unless you qualify for an exception to this prepayment rule.

Prepaid farm supplies include:

- Feed, seed, fertilizer, and similar farming supplies not consumed during the year (other than what is on hand at the end of the year but would have been consumed had it not been for fire, storm, flood, drought, disease, or other casualty).
- Poultry bought for use in your farm business that would be deductible in the following year if you had capitalized the cost and deducted it ratably over the lesser of 12 months or the useful life of the poultry.
- Poultry bought for resale and not resold during the year.

Prepaid farm expenses are deductible to the extent they do not exceed 50% of other deductible farm expenses in the year (including depreciation and amortization). Any prepaid expenses in excess of this limit are deductible in the following year.

**Example**

**In 2021, you bought fertilizer ($4,500), feed ($1,500), and seed ($750) for use in the following year for a total of $6,750. Your other farm expenses in 2021 total $12,000. You can deduct prepaid expenses up to $6,000 (50% of $12,000). The excess $750 is deductible in 2022, the year in which such items will be consumed.**

If you are *a farm-related taxpayer* (your main home is a farm, your principal business is farming, or a member of your family lives on the farm or has farming as his or her principal business), you are not subject to the 50% limit if:

- Your prepaid farm supplies expense is more than 50% of your other deductible farm expenses because of a change in business operations caused by unusual circumstances, or
- Your total prepaid farm supplies expense for the preceding 3 years is less than 50% of your total other deductible farm expenses for those 3 years.

### *Livestock Feed*

Generally, even though you are on the cash basis, feed must be deducted in the year that your livestock consumes it. However, if you meet all of the following 3 tests for the advance payment of feed, you can deduct in the year of payment the cost of feed your livestock will consume in a later year (subject to the prepaid farm supplies limit):

1. The expense is a payment for the purchase of feed and not a deposit. A binding contract for delivery shows this is not a deposit.
2. The prepayment has a business purpose and is not merely a tax avoidance scheme. A business purpose would include securing more favorable payment terms and prices.
3. The deduction of these costs does not result in a material distortion of income. For example, if this is your customary practice, then the deduction will have roughly the same impact on your income each year and will not produce a material distortion.

This limit on deducting the advance payment of feed does not apply to the purchase of commodity futures contracts.

### Labor and Related Costs

You can deduct reasonable wages that you pay for regular farm labor, piecework, contract labor, and other forms of labor hired to work your farm. This includes payments to your spouse or child as long as there is a true employer-employee relationship.

You can also deduct related costs including:

- The cost of maintaining houses and their furnishings for tenants or hired help (e.g., heat, light, insurance, depreciation, and repairs).
- Insurance related to the workers (e.g., health insurance and workers' compensation).
- Employer's share of FICA on farm wages.

You must reduce your deduction for wages by any employment tax credits you may be entitled to claim on such wages. These credits are explained in Chapter 7.

### Breeding Fees

Cash method farmers may deduct breeding fees as a farm business expense. Accrual method farmers must capitalize such fees and allocate them to the cost basis of the calf, foal, and so on to which they relate.

### Fertilizer and Lime

You have a choice of when to deduct the cost of fertilizer and lime used to enrich, neutralize, or enhance farmland.

- You can deduct it in the year you paid or incurred the expense (subject to the prepaid farm supplies rule discussed earlier in this chapter), or
- If the benefit from the material lasts more than one year, you can capitalize the cost and deduct a part of it each year in which the benefit lasts.

After you make your choice, you cannot change your reporting method without IRS consent.

### Depreciation

Property used in farming is generally subject to the same depreciation rules as property used in nonfarm businesses. The rules for depreciation are discussed in Chapter 14. However, certain farming property has special recovery periods. Table 20.1 shows the recovery periods for property used in farming.

**TABLE 20.1** Recovery Periods for Farm Property

| Type of Property | General Depreciation System | Alternative Depreciation System |
|---|---|---|
| Agricultural structures (single purpose)* | 10 | 15 |
| Automobiles | 5 | 5 |
| Cattle (dairy or breeding) | 5 | 7 |
| Cotton-ginning assets | 7 | 10 |
| Drainage facilities* | 15 | 20 |
| Farm buildings (other than single purpose)* | 20 | 25 |
| Farm machinery and equipment (new) | 5 | 10 |
| Farm machinery and equipment (used) | 7 | 10 |
| Fences (agricultural) | 7 | 10 |
| Goats and sheep (breeding) | 5 | 5 |
| Grain bins | 7 | 10 |
| Hogs (breeding) | 3 | 3 |
| Horses (age when placed in service) | | |
| Breeding and working (12 years or less) | 7 | 10 |
| Breeding and working (more than 12 years) | 3 | 10 |
| Race horses | 3 | 12 |
| Horticultural structures (single purpose)* | 10 | 15 |
| Logging equipment and machinery | 5 | 6 |
| Tractor units (over-the-road) | 3 | 4 |
| Trees or vines bearing fruit or nuts* | 10 | 20 |
| Trucks | | |
| Unloaded weight | | |
| 13,000 pounds or more | 5 | 6 |
| Weight less than 13,000 pounds | 5 | 5 |
| Water wells* | 15 | 20 |

*Large farming businesses (more than $26 million in average annual gross receipts in the 3 prior years) that elect out of the interest deduction limitation must use ADS for these assets.

Instead of depreciating certain farm-related property, you may claim a first-year expensing deduction (see Chapter 14). In addition to equipment and machinery used in farming, this deduction can be taken with respect to single-purpose agricultural or horticultural structures, grain bins, and drainage facilities.

### *Soil and Water Conservation Expenses*

Generally, soil and water conservation expenses must be capitalized. However, you can elect to deduct such expenses within limits. The deduction cannot be more than 25% of gross income from farming. Expenses must be consistent with a plan approved by the Natural Resources Conservation Service (NRCS) of the Department of Agriculture or a comparable state agency. Expenses eligible for this special write-off include:

- Treating or moving earth (e.g., leveling, conditioning, grading, terracing, contour furrowing, and restoration of soil fertility)
- Constructing, controlling, and protecting diversion channels, drainage or irrigation ditches, earthen dams, watercourses, outlets, and ponds
- Eradicating brush
- Planting windbreaks

They also include assessments by conservation districts for any of these expenses (but not more than 10% of your deductible share plus $500 and subject to the total limitation).

Endangered species recovery expenditures are included with soil and water conservation expenditures and land erosion expenditures to be currently deductible. Endangered species recovery expenditures are costs incurred for the purpose of achieving site-specific management actions recommended in recovery plans approved pursuant to the Endangered Species Act of 1973.

### Reforestation Expenses

You can deduct up to $5,000 annually ($10,000, if married filing jointly) in qualified reforestation expenses. Amounts in excess of this dollar limit can be amortized over 84 months. For further details, see Chapter 14.

### Miscellaneous Expenses

Ordinary and necessary business expenses common to all businesses (e.g., advertising costs or attorney's fees) are deductible. Other expenses specific to farming activities that may be deducted as ordinary and necessary expenses include:

- Chemicals
- Fuels and oil
- Freight and trucking
- Ginning
- Insect sprays and dusts
- Litter and bedding
- Livestock fees
- Storage and warehousing
- Tying materials and containers
- Veterinary fees and medicine

## Interest on Loans

The deduction for interest expense is limited if you are not a "small business." (The limitation is explained in Chapter 13.) For this purpose, a small business is one that meets the gross receipts test (i.e., for 2021, it means having average annual gross receipts in the 3 prior years not exceeding $26 million). However, even if a business does not qualify for this exception to interest expense limitation, it can still deduct all interest on business loans if it is a **farming business** and makes a "Section 163(j) election."

---

***Farming business*** **Any trade or business involving the cultivation of land, the raising or harvesting of any agricultural or horticultural commodity, the operating of a nursery or sod farm, or the raising or harvesting of trees bearing fruit, nuts, or other crops, or ornamental trees.**

---

If an election is made to escape the interest deduction limitation, then you must use the Alternative Depreciation System (ADS) for any property with a recovery period of 10 years or more (see Chapter 14).

## Qualified Business Income Deduction

If your farm is a pass-through entity (e.g., sole proprietorship, partnership, limited liability company, S corporation), you may be eligible for the 20% qualified business income deduction. The deduction, which is a reduction to the taxable income of the farm owner (not a business deduction or an adjustment to gross income) is explained in Chapter 21. It applies to income reported on Schedule F and Form 4835, as well as Schedule K-1 from a partnership or S corporation in the farming business.

But note that farming is not a specified service trade or business, so it is not subject to additional limitations that apply to a specified service trade or business. Special rules apply to a specified agricultural or horticultural cooperative and the patrons who sell their grain to them.

***Direct (non-coop) sales.*** For a farmer who sells grain directly (not through a cooperative), the 20% deduction applies, subject to the usual limits. Thus, the full deduction applies if taxable income in 2021 does not exceed $329,800 for married persons filing jointly, $164,925 for married persons filing separately, and $164,900 for singles and heads of households, with the wage and other limits applicable if taxable income is higher.

***Coop sales.*** For a farmer who sells grain through a cooperative in which he or she is a patron, there is a bifurcated calculation (not a straight 20% computation). This blends the old qualified domestic production activities deduction under Code Sec. 199 (which was repealed after 2017) with the qualified business deduction (Code Sec. 199A). The bifurcation calculation is complicated, but here's an overview:

- *Step 1*: Figure the deduction using the new 20% qualified business income deduction.
- *Step 2*: Subtract the smaller of (1) 9% of net income attributable to cooperative sales, or (2) 50% of W-2 wages paid to earn the income from the cooperative.
- *Step 3*: Add back an amount referenced by the qualified domestic production activities deduction, which ranges from 0% to 9% of the coop's qualified domestic production activities income attributable to the patron's sales.

***Cooperatives.*** Again, there is a complex computation. Essentially it boils down to a qualified business income deduction equal to an amount up to 9% of qualified domestic production activities income, subject to the usual limits for taxable income and 50% of W-2 wages. If this deduction is passed through to patrons, then there is a corresponding reduction for payments to patrons.

The IRS has provided guidance on W-2 wages for patrons receiving cooperative payments (see Revenue Procedure 2021-11).

## Farm Losses

If your deductible farm expenses exceed your farm income, you have a loss from the operation of your farm. The amount you can deduct of your farm loss may be limited by a number of rules. However, consider how the following rules may especially impact on farming activities.

### *Passive Activity Rules*

Losses from an activity in which you do not materially participate and any rental activity cannot exceed your income from passive activities. Thus, if you own the farm but do not work it yourself, you may not be able to deduct your losses.

### *At-Risk Rules*

These rules, which limit your deduction for losses to your economic investment, apply to farming activities in the same way in which they apply to nonfarming activities.

### *Hobby Loss Rules*

If you are not engaged in the farming activity with a realistic profit motive, then your losses are not deductible. They do not carry over to another year; they are gone forever. There is considerable litigation each year involving *gentlemen farmers*, and their success in deducting losses depends on demonstrating a profit motive. For details, see Chapter 27.

### *Farming Losses*

Farming losses cannot be used as a tax shelter. Before 2018, farming losses by those receiving subsidies under Title I of the Food, Conservation, and Energy Act of 2008, or Commodity Credit loans were limited in how much of those losses could be used to offset nonfarm income on Schedule F. The limit was the greater of $300,000 ($150,000 for married persons filing separately) or the net farm income received over the past 5 years, with excess losses carried forward. This rule is suspended for 2018 through 2025.

Losses that have been carried forward from pre-2018 years remain suspended and cannot be used until 2026. The IRS has not provided guidance on what happens if farm operations cease during this period.

### *Net Operating Losses*

For net operating losses (NOLs) arising in 2021, farmers are subject to special rules for NOL carrybacks. While most businesses cannot carry back any NOL arising after 2020, farmers may use a 2-year carryback for farming losses. Farming losses are the smaller of:

- The amount that would be the NOL for the year if only income and deductions attributable to farming businesses were taken into account, or
- The NOL for the year.

You can choose to forgo the carryback and simply carry forward the loss until it is used up. For farms operated through a partnership or S corporation, the losses pass through to the owners who claim the NOLs on their individual returns. Details on computing NOLs and claiming carrybacks and carryforwards are in Chapter 4.

## Farm-Related Tax Credits

Farmers may be entitled to claim the same tax credits available to other businesses (discussed in Chapters 7 and 23). For example, if they pay wages to certain types of workers, they may be eligible to claim employment credits. But, there are also credits unique to farmers.

### *Credits for Farming Activities*

In addition to credits available to nonfarm businesses, certain credits may be unique (or more relevant) to farmers. These include the following.

#### UNDYED KEROSENE AND UNDYED DIESEL FUEL FOR HOUSEHOLD USE

The credit is the amount of excise tax paid on kerosene used in your home for heating, lighting, and cooking.

#### FEDERAL TAX PAID ON FUELS

The credit is the amount of excise tax paid on gasoline, special motor fuels, diesel-water fuel emulsion, and compressed natural gas used on a farm for farming purposes. The credit is claimed by the ultimate purchaser, rather than the ultimate vendor—the farmer who bought the fuel and did not resell it.

#### FUELS USED IN OFF-HIGHWAY BUSINESS USE

The credit is for the amount of excise tax paid on fuels, including alternative fuels, used in running stationary machines (such as generators), for cleaning purposes, or in other vehicles not registered for highway use. However, if undyed diesel fuel or undyed kerosene is used on a farm, the fuel is not considered as being used in an off-highway vehicle.

### *Claiming a Credit or Refund*

You can claim the aforementioned credits for fuel-related excise taxes on your income tax return. The credits are claimed on Form 4136. Alternatively, you can claim a refund of the excise taxes you already paid. The claim for refund can be made for any quarter of your tax year for which you can claim $750 or more.

If for any quarter the excise tax paid on all fuels used for qualifying purposes is less than $750, you carry the amount over to the next quarter of your tax year to determine if you can claim at least $750 for that quarter. If you cannot claim at least $750 at the end of the fourth quarter of your tax year, you must claim a credit on your income tax return.

You can use Form 8849 to file a claim for refund. If you file Form 720, you can use the Schedule C portion of Form 720 for your claims, rather than Form 8849.

You must file a quarterly claim by the last day of the first quarter following the end of the last quarter included in the claim. If you do not file a timely refund claim for the fourth quarter of your tax year, you will have to claim a credit for that amount on your income tax return.

If you claimed taxes as an expense deduction that reduced your income, you must now include any credit or refund of excise taxes on fuels.

**Example**

**A cash basis farmer filed his 2020 Form 1040 return on April 15, 2021, on which he deducted gasoline that included $110 of excise tax. He then claimed a credit of $110 for excise tax paid on fuel. The $110 is reported as additional income in 2021.**

### *Who Claims a Credit or Refund?*

If fertilizer or pesticides are applied to your farm aerially or otherwise, the applicator is treated as having used the fuel. For kerosene used in aviation, the registered ultimate vendor is the claimant.

### *Exemption from Excise Tax on Fuels*

As a farmer, you can buy diesel fuel and kerosene excise tax free (and so are not eligible to claim any credit with respect to these fuels). To obtain tax exemption, you must provide the vendor with a signed certificate and keep a copy of it with your other business records. A Sample Exemption Certificate (Figure 20.1) is reproduced on page 400.

For more information about these special tax credits, see IRS Publication 510, *Excise Taxes (Including Fuel Tax Credits and Refunds)*.

## Nondeductible Farm-Related Expenses

Not every expense of the farm can be written off. Some expenses are personal in nature and are nondeductible. Other expenses may be subject to limitations. Nondeductible expenses include:

- Personal or living expenses that do not produce farm income (e.g., taxes, insurance, and repairs to the home). If you pay expenses (such as electricity) that is used for both personal and farm purposes, you must allocate the expenses accordingly (and deduct only the farm portion). While personal expenses are not deductible, there is one exception. You may claim a tax credit for the excise tax on kerosene used in your home for heating, lighting, and cooking (discussed earlier in this chapter). Also, a portion of the home may qualify for a home office deduction as discussed in Chapter 18.
- Expenses of raising anything consumed by you and your family.
- The value of animals or crops you raised that died. The costs of raising the animals or crops were separately deductible (under the rules discussed throughout this chapter).
- The cost of raising unharvested crops sold with land owned more than one year if you sell both at the same time to the same person. Instead, add these costs to the basis of the land for purposes of determining your gain or loss on the sale. Similarly, the cost of unharvested crops you buy with land is added to the purchase price of the land. This cost is then taken into account to determine your profit (or loss) when you later sell the land.
- Fines and penalties. However, penalties you pay for exceeding marketing quotas are deductible. If such penalties are paid by the purchaser of your crop, you simply report the net amount you receive as income (you do not claim a separate deduction for the penalties).

## Where to Claim Farming Expenses

### *Self-Employed*

Farming expenses are deductible in Part II of Schedule F (Form 1040 or 1040-SR). There are specific lines for various types of farming expenses. There is also a catchall line for reporting other expenses. If there are more than 6 other expenses, attach a statement to the return listing these other deductions.

**WAIVER FOR USE BY ULTIMATE PURCHASERS OF KEROSENE FOR USE IN COMMERCIAL AVIATION**

**(To support vendor's claim for a credit or payment under § 6427 of the Internal Revenue Code.)**

---

Name, address, and employer identification number of ultimate vendor

The undersigned ultimate purchaser ("Buyer") hereby certifies the following under penalties of perjury that the kerosene for use in aviation to which this waiver relates is purchased for use in commercial aviation (other than foreign trade).

This waiver applies to the following (complete as applicable):

________ This is a single purchase waiver:

1. ________ Invoice for delivery ticket number
2. ________ Number of gallons

________ This is a waiver covering all purchases under a specified account of order number:

1. Effective date ________
2. Expiration date ________ (period not to exceed 1 year after the effective date)
3. Buyer's account number ________

Buyer will provide a new waiver to the vendor if any information in this waiver changes.

If Buyer uses the kerosene for use in aviation to which this waiver relates for a use other than the use stated above, Buyer will be liable for tax.

Buyer understands that by signing this waiver, Buyer gives up its right to claim any credit or payment for the kerosene for use in aviation used in a nontaxable use.

Buyer acknowledges that it has not and will not claim any credit or payment for the kerosene for use in aviation to which this waiver relates.

Buyer understands that the fraudulent use of this waiver may subject Buyer and all parties making such fraudulent use of this waiver to a fine or imprisonment, or both, together with the costs of prosecution.

---

Printed or typed name of person signing

---

Title of person signing

---

Name of Buyer

---

Employer identification number

---

Address of Buyer

---

Signature and date signed

---

**FIGURE 20.1** Sample Exemption Certificate

### *Partnerships and LLCs*

Farming expenses are deductible in Part II of Schedule F. There are specific lines for various types of farming expenses. There is also a catchall line for reporting other expenses. Schedule F is attached to the partnership return, Form 1065.

Most expenses are not separately stated items passed through to partners and members. They are simply part of the entity's ordinary business income or loss. Therefore, partners and members in LLCs report their net income or loss from the farm on Schedule E.

### *S Corporations*

Farms operating as S corporations claim deductions on the corporation's return, Form 1120-S. Most expenses are not separately stated items passed through to shareholders. They are simply part of the corporation's ordinary business income or loss. Therefore, shareholders report their net income or loss from the farm on Schedule E.

### *C Corporations*

Farms operating as C corporations report their expenses on the corporation's return, Form 1120. This form contains separate lines for deducting certain costs. Other costs must be reported on the catchall line for "other deductions" with an explanation attached. Shareholders do not report any income (or loss) from the corporation.

### *All Taxpayers*

The credit for federal tax on fuels is figured on Form 4136, *Credit for Federal Tax Paid on Fuels*. Instead of claiming the credit on the current return, the taxpayer may be entitled to a refund. The refund is claimed on Form 8849, *Claim for Refund of Excise Taxes*.

CHAPTER 21

# Qualified Business Income Deduction


| | | | |
|---|---|---|---|
| General Rules | 402 | Other Limitations | 414 |
| Qualified Trade or Business | 403 | Partnerships and S Corporations | 414 |
| Qualified Business Income | 408 | Understatement Penalty | 414 |
| Basic Limitations | 410 | | |
| Specified Service Trades or Businesses | 411 | | |


When the Tax Cut and Jobs Act lowered the corporate tax rate to 21%, there was an attempt by Congress to reduce the tax rate for owners of pass-through entities in an indirect way. Instead of providing a special tax rate that these owners could apply to their business income, Congress instead created a special deduction that in effect lowers the tax rate (e.g., the top rate of 37% becomes an effective tax rate of 29.6% when the qualified business income deduction is applied), but only for some pass-through owners. The special deduction is called the "qualified business income (QBI) deduction." This deduction does not require any special outlay or action; you claim it if you are eligible.

## General Rules

The deduction may be claimed by owners of pass-through entities (subject to the limitations below). Pass-through entities include sole proprietorships (including independent contractors, freelancers, farmers, and other self-employed individuals), partnerships, limited liability companies, and S corporations. C corporations and their shareholders cannot claim the qualified business income deduction; they aren't a qualified business. Employees cannot take the deduction with respect to their wage income.

The deduction is not a business write-off on Schedule C, E, or F; and it is not a reduction from gross income to reduce adjusted gross income. The deduction is taken into account in figuring taxable income on which your applicable tax rate applies. It can be taken whether or not you itemize personal deductions.

Special rules for farmers are explained in Chapter 20.

***Deduction amount.*** The deduction is 20% of qualified business income (QBI). The full 20% deduction applies if your taxable income (not just business income) in 2021 is no more than $329,800 for married persons filing jointly, $164,925 for married persons filing separately, and $164,900 for singles and heads of households. This taxable income threshold applies regardless of your type of business, which means even if you are in a specified service trade or business (defined later), you get the full deduction.

**Example**

**You are an independent contractor with QBI of $50,000 (and taxable income of $95,000). Your business income deduction is $10,000 (20% of $50,000). In effect, you are paying income tax on $40,000 of profit (even though the deduction does not directly reduce the amount of profits subject to tax). The same is true if you are a bookkeeper operating as a sole proprietorship (a specified service trade or business).**

If your taxable income does not exceed the applicable threshold, then figure your QBI deduction on Form 8995, Qualified Business Income Deduction Simplified Computation (Figure 21.1; this is the 2020 version so check for an update).

If your taxable income exceeds the threshold for the type of return you file, then various limitations come into play. You can add 20% of qualified real estate investment trust (REIT) dividends and qualified publicly traded partnership (PTP) income to the 20% of QBI. These sources of income are not discussed further in this chapter.

If your taxable income exceeds the applicable threshold, then figure your QBI deduction on Form 8995-A, *Qualified Business Income Deduction* (Figure 21.2; this is the 2020 version so check for an update).

## Qualified Trade or Business

What constitutes a trade or business for purposes of the QBI deduction is based on standard tax law; nothing has been changed. Generally, each trade or business stands alone, meaning you look at the numbers from each to determine the deduction.

***Real estate activities.*** Regulations have a safe harbor for treating a **real estate enterprise** as a qualified trade or business.

***Real estate enterprise*** **An interest in real property held for the production of rents and may consist of an interest in multiple properties. Taxpayers must either treat each property held for the production of rents as a separate enterprise or treat all similar properties held for the production of rents as a single enterprise. But commercial and residential real estate can't be part of the same enterprise. And taxpayers may not vary this treatment from year to year unless there has been a significant change in facts and circumstances.**

If the safe harbor is not applicable, a taxpayer can still try to establish that the real estate activities amount to a trade or business.

There are 4 conditions for the safe harbor to apply:

1. Separate books and records are maintained to reflect income and expenses for each rental real estate enterprise (RPE).
2. For an RPE in existence for less than 4 years, 250 or more hours of rental services are performed per year with respect to the rental enterprise. For other RPEs, in any 3 of the 5

Form **8995**

Department of the Treasury
Internal Revenue Service

**Qualified Business Income Deduction Simplified Computation**

▶ Attach to your tax return.

▶ Go to *www.irs.gov/Form8995* for instructions and the latest information.

OMB No. 1545-2294

**2020**

Attachment Sequence No. **55**

| Name(s) shown on return | Your taxpayer identification number |
|---|---|
| | |

**Note.** *You can claim the qualified business income deduction* **only** *if you have qualified business income from a qualified trade or business, real estate investment trust dividends, publicly traded partnership income, or a domestic production activities deduction passed through from an agricultural or horticultural cooperative. See instructions.*
*Use this form if your taxable income, before your qualified business income deduction, is at or below $163,300 ($326,600 if married filing jointly), and you aren't a patron of an agricultural or horticultural cooperative.*

| 1 | (a) Trade, business, or aggregation name | (b) Taxpayer identification number | (c) Qualified business income or (loss) |
|---|---|---|---|
| i | | | |
| ii | | | |
| iii | | | |
| iv | | | |
| v | | | |

| | | | | | |
|---|---|---|---|---|---|
| 2 | Total qualified business income or (loss). Combine lines 1i through 1v, column (c) | 2 | | | |
| 3 | Qualified business net (loss) carryforward from the prior year | 3 | ( ) | | |
| 4 | Total qualified business income. Combine lines 2 and 3. If zero or less, enter -0- | 4 | | | |
| 5 | Qualified business income component. Multiply line 4 by 20% (0.20) | | | 5 | |
| 6 | Qualified REIT dividends and publicly traded partnership (PTP) income or (loss) (see instructions) | 6 | | | |
| 7 | Qualified REIT dividends and qualified PTP (loss) carryforward from the prior year | 7 | ( ) | | |
| 8 | Total qualified REIT dividends and PTP income. Combine lines 6 and 7. If zero or less, enter -0- | 8 | | | |
| 9 | REIT and PTP component. Multiply line 8 by 20% (0.20) | | | 9 | |
| 10 | Qualified business income deduction before the income limitation. Add lines 5 and 9 | | | 10 | |
| 11 | Taxable income before qualified business income deduction | 11 | | | |
| 12 | Net capital gain (see instructions) | 12 | | | |
| 13 | Subtract line 12 from line 11. If zero or less, enter -0- | 13 | | | |
| 14 | Income limitation. Multiply line 13 by 20% (0.20) | | | 14 | |
| 15 | Qualified business income deduction. Enter the lesser of line 10 or line 14. Also enter this amount on the applicable line of your return ▶ | | | 15 | |
| 16 | Total qualified business (loss) carryforward. Combine lines 2 and 3. If greater than zero, enter -0- | | | 16 | ( ) |
| 17 | Total qualified REIT dividends and PTP (loss) carryforward. Combine lines 6 and 7. If greater than zero, enter -0- | | | 17 | ( ) |

**For Privacy Act and Paperwork Reduction Act Notice, see instructions.** Cat. No. 37806C Form **8995** (2020)

Note: This form is the 2020 version.

**FIGURE 21.1 Form 8995, Qualified Business Income Deduction—Simplified Computation**

consecutive taxable years that end with the taxable year, 250 or more hours of rental services are performed with respect to the rental real estate enterprise in any 3 out of 5 consecutive years.

3. The taxpayer maintains contemporaneous records, including time reports, logs, or similar documents, regarding the following: (i) hours of all services performed; (ii) description of all services performed; (iii) dates on which such services were performed; and (iv) who performed the services. If services with respect to the rental real estate enterprise are performed by employees or independent contractors, the taxpayer may provide a description of the rental services performed by such employee or independent contractor, the amount of time such employee or independent contractor generally spends performing such services

for the enterprise, and time, wage, or payment records for such employee or independent contractor. Such records are to be made available for inspection at the request of the IRS.

4. You or the relevant pass-through entity (RPE) attaches a statement to a timely filed original return (or an amended return for the 2018 taxable year only) for each taxable year in which you or the RPE relies on the safe harbor. An individual or RPE with more than one rental real estate enterprise relying on this safe harbor may submit a single statement, but the statement must list the required information separately for each rental real estate enterprise.

Form **8995-A** — **Qualified Business Income Deduction** — OMB No. 1545-2294 — **2020**

Department of the Treasury Internal Revenue Service

▶ Attach to your tax return.

▶ Go to *www.irs.gov/Form8995A* for instructions and the latest information.

Attachment Sequence No. **55A**

Name(s) shown on return | **Your taxpayer identification number**

**Note:** *You can claim the qualified business income deduction* **only** *if you have qualified business income from a qualified trade or business, real estate investment trust dividends, publicly traded partnership income, or a domestic production activities deduction passed through from an agricultural or horticultural cooperative. See instructions. Use this form if your taxable income, before your qualified business income deduction, is above $163,300 ($326,600 if married filing jointly), or you're a patron of an agricultural or horticultural cooperative.*

**Part I — Trade, Business, or Aggregation Information**

*Complete Schedules A, B, and/or C (Form 8995-A), as applicable, before starting Part I. Attach additional worksheets when needed. See instructions.*

| 1 | (a) Trade, business, or aggregation name | (b) Check if specified service | (c) Check if aggregation | (d) Taxpayer identification number | (e) Check if patron |
|---|---|---|---|---|---|
| A | | ☐ | ☐ | | ☐ |
| B | | ☐ | ☐ | | ☐ |
| C | | ☐ | ☐ | | ☐ |

**Part II — Determine Your Adjusted Qualified Business Income**

| | | | A | B | C |
|---|---|---|---|---|---|
| 2 | Qualified business income from the trade, business, or aggregation. See instructions | 2 | | | |
| 3 | Multiply line 2 by 20% (0.20). If your taxable income is $163,300 or less ($326,600 if married filing jointly), skip lines 4 through 12 and enter the amount from line 3 on line 13 | 3 | | | |
| 4 | Allocable share of W-2 wages from the trade, business, or aggregation | 4 | | | |
| 5 | Multiply line 4 by 50% (0.50) | 5 | | | |
| 6 | Multiply line 4 by 25% (0.25) | 6 | | | |
| 7 | Allocable share of the unadjusted basis immediately after acquisition (UBIA) of all qualified property | 7 | | | |
| 8 | Multiply line 7 by 2.5% (0.025) | 8 | | | |
| 9 | Add lines 6 and 8 | 9 | | | |
| 10 | Enter the greater of line 5 or line 9 | 10 | | | |
| 11 | W-2 wage and UBIA of qualified property limitation. Enter the smaller of line 3 or line 10 | 11 | | | |
| 12 | Phased-in reduction. Enter the amount from line 26, if any. See instructions | 12 | | | |
| 13 | Qualified business income deduction before patron reduction. Enter the greater of line 11 or line 12 | 13 | | | |
| 14 | Patron reduction. Enter the amount from Schedule D (Form 8995-A), line 6, if any. See instructions | 14 | | | |
| 15 | Qualified business income component. Subtract line 14 from line 13 | 15 | | | |
| 16 | Total qualified business income component. Add all amounts reported on line 15 ▶ | 16 | | | |

**For Privacy Act and Paperwork Reduction Act Notice, see separate instructions.** Cat. No. 71661B Form **8995-A** (2020)

Note: This form is the 2020 version.

**FIGURE 21.2** Form 8995-A, Qualified Business Income Deduction

Form 8995-A (2020) Page 2

**Part III Phased-in Reduction**

*Complete Part III only if your taxable income is more than $163,300 but not $213,300 ($326,600 and $426,600 if married filing jointly) and line 10 is less than line 3. Otherwise, skip Part III.*

| | | | | | A | B | C |
|---|---|---|---|---|---|---|---|
| 17 | Enter the amounts from line 3 | | | 17 | | | |
| 18 | Enter the amounts from line 10 | | | 18 | | | |
| 19 | Subtract line 18 from line 17 | | | 19 | | | |
| 20 | Taxable income before qualified business income deduction | 20 | | | | | |
| 21 | Threshold. Enter $163,300 ($326,600 if married filing jointly) | 21 | | | | | |
| 22 | Subtract line 21 from line 20 | 22 | | | | | |
| 23 | Phase-in range. Enter $50,000 ($100,000 if married filing jointly) | 23 | | | | | |
| 24 | Phase-in percentage. Divide line 22 by line 23 | 24 | % | | | | |
| 25 | Total phase-in reduction. Multiply line 19 by line 24 | | | 25 | | | |
| 26 | Qualified business income after phase-in reduction. Subtract line 25 from line 17. Enter this amount here and on line 12, for the corresponding trade or business | | | 26 | | | |

**Part IV Determine Your Qualified Business Income Deduction**

| | | | | | |
|---|---|---|---|---|---|
| 27 | Total qualified business income component from all qualified trades, businesses, or aggregations. Enter the amount from line 16 | 27 | | | |
| 28 | Qualified REIT dividends and publicly traded partnership (PTP) income or (loss). See instructions | 28 | | | |
| 29 | Qualified REIT dividends and PTP (loss) carryforward from prior years | 29 | ( ) | | |
| 30 | Total qualified REIT dividends and PTP income. Combine lines 28 and 29. If less than zero, enter -0- | 30 | | | |
| 31 | REIT and PTP component. Multiply line 30 by 20% (0.20) | 31 | | | |
| 32 | Qualified business income deduction before the income limitation. Add lines 27 and 31 ▶ | | | 32 | |
| 33 | Taxable income before qualified business income deduction | 33 | | | |
| 34 | Net capital gain. See instructions | 34 | | | |
| 35 | Subtract line 34 from line 33. If zero or less, enter -0- | | | 35 | |
| 36 | Income limitation. Multiply line 35 by 20% (0.20) | | | 36 | |
| 37 | Qualified business income deduction before the domestic production activities deduction (DPAD) under section 199A(g). Enter the smaller of line 32 or line 36 ▶ | | | 37 | |
| 38 | DPAD under section 199A(g) allocated from an agricultural or horticultural cooperative. Don't enter more than line 33 minus line 37 | | | 38 | |
| 39 | Total qualified business income deduction. Add lines 37 and 38 ▶ | | | 39 | |
| 40 | Total qualified REIT dividends and PTP (loss) carryforward. Combine lines 28 and 29. If zero or greater, enter -0- | | | 40 | ( ) |

Form **8995-A** (2020)

**FIGURE 21.2** ***(Continued)***

Rental services include:

- Advertising to rent or lease the real estate;
- Negotiating and executing leases;
- Verifying information contained in prospective tenant applications;
- Collecting rents;
- Daily operation, maintenance, and repair of the property;
- Management of the real estate;
- Purchasing materials; and
- Supervising employees and independent contractors.

Rental services do not include:

- Financial or investment management activities (such as arranging financing; procuring property; studying and reviewing financial statements or reports on operations; planning, managing, or constructing long-term capital improvements).
- Hours spent traveling to and from the real estate.

Rental services may be performed by owners or by employees, agents, and/or independent contractors of the owners.

*Excluded rental real estate arrangements.* Certain types of arrangements are not treated as real estate enterprises, including:

- A taxpayer's home if it is rented out at any time during the year.
- Real estate rented or leased under a triple net lease (i.e., one that requires the tenant or lessee to pay taxes, fees, and insurance, and to be responsible for maintenance activities of a property in addition to rent and utilities).

***Relying on the rental real estate safe harbor.*** If a taxpayer or a real estate enterprise is relying on the safe harbor, a statement must be attached to the return on which the QBI deduction is claimed. The statement must be signed under penalty of perjury by the taxpayer or an authorized representative.

***Statutory employees.*** Being an employee is not treated as a trade or business for purposes of the QBI deduction. However, statutory employees who file Schedule C to report their income and deductions can use the QBI deduction. See IRS FAQs at https://www.irs.gov/newsroom/tax-cuts-and-jobs-act-provision-11011-section-199a-qualified-business-income-deduction-faqs (Q22).

***Employees turned independent contractors.*** The trade or business of being an employee does not make a taxpayer eligible for the QBI deduction (i.e., the QBI deduction cannot be based on wage income). Final regulations have a presumption that an employee who becomes an independent contractor and continues to provide the same services for the same company is still in the business of being an employee and is not in a trade or business for purposes of the QBI deduction. There is a 3-year lookback for purposes of this presumption.

***Aggregation of multiple trades or businesses.*** You can aggregate certain multiple trades or businesses for purposes of applying the W-2 wage and UBIA of qualified property deduction limit as long as at least one person in the ownership group holds at least 50% ownership, directly or indirectly, in each trade or business being aggregated. You make this decision regardless of what your co-owners, if any, decide to do.

This ownership test must be met for the majority of the year (including the last day of the year). What's more, the trades or businesses being aggregated must satisfy various tests, including 2 of the following 3 listed factors:

1. The businesses provide products, property, or services that are the same (for example, a restaurant and a food truck) or customarily provided together (for example, a gas station and a car wash);
2. The businesses share facilities or share significant centralized business elements (for example, common personnel, accounting, legal, manufacturing, purchasing, human resources, or information technology resources); or
3. The businesses are operated in coordination with, or reliance on, other businesses in the aggregated group (for example, supply chain interdependencies).

No aggregation is permitted with a specified service trade or business (SSTB).

The fact that there is no aggregation in one year does not preclude aggregation in a subsequent year. But the election must be made on an original return; it cannot be made on an amended return (other than for 2018 returns).

Once there is an election to aggregate, it must continue unless there is a material change in circumstances that would cause a change to the aggregation (e.g., common ownership falls below

50%). But disaggregation isn't permanent, although trades or businesses that are disaggregated by the IRS may not be re-aggregated for the 3 subsequent taxable years.

Schedule B, *Aggregation of Business Operations,* accompanying Form 8995-A (see Figure 21.2) is used to aggregate a group of business activities. Provide a description of the aggregated businesses and an explanation of the factors supporting aggregation. If you have more than one aggregated group, use a separate Schedule B for each one.

## Qualified Business Income

The 20% deduction is figured on "qualified business income." This is income from a trade or business in the United States (including Puerto Rico). QBI is determined for each of an owner's separate businesses. Only items of income, gain, deduction, and loss allowed in determining taxable income are taken into account for qualified business income. Capital gains and losses (including Section 1231 gains explained in Chapter 6), certain dividends, and interest income are excluded.

**Example**

**An S corporation with one shareholder has $100,000 of ordinary income from inventory sales, and makes an expenditure of $25,000 that must be capitalized and amortized over 5 years under applicable tax rules. Qualified business income is $95,000 ($100,000 minus $5,000, which is the current-year ordinary amortization deduction). Qualified business income is not reduced by the entire amount of the capital expenditure, only by the amount deductible in determining the business's net income for the year.**

QBI does not include amounts paid by an S corporation treated as reasonable compensation to the owner. So if an S corporation has income of $100,000 and pays out $40,000 as salary to the owner, only $60,000 is treated as QBI. Similarly QBI does not include guaranteed payments by partnerships/LLCs for services rendered by an owner.

***Payments to partners.*** QBI does not include guaranteed payments for the use of capital or payments to partners for services performed.

***Net capital gain.*** For purposes of QBI, net capital gain means the excess of the net long-term capital gain over the net short-term capital loss, plus any qualified dividend income.

***Losses and deductions previously disallowed.*** If you have a net QBI loss for the year, you cannot take any QBI deduction. The net loss carries over to the following year and is taken into account in the QBI deduction calculation. It does not affect the deductibility of losses for other tax purposes. If you own multiple pass-through entities and at least one of which has negative QBI, it must be allocated among all positive QBI businesses.

Many businesses experienced losses in 2020 and they impact the QBI deduction for 2021. You may use a worksheet (Figure 21.3) to track and compute previously disallowed losses or deductions to be included in the QBI deduction calculation.

Losses and deductions previously disallowed $329,800 for married persons filing jointly, $164,925 for married persons filing separately, and $164,900 for singles and heads of households. (e.g., at-risk losses, passive activity losses, and, excess business losses), which are allowed in

Keep for Your Records

**QBI Loss Tracking Worksheet**

Use this worksheet to track losses or deductions suspended by other provisions and attributable to QBI using the FIFO method.

Code __________ [Enter the Code section limiting your loss]

**Part I Suspended & Allowed Losses**

| | A. Total suspended losses in year of disallowance | B. QBI fixed percentage | C. Prior year suspended losses allowed | D. Allowed losses limited by other Code sections |
|---|---|---|---|---|
| 1. Pre-2018 | | 0.00 % | | |
| 2. 2018 | | % | | |
| 3. 2019 | | % | | |
| 4. 2020 | | % | | |
| 5. Total | | | | |

**Part II Non-QBI Suspended and Allowed Losses**

**Allocable to Non-QBI**

| | E. Suspended losses | F. Allocated prior year suspended losses allowed | G(i). Utilized 2018 | G(ii). Utilized 2019 | G(iii). Utilized 2020 | H. Remaining suspended losses |
|---|---|---|---|---|---|---|
| 1. Pre-2018 | | | | | | |
| 2. 2018 | | | | | | |
| 3. 2019 | | | | | | |
| 4. 2020 | | | | | | |
| 5. Total | | | | | | |
| 6. Allocation of allowed losses limited by other Code sections . . . . . . . . . . . . . . | | | | | | |

**Part III QBI Suspended and Allowed Losses**

**Allocable to QBI**

| | I. Suspended losses | J. Allocated prior year suspended losses allowed | K(i). Utilized 2018 | K(ii). Utilized 2019 | K(iii). Utilized 2020 | L. Remaining suspended losses |
|---|---|---|---|---|---|---|
| 1. Pre-2018 | | | | | | |
| 2. 2018 | | | | | | |
| 3. 2019 | | | | | | |
| 4. 2020 | | | | | | |
| 5. Total | | | | | | |
| 6. Allocation of allowed losses limited by other Code sections . . . . . . . . . . . . . . | | | | | | |
| 7. Total prior year suspended losses allowed that must be included in QBI . . . . . . . . . | | | | | | |

**FIGURE 21.3** QBI Loss-Tracking Worksheet

the current year, generally are taken into account for purposes of computing QBI to the extent the disallowed loss or deduction is otherwise allowed by Section 199A. These losses are used in order from the oldest to the most recent on a first-in, first-out (FIFO) basis. They are treated as losses from a separate trade or business. However, losses or deductions that were disallowed, suspended, limited, or carried over from taxable years ending before January 1, 2018, are not taken into account in a later taxable year for purposes of computing QBI.

***Owner's personal deductions.*** In general, deductions related to a trade or business are taken into account for the QBI deduction. These include one-half of self-employment tax, the self-employed health insurance deduction, and the deduction for qualified retirement plan contributions on behalf of self-employed individuals as entered on lines 14, 15, and 16 on Schedule 1 of Form 1040 or 1040-SR.

Other personal deductions taken into account in figuring the QBI deduction include the deduction for unreimbursed partnership expenses, the interest expense to acquire partnership and S corporation interests, and state and local taxes are attributable to a trade or business.

***Multiple activities.*** If you own multiple qualified trades or businesses, you must calculate QBI from each and then net the amounts unless you elect to aggregate your businesses (explained earlier).

## Basic Limitations

Having qualified business income is no guarantee you'll be able to take the 20% deduction. There are various limitations that curtail or bar the deduction.

### *Income Threshold*

If your taxable income is over your applicable threshold listed earlier in this chapter without taking the qualified business deduction into account, then limitations apply.

For those with taxable income over the thresholds noted above, the deduction is limited to the *lesser* of (1) 20% of qualified business income, or (2) the greater of (a) 50% of **W-2 wages**, or (b) 25% of W-2 wages *plus* 2.5% of the **unadjusted basis immediately after acquisition (UBIA)** of qualified property. This is referred to as the "W-2 limitation."

---

***W-2 wages*** **Wages subject to income tax withholding, elective deferrals to 401(k) and similar plans, and deferred compensation. It includes amounts for S corporation owner-employees.**

***Unadjusted basis immediately after acquisition (UBIA)*** **This is depreciable tangible property for which the "depreciable period" has not ended. The depreciable period starts on the date the property is placed in service and ends on the later of 10 years after that date or the last day of the year of the property's recovery period. Additions to or improvements of property are treated as separate qualified property.**

---

***W-2 wages.*** There are 3 methods for calculating W-2 wages for QBI purposes:

- *Method 1: Unmodified Box method.* This is a simplified calculation. It is the lesser of total wages in Box 1 or 5 of all Forms W-2 filed with the Social Security Administration.
- *Method 2: Modified Box method.* This is the amount under Method 1 adjusted by subtracting amounts that are not wages for federal income tax withholding purposes (e.g., supplemental unemployment benefits) and adding amounts reported in Box 12 of the W-2.
- *Method 3: Tracking wages method.* This is actual wages subject to federal income tax withholding with certain modifications. More specifically, W-2 wages under method 3 are amounts subject to federal income tax withholding reported on W-2s filed with the Social Security Administration, plus amounts reported in Box 12 which are coded D, E, F, G, and S.

Wages listed on Form W-2 for statutory employees are not treated as part of W-2 wages for the QBI deduction. Wages taken into account for the QBI deduction are not determinative for purposes of FICA and FUTA taxes. Wages for the QBI deduction include wages under Code Sec. 3401(a), elective deferrals, and designated Roth contributions.

If a business has a short taxable year, only take into account wages paid and employee elective deferrals made during that period. Method 3 must be used for this purpose.

Wages for agricultural cooperatives are explained in Chapter 20.

***UBIA.*** In the case of property contributed to a partnership or S corporation in a nontaxable transfer (e.g., upon the creation of an S corporation through the transfer of property in exchange for stock), the property retains its UBIA on the date it was first placed in service by the contributing partner or shareholder. In other words, the transferee's UBIA in the qualified property is the same as the transferor's UBIA in the property, decreased by the amount of money received by the transferee in the transaction or increased by the amount of money paid by the transferee to acquire the property in the transaction.

For like-kind exchanges, the UBIA of like-kind property that a taxpayer receives is the UBIA of the relinquished property. However, if a taxpayer either receives money or property not of a like kind to the relinquished property (other property) or provides money or other property as part of the exchange, the taxpayer's UBIA in the relinquished property is adjusted:

- Downward by the excess of any money or the fair market value of other property received by the taxpayer in the exchange over the taxpayer's appreciation in the relinquished property (excess boot). Appreciation for this purpose is the excess of the relinquished property's fair market value on the date of the exchange over the fair market value of the relinquished property on the date of acquisition by the taxpayer.
- Upward by the amount of money or the FMV of other property transferred to reflect additional taxpayer investment.

The same rules apply for involuntary conversions.

For qualified property acquired from a decedent and immediately placed in service, the UBIA generally is the FMV at the time of the decedent's death. Also, this begins a new depreciable period for the property.

**Example**

**You are single and the sole owner of an S corporation in the construction business. You have taxable income of $500,000 and QBI of $600,000. Your corporation's W-2 wages are $300,000 and it has $1 million of unadjusted basis immediately after acquisition (UBIA) in qualified property. Your QBI deduction is $120,000, which is the lesser of:**

- **20% of QBI ($600,000 × 20% = $120,000), or**
- **The greater of 50% of W-2 wages of $150,000 ($300,000 × 50%) or UBIA of $25,000 (2.5% of $1 million).**

## Specified Service Trades or Businesses

There's another rule that effectively limits or bars the 20% deduction for income from services performed in specified service trades or businesses. A specified service trade or business (SSTB) is one involved in the performance of services in the fields of health, law, accounting, actuarial science, performing arts, consulting, athletics, financial services, brokerage services, or any business where its principal asset is the reputation or skill of one or more of its owners or employees.

Architecture and engineering specifically are *not* SSTBs. Clearly, doctors, lawyers, accountants, consultants, financial advisers, actuaries, athletes, and performing artists are specified service trades or businesses. Proposed regulations amplify these terms. For example, a bookkeeper, a return preparer, and an enrolled agent are classified as part of accounting, which is an SSTB.

But not all businesses that would seem to be within these specified fields are treated as SSTBs. For example, SSTBs do not include:

- Health clubs and spas providing exercise or conditioning to customers
- Insurance agents and brokers
- Manufacturing and/or sale of pharmaceuticals or medical devices
- Medical research
- Medical testing
- Payment processing for doctors offices, law firms, accounting firms, etc.
- Provision of services to support the performing arts (e.g., those who broadcast or otherwise disseminate video or audio of performing arts to the public)
- Real estate agents and brokers

According to regulations, the government is narrowly construing the catchall phrase of the owner's reputation. For example, a bicycle sales and repair shop staffed by employees with years of substantial skill and reputation is not an SSTB. A business that turns on an owner's reputation but is not one of the listed SSTBs will be treated as one only if the individual or partnership:

1. Receives income for endorsing products or services,
2. Licenses or receives income for the use of an individual's image, likeness, name, signature, voice, trademark, or other symbol associated with the individual's identity, or
3. Receives fees or income for appearing at an event or on radio, television, or other media format.

The IRS gives this example: A well-known chef who is the sole owner of several restaurants receives an endorsement fee of $500,000 for the use of his name on a line of utensils and cookware. Although being a chef and owning restaurants is not one of the SSTBs listed earlier, he is in the business of receiving endorsement income. Thus, the endorsement fee income for his skill and reputation is an SSTB. But the restaurant is not tainted by this and remains a non-SSTB.

***De minimis rule.*** A business is not an SSTB if less than 10% of gross receipts (5% if gross receipts are greater than $25 million) are attributable to the performance of services in a specified service activity.

***No chopping.*** You can't chop up a business in order to create QBI that isn't from an SSTB. An SSTB includes any trade or business with 50% or more common ownership (directly or indirectly) that provides 80% or more of its property or services to an SSTB. Additionally, if a trade or business has 50% or more common ownership with an SSTB, to the extent that the trade or business provides property or services to the commonly owned SSTB, the portion of the property or services provided to the SSTB is treated as an SSTB so that the income is treated as income from an SSTB.

**Example**

**A dentist owns a dental practice and also owns an office building. He rents half the building to the dental practice and half the building to unrelated persons. The renting of half of the building to the dental practice is treated as an SSTB.**

Also, SSTB includes any trade or business that provides 80% or more of its property or services to an SSTB if there is 50% or more common ownership of the trades or businesses. If a trade or business provides less than 80% of its property or services to an SSTB and there is 50% or more common ownership of the trades or businesses, that portion of the trade or business of providing property or services to the 50% or more commonly owned SSTB is treated as a part of the SSTB.

**Example**

**A law firm is a partnership that provides legal services to clients, owns its own office building, and employs its own administrative staff. This divides into 3 partnerships: one to perform legal services to clients, a second to own the office building rented to the first partnership, and a third to employ the administrative staff that provides services to the first partnership. All three of the partnerships are owned by the same people (the original owners of the law firm). Because there is 50% or more common ownership of each of the 3 partnerships, with partnership 2 providing substantially all of its property to partnership 1, and partnership 3 providing substantially all of its services to partnership 1, all the partnerships are treated as one SSTB.**

If a trade or business that would not otherwise be treated as an SSTB has 50% or more common ownership with an SSTB, and has shared expenses with the SSTB (e.g., wages and overhead expenses), then it is treated as incidental to and, therefore, part of the SSTB if the gross receipts of the trade or business represents no more than 5% of the total combined gross receipts of the trade or business and the SSTB in a taxable year.

**Example**

**A dermatologist provides medical services to patients through Dermatology LLC. In addition to providing medical services, Dermatology LLC also sells skin care products to its patients. The same employees and office space are used for the medical services and sale of skin care products. The gross receipts with respect to the skin care product sales do not exceed 5% of the gross receipts of Dermatology LLC. Accordingly, the sale of the skin care products is treated as incidental to the LLC's SSTB of performing services in the field of health and is treated as part of such SSTB.**

When taxable income in 2021 exceeds the applicable threshold, then only a percentage of QBI, W-2 wages, and the unadjusted basis of property can be taken into account. The amount of QBI that can be taken into account phases out over the next $100,000 for joint filers or $50,000 for other filers. In other words, for owners of these SSTBs with taxable income within the phase-out range, only part of QBI can be taken into account. The amount of excess taxable income is converted into a percentage for determining the amount of QBI taken into account.

**Example**

**If a consultant who files a joint return has taxable income in 2021 of $375,000 so that excess taxable income is $45,200 ($375,000 – $329,800 threshold for joint filers), he'd be able to figure the deduction by using only 54.8% of qualified business income; the other 45.2% cannot be taken into account ($45,200 excess/$100,000 phase-out range).**

The deduction is lost entirely by those in an SSTB when taxable income in 2021 exceeds $429,800 for married persons filing jointly, $214,925 for married persons filing separately, and $214,900 for singles and heads of households; all qualified business income is disregarded. The limitation for a specified service trade or business is figured on Schedule D, *Specified Service Trades or Businesses*, of Form 8995-A.

## Other Limitations

Even after you jump through all of these hoops, the deduction cannot be more than 20% of taxable income minus net capital gains. And if an owner has a loss from one or more businesses, it's carried forward to the following year, and any 20% deduction allowed in the following year is reduced by the carryover loss.

## Partnerships and S Corporations

The deduction is computed at the owner level. Each partner takes into account his or her allocable share of each item of income, gain, deduction, and loss. Each shareholder takes into account his or her pro rata share of these items. Each owner also takes into account his or her share of W-2 wages (to the extent of the owner's share of wage expenses) and the unadjusted basis immediately after acquisition (to the extent of the owner's allocable share of depreciation).

Special partnership basis adjustments (under Code Secs. 734(b) or 743(b)) are not treated as separate qualified property.

The aggregation election to treat multiple businesses as one (as explained earlier in this chapter) is made by the owner and not by the entity.

## Understatement Penalty

If you claim the qualified business income deduction and have a substantial understatement of income tax, you may be subject to a 20% penalty. A substantial understatement for this purpose means that the understatement is more than 5% of the tax required to be shown on your return. The penalty is 5% of the proper tax, or $5,000, whichever is greater.

### *Self-Employed*

The QBI deduction is figured on the 2021 version of Form 8995, *Qualified Business Income Deduction Simplified Computation* (Figure 21.1), if your taxable income in 2021 is below $329,800 for married persons filing jointly, $164,925 for married persons filing separately, and $164,900 for singles and heads of households. If your taxable income is higher, use the 2021 version Form 8995-A, *Qualified Business Income Deduction* (Figure 21.2). There are 4 schedules accompanying this form:

1. Schedule A, *Specified Service Trades or Businesses*
2. Schedule B, *Aggregation of Business Operations*
3. Schedule C, *Loss Netting and Carryforward*
4. Schedule D, *Special Rules for Patrons of Agricultural or Horticultural Cooperatives*

The QBI deduction is entered on line 10, page 1 of Form 1040 or 1040-SR; it is subtracted from adjusted gross income to arrive at taxable income.

### Partnerships and LLCs

The information necessary to enable owners to figure their shares of this deduction is reported to them on Schedule K-1 (codes for this purpose are listed on page 2 of this schedule). Owners then figure the deduction (explained above) and enter it on line 10, page 1 of Form 1040 or 1040-SR.

### S Corporations

The information necessary to enable owners to figure their share of this deduction is reported to them on Schedule K-1 (codes for this purpose are listed on page 2 of this schedule). Owners then figure the deduction (explained above) and enter it on page 2 of Form 1040 or 1040-SR.

CHAPTER 22

# Miscellaneous Business Deductions


Other Business Expenses in General 417
Moving Expenses 417
Educational Expenses 418
Charitable Contributions Made by Your Business 420
Licenses and Permits 424
Dues and Subscriptions 425
Legal and Professional Fees 425
Bank and Merchant Fees 427
Supplies, Materials, and Office Expenses 428
Uniforms and Clothing 429
Insurance 430
Commissions 433
Outsourced Workers 433
Payments to Directors and Independent Contractors 433
Penalties, Fines, and Damages 433
Meal Costs for Day-Care Providers 434
Expenses of Persons with Disabilities 435
Dividends-Received Deduction 435
Foreign Housing Deduction 436
Other Expenses 438
Checklists of Deductible and Nondeductible Items 438


Some miscellaneous business items defy classification. They do not necessarily fall into categories for which there is a line on the tax return, nor into any of the other chapters in this book. Still, you may be able to deduct them.

Some of the deductions in this chapter apply only to individuals (and generally limited to those who are self-employed); others apply only to corporations. Review all of the categories to see which deductions may apply to you. Checklists of deductible and nondeductible expenses are found in Table 22.3, page 438.

For more information on other business expenses, see IRS Publication 535, *Business Expenses*.

## Other Business Expenses in General

You generally may deduct any business expense if it is considered ordinary and necessary. It need not fit neatly into a specific category as long as it meets 3 tests:

1. The expense must be related to the business you carry on (be it employment or a business you own).
2. The expense cannot be a capital expenditure. *Capital expenditures* are costs related to the acquisition of a capital asset. For example, you generally cannot deduct the cost of improvements to property. These costs are capital in nature. However, some capital expenditures can be recovered through deductions for depreciation or amortization or under special rules (see Chapter 14).
3. The expense must be **ordinary** and **necessary**.

---

***Ordinary*** **Common and accepted in your business.**

***Necessary*** **Helpful or appropriate to your business. To be necessary, an expense need not be indispensable. For example, if you send flowers to your employee in the hospital, you may deduct the cost of the flowers.**

---

Another requirement that applies to all deductions is that the expenses must be reasonable in amount. What is reasonable is a question of fact based on the particular situation. Checklists of various miscellaneous deductions related to your business status can be found toward the end of this chapter.

For 2018 through 2025, employees cannot take a deduction for unreimbursed employee business expenses, such as driving for work, maintaining a home office, or paying union dues. The miscellaneous itemized deduction subject to the 2%-of-adjusted-gross-income floor is suspended during this period.

## Moving Expenses

If you move your business to another location (e.g., you relocate your offices to larger quarters) or you move equipment to another location (e.g., you move machinery from one plant to another), your moving costs are deductible. There is no requirement that your new location be any special distance from the old one.

In general, if you personally move from one home to another, you cannot deduct the cost of moving your furnishings and family because these are personal expenses. Prior to 2018, there was a personal deduction allowed if the moving was required for work. However, this deduction has been suspended through 2025. (The only exception is for relocations of military personnel.)

If you are an employer who pays the cost of relocating an employee in 2021, you cannot treat the payments, including any reimbursements to the employee, as a tax-free fringe benefit. However, you can deduct the cost as wages because it is taxable compensation to the employee.

## Educational Expenses

If you are self-employed and take educational courses, you may be able deduct the cost as a business expense. If you are an employee, you can only deduct tuition and fees. Or you may qualify for tax credits, explained later under personal education incentives, whether or not you are an employee or self-employed. The tax law clearly states what types of educational courses are deductible and what types are not.

As a self-employed individual you can deduct education courses as a business expense that are primarily undertaken to:

- *Maintain or improve skills required in your business*. If you haven't worked in a while, education costs may not be deductible.
- *Meet the requirements of applicable law or regulations imposed as a condition of conducting your work*. For example, continuing professional education courses are deductible as business expenses.

You cannot deduct education courses designed to:

- *Meet minimum educational requirements*. This precludes you from deducting the cost of obtaining any professional degree in law, accounting, medicine, or dentistry. The fact that you may already be performing service in an employment status within the profession does not necessarily mean that you have met the minimum education requirements. For example, if a second-year law student is hired to do research, the cost of the third year of law school is not a deductible education expense since the student has not yet met the minimum education requirements to practice law (3 years of law school and admission to the bar). If new minimum requirements are imposed after you have met old minimum requirements, however, the cost of taking the additional courses is deductible.
- *Qualify you for a new business*. A mere change in duties is not treated as a new business if it involves the same general type of work. For example, a certified public accountant (CPA) who attends law school at night cannot deduct the cost of courses, since this leads to a new line of work—law. This is so even if the CPA never plans to practice law. A bookkeeper who takes courses to get a B.A. in accounting cannot deduct education expenses because the courses lead to a new business of being an accountant. However, a practicing attorney who takes courses toward an LL.M. can deduct expenses because the courses do not lead to a new line of work.
- *Relate to something that does not pertain directly to your business*. For example, an attorney could not deduct the cost of an English course that he argued would help him write better briefs. The courses were not directly related to his business of law even though they were helpful to his work.

### Deductible Expenses

If education costs are deductible, the following types of expenses may be deducted:

- Tuition and fees
- Books
- Travel costs to and from school. If you drive, you can use the standard mileage rate for business, which is 56¢ per mile in 2021.

These travel costs include going to or from home to school, as well as travel between work and school. If you attend a seminar at a resort, see Chapter 8 to determine whether or to what extent you may deduct your education-related travel costs.

However, you may not deduct the cost of travel as a form of education. Thus, for example, an architect cannot deduct the cost of a trip to Rome to look at ancient Roman architecture as an educational expense. However, if the architect takes education courses in Rome on architecture, then the cost of the trip may become deductible.

**NOTE**

**You cannot deduct your education costs if you claim an education credit for the same expenses, as explained later.**

### *Employer-Paid Education*

If an employer pays for the cost of the courses (and even student loan repayment through 2025), this may be a tax-free fringe benefit on which you are not taxed. Such benefits are discussed in Chapter 7. If you have a C corporation and the corporation pays your education costs, the corporation can deduct the costs whether or not you are taxed on the benefits.

### *Personal Education Incentives*

There are a number of personal tax incentives designed to encourage higher education, whether or not it is work-related. Here are some to consider:

- *American opportunity tax credit*. There is a credit per student of up to $2,500 for the cost of tuition and fees for the first 4 years of college (100% of the first $2,000 of these costs, plus 25% of the next $2,000). The full credit can be claimed for the taxpayer, spouse, or dependents, but only if modified adjusted gross income (MAGI) is not over $80,000 if single, or $160,000 on a joint return. The credit phases out for MAGI between $80,000 and $90,000 if single, or $160,000 to $180,000 on a joint return. No credit can be claimed if MAGI is over $90,000 if single, or $180,000 on a joint return. No credit can be claimed by a married person who files a separate return. The credit is 40% refundable (you can receive a refund for up to this portion even though it exceeds your tax liability for the year).
- *Lifetime learning credit*. There is a credit of up to $2,000 (20% of up to $10,000) per return for the cost of tuition and fees for any college, graduate school, or vocational training. Like the American opportunity credit, the lifetime learning credit can be claimed for the taxpayer, spouse, or dependents, but only if modified AGI for 2021 is below a threshold amount (the limits for the American opportunity credit apply for the lifetime learning credit). Unlike the American opportunity credit, there is no limit on the number of years you can claim this credit. This credit cannot be claimed if the American opportunity credit is elected for any student (but you can claim the credit for any other eligible student). For example, if your child begins college and you take a graduate course, you can elect the American opportunity credit for your child and the lifetime learning credit for yourself if your modified AGI is below the threshold amount.
- *Interest on student loans*. Interest of up to $2,500 on student loans is deductible as an adjustment to gross income on Form 1040 or 1040-SR. The full deduction can only be claimed if your AGI in 2021 is below a threshold amount ($70,000 for singles or $140,000 on a joint return). The deduction phases out over the next $15,000 of adjusted gross income for singles or $30,000 for joint filers, so that no deduction can be claimed once adjusted gross income exceeds $85,000 for singles or $170,000 on a joint return.

- *Penalty-free IRA withdrawals*. Withdrawals used to pay qualified higher education costs by those under age 59½ are not subject to the 10% premature distribution penalty. However, using IRA funds for education is still costly since the distribution is subject to regular income tax and you lose the opportunity for tax-free compounding.

## Charitable Contributions Made by Your Business

Your business may contribute cash or property to various charities. In general, the amount of your charitable contribution is deductible, but there are certain limits and requirements that must be followed. Donations of your time and effort are not deductible.

**Example**

**An attorney performs services for a charitable organization. She cannot deduct the value of her uncompensated legal services as a charitable contribution.**

Charitable giving and other activities can be a business plus even if no deduction is allowed. For example, donating items for which no deduction is allowed (as explained later), such as a fully depreciated computer or cell phone, can still benefit a charity and the people it serves. While you cannot deduct the value of your time spent when serving on the board of a nonprofit organization (you can claim only a personal charitable contribution deduction for your out-of-pocket expenses), you not only serve a cause but also gain visibility and make important connections in your community that can benefit your business in the long run.

Deductions for charitable contributions by individuals and corporations are limited by income. More specifically, a 2021 charitable deduction for cash donations made by a partnership, which is claimed by a partner on his or her personal return to the extent of the partnership interest, is up to 100% of adjusted gross income if so elected when itemizing personal deductions (or up to $300 per taxpayer if the standard deduction is claimed). The 100% limit must be elected and the deductible amount is reduced by other charitable contributions for 2021. Corporate deductions for cash donations are generally limited to 25% of taxable income (instead of the usual 10% limit). Special deduction limits apply to donations of conservation easements as explained later in this chapter.

### *Unincorporated Businesses*

Individuals may deduct up to $300 for cash contributions if they claim the standard deduction ($600 on a joint return), or elect to deduct cash contributions up to 100% of adjusted gross income contributions if they itemize deductions (AGI limits apply to other types of donations). For example, if you are a partner and the partnership makes a charitable contribution, the contribution is passed through to you as a separately stated item and if you itemize deductions, take the charitable contribution as a deduction on Schedule A of Form 1040 or 1040-SR. The same is true for members of LLCs and shareholders in S corporations. Self-employed individuals who file Schedule C do not take business-related charitable contributions as a business expense. Similarly, an employee who makes a charitable contribution at work (e.g., amounts are withheld from pay as contributions to the United Fund or another charity) deducts the contribution up to $300 or $600 if not itemizing or on Schedule A as a charitable contribution (this is not an employee business expense).

Donations of property by a partnership, limited liability company, or S corporation can affect the owner's basis in his or her business interest.

**Example**

**If a partnership owned equally by 2 individuals donates a painting worth $80,000 that the partnership bought for $50,000, each partner can deduct $40,000 on his or her individual return (50% of $80,000). Each partner must also reduce the basis in the partnership interest by $25,000 (50% of the property's basis). An S corporation shareholder's stock basis must be reduced by his or her pro rata share of the corporation's adjusted basis of the contributed property (not its value at the time of the donation).**

Sometimes it is not clear whether an expense is a charitable contribution or some other kind of business expense. For example, if you pay to run an ad in a journal of a tax-exempt organization, the expense may be an advertising expense rather than a charitable contribution.

Unincorporated businesses that donate food inventory can claim the same enhanced deduction as C corporations (explained later in this chapter).

Unused charitable contributions by noncorporate taxpayers can be carried forward for up to 5 years. For cash donations, the applicable limitation for carryforwards is 60% of adjusted gross income.

**NOTE**

**Employers that have leave-based donation programs in 2021 may take a charitable contribution deduction for cash donations of unused leave donated to organizations providing COVID-19 relief as explained in Chapter 7.**

### *Corporations*

Corporations may make charitable contributions and deduct them on their returns. The contributions must be made to public charities. The corporation cannot take a deduction if the organization receiving the contribution benefits any private shareholder or individual.

The corporation's accounting method may affect the timing of the deduction for a contribution. Cash method corporations deduct the contribution only in the year it is actually made. Corporations on the accrual method can choose to deduct contributions made within 2½ months after the close of its year as having been made in the prior year. To do this, the board of directors of the corporation must authorize the payment of the contribution within 2½ months after the close of the year. This authorization should be reflected in the corporate minutes.

As mentioned earlier, for 2021 a C corporation can deduct only charitable contributions that total no more than 25% of its taxable income. Taxable income for purposes of this limitation does not include the deduction for contributions, the deduction for dividends received and dividends paid, net operating loss (NOL) carrybacks for farming businesses, and capital loss carrybacks.

Contributions in excess of the 25% limit can be carried forward for up to 5 years. If the corporation makes contributions in the carryforward years, the current deductions are taken into account before the carryforwards. Carryforwards are limited to 10% of taxable income. Carryovers of excess charitable contributions cannot be deducted in a subsequent year if they increase a net operating loss carryover. Keep this rule in mind: NOL carryovers are used from the earliest year, while charitable contributions for the current year are taken into account first.

Corporations cannot claim a charitable contribution deduction for amounts given to an organization that conducts lobbying activities on matters of direct financial interest to their business.

***Special rule for S corporations.*** When an S corporation gives appreciated property, the shareholder can deduct his or her share of the fair market value of the property. However, under a special rule, the shareholder reduces his or her basis in stock of the corporation only by his or her share of the corporation's adjusted basis in the property given.

### Inventory

If you donate items from your inventory, the deduction is limited to the fair market value (FMV) of the property on the date of the contribution, reduced by any gain that would have been realized if you had sold the property at its FMV instead of donating it. Be sure to remove from opening inventory any contributions you make (namely, the costs for the donated property included in prior years). These costs are not part of the cost of goods sold for the year in which the contribution is made.

If you have excess or dated inventory that you wish to dispose of but do not know of an organization interested in it, consider working with an organization that can find a place for your inventory, such as:

- Good 360 at https://good360.org
- National Association for the Exchange of Industrial Resources at https://www.naeir.org/
- Waste to Charity at https://wastetocharity.org/

### Donations for the Ill, Needy, or Infants

If a C corporation donates items from inventory to a public charity or an operating foundation where the inventory will be used for the care of the ill, the needy, or infants, add to the deduction 50% of the difference between the basis and the FMV of the inventory (but not more than 200% of the basis of the property). The donations must be for necessities of life, such as food, clothing, and shelter, so donations of cosmetics won't qualify for this special inventory rule. This special inventory rule does not apply to S corporations.

### Certain Donations of Scientific Property and Computers

A C corporation can claim a larger deduction than ordinarily allowed if certain scientific property used for research is donated to an institution of higher education. This special rule allows the corporation to increase its deduction by 50% of the difference between its basis and the FMV of the property (but not more than 200% of the basis of the property). This special deduction is not allowed for S corporations, personal holding companies, or service organizations.

### Food Inventory Donations

Donations of food qualify for a deduction that's limited. Generally, it can be increased by 50% of the difference between its basis and the FMVI of the property (but not more than 200% of the basis of the property) and this is subject to a limit based on net income. For 2021 donations, the deduction is 25% of net income from the business (it declines to the usual 15% after 2021 unless Congress extends it). To qualify, food must be apparently wholesome and meet all labeling standards.

### Donations of Conservation Easement

Generally, a charitable deduction up to 50% of a contribution base is allowed for donations of conservation easements. A conservation easement is a restriction placed on real property for a public purpose to preserve the land or building for future generations. However, farmers and ranchers can claim a deduction up to 100% of their contribution basis (essentially adjusted gross income). And, if they cannot use up all of the deduction in the year of the contribution (because of adjusted gross income limits on contribution deductions by individuals), they can can effectively carry forward the excess for up to 15 years.

Syndicated conservation easements are being scrutinized by the IRS. They may be abusive, resulting in the loss of deductions for investors, plus penalties. They are not discussed further in this book.

### *Appraisal Rules for Corporate Donations*

All corporations that donate property valued at more than $5,000 must obtain a qualified appraisal. However, certain property donations are exempt from this requirement: donations of inventory, publicly traded stock, intellectual property, and vehicles for which a written statement is obtained from the charity. If the deduction for a donation is more than $500,000, the appraisal must be attached to the return.

### *Contributions of Intellectual Property*

All types of businesses may make charitable contributions of their intellectual property. The deduction for such contributions is limited to the lesser of the basis of the property or its fair market value. Intellectual property includes:

- Patents, copyrights, and trademarks
- Trade names, trade secrets, and know-how
- Software
- Other similar property or applications

#### ADDITIONAL DEDUCTION BASED ON INCOME

You can also deduct an amount based on the income derived by the charity from the intellectual property for up to 10 years. The amount of the additional deduction is the applicable percentage found in Table 22.1 (the table runs for 12 years because of the potential for a donee to have a fiscal year or a short tax year).

No additional deduction can be claimed after the legal life of the intellectual property ends or after the 10th anniversary of the donation, whichever happens first. Donations to private foundations do not qualify.

How will you know how much income the organization derived from your donated property? At the time you make the donation, inform the organization that you intend to claim the additional deduction. The organization is then required to file Form 8899, *Notice of Income from Donated Intellectual Property*, showing the income it derived from the property.

#### PLANNING FOR INTELLECTUAL PROPERTY

If you own intellectual property, should you sell it or donate it? Which produces the greater tax benefit? Clearly both personal and tax considerations come into play.

Keep in mind that a self-created patent, invention, model or design (whether or not patented), or secret formula or process is not treated as capital gain property. A sale of such property results in ordinary income (not capital gain). This treatment has long applied to other self-created intellectual property, including copyrights and literary, musical, or artistic compositions (although musicians can elect to treat their compositions and copyrights as capital gain property). All in all, planning for the transfer of intellectual property is complicated and you should seek professional advice.

**TABLE 22.1 Applicable Percentage for Additional Contribution**

| Tax Year | Deductible Percentage |
|---|---|
| 1 | 100% |
| 2 | 100% |
| 3 | 90% |
| 4 | 80% |
| 5 | 70% |
| 6 | 60% |
| 7 | 50% |
| 8 | 40% |
| 9 | 30% |
| 10 | 20% |
| 11 | 10% |
| 12 | 10% |

### *Special Deduction for Whaling Captains*

Those recognized by the Alaska Eskimo Whaling Commission as whaling captains charged with the responsibilities of sanctioned whaling activities can deduct reasonable and necessary whaling expenses as a charitable contribution deduction. The deduction is limited to $10,000 per year.

### *Payments Made Under State or Local Tax Credit Programs*

State and local workarounds created to allow residents to transform the limited federal income tax deduction for state and local taxes (SALT) into a federal charitable contribution is viewed by the IRS as *quid pro quos*, so that a federal charitable contribution deduction is barred (except for de minimis amounts). However, business taxpayers who make business-related payments to charities or government entities can deduct them in full as long as the payments are ordinary and necessary business expenses.

## Licenses and Permits

If you obtain licenses and permits in the course of your business, the cost is usually deductible. However, there are 2 exceptions:

1. Licenses for vehicles cannot be deducted if the deduction for vehicle expenses is based on the IRS standard mileage allowance (you must use the actual expense method to account for vehicle costs if you want to deduct licenses).
2. Permits obtained for the construction of realty are a capital cost added to the basis of the property and recovered through depreciation.

### *Customs Expenses*

If you import or export wares, you may incur special customs-related costs. These include customs fees, duties, and tariffs, as well as charges by customs brokers and international handlers. All of these fees are deductible. However, when they relate to inventory purchases, you may be able to add to inventory costs and recover them as part of the cost of goods sold.

## Dues and Subscriptions

### *Dues*

Certain dues are deductible; others are not. Dues paid to professional, business, service, or civic organizations are deductible (other than any portion allocable to lobbying activities as specified by organization), such as dues to:

- American Bar Association, American Institute of CPAs, American Medical Association, National Association of Enrolled Agents, and other professional associations
- Chambers of commerce, business leagues, trade associations, boards of trade, real estate boards, and business lunch clubs
- Civitan, Rotary, Lions, and other civic organizations

However, no deduction is allowed for dues if the principal purpose of the organization is to entertain or provide entertainment facilities for members or their guests. Examples of such nondeductible dues include dues paid for athletic, sporting, airline, hotel, or other recreational clubs, even though membership is for business.

### *Subscriptions*

The cost of subscriptions to business or professional publications is deductible. However, if you are on the cash basis and prepay subscriptions—that is, your subscription covers a period of more than one year—your deduction may be limited to the cost related to one year. You can deduct an allocable portion of the subscription cost in each succeeding year.

**Example**

**In January 2021, you pay for a 3-year subscription to a trade magazine. Your total cost is $150. (Assume you are on a calendar year for reporting your income and deductions.) In 2021, you can deduct $50 (one-third of your total cost). In 2022 and again in 2023, you can deduct $50, the remaining portion of your subscription cost.**

## Legal and Professional Fees

Legal and professional fees related to your business are deductible. Professional fees may include, for example, not only legal fees but also accounting fees, actuarial fees, systems analyst fees, and appraisal fees.

### Legal Fees

Legal fees for business matters generally are deductible as an ordinary and necessary business expense. Examples of deductible legal fees include fees incurred for:

- Assistance in collecting outstanding accounts payable
- Defending against or pursuing a claim of infringement of intellectual property
- Defending against charges of mismanagement of a retirement plan
- Defending against shareholder allegations of misconduct
- Defending against wrongful discharge actions
- Obtaining an IRS ruling
- Tax advice

Not all legal fees are currently deductible. Examples of nondeductible legal fees include fees incurred for:

- *Acquiring a capital asset*. The fees are added to the basis of the asset. For example, if you pay attorney's fees to handle the closing when you buy your office building, the fees become part of the basis of the office building and are recovered through depreciation.
- *Actions that are personal in nature*, such as legal fees to pursue a personal injury action, even if the injury occurred during a business trip; to prepare a will even if it includes a business; and to settle a divorce even if it relates to reserving your interest in a business. The portion of fees that can be allocated to tax advice, however, is deductible.
- *Incorporating a business or setting up a partnership or LLC*. These costs are treated as incorporation fees or organizational costs for a partnership, and are currently deductible up to a set dollar limit; excess amounts must be amortized, as discussed in Chapter 14.
- *Sexual harassment or abuse*. No deduction may be claimed for a settlement or payment, or legal fees related to it, for sexual harassment or sexual abuse if the matter is subject to a nondisclosure agreement.

### Accounting and Tax Preparation Fees

If you pay an accountant to show you how to set up the books for your business or to keep your books for you, the accounting fees are deductible. Also deductible are fees for accounting advice, such as advice on whether to change your method of accounting or your method of inventory. The same is true for fees for accounting representation at an IRS audit. If you use a regular accounting system, such as QuickBooks Online or Xero, or an automated bookkeeping service, such as Botkeeper, your monthly subscription costs are deductible.

If you pay an accountant or other tax professional (paid preparer) to complete your company's tax return or contest a tax deficiency for your business (Form 1065, Form 1120, or Form 1120-S), the cost is fully deductible on the appropriate return. If you are self-employed, the allocable cost of preparing Schedule C or contesting a tax deficiency related to it is a deductible business expense that can be claimed on Schedule C. The balance of tax preparation fees is not deductible as a miscellaneous itemized expense on Schedule A, because of the suspension of this itemized deduction for 2018 through 2025.

Accounting fees incurred in investigating whether to buy a business are not currently deductible but may qualify as start-up expenses. The treatment of start-up costs is discussed in Chapter 14.

### *Recovering Legal Fees and Other Costs from the Government*

If you are involved in a tax dispute with the IRS and you win, you may be able to make the government pay any reasonable costs of your tax contest. You must have exhausted your administrative remedies and have substantially prevailed in your tax dispute. The IRS has the burden of proving that its position in going after you was substantially justified. If the IRS did not follow published regulations, revenue rulings, revenue procedures, information releases, notices or announcements, private letter rulings, determination letters, or technical advice memoranda issued to you, then there is a rebuttable presumption that the IRS's position was not substantially justified. Also, the fact that the IRS has lost in other appellate courts on substantially similar issues must be taken into account in determining whether the IRS's position was not substantially justified. If you succeed, you can recover attorney's fees at the rate of $210 per hour in 2021. In limited circumstances, a higher award may be possible.

If you are successful in your claim to recover costs from the government (e.g., if the IRS fails to prove that it was substantially justified in its position), you cannot also take a deduction for these costs. If you have already taken a deduction for your costs, you must include the government's award in your income.

The opportunity to recover legal fees from the government is limited to an individual with a net worth below $2 million. When married persons file jointly, jointly petition the court for a recovery of costs, and incur the costs jointly, each spouse qualifies for a separate $2 million net worth limit. However, the limit will be evaluated jointly. When they file jointly but petition the court separately and have separate costs, the limit is evaluated separately. In the case of businesses, the net worth requirement is below $7 million and fewer than 500 employees.

### *Lobbying Costs*

Fees paid after December 22, 2017, through 2025, to professional lobbyists to influence legislation on the federal, state, or local level are not deductible. This bar includes lobbying local councils and other government bodies, which had been deductible prior to 2018.

## Bank and Merchant Fees

All banking fees for your business bank account are deductible. These include not only monthly account maintenance and check processing fees, but also ATM charges, check printing costs, online banking charges, account closing fees, and other special charges (e.g., returned check fees). These fees can amount to several hundred dollars a month. You can reduce or eliminate these costs by banking with an institution that is pro–small business (e.g., offers free business checking) or by maintaining a minimum monthly balance.

Like banking fees, merchant authorization costs to process credit and debit cards are deductible. These costs include an initial setup cost, processing fees per transaction, monthly account maintenance costs, and other charges.

**NOTE**
**Financial institutions processing merchant accounts, including PayPal and Amazon Payment, must report transactions to the IRS on Form 1099-K; there is a small business exception. For more details, see Appendix A.**

If you accept PayPal as a payment method for sales, you can deduct PayPal fees as well. While there are no setup or monthly fees, you pay a per-transaction charge of 30¢ plus a percentage of the transaction ranging from a high of 2.9% to a low of 1.9%, depending on the size of the transaction, with special charges for international transactions. Amazon Payments has a similar fee structure for merchants, with 30¢ per transaction, plus a percentage of the transaction up to 2.9% for domestic transactions (higher for cross-border processing).

If you accept payment in Bitcoin, BitcoinCash, or other digital payment, this is treated as a property transaction (not as if you accepted payment in currency). Processing fees are part of the cost of the transaction (i.e., are factored into basis or amount received).

## Supplies, Materials, and Office Expenses

**NOTE**
**The IRS has noted that overstated deductions for items, including supplies and materials, account for up to $30 billion in unpaid taxes each year, so expect careful scrutiny of a deduction for supplies if a return is examined.**

The cost of incidental supplies and materials used in your business is deductible as an ordinary and necessary business expense. This includes copy paper, cleaning supplies, and other miscellaneous costs. However, if you are on the cash basis and order such large quantities that the supplies or materials will last you more than a year, you can deduct only the portion of the cost related to supplies or materials expected to be used within the year.

Supplies used directly or indirectly in manufacturing goods are part of the cost of goods sold (see Chapter 4). The purchase of a capital asset (an item with a useful life greater than one year) cannot be written off merely by calling it a supply (although it, too, may be deducted through expensing, as explained in Chapter 14). Also, the cost of certain tangible property that might otherwise be capitalized and recovered through depreciation may be treated as currently deductible nonincidental materials and supplies by using a de minimis safe harbor for tangible personal property (also covered in Chapter 14). If this de mimimis safe harbor is used (and, like most small businesses, you do not have an applicable financial statement), then you can deduct up to $2,500 per item or invoice if you make an election on your return (i.e., attach your own election statement as described in Chapter 14).

**Example**

**You own a 30-room motel and buy ironing boards for each room at a cost of $40 each. Normally, these items must be capitalized and recovered through depreciation (or first-year expensing if applicable), but under the de minimis safe harbor you can treat the $1,200 ($40 per invoice × 30 rooms) as nonincidental materials and supplies.**

Usually, you need to retain receipts or other proof of any supplies and materials you deduct. However, the Tax Court in one case allowed a deduction for some office supplies based on the *Cohan* rule (explained in Chapter 4). Despite lack of receipts, the Tax Court estimated the amount of deductible expenses in this case.

### *Postage and Shipping*

The costs of postage, delivery charges, courier and messenger charges, and other mailing and shipping costs are deductible. However, freight charges to obtain inventory are part of the cost of goods sold. Similarly, freight charges for acquiring business assets, such as furniture or equipment, are added to the basis of these assets and recovered through depreciation.

The IRS has ruled privately that a business can deduct deposited funds for a postal meter as long as they relate to stamps that will be used within 3½ months of the end of the deposit year.

### *Books, Software, Apps, and Equipment*

Books, software, apps, and professional equipment that normally have a life of one year or less can be deducted. For example, if you buy a business book that is updated annually (such as this book), you can deduct its cost. By the same token, if you buy tax return preparation software that applies to one tax year, you can deduct its cost. However, if you buy a professional library or other equipment that can be expected to last for more than a year, its cost is subject to depreciation (also, Section 179 expensing, bonus depreciation, and the de minimis safe harbor rule may apply). See Chapter 14 for depreciation rules.

### *Office Expenses*

The cost of miscellaneous office expenses not deducted separately (such as rent and utilities) is deductible as long as the expenses are ordinary and necessary for your business. Examples of deductible office expenses include:

- Aquarium and its maintenance
- CDs for office sound system
- Cleaning and janitorial services
- Decorator fees
- Flowers and plants
- Hand sanitizer dispensers and other COVID-19-related supplies for customer convenience and safety
- Magazines and newspapers for the waiting room
- Snacks, coffee, tea, water, and other small refreshments (subject to a 50% limit)

## Uniforms and Clothing

The cost of uniforms required by the position generally is deductible. Thus, for example, the cost of uniforms for a self-employed doctor is deductible. If the medical office provides uniforms for nurses, the cost is also deductible. However, clothing that is adaptable to ordinary street use is not deductible even if used solely in business.

Nondeductible clothing costs cannot be transformed into deductible costs by calling the clothing something else. For example, an attorney cannot deduct the cost of business suits by claiming they are an advertising expense, even though a prosperous look is a way of attracting new clients.

**Example**

**A self-employed actor who buys a tuxedo for a role cannot deduct the cost because the tuxedo is adaptable to street use—in other words, it can be used in ways other than on-the-job uses.**

If the cost of the clothes is deductible as a business expense, then the cost of cleaning and altering the clothes is also deductible.However, an employee cannot deduct the cost of work clothing, because the miscellaneous itemized deduction is suspended for 2018 through 2025.

## Insurance

The cost of most types of business-related insurance is deductible. (Medical insurance is discussed in Chapter 19.) Examples of other deductible insurance include:

- *Accident and health insurance* (including long-term care insurance). The business can deduct this coverage for its employees, spouses, and dependents. Employees can exclude this benefit from their income (with a limited exclusion for long-term care insurance). Sole proprietors, partners, LLC members, and more-than-2% S corporation shareholders cannot enjoy this tax-free fringe benefit. Instead, self-employed persons and more-than-2% S corporation shareholders can deduct a percentage of their health insurance costs on their individual returns. (Deducting medical coverage is explained more fully in Chapter 19.)
- *Automobile insurance* on business cars. However, if you use the IRS's standard mileage rate to write off car expenses in lieu of deducting actual costs, you may not separately deduct car insurance. This expense is built into the standard mileage rate.
- *Business owners' policy (BOP)*. This comprehensive policy includes both casualty insurance (described below) and liability coverage (also described below).
- *Business interruption coverage*. Like overhead insurance, this type of coverage provides payment during a period in which a business is forced to close, such as during a natural disaster, a civil riot, or a terrorist attack.
- *Business umbrella coverage*. This provides coverage for liability claims above the limits on general liability, commercial auto, and employer's liability insurance.
- *Casualty insurance* to cover fire, storm, and other casualty destruction to property. Casualty insurance may include coverage for data recovery necessitated by destruction or damage to a computer system. This may be a separate policy or part of a comprehensive business owner's policy (BOP). Casualty insurance also covers loss of property by theft. Check to make sure your policy covers theft of laptop computers. If the policy does not provide this specific coverage, you can obtain a separate policy for this purpose. You may need separate coverage for certain casualties, such as floods, earthquakes, and wind damage.
- *Credit insurance* to cover nonpayment of debts owed to the business.
- *Cyber-liability coverage* to provide protection from data breaches, ransomeware, and other problems from hacking. Depending on the policy, it can also provide protection from copyright or trademark infringement or actions arising from misinformation on your website. This coverage may supplement professional liability or other coverage or act as a stand-alone policy. Why supplement professional liability coverage with cyber coverage? If you do not charge for advice or other information provided on your website, then your professional liability coverage will not protect you from claims because you do not have an attorney-client or doctor-patient relationship required as a condition of protection under your professional liability policy.
- *Directors and officers (D&O) coverage* provides financial protection for these people in case they are sued in connection with the performance of their duties to the company.
- *Disability insurance* beyond short-term disability insurance required by state law provides income replacement for those covered. If the business pays for such insurance for employees, it's fully tax deductible (but employees should be aware that benefits received under the policy will be taxable to them).

- *Employment practices liability (EPL)* protects employers from claims by employees based on sexual harassment, age discrimination, wrongful termination, or other similar work-related claims.
- *Environmental and pollution liability insurance* for coverage needed because of environmental contaminations, accidents, and compliance with stricter government regulations.Gardeners, building contractors, truck stop operators, and others should check on whether this coverage is advisable to provide protection to third parties from contamination or pollution they may produce.
- *Errors and omissions (E&O) insurance* to provide protection for doing or failing to do something in the line of work (similar to professional liability coverage but for nonprofessionals). Self-employed individuals can carry the coverage to protect themselves. Businesses can carry the coverage to protect themselves with respect to the acts of their employees.
- *Fidelity bonds* to protect clients and customers against theft or embezzlement by company employees.
- *Flood insurance*. Depending on your location, your BOP may not provide coverage for floods. You may be able to obtain separate flood insurance. Check with FEMA.gov.
- *Group-term life insurance* for employees. This type of coverage allows employees to name the beneficiaries who will receive the proceeds. What is more, up to $50,000 of coverage is not taxable to employees if the coverage is provided on a nondiscriminatory basis (coverage does not favor owners and top executives at the expense of rank-and-file employees). (This type of coverage is discussed in more detail in Chapter 7.)
- *Key person life insurance* for employees. This type of coverage protects the business from the loss of a key employee. The proceeds are payable to the business, allowing it to look for replacement help and to cover losses in the interim.
- *Liability coverage* protects clients and customers injured on your premises. It may be a separate policy or part of a business owner's policy (BOP).
- *Overhead insurance* to cover the costs of rent, salaries, and other overhead expenses during periods of illness by the owner.
- *Pension Benefit Guaranty Corporation (PBGC)* premiums for defined benefit plans to provide a minimum retirement benefit to employees if the plan goes under. (This premium amount is discussed in Chapter 16.)
- *Performance bonds* to ensure the faithful performance of employees, and bonds to ensure a company's performance on a contract. These are also called surety bonds.
- *Product liability coverage* to provide protection from claims that products you manufacture or sell are defective and have caused injury to the public.
- *Professional liability coverage* to provide protection from malpractice claims. However, premiums paid to physician-owned carriers may not be deductible unless most of the policyholders are not economically related to one another and none of them owns a controlling interest in the insuring company.
- *Workers' compensation*. Businesses are required to provide coverage for employees.In some states, sole proprietors and partners can opt to have this coverage for themselves.

Disability insurance you pay for your employees is deductible. But if you buy insurance coverage for yourself, you cannot deduct your premiums even though the insurance relates to your work.

Of course, if you receive benefits under a policy you took for yourself (in which premiums were nondeductible), you are not taxed on the benefits.

In most cases, insurance premiums are currently deductible in full. After all, most small business owners can't afford to pay for coverage that extends beyond the current year. However, if you are on the cash basis and your premium covers a period of more than 12 months, you may deduct only the portion of the premium related to the current year. The balance of the premium is deductible over the period to which it relates.

**Example**

**Your business reports on a calendar year basis, and you pay your business owner's policy (BOP) effective July 1, 2021, to cover you for a term of 3 years at a premium of $6,000. You can deduct $1,000 in 2021, $2,000 in 2022, $2,000 in 2023, and $1,000 in 2024.**

If, however, the premiums cover no more than 12 months or the end of the tax year after the year in which the payment is made, whichever is earlier, you can deduct the full premiums (the 12-month rule).

**Example**

**This example is the same as the preceding example, except you pay $2,000 for 1 year's coverage. Under the 12-month rule, you can deduct all of the $2,000 premium in 2021 because it covers a period of no more than 12 months (which is shorter than a period extending to the end of 2021, the end of the year after the year in which the payment is made).**

If you are a business owner and enter into a cross-purchase buy-sell agreement with other owners to acquire the interests of an owner who dies, the agreement may be funded with life insurance. In this instance, the cost of the premiums is not deductible. The reason: No deduction is allowed for premiums paid on life insurance if you are, directly or indirectly, the policy beneficiary.

**Example**

**A and B are partners in the AB Partnership. They have a buy-sell agreement that requires A to buy B's interest in the event of B's death, and vice versa. A takes out life insurance on B and will use the proceeds of the policy to buy out B's interest if B dies before A. Similarly, B takes out life insurance on A. Neither A nor B may deduct the premiums on this life insurance arrangement even though there is a business reason for the purchase.**

### *Interest on Life Insurance Policies*

If you take out a loan on a life insurance policy covering the life of anyone in whom you have an insurable interest, you may not deduct the interest on the loan. So, if you borrow on a policy maintained to fund a buy-sell agreement, you may not deduct the interest. Corporations (and other nonnatural persons) generally may not deduct a portion of interest on any of their outstanding loans to the extent of any *unborrowed policy cash value* (cash surrender value of the policy reduced by any loans). This interest deduction rule, however, does not apply if the business owns a policy covering only one individual who owns at least 20% of the business or is an employee, officer, or director of the company.

## Commissions

Payments you make to independent parties for services they perform for you are deductible. These payments can include commissions, finders' fees, referral fees, or other similar payments. There is no dollar limit on the amount you can deduct. If these payments are made to independent contractors and they total $600 or more for the year, they must be reported to the IRS (see Appendix A).

For the treatment of commissions paid to employees, see Chapter 7.

## Outsourced Workers

Fees paid to temporary agencies for temporary workers (who remain the employees of the agencies and are not your employees) are deductible. So, too, are fees paid to professional employer organizations (PEOs) that are co-employers of your workers; they are responsible for taxes and insurance, and you pay the PEOs a fee.

## Payments to Directors and Independent Contractors

Payments to directors and independent contractors are not treated as compensation. Rather, they are miscellaneous payments that are deductible as a business expense. Since they are not compensation, they are not subject to employment taxes. However, you must report nonemployee compensation of $600 or more on Form 1099-NEC (see Appendix A).

Individuals who work for their corporations and also serve as directors may receive both salary (as an employee) and self-employment income (as a director). Such individuals may be able to reduce the tax on directors' fees by setting up retirement plans based on this self-employment income. For a discussion of whether a worker is an employee or an independent contractor, see Chapter 1.

## Penalties, Fines, and Damages

You cannot deduct fines or penalties due to a violation of the law if the government is the complainant or investigator. This bar does not apply to payments that are compensation for damages, restitution, remediation, to come into compliance with the law, are paid to satisfy a court order where the government isn't a party, or are paid for taxes due.

Examples of nondeductible fines and penalties include:

- Parking tickets
- Amounts paid as penalties to plead no contest or to plead guilty to a criminal offense
- Penalties imposed by federal, state, or local law (e.g., additions to tax imposed by the Internal Revenue Code)
- Payments to settle actual or possible criminal litigation

- Fines for violation of housing codes
- Fines by truckers for violating state highway maximum weight limits or air quality laws
- Civil penalties for violating federal laws on mine safety or discharge into navigable waters

If you contract to perform work and are subject to penalty for noncompletion or lateness, you can deduct the penalty assuming it does not involve government fines or penalties.

**Example**

**You contract to remodel a customer's kitchen. The contract calls for a penalty if the job is not completed within a month. You do not bring the job in on time and must pay a penalty for each day beyond the month. You can deduct this penalty.**

If you lose a business lawsuit and must pay damages, you deduct your outlays. For example, if you lose a malpractice case and your insurance carrier pays 95% of the damages while you pay 5%, you can deduct your 5% payment.

### *Related Expenses*

Certain expenses related to nondeductible fines or penalties may themselves be deductible. For example, legal fees to defend your business against prosecution or civil action for a violation of a law imposing a fine or civil penalty are deductible.

## Meal Costs for Day-Care Providers

If you provide family day-care services and include meals to children you are caring for, you can deduct the cost of the meals. There are 2 ways to figure your deduction:

1. Your actual costs, for which you need records and receipts to support your deduction.
2. Reliance on an IRS per diem amount, for which you need only keep records of the number of children you care for and the meals they consume.

The per diem amounts are based on a per person rate. The rates for 2021 may be found in Table 22.2.

To use the standard rates, you must provide care in your home to minor children, other than children who are full-time or part-time residents in your home. If you opt to use the standard meal rates, you must do so for all food costs provided to eligible children during the year.

**TABLE 22.2 Standard Meal and Snack Rates for 2021**

| Your Location | Breakfast | Lunch and Dinner | Snack |
|---|---|---|---|
| States other than | | | |
| Alaska and Hawaii | $1.39 | $2.61 | $0.78 |
| Alaska | $2.22 | $4.24 | $1.26 |
| Hawaii | $1.62 | $3.06 | $0.91 |

*Source:* USDA.

## Expenses of Persons with Disabilities

Individuals with disabilities may incur certain expenses to enable them to work. For example, someone who is visually impaired may hire a reader. In general, the cost of work-related expenses of disabled persons is deductible.

Sometimes it may be difficult to decide whether the expense is a personal medical expense that is subject to an adjusted-gross-income floor or a business expense. If the expense is required for the individual to perform his or her job and the goods or services are not used primarily for personal purposes, the expense can be treated as a business expense. For example, attendant care services at the office generally are treated as business expenses. You must show a physical or mental handicap that results in a functional limitation to employment, such as blindness or deafness.

Work-related business expenses of persons with disabilities are itemized deductions that are not subject to the 2%-of-AGI floor (they are not barred by the suspension of miscellaneous itemized deductions subject to the 2%-of-AGI floor). However, they are subject to the reduction in itemized deductions for high-income taxpayers. If the person with the disability is self-employed, the expenses are deductible as any other business expense on Schedule C.

If you, as an employer, incur special costs because of compliance with the Americans with Disabilities Act, you may deduct these costs as ordinary and necessary business expenses. If they are capital in nature, you may be able to claim a special deduction or credit, as explained in Chapter 10.

## Dividends-Received Deduction

Corporations cannot deduct the dividends they pay out to shareholders. But C corporations may be able to claim a special deduction for a percentage of certain stock dividends they receive. This is called a dividends-received deduction. Other taxpayers—individuals, partnerships, LLCs, and S corporations—cannot claim this deduction.

### *Percentages of the Dividends-Received Deduction*

The percentage of the dividend that can be deducted depends on the amount of stock your corporation owns and the type of company paying the dividends. Other factors may operate to further limit the percentage.

#### FORTY-TWO PERCENT DEDUCTION

If your corporation owns less than 20% of the preferred stock issued before October 1992 of a taxable public utility, your dividends-received deduction is limited to 42% of the dividends received from that public utility. If your corporation owns more than 20% of the utility, the dividends-received deduction increases to 48%.

#### FIFTY PERCENT DEDUCTION

If your corporation owns less than 20% of the stock of the dividend-paying corporation, your dividends-received deduction is 50% of the dividends you receive from that corporation.

#### SIXTY-FIVE PERCENT DEDUCTION

If your corporation owns at least 20% of the stock of the dividend-paying corporation, your dividends-received deduction is 65% of the dividends you receive from that corporation.

#### ONE HUNDRED PERCENT DEDUCTION

If your corporation and the dividend-paying corporation are members of an affiliated group, all of the dividends received are deductible. The full deduction also applies to small business investment companies that receive dividends from domestic corporations.

### *Other Limits on the Dividends-Received Deduction*

In addition to the percentage limitation, other limits may apply to reduce or eliminate entirely the deduction.

#### LIMIT FOR DEBT-FINANCED PORTFOLIOS

If your corporation borrows to buy or carry a stock portfolio, the 50% and 65% dividends-received deductions must be reduced by the percentage related to the amount of debt.

#### OVERALL LIMIT

There is an overall limit on the deduction for dividends received. This limit is calculated on Schedule C of Form 1120.

#### NO DEDUCTION ALLOWED

Certain types of deductions do not qualify for the dividends-received deduction. These include dividends from:

- Foreign corporations (with limited exceptions).
- Real estate investment trusts.
- Corporations whose stock has been held for 46 days or less during the 90-day period beginning on the date that is 45 days before the date on which the shares become ex-dividend.
- Corporations whose stock has been held for 91 days or less during the 180-day period beginning on the date that is 90 days before the date on which the shares became ex-dividend, if the stock has preference as to dividends and the dividends received on it are attributable to a period of more than 365 days.
- Tax-exempt corporations.
- Corporations to which your corporation is obligated (pursuant to a short sale or otherwise) to make related payments for positions in substantially similar or related property.

## Foreign Housing Deduction

If you qualify for the foreign earned income exclusion on your self-employment income earned abroad (see Chapter 4), you may deduct a housing amount, which is the total of your housing expenses for the year minus the "base housing amount."

### *Base Housing Amount*

This amount is tied to the maximum foreign earned income exclusion. The base housing amount is 16% of the exclusion computed on a daily basis; this is multiplied by the number of days abroad (it's a little more technical than this, as explained in the instructions to Form 2555). Thus, because the exclusion in 2021 is $108,700, 16% of this is $17,392, which is $47.65 per day. If you're abroad and it counts toward your qualifying period (see Chapter 4), then your deduction depends on the days there.

**Example**

**You move to England on January 15, 2021, and work as a self-employed person for the rest of the year (and beyond), qualifying for the foreign earned income exclusion. Your maximum foreign housing deduction is limited to $16,775 ($47.65 × 350 days).**

### *Housing Expenses*

Housing expenses for the purpose of the deduction include reasonable costs for you (and your spouse and dependents, if they live with you) during the part of the year that you qualify for the foreign earned income exclusion). However, the amount of housing expenses taken into account cannot be more than 30% of the foreign earned income exclusion (this limit is explained below).

Housing expenses include:

- Rent
- Fair rental value of housing provided in kind by your employer
- Repairs
- Utilities (other than telephone charges)
- Real and personal property insurance
- Nondeductible occupancy taxes
- Nonrefundable fees for securing a leasehold
- Rental of furniture and accessories
- Residential parking

Housing expenses do not include:

- Expenses that are lavish or extravagant under the circumstances
- Deductible interest and taxes (including deductible interest and taxes of a tenant-stockholder in a cooperative housing corporation)
- The cost of buying property, including principal payments on a mortgage
- The cost of domestic labor (maids, gardeners, etc.)
- Pay television subscriptions
- Improvements and other expenses that increase the value or appreciably prolong the life of property
- Purchased furniture or accessories
- Depreciation or amortization of property or improvements

The amount of qualified housing expenses eligible for the housing deduction is limited. The limit is generally 30% of the maximum foreign earned income exclusion (computed on a daily basis), multiplied by the number of days in your qualifying period that fall within your tax year.

This works out to $32,610 (30% of $108,700), or $89.34 per day.

**Example**

**You qualify for the housing exclusion and live abroad for January through March 2021. Your exclusion is limited to $8,040.60 (89.34 × 90 days).**

If you incur housing expenses in a high-cost locality during 2021 (these are listed in the instructions to Form 2555), you can use housing expenses that total more than the standard limit on housing expenses of $32,610. High-cost localities change each year, so check for updates.

## Other Expenses

Not every cost made on behalf of a business fits neatly into a deduction category or, in fact, is even deductible. As long as the cost is ordinary and necessary for your business and is not designated as "nondeductible" by the tax law, you can deduct it in a catchall category called "other expenses." Examples of other expenses include:

- Prizes to customers or suppliers
- Research expenses (other than costs related to the research credit or capitalized and amortized over 60 or more months, as explained in Chapter 14)
- Trade show fees

## Checklists of Deductible and Nondeductible Items

Table 22.3 that follows is a checklist of deductible and nondeductible expenses. The table has separate entries for self-employed individuals and small corporations.

**TABLE 22.3 Checklists of Deductible and Nondeductible Expenses**

| Deductions for Self-Employed Individuals |
|---|
| Abandonment of assets, loss for |
| Accounting fees |
| Acquiring a lease, cost of |
| Actuary fees for defined benefit plans |
| Advertising |
| Agreement not to compete |
| Air transportation taxes |
| Alarm system monitoring fees |
| Allowances and returns |
| Amortization of acquired intangibles |
| Association dues |
| Attorney's fees |
| Automobiles (see Cars) |
| Bad debts |

**TABLE 22.3** *(Continued)*

| Deductions for Self-Employed Individuals |
|---|
| Bank fees |
| Black Lung benefit trust contributions |
| Bond premium |
| Bonuses to employees |
| Bookkeeping services and automated bookkeeping subscriptions |
| Breach of contract damages |
| Buildings, demolition of |
| Business conventions |
| Business interruption insurance |
| Capital losses |
| Cars |
| Casualty insurance |
| Casualty losses |
| Commissions paid to independent contractors |
| Computers |
| Conventions |
| Copyrights |
| Cruise ship, conventions on |
| Dependent care |
| Depreciation |
| Dues for professionals |
| Education expenses |
| Employee compensation |
| Employment taxes |
| Equipment |
| Excise taxes |
| Experimental costs |
| Fax machines |
| First-year expensing of equipment |
| Franchise fees (acquisition costs and annual payments) |
| Franchise taxes |
| Freight |
| Fuel taxes |
| FUTA tax for employees |
| Gifts |
| Going concern value |
| Goodwill |
| Handicapped, improvements for |
| Health insurance for employees |

**TABLE 22.3** *(Continued)*

| Deductions for Self-Employed Individuals |
|---|
| Health savings account contributions |
| Home office expenses |
| Insurance |
| business owner's policy |
| business interruption |
| car |
| casualty |
| cyber-liability |
| environmental and pollution liability |
| errors and omissions |
| health |
| liability |
| long-term care |
| malpractice |
| overhead |
| workers' compensation for employees |
| Intangible drilling costs |
| Interest |
| Internet-related fees |
| Involuntary conversions |
| Journals and other work-related publications |
| Labor costs |
| Lease payments |
| Legal fees |
| Liability insurance |
| Libraries |
| License fees |
| Maintenance costs (repairs) |
| Malpractice insurance |
| Materials |
| Meals for business |
| Medical insurance |
| Medical reimbursement plans |
| Merchant fees for credit card processing |
| Mortgages |
| Moving expenses for the business |
| Net operating losses |
| Office in home |
| Oil and gas wells |

**TABLE 22.3** *(Continued)*

| Deductions for Self-Employed Individuals |
|---|
| Organizational expenses |
| Outplacement services for employees |
| Overhead insurance |
| Patents |
| PayPal and Amazon Payment fees |
| Penalties (other than tax penalties and penalties paid to the government) |
| Pension plans |
| Pollution control facilities |
| Postage |
| Qualified business deduction |
| Qualified retirement plan contributions |
| Real estate taxes |
| Reforestation expenses |
| Registration fees |
| Removal of architectural barriers |
| Rent |
| Research costs |
| Retirement plan contributions |
| Royalty payments |
| Sales tax |
| Section 197 intangibles |
| Self-employment tax (employer portion) |
| SEP-IRAs |
| Sick pay to employees |
| SIMPLE plan contributions |
| Smartphones |
| Software |
| Start-up costs |
| Subscriptions |
| Supplemental unemployment benefits for employees |
| Supplies |
| Tax return preparation fees |
| Telephone charges and answering service |
| Thefts |
| Timber |
| Tools |
| Trade names |
| Trademarks |

**TABLE 22.3** *(Continued)*

| Deductions for Self-Employed Individuals |
| --- |
| Transportation expenses |
| Trucks (see Cars) |
| Travel expenses |
| Unemployment payments to state compensation fund for employees |
| Uniforms |
| Use tax |
| Utilities |
| Vandalism |
| Wages for employees |
| Work clothes |
| Workers' compensation for employees |
| **Deductions for Small Corporations** |
| Abandonment of assets, loss for |
| Accident and health plans, contributions to |
| Accounting fees |
| Acquiring a lease, cost of |
| Actuary fees for defined benefit plans |
| Advances for travel expenses |
| Advertising agreement not to compete |
| Air transportation taxes |
| Alarm system monitoring fees |
| Allowances and returns |
| Amortization of acquired intangibles |
| Amortization of premium on bonds |
| Appraisal fees |
| Association dues |
| Attorney's fees |
| Automobiles (see Cars) |
| Awards and prizes to employees |
| Bad debts |
| Bank fees |
| Black Lung benefit trust contributions |
| Bond premiums |
| Bonuses |
| Bookkeeping services and automated bookkeeping subscriptions |
| Breach of contract damages |
| Bribes |
| Buildings, demolition of |

**TABLE 22.3** *(Continued)*

| Deductions for Small Corporations |
|---|
| Business conventions |
| Business interruption insurance |
| Capital losses |
| Cars |
| Casualty insurance |
| Casualty losses |
| Charitable contributions |
| Commissions paid to independent contractors |
| Computers |
| Conventions |
| Copyrights |
| Cruise ships, conventions on |
| Dependent care |
| Depreciation |
| Disability insurance |
| Dividends-received deduction |
| Education expenses |
| Employee benefit plans |
| Employee compensation |
| Employment taxes |
| Equipment |
| Excise taxes |
| Experimental costs |
| Fax machines |
| FICA |
| First-year expensing of equipment |
| Foreign taxes |
| Franchise fees (acquisition fee and annual fees) |
| Franchise taxes |
| Freight |
| Fringe benefits |
| Fuel taxes |
| FUTA tax |
| Gifts |
| Going concern value |
| Goodwill |
| Group term life insurance |
| Handicapped, improvements for |

**TABLE 22.3** *(Continued)*

| Deductions for Small Corporations |
|---|
| Health plans, contributions to |
| Health reimbursement arrangement payments |
| Health savings account contributions |
| Incorporation fees |
| Insurance |
| business interruption |
| car |
| casualty |
| cyber-liability |
| employment practices liability |
| environmental and pollution liability |
| errors and omissions |
| flood |
| group term |
| health |
| key person life |
| liability |
| life |
| long-term care |
| malpractice |
| overhead |
| workers' compensation |
| Intangible drilling costs |
| Interest |
| Internet-related fees |
| Involuntary conversions |
| Journals and other work-related publications |
| Kickbacks |
| Labor costs |
| Lease payments |
| Legal fees |
| Liability insurance |
| Libraries |
| License fees |
| Life insurance |
| Maintenance costs (repairs) |
| Malpractice insurance |
| Materials |
| Meals for business |
| Medical insurance |

**TABLE 22.3** *(Continued)*

| Deductions for Small Corporations |
|---|
| Medical reimbursement plans |
| Medicare tax |
| Merchant account fees for credit card processing |
| Mortgages |
| Moving expenses for the business |
| Net operating losses |
| Oil and gas wells |
| Organizational expenses |
| Outplacement services |
| Overhead insurance |
| Patents |
| PayPal and Amazon Payments fees |
| Penalties |
| Pension plans |
| Pollution control facilities |
| Postage |
| Prizes to employees |
| Qualified retirement plan contributions |
| Real estate taxes |
| Reforestation expenses |
| Registration fees |
| Removal of architectural barriers |
| Rent |
| Research costs |
| Retirement plan contributions |
| Royalty payments |
| Salaries |
| Sales tax |
| Section 197 intangibles |
| SEP-IRAs, contributions to |
| Sick pay |
| SIMPLE plans, contributions to |
| Smartphones |
| Social Security tax |
| Software |
| Start-up costs |
| State income tax |
| Subscriptions |
| Supplemental unemployment benefits |
| Supplies |

**TABLE 22.3** *(Continued)*

| Deductions for Small Corporations |
|---|
| Tax return preparation fees |
| Telephone charges and answering service |
| Thefts |
| Timber |
| Tools |
| Trademarks |
| Tradenames |
| Transportation expenses |
| Travel expenses |
| Trucks (see Cars) |
| Unemployment payments to state compensation fund |
| Unemployment tax (FUTA) |
| Use tax |
| Utilities |
| Vacation pay |
| Vandalism |
| Wages |
| Workers' compensation insurance |
| Workforce in place |
| Worthless securities |
| **Deductions Not Allowed** |
| Additional Medicare tax on earned income over a threshold amount |
| Advances to one's corporation (they are loans or contributions to capital) |
| Anticipated liabilities |
| Architect's fees (generally capitalized) |
| At-risk, losses in excess of |
| Bad debt deduction for income not reported |
| Bar examination fees |
| Bribes |
| Car used for commuting |
| Club dues for recreational, social, and athletic clubs |
| Commuting expenses |
| Containers treated as part of inventory |
| Corporation's expenses paid by shareholder under no obligation to pay them |
| Demolition of entire buildings |
| Disability insurance for yourself |
| Dividend payments |
| Educational costs to meet minimum job requirements |

**TABLE 22.3** *(Continued)*

| Deductions Not Allowed |
|---|
| Embezzlement losses of income not yet reported |
| Entertainment expenses |
| Estimated tax penalties |
| Extortion payments |
| Federal income tax |
| FICA by employees |
| Fines |
| 401(k) contributions by employees |
| Gifts to business clients or customers over $25 |
| Hobby losses |
| Interest on life insurance policy loans funding buy-sell agreements |
| Inventory |
| IRA contributions by participants in qualified plans with AGI over set limit |
| IRA rollovers |
| Job-hunting costs for a first job |
| Kickbacks |
| Land costs |
| Loans (principal repayment) |
| Lobbying expenses |
| Net investment income tax on passive business activity income |
| Not-for-profit activity losses |
| Passive activity losses in excess of passive activity limits |
| Payments to a minister for prayer-based solutions to business problems |
| Penalties paid to the government |
| Political contributions |
| Reimbursed expenses (payments received by employees under accountable plans) |
| Related parties, losses on sales to |
| Roth IRA and designated Roth account contributions |
| Salary reduction contributions to retirement plans |
| Self-insurance reserve funds |
| Sexual harassment payments if there's a nondisclosure agreement |
| Spousal travel costs |
| State and local income taxes on self-employment income |
| Tax penalties |
| Travel costs as a form of education |
| Treble damage awards—two-thirds |

## Where to Deduct Miscellaneous Business Expenses

### Employees

In general, employee business expenses are not deductible, but there are some exceptions:

***Special rule for performing artists*.** Expenses are fully deductible from gross income if you meet certain tests:

- You must perform services as a performing artist as an employee for at least 2 employers.
- Your business deductions must exceed 10% of your gross income from the performance of services.
- Your income without regard to these business deductions must not exceed $16,000.

If you meet these tests to fully deduct your expenses, they are not claimed as itemized deductions on Schedule A, but rather as an adjustment to gross income on Schedule 1 of Form 1040 or 1040-SR.

***Individuals with disabilities*.** Business-related expenses of individuals with disabilities are itemized deductions that are not subject to the 2% of-AGI rule.

***Fee-based government officials and reservists*.** See pages 184 and 185.

***Education credits*.** The American opportunity and lifetime learning credits are figured on Form 8863, *Education Credits*.

***Foreign housing exclusion*.** The exclusion is figured on in Part VI of Form 2555, *Foreign Earned Income*.

### Self-Employed

Certain items discussed in this chapter are itemized on Schedule C. These include commissions and fees, insurance, and legal and professional services. Other miscellaneous business expenses discussed in this chapter are grouped together and deducted as other expenses on Schedule C. Other expenses are separately listed and explained in Part V of Schedule C.

For self-employed farmers, certain expenses discussed in this chapter, such as insurance, are listed on Schedule F. Other miscellaneous business expenses, such as legal and accounting fees, are grouped together and deducted as other expenses on Schedule F. Farming expenses are explained in Chapter 20.

The American opportunity and lifetime learning credits for higher education are personal credits claimed on Form 1040 or 1040-SR. You figure your credits on Form 8863, and then enter the credit amount on Schedule 3 of Form 1040 or 1040-SR.

The foreign housing exclusion is figured in Part VI of Form 2555, *Foreign Earned Income*.

### Partnerships and LLCs

All of the miscellaneous business expenses discussed in this chapter to which a partnership or limited liability company is entitled are entered on Form 1065 as other expenses. Attach a schedule to the return, itemizing these expenses.

Charitable contributions made by the partnership or LLC are subject to limitations and are treated differently. Contributions are reported on Schedule K and passed through to partners/members on Schedule K-1. These are separately stated because they are subject to limitation at the owner level. Partners/members report their net income or loss from the business on Schedule E. However, separately stated items are reported on the owner's personal return in the appropriate space. For example, charitable contribution deductions are reported on the owner's Schedule A.

### S Corporations

All of the miscellaneous business expenses discussed in this chapter to which the S corporation is entitled are entered on Form 1120-S as other deductions. Attach a statement to the return explaining these deductions.

However, deductions that are subject to special limitations at the shareholder level are separately treated items reported on Schedule K and passed through to shareholders on Schedule K-1. For example, charitable contributions by the S corporation are separately stated items because they are subject to limitation at the shareholder level. Shareholders report their net income or loss from the business on Schedule E. Separately stated items are reported on the shareholder's personal return in the appropriate space. For example, charitable contribution deductions are reported on the owner's Schedule A. But business expenses that a shareholder pays out-of-pocket are not deductible due to the suspension of miscellaneous itemized deductions.

### C Corporations

Miscellaneous business expenses are taken into account in determining the profit or loss of the C corporation on Form 1120. The corporation then pays tax on its net profit or loss. Shareholders do not report any income (or loss) from the corporation.

Charitable contributions by the corporation, as well as NOLs and special deductions for dividends received, are listed separately on Form 1120. All other miscellaneous deductions are grouped together and reported as other deductions. Attach a schedule to the return explaining these deductions.

If a corporation claims a dividends-received deduction, it must also complete Schedule C, *Dividends and Special Deductions*, of Form 1120. The net amount of the dividends-received deduction is then entered on page 1 of Form 1120 after any NOL has been taken. The dividends-received deduction is not part of the other deductions reported on this form.

### All Businesses

If your business makes payments of $600 or more to independent contractors for services during 2021, you are required to file an annual information return, Form 1099-NEC, *Nonemployee Compensation*. Also use this form to report payments to corporate directors. See Appendix A for details on furnishing and filing 1099s.

CHAPTER 23

# Roundup of Tax Credits


| | | | |
|---|---|---|---|
| Employment-Related Credits | 450 | Other Tax Credits | 456 |
| Work-Related Personal Credits | 454 | General Business Credit | 459 |
| Capital Construction—Related Credits | 455 | Credits Offsetting Employment Taxes | 461 |


Just as deductions offset business income, tax credits offset tax liability. Most credits offset income tax. Several credits offset employment taxes. In effect, tax credits are considerably more valuable than deductions since they offset taxes on a dollar-for-dollar basis.

Businesses may be entitled to a variety of credits that Congress created to encourage certain activities—hiring special workers, using alternative energy sources, pouring money into research, providing health coverage for your staff, providing relief during COVID-19, and so on. Not every business credit applies to small business owners, but most of the business-related credits are listed within this chapter to alert you to their existence.

Many of these credits have been discussed throughout this book in the chapter to which they relate. However, here you will find a roundup of business tax credits, a brief explanation of what they are all about, and where you can find more information on them within this book (see Table 23.1, page 451). Some personal credits that have a business connection are explained in this chapter, but personal education tax credits are explained in Chapter 22.

## Employment-Related Credits

The tax law encourages you to hire certain workers by permitting you to claim tax credits for certain wages you have paid. As mentioned earlier, some employment credits are offsets to income tax liability and are part of the general business. Some other credits are offsets to employment taxes (explained later in this chapter); they are not part of the general business credit.

**TABLE 23.1** Guide to Tax Credits

| Business Credits | Tax Form | More Info |
|---|---|---|
| Agricultural chemicals security credit | Form 8931 | Chapter 20 |
| Alcohol fuels credit | Form 6478 | |
| Alternative fuel vehicle refueling property credit | Form 8911* | Chapter 10 |
| Alternative motor vehicle credit | Form 8910 | Chapter 9 |
| Credit for FICA tax on tips | Form 8846 | Chapter 7 |
| Disabled access credit | Form 8826 | Chapter 10 |
| Employer-provided child care facilities and services credit | Form 8882 | Chapter 23 |
| Employer differential wage payment credit | Form 8932 | Chapter 7 |
| Energy-efficient home credit | Form 8908* | Chapter 23 |
| Enhanced oil recovery credit | Form 8830 | |
| Family and medical leave credit | Form 8994 | Chapter 23 |
| Federal excise tax on fuel | Form 4136 | Chapter 13 |
| Foreign tax credit | | |
| corporations | Form 1118 | Chapter 13 |
| individuals | Form 1116 | Chapter 13 |
| General business credit | Form 3800 | Chapters 7 and 23 |
| Indian employment credit | Form 8845* | Chapter 7 |
| Investment credit (rehabilitation credit, energy credit, advanced coal project credit, and qualifying gasification project credit) | Form 3468 | Chapter 10 |
| Minimum tax credit | | |
| corporations | Form 8827 | Chapter 26 |
| individuals | Form 8801 | Chapter 26 |
| New markets credit | Form 8874 | Chapter 23 |
| Orphan drug credit | Form 8820 | |
| Plug-in electric drive motor vehicle credit | Form 8834 | Chapter 9 |
| Renewal electricity production credit | Form 8835 | |
| Research credit | Form 6765 | Chapter 14 |
| Self-employed credit equivalent for paid sick leave and paid family leave | Form 7202 | Chapter 23 |
| Small employer health insurance credit | Form 8941 | Chapter 19 |
| Small employer automatic enrollment credit | Form 8881 | Chapter 16 |

TABLE 23.1 *(Continued)*

| Business Credits | Tax Form | More Info |
|---|---|---|
| Small employer pension plan startup costs | Form 8881 | Chapter 16 |
| Work opportunity credit | Form 5884 | Chapter 7 |
| **Personal Work-Related Credits** | **Tax Form** | **More Info** |
| Earned income credit | Form EIC | Chapter 7 |
| Education credits | Form 8863 | Chapter 22 |
| Dependent care credit | Form 2441 | Chapter 7 |
| Premium tax credit | Form 8962 | Chapter 19 |

*These credits expire at the end of 2021 but could be extended for 2022; check the Supplement for details.

## *Work Opportunity Credit*

The work opportunity credit applies for hiring workers from certain economically disadvantaged designated groups:

- Recipient of Temporary Assistance for Needy Families (TANF) (someone who is a member of a family receiving TANF or its predecessor, AFDC, for any 9 months during the past 18 months ending on the hire date).
- Qualified veteran (someone with a service-related disability who has been unemployed for any 6 months or more during a one-year period ending on the hire date).
- Qualified ex-felon (someone convicted of a felony under any statute of the United States or any state, who received food stamps for at least 3 months during the 12-month period ending on the hiring date, and is hired not more than one year after the date of conviction or release from prison).
- Designated community resident (someone at least age 18, but not yet 40, on the hiring date, who resides in an empowerment zone, enterprise community, renewal community, or rural renewal community).
- Summer youth employee (someone 16 or 17 years old who performs services between May 1 and September 15, and who resides in an empowerment zone, enterprise community, renewal community, or rural renewal community).
- Vocational rehabilitation referral (someone certified as having a physical or mental disability that constitutes a substantial hardship to employment, including an individual participating in the Ticket to Work and Self-Sufficiency Program).
- Food stamp recipient (someone at least age 18, but not yet 40, on the hiring date who received food stamps for at least 3 months during the 12-month period ending on the hiring date).
- Supplemental Security Income recipient (someone receiving SSI for any month ending within 60 days of the hiring date).
- Long-term family assistance recipient (a member of a family that received long-term family assistance for at least 18 months ending on the hiring date, or who is no longer eligible for assistance and is hired within 2 years of the expiration of eligibility).

- Returning heroes: 40% of the first $6,000 of wages (top credit of $2,400) for hiring a veteran who has been unemployed at least 4 weeks but less than 6 months in the year preceding the hiring date; 40% of the first $14,000 of wages (top credit of $5,600) for hiring a veteran who has been unemployed at least 6 months in the prior one-year period.
- Wounded warriors (those with a service-related disability): 40% of the first $12,000 of wages (a top credit of $4,800) for hiring any such veteran within a year of release from active duty; 40% of the first $24,000 of wages (top credit of $9,600) for hiring a veteran with service-connected disabilities who has been unemployed at least 6 months in the year preceding the hiring date.
- Long-term unemployed (someone who is unemployed at least 27 weeks and receiving government unemployment benefits).

To claim the credit, you must submit Form 8850, *Pre-Screening Notice and Certification Request for the Work Opportunity Credit,* to your state workforce agency within 28 days of the worker's start of employment. The IRS extended this period through November 8, 2021, for an employee hired before October 9, 2021, who is a designated community resident or a qualified summer youth.

As a good business practice, have all newly hired workers automatically sign the form (if applicable) when completing other paperwork (e.g., when signing Forms I-9 and W-4) so you can submit the form within the time limit. This will avoid forgetting to do so and enable you to meet the submission deadline.

### Employer Credit for FICA on Tips

If you own a food or beverage business, you may claim a credit for the employer portion of Social Security and Medicare taxes (FICA) on tips in excess of those treated as wages for purposes of satisfying the minimum wage provisions of the Fair Labor Standards Act. The credit applies to tips both on premises as well as off premises (e.g., earned for pizza deliveries). The credit is based on the old federal minimum wage rate of $5.15 per hour (even though the basic federal minimum wage rate is $7.25 per hour).

### Indian Employment Credit

This credit is 20% of the first $20,000 in wages and health care costs in excess of amounts paid in 2003 and may be claimed for employing Indian tribe members who live and work on a reservation. The top credit is $4,000 per employee.

**Looking Ahead**

**The Indian employment credit is scheduled to expire at the end of 2021. However, Congress may extend it; check the Supplement for any update.**

### Employer Differential Wage Payments Credit

If you continue some or all of the wages of employees called to active duty (called a differential wage payment), you can take a tax credit of 20% of the differential that does not exceed $20,000. This credit applies only to small employers (on average fewer than 50 employees) that have a written plan to provide the wage differential. No deduction for compensation can be claimed if the compensation is a differential wage payment used to determine this credit.

### Family and Medical Leave Credit

Federal law usually does not require employers to pay for family and medical leave, even though businesses with 50 or more employees must give time off for specified family and medical reasons. However, employers that choose to offer paid leave may be eligible for a tax credit that is part of the general business credit. Credits for mandated leave are discussed later in this chapter.

The credit can be claimed if (1) you give at least 2 weeks of family and medical leave (not merely sick, personal, or vacation days) under a written policy and (2) pay at least 50% of regular earnings. The amount of the credit ranges from 12.5% to 25% of the paid leave, depending on the percentage of preleave wages being paid.

For 2021, the credit may only be claimed for an employee who earned up to $75,000 in 2020. IRS FAQs on the credit are at https://www.irs.gov/newsroom/section-45s-employer-credit-for-paid-family-and-medical-leave-faqs.

### Credits for Sick Leave and Family Leave for Self-Employed Individuals

The American Rescue Plan Act extended employment tax credits for employers that pay on a voluntary basis certain sick leave and family leave to employees. An income tax credit equivalent to the employer credits applies to eligible self-employed individuals. The credit is only for qualified sick leave and family leave payments from January 1, 2021, through September 31, 2021. To be eligible, you must have regularly carried on a trade or business and would have been eligible to receive sick leave wages and/or family leave wages if you'd been an employee (see Chapter 7 for qualified wages).

If you and your spouse are self-employed and are each eligible for the credit, file 2 Forms 7202, *Credits for Sick Leave and Family Leave for Certain Self-Employed Individuals*, one for each spouse. And keep records to show you are an eligible self-employed individual.

## Work-Related Personal Credits

If you work as an employee or as a self-employed person, you may be eligible for certain personal tax credits.Personal credits for education are discussed in Chapter 22.

### Earned Income Credit

Workers with wages or self-employment income whose income is below threshold amounts may be eligible to claim an earned income credit. This credit is a type of negative income tax—it may be paid even though it exceeds tax liability. The amount of the credit depends on the number of qualifying dependents, if any, and AGI.

### Dependent Care Credit

Whether you are an employee or a business owner, if you hire someone to look after your child under age 13 or a disabled spouse or disabled child of any age so that you can go to work, you may claim a personal tax credit.

For 2021, special rules apply to this credit:

- The credit is up to 50% of work-related expenses, depending on adjusted gross income (AGI). The credit phases down and is completely phased out if AGI is more than $438,000.

- The maximum amount of work-related expenses that may be taken into account in figuring the credit is $8,000 if you have one qualifying person, or $16,000 if you have 2 or more qualifying persons. The expenses may not exceed earned income.
- The credit is fully refundable.

### Premium Tax Credit

Whether you are an employee or a self-employed individual, you must have minimum essential health coverage in order to avoid a penalty. If you do not have such coverage through an employer (yours or your spouse's) or a government plan (e.g., Medicare), and you cannot afford coverage, you may be eligible for a tax credit to help pay the premiums. The credit is explained in Chapter 19.

## Capital Construction—Related Credits

The tax law encourages certain types of construction.

### Disabled Access Credit

If you make capital improvements to make your premises more accessible to individuals with disabilities, you may qualify for a credit of 50% of expenditures over $250, but not over $10,250. Thus, the top credit is $5,000. If you claim this credit, you cannot claim depreciation on these costs.

### Low-Income Housing Credit

If you invest in the construction or rehabilitation of housing for low-income individuals, you may be eligible for a tax credit of 70% of new construction or 30% of federally subsidized buildings. The credit is claimed over a 10-year period.

### Rehabilitation Credit

If you rehabilitate or reconstruct certain buildings, you may claim a credit of 20% spread over 5 years. This credit applies if the building is a certified historic structure listed on the National Register of Historic Places. To qualify, your expenditures must be more than the greater of $5,000 or your adjusted basis in the building and its structural components.

### New Markets Credit

To encourage investments in certain economically disadvantaged areas, you may claim a credit for purchasing stock in a community development entity (CDE). A CDE is a domestic corporation or partnership that provides investment capital for low-income communities or persons, maintains accountability to the residents of the area, and has been certified as a CDE by the Community Development Financial Institutions (CDFI) Fund of the Department of the Treasury. The credit is claimed over a period of 7 years. The amount of the credit is the equity investment multiplied by 5% in years one through 3 and 6% in years 4 through 7. The credit is subject to recapture if the CDE ceases to be qualified, the proceeds cease to be used to make qualified investments, or the investment is redeemed by the entity (there is no recapture if you merely sell your investment).

### *Energy-Efficient Home Credit*

To encourage the construction of energy-efficient homes, contractors may qualify for a tax credit of up to $2,000 per dwelling unit for site-built homes or $1,000 or $2,000 (depending on energy conservation) for manufactured homes. To qualify for the credit, a home must be certified to provide a level of heating and cooling energy consumption that is at least 30 to 50% in the case of a manufactured home, and 50% for other homes, below that of a comparable home constructed in accordance with the standards of the 2004 Supplement to the 2003 International Energy Conservation Code. It must also have building envelope component improvements providing a level of heating and cooling energy consumption that is at least 10% below that of a comparable home.

**Looking Ahead**

**The energy-efficient home credit is scheduled to expire at the end of 2021. However, Congress may extend it; check the Supplement for any update.**

## Other Tax Credits

Other tax credits in the law are intended to encourage specific things—research, alternative energy improvements, and so on. Some other credits relate specifically to relief due to the pandemic.

### *Credit for Self-Employed Paid Sick Leave and Paid Family Leave*

Employers may choose to provide for a certain period paid sick leave and paid family leave to employees cover this cost through employment taxes (employer credits are explained in Chapter 7). Self-employed individuals may take a comparable benefit by means of a tax credit, which is fully refundable. More specifically, this is an income tax credit to offset income tax equal to a "qualified sick leave equivalent amount" or "qualified family leave equivalent amount."

For an eligible self-employed individual who is unable to work or telework due to COVID-19 (eligibility defined in Chapter 7 for employees applies to self-employed individuals), the qualified sick leave equivalent amount is equal to the number of days in 2021 during the period from January 1, 2021, through September 30, 2021, that the individual cannot perform services in the applicable trade or business, multiplied by the lesser of $511 or 100% of the "average daily self-employment income" for the year.

For an eligible self-employed individual who is unable to work or telework because of providing family care (again, eligibility defined in Chapter 7 for employees applies to self-employed individuals), the qualified family leave equivalent amount is equal to the number of days in 2021 that the individual cannot perform services in the applicable trade or business, multiplied by the lesser of $200 or 67% of the "average daily self-employment income" for the year.

The only days taken into account in determining the qualified sick leave equivalent amount are days occurring during the period beginning on January 1, 2021, through September 30, 2021. The maximum number of days a self-employed individual may take into account in determining the qualified sick leave equivalent amount is 10.

The credit is figured on Form 7202, *Credits for Sick Leave and Family Leave for Certain Self-Employed Individuals*. Be sure to maintain documentation establishing eligibility for this credit.

If a self-employed individual is also an employee and receives qualified sick leave or family leave from an employer, the qualified sick or family leave equivalent amounts are offset by the qualified sick or family leave wages specified in box 14 of the individual's Form W-2.

### *Small Employer Health Tax Credit*

If you pay more than half of your employees' health care costs and meet certain payroll limits, you may qualify for a tax credit of up to 50% of your premiums as long as you obtained the coverage through the Marketplace (a government exchange). This credit is explained in Chapter 19.

### *Credit for Employer-Provided Child Care Facilities and Services*

You can claim a credit for providing child care facilities and child care referral services. The credit is 25% of qualified facility expenses, plus 10% of referral service costs, for a maximum credit of $150,000. If a company builds a child care facility, the basis of the facility for purposes of depreciation must be reduced by the expenses taken into account in figuring the credit. If the facility ceases to be used for child care within 10 years, the credit is subject to recapture.

**NOTE**

**The IRS has said it would scrutinize all refund claims involving the research credit because it suspects many taxpayers do not have proper documentation or the credits are based on invalid assumptions. Erroneous refund claims may be subject to a 20% penalty.**

### *Research Credit*

If you engage in search and experimentation, you may claim a credit of 20% of increased research activities (increased costs this year compared with a base period).

For companies long in existence, the base period is 1984 to 1988 ("existing company rule"). For others, it is 3 years of a fixed base period ("start-up company rule"); this also applies to older companies that did not previously have research expenses.

Alternatively, you may claim an alternative simplified credit, which works best for a company that had little or no R&D spending in the previous 3 years. This credit is 14% of the amount of current-year R&D spending that exceeds 50% of the average spent in the previous 3 years. This alternative is figured without regard to gross receipts. The alternative simplified credit can be elected on an original or amended return.

The credit applies only to qualified research expenses (QREs). These include in-house expenses (e.g., wages, supplies) and contract research expenses (65% of the amount paid to nonemployees for qualified research).

***Special options for small businesses.*** Instead of using the research credit to offset regular income tax, there are two other offset options. Small businesses that do not have sufficient tax liability to benefit from the research credit may be able to use the credit as an offset to the employer's Social Security tax liability, up to $250,000. This is explained later in this chapter.

A second offset option is to use the research credit to offset alternative minimum tax liability (since there is no AMT for C corporations, this applies only to owners of pass-through entities). This option is available to businesses with average annual gross receipts of $50 million or less in the 3 prior years. For partnerships and S corporations, the owners must also satisfy this gross receipts test individually.

### *Alcohol Fuels Credit*

The credit applies to alcohol (ethanol and methanol) you sold or used as fuel in your business.

### Enhanced Oil Recovery Credit

The credit applies to certain oil recovery costs if you are in the oil and gas business.

### Federal Excise Tax on Fuels

The federal excise tax you pay on certain fuels used in your business (particularly farming activities) may be claimed either as a credit or a tax refund. The credit is the amount of this tax paid on fuel used in machinery and off-highway vehicles (such as tractors) and on kerosene used for heating, lighting, and cooking on a farm.

### Foreign Tax Credit

If you pay tax to a foreign country—on business income or investments made abroad—you may be eligible for a tax credit. The purpose of the tax credit is to prevent you from paying tax twice on the same income (once to a foreign country and again on your federal income tax).

### Energy Credit

There is an energy tax credit (which is part of the investment credit) for a specified percentage of the basis of each qualified energy property placed in service.

### Renewable Energy Production Credit

The credit is the cost of selling electricity produced from alternative energy sources within 10 years of placing the production facility in service.

### Alternative Fuel Vehicle Refueling Property Credit

If you install certain refueling property for your business for the purpose of storing or dispensing clean burning fuel or electricity, you may claim a credit of up to $30,000. Find details in Chapter 9.

**Looking Ahead**

**The alternative fuel vehicle refueling property credit is scheduled to expire at the end of 2021. However, Congress may extend it; check the Supplement for any update.**

### Credit for Small Employer Pension Plan Start-Up Costs

Small employers (those with no more than 100 employees who received at least $5,000 of compensation in the preceding year) may claim a tax credit for starting up a qualified retirement plan. This credit is explained in Chapter 16.

### Credit for Adopting an Automatic Enrollment Plan

Small employers (defined above) can claim a tax credit for choosing an automatic enrollment plan (i.e., setting up such a plan or changing an existing one to automatic enrollment). The credit is in addition to the credit above. The credit is explained in Chapter 16.

### Orphan Drug Credit

If your business engages in research on diseases and afflictions that are not widespread, you may claim a special credit for your related expenses.

### *Biodiesel Fuels Credit*

This credit is the sum of 2 tax credits: the biodiesel mixture credit and the biodiesel credit. There is a higher credit limit for agribiodiesel.

### *Low-Sulfur Diesel Fuel Production Credit*

Small business refiners can claim a credit for the production of low-sulfur diesel fuel that complies with the EPA's Highway Diesel Fuel Sulphur Control Requirements. A small refiner is one with an average daily domestic refinery run for a one-year period ending on December 31, 2002, that is 205,000 barrels or less and cannot employ more than 1,500 individuals on any day during the year.

### *Marginal Oil and Gas Well Production Credit*

The credit is $3 per barrel of qualified crude oil production and 50¢ per 1,000 cubic feet of qualified natural gas production.

### *Minimum Tax Credit*

If you paid AMT in a prior year, you may be eligible for a tax credit this year. Different rules apply to individuals and C corporations. (This credit is explained in Chapter 28.)

## General Business Credit

Most tax credits discussed in this chapter are part of the general business credit. This means that after figuring each separate credit, there is an overall limit to credits under the general business credit. Total credits in excess of these limits can be carried back and/or forward within limits.

The general business credit is composed of the following (some credits that are applicable only to large companies are not included here):

- Investment credit (rehabilitation credit, renewal energy credit, and the credit from cooperatives)
- Research credit
- Low-income housing credit
- Distilled spirits credit
- Disabled access credit
- Family and medical leave credit (not the mandatory COVID-related leave)
- Renewable electricity production credit
- Indian employment credit
- Orphan drug credit
- Credit for contributions to selected community development corporations
- Credit for employer-provided child care facilities and services
- Credit for small employer retirement plan start-up costs
- Credit for an automatic enrollment plan
- New markets credit
- Biodiesel and renewable diesel fuels credit

- Low-sulfur diesel fuel production credit
- Marginal oil and gas well production credit
- Energy-efficient homes credit
- Alternative motor vehicle credit
- Alternative fuel vehicle refueling property credit
- Credit for employer differential wage payments
- Plug-in electric drive motor vehicle credit
- Work opportunity credit
- Small employer health insurance credit

### *Credit Limitations*

First, you figure each separate credit of the general business credit and then total them. The total is then subject to special limits, determined by your regular and alternative minimum tax liability and certain other tax credits. Your limit is your net tax liability (regular tax reduced by certain personal credits, including the foreign tax credit), reduced by the greater of:

- Your tentative AMT liability (figured before comparing it with regular tax).
- 25% of regular tax liability (before personal tax credits) over $25,000.

**Example**

**In 2021, your regular tax liability is $12,000. You are entitled to claim $1,000 in personal tax credits. You have no AMT liability. Your general business credit is limited to $11,000 (net tax liability of $11,000, reduced by zero since you do not have any AMT liability and 25% of your regular tax does not exceed $25,000).**

#### ALTERNATIVE MINIMUM TAX

Eligible small businesses can use the research credit to offset AMT. An eligible small business is a privately held S corporation, partnership, or sole proprietorship with average annual gross receipts not exceeding $50 million in the 3 prior years (C corporations are not subject to the AMT). Partners and S corporation owners must meet the gross receipts test on their personal returns.

#### CARRYBACKS AND CARRYFORWARDS

If the credit limitation prevents you from claiming the full general business credit that you are otherwise entitled to, you do not lose the benefit of this excess amount—you simply cannot claim it in the current year. You may be able to use the excess credit to offset your tax liability in prior and/or future years.

You carry back the excess amount of credits for one year. You cannot waive this carryback. If there continues to be an excess, you may then carry forward the excess up to 20 years.

#### EXPIRED CARRYFORWARDS

If you still have unused amounts and the carryforward period expires or the business ceases (or you die), the unused amounts may be deducted in the year after the carryforward expiration or in the year of business cessation (or death). However, to the extent the credit relates to the research credit, it must be cut in half before deducting it.

## Credits Offsetting Employment Taxes

Some credits do not offset income tax and are not part of the general business credit. They are employment tax offsets taken into account on the employer's quarterly return, Form 941. Employment taxes are explained in Chapter 29.

### *Employee Retention Credit*

The employee retention credit originally created by the CARES Act in 2020 and expanded and extended by the American Rescue Plan Act in 2021 applies in 2021 through December 31, 2021 (or only September 30, 2021, if pending legislation is enacted; see the Supplement for any update). The credit is 50% of qualified wages called the employee retention credit applicable to wages paid in the applicable period. Up to $10,000 in wages per employee can be taken into account, which means a maximum credit of $5,000 per employee.

This employee retention credit is different than the employee retention credit applicable to employers impacted by serious disasters (explained in Chapter 17). It is not an income tax credit; it's an offset to employment taxes (explained below). Details of this credit are in Chapter 7.

### *Paid Sick Leave and Paid Family Leave Credits*

Businesses having fewer than 500 employees may claim a tax credit for the cost of providing employees with paid sick leave and paid family leave for reasons related to COVID-19, from January 1, 2021, through September 30, 2021. Small employers are not required to provide such paid leave, but get the credit if they do. These credits are explained in Chapter 7.

### *COBRA Assistance Credit*

Mandatory assistance from April 1, 2021, through September 30, 2021, are an employment tax offset. This credit is explained in Chapter 19.

### *Research Credit*

Instead of claiming the research credit as an offset to income taxes as explained earlier, you may use the credit to offset up to $250,000 of the employer's share of Social Security taxes.

To be eligible, the business must:

- Be a corporation or partnership, as well as any other person (such as a sole proprietor), with gross receipts for the current year of less than $5 million. If you carry on multiple businesses, their gross receipts are aggregated for this purpose.
- Have no gross receipts for any years prior to the 5 taxable years before the current year.

**Example**

**In 2021, X Corp., a calendar year corporation, has gross receipts of $4 million. Gross receipts in the prior 5-year period were $3 million in 2020, $2 million in 2019, $1 million in 2018, $500,000 in 2017, and $250,000 in 2016. It had no gross receipts before then. X is a qualified small business because its current year gross receipts are less than $5 million and it had no gross receipts in 2014 or before then (the years prior to the 5-year period ending before the current year).**

## Where to Claim Tax Credits

### *Self-Employed Individuals*

Employment tax credits are taken into account on Schedule C as a reduction to wages paid to employees. All credits—both business and personal—are claimed on Schedule 3 of Form 1040 or 1040-SR or directly on the return.

### *Farmers*

All credits, including the credit for federal excise tax on fuels, are also claimed on Schedule 3 of Form 1040 or 1040-SR or directly on the return.

### *Partnerships and LLCs*

All business credits pass through separately to owners and are claimed on their individual returns.

### *S Corporations*

The credit for the federal tax on fuels is claimed by the S corporation on Form 1120-S. All other business credits pass through separately to shareholders and are claimed on their individual returns.

### *C Corporations*

All tax credits are claimed on Form 1120. Some credits are taken into account on Form 1120, Schedule J, *Tax Computation*, in figuring tax liability while other credits are claimed directly on Form 1120 as an offset to tax liability.

### *All Taxpayers*

All taxpayers use the same form, Form 3800, *General Business Credit*, for figuring the general business credit, limitations, and carrybacks/carryforwards. However, if you have only one credit that is part of the general business credit, you need not complete Form 3800. Instead, complete the form for the specific credit and then figure the general business credit limitation on a separate attachment.

When claiming any carrybacks or carryforwards, you must attach your own explanation that includes the following information:

- The year in which the credit originated
- The amount of the credit
- The amount allowed in the year of origination
- The amount allowed in each carryback year
- The amount allowed in each carryforward year

See Table 23.1 for a guide to tax credits.

All taxpayers claiming the employee retention credit, the credits for paid sick leave and paid family leave, and the credit for COBRA premium assistance do so on Form 941, *Employer's Quarterly Federal Tax Return*. If they want an accelerated refund, they can file Form 7200, *Advance Payment of Employer Credits Due to COVID-19*.

# PART 4

# Tax Planning for Your Small Business

CHAPTER 24

# Income and Deduction Strategies


Tax-Saving Tips 465
Audit-Proofing Your Return 469
Common Errors and How to Avoid Them 472
Tax Assistance 475


Understanding what income you must report and the various business deductions you may claim is only half the job. You must also know when to report income and when to postpone it, when to claim certain deductions and when not to claim them. You should also be aware of the common traps that business owners often fall into with their income and deductions so you can audit-proof your return to the extent possible.

Tax planning is always complicated, but this is a time of particular confusion. While many of the tax changes made by recent legislation are permanent, many others are temporary. For example, the lowered individual income tax rates and the qualified business income deduction for owners of pass-through entities are set to expire at the end of 2025. Some of the COVID-19-related changes apply only for a portion of 2021. What's more, new legislation always contains uncertainties requiring technical corrections in Congress or IRS guidance. Finally, it is important to recognize that you should not always go at it alone. You may need to get the assistance of tax professionals or additional information from the IRS. You need to know how to obtain referrals to tax professionals. You also need to know some important IRS telephone numbers to call for assistance. This information is included throughout this chapter for your convenience.

## Tax-Saving Tips

### *Tax-Planning Decisions*

Some deductions are under your control because you can decide whether to incur the expenditure. Also, sometimes you are permitted to make tax elections on when to report income or when to claim write-offs. Here are some pointers that can help you minimize your income and maximize your deductions. Or, you can follow the reverse strategy if you already have losses for the year and want to accelerate income to offset those losses (and defer deductions).

- *Cash-basis businesses*. If you account for your expenses and income on a cash basis, you can influence when you receive income and claim deductions for year-end items. For example, you can delay billing out for services or merchandise so that payment will be received in the following year. In deferring income for services or goods sold, do not delay billing so that collection may be in jeopardy. Also factor in your tax bracket for this year and the bracket you expect to be in next year. If you will be in a higher tax bracket next year because your income will be greater or because of tax law changes, you may not want to defer income. You may prefer to bill and collect as soon as possible to report the income in the lower-tax year.

**NOTE**

**For cash basis businesses, in deciding whether to defer income and accelerate deductions, factor in the possibility of future tax rate increases.**

On the flip side, you can accelerate deductions by paying outstanding bills and stocking up on supplies. Again, determine whether accelerating deductions makes sense for you.

However, in accelerating deductions, do not prepay expenses that relate to items extending beyond one year. For example, if you pay a 3-year subscription to a trade magazine, you can deduct only the portion of the subscription (one-third) that relates to the current year; the balance is deductible in future years as allocated.

- *Accrual method businesses*. The board of directors of an accrual-basis C corporation can authorize a charitable contribution and make note of it in the corporate minutes. A current deduction can be claimed even if the contribution is paid after the end of the year (as long as it is paid no later than 2½ months after the close of the year). Charitable contributions are discussed in Chapter 22.

  Similarly, accrual method businesses can accrue bonuses and other payments to employees in the current year that are paid within 2½ months of the close of the year. However, this rule does not extend to payments to S corporation owner-employees—payments are deductible only when received by the owner-employees.
- *Owner participation*. If you own a business, be sure that your level of participation is sufficient to allow you to deduct all your losses under the passive loss limitation rules and avoid the 3.8% tax on net investment income. Increase your level of participation, and keep records of how and when you participated in the business. Passive loss rules and the various participation tests under these rules are discussed in Chapter 4.
- *Increase basis to fully utilize losses*. If you are an owner in a pass-through entity, your share of losses generally is deductible only to the extent of your basis in the business. Explore ways in which to increase your basis so that the losses can be fully utilized. For example, if you are an S corporation shareholder, you can increase basis by lending funds to your business. Alternatively, you can work with the corporation's lenders to restructure debt, making you primarily liable for the amount borrowed (which you then lend to the corporation and increase basis). Basis rules and their impact on deducting losses are discussed in Chapter 4.
- *Minimize FICA*. Owners who work for their corporations may be able to extract distributions on a FICA-free basis by arranging loans or rentals to the business and taking payments in the form of interest or rents. Of course, these arrangements must be bona fide. However, S corporation shareholders who perform substantial services for their corporation should not erroneously characterize compensation as dividends. And W-2 wages are important for optimizing the qualified business income deduction.

- *Review qualified plan selection.* If you are self-employed and use an IRA, SEP, SIMPLE, or other qualified plan to save for retirement, review your choice of plan annually to see if it optimizes your benefits while keeping costs down.

  Similarly, corporations should review existing plans to see whether terminations or other courses of action are warranted as cost-cutting measures. If you want to terminate one plan and begin another, do not do so without consulting a pension expert. You must be sure that your old plan is in full compliance with the tax laws before it is terminated.

- *Carry medical coverage for yourself and employees.* Buy the kind of coverage you can afford as long as it meets minimum essential coverage requirements. The business picks up the expense for your personal insurance protection. Even if you cannot receive this benefit on a tax-free basis (if, for example, you are a partner or S corporation shareholder who must include business-paid insurance in your income), you may deduct 100% of the coverage on your individual return.

  You can reduce the cost of coverage to the business by buying a high-deductible plan that allows employees to contribute to health savings accounts on a tax-deductible basis. Alternatively, you can make deductible contributions to an HSA on behalf of your employees. If you are not subject to the employer mandate under the Affordable Care Act, you can shift most of the cost of coverage to employees by adopting a premium-only cafeteria plan. Or you may be able to use a type of health reimbursement arrangement to help employees pay for their individually-obtained coverage.

  If you have a C corporation and are a shareholder-employee, you can institute a medical reimbursement plan to cover out-of-pocket medical costs not otherwise covered by insurance (such as dental expenses, eye care, or prescription drugs) as long as the plan conforms to Affordable Care Act requirements. Medical coverage strategies are discussed in Chapter 19.

  If you pay at least half the premiums for your employees and qualify as a small employer, you can claim a tax credit for a percentage of your payments (Chapter 19).

- *Institute other employee benefit plans.* If you have a C corporation that is profitable and you are a shareholder-employee, you may be able to turn your nondeductible personal expenses into deductible business expenses. For example, you can have the corporation institute a group term life insurance plan for employees and obtain tax-free coverage up to $50,000. Of course, in weighing the advantages and disadvantages of employee benefit plans, be sure to consider the cost of covering rank-and-file employees, since most benefit plans have strict nondiscrimination rules. Also, take into account the fact that employer-paid educational assistance and adoption assistance plans cannot give more than 5% of benefits to shareholders owning more than 5% of the stock, usually making such plans undesirable for closely held corporations. Employee benefits are discussed in Chapter 7.

- *Adopt reimbursement arrangements.* If your corporation reimburses you for travel, work-from-home expenses (e.g., internet access fees), and other business costs, be sure that the arrangement is treated as an *accountable plan*. This will ensure that not only does the corporation save on employment taxes but also that you are not taxed on reimbursements. With an accountable plan, the corporation deducts the expenses, and no income is reported to you. Reimbursement arrangements are discussed in Chapter 8.

- *Abandon versus selling of property.* If you have property that simply is of no value to the business, you may want to abandon it rather than sell it for a nominal amount. This will allow the business to take an ordinary loss deduction rather than a capital loss on a sale.

A sale of Section 1231 property may result in a capital or ordinary loss, depending on other Section 1231 transactions for the current year and prior Section 1231 losses. Abandonment of property and Section 1231 property are discussed in Chapter 6.

- *Take disaster losses in the prior year*. If you suffer a disaster loss to business property in an area declared to be eligible for federal disaster assistance, consider claiming the deduction on a return for the year preceding the year of the loss if this will give you needed cash flow or result in a greater benefit from the deduction. Disaster losses are discussed in Chapter 17.
- *Review the business structure*. Changes in the business climate, in business goals, tax laws, and state laws may warrant a change in the form of business organization. For example, your business may start as a sole proprietorship; later you may want to incorporate in order to take advantage of certain employee benefit plans. Review the options that will afford tax reduction and other benefits. Business organization is discussed in Chapter 1.
- *Do year-end planning*. Businesses have an opportunity to save on taxes with year-end planning. Well-timed expenditures for which tax credits or deductions are available may prove advantageous. Begin year-end planning well before the end of the year in order to have time to implement your decisions.
- *Stay abreast of tax law changes*. New opportunities are continually being created—through Congressional action, court decisions, and IRS rulings. As the economy recovers from the effects of COVID-19, expect new tax rules to be enacted and you need to know what these changes are in order to take advantage of them. Download a free Supplement to this book (available in February 2022) on tax developments affecting small businesses from https://www.jklasser.com and https://www.BigIdeasForSmallBusiness.com.

### *Post-Year Tax Elections to Cut Your Tax Bill*

Even though the tax year is over, there are still certain decisions that you can make after the year has ended to favorably impact your tax liability. Here are some elections and actions that can be helpful when you file your tax return for the current year:

- *Take optimum write-offs for business equipment purchases*. When the business can benefit from a larger deduction, instead of depreciating the cost of equipment over the life of the property, consider electing the Section 179 deduction or using bonus depreciation. Alternatively, when the business cannot benefit from a current deduction because it does not have sufficient income to offset it or you may be subject to the limit on excess noncorporate losses, consider other write-off options. Time business equipment purchases carefully in view of the mid-quarter convention. Depreciation, Section 179 expensing, bonus depreciation, and the de minimis safe harbor election are discussed in Chapter 14.
- *Installment sale*. If you sold property on an installment basis where at least one payment is due after the year of sale, you report the gain over the period in which payments are made. However, you may opt to report *all* of the gain in the year of sale, regardless of when payments are received. This is done simply by reporting the full amount of gain on the 2021 return. Reporting the full gain may be advisable if you have losses in the year of sale or loss carryovers to offset the gains. It may also make sense if you expect to be in a higher tax bracket when additional installment payments will be received.
- *Real estate professionals*.If you own multiple rental properties that produce a net loss, you can escape the passive activity loss limitation imposed on investors by aggregating the properties to qualify as a real estate professional. To do this, you must attach an election to your

return. Without the election, a reported net loss may be disallowed. What's more, unless qualifying as a real estate professional, income from real estate activities cannot escape the additional Medicare tax on net investment income if you are a high-income taxpayer.

- *Retirement plans*. If 2021 is a profitable year but you don't have a qualified retirement plan for your business, it may not be too late to create and fund one. You have until the extended due date of the return to set up a qualified retirement plan and add the deductible contribution for 2021, but watch pre-year-end deadlines for giving notice to employees where applicable.
- *File for refunds*. There are many situations in which you can obtain a tax refund from earlier years. This is explained in Appendix E.

### Track Carryovers

You may have tax write-offs that you are unable to use because of a dollar, a percentage, or some other limit. Be sure to keep track of the carryovers so you can use them in future years to the extent allowed. Here are some common carryovers to keep records on:

- *Capital losses*. Unused capital losses for individuals have an unlimited carryforward. Unused capital losses of C corporations have a 5-year carryover limit.
- *Charitable contribution carryover*. If charitable contributions are limited because of adjusted gross income (AGI) or taxable income, excess amounts can be carried forward for up to 5 years (15 years for contributions of conservation easements).
- *General business credit carryover*. If you have any unused general business credit, it can be carried forward for up to 20 years.
- *Home office deduction carryover*. If your home office deduction in 2021 (figured using the actual expense method) is limited because of your gross income from the home office activity, the excess deduction can be used on the 2022 return to the extent there is sufficient gross income from the home office activity. You do not have to be in the same home office in the carryover year in order to use the carryover. There is no time limit on the use of a home office deduction carryover. There is no carryover if your home office deduction for 2021 is figured using the simplified method.
- *Investment interest*. Unused investment interest by individuals has an unlimited carryover period. Investment interest may arise, for example, on borrowing to purchase stock in your incorporated business.
- *Net operating loss carryover*. If you have a pre-2018 net operating loss (NOL) carryover that has not been used up, carry it forward for up to 20 years. NOLs arising in 2018 and later years have an indefinite carryover. Keep track of each separate NOL. The NOL is reported as a negative figure on the "other income" line on Schedule 1 of Form 1040 or 1040-SR.

## Audit-Proofing Your Return

It is impossible to completely audit-proof your return. However, you can take steps to minimize your audit exposure.

Perhaps the number one audit trigger for small business is improper classification of workers. Small business owners may treat workers as independent contractors when they should be treated as employees. If the IRS successfully reclassifies workers as employees, you could owe back employment taxes, interest, and penalties as well as risk loss of qualified status for your retirement plan. In other words, the monetary risks of misclassification are substantial.

For employment tax purposes, you can rely on a safe harbor to avoid misclassification. You need to show that it is an industry practice to treat such workers as independent contractors. All company practices should be consistent.

- Contract terminology in any agreements with these workers should reflect independent contractor status.
- Form 1099-NEC should be issued to all your independent contractors for payments of $600 or more in 2021.
- Treat all workers on a consistent basis every year (independent contractors should remain independent contractors).
- Treat all workers with similar responsibilities on a consistent basis (all workers who handle a particular job should be treated *either* as employees *or* independent contractors, depending on the circumstances).

Many audit problems arise in connection with deductions. Your goal should be to claim all the deductions to which you are entitled in order to minimize your business income. At the same time, you want to *audit-proof* your return to avoid confrontations with the IRS. The following are some tips you can use to ensure that your write-offs will be allowed.

- *Report business income*. While there is an underground economy operating strictly for cash, do not join the ranks of those who do so to avoid taxes. The failure to report income can result in criminal charges punishable by fines and imprisonment. The IRS is becoming increasingly sophisticated about discerning unreported income. It has developed audit guides for various industries to enable its auditors to detect unreported income. For example, under an old audit guide, by examining the amount of flour ordered by a pizzeria, the IRS was able to determine how many pizzas had been sold—the failure to fall within reasonable parameters can lead to charges of failing to report income. And, in a couple of cases when merchants failed to report income, the IRS used Form 1099-Ks (information returns reporting merchant transactions on credit/debit cards and electronic payments) to reconstruct their income and tax them on it.
- *Keep good records*. You need proof to back up your deductions, such as when the expense was paid or incurred, the amount of the expense, and why you think it is deductible. If you develop good recordkeeping practices, you will automatically be assured of the necessary evidence to support your deductions. For example, if you want to claim deductions for travel expenses, you must have certain proof of expenditures. Using software or cloud solutions and apps on a computer or smartphone to keep your books and records can simplify both recordkeeping requirements and tax return preparation. Recordkeeping is explained in detail in Chapter 3.
- *Formalize agreements between corporations and shareholders*. If loans are made to or from shareholders, be sure that the interest rate, terms of repayment, and other particulars of the loans are written down. Have the note signed by all of the parties. Formal agreements should also be made if property is leased by a shareholder to the corporation. In addition to promissory notes, contracts, or other agreements between the parties, it is a good idea to put any agreements into the minutes of the corporation. Be sure that corporate minutes reflect any arrangements between corporations and shareholders (see Appendix C).

- *Be careful when claiming deductions and credits.* Make sure you meet eligibility requirements before taking write-offs. Be aware that the IRS may flag returns that claim excessive deductions, although there are no guidelines on what is excessive. However, even claiming modest deductions is no guarantee you will be free from being audited. Claim *all* deductions to which you are entitled. Even if the IRS examines your return, you can prove entitlement to your write-offs.
- *Supply all necessary information.* In completing business returns, be sure to fill out all forms and schedules required. Also include all required information for claiming certain deductions. For example, if you have a bad debt, you cannot simply deduct the loss. You must attach a statement to the return detailing the nature and extent of the bad debt. And also attach statements for any elections you are making (various election statements are contained in this book).
- *Review the IRS audit guide for your industry* (if such a guide has been released). This guide is used by IRS personnel to review returns of businesses within an industry and thus provides key information about what the IRS is on the lookout for. Currently, there are more than 3 dozen "Audit Technique Guides" available free from the IRS at https://www.irs.gov/businesses/small-businesses-self-employed/audit-techniques-guides-atgs.
- *Review special information for your industry.* The IRS has created industry-based guidance for farming, automotive, entertainment, fishing, gas retail, manufacturing, online auctions, real estate, restaurants, and some links for other industries and professions at https://www.irs.gov/ (search: "industries; professions").
- *Ask for the IRS's opinion.* If you are planning a novel transaction or want to take a deduction about which you are unsure, you may be able to get the IRS's view on the situation. You may want to request a private letter ruling. If the ruling is favorable, you can be confident of your position. If it is unfavorable, you may be able to modify the situation as the ruling suggests. The IRS charges a user fee for issuing letter rulings (the amounts vary and can be hefty). Before asking for a ruling, though, it may be better to discuss the situation with a tax professional who can research existing precedent and help you prepare a ruling request.
- *File on time.* If you delay filing, you face not only penalties and interest but also the loss of deductions in some situations. If you cannot meet the filing deadline, be sure to ask for a filing extension in a timely manner. File the correct form for claiming a filing extension appropriate to your business return. (See Table 24.1.) Also, check state income tax rules for filing extensions that may require a separate form.
- *Get good advice.* If you are unsure of whether you need to report certain income or whether you are entitled to claim a particular deduction, ask a tax professional. You may have special questions concerning the new tax law.

  Be sure to understand the protection you receive from attorney-client privilege. This privilege also applies to accountants and other federally authorized tax practitioners with respect to federal civil tax matters. But the accountant-client privilege does not apply to mere tax return preparation, state tax matters (unless your state extends similar protection), or other federal nontax matters (such as securities matters).
- *Use the right tax return preparer.* The IRS has stepped up its review of tax return preparers, looking for those who take questionable positions on clients' returns. If you use a preparer who falls in the IRS's net, your return may be examined.

If you do all you can to avoid an audit but are selected for one nonetheless, don't panic. Find guidance in Chapter 33.

TABLE 24.1 Forms for Filing Extensions

| If You File | Ask for an Extension On |
|---|---|
| Schedule C, Form 1040 or 1040-SR, for sole proprietors | Form 4868 |
| Schedule E, Form 1040 or 1040-SR, for partners and S corporation shareholders | Form 4868 |
| Schedule F, Form 1040 or 1040-SR, for farmers | Form 4868 |
| Form 1065, for partnerships and LLCs | Form 7004 |
| Form 1120, for C corporations | Form 7004 |
| Form 1120-S, for S corporations | Form 7004 |

### *Planning Ahead*

The ever-changing tax laws make it challenging to devise long-term tax strategies for your business. This is especially true at this time when political wrangling and historic budget deficits may result in the imposition of new or increased taxes and the elimination of some tax breaks; some changes could even be made retroactive. Still, it is important to be able to plan ahead so you can decide in which year it may be more favorable to purchase capital equipment, hire new workers, or take other actions that can affect your after-tax profits.

Many of the tax changes that take place each year are the result of cost-of-living adjustments (COLA). Others are the product of phased-in law changes, while still others are IRS devised. In Appendix D, you will find a listing of some common scheduled adjustments and law changes affecting small businesses over the next several years.

## Common Errors and How to Avoid Them

The IRS has identified the most common errors that businesses make on their returns. Having one or more of these errors can trigger a closer look by the IRS, which is something you want to avoid. Here are 25 of the most common errors on income tax, employment tax, and other returns:

1. Incomplete business name and address (e.g., use of individual name instead of the business name).
2. Missing or multiple tax periods on Form 941 (quarterly employment tax return).
3. Incomplete Schedule B of Form 941 (supplemental record of federal tax liability).
4. Entering the same amount from a previous return (e.g., entering the same amount on line 3 of Form 941, federal withheld from wages, tips, and sick pay).
5. Not filing Form 941-X to correct information.
6. Incomplete line 10 of Form 941 (total taxes after adjustments).
7. Missing or incorrect North American Industry Classification System (NAICS) code or incorrect principal business activity (PBA).
8. Incorrect sequencing of forms according to instructions to Forms 1120 (C corporations), 1120-S (S corporations), and 1065 (partnerships and limited liability companies) when paper returns are filed.

9. Unexplained short tax periods.
10. Missing or incomplete balance sheet.
11. Failing to properly apply limitations (e.g., 50% limitation on meals where applicable).
12. Missing number of partners.
13. Missing, incomplete, or invalid SSN, TIN, or PTIN of the preparer.
14. Improperly showing real estate rental income or expense on Schedule E. This belongs on Form 8825 for partnerships and S corporations.
15. Showing income and expenses from sources other than real estate on Form 8825.
16. Missing or incomplete Schedule K-1.
17. Missing Schedule K (partners' distributive share items) or Schedule L (balance sheet per books) for Form 1065.
18. Missing additional statement detailing line 7 (other income) or line 20 (other deductions) on Form 1065.
19. Late or inaccurate filing of Form 2553 (election by a small business corporation to be treated as an S corporation).
20. Missing number of shares in column L in Part I of Form 2553.
21. Missing Form 8869 (qualified subchapter S subsidiary election) when making such an election.
22. Missing or incorrect EIN.
23. Failing to elect association treatment on Form 8832 (entity classification election) when an LLC is electing S corporation status.
24. Missing or invalid effective date on line E of Form 2553.
25. Missing information in Part II of Form 2553 when selecting a tax year other than a calendar year.

Also pay special attention to the following areas.

### Salary of Corporate Officers

Some corporations have been claiming deductions for management or consulting fees paid to the corporation's owners. At the same time, these corporations have not claimed deductions for salary. This leads the IRS to conclude that the corporations are misclassifying payments to corporate officers as fees rather than compensation in order to avoid payroll taxes. Corporations may be liable for penalties for failing to withhold and deposit payroll taxes and for failing to file required payroll tax returns. Of course, sometimes payments to shareholders may very well be management or consulting fees for occasional outside assistance. But if these individuals conduct the actual business of the corporation—perform the services for which the corporation was organized or provide management services on a full-time or consistent basis—the payments look more like compensation.

S corporations especially may also fail to deduct compensation paid to owner-employees and instead call distributions to them *dividends*. The rationale for this strategy is to reduce the corporation's liability for payroll taxes. Again, the IRS has identified this strategy as a common error and has imposed penalties on S corporations that have followed it. If an owner-employee performs substantial services for the S corporation, some reasonable amount of payment for services must be treated as deductible compensation subject to payroll taxes. And the impact of the W-2 limitation for the qualified business income (QBI) deduction must be factored in when setting compensation to owner-employees.

### Below-Market Loans

Loans from shareholders to their corporations that bear an interest rate lower than the applicable federal rate (a rate set monthly by the IRS, which varies with the term of the loan) result in phantom or *imputed* interest. Shareholders must report this interest income; corporations can deduct the imputed interest. Of course, in today's low-interest rate environment, IRS attention to below-market loans may be minimal. Nonetheless, here are the rules to note. If the corporation fails to take an interest deduction, the IRS may conclude that the shareholder has not really made a loan but rather a contribution to the capital of the corporation, and no deduction for the corporation will be allowed.

Loans to shareholders from their corporations may also present tax deduction problems. Shareholders are entitled to deduct imputed interest in this case (as business or investment interest), with the corporation picking up the imputed interest as interest income. Unfortunately, some corporations are failing to report the income, but they are still showing the loan on their balance sheets. This is an unnecessary error for corporations to make. If the shareholders are also employees of the corporation, then the corporation can claim a deduction for compensation to the shareholder-employees to offset the imputed interest income. If, however, the shareholders are not employees of the corporation, the payments to them must be treated as dividends, which are not deductible by the corporation.

### Meals Deductions

Some businesses claim a full deduction for the cost of business meals. While business meals provided at restaurants in 2021 and 2022 are 100% deductible, other business meals are only 50% deductible. This problem commonly occurs for meals away from home, especially when using a per diem rate for meal costs that do not qualify for the 100% deduction in 2021 or 2022.

### Bad Debt Deductions

Some individuals are claiming bad debt deductions as ordinary losses rather than short-term capital losses. In other words, they are classifying the bad debt as a business bad debt when, in fact, it may be a nonbusiness bad debt. For example, if a shareholder has a bad debt for a loan to the corporation, the loan should be treated as a nonbusiness bad debt because it is not incurred in a trade or business; rather, it is made to protect one's investment as a shareholder.

### Casualty Losses

Some businesses fail to reduce deductions for casualty losses by any insurance reimbursements received. This results in an overstatement of casualty losses.

### Claiming Losses in General

Some taxpayers claim losses in excess of amounts that are otherwise allowed. They fail to observe the passive loss limitation rules that limit loss deductions for activities in which there is no material participation. Just because someone owns stock in an S corporation, for example, does not mean that he or she is a material participant in the business. The shareholder must meet special material participation tests to deduct losses in excess of passive income.

Other taxpayers may be treating hobby losses as business losses. If the activity is really a hobby, no expenses can be deducted.

Also, some shareholders in S corporations claim losses in excess of their basis in the corporation. Losses are deductible only to the extent of a shareholder's basis in stock and loans to the corporation. Basis is adjusted annually for various transactions—shareholder's distributive share of S corporation income that is taxable to the shareholder, distributions by the corporation, and losses claimed. Losses in excess of basis are not lost. They can be carried forward and used in a subsequent year when there is sufficient basis to offset them.

**NOTE**

**States may have different rules on the treatment of losses.**

## Tax Assistance

Your primary focus should be on running your business and making it profitable. This may leave you little or no time to attend to tax matters. It may be cost effective to use the services of a tax professional to maintain your books and records, file your returns, and provide needed tax advice.

There are many different types of tax professionals to choose from. The particular type of counsel you seek depends in part on your needs and what you can afford to pay for the services provided. The types of tax professionals you can consult include:

- Certified public accountants (CPAs)
- Enrolled agents
- Tax attorneys
- Tax return preparers who are not attorneys, CPA, or enrolled agents. The IRS's Annual Filing Season Program allows unenrolled return preparers to voluntarily complete certain continuing education that qualifies them for limited permission to practice before the IRS.

Storefront tax return preparation services may provide assistance with filing your returns. They generally are not staffed to provide tax guidance.

Keep in mind that any information you disclose to an attorney is completely confidential under the attorney-client privilege. This privilege has been extended to other federally authorized tax practitioners (such as accountants) in civil tax matters. However, it does not apply to the following situations:

- Tax return preparation
- Criminal tax matters
- State tax matters (unless there is a special state-created accountant-client privilege)
- Matters involving other federal agencies (such as the Securities and Exchange Commission)

If there is anything you absolutely want to remain confidential, then you must use an attorney. The attorney may hire an accountant to perform accounting tasks and, as the attorney's agent, tax information disclosed to the accountant in this situation remains completely confidential.

If you do not know the name of a specific individual to help you, ask business acquaintances for referrals or search the Internet. For example, you can search for a tax attorney at www.martindale.com. If you wish to check whether a particular CPA is licensed as claimed, contact your state Society of CPAs. Similarly, if you want to check on a particular attorney, call your state Bar Association. Do not hesitate to ask the professional what he or she charges for the services to be provided.

For more information about selecting and working with a tax return preparer, see Chapter 32.

### Help from the IRS

The IRS has a website exclusively for small business and self-employed individuals at https://www.irs.gov/businesses/small-businesses-self-employed. This site contains industry-specific information so, for example, if you are in construction you will find the hot issues relating to the construction industry. You will also find audit guides that tell IRS agents what to look for when examining returns of businesses within your industry. And there is a Self-Employed Individuals Tax Center at https://www.irs.gov/individuals/self-employed with help for Schedule C filers. You will also find links to other tax sites that may be helpful to you.

The IRS provides a number of publications, some of which have been mentioned throughout this book, that can give you important information on income and deductions. Table 24.2 lists some of these publications.

These publications are available directly from the IRS by calling (800) 829-3676 or by visiting your local IRS office, post office, or library. You may also download them from the IRS at https://www.irs.gov.

The IRS also offers the *Small Business Taxes: The Virtual Workshop* at https://www.irsvideos.gov/Business/virtualworkshop, which is composed of nine interactive lessons about tax rights and responsibilities for small business owners.

Another valuable source of assistance is the instructions for particular tax returns. For example, if your business is an S corporation, you can obtain guidance on claiming various tax deductions from the instructions for Form 1120-S.

You may want to attend a free IRS seminar offered to new business owners. Topics covered in these seminars include recordkeeping, tax filing requirements, employment taxes, and federal tax deposit rules. There are also special seminars for different types of businesses (e.g., S corporations). To find out about a seminar in your area, call the IRS's Taxpayer Education Coordinator (available through the IRS's general number, (800) 829-1040).

If you have questions, you may direct them to the IRS. There is a special telephone number to call for questions about your business return: (800) 829-4933. However, do not simply rely on statements made to you by someone in your local IRS office or over the telephone. If you want to rely on IRS advice, be sure to get it in writing (note the IRS employee's ID number). The IRS is not bound by oral advice, but it is bound by any written advice it may give you. If you can't resolve a problem with the IRS, the Taxpayer Advocate Service may be able to help; call (877)-777-4778 or visit https://www.irs.gov/advocate/local-taxpayer-advocate to find a Local Taxpayer Advocate.

If you have a thorny tax issue involving substantial dollars and are not sure how the IRS will rule on the subject, you may want to obtain a special ruling. You may ask for a private letter ruling without the assistance of a tax professional, but this may not be the best course of action. You need to frame your question appropriately. Also, you need to supply a great deal of information to the IRS before it will take any action. A tax professional can ensure that your request will receive the attention you desire. The procedure entails the payment of a user fee that must accompany your ruling request.

**TABLE 24.2** IRS Publications of Interest

| Publication Number | Title |
|---|---|
| 15 | Circular E, Employer's Tax Guide |
| 15-A | Employer's Supplemental Tax Guide |
| 15-B | Employer's Guide to Fringe Benefits |
| 51 | Circular A, Agricultural Employer's Tax Guide |
| 225 | Farmer's Tax Guide |
| 334 | Tax Guide for Small Business |
| 463 | Travel, Gift, and Car Expenses |
| 509 | Tax Calendars |
| 510 | Excise Taxes |
| 521 | Moving Expenses |
| 525 | Taxable and Nontaxable Income |
| 526 | Charitable Contributions |
| 531 | Reporting Tip Income |
| 535 | Business Expenses |
| 536 | Net Operating Losses for Individuals, Estates, and Trusts |
| 537 | Installment Sales |
| 538 | Accounting Periods and Methods |
| 541 | Partnerships |
| 542 | Corporations |
| 544 | Sales and Other Dispositions of Assets |
| 547 | Casualties, Disasters, and Thefts (Business and Nonbusiness) |
| 550 | Investment Income and Expenses |
| 551 | Basis of Assets |
| 560 | Retirement Plans for Small Business |
| 583 | Starting a Business and Keeping Records |
| 584B | Business Casualty, Disaster, and Theft Loss Workbook |
| 587 | Business Use of Your Home (Including Use by Day Care Providers) |
| 590-A | Contributions to Individual Retirement Arrangements (IRAs) |
| 590-B | Distributions from Individual Retirement Arrangements (IRAs) |
| 595 | Capital Construction Fund for Commercial Fishermen |
| 908 | Bankruptcy Tax Guide |
| 925 | Passive Activity and At-Risk Rules |
| 946 | How to Depreciate Property |
| 969 | Health Savings Accounts and Other Tax-Favored Health Plans |

**TABLE 24.2** *(Continued)*

| Publication Number | Title |
|---|---|
| 974 | Premium Tax Credit |
| 1544 | Reporting Cash Payments of Over $10,000 |
| 3402 | Taxation of Limited Liability Companies |
| 4681 | Canceled Debts, Foreclosures, Repossessions, and Abandonments |
| 4808 | Profit-Sharing Plans for Small Business |

CHAPTER 25

# Distributions from Your Business


Distributions from a Sole Proprietorship 479
Distributions from a Partnership 479
Distributions from an S Corporation 480
Distributions from a C Corporation 481


Let's face it. One of the main reasons you're in business is to be able to get something monetary out of it. From a tax perspective, distributions to you from your business may or may not be taxable, and if taxable, handled in various ways. It depends on the type of your business entity and other factors. Some of the rules for distributions are very complicated. The following is merely an overview of the tax treatment of distributions.

## Distributions from a Sole Proprietorship

As a sole proprietor, you pay tax on net income from the business, regardless of whether it's distributed to you. When you take money from your business bank account, it isn't taxable to you.

## Distributions from a Partnership

As in the case of a sole proprietorship, you pay tax on your share of net income from the partnership, whether or not it's distributed to you.In determining whether or to what extent a distribution is taxable to you, keep both your inside basis and outside basis in mind (explained in Chapter 3).

### *Current Distributions*

These distributions reduce your capital account but don't terminate your partnership interest. A distribution of cash or marketable securities is tax free to the extent of your outside basis. If the distribution exceeds your outside basis, the excess is taxed as capital gain.

A distribution of partnership property to a partner is not taxable. Instead the partner takes over the partnership's basis in the property; it reduces the partner's outside basis. If the fair market value of the property exceeds the partner's outside basis, then such basis is reduced to zero and the partner's basis in the distributed property becomes the partner's outside basis before the distribution. Taxable gain is the property's basis after subtracting the partner's outside basis.

**Example**

**You contribute $15,000 to a partnership (your outside basis). You receive a distribution of $10,000 cash. Because the cash distribution is less than your outside basis, it's not taxed to you; your outside basis is reduced to $5,000 ($15,000 – $10,000). Later, you receive a distribution of property with an inside basis of $8,000. Because your outside basis is only $5,000, your adjusted basis in the property becomes $5,000 and you have a gain of $3,000 ($8,000 – $5,000).**

If the distribution is unrealized receivables or substantially appreciated inventory items having a fair market value exceeding 120% of the partnership's adjusted basis in property, then the distribution is treated as a sale. And, if the inventory is disposed of within 5 years, ordinary income results. Special rules apply to a distribution to a retiring partner or a deceased partner's estate (or other successor in interest).

### *Liquidating Distributions*

These distributions end your ownership interest in the partnership. They can be done, for example, when you retire or you die and the partnership buys out your interest from your estate. A liquidating distribution can also occur if you simply want out of the partnership and this is accomplished by the partnership buying out your interest (rather than you selling your interest to other partners or third parties).

Cash distributions in liquidation produce gain to the extent they exceed the partner's outside basis. The value of marketable securities and decreases in the partner's share of partnership debt are treated as cash distributions.

Losses can be recognized on a liquidating distribution, but only if the distribution consists of cash, unrealized receivables of the partnership, or the partnership's inventory. If a partner's outside basis is greater than the cash plus the fair market value of property received, then the excess is a taxable loss.

## Distributions from an S Corporation

Payments to you in the form of salary, bonuses, and fringe benefits for services you perform are taxed in the same ways as payments to any non-owner employee (see Chapter 7). The one exception is health insurance, which is a taxable fringe benefit to you even though it's tax free to non-owner employees. You then deduct the premiums as a personal deduction from gross income (see Chapter 18).

### *AAA Account*

Because income is taxed to owners whether or not distributed, it's essential to keep tract of what's been taxed but not yet distributed so that distributions are not taxed twice. Therefore, S corporations must maintain an Accumulated Adjustment Account (AAA) account (referred to as the Triple A account) to keep tabs on amounts that were taxed to shareholders but not yet distributed. Distributions from the Triple A account to shareholders are tax free because they've already paid tax on these amounts.

When an S corporation terminates its election and becomes a C corporation, there is a post-termination transition period (PTTP) during which the Triple A account can be drained tax free. Once this period ends, distributions are taxable dividends from the C corporation to the extent there is earnings and profits (E&P). Generally, the PTTP is one year from the date that the election terminates. But the Tax Cuts and Jobs Act extended this period for an electing S corporation (ETSC). More specifically, if a distribution is made after the PTTP has ended, the distribution is treated as chargeable to the ETSC Triple A account and its accumulated E&P in a ratio (the amount of the ETSC's AAA bears to the amount of its accumulated E&P). Regulations use a "snapshot approach," which means the AAA and E&P accounts are those in effect on the date of revocation.

This extended distribution rule applies only if all of the following conditions are met:

- The corporation was an S corporation on December 21, 2017.
- The corporation revoked its S election during a 2-year period beginning on December 22, 2017.
- The owners of the stock of the corporation on December 22, 2017, are the same owners on the date of the revocation of the S election (although there are some limited circumstances where this requirement doesn't apply).

A federal district court in Oregon made it clear that the AAA account does not survive past the PTTP. In this case, the S corporation terminated its election to become a C corporation, and then later re-elected S status. The shareholders could not use the original AAA to make tax-free distributions to them under the re-election.

### *Redemptions*

The redemption of stock in an S corporation is taxed in the same manner as a redemption in a C corporation, explained below.

## Distributions from a C Corporation

Payments to you in the form of salary, bonuses, and fringe benefits for services you perform are taxed in the same ways as payments to any non-owner employee (see Chapter 7). You may also borrow money from your corporation. The loan proceeds are not taxable to you, assuming that the transaction is a bona fide loan and not a disguised taxable transaction. When borrowing from your corporation, be sure to follow formalities, including the use of a promissory note, carrying the loan on the corporate balance sheet, providing for a repayment date, and charging a reasonable rate of interest.

But other payments to you or for your benefit may constitute taxable dividends. Dividends are taxable to the extent they are paid out of current earnings and profits (E&P). If there is not enough current E&P, then distributions out of accumulated E&P are also taxable dividends. If the dividends are "qualified," you apply special tax rates (zero, 15%, or 20%, depending on your taxable income for your filing status).

If distributions exceed current and accumulated E&P, then they're treated as a return of capital to the extent of your basis in the stock of your corporation. This is not taxable to you, but you reduce the basis of your stock accordingly. If distributions exceed E&P and your basis in the stock, they are treated as taxable capital gain.

Even if there is no actual distribution to you, there are situations in which you are treated as having received a constructive dividend. This results, for example, if your corporation pays personal expenses for you, allows you or your family to use corporate property at no cost, or you buy corporate property at less than its fair market value. There doesn't have to be any formal dividend declaration by the corporation; a constructive dividend results merely because you receive a benefit from your corporation. Depending on the situation, some constructive dividends may be characterized as additional compensation (deductible by the corporation but subject to employment taxes). If not, they are nondeductible dividend payments.

### Redemptions

Your corporation may redeem some or all of your stock. The tax treatment of the distribution you receive from a redemption of your stock may be taxed as a dividend or capital gain from the sale of the stock (it's referred to as a redemption that's not equivalent to a dividend). In determining the tax treatment, stock owned by family members—directly or indirectly—is taken into account ("family attribution rules").

- ***Partial liquidation.*** If you sell part of your holdings to your corporation—a partial liquidation—the transaction is a dividend or a sale depending on the situation. For capital gain treatment on the sale to apply, the redemption must not be essentially equivalent to a dividend. This means it's not a dividend from the corporation's perspective and is pursuant to a plan adopted by the corporation. A partial liquidation may be viewed as a sale if it's a substantially disproportionate distribution. Your voting interest in the corporation must be reduced by more than 20% and you can no longer have a controlling interest in the corporation. Family attribution rules come into play here.
- ***Complete liquidation.*** If you sell all of your shares to your corporation—a complete redemption—this is treated as a sale of your stock as long as the family attribution rules don't apply. You have capital gains to the extent that what you receive is greater than your basis in the stock. You can waive the family attribution rules if you terminate your entire interest in the corporation (e.g., you no longer serve on the board of directors); you can continue to be a creditor of the corporation without violating this waiver.

CHAPTER 26

# Tax Strategies for Opening or Closing a Business


| | |
|---|---|
| Initial Tax Decisions to Make | 483 |
| Investing Your Own Resources | 484 |
| Debt versus Equity Financing | 485 |
| Tax Identification Numbers | 488 |
| Tax Reporting for the First Year | 490 |
| How to Write Off Start-Up Costs | 490 |
| Setting Up a Business Bank Account and Credit Card | 490 |
| Moving a Business | 490 |
| Aborted Business Ventures | 491 |
| Bankruptcy | 491 |
| Expenses of Winding Up a Small Business | 492 |
| Tax Reporting in the Final Year | 493 |


Two of the most challenging times of running a business are, perhaps, the start-up and close-down phases. Taxwise, there are certain opportunities that should not be overlooked. For further information, see IRS Publication 583, *Starting a Business and Keeping Records*.

## Initial Tax Decisions to Make

When you start a business of any kind, whether a full-time or part-time one, you need to make certain choices. Here is a checklist of the elections, choices, and decisions to make when commencing a business (the chapter in which the item is discussed is also noted):

- *Type of entity* (Chapter 1). Should you incorporate? Form an LLC?
- *Tax year* (Chapter 2). Should you use a calendar year? A fiscal year (and which fiscal year)?
- *Accounting method* (Chapter 3). Should you use the cash method? Accrual method? Some other method?
- *Investing your own resources*. When you add money or property to a start-up, are there any immediate tax results to you? To the business?
- *Financing* (see below). If you need more money beyond what you can add, should you borrow money to start up? Should you take in investors?

- *Equipment* (Chapter 14). Should you start with the things you already own? Buy new equipment? Lease new equipment?
- *Home office* (Chapter 18). Should you start from home? Rent space? Buy a facility?
- *Workers* (Chapter 7). Should you hire employees or use independent contractors to perform the work that the business needs to get done? Should you used leased employees?
- *Professional advisers* (Chapter 22). Who is going to be your company attorney? Accountant? Insurance agent? IT expert? Marketing expert? Business coach or mentor?

None of the decisions you make are initially carved in stone. You can make changes, but they often come with tax consequences (and the cost of professional fees if you need assistance in making a change). For instance, if you start as a corporation and then want to become a limited liability company, you may incur taxes upon the corporation's liquidation. Similarly, when you change tax years or accounting methods, you may have additional income to report from the changeover.

It is always a good idea to work with knowledgeable professionals to get started on the right foot. The money you pay for this advice can be considerably less than the cost of mistakes for doing things incorrectly on your own.

**NOTE**

**The following brief discussion is only an introduction to what can be a very complicated situation. You should work with a knowledgeable tax adviser when setting up a business and contributing property to it, so you get things right!**

## Investing Your Own Resources

Most small businesses are started with the owner's own resources. When you add cash to your start-up, there are no immediate tax consequences to you or your business. The cash you add becomes part of your tax basis for your interest in the business. The company includes the cash on its balance sheet as an asset as well as owner equity.

However, when you add property to a business, things get a little more complicated. The results can depend on whether the business is incorporated or is a partnership as well as whether there is any outstanding liability on the property (e.g., a mortgage on a building you contribute to your business).

### *Partnerships and Limited Liability Companies*

No gain or loss is recognized when you transfer property to a partnership or limited liability company (LLC) in exchange for an interest in the partnership or LLC. Gain may be recognized if your liabilities are assumed by noncontributing partners and these liabilities exceed your adjusted basis in the property you transfer to the business. Gain can also be recognized when a partnership or LLC interest is given in exchange for services you render.

***Business's basis in transferred property.*** The business's basis in the property received is the same as your basis (increased by any gain you may have had to recognize). The business's holding period in the property it received includes your holding period in the property.

***Owner's basis in partnership/LLC interest.*** Your basis in the interest is the same as your basis in the property transferred to the business, decreased by any liabilities you are relieved of and increased by any liabilities assumed by the business and any gain you recognize on the transfer.

**Example**

**You and your sister form a partnership. You contribute cash of $60,000 for a 60% interest in the capital and profits of the business. Your sister contributes equipment with a fair market value of $110,000 and an adjusted basis of $45,000 and subject to a $70,000 liability for a 40% interest.**

**Your partnership basis: $60,000 cash + (60% × $70,000) = $102,000**

**Your sister's basis: $45,000 – $70,000 + (40% × $70,000) = $3,000**

**Partnership's basis in equipment: $45,000**

### *Corporations*

No gain or loss is recognized if property is transferred to a corporation by you and other persons solely in exchange for stock in such corporation, and immediately after the exchange such person or persons are in control of the corporation (at least 80% of the total combined voting power of all classes of stock entitled to vote and at least 80% of the total number of shares of all other classes of stock of the corporation). So if you transfer your computer, office furniture, truck, and $10,000 cash to your corporation in exchange for 100% of its stock, you aren't taxed on the transfer of the property. You cannot recognize any loss on the transfer.

If any loans are transferred as part of the incorporation (e.g., a loan on the truck), there may or may not be immediate tax results to you. You must recognize gain to the extent that the sum of your liabilities assumed by the corporation exceeds your basis in the property transferred.

The corporation does not have any gain or loss when it issues its stock for money or other property received during the incorporation.

***Corporation's basis in transferred property.*** The corporation's basis in the assets you transfer to it is the same as your basis in the transferred property, increased by any gain recognized by you. The corporation's holding period in the property received includes your holding period in the property you transferred.

***Shareholder basis in stock.*** Your basis in the stock received equals the basis of the property you transferred to the corporation. Your holding period in the property transferred carries over to the stock received, so you may immediately have a long-term holding period (depending on when you acquired the property you transferred to the corporation).

## Debt versus Equity Financing

More than 80% of start ups require $10,000 or less of capital to get started. As mentioned earlier, most small business owners start with their own money, but some need additional financing. Even when credit is tight, you can still find the seed money you need if you know where to look. There are 2 main ways to get the capital you need for starting a business:

1. Debt (borrowing the money)
2. Equity (taking in investors)

You can use one financing method, the other method, or both. There are also alternative financing options. There are practical, legal, and tax considerations to your decision.

**NOTE**

**Some sites, such as IFUNDWOMEN (https://ifundwomen.com/), offer different financing options, including crowdfunding and grants.**

It's worth noting that in informal guidance, the IRS clarified the tax treatment of crowdfunding. Crowdfunding that constitutes loans, contributions to capital ("equity crowdfunding"), or gifts (without any quid pro quo) are not taxable to the business. However, amounts received through a crowdfunding portal for services rendered or gains from the sale of property are taxable.

### *Debt Financing*

Debt means borrowing money that must be repaid. For instance, you may go to a friend or a bank to raise the $10,000 you need to start up. The $10,000, plus interest, must be repaid to the lender (creditor) over a fixed period.

There are many places to look for loans: your own resources (e.g., using home equity loans), family and friends, and commercial loans (e.g., SBA-backed loans are obtained through commercial lenders and not directly from the SBA).

The positive thing about debt financing is that the relationship is limited in a couple of ways. First, the lender usually has no say in how you run your business. As long as you repay the loan on time, the lender is happy (you may be required to provide financial information on an ongoing basis to keep your loan in good standing). Second, the relationship has a limited duration. Once you've repaid the loan, you do not have to deal with the lender (unless you borrow new money).

The negative thing about debt is that it can be costly to you. Except when borrowing from family or friends in some cases, you must repay not only the amount you borrow ("principal"), but also interest. Typically, you will have to make money payments to the lender and this can be a drain on your cash flow.

Taxwise, you can deduct the interest you pay to the lender as a business expense. Repayment of principal is not deductible. You cannot disguise equity financing as debt in order to create an interest deduction. "Thin capitalization" (too much debt compared with equity) can raise IRS eyebrows and result in the disallowance of interest deductions.

There are a number of online ways to obtain loans for your business. For example, peer-to-peer lending may provide small amounts of needed capital. Sites include Lending Club (https://www.lendingclub.com), but there are many other crowdfunding sites offering loans. However, steer clear of fly-by-night, easy money offers.

Before borrowing, read the Small Business Borrowers' Bill of Rights at www.responsiblebusinesslending.org. Check here whether your prospective lender is a signatory to this bill of rights.

***Royalty financing.*** A twist on debt financing is an arrangement called royalty financing. It uses a percentage of a company's revenue over a set period of time to repay a loan; there usually is a ceiling on the amount that the lender will be paid.

### *Equity Financing*

Equity means ownership, so equity financing means sharing some ownership with an investor in exchange for money and/or property. For instance, say you need to raise $10,000 and you find an investor willing to provide it; you might give a 1%, 5%, or other interest in your business to the investor to secure this money.

There are a number of ways to find investors: Ask family or friends or look for angel investors (private individuals or groups who want to invest in small businesses). You can find interested angels through Angel Capital Association (www.angelcapitalassociation.org). Venture capital is typically used for start-ups with rapid, high-growth potential in such fields as biotechnology, information technology, and other emerging technologies, that need $500,000 and up to launch; it is usually not suitable for the average small business start-up.

The positive thing about equity financing is that you are not required to make any paybacks to the investor; the investor is gambling on your success and will share in that some time in the future. In other words, with an investor, there is no monthly drain on cash flow as there is with debt servicing.

The negative thing about equity financing is that you have to share your profits. You also have created a long-term relationship with your investor: There is no fixed end to the relationship as there is with debt, which ends when the loan is repaid. Depending on the size of the investor's interest in your business, the investor may have a say in your day-to-day operations.

Taxwise, there is usually no immediate tax impact when an investor joins you in the business. Neither you, nor the company is taxed on the capital contribution (money and/or property) made to the company.

***Equity crowdfunding.*** Small businesses may seek funding from small investors without having to go through extensive and costly government registration. Businesses cannot raise the funds directly from investors; they must use Securities and Exchange Commission (SEC)—approved portals (websites designed for this purpose).

Some equity crowdfunding sites include Crowdfunder (https://www.crowdfunder.com/), Fundable (https://www.fundable.com/), Equity Net (https://www.equitynet.com/), and WeFunder.com (https://www.wefunder.com).

Companies using equity crowdfunding to raise up to $1 million can offer shares to all types of investors, but investors' net worth and income may limit their investments. Those with annual incomes under $100,000 may invest 5% of their annual income or $2,000, whichever is less. Those with higher annual incomes can invest up to 10% of their annual income. Under SEC rules, companies may do "mini-IPOs"; the rules, which are governed by SEC Reg. A, are not explained here.

Some states have created an exemption from the federal rules to allow intrastate equity crowdfunding. This means residents can invest in businesses within their state through crowdfunding platforms in their state. Table 26.1 lists the states that have intrastate equity crowdfunding rules. If you are interested in raising capital through crowdfunding and are based in a state permitting intrastate equity crowdfunding, look for a platform in your state (a website dedicated to equity crowdfunding).

In informal guidance, the IRS clarified the tax treatment of crowdfunding. Crowdfunding that constitute loans, contributions to capital ("equity crowdfunding"), or gifts (without any quid pro quo) are not taxable to the business. However, amounts received through a crowdfunding portal for services rendered or gains from the sale of property are taxable.

**TABLE 26.1 States with Intrastate Equity Crowdfunding**

| | | |
|---|---|---|
| Alabama | Kansas | North Carolina |
| Alaska | Kentucky | Oregon |
| Arizona | Maine | South Carolina |
| Colorado | Maryland | Tennessee |
| Delaware | Massachusetts | Texas |
| District of Columbia | Michigan | Vermont |
| Florida | Minnesota | Virginia |
| Georgia | Mississippi | Washington |
| Idaho | Montana | West Virginia |
| Illinois | Nebraska | Wisconsin |
| Indiana | New Jersey | Wyoming |
| Iowa | New Mexico | |

### Other Financing

Debt and equity are not the only financing options for start-ups.

***Grants.*** Business-related grants usually are limited to companies that will create jobs within an economically distressed area or provide some other community benefit; the grant application process is complex, so this financing option is limited. However, during COVID-19, a number of localities offered business grants with simplified applications. Such grants were not designed for startups but rather to help keep existing companies in business. Grants are tax free. But some payments, called grants, may not be tax free (e.g., government assistance following natural disasters).

***Contests.*** Contests, usually sponsored by major corporations, can provide first-prize winnings of $5,000, $25,000, or more. There is no central listing for contests; just stay alert to these opportunities. Prize winnings are fully taxable.

***ROBS.*** Some businesses use an owner's 401(k) fund to get started. Rollovers as business start-ups (ROBS), which are being aggressively marketed to would-be entrepreneurs, have been identified by the IRS as *potential* abusive transactions, according to the Employee Plan Examinations Office. The IRS also has a compliance project for ROBS (go to www.irs.gov and search "rollovers as business start-ups compliance project"). Here's how ROBS work: An entrepreneur uses his/her 401(k) or other plan benefits to finance a new venture without paying taxes on the funds in the plan. The entrepreneur incorporates the business and sets up a qualified retirement plan into which the owner rolls over the 401(k); the funds in the new qualified plan are then used to buy company stock (i.e., put cash into the company). While the IRS hasn't gone so far as to define this arrangement as abusive, as said earlier it's on the IRS watch list, so entrepreneurs should beware! More concerns and issues related to ROBS are in Chapter 16.

***Crowdfunding donations.*** Raise money in small increments from complete strangers through websites designed for this purpose. These people essentially donate small amounts, typically, to help businesses with special projects. Websites for this purpose include GoFundMe (https://www.gofundme.com/discover/business-fundraiser), Kickstarter (https://www.kickstarter.com/), and many others.

Find general information about small business loans, grants, and other financing at SBA at https://www.sba.gov/loans-grants.

## Tax Identification Numbers

For personal returns, your Social Security number is your tax identification number. But for business, you may have several different numbers.

Your tax identification number is a 9-digit number unique to you. You use this number when filing tax returns, making tax deposits, opening a business bank account, applying for a loan, and setting up a qualified retirement plan. Usually, you use a federal employer identification number (EIN) obtained from the IRS as your tax identification number (even if you are not an employer because you do not have any employees). Special rules not discussed here apply to victims of identity theft who may be given special tax ID numbers.

If you are a sole proprietor (or the sole owner of a limited liability company), you can usually use your Social Security number as your tax identification number on your income tax return. But even this type of business must use an EIN for a business bank account, to report payroll taxes for employees, and to start a qualified retirement plan. And, in this era of identity theft, you may want to use an EIN if you are an independent contractor who is paid $600 or more for the year, so that you do not have to give your Social Security number to the business for which you are providing services.

### Where to Get Your EIN

You can obtain your federal EIN by completing IRS Form SS-4, *Application for Employer Identification Number*, online at https://www.irs.gov and search "EIN Online" (see Chapter 1).

When you apply online, the IRS automatically enrolls you in the Electronic Federal Tax Payment System (EFTPS) (https://www.eftps.gov). This electronic system enables you to make tax payments, including estimated taxes, online. After automatic enrollment, you will receive an enrollment confirmation, along with a PIN and instructions within a few days. Without a payroll, you are not required to use EFTPS, but may choose to do so for the convenience. Millions of small businesses have voluntarily signed on to use EFTPS.

### State EINs

States may assign their own tax identification numbers (also called business registration numbers) to your business for unemployment insurance reporting for employees and for other purposes, typically at the time you register to do business in your state. For more information about your state EIN, contact your state tax, revenue, or finance department.

If you do business in New York, Massachusetts, and South Carolina, you can register with the IRS and state in one step (go to https://www.irs.gov, search "state and federal online business registration," and click on the applicable state).

**NOTE**

**Changing the name of your business requires you to notify the IRS. How you do this depends on your entity type:**

- **Sole proprietors can simply write to the IRS about the change.**
- **Partnerships should mark the appropriate box on their return for the year (line G, box 3 of Form 1065).**
- **Corporations should mark the appropriate box on their return for the year (line E, box 3 of Form 1120 for C corporations and line H, box 2 of Form 1120-S for S corporations).**

**You may also need a new employer identification number in some cases (check with the IRS).**

### Sales Tax Permit

Business owners are responsible not only for income and employment taxes, but also for state and local sales taxes on the goods and services they sell. In order to properly remit sales tax that you collect to your state (or to states collecting sales tax from remote sellers and you transact business there) and to avoid paying sales tax on items you buy for resale, you need a resale number (states without sales tax—Alaska, Delaware, Montana, New Hampshire, and Oregon—do not issue resale numbers). Your state sales tax number (called a resale number, a seller's permit, or sales tax license) is *not* the same as your federal tax identification number.

Once you have your resale number, your state may permit you to continue to use it as long as you are in business; in other states, you must renew the resale number periodically. For information on obtaining a resale number, contact your state tax, revenue, or finance department as well as state in which you conduct remote transactions.

### Other Numbers

As a business, you may need other identification numbers:

- The D-U-N-S number is one assigned to you by D&B, a business credit rating service. This number is not used for tax purposes, but is required if you do any government contracting. Having this number also enables you to more easily build business credit. There is no cost for obtaining a D-U-N-S number. Register for your D-U-N-S number at https://www.dnb.com/duns-number/get-a-duns.html.
- State unemployment insurance may assign your business a number when you enroll to pay this tax.

## Tax Reporting for the First Year

Most businesses do not start on January 1, so the first year of business may be a "short year" (less than a full 12 months). From a tax-reporting standpoint, a return must be filed for the short year. For example, if a business that reports on a calendar-year basis starts to operate on August 10, 2021, it must file a return for 2021. It does *not* have to prorate deductions for the period in which it operates.

Indicate on the appropriate tax return that, being the first year of the business, this is the initial return.

## How to Write Off Start-Up Costs

Once you're in business, most expenses become deductible items (tax rules may affect when you can claim deductions or may place certain limits on the amount you can write off). Before you open your doors, you do not have a business in which to claim the deductions. Therefore, it is important to separate start-up costs from those incurred by an operating business.

Start-up costs may be deductible once you actually start your business, but they are not deductible during your preopening phase.

A complete discussion of items viewed as start-up costs and how to deduct them is found in Chapter 14.

## Setting Up a Business Bank Account and Credit Card

Once you have set up your business and obtained your tax identification number, it is highly advisable to set up a separate business bank account. Use this account exclusively to deposit business receipts and to pay business expenses. Do not commingle the funds in your business bank account with your personal money.

If you are self-employed, it is also advisable to set up another account for your personal estimated taxes. Use this account to set aside the funds needed to pay your quarterly estimated taxes. Often, small business owners who were formerly employees of large corporations that had withheld income taxes on their behalf are unfamiliar with estimated tax requirements on their share of business income and can fall short of the money needed to meet this tax obligation.

It is also a good idea to use a separate credit card solely for business purchases. Having both a separate business bank account and credit card simplifies recordkeeping for your business. Further, it helps to show that you are running your company in a businesslike fashion in case the IRS questions whether losses should be disallowed under the hobby loss rules (see Chapter 26). Some business advisers suggest that you have your credit card through a company that is separate from your bank so the card won't be charged if there are shortfalls in your bank account.

## Moving a Business

Businesses may relocate. The full cost of moving company property is deductible. Tax rules for deducting moving costs by self-employed individuals are in Chapter 22.

However, if your business receives relocation payments from a state agency under the federal Uniform Relocation Assistance and Real Property Acquisitions Act, you do not have to report the payments as income; you *cannot* deduct your moving costs.

Use Form 8822-B, *Change of Address or Responsible Party–Business*, to inform the IRS of a change of address or change of location.

## Aborted Business Ventures

What happens if you investigate the purchase of a business or the start of a venture but the deal never goes through? Or if you hire an architect to design a building but never get town approval for the construction? The costs of starting up and organizing a business are not immediately deductible in full (but may be amortized, as explained in Chapter 14). However, the costs of an aborted business venture are immediately deductible.

To deduct your costs, you must have proceeded beyond a general search. Once you focus on a particular business and the deal falls through, you can deduct your expenses. Mere investigatory expenses are not deductible; only those related to a specific business are. Thus, for example, if you travel to look at various business opportunities, you cannot deduct your travel costs. But once you select one particular business and begin drawing up contracts, your legal costs for the contracts are deductible even if they never get signed.

The Tax Court has allowed a deduction for a $25,000 fee paid to acquire a franchise where the purchaser decided to walk away rather than complete the deal after learning that the franchisor had flooded the area with stores, many of which were losing money.

## Bankruptcy

Bankruptcy, the "b" word, is a last resort for businesses on the ropes that cannot resolve things with their creditors. Bankruptcy is a legal process that may enable a company to stay in business ("reorganization" where a plan is used to provide partial satisfaction to creditors so the business can emerge after the process with a fresh start) or go out of business in an orderly fashion ("liquidation" where assets are sold and the proceeds used to pay off creditors to the extent possible).

### *Which Form of Bankruptcy to Use*

Your choices for bankruptcy protection depend on how your business is organized (entity type) and whether you want to stay in business, if possible.

- *Sole proprietors*. Owners are treated like other individuals. They can get a fresh start under Chapter 7 of the bankruptcy law, but most are forced to use a payment plan under Chapter 13.
- *Family farmers*. Farmers can use a simplified reorganization plan under Chapter 12 of the bankruptcy law if debts fall within a certain limit.
- *Other business entities*. The entities can be liquidated with proceeds distributed to creditors under Chapter 7, or can be reorganized under court supervision to continue operations under Chapter 11. Take note that general partners can be sued by the trustee in bankruptcy if partnership assets fall short of partnership debts.

Which type of bankruptcy solution is best for a business? It depends on the facts and circumstances. Sole proprietors may have no choice but to use the repayment plan, whether or not they continue the business operations.

Other entities may prefer to liquidate if they see the business as a failure (they have no heart for continuing the business); if the market is such that even if economic conditions recover, the business wouldn't be viable; or if the debts are so overwhelming that restructuring doesn't make economic sense.

### Tax Implications of Bankruptcy

If some or all of your debts are extinguished in bankruptcy, you are not taxed on the discharge (cancellation) of indebtedness.

Bankruptcy can provide some relief from taxes. First, filing for bankruptcy creates an automatic stay on collection activities (the IRS as well as state and local tax authorities must stop hounding you for money). Second, some outstanding taxes can be dischargeable; others cannot. This is a highly complex area, and you are advised to work with a knowledgeable tax adviser if you are considering filing for bankruptcy.

### Bankruptcy Alternative

If you want to continue your business without the cost of bankruptcy, you may try to DIY with a creditor composition agreement. Here, you and your creditors (e.g., vendors, landlord) negotiate a settlement. The creditors must come to a consensus about how the parties will be treated. It's advisable to have creditors sign a nondisclosure agreement so that you can share financial information without fear it will be leaked. You may want to bring your tax/financial adviser into the negotiations.

Alternatively, you may work with a credit professional to help restructure the company's debts. This lets you work your way out of debt in a manageable manner and avoid bankruptcy. For example, Corporate Turnaround (www.corporateturnaround.com) negotiates on your behalf with vendors, lessors, credit card companies, and other business creditors to set up a repayment plan that you can handle.

When you are seeking a company to help restructure your debt, look for members of the Turnaround Management Association (https://turnaround.org/about-tma), an international nonprofit association dedicated to corporate renewal and turnaround management. Members sign a code of ethics to provide professional, competent assistance.

### Tax Implications of Debt Forgiveness

If you don't file for bankruptcy and instead persuade creditors to accept partial payment, the amount of debt forgiven is treated as discharge (or cancellation) of indebtedness income. Whether such income is taxable to you depends on whether you are insolvent at the time of the forgiveness (insolvency means your liabilities exceed your assets). If you are insolvent, no tax consequences result from the discharge of indebtedness to the extent of your insolvency. If you are not insolvent, the forgiveness usually is taxable, but you can opt to adjust tax attributes so you'll effectively pay the tax later. See Chapter 5.

## Expenses of Winding Up a Small Business

Unfortunately, the cold statistics show that many small businesses fail. Some last longer than others, but a large number of ventures will reach a point where they are so unprofitable that the owners must simply give up. Certain expenses relate to the closing up of a small business. They are deductible business expenses.

### Unamortized Costs

If you have been amortizing certain items, such as organizational or incorporation fees or points on a commercial mortgage, you can deduct the unamortized amounts on a final return for the business. For example, say the business was formed in January 2019 and elected to amortize organizational costs above $5,000 over 180 months, but it goes under in 2021 after 30 months. You can deduct 150/180 of your organizational costs on the final return, in addition to any of the amortization allowed for the final year of the return.

### *Other Expenses*

You may incur special costs for going out of business. For example, a corporation may have to pay a special fee to the state corporation or franchise department when terminating. There may also be additional legal and accounting fees for winding up a business. Again, these costs are deductible business expenses.

Professionals who wind up their practice but continue to carry professional liability coverage to protect themselves from claims arising from work already performed can deduct the insurance premiums in full as a current deduction in the final year of the practice.

## Tax Reporting in the Final Year

As is the case in starting a business, most businesses do not shut their doors on December 31, so the final year of business may be a "short year" (less than a full 12 months). From a tax reporting standpoint, a return must be filed even though the business did not operate for the entire year. A business is treated as continuing from the time a decision to cease operations is made through the period in which assets are disposed of, liabilities addressed, and distributions made to owners. The business does *not* have to prorate deductions for the period in which it is still conducting business activities. For example, if the business winds up its closing 8 months after paying a one-year subscription, it can deduct the full 12 months, even though it enjoyed only 8 months' worth of magazines.

Indicate on the appropriate tax return that this is the final year of the business.

Obtain a *tax clearance* or *consent to dissolution* from your state to close your tax account. If you fail to do this, you may continue to be liable for annual filings and be subject to penalty for not doing so.

### *Special Rules for Corporations*

Corporations must notify the IRS of their termination. This is done by filing Form 966, *Corporate Dissolution or Liquidation*, with the IRS within 30 days after the plan or resolution of liquidation is adopted.

The corporation must recognize gain or loss on the distribution of its assets to shareholders in complete liquidation. In determining gain or loss, the assets are valued at their fair market value on the date of the distribution. Thus, a C corporation should retain sufficient cash to cover its tax liability resulting from a liquidation.

Shareholders are taxed on the liquidation distribution of money and assets. Their gain (or loss) is the difference between their basis in the stock of the corporation and what they receive. This is the final so-called double tax, because a C corporation pays tax on the liquidation and then the shareholders do, too, on the net amount they receive.

You must also follow state rules for dissolving your corporation. Even if you shut your doors for business, you have to formally terminate the corporation under state law in order to avoid continuing tax and fee obligations to the state. In order to dissolve the corporation, your state tax obligations must be up to date; you cannot dissolve the corporation if you owe the state any money. Check with your state's finance/revenue/Treasury department.

**TABLE 26.2** Checklist of Actions for Closing a Business

| Done | N/A | Action |
|---|---|---|
| | | Cancel business credit cards |
| | | Cancel business insurance policies; obtain refunds of premiums paid |
| | | Cancel permits, licenses, and registrations |
| | | Close business bank accounts after all business matters have been concluded |
| | | Close telephone numbers (including toll-free numbers) |
| | | Get out of leases for office/store space, rented equipment, and business vehicles |
| | | Keep records safe (e.g., retain tax returns, employment records, corporate minutes, and other necessary documentation) |
| | | Notify employees, customers, and suppliers |
| | | Notify the state unemployment division |
| | | Resolve outstanding financial obligations (settle debts; pay bills that are owed) |
| | | Take down website and social media presences |

### Other Details

Once the business has been terminated and a final return filed, be sure to wind up all other matters for the company (see the checklist of actions to take in Table 26.2). This includes notifying suppliers, canceling leases and permits, and closing bank accounts and business credit cards.

Be sure to retain business records even after you have closed your doors. Follow basic recordkeeping rules. This means retaining income tax–related records for a minimum of 3 years and employment tax–related records for a minimum of 4 years.

### Special Tax Issues for Pass-Through Owners

Aside from filing a final return for the business, owners of pass-through entities may continue to feel the effects on their personal returns for the final year of the business and for years to come.

- ***Reporting gain or loss.*** If the business liquidates its assets and distributes cash to an owner, the owner may recognize a loss. If, however, the business distributes assets, the owner may recognize a loss only when the asset is sold at a loss.
- ***Carryovers.*** If an owner has net operating loss carryovers, the owner can continue to claim them on a personal return.
- ***Cancellation of debt.*** If an owner is personally liable on debt that is forgiven when the company closes, the owner must report ordinary income from the cancellation of this debt (unless an exception to such income, such as insolvency, applies). If an owner is not personally liable or even a guarantor but pays off a business debt, this may be treated as a contribution to capital, which would increase the owner's basis and reduce the gain, if any, on the termination of the business.

### IRS Guidance

The IRS has Fact Sheets at https://www.irs.gov/newsroom/fact-sheets on filing requirements when going out of business:

- Sole proprietorships: FS-2020-16
- Partnerships: FS-2020-15
- Corporations: FS-2020-14

CHAPTER 27

# Tax Strategies for a Sideline Business


| | | | |
|---|---|---|---|
| Reporting Sideline Business Income | 495 | Business Expenses | 498 |
| Hobby Activities | 496 | | |


Millions of Americans today have a sideline business, especially today when many have only part-time jobs or are underemployed. Having a sideline business has become easy with the advent of eBay, Etsy, and other online marketplaces. The "gig" economy, with options for part-time and freelance work through Uber, TaskRabbit, Upwork, Takl, and others, also provides sideline business opportunities (assuming state law does not treat you as an employee of the platform). But sideline businesses, such as dog breeding and gentleman farming, have been around for years.

Starting and running a sideline business can be a savvy move. It can be a way to supplement your current income. It can be a safety net in case of a job dislocation. It has been helpful for many who have had reduced hours or were furloughed due to COVID-19. And it can be a way to test the waters for a full-time business in the future, say, on retirement.

For a further discussion of business expenses, see IRS Publication 535, *Business Expenses*.

## Reporting Sideline Business Income

There's a basic rule when it comes to income from a sideline business: You must report it. There is no minimum revenue or number of sales you must have before income becomes reportable. You must report income, whether or not it is reported to the IRS (such as on Form 1099-NEC for payments to independent contractors or Form 1099-K for merchant transactions).

Of course, all of the revenue you take in may not necessarily be profit. You can deduct expenses (subject to the limits explained throughout this book as well as the hobby loss limit, discussed next), which may mean that there is no income subject to tax.

The IRS has the Gig Economy Tax Center at https://www.irs.gov/businesses/small-businesses-self-employed/sharing-economy-tax-center to help explain income reporting and other requirements for those engaged in sideline activities.

## Hobby Activities

If your unincorporated business sustains losses year after year, you may not be able to deduct the expenses unless you can show that you have undertaken the business in order to make a profit. This limitation on deducting expenses is called the *hobby loss rule*, because it is designed to prevent individuals who collect coins and stamps, breed dogs or cats, or carry on other hobby activities from deducting what the tax law views as personal expenses. Any activity you do mainly for recreation, sport, or personal enjoyment is particularly suspect.

But the hobby loss rule is not limited to these types of activities. It can apply to any activity—even investment activities intended to produce only tax losses for investors. In fact, the IRS even tried to apply the hobby loss rule to a young attorney just starting her practice. The IRS argued that the losses she sustained were not deductible because of the hobby loss rule. The attorney was able to show a profit motive (proof of a profit motive is explained later), and she was allowed to deduct her losses.

The hobby loss rule applies to individuals (including partners and LLC members) and S corporations. It does not apply to C corporations. For partnerships, LLCs, and S corporations whose business losses pass through to owners, the determination of whether there is a profit motive is made at the business level rather than at the owner level. In other words, the business itself must have a reasonable expectation of making a profit. The fact that an individual owner has a profit motive does not transform a hobby activity into a deductible business expense if the business does not reasonably have a profit motive. A business may be able to establish a profit motive in one year even if this cannot be done for another year.

### Impact of Hobby Classification

If your business is classified as a hobby, then you can't deduct any expenses. You must report all of the income from the activity (it's treated as "other income" on Form 1040 or 1040-SR). But expenses cannot be deducted because of the suspension of miscellaneous itemized deductions for 2018 through 2025. In previous years (and for years after 2025), expenses for a hobby activity are deductible only to the extent of income from the activity. Expenses in excess of these rules are never deductible; the tax benefit of these expenses is lost forever.

### Proving a Profit Motive

There is no hard and fast way for proving that you have *profit motive*. Rather, a profit motive is something that is inferred on the basis of various factors. The burden of proof is on you, the taxpayer. No single factor is determinative. Some or all of the factors used to determine profit motive include:

- *Whether you carry on the activity in a businesslike manner*. This means that you keep good books and records separate and apart from your personal records, and have a business bank account, telephone, stationery, and other indices of a business. Having a written business plan and marketing plan is also helpful. Some tax experts also believe that taking the formal steps to create a limited liability company or an S corporation helps to prove a profit motive.
- *Whether the time and effort you put into the activity shows that you intend to make a profit*. If you spend only a small amount of time on it, this may show that there is no realistic way in which you can make a profit.
- *Whether you depend on the income from the activity for your livelihood*. If you do, then obviously you hope to make a profit to live on.

- *Whether you change methods of operation to improve profitability*. If you get the advice of experts, this shows you want to make a profit.
- *Whether the activity is profitable in some years, and how much profit is realized in those years*. Certainly, an activity may not always be profitable, but if there has already been a profit in some years and that profit is substantial, this shows an expectation of continued profit.
- *Whether you or your advisers have the know-how needed to carry on your business at a profit*. If you undertake some activity that you enjoy but know nothing about, this may indicate a lack of profit motive.
- *Whether you can expect to see a profit from the appreciation of the assets used in the activity*. You may not necessarily realize profit from the operations of the business, but its assets may prove to be profitable. A realistic expectation of this profit from the appreciation of business assets shows profit motive.

The Court of Federal Claims has allowed a taxpayer with multiple activities to aggregate them in order to establish a profit motive. In other words, if one activity has a loss but is part of an overall plan to make a profit, the loss may be allowed.

Aggregation of multiple activities is permitted when the facts and circumstances support it. The most significant factors enumerated in Reg. §1.183-1(d)(1) for aggregation are:

- The degree of organizational and economic interrelationship of the activities
- The business purpose served by carrying on the activities separately or together
- The similarities of the activities

### Presumption of a Profit Motive

Your business may not be profitable, particularly in the early or start-up years. The tax law gives you a special presumption on which you can rely to show a profit motive (and delay an IRS inquiry into your activity). An activity is presumed to be engaged in for profit if you have a profit in at least 3 out of 5 years. If the activity is breeding, training, showing, or racing horses, the presumption period is 2 out of 7 years. If you meet this presumption, then the hobby loss rules do not apply, and your losses in the off years can be claimed in excess of your income from the activity.

You can rely on this presumption and avoid having the IRS question your losses by filing Form 5213, *Election to Postpone Determination as to Whether the Presumption Applies that an Activity Is Engaged in for Profit*. In effect, the form asks the IRS to delay a determination of your profit motive until the end of the 5-year (or 7-year) period.

Generally, you must file Form 5213 within 3 years of the due date of the return for the year in which you first carry on the activity. You should know within this time whether you can reasonably expect to be profitable and avoid the hobby loss rules or whether you need to rely on the presumption to gain additional time for the business to make a profit.

The downside to filing this form is that it extends the statute of limitations (the period in which the IRS can question your return and assess additional taxes). In this case, the statute of limitations is extended to 2 years after the due date of the return for the last year of the presumption period. However, it is extended only for deductions from the activity and any related deductions. Other items on your return, such as your personal itemized deductions, are not affected by this extension of the statute of limitations.

Is it a good idea to file Form 5213 and raise the presumption? Doing so is almost a guarantee that the IRS will look closely at your return. Should you not show a profit in the required number of years during the presumption period, you will be forced to argue that you have a profit motive despite recurrent losses. Thus, you are probably no better off than if you had not filed the form.

## Business Expenses

Any type of expense you could deduct for a full-time business applies to a sideline activity as well. The only question is whether the hobby loss rule limits your annual write-off.

### *Home Office Deduction*

If you run a sideline activity from your home, you can claim a home office deduction as long as you meet the home office rules (see Chapter 18). The office need not be used for a full-time activity. As long as it is your principal place of business for a sideline activity, you can deduct related expenses.

### *Other Business Expenses*

From start-up to shut-down and in between, expenses incurred in a sideline activity are viewed as deductible costs just as if it were a full-time business. There are *no* deductions barred to you merely because you do not work full-time at this activity.

# Where to Report Sideline Income and Expenses

Income from a hobby activity is reported as "Other Income" on Schedule 1 of Form 1040 or 1040-SR. There is no additional form or schedule to complete, although you can attach your own statement explaining the income. No deductions can be claimed or carried over. Income and expenses from any sideline activity that is not a hobby is reported as explained throughout this book.

CHAPTER 28

# Tax Strategies for Multiple Businesses


Advantages and Disadvantages of Multiple Entities 499
When to Run Multiple Activities within One Business 500
Treatment of Multiple Corporations 501
Tax Rules for Owners of Multiple Businesses 502


"Multiple businesses" connotes multinational corporations with intertwining ownership of many entities. But small business owners may conduct different activities through various entities. These entrepreneurs simultaneously own and usually run 2 or more businesses.

There may be sound legal, business, and tax reasons for using multiple businesses rather than funneling all activities through a single entity. Liability issues, for example, are one good reason for operating separate activities through more than one business. This chapter focuses primarily on the tax implications of running multiple businesses.

## Advantages and Disadvantages of Multiple Entities

Some activities can naturally and logically exist within a single entity. For example, a beauty salon can provide grooming services and sell beauty products using a single business. This makes sense. This can be done, for example, using a single entity or a holding company, with different activities run by different divisions, each with its own name.

For other situations, however, conducting different activities through separate entities makes more sense. Here are some pros and cons to using multiple entities. (The impact on the hobby loss rule of conducting separate activities is explained in Chapter 27.)

### *Legal Reasons*

There are usually no legal bars under state law to operating different activities within a single business. But separate entities are a way to create the utmost liability protection. Typically, building owners form separate LLCs or corporations for each property. In this case, it is not the owner's personal liability that is being protected in case of lawsuits, but rather the assets of the properties on which the liability did *not* arise. For instance, say an individual owns 2 small motels.

If there is a legal action against one motel, the other can be at risk unless each is a separate legal entity.

### *Business Reasons*

Administratively, it may be easier and less costly to run a single entity, but the activities may not be suitable to be joined in a single business. For example, say a computer consultant operating as a single-member LLC also has an active eBay business. From a marketing perspective, it does not make good business sense to conduct the eBay activities through the same LLC; they can be run as a sole proprietorship or other entity formed exclusively for online selling.

### *Tax Reasons*

There may be tax reasons for separating businesses into different entities. Depending on the nature of each activity, one might be better operated on a calendar year, while it makes better sense to use a fiscal year for another.

It is usually wise to use a separate entity to own real estate that will be used by the business. This allows the owner to make decisions regarding the real estate without involving the business. For example, a single owner of a dental practice run as a professional corporation may buy a professional building, using an LLC. The practice can lease space from the LLC, but the owner can decide when or if to sell the building. Or, for estate planning reasons, the owner may decide to gift interests in the LLC to family members and cede ownership and/or control to younger relatives. As long as the terms of the lease are fair (i.e., a reasonable rent is charged), the practice can deduct its lease payments even though it is the dentist who is ultimately receiving the rents as owner of the LLC.

In deciding between a single entity or multiple entities, factor in the passive activity loss rules. If you are a silent partner in one activity and active in the other, losses from the silent (passive) activity cannot be used to offset income from the active business; if these separate activities were run within a single entity, income could be offset by losses, and it might be possible that no activity would be viewed as a passive activity because of your level of participation in the overall business.

If you have multiple businesses, you may be able to aggregate them to maximize the QBI deduction (see Chapter 21).

In deciding between a single entity or multiple entities, take state taxes into account. The added cost of additional state taxes for multiple entities may make using a single entity preferable.

## When to Run Multiple Activities within One Business

It is not always better to use multiple businesses. Sometimes a single entity can meet business needs, with no tax disadvantages. Here are some reasons to opt for a single entity:

- *Savings on legal and accounting costs*. A single entity cuts down on the cost for entity formation as well as ongoing costs for accounting and tax return preparation. Series LLC (also referred to as cell LLCs), which is a group of individual LLCs, may be formed in a number of locations (see Table 28.1). Some states don't permit formation but recognize those formed in other states ("foreign LLCs"). In this type of organization, the debts and liabilities of each LLC remain separate from those of the other LLCs. But using a master LLC makes things administratively easier and less costly.

**TABLE 28.1** Locations Where Series LLCs May Be Formed

| | | |
|---|---|---|
| Alabama | Kansas | Tennessee |
| Arkansas | Missouri | Texas |
| Delaware | Montana | Utah |
| District of Columbia | Nebraska | Virginia |
| Illinois | Nevada | Wisconsin |
| Indiana | North Dakota | Wyoming |
| Iowa | Oklahoma | |

- *State tax savings*. Where state law imposes a tax, a single entity reduces franchise or other annual tax costs. For example, California charges an annual fee for LLCs (in addition to the annual fee on their revenues), so using separate entities can get pricey.

## Treatment of Multiple Corporations

C corporations that have certain intertwining ownership are called "controlled corporations" and are subject to special tax treatment. There are 2 types of controlled corporations:

1. *Parent-subsidiary controlled group*. One corporation owns (directly or indirectly) at least 80% of the stock of one or more other corporations.
2. *Brother-sister controlled group*. Two or more corporations are owned by 5 or fewer persons (persons include not only individuals, but also estates and trusts), who together possess at least 50% of the total voting power or value of the corporation and more than 50% of the combined voting power or value of all stock.

**Example**

**An individual owns all the stock of Corporation A and 75% of the stock of Corporation B. A and B are a brother-sister controlled group.**

The status of a group can change from year to year. For instance, in the brother-sister situation, a sixth shareholder can enter the picture so that the group of corporations is no longer a controlled group.

### *Advantages and Disadvantages*

There are both advantages and disadvantages of a controlled group.

Advantages include:

- Minimizing payroll taxes when an employee works for more than one related corporation. Under the "common paymaster rule," one corporation is designated as the paymaster responsible for payroll taxes so that each corporation does not pay payroll taxes that could have been avoided. For instance, in 2021, if a shareholder works for his 2 controlled corporations, earning $150,000 from each, one is designated as a paymaster and pays the employer's Social Security portion of FICA on wages up to $142,800, a tax of $8,853.60. Without a common paymaster, each corporation would owe this tax.

- Flexibility to sell off property or business units without selling the entire business. But if a member of a brother-sister group sells property at a loss to another member of the group, the loss is not deductible in the year of sale but is postponed until the property is sold outside the group.
- State tax simplification (filing a single return for the group).
- Ability to attract investors or obtain financing.
- Different tax elections (accounting method and tax year) are still allowed.

Disadvantages include:

- Allocation required for various tax breaks, including the Section 179 expensing deduction, the accumulated earnings tax exemption, the disabled access credit, and certain other tax breaks.
- Postponement of loss recognition on intergroup sales.
- Employees of each corporation are treated as a group for purposes of employee benefits and retirement plans (e.g., testing for nondiscrimination of a plan must take employees of all group members into account).
- Full-time and full-time equivalent employees are aggregated for determining whether a company is an applicable large employer for purposes of the Affordable Care Act's employer mandate.

The losses of one corporation cannot be used to offset the profits of another unless the group files a consolidated corporate income tax return.

## Tax Rules for Owners of Multiple Businesses

The tax impact of multiple businesses is not limited to controlled corporations. There may be special rules or limitations on owners of multiple businesses.

### *Tax Returns*

Each entity is required to file separate federal income tax returns. For example, a sole proprietorship for consulting and another for a gift basket business must each complete a separate Schedule C.

Separate returns are also due at the state level in states that impose an income tax or annual filing requirement.

Entities that own or are owned by other entities may have to disclose this information on their tax returns. For example, corporations must include detailed information about ownership in Schedule K of Form 1120 if any foreign or domestic corporation, disregarded entity, partnership, or trust owns (directly or indirectly) 20% or more of the total voting power of all classes of the corporation's stock entitled to vote. Such information includes the name of the entity, its employer identification number, type of entity, country of organization, and percentage owned of the voting stock.

### *First-Year Section 179 Expensing*

The Section 179 deduction applies at the owner level for pass-through entities. Thus, individuals who own more than one such business must use care to optimize this write-off.

**Example**

**An individual has a sole proprietorship and is a 50% member of a limited liability company. In 2021, the sole proprietorship buys equipment costing $100,000 and elects Section 179 expensing. The LLC also buys equipment costing $400,000 and elects the full expensing amount. As a result, the individual's Schedule K-1 from the LLC allocates $200,000 to her (50% of the $400,000 deduction). If her taxable income is only $175,000, she can't claim all of the Section 179 expensing allocable to her.**

### *Retirement Plans*

Having separate entities can help owners boost their retirement savings.

**Example**

**B has a sole proprietorship and an LLC. Each is highly profitable. Each business can set up a simplified employee pension (SEP) plan and add for 2021 up to $58,000 on behalf of B, so that the owner's retirement savings for the year is $116,000.**

But owners of multiple businesses are subject to an overall limitation on salary reductions, the so-called employee share of contributions, to 401(k) plans and SIMPLE plans. In 2021, for example, the maximum employee contribution to a 401(k) plan is $19,500 ($26,000 for those 50 and older by year-end). If an owner's multiple businesses each maintains 401(k) plans, the most he or she can add in 2021 is this dollar limit.

**Example**

**C, age 45, has a sole proprietorship with a solo 401(k) and is a 50% owner of an S corporation that maintains a 401(k) plan. If he contributes $19,500 to his sole proprietorship's plan, he cannot make any salary reduction contributions to the S corporation's plan. In this situation, the salary reduction should be made to the plan that provides the greater employer contribution.**

Multiple businesses with common ownership are treated as a single business for qualified retirement plan rules (see Chapter 16).

### *Employer Mandate*

In determining whether you are an applicable large employer (ALE) subject to the employer mandate (assuming it is in place), all employees of your multiple businesses are taken into account using the same rules that apply to retirement plans (see above).

CHAPTER 29

# Alternative Minimum Tax


| | | | |
|---|---|---|---|
| Alternative Minimum Tax Basics | 504 | Credit Offsets | 506 |
| Deduction Limits for Alternative Minimum Tax | 505 | Minimum Tax Credit | 507 |


Reducing regular tax is only part of the battle that a small business owner wages to increase after-tax returns. Minimizing or avoiding alternative minimum tax (AMT) where applicable is another important front that must be addressed. Some business owners may find themselves subject to AMT if they have certain substantial deductions and/or credits. C corporations are not subject to the AMT, so the balance of this chapter refers to the AMT for individuals (i.e., owners of pass-through entities).

## Alternative Minimum Tax Basics

*Alternative minimum tax* is designed to ensure that all taxpayers pay at least some tax. Years ago, with tax shelters and other loopholes, wealthy individuals and corporations often paid little or no tax. In an effort to make all taxpayers share the tax burden, an AMT was imposed.

The AMT is a separate tax system, with its own deductions and tax rates. A taxpayer computes the regular income tax as well as a tentative AMT. The extent to which the tentative AMT exceeds regular tax liability is reported as AMT.

Alternative minimum tax liability for individuals can be reduced by certain personal tax credits, including a limited foreign tax credit (corporations can reduce their AMT liability only by a limited foreign tax credit).

Individuals have a two-tier AMT rate structure of 26% on the first $199,900 of income subject to AMT in 2021 (called alternative minimum taxable income, or AMTI), plus 28% on any excess amount. For married persons filing separately, the 26% rate applies to AMTI up to $99,950. The amount subject to these tax rates is reduced by an exemption amount. This exemption amount is phased out for high-income taxpayers.

The AMT exemption amounts for 2021 are listed in Table 29.1.

**TABLE 29.1 2021 Exemption Amounts**

| Filing Status | Exemption |
|---|---|
| Married filing jointly/surviving spouse | $114,600 |
| Single/head of household | $73,600 |
| Married filing separately | $57,300 |

The exemption for individuals begins to phase out when AMTI exceeds a threshold amount that depends on your filing status. For 2021, the thresholds are:

- $1,047,200 for married persons filing jointly and surviving spouses
- $523,600 for other filers

Fortunately, AMT liability can be offset by nonrefundable personal credits.

Who is subject to the AMT? Owners of pass-through entities (partnerships, LLCs, and S corporations) figure AMT on their individual returns. They include business items passed through to them and identified as AMT items on their Schedule K-1.

## Deduction Limits for Alternative Minimum Tax

Certain deductions that were allowed for regular tax purposes may be disallowed or modified for AMT. If you claimed an itemized deduction for state and local taxes and foreign income taxes on Schedule A (Form 1040 or 1040-SR), you need to make an adjustment in figuring your alternative minimum taxable income.

The following deductions that were claimed on individual returns must also be modified for AMT purposes:

- Investment interest.
- Depreciation.
- Net operating losses (NOLs).
- Mining exploration and development costs (the regular tax deduction must be amortized over 10 years).
- Research and experimentation expenditures (costs must be amortized over 10 years if you are not a material participant in the business).
- Passive activity losses from nonfarming activities (losses are adjusted for items not deductible for AMT purposes).

### *Adjustments for Depreciation*

The depreciation method that you use for regular tax purposes may require that an adjustment be made for AMT purposes. For AMT purposes, you are allowed only a limited depreciation deduction. If you claimed more for regular tax purposes, you must adjust your AMT income accordingly.

For property (other than real property) acquired after 1986, your AMT depreciation is limited to the 150% declining balance method, switching to straight line when a larger depreciation deduction results. For real property paced in service after 1986 but before 1999, your AMT depreciation is limited to straight line over 40 years.

**NOTE**
**Different adjustments apply to property placed in service before 1987. Follow the instructions to Form 6251.**

For real property placed in service after December 31, 1998, an AMT adjustment is no longer required. For personal property placed in service after this date, a depreciation election can be made to use the same depreciation method for regular and AMT purposes so that an AMT adjustment is avoided. By making this election, depreciation is figured using the 150% declining balance method over the regular tax recovery period (instead of the 200% declining balance method). For an explanation of these depreciation methods, see Chapter 14.

### *Preference Items*

Certain items that may have escaped the regular tax are subject to AMT. These include:

- Tax-exempt interest on private activity bonds issued after August 7, 1986.
- Exclusion of 50% of the gain on the sale of certain small business stock (see Chapter 5).
- Oil and gas preferences.
- Accelerated depreciation on real property acquired before 1987.

### *Net Operating Losses*

The NOL deduction for regular tax purposes must be adjusted for AMT. This is because only a limited NOL deduction is allowed for AMT purposes by individuals. The NOL for AMT purposes is the regular tax NOL except that the nonbusiness deduction adjustment includes only AMT itemized deductions (i.e., state and local taxes and certain other deductions cannot be used to figure the NOL deduction).

You may be able to eliminate your AMT liability because of your NOL deduction. However, the NOL deduction cannot be more than 90% of AMT income (without regard to the NOL deduction). If you cannot use all of your NOL because of the 90% limit, you may carry it forward indefinitely (explained in Chapter 4). However, the carryback and carryforward are also subject to the 90% limit.

### *Other Adjustments and Preferences*

In figuring AMT income on which AMT tax is imposed, certain income items are also given special treatment. These include incentive stock options, long-term contracts, tax-exempt interest on private activity bonds, and basis adjustments for AMT gain or loss.

## Credit Offsets

Only certain tax credits can be used to offset AMT liability. Components of the general business credit *cannot* be used to offset this tax. In 2021, the credits that can offset AMT liability include:

- *Foreign tax credit.*
- *Research credit.* This offset option applies only to a business with average annual gross receipts of $50 million or less in the 3 previous years. For partnerships and S corporations, this test must also be met at the owner level.
- *Certain personal tax credits.* Nonrefundable personal credits can be used to offset the AMT.

## Minimum Tax Credit

If you paid AMT last year, you may be eligible for a tax credit this year. Different minimum tax credits apply for individuals and corporations.

### *Individuals*

You qualify for a minimum tax credit if you meet any of the following 3 conditions:

1. You paid any AMT in 2020.
2. You had an unused minimum tax credit that you carried forward from 2020 to 2021.
3. You had certain unallowed business-related credits in 2020.

The credit is the amount of AMT paid in 2020 reduced by the part of the tax related to exclusion items (standard deduction, medical expenses, taxes, gains on small business stock, tax-exempt interest from private activity bonds, and depletion). The credit may be increased by minimum tax credit carryforwards, and unallowed credits for nonconventional-source fuel, and orphan drugs.

Compute the credit on Form 8801 *Credit for Prior Year Minimum Tax–Individuals, Estates, and Trusts*. If the credit exceeds your AMT liability for 2021, the excess amount may be carried forward and used to offset AMT liability in a future year. There is no limit on the carryforward period.

### *Corporations*

While the corporate AMT has been repealed, there is still an opportunity for corporations to use minimum tax credits. Unlike an individual's minimum tax credit which is limited to exclusion items, corporations that paid AMT in a prior year may claim a tax credit in 2021. The credit applied against income tax (reduced by nonrefundble credits) is refundable. More specifically, the credit is 100% refundable in 2021 if it hasn't yet been used up.

Of course, since small corporations were exempt from AMT, only large corporations can have a minimum tax credit.

## Where to Figure Alternative Minimum Tax

### *Self-Employed*

If you have any adjustments or preference items, you must complete Form 6251, *Alternative Minimum Tax—Individuals*. The amount of AMT liability is entered on Schedule 2 of Form 1040 or 1040-SR. You may or may not have any AMT liability.

If you are eligible for the minimum tax credit, it is figured on Form 8801, *Credit for Prior Year Minimum Tax—Individuals, Estates, and Trusts*. Also use this form to figure any credit carryforward to the next year.

### *Partnerships and LLCs*

The business reports an owner's share of AMT items on Schedule K-1. As an owner, you must complete Form 6251 to see if you owe any AMT.

### S Corporations

The business reports an owner's share of AMT items on Schedule K-1. As an owner, you must complete Form 6251 to see if you owe any AMT.

### C Corporations

Even though a C corporation is no longer subject to the AMT, if it has an unused minimum tax credit carryforward, use Form 8827, *Credit for Prior Year Minimum Tax—Corporations,* to figure the refundable portion that can be claimed for 2021.

# CHAPTER 30

# Other Taxes


State Income Taxes 509
Employment Taxes 512
Self-Employment Tax 519
Additional Medicare Taxes for Individuals 523
Sales and Use Taxes 524
Excise Taxes 525


Federal income taxes may be your primary concern and your greatest tax liability, but as a business owner, you may have other tax obligations as well. You may owe state income and franchise taxes, employment taxes, sales and use taxes, and excise taxes.

Estimated taxes, which are not a separate tax but rather a way in which to pay taxes, are discussed in Chapter 31.

For more information about various other taxes, see IRS Publication 15, *Circular E, Employer's Tax Guide*; IRS Publication 15-A, *Employer's Supplemental Tax Guide*; IRS Publication 15-B, *Employer's Guide to Fringe Benefits*; and IRS Publication 510, *Excise Taxes*.

## State Income Taxes

You may owe state income taxes on your business profits in each state in which you do business. Your obligation does *not* depend on where the business is set up. For example, if you incorporate your business in Nevada but operate in California, you owe income taxes to California, the state in which you do business. (And you may owe a tax or fee to Nevada as well.)

Generally, state income taxes usually depend on having a nexus (connection) to the state. This is based on having a physical presence there, which may be evidenced by maintaining an office or sending a sales force into the state; merely shipping goods into the state without some additional connection is not enough to establish a business presence within the state. You may have a nexus to more than one state, no matter how small your business is.

If there is a business connection to more than one state, the business income is apportioned among those states. Apportionment is based on a sales factor, a payroll factor, and a property factor (each state has different apportionment formulas). The apportionment rules are highly complex, but there is some flexibility that permits you to shift income into the state with the lower taxes within certain limits.

Some states are moving toward a commercial or financial nexus as a basis for imposing state income tax. Doing business with consumers and companies in other states may expose you to taxes that you never dreamed of. States are reaching out across their borders to grab revenue from out-of-state businesses in any way they can.

### Tax on Services Revenue

There are two main ways in which revenue on services is taxed: market-based method and cost-of-performance (COP) method. The trend is in favor of market-based performance.

- ***Market-based method.*** This is a tax sourced where the economic benefit of the activity results. For example, an advertising firm based in Connecticut provides services for a business in California. The California imposes a tax, to be paid by the Connecticut firm, on the services that benefit the California business. A business can be subject to double taxation—income tax on revenue earned in its state plus the sourcing of services tax on the benefits received in another state. There is no credit that can be claimed for the out-of-state taxes; they are, however, deductible. This type of income tax applies in Alabama, Arizona, California, Connecticut, District of Columbia, Georgia, Illinois, Iowa, Louisiana, Maine, Maryland, Massachusetts, Michigan, Minnesota, Missouri, Nebraska, New York, Oklahoma, Pennsylvania, Rhode Island, Tennessee, Utah, Washington, and Wisconsin.
- ***Cost-of-performance (COP) method.*** This is a tax on services sourced to where the activities are performed. States following this method include Alaska, Colorado, Delaware, Florida, Hawaii, Idaho, Kansas, Kentucky, Mississippi, Montana, New Hampshire, New Jersey, New Mexico, North Carolina, North Dakota, Oregon, South Dakota, Texas, Vermont, Virginia, and West Virginia.

### Gross Receipts Tax

**NOTE**

**Some states have both an income tax and a gross receipts tax.**

A tax that differs from a state income tax is a gross receipts tax. This is a tax on a company's gross sales without taking into account any deductions for expenses. A state may call the tax something other than a gross receipts tax (e.g., "business and occupation tax," "commerce tax," "margin tax"). States with a gross receipts tax include: Delaware, Nevada, Ohio, Oregon, Tennessee, Texas, and Washington.

### Reporting State Taxes

If you are a sole proprietor or an owner of a pass-through entity, you must file a state income tax return in every state in which your company does business (if such state has a personal income tax). For example, if an LLC does business in 12 states, all of which impose an income tax, each member of the LLC must file a personal income tax return in those 12 states.

Of course, even if you do business within a state, there may be no tax liability. For example, Wyoming does not have a personal or corporate income tax, so there is no tax even if you do business in this state.

The filing deadlines for state business returns are not the same as the federal deadlines in all cases, so check with your state tax authority for the forms to file and when to file them. You may also need to obtain a state tax identification number for your business.

### Corporations

Corporations may owe state corporate income tax. Only 6 states—Nevada, Ohio, South Dakota, Texas, Washington, and Wyoming—have no corporate income tax. Again, check for "nexus" to determine whether your corporation is subject to state corporate income tax. For example, Pennsylvania is now using economic nexus. In some states, this is called a **franchise tax**.

---

***Franchise tax*** **State tax imposed on a state-chartered corporation for the right to do business under the corporate name within the state (it has nothing to do with whether the business is a franchise).**

---

S corporations in most states are taxed in the same way as they are taxed for federal income tax purposes (i.e., income, losses, etc., pass through to shareholders to be reported on their personal income tax returns). In jurisdictions where the S election is not recognized (e.g., District of Columbia, New Hampshire, New York City, and Tennessee), an S corporation is taxed the same as a C corporation. However, if the S election is recognized and the corporation has shareholders who are not residents of the state, special rules may apply (for example, the corporation may be required to make tax payments on behalf of these shareholders).

In most states, the S election for state tax purposes is automatic if a federal election is filed. However, in about half a dozen states you must file a separate state tax election for S corporation status (merely filing the federal election is not sufficient for state tax purposes).

Some states, such as California, New York and Rhode Island, allow S status but also impose an annual corporate-level tax for the privilege of being an S corporation. The corporate-level tax applies even though the income and deductions of the corporation pass through to shareholders and are taxed on their personal returns.

Some states that recognize S status still tax some of the S corporation's income (e.g., S corporations in Indiana and Kentucky pay tax on their capital gains and excess passive income, while Massachusetts taxes the corporation on net profits over a certain amount but shareholders are not taxed on these profits).

For more information about the state income taxes, contact the tax or revenue departments of each state in which you do business. You can find contact information through https://www.statelocalgov.net.

### Other Income-Based State Taxes

States seem to be able to dream up new taxes when there is a need for revenue. For example, in New York, there is a Metropolitan Commuter Transportation Mobility tax imposed on self-employed individuals and business owners in New York City and the 7 counties that surround it. For self-employed individuals, the tax is 0.0034 of net earnings from self-employment, even if they do not venture into New York City. The tax is paid by self-employed individuals along with their state income tax returns. Businesses with payroll exceeding a set amount in a calendar quarter are required to pay the tax (ranging from 0.11% to 0.34%, depending on the payroll expense) and remit it to the state on a quarterly basis. Find information about this tax at https://www.tax.ny.gov/bus/mctmt/.

Seattle imposes a tax on businesses with at least $7 million in annual payroll expenses. The payroll tax ranges from 0.7% to 2.4% of salary amounts over $150,000 paid to Seattle-based employees.

## Employment Taxes

You may be liable for the payment of certain taxes with respect to the compensation you paid to your employees. If you own a corporation, these obligations apply even if you are its *only* employee. If you are a single member limited liability company, you are treated as a separate entity for employment taxes, even though you are a "disregarded entity" for reporting and paying your own income taxes; you must report employment taxes on wages paid to employees, under your entity name and using an employer identification number (not your Social Security number). As a small business owner, you need to know what taxes you are responsible for, where and when to deposit the taxes, and what returns you must file for employment taxes. The returns you must file are discussed later in this chapter. In this section you will learn about employment taxes and where to deposit them. The deductibility of these taxes is discussed in Chapter 13.

*Employment taxes* (also called *payroll taxes*) is a term that collectively refers to an employer's tax obligations with respect to employee compensation. Employment taxes include income tax withholding (both federal and, where applicable, state), FICA (the employer and employee share, as explained later), FUTA (federal unemployment tax, as explained later), and state unemployment tax. There may also be state disability taxes.

You may find assistance on employment tax obligations for small businesses at www.irs.gov and search "small business and self-employed tax center." You should also contact your state tax department to learn about your state employment tax obligations.

### *Employment Tax Obligations*

The Federal Insurance Contribution Act (FICA) set up a (Social Security and Medicare) system to provide for old age, survivors, disability, and hospital insurance of workers. Both you, the employer, and your employees contribute to this system. The Federal Unemployment Tax Act (FUTA), together with state unemployment systems, provides payment to workers in the event of unemployment. Only employers pay this tax.

You must withhold from your employees' wages income tax and the employee portion of Social Security and Medicare taxes. These taxes are referred to as *trust fund* amounts because you, as employer, are holding the funds in trust for your employees. You must pay over these amounts to the IRS. You must also pay the IRS the employer portion of Social Security and Medicare taxes, which is the same amount that the employee paid, plus FUTA.

Severance payments to terminated workers are wages for employment tax purposes.

Employment taxes must be figured to the penny. You cannot round off employment taxes to the nearest dollar (as you can with income taxes).

**NOTE**

**The U.S. Justice Department's Tax Division has indicated it will aggressively pursue unpaid employment taxes, which can include paying employees in cash so that wages are unreported. A willful failure to collect or pay employment taxes is punishable by fines up to $250,000 for individuals and/or jail time up to 5 years.**

#### FICA

The tax rate for the Social Security portion of FICA is 6.2% of the first $142,800 of wages in 2021. This wage base is adjusted annually for inflation. Both the employer and employee pay this tax rate on the taxable compensation up to the wage base limit. The tax rate for the Medicare portion of FICA is 1.45% on all compensation. There is no wage base ceiling for purposes of computing this tax. You must withhold this amount from the employee's compensation and pay a similar amount as the employer. Usually, FICA is paid on deferred compensation when it is earned, not when it is paid.

***Deferral***. Employers that elected to defer the employer share of Social Security taxes required to be made on taxable compensation paid from March 27, 2020, through December 31, 2020, must pay 50% of the taxes by December 31, 2021, and the other 50% by December 31, 2022. No interest is charged on the deferred taxes.

Employers were permitted (but didn't have to) defer the employees' share of Social Security taxes for September 1, 2020, through December 31, 2020, if their bi-weekly pay period compensation was less than $4,000. Deferred amounts must be paid between January 1, 2021, and December 31, 2021; interest, penalties, and additions to tax begins to accrue on employers thereafter. Employers remain fully responsible for the deferred taxes (see IRS Q&As at https://www.irs.gov/newsroom/deferral-of-employment-tax-deposits-and-payments-through-December-31-2020).

***Certain employment tax credits***. The employee retention credit and, the mandatory paid sick leave and paid family leave credits, and the COBRA assistance credit are offsets to employment taxes. See Chapter 7 for an explanation of these credits.

### FUTA

The tax rate for FUTA is 6.0% of the first $7,000 of each employee's wages. However, you may claim a credit for payments to state unemployment funds of up to 5.4% of taxable wages if all state payments were made in a timely fashion. Thus, the effective FUTA rate in most cases is 0.6% of the first $7,000 of each employee's wages, which is $42.

States that owe the federal government money borrowed to pay unemployment benefits give employers a reduced credit. Information about credit reduction states for 2021 can be found in Chapter 13.

### INCOME TAX WITHHOLDING

In addition to FICA and FUTA tax you may owe, you may also be required to withhold income taxes from employee compensation. Your withholding is based on each employee's dependents (impacting eligibility for the child tax credit), other adjustments, and marital status as reported to you on Form W-4, *Employee's Withholding Certificate*. This form should be completed when employment commences and need not be updated each year (unless the employee chooses to do so). Because Form W-4 has been revised for 2021, employees may want to submit a new form. If an employee fails to complete Form W-4, then withhold based on the employee's old Form W-4 on file with you. Employers must retain these forms and make them available to the IRS, if requested.

It is important to note that the definition of compensation is, in some instances, different for purposes of income taxes and employment taxes. For example, a salary reduction that is contributed to an employee's 401(k) plan or Savings Incentive Match Plan for Employees (SIMPLE) plan is not treated as compensation subject to income tax. However, the salary reduction is still subject to FICA and FUTA.

**NOTE**

**The IRS looks closely at family hiring. Make sure that the wages are reasonable for the work performed. Keep timesheets as proof of work performed by your relatives.**

Wage differential payments made to employees while they are on active duty for more than 30 days are subject to income tax withholding but not to FICA and FUTA. Withholding on wage differential payments, viewed as "supplemental wages," can be made by using withholding tables, or ordinary pay can be aggregated with wage differential payments and subjected to a flat 22% withholding, as long as this compensation is less than $1 million.

Table 30.1 can be used to determine your employment tax obligations for various fringe benefits you may provide to employees in 2021.

**TABLE 30.1** Your Employment Tax Obligation on Common Fringe Benefits for 2021

| Fringe Benefit | Withhold Income Tax | Pay Social Security and Medicare Taxes | Pay Federal Unemployment Tax (FUTA) |
|---|---|---|---|
| Achievement awards (within limits) | No | No | No |
| Adoption assistance up to $14,440 | No | Yes | Yes |
| Athletic facilities | No | No | No |
| Company car personal use | Yes | Yes | Yes |
| De minimis benefits | No | No | No |
| Dependent care assistance up to $10,500 | | | |
| Rank-and-file employees | No | No | No |
| HCEs* (if plan discriminates) | Yes | Yes | Yes |
| Differential wage payments | Yes | No | No |
| Education assistance up to $5,250—not job related | No | No | No |
| Any job related | No | No | No |
| Elective deferrals to 401(k), SEP, or SIMPLE plans | No | Yes | Yes |
| Employee discounts | | | |
| Rank-and-file employees | No | No | No |
| HCEs* (if plan discriminates) | Yes | Yes | Yes |
| Flexible spending arrangement salary contribution | No | No | No |
| Group term life insurance | No | No up to cost of $50,000 of coverage | No |
| Health insurance | | | |
| Rank-and-file employees | No | No | No |
| More-than-2% S corporation shareholders | Yes | Yes | Yes |
| Health reimbursement arrangements (HRAs) | No | No | No |
| Health savings account contributions | No | No | No |
| Lodging on the premises | No | No | No |
| Meals on the premises | No | No | No |
| Medical care reimbursements under a self-insured plan | No | No | No |
| No-additional-cost services | No | No | No |
| Paid sick leave and paid family leave | Yes | Yes | Yes |
| Stock options | | | |
| ISOs | No | No when granted; yes when exercised | No when granted; yes when exercised |
| Employee stock purchase plans | No | No when granted; yes when exercised | No when granted; yes when exercised |
| Nonqualified stock options | Yes when exercised | Yes when exercised | Yes when exercised |

**TABLE 30.1** ***(Continued)***

| Fringe Benefit | Withhold Income Tax | Pay Social Security and Medicare Taxes | Pay Federal Unemployment Tax (FUTA) |
|---|---|---|---|
| Supplemental unemployment compensation plan benefits | Yes | No | No |
| Transportation benefits | | | |
| Rank-and-file employees | No | No | No |
| More-than-2% S corporation shareholders | Yes | Yes | Yes |
| Vacation pay | Yes | Yes | Yes |
| Working condition benefit | No | No | No |

*HCEs are highly compensated employees—owners and employees earning over a set dollar limit that adjusts annually for inflation.

Income tax withholding usually is based on IRS withholding tables. There are separate tables for married employees and for those who are single (including heads of households). As a practical matter, very few small businesses still figure withholding manually; software or an outside payroll service is used for this purpose.

For supplemental wages, such as bonuses, commissions, overtime pay, payments for accumulated sick leave, severance pay, awards, prizes, back pay, retroactive pay increases, differential wage payments to reservists, and payments for nondeductible moving expenses, you have a choice:

- Add payments to regular wages and figure withholding on the total in the usual way.
- Withhold on the supplemental wages at the rate of 22%. (A 37% withholding rate applies to supplemental wages exceeding $1 million, which isn't likely to occur in a small business.)

#### EMPLOYING FAMILY MEMBERS

If you are self-employed and employ your child who is under age 18, his or her wages are not subject to FICA. If you employ your spouse in your business, his or her wages are fully subject to FICA. If you have a corporation that employs a child under age 18, his or her wages are still subject to FICA. Your child's wages are exempt from FUTA until he or she reaches age 21.

#### LEASED EMPLOYEES

If you lease employees from a corporation that supplies workers for your business, the employees may be treated as in the employ of the corporation that does the leasing rather than as your employees. The leasing corporation, and not you, is responsible for the payment of employment taxes.

### *Special Rules for Tips*

Tips that employees receive are taxable wages for purposes of employment taxes. Employees are *supposed* to report their tips to employers so that employment taxes can be applied. However, as a practical matter, this is not always the case.

The U.S. Supreme Court has said that the IRS can use an estimated aggregation of unreported tips to assess FICA tax on employers; the IRS does not have to audit each employee to determine actual unreported tips for purposes of determining the employer share of FICA.

To avoid this forced rate upon employers, the IRS has developed voluntary compliance agreements for industries, such as the restaurant industry, where tipping is customary. These agreements are designed to enhance tax compliance among tipped employees through education and avoid employer examination during the period that the agreements are in place. They include:

- Tip reporting alternative commitment (TRAC)—avoids the establishment of a tip rate, requires all employers to educate employees on tip reporting requirements, requires employees to report monthly to employers, and provides for audits of those employees who underreport.
- Tip rate determination agreement (TRDA)—sets a tip rate through employers cooperating with the IRS; requires employees to sign a Tipped Employee Participation Agreement with the employer (75% of whom must sign).
- Employer-designed tip reporting alternative commitment (EmTRAC)— solely for those in the food and beverage industry whose employees receive both cash and charged tips, this program generally follows the TRAC program.
- Gaming Industry Tip Compliance Agreement (GITCA)—solely for the gaming (casino) industry (details are in Publication 4932, Gaming Industry Tip Compliance Agreement). The IRS modified the program so the agreement may now run for 5 years (see Revenue Procedure 2020-47).

### SERVICE CHARGES

Restaurants that have an 18% service charge for large groups (e.g., 8 or more people) or other similar charge cannot treat the charge as a tip. Instead, service charges are considered wages subject to the usual income tax and FICA withholding. This means that the service charges are not taken into account by employers when figuring the credit for FICA on tips (see Chapter 23).

Sometimes it's not easy to distinguish between a tip and a service charge. A customer's payment can be treated as a tip only if *all* of the following conditions are met:

1. The payment is made free from compulsion
2. The customer has the unrestricted right to determine the amount
3. The payment is not the subject of negotiation or dictated by the employer's policy
4. The customer has the right to determine who receives the payment

If you show computations of various percentages as tips possibilities, this does not create a service charge

**Example**

**The customer's bill comes to $68.43. The printed bill presented to the customer shows a calculation for a 10% tip of $6.84, a 15% tip of $10.26, and an 18% tip of $12.32. It's up to the customer what, if anything, to add to the bill for the server. Whatever is added is a tip.**

**The customer's bill comes to $142.58 for a party of 6. As is the practice in the restaurant, 18% is automatically added to the bill, bringing the total to $168.24 ($142.58 + $25.66). The 18% addition to the bill is a service charge representing wages for the server.**

### *Paying Employment Taxes*

When employment taxes must be paid to the IRS is determined in part by the size of the tax liability. The largest employers (more than $50,000 in employment taxes in the previous calendar quarter) pay ("deposit") their employment taxes semiweekly (every 2 weeks); those that are not quite as large ($50,000 or less in employment taxes) do so every month. Employers of very small businesses (less than $2,500 in employment taxes in the calendar quarter or previous calendar quarter) can submit their employment taxes along with their quarterly employer tax returns. The smallest employers ($1,000 or less for income tax withholding and FICA or a FUTA payment under $500) can pay annually. For FUTA, this means employers with 8 or fewer employees qualify for making one annual payment.

All employers, other than those that pay their taxes with returns, must deposit taxes electronically using the Electronic Federal Tax Payment System (EFTPS) (https://www.eftps.gov). With EFTPS, funds are transferred from your bank directly to the U.S. Treasury.

Very small employers that are not required to use EFTPS can voluntarily do so. One benefit of doing so is the ability to schedule payments in advance. Note that using EFTPS does not give the IRS access to your bank account. If you wish to voluntarily enroll, you can do so online at https://www.eftps.gov or call 800-945-8400 or 800-555-4477.

#### DEPOSIT DATES

Depending on the size of your payroll, you are put on one of 2 deposit schedules, *monthly* or *semiweekly*. (See Table 30.2.) The IRS notifies all employers each November of their schedule for the coming calendar year. The determination of your deposit schedule is based on your employment taxes during a lookback period (2 years prior to the upcoming year). If your employment taxes were $50,000 or less in the lookback period, you are on a monthly deposit schedule. If your employment taxes exceeded $50,000 in the lookback period, you are on a semiweekly deposit schedule. It is important to note that even if you are put on a monthly deposit schedule, you need not file the quarterly employment tax return monthly or more frequently unless the IRS instructs you to file Form 941-M, *Employer's Monthly Federal Tax Return*. Remember, the amount of your employment taxes, not the time you pay your employees (i.e., weekly, semimonthly, monthly), determines your depositor status.

**NOTE**

**If you fall behind in a deposit, the IRS may send a reminder letter. This letter is designed to prompt you to take action, or if you use an outside payroll company, inform you that your deposits are not being made.**

**TABLE 30.2 Deposit Schedule**

| Type of Deposit Schedule | Due |
|---|---|
| Monthly | 15th day of the following month |
| Semiweekly | |
| Payment on Wednesday, Thursday, and/or Friday | Following Wednesday |
| Payment on Saturday, Sunday, Monday, and/or Tuesday | Following Friday |

#### PAYMENT WITH RETURNS

Instead of depositing employment taxes, you can pay them directly to the IRS along with your return if your net tax liability for the quarterly return is less than $2,500. Thus, for example, if you have one employee who earned only $10,000 for the quarter, employment taxes will be under $2,500, so you can pay them directly to the IRS when you file your return, Form 941. If you are not sure whether your quarterly employment taxes will cross the $2,500 threshold, it is advisable to deposit the taxes monthly in order to avoid a penalty.

For FUTA taxes, the deposit threshold is $500. This means that companies with 8 or fewer employees can pay this tax annually when the annual FUTA return is filed.

You can pay employment taxes by credit card to cover any balance due on the return. There is a convenience fee charged by the credit card service provider:

- Pay 1040 at https://www.pay1040.com/
- ACI Payments at https://fed.acipayonline.com/
- PayUSAtax at https://payusatax.com/

### Payroll Tax Credits

Certain credits can be offsets to some employment taxes. These credits are listed in Chapter 23.

### Penalty for Failure to Pay Employment Taxes

As an employer, you are required to deduct and withhold income taxes and FICA from your employee's compensation. If you fail to do so, or if you withhold an insufficient amount, you are still liable for the correct amount.

There is a 100% penalty imposed on persons who are responsible for paying employment taxes but willfully fail to do so. This penalty, called the *trust fund recovery penalty* (because an employer pays income tax withholding and the employee's share of Social Security and Medicare taxes into a trust fund maintained by the government for the employee's benefit), is a personal one against an owner, officer, or other responsible person. Thus, for example, a shareholder in a corporation who serves as company president may be personally liable for this penalty even though a shareholder generally is not liable for corporate debts.

Even if there is more than one responsible person, the IRS can collect the entire tax and penalty from one person. It is up to that one person to try to recover a portion of the payment from other responsible persons. If you make a written request, the IRS must notify you of the name of the person who it has determined to be responsible and whether it has attempted to collect the penalty from other responsible persons. There is *federal right of contribution* (to collect a share of the penalty by someone who has paid it from someone else who is also responsible) where there are multiple responsible persons.

The second test for the trust fund recovery penalty (the first is being a responsible person) is willfulness to deposit the funds. Willfulness doesn't require any evil or bad intent. Understanding the responsibility to make the deposit and using the funds for any other purpose (even paying the rent, utilities, or vendors in order to stay in business) is treated as willfulness.

### Penalty for Delinquent Deposits

Unless you can show reasonable cause for failing to deposit required amounts or paying deposits directly to the IRS instead of depositing the employment taxes, you will be subject to a penalty. The penalty schedule is designed to encourage employers to comply with deposit requirements as quickly as possible. The penalty for delinquent deposits and penalty relief are explained in Appendix B.

In view of this substantial penalty, it is essential that employment taxes be paid. If you are experiencing a cash crunch, see that these taxes are paid before satisfying other creditors.

### State Employment Tax Obligations

As mentioned earlier in this chapter, as an employer, you should check out your obligation, if any, for state employment taxes.

## Self-Employment Tax

Self-employed individuals—sole proprietors, general partners, and LLC members who are not treated as limited partners—are not employees of their businesses even though they may be compensated for their services. Thus, they are not subject to FICA. However, self-employed individuals bear the same tax burden as owners who work for their corporations; they pay self-employment tax.

As a general rule, self-employed individuals pay self-employment tax on net earnings from self-employment. This includes a sole proprietor's net profit reported on Schedule C or Schedule F, and a general partner's self-employment earnings reported on Schedule K-1 of Form 1065, plus any guaranteed loans to them. This means self-employed individuals pay self-employment tax on more than just what might be viewed as compensation for their services; they pay the tax on a full share of their net profits (even if they don't actually receive this as payment). This is so even if they do no work at all for their business and hire someone else to run it.

Net earnings from self-employment tax include earnings abroad, even if they qualify for the foreign earned income exclusion.

Net earnings not subject to self-employment tax are investment income (dividends, interest, and capital gains); rentals from real estate by someone who is not a real estate dealer (even if the rentals are treated as qualified business income for purposes of the QBI deduction); income received as a retired partner; and Conservation Reserve Program (CRP) payments to a retired or disabled farmer.

A federal appeals court held that CRP payments to nonfarmers are not treated as self-employment income subject to self-employment tax. However, the IRS announced it would not acquiesce (agree to follow) to the decision. This means that CRP payments to nonfarmers are exempt from self-employment tax only in Arkansas, Iowa, Minnesota, Missouri, Nebraska, North Dakota, and South Dakota unless the matter is litigated and decided the same way in other federal circuits (applicable in other states).

Self-employed individuals pay both the employee and employer portion of FICA, called self-employment tax (SECA). The rate for self-employment tax is 12.4% on net earnings from self-employment (technically 92.35% of earnings) up to $142,800 in 2021 and 2.9% on all net earnings from self-employment tax. To more closely equate self-employed individuals with corporations, self-employed individuals may claim a deduction for the "employer share" of self-employment tax (what amounts to the employer portion of FICA). For 2020, self-employed individuals had the option of deferring the "employee share" of Social Security taxes on net earnings from self-employment from March 27, 2020, through December 31, 2021. If they did half of the deferred taxes must be paid by December 31, 2021, and other half by December 31, 2022. You were able to use any reasonable method to allocate 50% of the Social Security portion of self-employment tax attributable to net earnings from self-employment during this period. The maximum deferral was figured in Part III of 2020 Schedule SE (Form 1040 or 1040-SR).

Farmers who have low net earnings or even losses from farming activities can opt to create Social Security credits by using a farm optional method to report self-employment earnings. A similar option is available to nonfarmers. The tax is figured on Schedule SE, *Self-Employment Tax*, of Form 1040 or 1040-SR (see Figure 30.1).

Those with a loss or minimal earnings who want to contribute more to the Social Security system in order to build up retirement income can use the optional methods in Part II of the schedule to figure net earnings on which the self-employment tax is based.

- ***Optional farm method.*** You can use this method to figure your net earnings from farm self-employment if your gross farm income was $8,820 or less or your net farm profits were less than $6,367. Under this method, report two-thirds of your gross farm income, up to $5,880, as your net earnings for figuring self-employment tax. There is no limit on the number of years that you can use this method.
- ***Optional nonfarm method.*** You can use this method to figure your net earnings from nonfarm self-employment if your net nonfarm profits were less than $6,367 and also less than 72.189% of your gross nonfarm income. To use this method, you must also be regularly self-employed. You meet this requirement if your actual net earnings from self-employment were $400 or more in 2 of the 3 years preceding the year you use the nonfarm optional method. Under this method, report two-thirds of your gross nonfarm income as your net earnings, but not less than your actual net earnings from nonfarm self-employment. Use of the nonfarm optional method from nonfarm self-employment is limited to 5 years, but the 5 years do not have to be consecutive.

Limited partners (and LLC members treated as limited partners) are not subject to self-employment tax on their distributive share of partnership income. They are viewed as mere investors. At the present time, there is no guidance on how to treat LLC members for purposes of self-employment tax. The IRS was prevented, by law, from issuing regulations on this issue before July 1, 1998, but have not yet been issued. There have been cases in which courts have treated member-managers of LLCs as general partners subject to self-employment tax on their distributive shares of partnership income.

Unlike FICA, self-employment tax is not deposited through the Federal Electronic Tax Payment System (EFTPS.gov). Instead, it is paid along with income taxes. This means that self-employed individuals must ensure that quarterly estimated taxes cover not only their income tax obligations but also their self-employment tax for the year.

Self-employed individuals are not subject to FUTA. They cannot cover themselves for periods of no work because, by definition, self-employed persons are never employed.

However, due to COVID-19, self-employed individuals who are out of work may obtain unemployment benefits. States can provide Pandemic Unemployment Assistance (PUA) to self-employed individuals for up to 14 weeks in 2021. Self-employed individuals do not pay any federal or state unemployment tax, but are taxed on the receipt of the benefits.

### State Income Tax Withholding

If your business is located in a state that imposes a personal income tax, you are required to withhold state income tax from your employees' compensation. You can obtain information about state withholding rates by contacting your state tax authority.

**SCHEDULE SE (Form 1040)**

Department of the Treasury Internal Revenue Service (99)

# Self-Employment Tax

▶ Go to *www.irs.gov/ScheduleSE* for instructions and the latest information.
▶ Attach to Form 1040, 1040-SR, or 1040-NR.

OMB No. 1545-0074
**2021**
Attachment Sequence No. **17**

Name of person with self-employment income (as shown on Form 1040, 1040-SR, or 1040-NR) | Social security number of person with **self-employment** income ▶

## Part I Self-Employment Tax

**Note:** If your only income subject to self-employment tax is **church employee income,** see instructions for how to report your income and the definition of church employee income.

**A** If you are a minister, member of a religious order, or Christian Science practitioner **and** you filed Form 4361, but you had $400 or more of **other** net earnings from self-employment, check here and continue with Part I . . . . . . . . . ▶ ☐

Skip lines 1a and 1b if you use the farm optional method in Part II. See instructions.

| | | | |
|---|---|---|---|
| **1a** | Net farm profit or (loss) from Schedule F, line 34, and farm partnerships, Schedule K-1 (Form 1065), box 14, code A . . . | **1a** | |
| **b** | If you received social security retirement or disability benefits, enter the amount of Conservation Reserve Program payments included on Schedule F, line 4b, or listed on Schedule K-1 (Form 1065), box 20, code AH | **1b** | ( ) |
| | Skip line 2 if you use the nonfarm optional method in Part II. See instructions. | | |
| **2** | Net profit or (loss) from Schedule C, line 31; and Schedule K-1 (Form 1065), box 14, code A (other than farming). See instructions for other income to report or if you are a minister or member of a religious order | **2** | |
| **3** | Combine lines 1a, 1b, and 2 . . . | **3** | |
| **4a** | If line 3 is more than zero, multiply line 3 by 92.35% (0.9235). Otherwise, enter amount from line 3 . **Note:** If line 4a is less than $400 due to Conservation Reserve Program payments on line 1b, see instructions. | **4a** | |
| **b** | If you elect one or both of the optional methods, enter the total of lines 15 and 17 here . . . . . | **4b** | |
| **c** | Combine lines 4a and 4b. If less than $400, **stop;** you don't owe self-employment tax. **Exception:** If less than $400 and you had **church employee income,** enter -0- and continue . . . . . . . ▶ | **4c** | |
| **5a** | Enter your **church employee income** from Form W-2. See instructions for definition of church employee income . . . . . **5a** | | |
| **b** | Multiply line 5a by 92.35% (0.9235). If less than $100, enter -0- . . . | **5b** | |
| **6** | Add lines 4c and 5b . . . | **6** | |
| **7** | Maximum amount of combined wages and self-employment earnings subject to social security tax or the 6.2% portion of the 7.65% railroad retirement (tier 1) tax for 2021 . . . | **7** | 142,800 |
| **8a** | Total social security wages and tips (total of boxes 3 and 7 on Form(s) W-2) and railroad retirement (tier 1) compensation. If $142,800 or more, skip lines 8b through 10, and go to line 11 . . . **8a** | | |
| **b** | Unreported tips subject to social security tax from Form 4137, line 10 . . . **8b** | | |
| **c** | Wages subject to social security tax from Form 8919, line 10 . . . . . **8c** | | |
| **d** | Add lines 8a, 8b, and 8c . . . | **8d** | |
| **9** | Subtract line 8d from line 7. If zero or less, enter -0- here and on line 10 and go to line 11 . . . ▶ | **9** | |
| **10** | Multiply the **smaller** of line 6 or line 9 by 12.4% (0.124) . . . | **10** | |
| **11** | Multiply line 6 by 2.9% (0.029) . . . | **11** | |
| **12** | **Self-employment tax.** Add lines 10 and 11. Enter here and on **Schedule 2 (Form 1040), line 4** . . | **12** | |
| **13** | **Deduction for one-half of self-employment tax.** Multiply line 12 by 50% (0.50). Enter here and on **Schedule 1 (Form 1040), line 15** . . . **13** | | |

## Part II Optional Methods To Figure Net Earnings (see instructions)

**Farm Optional Method.** You may use this method **only** if **(a)** your gross farm income[1] wasn't more than $8,820, **or (b)** your net farm profits[2] were less than $6,367.

| | | | |
|---|---|---|---|
| **14** | Maximum income for optional methods . . . | **14** | 5,880 |
| **15** | Enter the **smaller** of: two-thirds (2/3) of gross farm income[1] (not less than zero) **or** $5,880. Also, include this amount on line 4b above . . . | **15** | |

**Nonfarm Optional Method.** You may use this method **only** if **(a)** your net nonfarm profits[3] were less than $6,367 and also less than 72.189% of your gross nonfarm income,[4] **and (b)** you had net earnings from self-employment of at least $400 in 2 of the prior 3 years. **Caution:** You may use this method no more than five times.

| | | | |
|---|---|---|---|
| **16** | Subtract line 15 from line 14 . . . | **16** | |
| **17** | Enter the **smaller** of: two-thirds (2/3) of gross nonfarm income[4] (not less than zero) **or** the amount on line 16. Also, include this amount on line 4b above . . . | **17** | |

[1] From Sch. F, line 9; and Sch. K-1 (Form 1065), box 14, code B.
[2] From Sch. F, line 34; and Sch. K-1 (Form 1065), box 14, code A—minus the amount you would have entered on line 1b had you not used the optional method.
[3] From Sch. C, line 31; and Sch. K-1 (Form 1065), box 14, code A.
[4] From Sch. C, line 7; and Sch. K-1 (Form 1065), box 14, code C.

**For Paperwork Reduction Act Notice, see your tax return instructions.** Cat. No. 11358Z **Schedule SE (Form 1040) 2021**

**FIGURE 30.1** Schedule SE

**NOTE**
**With more and more employees working remotely, be sure to check on withholding requirements if these workers are in a state that is different from your business location.**

If you have employees who live in another state, usually you are required only to withhold tax for the state in which your business is located. (The employees may be entitled to a credit for taxes paid to another state.) However, you *may* withhold state income tax for the state in which the employees reside so that they do not have to grapple with state estimated taxes. If you make such an accommodation, you must still withhold state taxes for the state in which your business is located. If you do business in more than one state and have employees who work in more than one location, you must withhold state income tax in each state in which they work. In one case, for example, withholding was required for a professional baseball player for each state in which he played ball, not just in his home state. Withholding in this case was based on the number of days he played in each of these other states.

### *Employment Tax Filing for All Businesses*

If you have employees (even if you are your corporation's only employee) and your annual taxes exceed $1,000, you must report quarterly to the IRS. Use Form 941, *Employer's Quarterly Federal Tax Return*, to report any income tax withholding and FICA withholding and payments made during the quarter. Employers seeking an advance due to certain COVID-19-related tax credits could file Form 7200, *Advance Payment of Employer Credits Due to COVID-19*.

If your annual employment taxes are anticipated to be no more than $1,000 (total compensation is about $4,000), you may qualify to file annually, rather than quarterly. The IRS notifies eligible employers that they do not have to file quarterly on Form 941 but instead can file Form 944, *Employer's Annual Federal Tax Return*. Once you have been notified by the IRS to file Form 944, you continue to do so until you are notified that you are no longer eligible for this form. If you think you qualify for annual filing but have not received notification from the IRS, you should contact the IRS and say you want to file annually. Even if you qualify to file annually, you can opt out of using Form 944 and instead file quarterly if you follow simple IRS guidelines. If you are a farmer required to file Form 943, *Employer's Annual Federal Tax Return for Agricultural Employees*, you cannot use Form 944 in any event, even if you meet the definition of a small employer.

You must also file an annual return to report the payment of federal unemployment insurance. Use Form 940, *Employer's Annual Federal Unemployment (FUTA) Tax Return*.

**NOTE**
**Reporting for employment tax obligations is separate from income tax reporting.**

Employment tax forms can be signed by facsimile, including alternative signature methods such as computer software programs or mechanical devices.

If you discover an error in a previously filed Form 941 or 944, correct the error using Form 941-X, *Adjusted Employer's QUARTERLY Federal Tax Return or Claim for Refund*, or Form 944-X, *Adjusted Employer's ANNUAL Federal Tax Return or Claim for Refund*. There is no "X" form for amending Form 940; simply use Form 940 and check the "amended return" box at the top of the return.

If you overpaid FICA taxes, you can adjust future required payments as an offset. If you want a refund, you must obtain employee consent or be limited to a refund of the employer share of FICA. Details about obtaining consent are in Rev. Proc. 2017-28.

#### SPECIAL REPORTING FOR EMPLOYING A WORKER IN YOUR HOME

If you are a sole proprietor and have a nanny or other household employees, as well as regular business employees, you can report the FICA and FUTA taxes for your household employee on

Schedule H and pay the taxes with your Form 1040 or 1040-SR. Alternatively, you can report and pay the FICA taxes for your household employee with the quarterly reports for your regular business employees on Form 941, and you can pay the FUTA taxes on Form 940.

## Additional Medicare Taxes for Individuals

There are 2 additional Medicare taxes imposed on individuals when income (explained below) exceeds set amounts:

- 0.9% on earned income over the applicable threshold amount in Table 30.3
- 3.8% on net investment income

You may be subject to one or both of these taxes.

***Threshold amounts.*** The same threshold amounts listed in Table 30.3 apply for both additional Medicare taxes. The thresholds are not adjusted annually for inflation.

***Definition of earned income.*** Earned income for purposes of the 0.9% additional Medicare tax means taxable compensation and net earnings from self-employment. Whether an owner materially participates in a business is not determinative; all income constituting net earnings from self-employment are taken into account.

***Definition of net investment income (NII).*** In general, investment income includes, but is not limited to: interest, dividends, capital gains, rental and royalty income, non-qualified annuities, income from businesses involved in trading of financial instruments or commodities, and businesses that are passive activities to the taxpayer. Whether business income is treated as derived from a passive activity depends on the application of the passive activity loss rules (see Chapter 4). Thus, a partner who materially participates in the daily activities of the business does not count his/her distributive share of partnership income as investment income for purposes of the NII tax. Gains from the sale of interests in partnerships and S corporations (to the extent the partner or shareholder was a passive owner) are treated as NII.

***Other rules.*** No deduction may be claimed by individuals paying one or both additional Medicare taxes. These taxes should be factored into estimated taxes (Chapter 31).

Employers are required to withhold the 0.9% on employee wages once taxable compensation exceeds $200,000 (regardless of the employee's marital status). There is no employer matching contribution for this tax.

The 0.9% additional Medicare tax is figured on Form 8959, *Additional Medicare Tax*. The NII tax is figured on Form 8960, *Net Investment Income Tax–Individuals, Estates, and Trusts*.

**TABLE 30.3** **Threshold Amounts for Additional Medicare Taxes**

| Filing status | Threshold amount |
|---|---|
| Married filing jointly | $250,000 |
| Married filing separately | $125,000 |
| Single | $200,000 |
| Head of household | $200,000 |
| Qualifying widow(er) with dependent child | $200,000 |

## Sales and Use Taxes

There is no federal sales or use tax. But there are more than 10,000 states, counties, cities, and towns with their own sales taxes, in many cases generating the greatest revenue for these jurisdictions. Many also impose a **use tax**.

***Use tax*** **Tax imposed on the purchaser of certain goods from out-of-state vendors.**

The rules for these taxes vary considerably from one locality to another. For example, the sale of one type of product may be subject to sales tax in one state but exempt in another. Because these taxes produce significant revenue in some places, taxing authorities may be aggressive in their collection activities, so you should understand your responsibilities.

### *Sales Taxes*

If you sell goods or provide certain services within a state that has a sales tax, as the vendor, you are required to collect the tax from the purchaser and remit the tax to the state agency. Generally, the same test used for state income tax purposes to determine whether you do business within a state applies for sales tax purposes as well.

Following the Supreme Court's 2018 decision in *South Dakota v. Wayfair*, most states began requiring remote sellers to collect and remit sales tax. States have an exemption for small sellers, which varies from state to state (e.g., sales of no more than $100,000 in some states or $250,000 in others, or 200 or more separate transactions; Massachusetts has a $500,000/100 transaction exception).

**NOTE**

**States are permanently barred from imposing sales tax on Internet access.**

The Streamlined Sales and Use Tax Agreement, which took effect in some states on October 1, 2005, attempts to simplify and standardize some sales tax rules to make it easier for businesses to collect this important revenue. For information about states participating in the agreement, go to www.streamlinedsalestax.org. Various proposed in Congress would require most online sellers to collect sales tax on sales to out-of-state customers. Check the Supplement for any update on these measures.

Familiarize yourself with how the sales tax works. For example, some states impose an origin-based sales tax while others have a destination-based tax. If goods are returned and you refund the purchaser's money, you may be entitled to a deduction or credit for the sales tax you originally collected.

*When* you must remit sales tax to the state depends on how much you collect. You must also file certain returns reporting your collection activities.

Contact your state tax authority to request a sales tax package. This will explain whether you must collect tax (and how much) and when to pay it to the state and file sales tax returns. You can simplify your sales tax obligations by using a Certified Service Provider (CSP), a company approved by the governing board and currently offering service:

Avalara (https://www.avalara.com/)
Accurate Tax (https://www.accuratetax.com/)
Sovos (https://sovos.com)
TaxCloud (https://taxcloud.net)

The CSP will provide technology assistance to ensure proper collection and remittance of the tax to the CSP for payment to the appropriate state or states. There is no cost to you for using a CSP (it is paid by the states), and you are insulated from a state audit on sales tax (the state can audit only the CSP with respect to your collections).

### *Use Taxes*

If you buy goods out-of-state, you may be liable for a use tax on the purchase. (In effect, your state is collecting the sales tax you would have paid had you made the purchase in-state.) Generally, the tax is imposed on the purchaser (though some states may collect the tax from the seller).

Before you pay any use tax, check to see if the sale is exempt from the tax. Exemptions often exist for items that will be resold (including components of products for resale), used for capital improvements, or used in research and development.

Even if the vendor does not charge a use tax because it has no responsibility to pay the tax to your state, you may still be liable for it. In effect, you may be required to "self-assess" the tax.

## Excise Taxes

An excise tax is a tax imposed on the manufacture and distribution of certain nonessential consumer goods, such as spirits and tobacco, although it now applies to many essential goods and services as well (such as gasoline and telephone service). Until the advent of the income tax in 1913, the federal government ran entirely on excise taxes. Today, excise taxes are only a small part of the government's revenue, but may still be an obligation for you. Excise taxes include:

- Environmental taxes on the sale or use of ozone-depleting chemicals
- Coal tax
- Communications and air transportation taxes
- Fuel taxes
- Manufacturers' taxes on various items (including sport fishing equipment, bow and arrow components, etc.)
- Retail tax on the sale of heavy trucks, trailers, and tractors (imposed on the seller)
- 10% excise tax on indoor tanning salon services. Salon owners must collect this tax from patrons and pay the tax to the IRS in quarterly installments, along with Form 720, *Quarterly Federal Excise Tax Return*.
- Patient-centered outreach research institute (PCORI) fees. This applies to certain health policies and self-insured health plans. The annual fee for plan years ending after September 30, 2021, and before October 1, 2021, is $2.66 per person covered by the plan (e.g., employee, spouse, dependent, retiree). This fee is reported in Part II of Form 720. Check the Supplement for any fee increase effective October 1, 2021.
- Sports wagering. There is a federal excise tax on wagering, regardless of whether the activity is allowed by the state.

Many small companies have no liability for excise taxes because of the nature of their business. However, there are no specific exemptions from these taxes because a business is a small one. For example, small farmers are subject to certain fuel taxes, although they may be entitled to a credit or refund, and an owner of a heavy truck (one with a gross taxable weight of 55,000 pounds or more) is subject to a use tax for the vehicle. Disregarded entities (e.g., one-member LLCs) must pay the tax under the entities' tax identification numbers; the entities and not their owners are liable for excise taxes.

Businesses with 25 or more trucks, tractors, or other heavy vehicles used on highways are now required to make their excise tax filings electronically. Form 2290, *Heavy Highway Vehicle Use Tax Return*, is used for this purpose and is generally due by August 31.

The deduction for excise taxes is discussed in Chapter 13. Tax credits for certain farm-related excise taxes are discussed in Chapter 20.

CHAPTER 31

# Filing Tax Returns, Paying Taxes, and Making Refund Claims


| | | | |
|---|---|---|---|
| Income Tax Deadlines and Extensions | 527 | Estimated Taxes | 530 |
| Online Filing of Business Income Tax Returns | 529 | Making Tax Payments | 533 |
| | | Claiming Refunds | 535 |
| | | Filing Other Business Returns | 538 |


It's one of the facts of a business owner's life to file returns and pay taxes. The filing deadlines and tax payment rules for businesses and their owners may be different from those for individuals. Making sure you comply with filing and payment requirements is essential for avoiding unnecessary penalties and interest.

For more information about the electronic federal tax payment system, see IRS Publication 966, *Electronic Federal Tax Payment System*.

## Income Tax Deadlines and Extensions

The date by which your business return must be filed depends on your type of entity and tax year. The information in Table 31.1 applies for 2021 returns to businesses reporting on a calendar-year basis. Do not anticipate automatic extensions like the ones provided by the IRS during the pandemic in 2021.

Partnerships, limited liability companies, and S corporations must also furnish owners with a Schedule K-1 by the due date.

For corporations on a fiscal year ending other than June 30, the due date is 3½ months after the close of their fiscal year. For example, a C corporation on a fiscal year ending on July 31 has a filing deadline of November 15. For C corporations with a fiscal year ending June 30, the filing due date is September 15.

For all other entities on a fiscal year, the due date is 3½ months after the close of their fiscal year. For example, a limited liability company reporting on a fiscal year ending September 30 has a filing deadline of January 15 of the following year.

If any due date falls on a Saturday, Sunday, or legal holiday, the due date becomes the next business day. For example, the deadline for calendar year partnerships and S corporations to file

**TABLE 31.1** Usual Filing Deadlines

| Type of Entity* | Income Tax Return | Return Due Date |
|---|---|---|
| Sole proprietorship | Schedule C of Form 1040 or 1040-SR | April 15 |
| Partnership | Form 1065 | March 15 |
| Limited liability company | Form 1065 | March 15 |
| S corporation | Form 1120-S | March 15 |
| C corporation | Form 1120 | April 15 |

*Assuming the business reports on a calendar year basis.

**TABLE 31.2** Usual Filing Extensions

| Type of Entity | Form to Request Filing Extension | Extended Due Date |
|---|---|---|
| Sole proprietorship | Form 4868 | October 15 |
| Partnership | Form 7004 | September 15 |
| Limited liability company | Form 7004 | September 15 |
| S corporation | Form 7004 | September 15 |
| C corporation | Form 7004 | October 15 |

their 2019 income tax return was March 16, 2020 (March 15 was on a Sunday). For 2021 returns, the deadline is March 15, 2022, because it does not fall on a weekend or holiday.

### Filing Methods

Small business owners can choose to file paper returns or file electronically; certain large entities must file electronically (explained later in this chapter). The filing method does not affect the filing deadline.

### Filing Extensions

If, for any reason, you are unable to file on time, you can avoid penalties by requesting an automatic 6-month filing extension. The request must be made no later than the due date of the return (see Table 31.1). The form used to request the extension and the extended due date for 2021 returns depends on your type of entity, as shown in Table 31.2 (for calendar-year businesses).For fiscal year entities, the extended due date is 6 months after the filing deadline.

There are no extensions available beyond the extended due date, regardless of the reasons involved; returns filed after the extended due date are usually subject to penalty. The only exception to the rule against having more time to file is a blanket extension granted by the IRS to taxpayers located in certain areas affected by extreme disasters. There is an automatic 60-day extension for individuals with a principal residence in a federally-declared disaster area or a principal place of business in such area, but the IRS has discretion to grant extensions for up to one year. Find news about this on an IRS landing page titled "Tax Relief in Disaster Situations" at https://www.irs.gov/uac/tax-relief-in-disaster-situations.

### *Late Filing Penalties*

If you fail to file your return on time—by the due date or the extended due date if you obtain a filing extension—you will be subject to a late filing penalty. Late filing penalties, and how to get the IRS to waive them, are discussed in Appendix B.

## Online Filing of Business Income Tax Returns

Today, the vast majority of tax returns for individual business owners as well as their business entities are filed e-filed with the IRS and with state tax or revenue departments. While e-filing is not mandatory for all taxpayers, there are compelling reasons to submit returns in this way:

- *Faster refunds*. Those who are owed a refund can expect to receive it in about half the time that it would take had the return been filed the traditional way in paper form. With electronic filing of returns and direct deposit of refunds, you can receive a refund in as little as 7 days.
- *Accuracy*. There is a less than 1% error rate with electronically filed returns (compared with a more-than-20% error rate for paper returns). This is because the IRS reviews the return before accepting it. The IRS acknowledges acceptance of a return within 48 hours of submission. This acknowledgment is your proof of filing and assurance that the IRS has your return information.
- *Convenience*. You can use your personal computer to file your return 7 days a week, 24 hours a day. If you lack the software to *e-file*, you can use an authorized IRS *e-file* provider (for a modest fee). In 37 states, you can file your federal and state returns simultaneously. If you owe taxes, you can file early and postpone payment until the return's due date. (Payment can be made by authorizing an automatic withdrawal [direct debit] from a savings or checking account through IRS Direct Pay, an electronic transfer through EFTPS.gov, payment by credit or debit card [American Express, Discover, Mastercard or Visa], or by mailing a check payable to the United States Treasury along with Form 1040-V, *Payment Voucher*, to your service center.)
- *Preparers required to e-file*. Paid tax return preparers are required to e-file client returns if they expect to file 11 or more Forms 1040, 1040-SR, and 1041, so if you use a paid preparer, your return will likely be e-filed.

If you *e-file*, then you do not have to attach any information returns that would otherwise be required. For example, if you are a sole proprietor but your spouse is an employee with a W-2 form, that form need not be sent to the IRS if you file your return electronically.

#### ELECTRONIC SIGNATURES

To e-file, the signature of an electronically filed self-prepared return is handled through a *self-select personal identification number* (PIN). This is a self-created 5-number code that is used in conjunction with your prior year's adjusted gross income, total tax, and date of birth to verify that the return being filed is your own. You do not have to register your PIN number, nor even notify the IRS. But if you are a sole proprietor filing a joint return, both you and your spouse need separate PINs. Tax professionals filing clients' returns electronically use their PTINs.

#### DEEMED FILING DATE

An electronically filed return is deemed timely if it is transmitted on or before the due date *and* an acknowledgment of processing by the IRS is issued.

### Sole Proprietorships

You can *e-file* your income tax return if you are a sole proprietor filing a Schedule C or F. Virtually all the forms and schedules you need can be filed electronically.

### Partnerships and LLCs

Partnerships filing 100 or more returns in 2022 must *e-file* their 2021 Form 1065. According to the *2020 IRS Data Book*, more than 4.2 million partnership returns were filed electronically.

### S Corporations

S corporations with 100 or more returns filed annually (including income tax, excise tax, information—W-2 and otherwise—and employment tax returns) *must* file Form 1120-S electronically. Smaller S corporations can opt to e-file. According to the *2020 IRS Data Book*, more than 4.7 million S corporations filed their returns electronically. Whether *e-file* is used, if the corporation owes any income tax, it must deposit it electronically if it is otherwise required to use EFTPS as explained later in this chapter.

S corporation shareholders can, however, file their personal tax returns electronically, even if the corporation files by mail (and vice versa). Thus, they can obtain the benefit of *e-filing* on their share of business items.

### C Corporations

The return can be filed under the 1120/1120-S *e-file* program. C corporations with 100 or more returns filed annually (including income tax, excise tax, information—W-2 and otherwise—and employment tax returns) *must* file Form 1120 electronically. According to the *2020 IRS Data Book*, more than 1.43 million C corporations filed their returns electronically. Whether *e-file* is used, you must still deposit corporate income taxes electronically if you are required to use EFTPS as explained later in this chapter.

## Estimated Taxes

Estimated taxes are not separate tax obligations; they are a method of paying throughout the year what you expect to owe when you ultimately file your return. Estimated taxes are paid by individuals (including owners of partnerships, limited liability companies, and S corporations on their share of business income) and C corporations. If you do not pay enough estimated taxes (plus withholding taxes on wages and certain other payments), you may be subject to penalties.

#### INDIVIDUALS

Estimated taxes cover:

- Regular income tax (including income taxes on your share of business income)
- Alternative minimum tax for high-income taxpayers (see Chapter 29)
- Self-employment tax (discussed earlier in this chapter)
- Additional Medicare taxes on earned income and net investment income (see Chapter 30)

- Employment taxes on a household employee
- Additional tax on IRAs, qualified retirement plans, and other tax-favored accounts figured on Form 5329

You must pay estimated taxes if you expect tax liability for the year to be at least $1,000 and you do not meet a safe harbor test (or file your return and pay the tax in full by January 31). The safe harbor test means that your withholdings and tax credits (e.g., applying an excess payment from last year toward this year's taxes) are less than the smaller of:

- 90% of the tax shown to be on this year's return (66% for farmers and commercial fishermen), or
- 100% of the tax shown on last year's return (110% if your adjusted gross income last year is more than $150,000, or $75,000 if married filing separately).

There is a special estimated tax rule for farmers and commercial fishermen. No estimated tax penalties are owed if the income tax return is filed and any taxes paid by February 28. If you don't file by this date, then any estimated tax penalties will be figured from only one payment date—January 15.

Use the Estimated Tax Worksheet (Figure 31.1) to figure what you must pay in order to avoid penalties for 2021 (if you still have time to make an installment for 2021). An updated version should be used for 2022 estimated taxes. If you have wages and also receive self-employment income, you may also use the IRS's Tax Withholding Estimator tool at https://www.irs.gov/individuals/tax-withholding-estimator, which takes into account the self-employed health insurance deduction, contributions to a SEP or other retirement plan, and one-half of self-employment tax.

Estimated taxes are due on April 15, June 15, September 15, and January 15 of the following year (the due date is extended to the next business day if any payment date falls on a Saturday, Sunday, or legal holiday).

Estimated taxes can be paid in several ways: by check made payable to the U.S. Treasury, along with Form 1040-ES, *Estimated Tax for Individuals*, by charging the payment to a major credit card, by transferring funds from your bank account through the IRS's Direct Pay!, or by transferring funds using EFTPS.gov.

If you do not pay enough through estimated taxes, figure your penalty on Form 2210, *Underpayment of Estimated Taxes by Individuals, Estates, and Trusts* (Form 2210-F, *Underpayment of Estimated Tax by Farmers and Fishermen*).

### CORPORATIONS

S corporations are usually not separate taxpayers and therefore need not be concerned with estimated taxes (shareholders pay estimated taxes). C corporations are separate taxpayers and must meet estimated tax payment obligations to avoid penalties.

Corporations are required to prepay current tax liabilities by making estimated tax payments during the year if the tax liability is $500 or more. Estimated tax for corporations covers the regular corporate income tax, alternative minimum tax, and the tax on gross transportation income of foreign corporations from U.S. sources. C corporations must base estimated taxes on their actual tax liability to avoid underpayment penalties. However, *small* C corporations can base their estimates on the prior year's tax liability and are not penalized even if this falls short of

## 2021 Estimated Tax Worksheet

*Keep for Your Records*

| | | |
|---|---|---|
| 1 | Adjusted gross income you expect in 2021 (see instructions) | 1 |
| 2a | Deductions<br>• If you plan to itemize deductions, enter the estimated total of your itemized deductions.<br>• If you don't plan to itemize deductions, enter your standard deduction. | 2a |
| b | If you can take the qualified business income deduction, enter the estimated amount of the deduction | 2b |
| c | Add lines 2a and 2b ▶ | 2c |
| 3 | Subtract line 2c from line 1 | 3 |
| 4 | **Tax.** Figure your tax on the amount on line 3 by using the **2021 Tax Rate Schedules.**<br>**Caution:** *If you will have qualified dividends or a net capital gain, or expect to exclude or deduct foreign earned income or housing, see Worksheets 2-5 and 2-6 in Pub. 505 to figure the tax* | 4 |
| 5 | Alternative minimum tax from **Form 6251** | 5 |
| 6 | Add lines 4 and 5. Add to this amount any other taxes you expect to include in the total on Form 1040, line 16 | 6 |
| 7 | Credits (see instructions). **Do not** include any income tax withholding on this line | 7 |
| 8 | Subtract line 7 from line 6. If zero or less, enter -0- | 8 |
| 9 | Self-employment tax (see instructions) | 9 |
| 10 | Other taxes (see instructions) | 10 |
| 11a | Add lines 8 through 10 | 11a |
| b | Earned income credit, additional child tax credit, fuel tax credit, net premium tax credit, refundable American opportunity credit, and refundable credit from Form 8885* | 11b |
| c | **Total 2021 estimated tax.** Subtract line 11b from line 11a. If zero or less, enter -0- ▶ | 11c |
| 12a | Multiply line 11c by 90% (66⅔% for farmers and fishermen) — 12a | |
| b | Required annual payment based on prior year's tax (see instructions) — 12b | |
| c | **Required annual payment to avoid a penalty.** Enter the **smaller** of line 12a or 12b ▶ | 12c |
| | **Caution:** *Generally, if you do not prepay (through income tax withholding and estimated tax payments) at least the amount on line 12c, you may owe a penalty for not paying enough estimated tax. To avoid a penalty, make sure your estimate on line 11c is as accurate as possible. Even if you pay the required annual payment, you may still owe tax when you file your return. If you prefer, you can pay the amount shown on line 11c. For details, see chapter 2 of Pub. 505.* | |
| 13 | Income tax withheld and estimated to be withheld during 2021 (including income tax withholding on pensions, annuities, certain deferred income, etc.) | 13 |
| 14a | Subtract line 13 from line 12c — 14a<br>Is the result zero or less?<br>☐ **Yes.** Stop here. You are not required to make estimated tax payments.<br>☐ **No.** Go to line 14b. | |
| b | Subtract line 13 from line 11c — 14b<br>Is the result less than $1,000?<br>☐ **Yes.** Stop here. You are not required to make estimated tax payments.<br>☐ **No.** Go to line 15 to figure your required payment. | |
| 15 | If the first payment you are required to make is due April 15, 2021, enter ¼ of line 14a (minus any 2020 overpayment that you are applying to this installment) here, and on your estimated tax payment voucher(s) if you are paying by check or money order | 15 |

*If applicable.

**Note: This is the 2021 version and should not be used for your 2022 estimated taxes.**

**FIGURE 31.1 Estimated Tax Worksheet**

actual liability for the year. A small C corporation for this purpose is one with taxable income of less than $1 million during any of the 3 immediately preceding taxable years.

Estimated tax is figured on Form 1120-W, *Estimated Tax for Corporations*. This form is not filed with the IRS. Instead, payments are made through deposits at federal depositories or through electronic transfers (whichever method is required or selected). The payment slip accompanying the deposit or transfer can be checked off to indicate that it is for estimated tax purposes.

Corporations must pay 25% of the "required annual payment" in each of 4 installments. For a corporation other than a "large corporation," the required payment is either 100% of the tax shown on the current year's return or 100% of the tax on the preceding year's return. However, there are other methods that can be used to satisfy payment requirements while avoiding penalties. For calendar-year corporations, these are due April 15, June 15, September 15, and December 15.

#### ESTIMATED TAX STRATEGIES

It can be challenging for individuals and businesses to have the funds on hand to pay estimated taxes on time. It is advisable to set aside funds on a regular basis for this purpose. For example, say a sole proprietor with fee income is in the 24% tax bracket. It might make sense to deposit 10% to 20% of fee income (taking into account the fact that deductions reduce the income that's taxable) into a separate bank account for estimated taxes so that it is available for making timely estimated tax payments.

However, when figuring estimated taxes, it is not advisable to overpay so that you are making an interest-free loan to the government. In the current low-interest environment, it is probably better to err on the side of underpaying so that you have the use of your money now and do not have to wait until you file a return to recoup an overpayment.

If you find that you have overpaid estimated taxes, you can recover the money by:

- Filing your tax return as quickly as possible to receive a refund.
- Applying your overpayment to next year's taxes, thus reducing your out-of-pocket payments for estimated taxes for next year. Just indicate this choice on your tax return to apply some or all of the overpayment to next year's taxes. Usually, this will allow you to skip one or two estimated tax payments (depending on the size of your overpayment and your projections for next year's taxes).

## Making Tax Payments

There are several ways to pay taxes: By check, by transferring payment using the Electronic Federal Tax Payment System (EFTPS), by charging payment to a major credit card, and by using IRS Direct Pay.

### *Paying by Check*

Most small business owners can pay their tax bill via check made payable to the United States Treasury. Remember that the bulk of the taxes should have been paid through estimated taxes; the check that accompanies the return should be modest.

Corporations cannot pay their income taxes by writing a check to accompany their tax return. They must pay amounts owed by depositing them with an authorized depository (explained below) or by transferring funds through EFTPS.

**NOTE**

**The IRS may not access your account via EFPTS.gov to collect unpaid taxes. Using EFPTS.gov is a one-way street for sending taxes to the U.S. Treasury.**

### *Paying through EFTPS*

Some businesses *must* deposit their taxes through the Electronic Federal Tax Payment System (EFTPS) while others may choose to do so. According to information from several years ago (no updated information is available), EFTPS processes over 100 million transactions per year, totaling nearly $2 trillion, with an error rate of 0.18%. Under this payment method, you authorize the transfer of funds from your bank account by using your telephone or personal computer. This payment method can be used whether or not returns are filed electronically and enables you to designate up to 120 days in advance the amount of payment to be made and the time of payment (365 days for estimated taxes by individuals). As long as the transfer is initiated at least one business day before the due date of the deposit, the electronic funds transfer is considered timely. If you use an outside payroll service that uses EFPTS to deposit your taxes, you automatically receive an EFTPS Inquiry PIN. Use this to check that your payroll provider is timely depositing the taxes on your behalf.

#### REQUIRED USE OF EFTPS

Nearly all federal tax deposits are now made electronically. The use of federal tax coupons allowing deposits to certain banks can no longer be used; all deposits (with some exceptions) must be made using EFTPS.

Payment can be made with the tax return and is not required to be deposited electronically if employment taxes are less than $2,500 per pay period.

You can enroll online at https://www.eftps.gov. If you prefer to submit a paper application, file Form 9779, *EFTPS Business Enrollment Form*, with the EFTPS Enrollment Processing Center (it can take several weeks to process a paper application).

#### VOLUNTARY USE OF EFTPS

Even if you are *not* required to use EFTPS, you may wish to do so—for convenience. You initiate payment so you remain in control of your funds until you want them disbursed to the government. You receive an acknowledgment number as a record of your payment.

You may voluntarily participate in EFTPS. To obtain more information on EFTPS or to enroll in the system, call (800) 555-4477 or (800) 945-8400. If you enroll, you can use the Internet or receive free Windows-based software for use on your PC. You also receive a PIN to use when making payments.

You can update existing passwords (to make them *more* secure) at "My Profile" at https://www.eftps.gov.

### *Credit Card Charges*

Businesses can pay taxes via credit card (American Express, Discover, Mastercard, or Visa) in some, but not all, instances. Balances owed with respect to employment tax returns (Forms 940, 941, and 944) can be charged to a credit card. However, federal tax deposits cannot be made by credit card.

Taxes owed on income tax returns of sole proprietors and owners of pass-through entities on Form 1040 or 1040-SR can also be charged to a credit card.

As of now, taxes owed on Form 1120 or Form 1120-S (in those limited situations where an S corporation owes tax) cannot be charged to a credit card. This could change in the future.

There are only 3 credit card processors authorized by the IRS to process tax payments:

- Pay1040 at https://www.pay1040.com/
- ACI Payments at https://fed.acipayonline.com/
- PayUSAtax at https://payusatax.com/

These companies charge a convenience fee (currently up to 1.99% of the amount charged); the IRS does not impose any additional cost for charging taxes.

The Taxpayer First Act authorized the IRS to accept credit/debit card payments directly if the taxpayer pays the fee. As yet, there are no details on how this will work; check the Supplement for an update.

### IRS Direct Pay

You can transfer funds from your checking or savings account using this online payment method. There is no registration or fee required. Go to https://www.irs.gov/payments/direct-pay for details.

### Late Payment Penalties

If you fail to pay the taxes due on time, you can be subject to late payment penalties and interest on the outstanding amount. Taxes must be paid in full by the due date of the return to avoid penalties and interest. Obtaining an extension of time to file the return does not give you more time to pay your taxes.

The penalty is 0.5% of the tax due, per month, with a maximum of 25%. In addition, interest is charged at the IRS interest rate, which adjusts quarterly. For news releases of IRS quarterly interest rates, go to https://www.irs.gov and search "news releases," and fact sheet archives.

The penalty may be waived if you can show that lateness was due to reasonable cause and not to willful neglect. You can also ask the IRS to waive the penalty under its first-time penalty abatement (FTA) program. To qualify, you must not have been delinquent in tax deposits in the prior 3 years and are other-wise in compliance with filing and payment requirements.

## Claiming Refunds

If you overpaid your taxes on a previously-filed income tax return, you may be able to make a claim for a refund of the overpayment. Refunds may result from failing to claim deductions or credits in previous years, using carryback opportunities, or taking advantage of retroactive law changes. Various refund opportunities are listed later in this chapter.

In filing for a refund, keep the statute of limitations in mind, which is the period during which a refund claim can be made. If you submit a claim after this period has expired, no refund can be obtained even though it would have been allowed if a timely request had been submitted.

### Statute of Limitations on Refund Claims

In general, a refund claim must be filed within 3 years from the time the return was filed or 2 years from the time the tax was paid, whichever of such periods expires the later, or if no return was filed by the taxpayer, within 2 years from the time the tax was paid. A 7-year period applies to refunds related to a bad debt or a loss from a worthless security. There was a special 5-year carryback for net operating losses arising in 2018, 2019, and 2020, meaning that the refund period was extended accordingly.

The statute of limitations can be tolled (suspended) only where a taxpayer is unable to manage his or her financial affairs due to a physical or mental impairment expected to result in death or that as lasted or is expected to last for a continuous period of not less than 12 months. To use this suspension, the taxpayer is not treated as financially disabled if there is a spouse or other person authorized to act in the taxpayer's financial matters.

### How to File for an Income Tax Refund

Generally, a claim for refund of income tax is made by filing an amended return. The form to file depends on the business entity. The form to use is in Table 31.3.

***Special rule for partnerships and LLCs.*** Small partnerships (and LLCs filing partnership returns) that elect out of the Bipartisan Budget Act audit regime file Form 1065 and check the box for "amended return." Other partnerships file Form 1065-X. However, the IRS granted relief

**TABLE 31.3** Forms for Amended Income Tax Returns

| Type of Entity | Form to Make a Refund Request |
|---|---|
| Sole proprietorship/1-member LLC | Form 1040-X |
| Partnership/LLC | Form 1065 or Form 1065-X |
| S corporation | Form 1120-S (check box H4) |
| C corporation | Form 1120X |

to non-electing partnerships to also use Form 1065 for net operating loss carrybacks and certain other COVID-19-related law changes. For these partnerships filing Form 1065, in addition to checking the box for "amended return," write at the top of the return "Filed Pursuant to Rev. Proc. 2020-23."

***Amended Schedule K-1s.*** Partnerships filing Form 1065 as well as S corporations must issue owner's amended Schedule K-1s. Check the box at the top of the form for "Amended K-1."

***Quick refunds.*** Instead of filing an amended return, taxpayers can obtain a quick refund for overpayments resulting from a net operating loss (NOL) carryback, a carryback of an unused general business credit, and an overpayment of tax due to a claim of right adjustment (explained in Internal Revenue Code Section 1341(b)(2)) by filing:

- Form 1045, *Application for Tentative Refund,* for individuals (owners of pass-through entities)
- Form 1139, *Corporation Application for Tentative Refund,* for C corporations

**NOTE**
**Although the IRS may issue a tentative refund, a later audit could show that the refund was excessive and that a deficiency is owed.**

Generally, the quick refund must be filed within one year after the end of the year in which the carryback arose, but not before the income tax return for the year in which the NOL arose has been filed. Also, the entity can elect to exclude Section 965(a) inclusion years (related to the transition tax) in the net operating loss 5-year carryback.

The IRS generally will act on the refund within 90 days of thedate the form is filed or the last day of the month that includes the due date (including extensions) of the tax return for the loss year, whichever is later.

When you carry back an NOL, you may have to recalculate certain deductions, credits, and other items in the carryback years. For individuals, these are items figured with respect to adjusted gross income. For example, the NOL will lower your adjusted gross income in the carryback years and therefore allow for greater itemized deductions that have an adjusted-gross-income floor. You may also have to recalculate alternative minimumtax. However, do not recalculate self-employment tax; the NOL applies only for income tax purposes.

### *Refund Opportunities*

A review of a previously filed return may show that deductions or credits were omitted, income was overstated, carrybacks were overlooked, or other reasons why there was an overpayment on the older return. Determine whether it's advisable to file for a refund, factoring in the cost of filing an amended return if you pay a CPA or other professional to do it versus the taxes that can be recouped. Also consider whether you want to draw IRS attention to an older return if you took tax positions that could be questioned after greater scrutiny.

The following is a list of certain specific situations that may present refund opportunities, assuming the statute of limitations has not yet passed. The list is not exclusive.

- ***Bad debts.*** If you learn that money owed to the business is uncollectible (e.g., outstanding receivables; loans), you may be able to obtain a refund of taxes for the year in which the debt went bad. (Remember that cash basis businesses with uncollected receivables cannot take a bad debt.) Business bad debts can be deducted if partially worthless, but nonbusiness bad debts must be wholly worthless to be deductible. You must determine the year of worthlessness and file for a refund with respect to that year. See Chapter 11.
- ***Business interest expense.*** For 2019 and 2020, the net interest expense for businesses that was not exempt from this limitation is 50% of adjusted taxable income (it was supposed to be 30% and is 30% in 2021). Taxpayers who filed 2019 returns before enactment of the CARES Act and used the 30% limitation may be eligible for a greater interest expense deduction; they may still file for a refund. See Chapter 13.
- ***Energy-efficient commercial buildings.*** The deduction for energy-efficient commercial buildings up to $1.80 per square foot was retained for 2018, 2019, and 2020 (it's now permanent and the dollar amount may be adjusted for inflation after 2021). If you were eligible for it but didn't claim it on a prior return, you can file for a refund. See Chapter 10.
- ***Excess business losses.*** If you were a "noncorporate taxpayer" (e.g., owner of a pass-through entity) and had losses in 2018 or 2019 that you did not claim due to the limit on excess business losses, you can amend returns to take the full loss. Losses had been limited to the excess of all your trade or business deductions for the year over all your trade or business gross income, plus an amount based on your filing status. See Chapter 4.
- ***General business credit carryback.*** The total of business tax credits in excess of the general business credit limitation is carried back for one year. See Chapter 23.
- ***Net operating losses.*** If you had a net operating loss in 2018, 2019, or 2020, you can carry back the loss for five years to offset 100% of taxable income in those years. See Chapter 4.
- ***Qualified improvement property.*** If you were a restaurant, retail store, or other business that acquired or placed in service any "qualified improvement property" after September 27, 2017, you may be eligible for a refund. Such property now has a 15-year recovery period so that it qualifies for 100% bonus depreciation. Previously, due to a drafting error in the Tax Cuts and Jobs Act of 2017, it had a 39-year recovery period, making it ineligible for bonus depreciation. See Chapter 14.
- ***Recovery periods for certain property.*** For depreciation purposes, in addition to the change for qualified improvement property, the 3-year period was retained for 2018, 2019, and 2020 for race horses and the 7-year period for motorsports entertainment complexes. The 3-year period for race horses expires at the end of 2021; the 7-year period for motorsports entertainment complexes expires at the end of 2025. See Chapter 14.
- ***Tax credits.*** Certain business tax credits that had expired at the end of 2017 were extended for 2018, 2019, and 2020 (and beyond except where noted). If they weren't claimed on prior returns, you may be able to claim a refund. These credits include: Empowerment

Zone employment credit (which was not extended beyond 2020), Indian employment credit, energy-efficient homes credit, biodiesel and renewable diesel tax credit, alternative fuel refueling property credit, and credit for electricity produced by certain renewable sources.

- ***Worthless securities.*** If you own stock or a bond that has become worthless, you can take a write-off. Usually, the loss is a capital loss, but Section 1244 losses (special stock of a small business) can result in an ordinary loss up to a set dollar limit. See Chapter 5.

## Filing Other Business Returns

There are other tax returns that may have to be filed in addition to income tax returns. At present, employment tax returns are not required to be filed online. Certain information returns *must* be filed online by certain taxpayers—others who are not required to do so may choose to file online.

### *Employment Tax Returns*

Employment tax returns may be filed electronically. These include:

- Form 940, *Employer's Annual Federal Unemployment (FUTA) Tax Return*
- Form 941, *Employer's Quarterly Federal Tax Return*
- Form 944, *Employer's Annual Federal Tax Return*

Employment tax returns are filed only by businesses that have employees. However, they must be filed even if no wages are paid. For example, an S corporation with one employee (the sole shareholder) that pays wages of $30,000 must file Form 941 for all quarters even though all of these wages are paid in the final quarter of the year. You can e-file employment tax returns through a third-party transmitter using the 940, 941, and 944 On-Line Filing Program. Or you can authorize a reporting agent to prepare, sign, and e-file for you. Find out more about your e-file options for employment tax returns from the IRS at https://www.irs.gov/uac/Employment-Taxes—Electronic-Filing-and-Payment-Options.

Looking for a company to transmit your employment tax returns for your company? You can find a list of IRS-approved e-file Business Providers at https://www.irs.gov/tax-professionals/e-file-providers-partners/approved-irs-e-file-for-business-providers.

#### DUE DATE OF EMPLOYMENT TAX RETURN

Whether filing electronically or on paper, employment tax returns must be filed by the date in Table 31.4. The annual returns are due by the end of the first month following the close of the quarter or tax year, depending on which period is applicable.

#### AMENDING EMPLOYMENT TAX RETURNS

If an employer makes a mistake on an employment tax return, the mistake should be corrected. To correct:

- Form 940: File amended Form 940 (check the box on the return indicating that it is an amended return).

**TABLE 31.4 Filing Deadlines for Employment Tax Returns**

| Type of Return | Filing Period | Return Due Date |
|---|---|---|
| Form 940 | Annual | January 31 |
| Form 941 | Quarterly | April 30, July 31, October 31, January 31 |
| Form 944 | Annual | January 31 |

- Form 941: File Form 941-X, *Adjusted Employer's QUARTERLY Federal Tax Return or Claim for Refund*.
- Form 944: File Form 945-X, *Adjusted Employer's ANNUAL Federal Tax Return or Claim for Refund*.

Filing an amended return in some cases may require an adjustment or refund claim to correct the amount of employment taxes previously claimed. This may also mean repaying or reimbursing employees for excess FICA taxes withheld and obtaining their written statement that they will not make a claim for refund or credit of these taxes.

From time to time, law changes may necessitate the filing of an amended return. If Congress makes any retroactive changes for 2021 that impact employment taxes for earlier years, similar action may be required.

## *Information Returns*

You may choose to submit certain information returns to the IRS electronically even though you must provide paper returns to your employees or others. You *must* file electronically in 2022 if you file 1009 or more information returns (Forms 1042-S, 1098, 1099, 5498, 8027, W-2, or W-G).

You do not have to be concerned about the security of the information you submit in this manner. The IRS has set up FIRE (Filing Information Returns Electronically) to protect the confidentiality of the data you submit. Changes effective September 10, 2021, affect the login for those using FIRE. To learn more about FIRE, go to https://www.irs.gov/tax-professionals/e-file-providers-partners/filing-information-returns-electronically-fire or call the Martinsburg Computer Center at (304) 263-8700.

You can provide information returns to payment recipients electronically *if* they consent to receive them in this manner. So, for example, if you paid an independent contractor $600 or more in 2021 and want to send the Form 1099-NEC to her electronically, you must obtain her consent to do so.

### EMPLOYEE BENEFIT RETURNS

Forms in the 5500 series must now be filed electronically with the Department of Labor (not with the IRS). (There is an exception for small plans.) For information about EFAST (ERISA Filing Acceptance System) and EFAST *e-filing* employee benefit returns, see https://www.efast.dol.gov/welcome.html.

### DUE DATE OF ELECTRONICALLY FILED INFORMATION RETURNS

In the past, transmittals for certain types of information returns (e.g., W-2s, 1099s) had an extended filing deadline for electronic submissions. For 2021 returns filed in the 2022 filing season, transmittals for Forms W-2 and 1099-NEC are due to the Social Security Administration and the IRS, respectively, on January 31, 2022 (the same date that the forms are furnished to employees and independent contractors), whether filing on paper or electronically. Most other Forms 1099 are due February 28, but March 31 if filed electronically. Of course, if the due date falls on Saturday, Sunday, or a legal holiday, the due date of an electronically filed return is extended to the next business day.

### *Excise Tax Returns*

Under the ExSTARS (Excise Summary Terminal Activity Reporting System), terminal operators and bulk fuel carriers can file their monthly information returns (Fuel Transaction Reports) electronically instead of using paper returns.

CHAPTER 32

# Retirement and Succession Planning


| | | | |
|---|---|---|---|
| Retirement Planning | 541 | Consulting Agreements | 546 |
| Social Security Planning | 544 | Estate Taxes | 546 |
| Exit Strategies | 545 | Estate Planning Concerns | 547 |
| Financing Options to Fund Buyouts | 546 | | |


What happens to your business when you retire or die? For many business owners, the pandemic has brought this question to the forefront. Have you made any decisions about whether to sell your interest, pass it on to children, or make other arrangements? Over 50% of all businesses in the U.S. are family owned, yet only 15% of them have any succession plan in place, according to a survey by the National Bureau of Economic Research's Family Business Alliance. If you are planning to retire, will the sale of your business provide you with sufficient funds for a comfortable retirement? The plans you make will have practical and tax implications for you, your family, and your business.

Succession planning is a complex and ongoing process involving both practical (business) and legal concerns. This chapter is designed to acquaint you with some of the issues you'll need to address in succession planning; it does not address every issue that may apply to you. For more general information about succession planning, you can take a free online course from SCORE at https://www.score.org/event/simple-steps-exiting-your-business-succession-planning. Work with a knowledgeable adviser to help you structure, monitor, and modify your succession plans.

## Retirement Planning

Looking ahead to the day when you can stop working and retire may be a pleasurable notion, and something to keep you going when you're working round the clock, dealing with business crises, and worrying about how you'll meet the next payroll. Many business owners expect that the sale of their business will provide them with the funds to have a financially secure retirement. Unfortunately, this doesn't always happen, especially if they sell during an economic downturn or their industry falls out of favor.

The best way to make sure you have the money to provide you with a comfortable retirement is to optimize your retirement savings. As long as you continue to work, you can continue to save money through a qualified retirement plan or IRA (the age cap on IRA contributions has been repealed). Chapter 16 discusses your retirement plan options, the rules for making annual contributions, and annual reporting requirements. Now let's focus on ways to optimize the returns from your retirement plans.

### Rollovers

You can change investments solely within your discretion in order to make the most of your retirement plan contributions. One way to do this is to change financial institutions. The best way from a tax perspective is to make a trustee-to-trustee transfer of the funds from one retirement plan account to another. (There is no need to transfer assets; you can liquidate one account and, if desirable, reacquire the same investments in the new account, because gains and losses within retirement plans are not taxed.) With a direct transfer, you never get your hands on the money; it goes from one financial institution directly to another. This is called a *direct rollover*, and you can do it as often as you deem advantageous. There are no tax consequences to a direct rollover. However, check with the financial institution from which you're taking the funds for any fees or penalties that may apply.

Alternatively, you can take a distribution from one account and roll it over to another. As long as you deposit the withdrawn funds into a new rollover account within 60 days, the distribution is not taxable to you (with the exception of a rollover to a Roth IRA or designated Roth account, which is taxable). If you fail to replace the funds within 60 days, you are taxed on the distribution. And if you're under age 59½, you'll also owe a 10% early distribution penalty.

You can shift funds from your qualified retirement plan to an IRA or other types of plans. Table 32.1 shows the rollover options for various types of qualified retirement plans (the chart omits 403(b) plans for tax-exempt organizations and 457 government plans). The term "in-plan rollover" means a rollover from a 401(k) plan to a designated Roth account of the same plan.

### Plan Loans

A qualified retirement plan can allow you to take a loan. You can use the funds for any business or personal purpose, such as paying for business expansion plans. The plan document must permit you (and other plan participants) to take a loan. And the tax law limits the amount of the loan you can take. The loan generally cannot be greater than 50% of your vested account balance or $50,000, whichever is less. The loan must contain a reasonable rate of interest, and repayment must be made ratably over 5 years (with an exception for loan proceeds used to buy a principal residence).

**NOTE**

**Special rules apply to coronavirus-related plan loans in 2020 and certain disaster-related loans in 2021. See Chapters 16 and 17.**

Loans are only permissible from qualified retirement plans. You cannot take a loan from IRAs and IRA-like plans, such as SEPs and SIMPLE-IRAs. However, you can make use of funds in your plan for a limited time without adverse tax consequences. If you take a distribution and replace the funds within 60 days, you effectively have made a short-term loan to yourself, and the distribution is not taxable. But use extreme caution here: As mentioned earlier in connection with rollovers, if you fail to replace the funds within 60 days, you are taxed on the distribution. And if you're under age 59½, you'll also owe a 10% early distribution penalty (unless some penalty exception applies).

**TABLE 32.1** Rollover Options

| | Roll To | | | | | |
|---|---|---|---|---|---|---|
| **Roll From** | **Traditional IRA** | **Roth IRA** | **SIMPLE-IRA** | **SEP** | **401(k) or Other Qualified Plan** | **Designated Roth Account** |
| Traditional IRA | Yes | Yes | No | Yes | Yes | No |
| Roth IRA | Yes | No | No | No | No | No |
| SIMPLE-IRA | Yes (after 2 years) | Yes (after 2 years) | Yes | Yes (after 2 years) | Yes (after 2 years) | No |
| SEP | Yes | Yes | No | Yes | Yes | No |
| 401(k) or other qualified plan | Yes | Yes | No | Yes | Yes | Yes, if it's an in-plan rollover |
| Designated Roth Account | Yes | No | No | No | No | Yes, if made via direct trustee to trustee transfer |

### Work with Professionals

Discuss your current retirement plan holdings and your plans for retiring with a financial planner or other expert. This person can help you craft retirement planning strategies so you can achieve your goals.

## Social Security Planning

In addition to personal savings and funds from qualified retirement plans and IRAs, Social Security benefits are important for retirement income for small business owners. The Social Security benefits you receive are based on your earnings from a job (e.g., your salary from being your corporation's president) or self-employment.

### When to take benefits

You can begin to take Social Security benefits at age 62 (a younger age applies for certain widows and divorced spouses). If you sell your business and retire early, you can commence benefits at age 62 if you want to. However, if you commence them before your full retirement age (see Table 32.2), your benefits are permanently:

**TABLE 32.2** Full Retirement Age

| Year of birth | Full retirement age |
|---|---|
| 1943–1954 | 66 years |
| 1955 | 66 years and 2 months |
| 1956 | 66 years and 4 months |
| 1957 | 66 years and 6 months |
| 1958 | 66 years and 8 months |
| 1959 | 66 years and 10 months |
| 1960 and later | 67 years |

**Example**

**Your full retirement age is 67. If you begin benefits at age 62, your monthly benefit is reduced by about 30%. This reduction continues for the rest of your life.**

You can increase your monthly benefit by delaying the receipt of benefits past full retirement age. For those born in 1950 and later, the monthly rate of increase is 2/3 of 1% (8% per year). But the increase only runs to your 70th birthday. No additional percentage applies after that. There's a Social Security Administration online calculator to see the impact of delayed retirement credits at https://www.ssa.gov/OACT/quickcalc/early_late.html.

### Impact of working on receiving benefits

If you are under the full retirement age and are receiving Social Security benefits, the amount of benefits is reduced if earnings exceed a set amount. For example, in 2021, if you receive benefits and are under the full retirement age, the earnings limit is $1,580 per month ($18,960 for the year). If earnings exceed this limit, then benefits are reduced by $1 for each $2 of excess earnings. For the year in which you reach full retirement age, the earnings limit is $4,210 per month ($50,520 for the year). If earnings for the month prior to attaining full retirement age exceed the limit, benefits are reduced by $1 for each $3 of excess earnings. Check the Supplement for the earnings limits in 2022.

Once you attain full retirement age, your earnings from continuing to work have no impact on the benefits you receive. This is effective beginning in the month you attain full retirement age.

As long as you continue to work, you continue to pay Social Security taxes (the portion of FICA if you are an employee; the portion of self-employment tax if you're self-employed). Because of the way in which the amount of Social Security benefits are computed (based on the highest 35 years of earnings), continuing to work can have a positive impact on benefits received. This means that if your current earnings are higher than in earlier years (which are adjusted in some way), your benefits increase in addition to any cost-of-living increases.

## Exit Strategies

There may be a variety of reasons why you leave your company. They include retirement, disability, being a serial entrepreneur (selling this company to start another one), or death. Whatever the reason, there are several exit strategies.

Before you make any plans, it is a good idea to determine what the business is worth now (the value may change in the future, but plans can be adapted to accommodate valuation shifts). This is done by obtaining a business appraisal. There are various formulas used to determine the value of a business:

- Asset and earnings valuations (factoring in intangibles such as goodwill)
- Asset-based formulas (based on book value or liquidation value)
- Comparable sales of similar businesses
- Earnings (revenue) formulas (multiples of revenue or capitalization of earnings)

Resources to help you find a qualified appraiser (someone with the requisite professional experience who meets certain standards) include the following:

- American Business Appraisers (https://www.businessval.com/)
- American Institute of CPAs—Accreditation in Business Valuation (https://account.aicpa.org/eWeb/dynamicpage.aspx?webcode=referralwebsearch) (search by "Accredited Business Valuation (ABV) Credential Holders")
- American Society of Appraisers (www.appraisers.org/BVhome.aspx)
- Institute of Business Appraisers (www.go-iba.org)

You can use free online tools to learn the approximate valuation of your business. These tools are no substitute for an actual valuation by a qualified appraiser. Free tools are available from:

1. BizEquity (https://www.bizequity.com) (you can only view results for a limited time and then need a subscription)
2. BizEx (www.bizex.net/business-valuation-tool)
3. Free Valuations Online (https://freevaluationsonline.com/)

## Financing Options to Fund Buyouts

Buying out the interest of a departing owner can be paid for in a variety of ways. Most common are:

- *Company buyouts*. The interest of the departing owner is acquired by the business, leaving the remaining owners with greater ownership interests. The company may set aside money for this purpose (e.g., a corporation may use retained earnings to buy out a retiring owner). Alternatively, the company may pay for the departing owner's interest through profits over time. If the company buying the interest of a departing owner is incorporated, this is referred to as a stock redemption.
- *Life insurance*. Usually, insurance is used to buy out a deceased owner's interest. However, insurance can also be used to pay for a retiring owner. Work with a knowledgeable insurance agent to structure insurance financing for a buyout.
- *Installment sales*. A departing owner may sell an interest under an installment payment agreement.
- *ESOP*. An employee stock ownership plan (ESOP) can be used for a corporation (C or S) as a way to buy out the shares of a departing owner. ESOPs are explained in Chapter 16.
- *Employee stock option plans*. If the business is incorporated, there are a variety of stock option plans that may be used to transfer some ownership to employees. Stock option plans are explained in Chapter 7.

In the past, private annuities were often used in family situations to transfer ownership to the younger generation at favorable transfer tax costs. However, changes in the tax treatment of private annuities mean this method is no longer used.

## Consulting Agreements

If you retire but want to continue your association with the company, negotiate a consulting agreement. Being a consultant means you are a self-employed individual who is paid a fixed amount for consulting services over a set period (typically 2 to 5 years following a buyout).

From the company's perspective, consulting fees it pays to you are fully tax deductible. There are no payroll taxes with respect to consulting fees.

## Estate Taxes

If your net worth (the value of your personal assets, including your business interests) are more than the federal estate tax exemption amount ($11.7 million in 2021, but may be reduced; check the Supplement for any update), then succession planning must include estate tax concerns. Some states have no death taxes, but your state may have one that is imposed on estates valued at less than the federal exemption amount in 2021 (e.g., $1 million in Massachusetts and Oregon; $1,595,156 in Rhode Island), making tax planning important even for more modest estates. If you fail to address estate taxes, your family may be forced to sell your business (or your ownership interest) at a fire sale price in order to raise the cash needed to pay the estate tax bill.

## Estate Planning Concerns

When you die, if you have not made any special plans, your business interest passes to your heirs according to the terms of your will or state law governing intestacy when there is no will. However, you are free to make whatever plans you want when it comes to your business interest.

***Factors in estate planning decisions.*** Is there a relative (e.g., spouse or child) who already works in the business and is your natural successor to run the business when you die? Or does your family want nothing to do with your business after your death? Do co-owners prefer to take over your ownership interest? Answering these questions can help direct you toward the best way to decide now what will happen to your interest when you die.

***Buy-sell agreements.*** These are contracts among co-owners of a business to fix the actions that will be taken when one owner dies. There are 2 basic types of buy-sell agreements:

1. *Redemption-type agreements (also called the entity plan).* Here the business buys back the deceased owner's interest, leaving the remaining owner or owners with greater interests. For example, say there are 2 co-owners who each own half of a limited liability company. When one owner dies, assets of the company are used to buy back the deceased owner's interest, leaving the remaining owner with 100% control. If the business is incorporated, the buy-back is done through a redemption of the deceased owner's stock.
2. *Cross-purchase agreements.* Here, each remaining owner buys out the deceased owner's interest. Say there are 3 equal co-owners in a corporation. When one owner dies, the remaining 2 buy half of the deceased owner's stock, leaving each remaining owner with a 50% ownership interest.

There are also hybrid agreements that use elements of each type of basic agreement to accomplish their goals.

From a tax perspective, as long as the buy-back is fixed and there is a mechanism for setting the buyout price, the IRS will usually respect the agreement. This means that the price paid under the agreement can be used to set the value of the ownership interest for estate tax purposes.

***Funding buy-sell agreements.*** In most cases, life insurance is used to pay for the buyout at death. If the corporation receives the life insurance, use care to avoid unwarranted income tax effects.

From your perspective, consulting fees are earned income for purposes of the 0.9% additional Medicare tax. You may want to set the consulting fees below your threshold amount ($200,000 if single; $250,000 if married filing jointly; $125,000 if married filing separately), factoring in any other earned income you may receive.

***Special estate tax rules.*** If a business owner's estate is sizable, meaning more than the applicable estate tax exemption amount ($11.7 million in 2021 unless changed; check the Supplement for any update), there may be federal estate tax as well as state death taxes. These taxes typically must be paid within 9 months after the date of death. However, estates of business owners enjoy certain special tax breaks:

- *Special valuation for closely held business real property.* Instead of valuing the realty at its highest and best use, it can be valued according to its actual use. This can considerably reduce the value of the property included in the owner's estate.
- *Tax deferral.* If the decedent's interest in a closely held business exceeds 35% of the adjusted gross estate, the estate can elect to defer the payment of estate taxes. Deferral means that

only interest is due during the first 4 years; taxes plus interest are then paid over the following 10 years (for a total deferral period of 14 years). A 2% interest rate applies to the tax attributable to the first $1,590,000 of the taxable estate for owners dying in 2021 (this dollar amount may be adjusted in the future).

- *Stock redemption to pay estate tax*. If the closely held business interest exceeds 35% of the gross estate (minus certain deductions) and the business interests remain with the family, then the estate can elect to have the stock redeemed in order to pay estate taxes. This can be done without incurring income tax liability on a partial redemption of the stock.

CHAPTER 33

# Working with CPAs and Other Tax Professionals


| | | | |
|---|---|---|---|
| Types of Tax Professionals | 549 | Tips for Selecting a Tax Professional | 552 |
| Finding a Tax Professional | 551 | | |


According to the NFIB, 93% of small businesses use an external tax practitioner to prepare their returns; only 7% do it in-house (by owners or staff). And given the numerous changes to tax rules in recent years, the percentage of owners turning to professionals is likely to increase. There are several compelling reasons for this: the complexity of tax rules; continual changes in tax rules; the variety of tax returns that must filed for income, employment, and excise taxes; and the time it takes to address tax responsibilities. Due to the sweeping changes in the tax law, it's likely that even more small businesses will use tax professionals for return preparation and advice.

If you work with a tax pro or are thinking of doing so, be sure you select the appropriate professional for your situation. This chapter explains what to look for. It also provides important tips in finding and vetting a tax professional.

All paid tax preparers are required to have a Professional Tax Identification Number (PTIN), which must be renewed annually.

## Types of Tax Professionals

There are various types of tax professionals. They have different levels of education, skills, and continuing education requirements. They also have different representation rights in dealing with the IRS.

### *Attorneys*

Attorneys are licensed by state courts, the District of Columbia or designees of courts of the states or the District of Columbia, such as the state bar. Usually, they have earned a degree in law and have passed a bar exam. Attorneys generally have ongoing continuing education and professional character standards.

Attorneys may offer a range of services. Some attorneys specialize in tax preparation and planning; others may litigate tax cases. Any information you share with an attorney is privileged; the IRS cannot obtain this information.

Attorneys have unlimited representation rights before the IRS. This means they may represent their clients on any matters including audits, payment/collection issues, and appeals.

### CPAs

Certified public accountants (CPAs) are licensed by state boards of accountancy, the District of Columbia, and U.S. territories. CPAs have passed the Uniform CPA Examination after having completed a program of study in accounting at a college or university. They must also meet experience and good character requirements established by their respective boards of accountancy. In addition, CPAs must comply with ethical requirements and complete specified levels of continuing education in order to maintain an active CPA license.

CPAs may offer a range of services. Like attorneys, some CPAs specialize in tax preparation and planning. Like attorneys, they have unlimited representation rights before the IRS.

CPAs have only limited confidentiality with respect to information you share with them. Under a federal statute (Code Sec. 7216), confidentiality extends only to communications regarding federal taxation that would be confidential if made between you and an attorney. The American Institute of CPAs (AICPA) offers guidance to its members on the scope of this privilege (AICPA Code of Professional Conduct at Section 1.700.001). However, some states, such as Florida and Texas, recognize some form of accountant-client privilege.

### Enrolled Agents

Enrolled agents are tax professionals licensed by the IRS. Enrolled agents are subject to a suitability check and must pass a 3-part Special Enrollment Examination, which is a comprehensive exam that requires them to demonstrate proficiency in federal tax planning, individual and business tax return preparation, and representation. They must complete 72 hours of continuing education every 3 years. Like attorneys and CPAs, they have unlimited representation rights before the IRS.

### Annual Filing Season Program Participants

This voluntary program recognizes the efforts of return preparers who are generally not attorneys, certified public accountants, or enrolled agents. It was designed to encourage education and filing season readiness. The IRS issues an Annual Filing Season Program Record of Completion to return preparers who obtain a certain number of continuing education hours in preparation for a specific tax year.

They may only represent clients whose returns they have prepared and signed, and only before revenue agents, customer service representatives, and similar IRS employees, including the Taxpayer Advocate Service. They cannot represent clients whose returns they did not prepare and they cannot represent clients regarding appeals or collection issues even if they did prepare the return in question.

### Other PTIN Holders

Tax return preparers who have an active preparer tax identification number (PTIN), but no professional credentials and do not participate in the Annual Filing Season Program, are authorized to prepare tax returns for compensation.

This is the only authority they have. They have no authority to represent clients before the IRS (except regarding returns they prepared and filed prior to this date).

### Payroll Providers

Payroll services and professional employer organizations may file employment tax returns for small businesses; they do not prepare income tax returns.

## Finding a Tax Professional

You know you need a tax professional, but how do you find one? As with a family doctor, it's always wise to get a referral from someone you know and trust (perhaps your banker or insurance agent). If you don't have such a referral, here are some other ways to find professionals.

### Local Chamber of Commerce

If you belong to a local chamber of commerce or other trade association, there is usually a directory of members. Check for tax return preparers or firms providing the services you seek.

### Professional Organizations

Attorneys, CPAs, and enrolled agents have various professional organizations that you can contact, directly or online, to find a professional near you. These organizations include:

- American Academy of Attorneys—CPAs at https://www.attorney-cpa.com/connect/find-attorney-cpa/. The members of the AAA-CPA are dually qualified as attorneys and CPAs.
- American Institute of Certified Public Accountants at https://www.aicpa.org/forthepublic/findacpa.html. This is the largest member association for CPAs. CPAs in this organization may hold special credentials in such areas as financial planning and business appraisal.
- National Association of Enrolled Agents at https://taxexperts.naea.org/. This is a professional society for enrolled agents.
- National Association of Tax Professionals at https://www.natptax.com/AboutNATP/Pages/Find-a-Tax-Preparer.aspx. This is a nonprofit organization representing tax preparers who engage in federal tax return preparation.
- National Conference of CPA Practitioners at https://go.nccpap.org/info/cpareferral. This is another organization representing tax preparers.
- National Society of Accountants at https://connect.nsacct.org/network/members. This organization represents tax professionals providing accounting, tax, auditing, and other services.

### IRS

The IRS has a directory of preparers with PTINs at https://irs.treasury.gov/rpo/rpo.jsf. Preparers listed here include attorneys, CPAs, enrolled agents, and annual filing season program participants (those who have completed certain continuing education and other requirements set by the IRS). The directory does not include preparers who have PTINs but no other credentials. You can search the directory by the credentials you are seeking, by zip code, or by the distance from you.

The IRS has another directory for professional employer organizations (PEOs) that obtain certification under an IRS program. The listing can be found at https://www.irs.gov/pub/irs-utl/list_of_cpeos.pdf.

### Storefront and Online Preparers

Some preparers operate storefront businesses where customers can simply walk in and get their returns prepared. There are several reputable storefronts, such as H&R Block and Liberty Tax. There are numerous local storefronts that are one-person businesses, and many of these operate only during the tax-filing season.

In addition to storefront preparers, there are also online preparers such as 1-800Accountant (https://1800accountant.com) and eFile4Biz (https://www.efile4biz.com/ for W-2s and information returns) offering their services to small businesses.

The credentials of any such preparer assigned to you can run the gamut of tax professionals. Most preparers in storefronts are enrolled agents, but some may be preparers with PTINs but no credentials. There may be some CPAs, often acting as supervisors or to whom more complex tax returns are assigned. Be sure to ask about credentials so you know who you're dealing with.

If you prepare your own return using software or online solution, such as TurboTax, H&R Block, and TaxAct, you may be able to get personal assistance from a tax adviser 24/7 through the software or online solution (e.g., you may be able to connect live with a CPA through your program).

## Tips for Selecting a Tax Professional

Decide what you need done by a tax professional and select the type who has the credentials that meet your needs. Take into account the cost of the services you'll obtain. Cost varies with the preparer's expertise and location. Learn whether you'll be charged a flat fee for the job (e.g., a fixed amount for the preparation of a tax return) or an hourly rate.

When considering a tax professional, steer clear of anyone with shady practices as listed below. You may save money up front but it can expose to you IRS scrutiny later on. When the IRS identifies unscrupulous preparers, the IRS often examines these preparers' clients. Here are some tipoffs that a preparer should be avoided:

- Basing his/her fee on a percentage of your tax refund. Such action is a violation of the IRS's code of ethics for preparers.
- Guaranteeing you a refund without regard to your actual situation.
- Offering to cash your refund check. This practice is prohibited and preparers can be subject to IRS penalties for doing so.
- Willing to prepare your tax return without seeing any records or documentation.

CHAPTER 34

# Handling Audits with the IRS


| | | | |
|---|---|---|---|
| Types of Audits | 553 | Taxpayer Bill of Rights | 556 |
| Appeals | 555 | Taxpayer Advocate Service | 556 |
| Litigation | 555 | Special Audit Rules for Partnerships | 556 |
| Mediation | 555 | | |


The word "audit" sends shivers up the spine of a small business owner, and for good reason. Tangling with the IRS diverts the owner's attention from running the business now to hashing over old taxes. An audit may also wind up costing the owner hefty professional fees for representation and additional taxes, penalties, and interest. The good news is that audit rates for most types of businesses are down, although the IRS has indicated it plans to increase audits of small businesses by 50% in 2021 (see Chapter 1 for audit statistics). Still, if you are selected for examination by the IRS, these statistics are little comfort to you. When you receive a letter from the IRS stating that you are under examination, you need understand what it means and what you can or should do.

This chapter is intended to give you only an overview of the audit process and your options for dealing with it. For further information about tax audits, see IRS Publication 1, *Your Rights as a Taxpayer;* IRS Publication 556, *Examination of Returns, Appeals Rights, and Claims for Refund*; IRS Publication 3498, *The Examination Process;* and IRS Publication 3498-A, *The Examination Process (Audits by Mail)*.

## Types of Audits

The IRS is the tax collector for the federal government. If the IRS thinks you have underreported your income or made other errors that caused an underpayment of taxes, it will seek recovery. To do this, it must audit you. IRS audits are conducted by mail or in person (never online). Audits can be:

- Examinations by mail (correspondence audits)
- Online audits under a pilot program for Schedule C income and expenses

- Office audits conducted in IRS offices
- Field audits conducted in a taxpayer's home or at a place of business

### Correspondence Audits

The most common type of audit is by U.S. mail. According to the *2020 IRS Data Book*, 72.6% of all examinations conducted in the government's 2020 fiscal year were correspondence audits. This type of examination is typically a request for additional information about items shown on a return (e.g., substantiation for a charitable contribution of $250 or more claimed). In some cases, it may be a request for additional taxes resulting from an omission of income that was reported to the IRS on an information return. For example, say Form 1099-NEC was issued to an independent contractor, showing $1,000 of nonemployee compensation in 2021, but such amount was not on the taxpayer's return. The letter may adjust the contractor's taxes to take the $1,000 into account.

**NOTE**

**The IRS *never* initiates contact with a taxpayer through a telephone call or e-mail. Any such contact purported to be from the IRS is an identity thief or scammer seeking money or your personal information. DO NOT RESPOND TO ANY SUCH TELEPHONE CALL OR E-MAIL. DO NOT OPEN ANY ATTACHMENT TO SUCH AN E-MAIL.**

Depending on the letter received, you may want to handle it yourself or turn to a tax professional, such as the CPA who prepared your return, or a tax attorney. If you checked the box on your return saying that the IRS may discuss the return with the preparer listed on the return, the preparer may talk to the IRS on your behalf about return processing issues, such as missing information, math errors, or payments and refunds. If you want to use a different professional from the one who prepared your return or if you have issues beyond return processing issues, you must complete Form 2848, *Power of Attorney and Declaration of Representative,* so the IRS can speak with your representative.

### Online Audits

Instead of corresponding by mail, the IRS has a pilot audit program called the Security Messaging Taxpayer Digital Communications program. You can communicate with an examiner through an online portal (which effectively becomes your own mailbox) to respond to questions, attach requested documents, and try to resolve outstanding issues. The program had been limited to various individual tax matters (itemized deductions, education credits), but has now been expanded to include Schedule C income and expenses.

Use of this program was by invitation only (the IRS invited more than 50,000 taxpayers to participate in 2019 [https://content.govdelivery.com/accounts/USIRS/bulletins/24b4fcf]). A taxpayer must receive an audit letter asking whether he or she wants to participate and providing instructions on registering for Secure Messaging before accepting the invitation. In 2020, the IRS expanded the program for its Large Business and International Division, but not to its Small Business/Self-Employed Division.

### Office Audits

The letter inviting you to an IRS office for an examination usually focuses on specific matters from your return. The letter lays out what additional documentation the IRS is seeking; you need to bring this with you when you appear.

Make sure you understand how an office audit works, and your rights during the process. It is usually a good idea to have a professional with you or representing you so you don't say anything or show anything that can induce the IRS to expand its audit focus.

### Field Audits

This type of audit is the most invasive because of its location. When the IRS does an in-person audit of a self-employed person, it is usually a field audit. While the IRS is usually looking at specific issues on a return, it may expand its focus after observing your operation. These audits were essentially suspended during the pandemic because of health concerns, with no indication of when they're likely to resume.

You should have professional representation during a field audit.

## Appeals

At the end of an examination, you can agree with any adjustment that the IRS proposes to make to your tax bill. If so, you pay up or arrange for payment and the matter is closed. If you don't agree with the proposed adjustment, you can appeal. Here you have the opportunity to explain your position to a different IRS agent, who may be persuaded to agree with you.

Beyond appeals handled by the IRS Examination and Collection Office, there is an Independent Office of Appeals that is separate and independent from the IRS Examination and Collections function. Its mission is to help settle disputes without favoring either the government or the taxpayer. You can reach the office at 559-233-1267.

## Litigation

If you've exhausted your administrative options, you can go to court.

- Tax Court allows you to argue your case without having to pay what is in dispute up front. If the taxes, penalties, and interest are less than $50,000, you can use a small case procedure in Tax Court. This is more expeditious and may be less expensive, but if you lose, there is no appeal from a small case decision.
- U.S. District Court may hear your case, but only after you pay what the IRS says you owe and you then sue for a refund.
- Federal Claims Court is another federal court option, which also requires payment so that you are suing for a refund.

The IRS may offer a settlement option even after a case has proceeded to litigation. For example, the IRS has a settlement program for syndicated conservation easement cases already docketed in Tax Court (see IR-2020-130).

## Mediation

This is a process in which both parties agree to work out their differences using a skilled third party, called a mediator. The results are not binding on the parties, but they are usually adopted.

The IRS offers mediation for tax matters for small businesses and self-employed individuals. The Fast Track Settlement Program at https://www.irs.gov/appeals/fast-track, can produce a settlement within 60 days. The mediator is a trained IRS professional. If you want to use an outsider, you'll have to pay for it, and the IRS must agree to it.

Opting for mediation does not eliminate your other rights, such as going to IRS Appeals or having a conference with an IRS manager. You can still pursue litigation if you can't resolve your issues.

If you want to use this program, you must apply and be accepted. Use Form 14017, *Application for Fast Track Settlement*. Attach to it your own statement explaining your position on issues in dispute. You cannot use mediation for collection cases, frivolous issues, and certain other matters.

## Taxpayer Bill of Rights

By law, as a taxpayer you have certain rights. Many of these rights relate to audits. These rights are:

1. The right to be informed
2. The right to quality service
3. The right to pay no more than the correct amount of tax
4. The right to challenge the IRS's position and be heard
5. The right to appeal an IRS decision in an independent forum
6. The right to finality
7. The right to privacy
8. The right to confidentiality
9. The right to retain representation
10. The right to a fair and just tax system

## Taxpayer Advocate Service

If you have an ongoing issue with the IRS that you've been unable to resolve and need immediate help, contact the National Advocate Service. For example, if the IRS has placed a lien on property that is causing you a hardship and you can't wait to address the issue through normal processes, the National Advocate Service may be able to help.

You can contact the National Advocate Service by calling 877-777-4778 or filing Form 911, *Request for Taxpayer Advocate Service Assistance*. Find more information at www.irs.gov/Advocate.

## Special Audit Rules for Partnerships

Effective for partnership returns filed after 2018, there is a centralized partnership audit regime (referred to as the BBA regime because it was created by the Bipartisan Budget Act). Under this regime, the partnership (rather than individual partners) is audited and adjustments are made at the partnership level; the partnership pays the adjustments unless it opts to push them out to partners by providing amended Schedule K-1s to them.

A "small partnership" can elect out of the BBA regime if both of the following conditions are met:

- All of the partners are individuals, C corporations, S corporations, or the estate of a deceased partner. Partnerships with partners that are disregarded entities (e.g., one-member limited liability company) cannot elect out of the BBA regime.
- The partnership is required to file 100 or fewer Schedule K-1s.

**Example**

A partnership has 95 partners who are individuals, plus one partner that is an S corporation. The S corporation-partner has 5 shareholders. The partnership is ineligible to elect out of the BBA regime because a total of 101 Schedule K-1s are filed (96 for the partners [95 individuals + 1 S corporation] plus 5 that the S corporation files for its shareholders).

APPENDIX A

# Information Returns


| | | | |
|---|---|---|---|
| Dividends | 559 | Retirement and Employee Benefit Plans | 562 |
| Large Cash Transactions | 560 | Small Cash Transactions | 563 |
| Payments to Independent Contractors | 561 | Wages | 563 |
| Pension and Retirement Plan Distributions | 561 | Merchant Transactions | 565 |
| | | Foreign Accounts | 565 |


Businesses are in a unique position to monitor certain activities with which they are involved, and the federal government has harnessed this power by requiring certain reporting for tax and financial purposes. Reporting enables the government, where possible, to make sure that income is reported as it should be and to keep tabs on certain monetary activities.

Reporting requirements vary from return to return. Filing deadlines are completely independent of your tax year (when you file your income tax return), and many of these deadlines have been changed for information returns required to be filed for the 2021 tax year (i.e., filed in 2022). If a filing deadline falls on a Saturday, Sunday, or legal holiday, then the deadline becomes the next business day that is not a Saturday, Sunday, or legal holiday.

The following is a review of the most common business-reporting requirements, some or all of which may apply to you. (Some of these responsibilities are explained in greater detail within the book as indicated.) Penalties for making mistakes, filing late, or not filing at all, are explained in Appendix B.

## Dividends

### *Who Must Report*

If your corporation pays out dividends or distributions to shareholders (including yourself), payments of $10 or more ($600 or more for liquidations) must be reported to the IRS and to the recipient.

File Form 1099-DIV, *Dividends and Distributions*. Request the forms from the IRS at 800-829-FORM or purchase them from an office supply company (the form is a triplicate form that cannot be downloaded from the IRS website). The IRS copy of Form 1099-DIV must be accompanied by Form 1096, *Annual Summary and Transmittal of U.S. Information Returns*.

### When to Report

Furnish the recipient with a copy of the form no later than January 31 of the year following the year in which dividends or distributions were paid.

File the form with the IRS no later than February 28 of the year following the year in which the dividends or distributions were paid. But if you file the form electronically, you have an additional month (to March 31) to file with the IRS.

### Where to Report

The filing location you use depends on where your corporation is located—there are 4 IRS service centers in which this information return is filed.

## Large Cash Transactions

### Who Must Report

If you receive more than $10,000 in cash in one or more related transactions in the course of your business, you must report the transaction to the IRS. You must also report your reporting to the party that paid you. "Cash" for reporting purposes does not mean only currency; it includes cashier's checks, money orders, bank drafts, and traveler's checks having a face amount of $10,000 or less received in a transaction used to avoid this reporting requirement.

In the past, the IRS could seize the bank accounts of owners suspected of structuring deposits or transactions in order to avoid the $10,000 reporting threshold. However, there is protection for small business owners. If there are seizures for structuring, there are more due process protections in place:

- Seizure for structuring is permissible only if derived from an illegal source or to conceal criminal activity.
- An owner who has funds seized for structuring can request a hearing in federal court (essentially to refute any basis that the IRS had for seizure).
- The hearing must be held within 30 days.
- If the court does not find probable cause for the structuring seizure, the funds must be returned.

File Form 8300, *Report of Cash Payments Over $10,000 Received in a Trade or Business*.

### When to Report

The form must be filed with the IRS by the 15th day after the date the cash was received. For example, if you receive a payment of $12,000 on February 1, 2022, you must report it by February 15, 2022. If the deadline falls on a Saturday, Sunday, or legal holiday, file by the next business day.

You must give a written statement to the party who paid you, but you have until January 31 of the year following the year in which the cash was received to do so. For example, on that February 1, 2022, cash payment, your written statement must be furnished by January 31, 2023.

### *Where to Report*

File Form 8300 with the IRS, Detroit Computing Center, P.O. Box 32621, Detroit, MI 48232 (regardless of where you file your business return). You can e-file the form at no cost with the BSA E-Filing System at https://bsaefiling.fincen.treas.gov/main.html. You must create an account to use this option.

## Payments to Independent Contractors

### *Who Must Report*

If you use independent contractors, freelancers, or subcontractors in your business and pay them $600 or more within the year, you must report these payments to the IRS as well as the contractors. In most cases, payments to corporations are not subject to this reporting requirement. However, you are required to report payments in the course of your business to incorporated attorneys and law firms.

File Form 1099-NEC, *Nonemployee Compensation*. Request a copy of the form from the IRS at 800-829-FORM or purchase it from an office supply company (the form is a triplicate form that cannot be downloaded from the IRS website). The IRS copy of Form 1099-NEC must be accompanied by Form 1096, *Annual Summary and Transmittal of U.S. Information Returns*.

### *When to Report*

You must furnish a copy of the form to the independent contractor no later than January 31 of the year following the year in which the payments were made.

You must also send copies to the IRS by the same date. This deadline applies whether you submit copies to the IRS on paper or electronically.

If you need additional time to file, extensions are not automatic. You can request a 30-day extension by submitting Form 8809, *Application for Extension of Time to File Information Returns*. You must give a reason why you need more time to file. The IRS will grant an extension only in extraordinary circumstances or catastrophe.

### *Where to Report*

The filing location you use depends on where your business is located—there are 4 IRS service centers in which this information return is filed.

## Pension and Retirement Plan Distributions

### *Who Must Report*

You must report any distributions from qualified retirement plans to the recipient of the distributions as well as to the IRS.

Furnish Form 1099-R, *Distributions from Pensions, Annuities, Retirement or Profit-Sharing Plans, IRAs, Insurance Contracts, Etc.*, and file Copy A of this form with the IRS. Submit the copy with Form 1096, *Annual Summary and Transmittal of U.S. Information Returns*.

### *When to Report*

You must furnish a copy of the form to the distribution recipient no later than January 31 of the year following the year in which the payments were made.

You must provide the IRS with its copy no later than February 28 of the year following the year of payment. But if you file the form electronically, you have an additional month (to March 31) to file with the IRS.

If you need additional time to file, request a filing extension on Form 8809, *Request for Extension of Time to File Information Returns.*

### *Where to Report*

The filing location you use depends on where your business is located—there are 4 IRS service centers in which this information return is filed.

## Retirement and Employee Benefit Plans

### *Who Must Report*

If you have a qualified retirement plan, such as a profit-sharing plan, or an employee benefit plan, such as a funded deferred compensation plan, you must report annually on the plan's activities. Reporting includes information on annual contributions, distributions, and the number of participants.

File Form 5500, *Annual Return/Report of Employee Benefit Plan.* For plans with 25 or fewer participants, there is simplified reporting (you can choose not to file Schedules D and R, and to provide limited information on Schedule A of Form 5500).

If you are self-employed and the only participant is you (or you and your spouse, or you and your partners and spouses), you can file Form 5500-EZ, *Annual Return of One-Participant (Owners and Their Spouses) Retirement Plan or A Foreign Plan*, a simplified form. You do not have to file *any* form if you qualify to file Form 5500-EZ and plan assets did not exceed $250,000 at the end of the plan year. And you must file this form, regardless of the amount of plan assets, for the final year of the plan.

### *When to Report*

The form is due on the last day of the seventh month following the close of the plan year (for example, for the 2021 plan year that was on a calendar year, August 1, 2022, because July 31 is a Sunday).

If you need additional time to file, obtain an automatic 2½-month filing extension on Form 5558, *Application for Extension of Time to File Certain Employee Plan Returns.* If you obtained an automatic 6-month filing extension for your personal income tax return, you automatically have until October 17, 2022, to file Form 5500 or 5500-EZ for 2021 (attach a copy of your personal extension when you file the form).

### *Where to Report*

File the form with the Employee Benefits Security Administration (not with the IRS). Forms must be filed electronically, with an exception for undue hardship. For plans with 25 or fewer participants, there is simplified reporting.

The form can be *e-filed* through a filing professional. For more information, click on https://www.efast.dol.gov.

## Small Cash Transactions

### Who Must Report

If you are in a business that sells or redeems money orders or traveler's checks in excess of $1,000 per customer per day or issues your own value cards, you are asked by the government to report suspicious transactions that exceed $2,000. Such businesses include convenience stores, groceries, liquor stores, travel agencies, courier services, and gas stations.

Suspicious activities include a customer who:

- Attempts to bribe or threaten you or your employee
- Buys multiple money orders in even hundred-dollar denominations or in unusual quantities
- Provides false or expired identification
- Refuses to proceed with a transaction once you notify him/her that a form will be completed
- Tries to keep the transaction from being reported or asks you how to avoid reporting requirements
- Works with one or more other individuals who split up to conduct separate transactions that combine for more than $3,000

All reporting is done electronically. First, you must submit Registration of Money Services Business (RMSB) form on FinCEN Form 107 through the BSA e-filing system (https://bsaefiling.fincen.treas.gov/main.html). Then you must renew this registration every two years. When reporting suspicious activity, file FinCEN Form 109, *Suspicious Activity Report by Money Services Businesses*. Filing the form does not give you any financial exposure; you have complete protection from civil liability (the person you report cannot sue you for damages).

### When to Report

File the form within 30 days of the suspicious activity. However, because this filing is voluntary, there are no penalties for nonfiling or late filing.

### Where to Report

File the form with the U.S. Treasury Department's Money Services Businesses Division, through the BSA e-filing system at https://bsaefiling.fincen.treas.gov/main.html. You need to create an account to e-file.

## Wages

### Who Must Report

If you have any employee (including yourself if your business is incorporated), you must report annual compensation and benefits to the employee and to the Social Security Administration. Information about what compensation is reportable is explained in Chapter 7.

File Form W-2, *Wage and Tax Statement*, with the Social Security Administration and furnish a copy to the employee. Also file Form W-3, *Transmittal of Income and Tax Statement*, with the Social Security Administration. Employers filing 100 forms in 2022 must file electronically. Smaller employers can continue to file paper forms, but are encouraged to file electronically.

The IRS lists the following as common errors on Forms W-2, some of which are relevant only to paper returns and not to those prepared and filed electronically. Do not:

- Omit or incorrectly enter an employee's name, Social Security number, or address.
- Omit the decimal point and cents from entries.
- Make entries using ink that is too light. Use only black ink.
- Make entries that are too small or too large. Use 12-point Courier font, if possible.
- Add dollar signs to the money-amount boxes. They have been removed from Copy A and are not required.
- Report an incorrect amount in box 12, Code DD (aggregate cost of health insurance).
- Inappropriately check the "Retirement plan" checkbox in box 13.
- Misformat the employee's name in box e. Enter the employee's first name and middle initial in the first box, his or her surname in the second box, and his or her suffix (such as "Jr.") in the third box (optional).
- Cut, fold, or staple Copy A paper forms mailed to SSA.
- Download Copy A of Forms W-2, W-2AS, W-2GU, W-2VI, W-3SS, or Form W-3 from IRS.gov and file with SSA. Copy A posted on the IRS website is for information purposes only.

### When to Report

Forms W-2 must be furnished to employees by January 31 of the year following the year in which the wages were paid. The same deadline applies for sending copies of the forms to the Social Security Administration (SSA), whether filing on paper or electronically.

If you need more time to provide the forms to employees, you can request an extension from the IRS. If approved, the extension is usually for no more than 15 days from the due date, unless a need for a 30-day extension is shown. To obtain this extension, you must write your own letter to the IRS, Attn: Extension of Time Coordinator, 240 Murall Drive, Mail Stop 4360, Kearneysville, WV 25430. The letter must include your name, address, and EIN, a statement that you need more time to furnish Forms W-2 to employees and the reason why, and your signature or that of an authorized agent.

**NOTE**

**Employers must report on Form W-2 certain tax-free fringe benefits. Use the appropriate codes for these items found in the instructions to Form W-2.**

If you need more time to submit copies to the SSA, you can request a 30-day extension from the IRS (not SSA). Submit Form 8809, *Application for Extension of Time to File Information Returns*. You must give a reason why you need more time to file. The IRS will grant an extension only in extraordinary circumstances or catastrophe, such as a natural disaster or fire that destroyed the books and records needed for filing the forms. No additional extension will be granted.

### Where to Report

File forms electronically using the Social Security Administration's Business Services Online at https://ssa.gov/employer. You can find a list of vendors who can file forms electronically for you. You can also file up to 5 W-2s for free using W-2 Online at https://ssa.gov/employer/bsohbnew.htm. File paper forms (copy A of W-2 and the entire page of W-3) with the Social Security Administration, Data Operations Center, Wilkes-Barre, PA 18769-0001. If you use certified mail, change the ZIP code to 18769-0002. If you use an IRS-approved private delivery service, add "Attn.: W-2 Process, 1150 E. Mountain Drive" to the address and change the ZIP code to 18702-7997.

## Merchant Transactions

Payment settlement companies that process credit cards, debit cards, and electronic payments (such as PayPal and Amazon Pay) must report the gross amount of these transactions, broken down monthly, to the IRS and merchants. Form 1099-K, *Merchant Card and Third-Party Payments*, is used for this purpose.

Gross amounts do not take into account any adjustments for credits, cash equivalents, discount amounts, fees, chargebacks, refunded amounts, or any other amounts. It will be up to you as a seller to report your income accurately on your return, but you do not have to reconcile it with amounts reported on Form 1099-K.

***Small merchant exception.*** Reporting is not required for merchants with annual gross sales on merchant cards of no more than $20,000 or 200 or fewer transactions; reporting is required only if gross amounts for the year exceed $20,000 *and* there are more than 200 transactions.

**Looking Ahead**

**Effective for transactions processed after December 31, 2021, Schedule 1099-K must be issued for transactions totaling $600 or more. The number of transactions no longer is taken into account.**

## Foreign Accounts

### *Who Must Report*

Any "United States Person" with signature authority over at least one financial account located outside the United States with an aggregate value exceeding $10,000 at any time during the year must report certain information to the U.S. Treasury. This reporting, which is required by the Bank Secrecy Act, is known as FBAR reporting. A United States Person includes:

- An individual who is a U.S. citizen or resident
- A domestic corporation
- A domestic partnership
- A domestic limited liability company

### *When to Report*

A report for 2021 is due by April 18, 2022. There is an automatic filing extension of up to 6 months.

### *Where to Report*

FinCEN Report 114, *Report of Foreign Bank and Financial Accounts,* is filed electronically through the Treasury's BSA e-filing system at https://bsaefiling.fincen.treas.gov/main.html. You must create an account to e-file. It cannot be filed by paper. It is not filed with the IRS or attached to a tax return.

APPENDIX B

# Tax Penalties


Failure to File a Tax Return or Pay Tax 566
Failure to File Retirement Plan Returns and Notices 567
Failure to File Correct Information Returns 567
Failure to File Correct Payee Statements 568
Accuracy-Related Penalties 568
Preparer Penalties 569
Penalty Relief 570


Most taxpayers try to do the right thing, but needless to say, taxes are confusing and tax responsibilities can be overwhelming. As Wernher von Braun, the father of the U.S. space program, said "We can lick gravity, but sometimes the paperwork is overwhelming." If you make mistakes, you don't file on time, or you don't file at all, you can be penalized. In addition, interest may accrue on the penalties as well as on any unpaid taxes.

In recent years, many of the penalty rules have changed. Amounts have increased, and new rules have been added. What's more, many penalties with dollar amounts can be adjusted annually for inflation. This appendix contains a roundup of common civil penalties. Criminal penalties are not discussed here.

## Failure to File a Tax Return or Pay Tax

If you fail to file your return on time—by the due date or the extended due date if you obtain a filing extension—you will be subject to a late filing penalty. A penalty can apply in some cases even if you have deposited your taxes on time and owe no additional tax with your return.

The late filing penalty is usually 0.5% of the amount due for each month or part of a month that the return is late, up to a maximum of 25% of the tax due.

However, the penalty increases to 15% of the amount due for each month or part of a month that the return is late, up to a maximum of 75% of the tax due, if the failure to file is fraudulent. If the 2021 return is more than 60 days late, the minimum penalty is $435 or 100% of the tax shown on the return, whichever is less. The dollar amount may be adjusted for inflation. Check the Supplement for any changes in the penalty for 2022 returns filed in 2023.

### *Failure of a Partnership to File a Return*

For 2021 returns, the penalty is $210 multiplied by the number of partners during any part of the year. The penalty is per month (or part-month) that the return is late, up to a maximum of 12 months.

**Example**

**A limited liability company with 4 members files its tax return (Form 1065) 10 months late. The penalty is $8,400 ($210 × 4 × 10).**

### *Failure of an S Corporation to File a Return*

For 2021 returns, the penalty is $210 multiplied by the number of shareholders during any part of the year. The penalty is per month (or part-month) that the return is late, up to a maximum of 12 months.

## Failure to File Retirement Plan Returns and Notices

For late filings after 2019, the penalty for failing to timely file Form 5500 (any in the series) is up to $250 per day (a maximum of $150,000 per plan year). The penalty for failing to provide income tax notices is up to $100 for each failure (a maximum of $50,000 for the calendar year).

## Failure to File Correct Information Returns

As a small business owner, you may have to file various information returns, including W-2s for employees and 1099-NEC for independent contractors for payments in 2021. Information return obligations are explained in Appendix A. Table B.1 shows the penalty amounts for delinquencies for small businesses with average annual gross receipts for the most recent 3 years of $5 million or less (penalties for businesses with higher gross receipts are not covered here). As you can see, the quicker you correct a problem, the lower your penalty amount will be. These are the penalty amounts for 2021 returns filed in 2022.

If the failure to file correct information returns is due to intentional disregard of the filing requirements (or the correct information reporting requirements), different penalty amounts apply; there is no limit on such penalty.

**TABLE B.1** Penalties for Small Businesses for Information Returns

| Scenario | Daily Penalty | Maximum Penalty |
|---|---|---|
| General rule | $280 | $1,142,000 |
| Corrected on or before 30 days after required filing date | $50 | $199,500 |
| Corrected after 30th day but on or before August 1 | $110 | $571,000 |

### De Minimis Exception

Usually, if there is an error on Form W-2 it must be corrected on Form W-2c. However, no correction is needed and no penalties are imposed for de minimis errors. This is defined as amounts less than $100 for Social Security and Medicare taxes, or $25 for income tax withholding. However, an employee can request a corrected form, and an employer must comply with the request or be subject to a penalty.

## Failure to File Correct Payee Statements

If you are required to provide employees with Form 1095-B or 1095-C but fail to do so or are late in doing so, you may be subject to a penalty unless the de minimis exception described earlier applies. Table B.2 shows the penalty amounts for small businesses with average annual gross receipts for the most recent 3 years of $5 million or less (penalties for businesses with higher gross receipts are not covered here). As you can see, the quicker you correct a problem, the lower your penalty amount will be. These are the penalty amounts for 2021 returns filed in 2022.

If the failure to file correct payee statements is due to intentional disregard of the filing requirements (or the correct information reporting requirements), different penalty amounts apply; there is no limit on such penalty.

## Accuracy-Related Penalties

If you make certain mistakes, you may owe a tax penalty. Penalties for these mistakes are called accuracy-related penalties. They include:

**NOTE**

**A 75% penalty applies instead of the basic accuracy-related penalty if an understatement of tax results from fraud.**

1. Negligence or disregard of IRS rules and regulations
2. Substantial understatement of tax liability
3. Overvaluation penalty
4. Undervaluation of property on a gift tax or estate tax return
5. Claim of benefits from a transaction lacking economic substance
6. An undisclosed foreign asset
7. Claiming a basis of property in excess of the amount reported on an estate tax return

### Negligence or Disregard of IRS Rules and Regulations

The penalty for failing to make a reasonable attempt to comply with the tax law is a penalty of 20% of the portion of an underpayment attributable to the negligence. If you take a position contrary to IRS revenue rulings, notices, or regulations, you can avoid the penalty by having a reasonable

**TABLE B.2** Penalties for Small Businesses for Payee Statements

| Scenario | Daily Penalty | Maximum Penalty |
|---|---|---|
| General rule | $280 | $1,142,000 |
| Corrected on or before 30 days after required filing date | $50 | $199,500 |
| Corrected after 30th day but on or before August 1 | $110 | $571,000 |

basis for your position *and* telling the IRS so on Form 8275 (for a position contrary to IRS rulings or notices) or 8275-R (for a position contrary to regulations). Even if you don't file this form, you can still avoid the penalty if you can show you had reasonable cause, explained later in this appendix.

### Substantial Understatement of Tax Liability

If you understate your tax liability by overstating your deductions or omitting income, you may owe a 20% penalty. An understatement is defined as substantial if it exceeds the greater of $5,000 or 10% of the proper tax (5% of the proper tax when it comes to the qualified business income deduction). Alternatively, you may be subject to the negligence penalty explained earlier.

### Overvaluation Penalty

If you donate property to charity and the value claimed on your return is 150% or more of the correct value that results in an underpayment exceeding $5,000, you may owe a penalty of 20% of the underpayment. If the overvaluation is 200%, the penalty becomes 40% of the underpayment.

The 20% penalty is avoided if you based your claimed deduction on a valuation from a qualified appraiser. However, this action does not avoid the 40% penalty.

### Undervaluation of Property on a Gift Tax or Estate Tax Return

If you give an interest in your business to your children or others and you undervalue the interest that results in an underpayment of more than $5,000, you may incur a penalty of 20% of the underpayment.

### Claim of Benefits from a Transaction Lacking Economic Substance

If you engage in a tax transaction that makes no sense economically, you may owe a penalty of 20% of the underpayment. The penalty doubles to 40% if you did not adequately disclose the transaction on your return. You may avoid the 20% penalty if you have reasonable cause (explained later), but you can't escape the 40% penalty by showing reasonable cause.

### An Undisclosed Foreign Asset

If you do not disclose specified foreign assets on Form 8938, you may owe a 40% penalty. The penalty is based on any underpayment resulting from the nondisclosure.

### Claiming a Basis of Property in Excess of the Amount Reported on an Estate Tax Return

Executors filing estate tax returns must provide to heirs the value of the property they inherit. This information is on Schedule A of Form 8971. The value reported to them (and the IRS) becomes their tax basis. If they use a higher basis when they sell or otherwise dispose of the property, they face a basic 20% penalty.

## Preparer Penalties

If you are a tax return preparer, you face an array of penalties with respect to your professional duties. Table B.3 shows the penalty amounts for various failures. These are the penalty amounts for 2021 returns filed in 2022.

**TABLE B.3** Tax Return Preparer Penalties

| Scenario | Daily Penalty | Maximum Penalty |
|---|---|---|
| Failure to furnish copy to taxpayer | $50 | $27,000 |
| Failure to sign return | $50 | $27,000 |
| Failure to furnish identifying number | $50 | $27,000 |
| Failure to retain copy or list | $50 | $27,000 |
| Failure to file correct information returns | $50 per return or item in return | $27,000 |
| Negotiation of check | $545 per check | No limit |
| Failure to be diligent in determining eligibility for refundable credits | $545 | No limit |

## Penalty Relief

Even if you've incurred penalties, you may be able to get them lifted. In tax parlance, this is called penalty abatement. Generally, penalty relief falls into 4 categories: reasonable cause, penalty exceptions created in the Tax Code, administrative waivers from the IRS, and correction of IRS errors.

### *Reasonable Cause*

Reasonable cause is based on the facts and circumstances in each situation and allows the IRS to provide relief from a penalty that would otherwise be assessed. Reasonable cause relief is generally granted if you exercised ordinary business care and prudence in determining your tax obligations but nevertheless failed to comply with those obligations. Ordinary business care and prudence requires you to make reasonable effort to determine your tax obligations. In assessing whether you exercised reasonable care, the IRS looks at the reason given, your past compliance history, the time between the event that triggered the noncompliance and subsequent compliance, and whether there were circumstances beyond your control (e.g., serious illness, fire, or storm).

For small partnerships and S corporations (those with 10 or fewer owners), reasonable cause is met *automatically* if all owners are natural persons (and not nonresident aliens), all owners receive equal allocations of each entity item, and all owners have reported these items on their personal returns.

Ignorance of the law is no excuse.

Whether your reliance on erroneous advice from a CPA or other tax professional constitutes reasonable cause depends on the penalty. Reasonable cause relief is not available for all penalties, but other types of relief may be available.

### *Waivers in the Tax Code*

The law may create a penalty exception upon which you can rely. Examples:

- Postponing filing deadlines by reason of a federally declared natural disaster or for other reasons.
- Relying on the written advice of the IRS, which turns out to be incorrect.

There is also an opportunity to avoid penalties for employment taxes when workers you've been treating as independent contractors are reclassified as employees. Section 530 of the Revenue Act of 1978 creates this relief. Find details at https://www.irs.gov/government-entities/worker-reclassification-section-530-relief.

### *Administrative Waivers*

The IRS has created a number of programs that taxpayers can use to avoid penalties. Examples are:

- Employee Plans Compliance Resolution Program (EPCRS) can be utilized to self-correct errors in qualified retirement plans. See https://www.irs.gov/pub/irs-pdf/i8950.pdf.
- The penalty relief program for Form 5500-EZ can be used to obtain penalty relief for an overdue return. Information is available at https://www.irs.gov/retirement-plans/penalty-relief-program-for-form-5500-ez-late-filers.
- Underpayments of employment taxes can be self-corrected without interest (although penalties may apply). The amount of the underpayment must be paid by the time an adjusted return (e.g., Form 941-X, *Adjusted Employer's QUARTERLY Federal Tax Return or Claim for Return*) is filed.
- Undue hardship relief for failing to pay taxes on time can be granted by filing Form 1127, *Application of Extension of Time for Payment of Tax Due to Undue Hardship*.
- For the Voluntary Classification Settlement Program (VCSP) for reclassifying independent contractors as employees, go to https://www.irs.gov/businesses/small-businesses-self-employed/voluntary-classification-settlement-program.

The Small Business/Self-Employed Division of the IRS is working on a new program to enable taxpayers to self-correct errors on their tax returns, which will help to minimize or possibly avoid penalties. The program is not yet up and running. Check the Supplement for further details.

### *First-Time Abatement Program*

You may be able to escape a penalty under IRS's first-time abatement (FTA) penalty waiver program. To qualify, you must have done things right in the past 3 years and be otherwise in compliance with all filings and payment requirements. Find details at https://www.irs.gov/irm/part20/irm_20-001-001r-cont01.html (see 20.1.1.3.3.2.1 in Part 20).

APPENDIX C

# Checklist of Tax-Related Corporate Resolutions

If you own a corporation (whether it is a C or S corporation), it is important to keep good records on actions taken by shareholders and/or your board of directors at their meetings. The reason: If your corporation fails to act like a corporation, creditors can "pierce the corporate veil" and hold you personally liable. Retain these records in the corporate minutes book.

The following is a listing of key votes that should be taken for tax actions. Some apply only to C corporations, while others apply to both C and S corporations.

- Adopting a fiscal year.
- Adopting an accounting procedure for the de minimis safe harbor rule (see Chapter 14).
- Adopting any of the following employee benefit plans:
  - Accountable plan.
  - Adoption assistance plan.
  - Deferred compensation plan.
  - Cafeteria plan (including FSAs for health and/or dependent care).
  - Educational assistance plan.
  - Employee stock ownership plan (ESOP).
  - Group legal services plan.
  - Medical reimbursement plan.
  - Qualified retirement plan.
  - Stock option plan.
- Authorizing a sale/leaseback transaction.
- Authorizing compensation and bonuses to employees (including shareholder-employees) and payments to corporate directors. To justify larger compensation to C corporation shareholder-employees, note in the minutes why the payment is reasonable under the circumstances (e.g., the payment reflects a catch-up for years in which little or no

compensation was paid). Also, if desired, include a resolution requiring officers to repay excess compensation (amounts determined to be nondeductible because they are unreasonable).

- Authorizing a reimbursement arrangement for officers' expenses.
- Declaring dividends.
- Making or terminating an S corporation election.
- Retaining earnings. C corporations that want to amass funds for future projects rather than distribute earnings currently to shareholders should use corporate minutes to reflect the reason for accumulating earnings to avoid a penalty on excess accumulations. These are earnings over a set limit ($250,000, or $150,000 for personal service corporations). However, to the extent earnings are retained for *specific* reasons spelled out clearly in corporate minutes, the penalty can be avoided if the accumulations are reasonable. For example, if funds are being accumulated to purchase property, to build a factory, or to buy out the interest of an owner who dies or is about to retire, the penalty will not be imposed as long as there is a record of this purpose and the amount of the set-aside is appropriate to the reason.
- Authorizing the purchase of the assets of another company.
- Transactions between the corporation and shareholder (e.g., a lease of property by the shareholder to the corporation; an interest-free loan from the corporation to the shareholder).

Other corporate resolutions that you might consider include:

- Acquiring assets or shares of stock in another business.
- Adopting a trade name.
- Assigning a lease, terminating a lease, or subletting space.
- Authorizing banking activities, including setting up a bank account, obtaining a corporate credit card, and establishing a line of credit.
- Borrowing money from outside parties, including individuals related to owners.
- Commencing litigation.
- Factoring accounts receivable.
- Filing for bankruptcy protection and approving a reorganization plan under Chapter 11 of the Bankruptcy Code.
- Issuing a guarantee or indemnification.
- Leasing equipment (including vehicles).
- Purchasing large equipment and realty.
- Retaining an outside professional (accountant, attorney, business broker, consultant).
- Selling corporate assets or shares.
- Terminating contracts, leases, and certain employees.

# List of Dollar Limits and Amounts Adjusted for Inflation

Taxes are a moving target because many dollar limits and percentages change annually due to increases in inflation. However, some limits and amounts are fixed in the Tax Code and cannot be changed without an act of Congress. Still others are set by the IRS for administrative convenience and are not adjusted annually but could change at the IRS's whim. To help you plan ahead and to figure estimated taxes for 2022, where necessary, lists of items that may or may not change for the next tax year follow. The adjustments for 2022 are listed in the Supplement to the extent that these are available in February 2022.

## Items Adjusted Annually for Inflation

***401(k) plans***—the annual contribution limit through salary reductions as well as the additional contribution limit for those age 50 and older by year end.

***Adoption assistance***—excludable employer-provided adoption assistance for employees ($14,440 for 2021).

***Archer medical savings accounts (MSAs)***—the dollar limit on contributions for plans established before 2008.

***Energy-efficient commercial buildings***—the dollar amount per square foot that can be deducted. For 2021, this is $1.80 per square foot (or 60¢ per square foot where applicable).

***Excepted benefit health reimbursement accounts***—the dollar limit, initially fixed at $1,800, is unchanged for 2021.

***First-year expensing (Sec. 179 deduction)***—the dollar limit on the deduction, as well as the phase-out on property placed in service. For 2021, the limits are $1,050,000 and $2,262,000, respectively.

***Foreign earned income exclusion***–the amount of wages or self-employment income earned abroad eligible for the exclusion is limited ($108,700 in 2021).

***Health savings accounts (HSAs)***—the dollar limit on contributions as well as the definition of a high-deductible health plan (HDHP).

***IRAs and Roth IRAs***—the contribution limits as well as the income limits on making contributions in certain situations.

***Medical flexible spending accounts (FSAs)***—the most that employees can add annually on a pretax basis is capped at $2,750 for 2021. The permissible carryover if the plan allows it is $550 for 2021 (or all unused amounts if the plan allows it).

***Penalties***—the amount imposed for late filing, underpayments, or other failures to comply with the tax law.

***Per diem rates for travel costs***—the special transportation industry meals and incidental expenses, incidental expenses only, and the high cost localities for purposes of the high-low substantiation method.

***Qualified small employer health reimbursement arrangements (QSEHRAs)***—the maximum annual reimbursement to employees for self-only or family coverage in 2021 is $5,300 and $10,700, respectively.

***Retirement plan contributions and benefits***—the limits on making tax-advantaged contributions to qualified retirement plans.

***Shared responsibility payment***—there is no penalty if the cost of employer health coverage is deemed to be unaffordable, which, in 2021, is 9.83% of household income.

***Small employer health insurance credit***—the amount of average compensation, originally fixed at $25,000, is $27,800 for 2021.

***Social Security wage base***—the amount that is used to figure the Social Security portion of FICA and self-employment tax ($142,800 for 2021).

***Tax brackets for individuals***—the amount of taxable income within each bracket may be increased annually; this impacts sole proprietors and owners of pass-through entities.

***Transportation fringe benefits***—the amount excludable for free parking, and the aggregate amount excludable for transit passes or van pooling, is $270 per month in 2021.

## Items Fixed by the Tax Code

***Additional Medicare tax on earned income***—the threshold above which earned income is subject to this 0.9% tax is fixed according to filing status; the threshold does not change annually.

***Cruise ship travel***—the cost of business meetings held on cruise ships is deductible up to $2,000 if certain requirements are met.

***Dependent care assistance***—employer-paid dependent care assistance is excludable up to $5,000 annually.

***Disabled access credit***—the maximum amount of expenses that can be taken into account in figuring the credit is between $250 and $10,250.

***Education assistance***—employer-paid education assistance for employees is capped at $5,250.

***Gifts***—the deduction for business gifts is limited to $25 (exclusive of shipping).

***Group term life insurance***—the tax-free portion is coverage up to $50,000.

***Net investment income tax***—the 3.8% net investment income (NII) tax depends on modified adjusted gross income over a threshold amount that varies with filing status but the threshold does not change annually.

***Prizes and awards to employees***—the maximum deduction for nonqualified award to any one employee is capped at $400 per year. Total awards (qualified and nonqualified) to any one employee is limited to $1,600 per year.

***Reforestation expenses***—up to $5,000 ($10,000 if married filing jointly) can be expensed.

***Start-up costs***—up to $5,000 can be deducted in the first year of business.

## Items Set by the IRS

***Annual reporting by retirement plans***—one-participant plans are exempt from reporting if plan assets at the end of the year do not exceed $250,000 (and this is not the final year of the plan).

***Below market loans***—low- and no-interest loans can trigger taxable income to the lender; the interest rate for determining whether a loan is below the market rate is fixed by the IRS. An annual blended rate applies for below market loans outstanding for the full year (e.g., 0.13% for 2021).

***Building improvements***—under a safe harbor method for small taxpayers, they can be capitalized if they do not exceed the lesser of $10,000 or 2% of the unadjusted basis of the building as long as the building's unadjusted basis is no more than $1 million.

***Dollar limits on depreciating vehicles under 6,000 pounds***—the amount of depreciation each year that the vehicle is owned is capped (the year in which the vehicle is placed in service affects the applicable cap for the remainder of the period of ownership).

***Deemed depreciation for business vehicles***—if expenses for business use of a personal vehicle owned by the taxpayer is figured using the IRS's standard mileage allowance, then the basis of the vehicle is reduced by a set amount per mile (e.g., 26¢ per mile in 2021).

***Home office deduction***—under the simplified method, the deduction is figured at $5 per square foot up to 300 square feet of space.

***Inclusion amount***—the amount of income taken into account for business use of a vehicle that is leased.

***Mileage allowance***—the rate per mile used to determine the deduction for business use of a personal vehicle instead of deducting the actual costs (56¢ per mile in 2021).

***Per diem travel rates***—the IRS sets the rate for a daily deduction covering lodging, meals, and incidental expenses for travel to high-cost areas and all other areas within the continental U.S. The General Services Administration also has per diem rates.

***Travel costs***—no receipt is required for the cost of travel expenses under $75. However, a receipt is required for lodging costs, regardless of amount.

# Index


Abandonment, 89, 113, 271, 284, 438, 442, 468, 478
  disposal of property by, 119–121, 467–468
Aborted business ventures, 491
Above-market loans, 257, 258
ABP test, 302
Abusive transactions, 326, 330, 488
ACA. *See* Affordable Care Act
Accelerated depreciation, 116, 190, 506
  under MACRS, 189
Access to capital and business organization, 27, 28
Accident and health insurance, 376, 430
Accident insurance, 154
Accountable plans
  car, 188
  travel, 180
Accounting fees, 425–427, 438, 442, 448, 493
Accounting methods
  about, 36
  accrual, 43
  cash, 40–42
  change in, 50
  for discounts, 48
  installment method, 47–48
  for long-term contracts, 46–47
  mark-to-market accounting, 48
  repairs and maintenance, 217
  tax year and, 36–50
Accounting periods
  about, 36–40
  business purpose for fiscal year, 37–38
  change in tax year, 39
  limits on use of fiscal year, 37
  pass-through business on fiscal year, 38–39
  restrictions on, 31
  seasonal businesses, 37
  Section 444 election for fiscal year, 38
  short tax years, 37, 39
Accrual accounting method, 43
Accrual method, x, 19, 31, 42–45, 47, 49, 66, 75, 78, 133, 134, 228, 247, 288, 375, 393, 421, 466, 483
Accumulated earnings tax, 26, 502
Accuracy-related penalties, 53, 568–569
Acquisitions, debt-financed, 255
Activated reservists, 157, 163
  employer wage credit for, 157, 163
Active participation, 88
Actual expense method
  about, 186
  business use, 188–190
  conventions, 190–193
  depreciation allowance, 189
  depreciation deduction, 193–195
  dollar limit on depreciation deduction, 193–195
  for home office deduction, 362–364
  Section 179 deductions, 193

Actual expense method (*Continued*)
  standard mileage allowance *versus*, 195–196
Actual receipt, 40, 344
Actuarial costs for defined benefit plans, 309
ADA (Americans with Disabilities Act), 216, 217, 387, 435
Additions to property, 97, 274
Adjusted basis, defined, 96, 117, 341
Adjusted basis, involuntary conversions and, 117
Adjusted gross income (AGI), 14, 19, 57, 77, 79, 88, 143, 179, 184, 203, 206, 207, 314, 319, 322, 376, 389, 402, 414, 419–421, 423, 435, 447, 454, 469, 529, 531, 536, 575
Administrative waivers, 570–571
Adoption assistance, 29, 128, 143, 157, 467, 514, 572, 574
ADS. *See* Alternative Depreciation System; Depreciation
Ad valorem taxes, 249
Advance payments, 41, 44, 71, 196, 243, 392, 393
Advance rents, 238
Advances, 41, 66, 73, 160, 163, 178, 180, 202, 226–229, 231, 234, 244, 350, 372, 389, 442, 446, 517, 522, 534
Advertising expenses, 294–299, 421, 429
Advocate service, taxpayer, 476, 550, 556
Affordable Care Act (ACA), 259, 303, 378, 387, 388, 467, 502
AFR (applicable federal rate), 101, 257, 474
Agricultural payments from government programs, 68
Aircraft, flights on employer-provided, 150
Alcohol fuels credit, 451, 457
ALEs (applicable large employers), 372, 387, 390, 502, 503
All events test, 43
Alternative Depreciation System (ADS), 255, 271, 272, 276, 279–281, 289, 396
Alternative fuel vehicle refueling property credit, 222, 451, 458, 460
Alternative minimum tax (AMT), 80, 108, 137, 157, 158, 200, 279, 280, 287, 380, 457, 460, 504-508, 530, 531
  exemption amount, 504, 505
Alternative minimum taxable income (AMTI), 504, 505
ALV (annual lease value), 147–149
Amazon Payments, 41, 428, 441, 445
Amended tax returns
  depreciation and, 270
  disaster losses, 347, 351
  employment tax, 522, 538–539
  net operating losses, 535
  replacement property, 123
  worthless securities, 111, 124
American opportunity tax credit, 419
Americans with Disabilities Act (ADA), 216, 217, 387, 435
Amortization
  of bond premiums, 286–287
  business start-up costs and organizational expenses, 284
  claiming, 289–293
  of computer software, 286
  defined, 262
  intangibles, 282–284
  leases and, 241–242, 287
  of reforestation costs, 287
  research and experimentation cost, 286
  Section 197 intangibles, 103
  of self-created intangible, 284
Amount received, defined, 96
AMT. *See* Alternative minimum tax
AMTI (alternative minimum taxable income), 504, 505
Angel investors, 486
Annual determination, 373
Annual Filing Season Program participants, 550, 551
Annual lease value (ALV), 147–149
Antichurning rules, 283
Antiques, 67, 269
Appeals, xiii, 129, 388, 519, 550, 555, 556
Applicable federal rates (AFR), 101, 257, 474
Applicable large employers (ALEs), 372, 387, 390, 502, 503
Apportionment, 76, 509–510

Appraisals, 56, 97, 272, 341, 349, 367, 423, 425, 442, 545, 551
Apps, 52, 53, 55, 183, 203, 297–298, 429, 470
 costs of, 183, 297, 298, 429
Archer Medical Savings Accounts (Archer MSAs), x, 144, 382, 385–386, 388, 389, 574
Architectural barriers, removal of, 266, 441, 445
Artists, performing, 184, 207, 411, 448
Assets. *See also* Recovery periods
 capital, 96
 sale of all, 121–122
 transfer of, 99, 485
Assistance programs, 118, 143
Association retirement plans (ARPs), 332
Athletic facilities, expenses for, 153
At-risk basis, 86
At-risk losses, 57, 408, 446
At-risk rules
 calculating limitation, 86
 defined, 83
 farm losses, 397
 limitations on business losses, 83–86, 94
 limits on write-offs from partnerships and LLCs, 14
 partnerships and LLCs passive activity losses and, 88–89
 real estate financing, 86–88
Attorney-client privilege, 471, 475
Attorneys, 9, 30, 65, 66, 97, 100, 178, 229, 234, 268, 284, 296, 342, 355, 357, 366, 395, 418, 420, 426, 427, 429, 430, 438, 442, 475, 476, 484, 496, 549–551, 554, 561, 573
Audit guides, 470, 471, 476
Audit-proofing returns, 469–472
Audits
 about, 553
 appeals and, 555
 audit chances, business organizations, 31–32
 corporations, strategies and, 136
 litigation and, 555
 mediation, 555–556
 partnership centralized regime, 556–557
 taxpayer advocate service, 556
 Taxpayer Bill of Rights and, 556
 types of, 553–555
Automatic enrollment in retirement plans, 303–305, 309, 310
Automobile insurance, 430
Average benefit percentage test (ABP test), 302
Awards for employees, 134, 297, 442, 514, 575
Away from home rule, 167

Bad debts. *See also* Debt
 about, 225
 accrual taxpayers, 232
 business *versus* nonbusiness, 228–229
 collection of, 228, 234
 debtor-creditor relationship, 226–227
 deducting, 234, 474
 guarantees resulting in, 231–232
 loans by shareholder-employees, 229–231
 loss sustained due to, 228
 nonaccrual-experience method, 232
 reporting on tax return, 232–233
 valuing, 229
 worthlessness, 227–228
Bank accounts, business start-up and, 490
Bank and merchant fees, 427–428
Bank fees, 439, 442
Bankruptcy, 9, 29, 33, 73, 97, 110, 227, 234, 477, 491–492, 573
Barriers for disabled persons, removal of, 217, 223
Bartering, 64
Basis
 adjusted, 97, 117, 341
 assets transferred to business, 484
 at-risk, 83–86
 car, 189
 casualty and theft losses, 345
 defined, 269
 depreciation and, 269–271
 losses, limitations on, 80
 recordkeeping for, 57
 S corporation shareholder's, 57
 shareholder, 485
 tax planning and, 466
Bed and breakfasts, 366
Below-market loans, 72, 133, 257–258, 474
Benefit funds, state, 250–251
Benefits. *See* Employee benefits
Bicycle commuting, 152
Bill of Rights, taxpayer, 556
Biodiesel fuels credit, 459
Bitcoin, 41, 64, 135, 428
Black Lung benefit trust contribution, 133, 439, 442

Bonding requirement for retirement plan, 308
Bond premiums, 97, 282, 286–287, 439, 442
Bonus depreciation, 190, 193–195, 213, 261, 262, 265, 267, 268, 275, 281, 295, 468, 537
Bonuses, 30, 68, 128, 131, 133, 134, 139, 240, 332, 439, 442, 466, 480, 481, 515, 572
Books, cost of, 429
Boot, 100, 111, 213, 411
BOP (business owner's policy), 430–432, 440
Borrowing. *See* Loans
Breeding fees, 393
Brother-sister controlled groups, 501
Built-in capital gains, 75, 111
Built-in gains, 17, 33, 75, 78, 93, 111
Built-in gains taxes, 17, 33, 111, 252
Business bad debts, 228–231, 474
Business days, counting, 172
Business equipment, optimum write-offs for, 468
Businesses controlled
  incorporation of, 285, 426, 492
  losses, deducting, 339
  multiple, 499–503
  seasonal, 37, 373
  tax credits, 460
  tax preparers, 551
  unincorporated, 20–421
Businesses, opening and closing, 355
Business expenses. *See* Expenses
Business gifts, 164, 178–179, 185, 575
Business income. *See* Income
Business interest limitation, 255
Business interest, sales of, 33, 105–106
Business interruption coverage, 430
Business losses, limitations on, 80–89
Business mileage logs, 204
Business name, 4, 472
Business organization. *See also specific business organization*
  about, 3
  access to capital, 28
  audit chances, 31–32
  C corporations, 18–26
  changing form of, 35
  choosing form of, 27–33
  comparing forms of, 33, 34
  employees, 27
  exit strategy, 32–33
  filing deadlines and extension, 32
  fringe benefits, 29
  lack of profitability, 28–29
  multistate operations, 31
  nature and number of owners, 29
  owner's payment of company expenses, 31
  personal liability, 27–28
  restrictions on accounting periods and accounting methods, 31
  S corporations, 16–18
  social security and Medicare taxes, 30
  sole proprietorships, 4–9
  tax rates, 30
  unincorporated, charitable contributions and, 420–421
Business owner's policy (BOP), 430–432, 440
Business purpose, 54, 55, 142, 149, 166, 182, 184, 203–205, 239, 296, 354, 355, 366, 393, 497
Business purpose for fiscal year, 37–38
Business start-up costs, 266, 282, 284–285, 490
Business stock, sales of qualified, 107–108
Business structure, review of, 468
Business use of home. *See* Home office deductions
Buyouts, financing options to fund, 546
Buy-sell agreements, 432, 447, 547

Cafeteria plans
  benefits allowed/not allowed under
  flexible spending accounts and
    medical coverage
    simple
Calendar year, 16, 18, 19, 31, 32, 36–40, 44, 45, 76, 106, 150, 168, 198, 247, 275, 277, 279, 324, 336, 348, 373, 425, 432, 461, 473, 483, 490, 500, 517, 527, 528, 533, 562, 567
Cancellation of debt (COD), 73, 74, 119, 494
Cancellation payments, 73–74
Capital, access to, 27, 28
Capital assets, 96, 98, 102, 105, 234, 258, 284, 285, 417, 426, 428
Capital construction-related tax credits, 455–456, 477

Capital expenditures, 65, 74, 209–211, 262, 282, 284, 289, 408, 417
Capital gains
- about, 95
- adjusted basis and, 96–98
- amount of, determining, 96–98
- built-in, 75
- business interest, sales of, 105–106
- capital assets and, 96
- C corporations, 103, 111
- holding period, 98–99
- installment sales, 100
- for partnerships and LLCs, 111
- for pass-through identities, 101–103
- reporting, 110–112
- sale of business interests, 105–106
- sale of qualified business stock, 107–108
- sale or exchange requirement, 98
- Section 1202 gains, 103
- Section 1244 losses, 108–109
- Section 1231 property, 113–115
- for self-employed persons, 110
- special situations, 107–110
- tax-free exchanges, 99–100
- tax rates on, 102
- tax treatment of, 103
- on worthless securities, 109–110

Capital improvements, 56, 57, 210, 211, 213, 214, 217, 220–221, 406, 455, 525
Capitalization rules. *See* Uniform capitalization rules
Capitalized costs, xiii, 46, 49, 57, 197, 210
Capital losses
- about, 95
- adjusted basis and, 96–98
- amount of, determining, 98
- business interest, sales of, 105–106
- capital assets and, 96
- carryovers, 57–59
- holding period, 98–99
- limitations, 103–105
- for pass-through identities, 101–103
- reporting, 110–112
- sale or exchange requirement, 98
- special situations, 107–110

Career counseling, 133
Car expenses
- about, 186
- actual expense method, 187–195
- arranging ownership, 199–200
- business use, 189–190
- commuting vehicles, 150
- company car, employee use of, 147–150
- deducting, 186–187, 206–208
- depreciation and, 188, 208
- heavy SUVs, 195
- hybrid purchase incentive, 134
- insurance, 349, 430
- leasing, 242–243
- plug-in electric vehicles credit, 200
- recordkeeping for, 203
- reimbursement arrangements, 202–203
- standard mileage allowance, 195–196
- substantiation requirement, 54–55
- trade-ins, 201–202
- trucks and vans, 200

Car insurance, 203, 349, 430
Carrybacks, 58, 59, 78–80, 92, 105, 157, 163, 248, 264, 391, 397, 421, 460, 462, 506, 535–537
Carryforwards, 58, 59, 78–80, 92, 101, 105, 111, 252, 260, 264, 362, 397, 414, 421, 460–462, 469, 506–508
Carryovers, 56–59, 73, 74, 78–79, 86, 89, 104, 142, 145, 163, 248, 367, 381, 414, 421, 468, 469, 494, 575
Cars. *See also* Car expenses
- "blue book value," 342
- casualty and theft losses, 188, 202
- defined, 186–187
- electric, plug-in, 200
- fair market value, 147, 149, 197–199, 243
- leasing *versus* buying, 199, 242–243
- sale of, 201

Cash
- large transactions, 560–561
- small transactions, 563

Cash basis and prepayment, carryover period for, 58
Cash-basis businesses, tax planning and, 466
Cash method, 19, 40–42, 50, 67, 75, 288, 375, 393, 421, 483
Cash method of accounting
- about, 40–42
- corporate exceptions, 42
- PSC exception, 42
- restrictions on use of, 42–43

Cash method of accounting (*Continued*)
small business exception, 42
small inventory-based business exception, 42–43
Cash transactions, 560–561, 563
Casualties, 53, 57, 67, 77, 97, 114, 117, 123, 124, 188, 202, 210, 211, 339–353, 360, 392, 430, 439, 440, 443, 444, 474, 477
Casualty and theft losses
about, 339
adjusted basis and, 341
appraisals and, 349
basis, 345
calculating, 343
cars, 188, 202
casualties, defined, 340
casualties, examples of, 340
casualties, proof of, 340
condemnations and, 345
coordination with repairs deducting, 345
determination of, 341–343
disaster assistance, 349–351
disaster losses, 347–348
fair market value and, 341
insurance and, 344, 348–349, 430
inventory and crops, 344
recovered property, 344
repairs and, 345
severance damages, 346–347
special assessments, 346, 347
theft, defined, 340
theft, proof of, 341
year of loss, 345
CCC (Community Credit Corporation) loan, 69, 70
C corporations
about, 14–26
audit strategies, 136
bad debts, 234–235
business expense deduction, 448–449
business income, 95
capital gains and losses, for, 101–105, 111
car expenses, 206–208
casualty and theft losses, 352
compensation payment strategy, 162–163
controlled corporations, 501
depreciation, amortization, and depletion, 293
dividends and, 72
e-filing and, 530
farming expenses, 401
gains and losses, 124
health insurance deductions, 389
owners, compensation to, 136
rent deductions, 244–245
repairs and maintenance, 299
reporting income/benefits, 161–162
retirement plan deductions, 336
sales of business interests, 105–106
special income items for, 75–76
tax credits, 462
taxes and interest, 260
tax treatment of capital gain, 103
travel expenses, 185
CDEs (community development entities), 455
Cellular phones. *See* Smartphones
Cents-per-mile special rule, 150
Certified public accountants (CPAs), vii, 330, 331, 418, 425, 475, 476, 537, 545, 549–552, 554, 570
Certified Service Provider (CSP), 524, 525
Change
in form of business, 35
in tax laws, 468
Change in control, 140
Charge off method, specific, 232
Charitable contributions
about, 420
carryovers and, 57, 469
computers, 422
conservation easements, 422–423
corporations, 421–422
food inventory, 422
for ill, needy, infants, 422
intellectual property, 423
inventory, 422
pass-through, 14
scientific property, 422
special substantiation requirements, 56
unincorporated businesses, 420–421
Charitable contributions, 14, 53, 56, 57, 77, 83, 351, 420-424, 443, 448, 449, 466, 469, 477, 554. *See also* Donations
Checklist, deductions, 438–447
Checks
cash method of accounting and, 40–42

paying taxes by, 246–247, 533–535
Child care facilities and services, 451, 457, 459
employer-provided, 457
Classification of workers, 469
Cliff vesting, 305
Closely held business real property, special valuation for, 547
Closing businesses
tax reporting in final year, 493–494
unamortized costs, 492–493
Clothing, costs of, 429
Club dues, 150, 153, 178, 446
COBRA, 376–378, 462
COBRA coverage, 374, 386–387
COD (cancellation of debt), 73, 74, 119, 494
COD income, 73, 74
COGS (cost of goods sold), 48, 65–68, 74, 92, 93, 127, 146, 151, 289, 292, 293, 344, 348, 349, 352, 392, 422, 425, 428, 429
Cohan rule, 56, 183, 428
COLA (cost-of-living adjustments), 472
Collection agencies, 227, 234
Commerce tax, 510
Commercial buildings, energy improvements to, 221–222
Commercial fishing, 70, 94
Commissions, 5, 30, 60, 65, 68, 127, 240, 285, 286, 433, 439, 443, 448, 515
Commitment fees, 258–259
Commodity Credit Corporation (CCC) loan, 69–70
Community development entities (CDEs), 455
Community renewal property, zero percent gain from, 108
Commuting costs, xiv, 165
Commuting vehicles, 150
Company buyouts, 546
Compensation limit for retirement plan, 306, 312, 328
Compensation. *See* Employee compensation
Compensatory damages, 433–434
Completed-contract method, 46
Computers
donations of, 422
first-year expensing, 262
home office deductions and, 359
Computer software, 267, 273, 283, 286, 522
Condemnation
casualty and theft losses, 345–346
defined, 117
Condemnation awards, 117, 118, 346, 347
Conferences, 295, 555
Conservation easement donations, 420, 422–423, 469
Conservation Reserve Program (CRP) payments, 68, 519
Consignments, 65
Construction, energy-efficient home credit, 451, 456
Constructive dividends, 132, 139, 482
Constructive receipt, 40
Consulting agreements, 300, 546
Contests, 246, 297, 426, 427, 433, 488
Continuation coverage. *See* COBRA coverage
Contractors, energy-efficient home credit, 451, 456
Contracts, long-term, 44, 46, 66, 68, 506
Contributions
federal right of, 518
to health savings account, 385
to qualified retirement plans, 307
to retirement plans, 323–324
to self-employed qualified retirement plans, 335
Control employees, 150
Controlled entities
C corporations as, 501
defined, 114
health care mandates for, 373–374
multiple corporations, treatment as, 501–502
CONUS per diem rate, 168
Conventions (conferences), 172–174
Conventions (depreciation write-off rules)
half-year convention, 190, 275
mid-month convention, 278
mid-quarter convention, 192–193, 275
Conversions from C status to S status, last-in, first-out inventor, 75
Conversions, involuntary, 71, 113, 117–119, 268, 352, 411, 440, 444
Corporate debt, 74, 81, 229, 256–257, 518
Corporate officers, salary of, 473–474

Corporate resolutions, tax-related, vi, 572–573
Corporations. *See also* S corporations
agreements between shareholders and, 470
amortization of organizational costs for, 285–286
capital loss limits on, 104–105
charitable contributions from, 421–422
checklist of deductions for, 438–447
closing, 492–493
controlled, 501
deductions checklist, 438–447
estimated taxes, 530–533
golden parachute payments, 140
indebtedness to shareholder, 256
loans between shareholders and, 256
net operating losses, calculating, 78
renting to, 236
small. *see* Small corporations
state income taxes, 511
termination or dissolution of transferred property and, 485
Correspondence audits, 553, 554
Cost depletion, 288, 289
Cost of goods sold (COGS), 48, 65–68, 74, 92, 93, 127, 146, 151, 289, 292, 293, 344, 348, 349, 352, 392, 422, 425, 428, 429
Cost of living, 132, 472, 545
Cost-of-living adjustments (COLA), 472
Cost segregation, recovery periods, 274
Costs of performance (COP), 510
Costs. *See also* specific costs
capitalized, 49
direct, 49
indirect, 49
organizational, 285
qualified, 145
unamortized, 492–493
Country club dues, 150
CPAs (certified public accountants), vii, 330, 331, 418, 425, 475, 476, 537, 545, 549–552, 554, 570
Credit cards
business start-up and, 490
cash method of accounting and, 42–43
merchant income on, 93
paying taxes by, 533–534
Credit checks, 233
Credit for federal taxes on fuels, 74, 251, 401, 462
Credit for paid family and medical leave, 157, 454
Credit, fuel-related excise taxes, 398
Credit insurance, 430
Credit offsets, alternative minimum tax and, xi, 506
Credit policies, 233
Credit reduction states, 250, 513
Credits. *See* Tax credits Crop insurance and crop disaster payments
Crops, casualty and theft losses to, 352
Crop shares, 69, 92
Cross-purchase agreements, 547
Crowdfunding, 28, 486–488
CRP (Conservation Reserve Program) payments, 68, 519
Cruise ships, conventions or meetings on, 173–174, 439, 443
CSP (Certified Service Provider), 524, 525
Customers
bankruptcy of, 234
credit policies and, 233
Customs expenses, 425
Cyber-liability coverage, 430

Damages, 68, 74, 118, 211, 339–342, 345–347, 349, 360, 430, 433–434, 439, 442, 447, 563
Day-care, 161, 355, 364, 366
Day-care facilities
about, 364–365
calculating deduction, 365–366
meal costs, 434
Day-care providers, 365, 434
Day traders, 6, 48
DBA (doing business as), 4, 31
D&B business credit rating service, 489
Deadlines, filing, xiv, 27, 32, 33, 390, 471, 510, 527, 528, 539, 559, 570
Death tax, 546, 547
Debt-financed acquisitions, 255
Debt-financed distributions, 256
Debt-financed portfolios, 436
Debt financing, 486
Debt forgiveness, 73, 97, 492
Debtor-creditor relationship, 225–228
Debt. *See also* Bad debts; Loans
cancellation of, 73–74

corporate, 356–357
nonrecourse, 120
recourse, 120
worthless, 227–228
Deductible employee compensation
defined, 131
limits on, 134
noncash payments, 135
restricted property, 135
rules for, 131–133
types of, 133–134
Deductible expenses
checklist of allowed, 438–447
checklist of not allowed, 442–443
temporary assignments and, 175
Deductible interest, 253–258, 437
Deductions
bad debt, 448–449
business equipment, 468
business, miscellaneous, 448–449
casualty and theft losses, 351–352, 474
checklist of, 438–447
claiming, 471
disaster losses and, 351
dividends-received, 72, 435–436
foreign housing, 436–438
not allowed, 442–443
removal of architectural or transportation barrier, 218
temporary assignments and, 175
transportation costs, 164–166
travel expenses, 167
whaling expenses, 424
Deductions checklist, 438-447. *See also* Income and deduction strategies; *specific deductions*
Deemed depreciation, 187, 201, 576
Deemed filing date, 530
Deemed NOL, 74
Deferrals, elective, 144, 302, 304, 312, 314, 316–318, 324, 410, 514
Deferred compensation, 134, 139, 302, 332, 410, 512, 562, 572
Defined benefit plans, 301, 306–309, 323, 327–328, 336, 431, 438, 442
Defined contribution plans, 301, 302, 306–308, 316, 322, 323, 327–328, 332
De minimis exception, 49, 568
De minimis fringe benefits, 142, 146, 147, 152, 176–178, 387
De minimis safe harbor rule, 262, 281, 429, 572
Demolition and removal expense, 213
Demolition costs, 213
Dependent care assistance, 29, 128, 142, 143, 154, 381, 514, 575
Dependent care credit, 128, 161, 452, 454
Depletion
cost depletion, 288
deduction of, 289
defined, 262, 287
methods, 288
partnership oil and gas properties, 288–289
percentage depletion, 288
Deposits, 28, 38, 40, 41, 53, 59, 60, 70, 73, 86, 94, 121, 238, 239, 259, 287, 288, 324, 326, 346, 350, 384, 385, 393, 429, 473, 476, 488, 490, 512, 517–519, 529, 530, 532–535, 542, 560
penalty for delinquent, 518–519
Depreciable property, installment sales and, 101
Depreciation
accelerated, 189
actual expense method, 188
allowance, 189
alternative depreciation system (ADS), 271
alternative recovery system, 279–280
basis, 189
bonus, 261, 267–268
of car, 207
claiming, 275
conventions, 190–192
deemed, 201
defined, 261
de minimis safe harbor rule, 262
dollar limits on, 193–195
excess, 190
farming and, 393
first-year expensing, 195
general rules, 268–271
home office deductions, 365
listed property, limitations of, 280–281
methods, 276–280
personal property put to business use, 281–282
property not eligible for, 269
recaptured, 143
record keeping for, 58
straight-line, 189

Depreciation (*Continued*)
unrecaptured, 116
write-off limits. *see* Conventions (depreciation write-off rules)
Designated Roth accounts, 316–318, 447, 542, 543
Diaries
of business mileage, 203–205
of travel expenses, 183
Differential wage payment tax credit, x, 157, 163, 451, 453
Direct costs, 49, 170
Direct gifts, 179
Directors and officers (D&O) coverage, 430
Directors, payments to, 433
Direct rollovers, 542
Direct sellers, other income for, 68
Disability insurance, 251, 430, 431, 443, 446
Disabled access credit, x, 59, 217, 218, 223, 451, 455, 459, 502, 575
Disabled persons
car expense, 184
expenses of, 435
repairs and maintenance for, 203
special rules for improvements for, 216–220
travel expenses, 184
Disallowance repayment agreements, 132, 139–140
Disaster assistance, 347–352, 468
Disaster losses
amended returns and, 348
casualty and theft losses, 348–349
tax planning and, 468
Disaster victims, certain, 78
Discharge of indebtedness, 74, 492
Discounts
accounting for, 48
qualified employee, 151
Disqualified person, 140, 325, 326
Distressed companies, contribution reduction for, 314
Distributions
debt-financed, 256
pension and retirement plan, 561–562
required, 38
Dividends
as business income, 72
C corporations and, 72
constructive, 139
information returns, 559–560
patronage, 69
S corporations and, 473
Dividends-received deduction, 72, 78, 93, 435–436, 443, 449
D&O (directors and officers) coverage, 430
Documentary evidence, 54, 56, 180, 182, 184
Doing business as (DBA), 4, 31
Dollar limits
inflation adjustment for, 574–575
IRS, fixed by, 576
tax code, fixed by, 575–576
Domain names, 283, 297
Dominant motive for loans, 229–231
Donations. *See also* Charitable contributions
crowdfunding, 488
Double taxation, 19, 30, 510
Draws, 127, 136, 144, 350, 537
Dues, 150, 153, 178, 298, 417, 425, 438, 439, 442, 446
DUNS number, 489

Earned income credit (EIC), 128, 160, 452, 454
Eating facilities, employer-operated, 146, 178
Economically disadvantaged designated groups, 452
Economic performance test, 43–44
Educational expenses
deducting, 418–419
employer-paid, 152, 419, 575
personal education incentives, 419–420
Education credits, 419, 448, 452, 554
EEOC (Equal Employment Opportunity Commission), 60, 387
E-file providers, 529, 539
E-filing, 529, 530, 539, 561, 563, 565
E-filing tax returns, 529, 530, 538
tax preparers and, 549, 551
EFTPS.gov, 520, 529, 531
EFTPS. *See* Electronic Federal Tax Payment System
EIN. *See* Employer identification number
Elderly persons
day care facilities for, 364–365
improvements for, special rules, 216–220

Elected farm income, 70
Election to postpone gains, 118
Elective deferrals, 144, 302, 304, 312, 314, 316–318, 324, 410, 514
Electric vehicles, plug-in, 97, 200, 208
Electronic Federal Tax Payment System (EFTPS)
paying taxes online, 533
required use of, 534
voluntary use of, 534–535
Electronic filing of tax returns, 529, 529, 538
Electronic imaging systems, 54
Electronic payment methods, 41
Electronic signatures, 529
Elcctronic transfer of funds to pay taxes, 529, 532
Eligible terminated S corporation, 75, 76
E-mail, IRS not contacting by, 554
Employee achievement awards, 134
Employee benefit plans
reporting, 562
tax planning and, 467
Employee benefits. *See also* Fringe benefits
about, 141
adoption assistance, 143
athletic facilities, 151
business organization and, 29
cafeteria plans, 144–145
cellular phones, 141–142
commuting vehicles, 150
company car, employee use of, 147–150
country club dues, 150
dependent care assistance, 142
discount, qualified employee, 151
educational assistance, 143
employment tax credits, 163
flexible spending account, 144–145
flights on, employer-provided aircraft, 150
frequent flyer miles, 153
golden parachute payments, 140
group-term life insurance, 142–143
health reimbursement accounts, 144
Health Savings Accounts, 144
housing relocation costs, 147
identity theft protection, 151
life insurance on individual basis, 150–151
meals and lodging, 146–147
medical insurance coverage, 141
moving expenses, 147, 417
no-additional-cost service, 151
retirement planning advice, 144
smartphones, 141–142
split-dollar life insurance, 151
supplemental unemployment benefit, 145
travel costs, 147
working condition fringe benefit, 151–152
Employee compensation. *See also* Employee benefits
about, 127–128
bonuses, 133
deductible, 131–135
deducting, 157–158
deferred compensation, 139
disallowance repayment agreements, 139–140
employment tax credits. *see* Employment tax credits
outsourced workers, 130
owners, compensation to, 135–136
stock options and restricted stock, 136–138
temporary workers, 130
worker classification, 128–130
Employee discounts, qualified, 151
Employee Plans Compliance Resolution System (EPCRS), 325
Employee records, retention of, 60
Employee relations expense, 179
Employees
about, 16–17
bad debts, 234
bonuses, 128
business expense deductions, 448–449
capital gains and losses, 96–98
car expense deductions, 206–208
casualty and theft losses, 339
health insurance deduction, 390
highly compensated, 303
home office deductions, 367
household, 161

Employees (*Continued*)
leased, 515–516
meal costs and, 176
outsourced, 433
rent deductions, 244–245
repairs and maintenance, 223
retirement plan deductions, 334
statutory, 5
taxes and interest, 259–260
temporary, 130
travel expenses, 54–55
Employee stock ownership plans (ESOPs), 29, 33, 45, 133, 328–329, 546, 572
Employee stock purchase plan, 137, 514
Employer differential wage payments credit, x, 157, 163, 453
Employer identification number (EIN)
obtaining, 489
state, 489
Employer mandate, x, 141, 371–374, 378, 387, 467, 502, 503
Employer-operated eating facilities, 146, 178
Employer-paid educational expenses, 467
Employer-paid parking, 152
Employer-provided aircraft, flights on, 150
Employer-provided child care facilities and services, 451, 457, 459
Employers
COBRA health coverage, 386, 387
eating facilities operated by, 146, 178
educational expenses paid by, 419
employment-related tax credits, 128, 155
health care mandate, 372
records retention, 60
small, xi, 131, 143, 144, 154, 157, 288, 301, 309, 310, 313, 315, 318, 323, 336, 372, 373, 379, 380, 385, 386, 390, 451–453, 457–460, 467, 481, 517, 522, 575
wage credit for activated reservists, 157, 163
Employment agency fees, 134
Employment practices liability insurance, 431
Employment-related tax, 128, 131, 155, 160
Employment-related tax credits, 128, 131, 155, 160
Employment tax credits
activated reservists, employer wage credit for, 157
for all businesses, 163
dependent care credit, 161
earned income credit, 160
employee's employment-relate, 160
employer credit for FICA on tips, 156
employer's employment-related tax credits, 155
employer wage payment credit for activated reservists, 157
empowerment zone employment credit, 537–538
general business credit, 157
Indian employment credit, 156
work opportunity credit, 155–156
Employment taxes
about, 250
deposit dates, 517
estimated taxes, 530
failure to pay, 518
federal, 5
Employment tax returns
amending, 538–539
due dates, 538
filing extensions, 528
returns for, 538
Empowerment zone employment credit, 537–538
Endangered species recovery expenditure, 395
Energy credit, 223, 458, 459
Energy-efficient home credit, 451, 456
Energy improvements, 209–224
Energy, tax credits and, 458
Enhanced oil recovery credit, 451, 458
Enrolled agents, 411, 425, 475, 550–552
Entertainment expenses
about, 220
club dues, 150
deducting, 186–187
ordinary and necessary, 391
recordkeeping requirements, 182
Entertainment. *See* Travel expenses
Entity plans, 547
Environmental and pollution liability insurance, 431
Environmental cleanup costs, 211

E&O (errors and omissions insurance), 431
EPCRS (Employee Plans Corrections Resolution System), 325, 333, 571
Equal Employment Opportunity Commission (EEOC), 60, 387
Equipment. *See also* Rents; *Repairs and maintenance*
  cost of, 429
  repossession of, 120
Equity crowd funding, 487
Equity financing, 485–488
Errors and omissions (E&O) insurance, 431
Errors, common
  avoidance of, 472–473
  retirement plans, 325–326
  W-2 forms and, 564
ESOPs (employee stock option plans), 29, 546
Estate planning
  buy-sell agreements and, 547–548
  factors in decision-making, 547
Estate taxes
  special rules for, 547
  succession planning and, 547
Estimated taxes, x, v, 6, 160, 161, 259, 350, 447, 489, 490, 509, 520, 522, 523, 530–533, 574
Excess business losses, 76–77, 80, 408, 537
Excess depreciation, 190
Excess net passive income, 75
Exchanges, tax-free, 95, 99, 111, 201, 202, 266, 271
Excise taxes
  about, 525–526
  credits, claiming, 398
  excess contributions, 325
  excess parachute payment, 140
  farmers and, 462
  on fuels, 251
  prohibited transactions, retirement plans, 325–326
Excise tax returns, 350, 540
Excluding gain, 107
Exclusive use test for home office, 354
Exit strategies, 32, 39–40, 680
Expenses
  advertising. *see* Advertising expense
  bank and merchant fees, 427–428
  business equipment, 468
  business, in general, 417
  car and truck, 186–187
  charitable contributions, 420
  checklist of deductible and nondeductible expenses, 438–447
  clothing, 429–430
  commissions, 433
  customs, 425
  deducting, 448–449
  depletion, 287–288
  disabled persons and, 435
  dues and subscriptions, 425
  educational, 418–419
  farming, 397
  fines, 433–434
  first-year expensing, 261
  insurance, 430–433
  interest. *see* Interest legal fees
  licenses and permits, 424–425
  lobbying, 296–297
  meal costs, day care providers, 434
  meals. *see* Meal and entertainment expenses
  moving, 417
  nondeductible, 296
  office, 428
  ordinary and necessary, 294–295
  other, 438
  outsourced workers, 433
  passive activity loss rules and deductions, 87–88
  payments to directors and independent contractors, 433
  penalties, 433
  postage, 429
  prepaid. *see* Prepaid expenses
  professional fees, 425–427
  rents, 72
  shipping, 429
  sideline businesses, 498
  supplies and materials, 428–429
  telephone, 361
  uniforms, 429–430
  write-offs and, 465
Expensing, 14, 57, 74, 97, 190, 195, 201, 213, 261–293. *See also* First-year expensing
Experimentation costs, deducting, 505
Extensions, filing, 27, 32, 33, 48, 90, 91, 144, 323, 324, 336, 471, 472, 528, 529, 561, 564, 565

Fair Labor Standards Act (FLSA), 156, 453
Fair market value (FMV)
  bad debts, 229
  cars, 147

Fair market value (FMV) (*Continued*)
  casualty and theft losses, 340–341
  charitable contributions and, 420
  incentive stock options and, 137
Family and medical leave credit, 454, 459
Family members, employed, 515
Farmers Home Administration (FHA), 342
Farm income averaging, 70, 92
Farming
  about, 391
  business income, 92
  claiming credits/refunds, 398
  conservation easements, 422
  elected farm income, 70
  expenses, 391, 399–401, 448
  expenses, nondeductible, 399
  fuels, exemption from excise tax on, 399
  fuels tax credits, 398
  home office deductions, 354–355
  income averaging, 92
  income from, 68–70
  losses, 397
  passive activity loss rules and, 89
  self-employment tax, 519
  tax credits, 398–399
  timber gains, 395
Farm-related taxpayer, 392
Farm Services Agency (FSA), 351
Fast Track Settlement Program, 555
FAVR (fixed and variable allowance), 150
FBAR reporting, 565
FBN (fictitious business name), 4
Federal Emergency Management Association (FEMA), 339, 341, 351, 431
Federal employment taxes, 5
Federal excise tax on fuels, 251, 458, 462
Federal Insurance Contribution Act (FICA), 5, 28, 128, 135, 136, 156, 157, 159, 248, 250, 252, 316, 376, 381, 382, 393, 410, 453, 466, 501, 512, 513, 515–520, 522, 523, 539, 545, 575
Federal Insurance Contribution Act. *See* FIC
Federally-declared disaster areas, 32, 528
Federal right of contribution, 518
Federal Unemployment Tax Act (FUTA)
  credit reduction states, 250
  employment tax and, 250
  filing, for all businesses, 522
  household workers and, 161
  income tax withholding, 513
  obligations, 512
  paying, 517–518
  penalties, 518–519
  records retention, 60
  self-employed persons and, 519–523
  service charges, 516
  state income tax withholding, 520
  states and, 512
  tips, special rules for, 515–516
  types of, 512
Feed assistance and payment, 69
Feed, livestock, 392–393
FEMA (Federal Emergency Management Association), 339, 341, 351, 431
Fertilizer, 251, 267, 392, 393, 399
Fertilizer and lime, 393
FHA (Farmers Home Administration), 342
FICA (Federal Insurance Contribution Act), 5, 28, 135, 136, 156, 157, 159, 248, 250, 252, 316, 376, 381, 382, 393, 410, 453, 466, 501, 512, 513, 515–520, 522, 523, 539, 545, 575
  employer credit for tips, 531
  employer portion, 156
  employment tax and, 250
  tax planning and, 465
  withholding wages for, 512
Fictitious business name (FBN), 4
Fidelity bonds, 431
Fiduciary rule, 305
Field audits, 554, 555
FIFO (first-in, first-out), 67, 68, 409
15-year property, 273, 276
Filing deadlines and extension
  business organization and, 32
  filing extensions, 528
  filing methods, 528
  IRS forms for. *see* IRS Form
  late filing penalties, 529

Filing extensions, IRS Forms for, 472
Filing online, 529–530
Filing tax returns. *See also* Filing extensions
employment taxes, 527–528
excise taxes, 549
failure to, 567
information returns, 565
online, 529–530
on time, 471
Film or television productions, expensin, 267
Financial planner, 544
Financing
for buyouts, 546
debt, 486
equity, 486–487
options, other, 488
real estate, 86
royalty, 486
Fines, payment of, 433
First in, first-out (FIFO), 38, 67, 409
First-time abatement (FTA) program, 535, 571
First-year expensing
about, 261
for cars, 189
defined, 261
disposition of property, 265–266
election, 265
limits on, 264–265
multiple businesses, 499–500
revocation of election of, 265
First year of business, tax reporting, 490
Fiscal year, 10, 16, 18, 19, 31, 36–39, 168, 247, 264, 423, 483, 500, 527, 528, 554, 572
Fishing, commercial, 70, 94
5-year property, 189, 190, 267, 272, 273, 276
Fixed and variable rate (FAVR) allowance for personal use of company cars, 150
Fleet valuation method, 147, 150
Flexible spending accounts (FSAs), 142, 144–145, 161, 351, 381, 384, 388, 571, 574
Flexible spending arrangements (FSAs), 42, 375, 381
Flights on employer-provided aircraf, 150
Flood insurance, 343, 349, 431
Floor plan financing, 254
FLSA (Fair Labor Standards Act), 156, 453
FMV. *See* Fair market value Food inventory donations
Foreclosure, 119–121
Foreclosure on or repossession of propert
equipment and other personal property, 121
lender's perspective, 120
real property, 120–121
Foreign accounts, information returns, 565
Foreign conventions, 173
Foreign earned income exclusion, 89–92, 436, 437, 519, 574
Foreign housing deduction
base housing amount, 436
housing expenses, 436–437
Foreign housing exclusion, 91, 448
Foreign investments, 94
Foreign tax credit, 74, 91, 157, 252, 259, 260, 458, 460, 504, 506
Foreign taxes, vii, 74, 91, 157, 252, 259, 260, 458, 460, 504, 506
Foreign travel
counting business days, 172
entirely for business, 170–171
primarily for business, 172
primarily for vacation, 173
Forest health protection payments, 69
Form of business organization, vi, xiii, 19, 27–33, 35, 36, 40, 111, 112, 289, 468
Forms. *See* IRS Forms
401(k) plans
"in-plan rollover," 317
investment choices and fees, 318
loans from, 317
one-person, 317
Franchise taxes, 248, 251, 509, 511
Frequent flyer miles, 153, 167
Fringe benefits. *See also* Employee benefits
business organization and, 28–29
de minimus (minimal), 188
employment tax obligations on, 512
limits on, for owners, 152–153
medical coverage as, 375
qualified transportation, 152
working condition, 152
FSA (Farm Services Agency), 351

FSAs (flexible spending accounts), 144, 388, 575
FTA (first-time abatement), 535, 571
FTEs (full-time equivalent employees), health care mandate, 372
  small employer health insurance credit, 379–380
Fuels
  exemption from excise tax on, 399
  tax credits on, 222
Fuel taxes, 75, 251, 399, 525
Full-time equivalent employees (FTEs), health care mandate, 372
  small employer health insurance credit, 379–380
FUTA. *See* Federal Unemployment Tax Act

Gains. *See also* Capital gains
  about, 113–114
  built-in, 17
  built-in gains tax and, 252
  community renewal property and, 108
  equipment and other personal property, 121
  excluding, 107
  installment sales, 100–101
  involuntary conversions, 117–118
  net, 103
  postponing, 118
  real property, 120–121
  recapture, 117
  reporting, 123
  sale-leasebacks and
  sale of all assets, 121–124
  Section 1202, 103
  Section 1231, 58, 69, 106
  short-term, 102–103
  timber, 114
  unrecaptured, 102
GDS (General Depreciation System), 271, 272, 276, 279
General business credit
  carryovers and, 469–470
  employment tax credits and, 163
  limitations on, 460
General Depreciation System (GDS), 271, 272, 276, 279
General partnerships, 9, 10, 37, 259
Gift cards, 43, 44, 66, 134, 387
Gift-leasebacks, 238, 239
Gift loans, 258
Gifts
  business, 178–179
  record keeping, 220
  requirements, 184
  substantiation requirement, 54–55
Gig economy, ix, 4, 495
Golden parachute payments, about, 140
Goodwill, promotion of, 295–296
Grants, 71, 91, 131, 134, 137, 138, 308, 347, 350, 486, 488, 528, 561, 564
Gross income, home office deductions and, 361–362
Gross profit percent, 151
Gross profit percentage, 101, 121
Gross profits, 68, 92, 93, 101, 120, 121, 151
Gross receipts
  cash method of accounting and, 42–43
  defined, 42
  from sale of goods, 76
Gross receipts tax, 76, 510–511
Gross receipts test, 19, 42, 47, 49, 67, 255, 395, 457, 460
Group-term life insurance, 142–143, 154, 431
Guaranteed payments to partners, 136, 153, 162, 376
Guarantees resulting in bad debt, 231–232

Half-year convention, 190, 191, 194, 275, 276, 287
Handicapped persons. *See* Disabled persons
HCEs (Highly compensated employees), 134, 140, 178, 302, 303, 309, 333, 515
Health care mandates
  annual determination, 373
  controlled businesses, 373
  employer mandate, 372–373
  information reporting, 374
  off-time counts, 373
  penalties, 373–374
  seasonal businesses, 373
  self-employed individuals, 372
Health insurance. *See* Medical coverage
Health reimbursement arrangements (HRAs), 144, 378, 467
  Excepted Benefit HRAs, 378
  Individual Coverage HRAs, 378
  Qualified Small Employer HRAs (QSEHRAs), 379

Health Savings Accounts (HSAs)
  about, 144
  benefits of, 387
  contributions, 383
  eligibility, 382
  Medical Savings Accounts and, 382, 385
  taxation of, 381
Heavy SUVs, 193, 195, 196
Help-wanted ads, 297
High-deductible plans, 382, 386, 467
High-low substantiation method, 168, 575
High-low substantiation rates, 169, 181
Highly compensated employees (HCEs), 134, 140, 178, 302, 303, 309, 333, 515
Hobby losses
  farming, 397
  hobby classification and, 496
  profit motive and, 496–497
Holding period, 98–99, 137, 320, 334, 484, 485
Home
  employing worker in your, 522
  energy-efficient home credit, 456
  living away from on temporary assignment, 174
  rental of portion for business use, 242
  tax home, defined, 165
Home office, xii, 57, 116, 118, 132, 153, 166, 175, 242, 244, 245, 258, 268, 274, 279, 280, 349, 353–370, 399, 417, 469, 484, 498, 576
Home office deductions
  about, 353–354
  actual expense method, 358–359
  ancillary benefits of claiming, 367
  bed and breakfasts, 366
  carryovers, 57, 469
  day-care facilities, 364–365
  deducting, 367–368
  exclusive and regularize, 354
  home mortgage interest and, 258
  homeowner's insurance, 360
  home sales, impact of, 367–368
  meeting with patients, clients, or customers, 356–357
  mobile offices, 366
  principal place of busines, 355–356
  separate structure, 357–358
  sideline businesses, 356, 495
  simplified method, 358, 362–363
  special business uses of home, 364–366
  storage space, 365
Home office depreciation, 364–365
Homeowners insurance, 360
Home sale exclusion, 116, 367
Homestead protection, 4
Household employees
  nanny tax, 161
  special reporting for, 522–523
Housing expenses, foreign housing deduction, 436–438
Housing relocation costs, 147
HRAs (health reimbursement accounts), 144, 388, 574
HRAs (health reimbursement arrangements), 372, 377–380, 467
HSAs. *See* Health Savings Accounts

Identity theft protection, 151
Ill, donations for, 422
Imaging systems, electronic, 54
Improvements. *See also* Capital gains
  capital, 210–211
  energy, 221–222
  leasehold, 242
  restaurant, 210, 242
  retail, 211, 242
Improvements to property
  deductions for, 209–210
  disabled access credit, 217
  for elderly and, 216
  people with disabilities, 216–220
  qualifying expenditures, 217
  recordkeeping, 220
  recovery periods, 274
Imputed income, 142
Imputed interest
  Incentive stock options (ISOs), 137
  Incidental property, 100
Incidental rate, 181
Incidental travel costs, 169, 182
Inclusion amount, 167, 197–199, 242, 243, 576
Income
  about, 63–64
  COD income, 73–74
  dividends, 72
  earned income credit, 160

Income (*Continued*)
- excess net passive, 75
- farming, 68–70
- foreign earned, 89–90
- imputed, 143
- interest, 72
- investment-type, 72
- miscellaneous business, 74–76
- rentals, 71
- reporting, 565
- sale of goods, 66–68
- service businesses, 65–66
- state taxes on, 76

Income and deduction strategie

Income and deduction strategies
- about, 465
- audit-proofing returns, 469–471
- carryovers, tracking, 469
- errors, common, 472–475
- post-year tax elections, 468
- tax-planning decisions, 465–469

Income averaging, 70

Income tax deficiencies, interest paid on, 259

Income taxes
- estimated, 509
- federal, 509
- nexus to state and, 31, 76
- state, 509

Income tax withholding, 28, 60, 69, 128, 157, 159, 410, 512, 513, 515, 517, 518, 520, 522, 568
- records retention, 59

Incorporation of business
- business income, 92
- payments to, 433
- reporting payments to, 560

Indian employment credit, 156, 453

Indirect costs, 49

Indirect gifts, 179

Individual retirement accounts (IRAs)
- about, 318–319
- converting to Roth, 321–322
- and other retirement plans, 318–322
- prohibited transactions, 325–326
- spousal, 320

Individuals
- capital loss limits on, 101–102
- estimated taxes, 530
- net operating losses, calculating, 77
- whaling captains, deduction for, 424

Industry-based guidance, 471

Infants, donations for, 422

Inflation, items adjusted for information return
- about, 529
- cash transactions, 560
- dividends, 559
- due dates, electronically filed, 539–540
- e-filing and, 316
- failure to file correct, 567–568
- filing, 538
- foreign accounts, 565
- health care mandates and, 372
- health coverage, 575
- independent contractors, payments to, 561
- large cash transactions, 560–561
- merchant transactions, 565
- online filing of, 529
- pension distributions, 561–562
- retirement plan distributions, 561–562
- small cash transactions, 563
- wages, 563–564

Information returns, vi, xiv, 10, 41, 162, 324–325, 328, 336, 350, 449, 470, 529, 538, 539–540, 552, 554, 559–565, 567–568

"In-plan rollover," 317, 542

Insolvency, 73, 97, 109, 228, 492, 494

Installment method accounting, 47–48

Installment reporting, election out of, 47, 101, 123

Installment sales
- buyouts and, 546
- capital gains from, 95
- depreciable property, 101
- election out of reporting, 101
- gains and losses, 114–115
- interest on deferred payments, 101
- reporting, election out of, 101
- tax planning and, 468

Insurance. *See also* Medical coverage; *specific insurance types*
- accident and health, 430
- business interruption, 430
- business owners' policy (BOP), 430
- car, 349, 430
- casualty and theft losses, 348–349
- credit, 430
- crop, 68
- cyber-liability, 430
- deductible costs of, 429
- directors and officers, 430
- disability, 430, 431
- employment practices liability, 431

environmental and pollution liability, 431
errors and omissions, 431
fidelity bonds, 431
flood, 431
group-term life, 146, 431
homeowners, 360
key person, 431
liability, 431
life. *see* Life insurance
long-term care, 375
overhead, 431
Pension Benefit Guaranty Corporation, 431
performance bonds, 431
product liability, 431
professional liability coverage, 431–432
use and occupancy, 349
workers' compensation, 431

Insurance premiums, cash basis and prepayment, 58

Intangible property
amortization of, 282
defined, 269
self-created, 284

Intellectual property
donations of, 420–423
suing for infringement, 426

Intent, and option to buy, 237

Interest
about, 246
in business, debt incurred to buy, 255–256
on condemnation awards, 117
deductible, 253–258
deducting, 259–260
imputed, 72, 257, 474
on income tax deficiencie, 259
investment. *see* Investment interest
on life insurance policies, 432
limit on deduction, 254
nondeductible, 253
personal, 253
prepaid, 58
reasonable rate of, 101
on student loans, 419
tax-exempt income and, 259

Interest-free loans, 72, 133

Interest income, vi, 72, 92, 98, 104, 109, 118, 254, 255, 408, 474

Intermediaries, qualified, 100

Inventory
casualty and theft losses to, 339
charitable contributions of, 420
depreciation not allowed for, 281
disasters and, 348
food, donations of, 422–423
storage of in homes, 365

Investment advice, retirement plan, 308

Investment income, passive, 17

Investment interest
carryovers, 58
general rules, 253–254

Investment limit on first-year expensin, 263

Investments
foreign, 94
for 401(k) plans, 317

Investment-type income, 72

Involuntary conversions, 71, 113, 117–119, 268, 352, 411
gains and losses from, 117–119

IRAs (individual retirement accounts), 4, 77, 91, 301, 312–314, 317–326, 329–331, 334–336, 351, 384, 388, 420, 467, 531, 542, 544, 561, 575
penalty-free withdrawals, 420

IRS. *See also* IRS Forms
assistance from, 475
audit guides, 471
e-file system, 529
opinions from, 471
private letter rulings, 427
publications of, 476

IRS Direct Pay, 529, 531, 533, 535

IRS Forms
8832, Entity Classification Election, 12–13
1099-MISC, *Miscellaneous Income*, 495
1099-NEC, 433, 449, 470, 539, 554, 567
1040 or 1040-SR, Schedule, 6
1040 or 1040-SR, Schedule SE, 519
1065, Schedule K-1 of, 10–11
5304-SIMPLE, Savings Incentive Match Plan for Employees of Small Employers, 315
1065, U.S. Return of Partnership Income, 10, 92, 389
W-2, Wage and Tax Statement, 563

IRS letters, 60

IRS tax preparers, 549

ISOs (incentive stock options), 28, 137, 506

Job assignments, change in, 175
Job locations, major and minor, 169
Joint ventures, spousal, 6, 9

Kay Bailey Hutchinson IRAs, 320
Kerosene fuel tax credit, undyed, 398
Key-person life insurance, 431
Kickbacks, 65, 74
Kiddie tax, 239

Labor costs for farming, 392
Land, as not depreciable, 269
Large cash transactions, 560–561
Last-in, first-out (LIFO), 18, 67, 68, 75, 87, 93
Late filing penalties, 529, 566
Late payment penalties, 535
Lawyers, 4, 411
Lease bonus payments, 73
Leased employees, 484, 515
Lease payments, 115, 150, 195–197, 236, 237, 239, 242–245, 286, 500
Leases. *See also* Rents
  amortization of costs of acquiring, 287
  annual lease value, 147–149
  business cars, 196–197
  buying *versus,* 196, 197, 199
  car, 196–197
  costs of acquiring, modifying, or canceling, 240–241
  gift-leasebacks, 239
  improvements to leased property, 241
  inclusion amount, 197
  leveraged, 243–244
  with option to buy, 196
  qualified leasehold, restaurant, and retail improvement, 242
  sale-leasebacks, 115
Legal fees, 97, 117, 120, 285, 425–427, 434
Leveraged leases, 243–244
Liability coverage, 28, 349, 430, 431, 493
Licenses, 122, 154, 203, 259, 260, 283, 365, 412, 424, 489, 550
Licenses and permits, 424
Life insurance
  buyouts and, 546
  group-term, 142, 431
  on individual basis, 150
  interest on policies, 432–433
  key-person, 431
  split-dollar, 151
Lifetime learning credit, 419
LIFO (last-in, first-out), 18, 67, 68, 75, 93
Like-kind exchanges
  property acquired in, 274
  timing of, 100
Like kind or class, 99, 100, 111, 268, 274, 411
Lime and fertilizer, 393
Limited liability companies (LLCs)
  about, 9–16
  alternative minimum tax, 507
  bad debts, 235
  basis determination, 14
  business expense deduction, 448
  business income, 66
  capital gains and losses, 111
  car expenses, 207
  casualty and theft losses, 352
  depreciation, amortization, and depletion, 289
  domestic production activities deductions, 396
  e-filing and, 530
  farming expenses, 399
  gains and losses, 124
  health insurance deductions, 389
  home office deductions, 353
  losses, limitations on, 80–81
  one-member, 8
  owners, compensation to, 136
  rent deductions, 244
  repairs and maintenance, 223
  required year and, 37
  retirement plan deductions, 335
  sales of business interests, 105
  series LLCs, 501
  tax credits, 462
  taxes and interest, 500
  transfer of assets to, 99
  transferred property and, 484
Limited liability limited partnerships (LLLPs), 9
Limited liability partnerships (LLPs), 9
Limited partnerships (LPs), 9, 10, 81
Limited use property, defined, 244
Listed property, limitations on, 280–281
Litigation, audits and, 555
Livestock feed, 392–393
Livestock sales, 69
LLCs. *See* Limited liability companies
LLPs (limited liability partnerships), 9

Loans. *See also* Debt; Mortgages
above-market, 258
bad debts, 225–226
below-market, 133, 257–258, 474
commitment fees for, 258
Commodity Credit Corporation (CCC), 69
dominant motive for, 229
gift, 258
interest-free, 133
long-term, 257
mid-term, 257
peer-to-peer, 486
repayment of, 70
by shareholder-employees, 229–230
from shareholders, 258
short-term, 257
student, 419
Lobbying expenses, 296–297
Local income taxes, 248, 359, 360
Local transportation costs, 164–165, 167
Location tax incentives, 72, 247
Lodging expenses
about, 146–147
deducting, 168
for employees on premises, 146
high-low method for, 168
local overnight stays, 166
travel within U.S. and, 166
Logs for expenses, 180
Long-term care insurance, 388
Long-term contracts, 44, 46, 66, 68, 506
Long-term loans, 320
Look-back method for long-term contract, 46
Losses. *See also* Capital losses; Casualty and theft losses; Disaster losses; Net operating losses; Passive activity losse
about, 57
at-risk, 83
bad debts, 227–228
basis and, 80
disasters and, 468
equipment and other personal property, 121
limitations on, 80–81
reporting, 123
sale of all assets, 121–122
Section 1231, 113–114
Section 1244, 108–109
tax planning and, 465
Low-income housing credit, 455
Low-sulfur diesel fuel production credit, 459, 460
LPs (limited partnerships), 9, 10, 81
Luxury taxes, 249–250

Machinery
replacement property, 99
spare parts, rotable, 215–216
write off costs and, 261
MACRS. *See* Modified Accelerated Cost Recovery System
Maintenance. *See* Repairs and maintenance
Mark-to-market accounting, 48
Material participation, 69, 87, 88, 474, 475
Material participation, defined, 87
Materials, cost of, 428
Materials, nonincidental, 281
Meal allowance, standard, 168, 169, 181, 365
Meal and entertainment expenses
about, 164, 175
club dues, 178
employer-operated eating facility, 146–147
gifts and, 178
limit, 178
missing, lost, inadequate records, 183
recordkeeping requirement, 182
reimbursement arrangements, 182
Meals
day-care providers, costs for, 434
standard meal allowance, 168
travel within U.S. and, 167
Mediation, 555–556
Mediation with IRS, 555
Medical coverage
about, 371
accident and health insurance, 430
Affordable Care Act, 259, 376
Archer Medical Savings Accounts, 385–386
cafeteria plans, 388
COBRA coverage, 386–387
deducting, 374–376
employees and, 141–142
employer mandate, 372–374
flexible spending arrangement, 381
FTEs and, 380
health care mandates, 372–374
health reimbursement arrangements, 379

Medical coverage (*Continued*)
  Health Savings Accounts (HSAs), 382–385, 388
  information returns, 561
  premium-only plans, 382
  reporting, 387
  S corporation shareholders, 376
  self-employed individuals, 377
  shifting costs to employees, 380–381
  tax credit for, 379–380, 456
  tax planning and, 465
  wellness programs, 387
Medical reimbursement plans
  EBHRAs, 378
  health reimbursement arrangements, 144, 372, 377, 379, 380, 467, 514
  ICHRAs, 378–379
  QSEHRAs, 379
  special reimbursements, 376
Medical Savings Accounts (MSAs), Health Savings Accounts and, 574
Medicare coverage, Part B premium, 375
Medicare taxes. *See also* FICA
  employer portion, 453
  records retention, 60
Merchant fees, 427
Merchant income on credit cards, 93
Merchant transactions, information returns, 565
Metropolitan area, defined, 165
Mid-month convention, 276, 278
Mid-quarter convention, 190–194, 275–277, 279, 468
Mid-term loans, 257
Mileage allowance. *See* Standard mileage rate
Military, employer wage credit for activated reservist, 453
Mineral properties, 287, 288
Mini-COBRA rules, 386
Minimum essential health coverage, 372–374, 455
Minimum tax credit, 73, 74, 111, 459, 507, 508
Miscellaneous business deductions, vi, 416–449
Miscellaneous business income, 74
Mobile offices, 466
Modified Accelerated Cost Recovery System (MACRS)
  Alternative Depreciation System (ADS), 279
  basic system, 286
  conventions, 274–275
  General Depreciation System (GDS), 271
  half-year convention, 275
  improvements to leased property, 241
  mid-month convention, 276
  mid-quarter convention, 275–276
  recovery periods, 272–273
Modified taxable income, 79
Money purchase plans, 302, 333
Mortgages
  home office deduction and, 258
  paying off, 72
Moving a business, 490–491
Moving expenses
  about, 417
  business deductions, miscellaneous, 448
  employer reimbursement of, 146
  employment status change, 146
MSAs (Medical Savings Accounts), 144, 382, 385–386, 388, 389, 574
Multiple businesses
  advantages and disadvantages of multiple entities, 499–500
  controlled corporations, 501
  employer mandate, 503
  first-year expensing, 626–627
  retirement plans, 503
  running multiple activities within one business compared to, 500
  tax rules, 502
Multistate operations and business organization, 31

NAICS (North American Industry Classification System), 43, 472
Nanny tax, 161
National Taxpayer Advocate Service, 556
Natural disasters, 344, 430, 488, 564, 570. *See also* Disaster losses
Nature and number of owners, business organization and, 29
Necessary expenses, 131, 177, 310, 395
Needy, donations for, 422
Negligence penalty, 54, 569
Net gains, 103, 111, 113, 352

Net investment income (NII)
investment interest and, 253
Medicare taxon, 248
Net investment income tax, 87, 252, 523, 575
Net operating losses (NOLs)
about, 64, 77–80
alternative minimum tax and, 504
calculating, 77
carrybacks, 78–79
carryovers, 78–79, 469
corporations, 78
deemed, 74
disasters and, 348
farming, 397
individuals, 77
Net passive income, excess, 75
Netting process, 114
New markets credit, 455, 459
Nexus to state and income taxes, 31, 509
No-additional-cost services, 151
Nonaccountable plans
car, 203
travel, 181
Nonaccrual-experience method for bad debts, 232
Nonaccrual method, 232
Nonbusiness bad debts, 228–231, 234, 235, 474, 537
Noncash payments to employees, 135
Nondeductible taxes, 252–253
Nonhighly compensated employees, 302
Nonqualified achievement awards, 134
Nonqualified employee stock options, 137
Nonqualified retirement plans, 331–332
Nonrecaptured losses, 58, 115
Nonrecourse debt, 120
Nonresidential realty, recovery period, 274
North American area, 173
North American Industry Classification System (NAICS), 43, 472

Obamacare. *See* Affordable Care Act
Occupational Safety and Health Administration (OSHA), 60
Office audits, 554
Office expenses, 153, 244, 245, 353, 356, 357, 361, 364, 365, 367, 428–429, 440
Officers of corporations
directors and officers coverage, 430
salary, 473–474
Office supplies, 43, 428, 560, 561
Off-time counts, 373
Oil and gas properties
partnerships, and depletion allowance, 288
refiners, 459
S corporations, and depletion allowance, 289
tax credits for, 459
Oil recovery credit, enhanced, 451, 458
150% declining balance rate, 276
One-member limited liability companies, 6, 512, 556
One-person 401(k) plans, 317
Online payment of taxes
investing resources in, 484–485
tax decisions, initial, 483–484
Optional farm method for self-employment tax, 520
Optional nonfarm method for self-employment tax, 520
Options, stock. *See* Stock options and restricted stock
Ordinary advertising expenses, 294–295
Ordinary and necessary business expenses, xii, 131, 133, 141, 145, 294, 297, 308, 310, 367, 391, 395, 424, 426, 428, 435
Ordinary loss deduction, limit on, 109
Ordinary loss treatment, qualifying for, 109
Ordinary repairs, 209–212
Organizational costs
corporations, 285
partnerships, 285–286
Orphan drug credit, 451, 458, 459
OSHA (Occupational Safety and Health Administration), 60
Outplacement services, 133, 152, 441, 445
Outsourced workers, 433
Overhead insurance, 430, 431, 441, 445
Overnight stays, local, 166
Owners
payment of company expenses, 31
tax planning and, 465

Parent-subsidiary controlled groups, 501
Parking, employer-paid, 152

Part B premium, Medicare, 377
Partial days of travel, 182
Partnerships
about, 9
alternative minimum tax, 507
amortization of organizational costs for, 285–286
audit regime, 556
bad debts, 235
basis determination, 17
business expense deductions, 448–449
business income, 51
capital gains and losses, 111
car expense deductions, 55
casualty and theft losses, 351–352
charitable contributions, 14
deductions, in general, 6
depreciation, amortization, and depletion, 289
distributive share of expenditures, 311
domestic production activities deductions, 402
e-filing and, 529
failure to file a return, 529
farming expenses, 401
gains and losses, 124
general, 9
guaranteed payments to partners, 136
health insurance deductions, 376
home office deductions, 370
losses, limitations on, 80
medical coverage, 375
oil and gas properties, and depletion, 289
owners, compensation to, 136
repairs and maintenance, 223
income/benefits, 301
required year and, 37
taxes and interest, 5
tax treatment, 246
transferred property and, 484
types of, 9
Passive activity, defined, 57
Passive activity losses (PAL)
at-risk rules and, 89
carryover period for, 58
deductions for expenses and, 86
farm losses and, 89
real estate exceptions, 88
Passive investment income, 17
Pass-through entities
bonuses to owners of, 133
capital gains and losses, 101
defined, 3
dividends and, 72
domestic production activities deduction, 396
first-year expensing, 261
partnerships as, 9
state income taxes and, 509
Patronage dividends, 69
Payee statements, failure to file, 568
Payments. *See also* Prepaid expenses
agricultural, 68
cancellation, 73–74
cash method of accounting and, 42
Conservation Reserve Program, 68
crop insurance and crop disaster, 68–69
deferred compensation, 139
to directors, 134
employment taxes, 128
feed assistance, 69
forest health protection, 69
guaranteed, 136
interest on deferred, 101
in kind, 64
lease bonus, 73
methods of, 64
prepayments, 41
relocation, 118
required, 38
in services, 65
Payments in kind, 64
Payments in services, 65
PayPal, 41, 64, 428, 441, 445, 565
Payroll providers, 534, 551
Payroll tax credit, 518
Payroll taxes. *See* Employment taxes
PBA (principal business activity), 43, 472
PBGC (Pension Benefit Guaranty Corporation), 309, 327, 331, 334, 336, 431
Peer-to-peer lending, 486
Penalties
accuracy-related, 568
employment taxes, 538–539
fines, damages and, 433–434
health care mandates and, 372
information returns and, 567
late filing, 563
negligence, 568–569
payee statements and, 568
preparer, 569–570
relief, 570–571
trust fund recovery, 518

Penalty abatement, 535, 570
Penalty-free IRA withdrawals, 420
Pension and Welfare Benefits Administration (PWBA), 336
Pension Benefit Guarantee Corporation premiums, 309
Pension Benefit Guaranty Corporation (PBGC)
Pension plans, 301, 306, 309, 310, 322, 333, 335, 336, 441, 445, 452, 458
PEOs (professional employer organizations), 130, 433, 551
Percentage depletion, 288
Percentage-of-completion method, exceptions from, 46
Percentage test, 302
Per diem rates
  recordkeeping for, 182
  reimbursement at, 181
Performance bonds, 431
Performing artists, 184, 207, 411, 448
Permits, 9, 10, 26, 35, 42, 57, 122, 123, 144, 153, 203, 220, 265, 283, 305–307, 317, 323, 332–334, 381, 424, 489, 494, 500, 510, 542
Personal education incentives, 418–420
Personal holding company penalty, 19
Personal holding corporation (PHC), 19
Personal identification number (PIN), 489, 529, 534
Personal interest, 188, 253, 256, 259
Personal property
  business use of, 281
  defined, 268
  removal costs, tangible, 211
  repossession of, 119
Personal property taxes, 188, 195, 249
Personal service corporations (PSCs)
  accounting period and, 37
  cash method of accounting and, 42
PHC (personal holding corporation), 19
Phones, cellular. *See* Smartphones
PIN (personal identification number), 489, 529, 534
Placed in service, 86, 116, 189–192, 194, 195, 197, 200, 207, 212, 222, 244, 262, 266–270, 272–280, 282, 289, 293, 364, 394, 410, 411, 458, 506, 537, 574, 576
Planning
  ahead, 472
  estate, 531
  retirement. *see* Retirement plans
  tax, 467
  year-end, 468
Plug-in electric vehicles
  2-wheel, 200
  4-wheel, 200
Pollution control facilities, amortization of, 282
Pollution liability insurance, 431
Portfolios, debt-financed, 436
Postage and shipping, 429
Postponing gains, 118
Post-year tax elections to cut bills, 468–469
Preference items, 506, 507
Premium-only medical plans, 382
Premium tax credit, 372, 374, 379, 389, 452, 455, 478
Prepaid expenses
  advance payments as, 41
  cash method of accounting and, 41
  deduction of, 56
  farm supplies, 392
  as income to service businesses, 65–66
  rent, 58
Prepaid interest, 41, 58, 258, 259
Preparer penalties, 569, 570
Preparers, tax return, 471, 475, 476, 529, 550, 551, 569, 570
Principal business activity (PBA), 43, 472
Principal place of business, 166, 354–356, 362, 498, 528
Private letter rulings, xiii, 427, 471, 476
Prizes
  as advertising expenses, 297
  for employees, 134
Produce, sales of, 68, 69
Product liability coverage, 431
Professional employer organizations (PEOs), 130, 433, 551
Professional fees, 285, 286, 309, 329, 425–426, 484, 553
Professional liability coverage, 430, 431, 493
Profitability, lack of, 27–29, 497
Profit motive and sideline businesses, 497

Profit-sharing plans, 302, 309–312, 317, 324, 328, 334, 335, 478, 561, 562
Promotional activities, 176, 294, 297
Property. *See also* Casualty and theft losses; Property, business, sale of; Rents; Repairs and maintenance
  abandonment of, 119
  additions to, 274
  community renewal, 108
  deduction of rents, 232
  depreciable, 101
  exchange of, 99
  foreclosure on, 119–120
  incidental, 100
  intellectual, 423
  limited use, 244
  listed, limitations on, 280
  oil and gas, 287
  personal, 211
  placed in service, 269
  qualified improvement, 210
  recovery periods, 272
  replacement, 99
  restricted, 135
  Section 1231 property, 114
  tangible, 269
  transfer of, 484
  unit of, 210
Property, business, sale of
  involuntary conversions, 117–118
  sale of all assets of business, 121–122
Property insurance, 236, 348–349, 437
PSCs (personal service corporations), 18–19, 26, 37, 38, 42, 45, 79, 573
PTIN holders, 550
QSEHRA (Qualified Small Employer Health Reimbursement Arrangement), xi, 144, 379, 380, 388, 575
Qualified achievement awards, 134
Qualified business income (QBI) deduction, vi, 9, 10, 17, 30, 57, 59, 63, 87, 128, 136, 264, 265, 396, 402–415, 465, 466, 474, 500, 519, 569
Qualified business stock, sale of, 107–108
Qualified cost, defined, 145
Qualified default investment alternatives (QDIAs), 305, 334
Qualified employee discounts, 151
Qualified equity grants, 138
Qualified improvement property, 210, 213, 242, 263, 273, 537
Qualified intermediaries, 100
Qualified medical expenses, 381, 388
Qualified performing artists (QPAs)
  car expenses, 185
Qualified personal service corporation (PSC)
  defined, 42
Qualified retirement plans
  approval, obtaining and maintaining, 306
  automatic enrollment feature of, 303
  borrowing from, 307
  comparison of, 326–328
  compensation limit, 306
  contribution limit, 307
  coverage for employees, 323
  disparity, permitted, 306
  excess contributions, 325
  filing information returns, 324
  loans from, 542
  obtaining and maintaining approval, 306
  participation in, 303
  permitted disparity, 306
  plan errors, 325
  prohibited transactions, 325–326
  for self-employed individuals, 310
  tax planning and, 465
  types of, 301–302
  vesting, 305
Qualified Small Employer Health Reimbursement Arrangement (QSEHRA), xi, 144, 379, 380, 388, 575
Qualified transportation fringe benefits, 152–153

Rabbi trusts, 332
Ranches. *See* Farming
Ratio test, 302
Real estate professionals, 88, 468, 469
Real estate/real property
  estate planning and, 547
  financing, at-risk rule for, 86
  gain on, 120
  home sale exclusion, 367
  rehabilitation credit, 455
  rents, 72
  taxes on, 247
Realty components, recovery periods, 273
Realty, nonresidential, 116, 274, 276–279, 367
Realty, recovery periods for, 272–274
Reasonable cause, 518, 535, 569–570

Reasonable compensation, xi, 132, 134, 408
Reasonable rate of interest, 101, 256, 307, 481, 542
Recapture
  by C corporations, 102
  of depreciation, 367
  first-year expensing, 261
  installment sales and, 177
  LIFO, 75
Receivables, unrealized, 105, 480
Recordkeeping. *See also* Documentary evidence
  about, 51
  audit exposure, minimizing, 469
  basis, 57
  car expenses, 203
  carryover, 56–59
  depreciation, 56
  diaries or logs, 183
  disposal of records and, 60
  general, 51–54
  importance of good, 470
  missing, lost, inadequate records, 183
  per diem rates, 184
  relief, 55–56
  repairs and maintenance, 203
  retention of records, 59
  special substantiation requirements certain expenses, 183
  technology for, 52–53
  travel expenses, 53
Recourse debt, 9, 120
Recovered property, 344
Recovery periods, 103, 194, 201, 211, 241, 242, 267, 270–276, 279–281, 360, 393, 394, 396, 410, 506, 537
Recreational vehicles (RVs), 366
Recurring items, 44
Redemption-type agreements, 547
Redemption-type buy-sell agreements, 547
Refiners, 459
Reforestation expense, 267, 287, 395, 441, 445, 576
Refunds
  from carrybacks, 80
  fuel-related excise taxes, 398
Rehabilitation credit, 223, 451, 455, 459
Rehabilitation doctrine, 212
Rehabilitation plans, 212–213
Reimbursement arrangements
  accountable plans, 179–180
  car, business use of, 186
  incidental rate, 181
  nonaccountable plans, 181
  partial days of travel, 182
  per diem rates and, 184
  tax planning and, 539–540
Reimbursement plans, 29, 35, 141, 371, 376–379, 440, 445, 467, 572
Related parties, 45, 86, 103, 104, 114, 118, 226, 237, 447
Relocating businesses, 147
Relocation, housing relocation costs, 147
Relocation payments, 118, 490
Removal costs, tangible personal property, 213
Renewable energy production credit, 458
Rental real estate exception to passive activity losses, 88
Rents
  about, 294
  advance, 238
  car leases, 242
  to corporations, 237
  cost of leases, 241
  deducting, 236–237
  defined, 236
  as farm income, 68
  gift-leasebacks, 238
  improvements to leased property, 242
  as income, 68
  leveraged leases, 243–245
  miscellaneous rentals, 239
  with option to buy, 242
  of portion of home for business, 242
  prepaid, 73
  real estate, 73
Repairs, 49, 50, 52, 88, 150, 188, 195, 202, 203, 209–224, 247, 252, 342, 343, 345, 353, 358, 360, 393, 399, 406, 412, 437, 440, 444, xi, xii
Repairs and maintenance
  about, 209
  accounting method, change in, 217
  capital improvements, list of deductible, 210
  capital items compared to, 210
  deducting, 209–210
  disabled access credit, 217
  improvements for elderly and handicapped, 217
  ordinary repairs, 209
  rehabilitation plans, 212
  removal of architectural or transportation barriers, 218

Repairs and maintenance (*Continued*)
repairs, list of deductible, 209
rotable spare parts, 215–216
small business safe harbors, 214–215
Replacement property
defined, 118
S corporations, 124
self-employed individuals, 110
tax-free exchanges and, 99
Replacement time limits, 119
Repossession. *See* Foreclosure on or repossession of property
Required distributions, 38, 334
Required payments, 38, 231, 522, 532
Required year, 37
Resale numbers, 249, 489
Research costs, deducting, 441, 445
Research credits
orphan drug credit, 458
research credit, 456–457
Resellers, xi, 49, 67
Residential rental realty, recovery period, 274
Restricted property, 135
Restrictions on accounting periods and accounting methods, 27, 31
Retirees, medical coverage, 376
Retirement planning
about, 541–542
plan loans, 542
professionals and, 544
rollovers, 542
Retirement plans. *See also specific plan type*
about, 301
added costs for, 308–309
advice, as employee benefit, 144
amendments to, 308
annual reporting requirements, 562
bonding requirement, 308
contributions, 323–324
deductions for, 335
defined benefit plans, 302
errors, common, 325
ESOPs (employee stock option plans), 329
filing information returns, 562
investment advice, 308
IRAs, 319
monitoring investments, 325
nonqualified, 331–332
owning your business, 330
plan maintenance cost, 308
qualified, 301
reporting distributions, 561
reporting requirements, 336
for self-employed individuals, 310–311
setting up, 323
start-up cost tax credit, 309
state-sponsored plans for private sector, 323
terminology for, 332–333
Returns, 538–540. *See also* Information returns; Tax returns
ROBS (rollovers as business start-ups), 330, 334, 488
Rollovers as business start-ups (ROBS), 330, 334, 488
Rollovers, retirement planning and, 542
Rotable spare parts, 215–216
Roth IRAs
converting to, 321–322
designated Roth accounts, 333
"in-plan rollover," 542
Roth 401(k) retirement plans, 317
Royalty financing, 486
Rulings, private letter, xiii, 427, 471, 476
RVs (recreational vehicles), 366

Safe harbor rules
bonus depreciation previously used for vehicle, 194
classification of workers, 130
de minimis (minimal), 262
home office deductions maintenance, routine, 353
small building, 214
small business, 210
Salary
continuations, 133–134
of corporate officers, 473–474
Salary reduction arrangements in SEPs (SARSEPs), 313, 334
Sale. *See also* Resellers
of cars, 201
exchange requirement or, 98
installment. *see* Installment sales
Sale-leasebacks, 115–116, 236, 238, 572

Sales and use taxes, 249, 509, 524–525, v, vi
Sales of business interests, 33, 105–106
Sales revenue, sourcing of Sales taxes
  resale number, 151
  use taxes and, 249
Sales tax, 53, 64, 188, 249, 250, 268, 272, 441, 445, 489, 524, 525, xiv
SARSEPs (Salary reduction arrangements in SEPs), 313, 334
Savings Incentive Match Plans for Employees (SIMPLEs), 302, 310, 313–315, 319, 322–324, 327, 328, 333–336, 441, 445, 467, 503, 513, 514, 542, xi
SBA (Small Business Administration), 28, 71, 127, 131, 231, 233, 342, 350, 351, 353, 486, 488
Scientific property donations, 422
S corporations
  about, 16
  alternative minimum tax, 507
  audit strategies, 136
  bad debts, 235
  business expense deductions, 449
  business income, 75
  cancellation of debt income for, 74
  capital gains and losses, 111
  car expenses, 55
  casualty and theft losses, 352
  charitable contributions from, 422
  depreciation, amortization, and depletion, 293
  dividends and, 451
  domestic production activities deductions, 396
  e-filing and, 529
  farming expenses, 401
  gains and losses, 96
  health insurance deductions, 389
  losses, limitations on, 80
  medical coverage, 376
  oil and gas properties, and depletion allowance, 376
  owners, compensation to, 133–134
  rent deductions, 240
  repairs and maintenance, 219
  reporting income/benefits, 157
  required year and, 37
  retirement plan deductions, 329
  sales of business interests, 106
  special income items for, 75
  tax credits, 447
  taxes and interest, 255
  travel expenses, 183
Seasonal businesses, 37, 373
SECA (self-employment tax), 5, 6, 30, 71, 77, 79, 91, 92, 136, 155, 162, 248, 249, 264, 311, 312, 317, 377, 409, 441, 519–523, 530, 536, 545, 575, xii
Section 179 deduction, 188, 193, 194, 210, 213, 222, 261–266, 268, 282, 286, 292, 293, 468, 502
Section 83(i) election, 138
Section 936 election, 108
Section 444 election for fiscal year, 38
Section 83(b) elections, 137–138
Section 1202 gains, 103
Section 1231 gains and losses, 58, 113–115, 123, 124, 264
Section 197 intangibles, 103, 283, 284, 441, 445
Section 1244 losses, xi, 33, 108–109, 538
Section 1231 property, 58, 69, 95, 96, 111–114, 123, 352, 468
Section 530 relief, 130, 570
Section 1202 stock, 103, 107, 108
Securities
  deferring gain and, 109
  defined, 109
  worthless, 109–110
Self-created intangibles, 284
Self-employed individuals. *See also* Independent contractors
  alternative minimum tax, 507
  bad debts, 67
  business expense deductions, 448
  business income, 92
  capital gains and losses, 110
  car expenses, 207
  casualty and theft losses, 352
  checklist of deductions for, 438–439
  COBRA payments, 377
  compensation paid to, 161
  depreciation, amortization, and depletion, 289–293

Self-employed individuals. *See also* Independent contractors (*Continued*)
farming deductions, 399
gains and losses, 123
health insurance deductions, 390
home office deductions, 367
medical coverage, 372
rent deductions, 253
repairs and maintenance, 222
reporting, income/benefits, 135–136
retirement plan deductions, 335
retirement plans, 335
self-employment tax, 248–249
tax credits, 127
taxes and interest, 299
travel expenses, 185
Self-Employed Qualified Plans
about, 310
contributions to, 311
Self-employment tax (SECA)
employer portion, 390
Self-insured, 141, 390, 514, 525
Self-select personal identification number (PIN), 529
SEPs. *See* Simplified employee pensions
Series LLC, 10, 14, 500, 501
Service businesses, income for, 65–66
Service charges, 141, 252, 361, 516–517
Service revenue, apportionment methods, 76
Services
no-additional-cost, 151
payments in, 65
7-year property, 266, 273, 275–277
Severance damages, 118, 346–347
Severance pay, 133, 515
Shareholders
compensation paid to, 133
formalizing agreements between corporations and, 458
guarantees of corporate debt, 250
more than 2%, 139, 153
Shipping costs, 429
SHOP (Small Business Health Options Program), 372, 380
Short tax years, 37, 39, 423
Short-term gains, 102, 104
Short-term loans, 257, 542
Shrinkage, 67, 340, 344
Sideline businesses
business expenses, 357
business expenses and, 357
hobby losses, 496
profit motive and, 496
reporting income, 495
reporting income and expenses, 498
Signatures
electronic, 529
signing return, 522
Significant participation activity, 88
SIMPLE (Savings Incentive Match Plans for Employees), xi, 302, 310, 313–315, 319, 322–324, 327, 328, 333–336, 441, 445, 467, 503, 513, 514, 542
SIMPLE-IRA *versus* Self-Employed Qualified Plan or, 328
Simplified employee pensions (SEPs)
contributions to, 469
covering employees in, 312
defined, 312
qualified plan *versus,* 328
salary reductions for, 312
Simplified expense method, for home office deduction, 362–363
Simplified method, 49, 57, 239, 240, 353, 358, 362–364, 370, 576
6-year graded vesting, 306
Sleep or rest rule, 167
Small building safe harbor election, 224
Small Business Administration (SBA), 28, 71, 127, 131, 231, 233, 342, 350, 351, 353, 486, 488
Small businesses
defined, 107
qualified business stock, sale of, 107
tax credits for, 456
Small business exception, cash method of accounting and, 421
Small Business Health Options Program (SHOP), 372, 380
Small cash transactions, reporting on, 563
Small corporations
alternative minimum tax, 507
checklist of deductions for, 438
Small employer health tax credit, 457

Small employer pension plan start-up costs, credit for, 336, 458
Small employers, SIMPLE plans and, 313
Small inventory-based business exception, 42, 43
Smartphones. *See also* Telephone expenses
 as employee benefit, 141
 golden parachute payments and, 140
 home office deductions and, 353
 recordkeeping and, 51–52
Social media, 298–299, 494
Social Security number, sole proprietorships and, 60
Social Security taxes
 business organization and, 30
 employer portion, 250
 records retention, 60
Software
 amortization of, 286
 cost of, 428
Soil and water conservation, 394–395
Soil conservation expenses, 394–395
Sole proprietorships
 about, 4
 day traders, 6
 e-filing and, 529
 husband-wife joint ventures, 6
 independent contractors, 4–5
 IRS Form 1099-NEC, 40, 65
 IRS Form 1040 or 1040-SR, Schedule C, 6
 one-member limited liability companies, 6
 reporting income, 5
 sales of business interests, 105
 spousal joint ventures, 6
 state income taxes and, 509
 statutory employees, 5
 tax treatment of, 4
Solo 401(k)s, 503
Spare parts, rotable, 215–216
Special assessments, 117, 346, 347
Special rulings from IRS, 476
Special substantiation requirements
 charitable contributions, 56
 travel expenses, 54–55
Specific charge-off method, 232
Specific identification method, 67
Specified service trade or business (SSTB), 52, 265, 396, 403, 407, 411–414
Split-dollar life insurance plans, 151
Spousal joint ventures, 6, 9
Spouses
 indirect gifts, 179
Standard meal allowance, 168, 169, 181, 365
Standard mileage allowance, 186, 187, 195–196, 201, 203, 349, 424, 576
Standard mileage rate
 about, 196
 actual expense method compared to, 188
 barred, 196
 recordkeeping for, 187
Start-up costs, 266, 282, 284–285, 309–310, 336, 427, 441, 445, 458, 459, 490, 575
Start-up of business
 amortization of organizational costs for, 293
 financing for, 485–488
 first year tax reporting, 490
 initial tax decisions, 483
 investing own resources, 484
 setting up bank accounts and credit cards, 490
 tax identification number, 488–489
 writing-off costs of, 490
State benefit funds, 250–251
State income taxes
 on business income, 76
 corporations, 511
 e-filing and, 529
 gross receipts tax, 510
 sourcing of services revenue, 510
 withholding of, 522
State-sponsored retirement plans for private sector, 323
State taxes
 income-based, other, 511
 multiple businesses and, 500
 nexus to state and income taxes, 31
 tax authorities, 492
Statute of limitations, 59, 98, 270, 497, 535, 537
Statutory employees, 5, 6, 161, 185, 407, 410
 travel expenses, 184
Stock
 in qualified small businesses, 106
 redemption, estate tax and, 548
 shareholder basis in, 511
 worthless securities, 110

Stock options and restricted stock
incentive stock options, 137
nonqualified employee stock options, 137
qualified equity grants, 138
Storage
of inventory and samples in homes, 365
of records and files, 59–60
Straight-line depreciation, 102, 116, 189, 280
Straight-line mid-quarter convention, 192, 278
Student loans, interest on, 253, 419
Subscriptions
cash basis and prepayment, 58
deducting, 425
Substantially vested, defined, 135
Substantial portion, rehabilitation and, 212
Substantiation methods, travel expenses, 183
Succession planning, 541–548
Supplemental unemployment benefits, 145, 410, 441, 445
Supplies
cost of, 428
nonincidental, 281
Surety bonds, 431
Suspended losses, carryover period and, 89
Sustainability perks, 134

TANF (Temporary Assistance for Needy Families), 155, 452
Tangible property, defined
Taxable income limit, 57, 264, 286
Taxable income, modified, 79
Tax adviser, vi, xii, xiii, 130, 239, 326, 484, 492, 552
Tax assistance, 475–479, vi
Tax attributes, 73, 74, 492
Tax credits
about, 450
alternative minimum tax and, 460, 504
American opportunity, 419
capital construction related, 455–456
claiming, 460, 470
credit limitations, 460
disabled access, 217, 223, 455
educational, 419, 448
employee health coverage contributions, 379–380
employment-related, 450–454
energy, 223
energy improvements, 222
farming, 398–399
general business, 459
guide to, 451
lifetime learning, 419
minimum, 459, 507
payroll, 518
plug-in electric vehicles, 200
rehabilitation, 223
rehabilitation costs, 212, 455
retirement plan set-up, 309
Tax deferral, estate planning and, 547
Tax deficiencies, interest paid on, 259
Taxes. *See also* Alternative minimum tax
about, 246
accumulated earnings tax, 26
built-in gains, 252
death, 546, 547
deducting, 246–252, 259–260
employment, 250
estate, 546
estimated, 533
excise, 525
floor, 249
foreign, 252
franchise, 251
fuel, 251, 458
gross receipts, 510
kiddie, 239
law changes and, 466
local income, 248
luxury, 249–250
Medicare, 249
multiple businesses and, 499–450
net investment income, 575
nondeductible, 252–253
payroll. *see* Employment taxes
personal property, 249
real estate, 247
reporting, all taxpayers, 123, 289–293
sales and use, 249, 524
self-employment, 248
Social Security, 30
state benefit funds, 250–251
state income, 248
trust fund, 28
Tax-exempt income, interest related to, 259
Tax forms. *See* IRS Forms
Tax Foundation

Tax-free exchanges, 95, 99–100, 111, 201, 202, 266, 271
capital gains and losses for, 110
Tax home, defined, 164, 165
Tax identification numbers
business organization and, 35
employer identification numbers. *see* Employer identification number
resale numbers *versus*, 489
Tax law changes, 48, 466, 468
Taxpayer Advocate Service, 476, 550, 556
Taxpayer Bill of Rights, 556
Tax payments. *See* Payments Tax planning
Tax penalties, 19, 98, 130, 161, 259, 441, 447, 531, 566–571, vi. *See also* Penalties
Tax preparation fees, 426–427
Tax preparers, e-filing and, 551
Tax professionals, vi, 35, 53, 113, 244, 253, 330, 426, 465, 471, 475, 476, 529, 549–552, 554, 570
Tax professionals, assistance from, 244, 465, 475–478
Tax rates, 3, 9, 17–19, 27, 28, 30, 35, 38, 47, 72, 76, 91, 102, 104, 116, 139, 248, 250, 330, 402, 465, 466, 481, 504, 512, 513
Tax returns
amended. *see* Amended tax returns
audit-proofing, 469–472
e-filing, 529–530
employment, 538
final year of business, 493
first year of business, 490
online filing, 529–530
payment of employment taxes, 517
preparers of, 471
retention of, 60
Tax-saving tips, 465–469
Tax year
about, 36
accounting methods, 40–48
accounting periods, 36
change in, 40
defined, 36
uniform capitalization rules, 49
Technology for recordkeeping. *See also* Smartphones
about, 52
electronic imaging systems, 53
Telephone
IRS not contacting by, 554
Temporary agencies, 130, 433
Temporary assignments, living away from home on, 174–175
Temporary Assistance for Needy Families (TANF), 155, 452
Temporary, defined, 165
Temporary travel, defined, 167
Temporary workers, 130, 378, 433
Temporary work sites
1099 income, 65–66
10-year property, 273
Termination of business, 32, 33
Theft. *See also* Casualty and theft losses
identity theft protection, 151
Timber gains, 69
Timber, sales of, 69
Tips
employer credit for FICA on, 156, 453
special rules for, 515–516
Total income or loss, 92, 101
Trade-in of cars, 342
Transfers
of assets to business, 90
of property, 484
Transit passes, 152, 153, 575
Transportation costs, travel within U.S. and, 167
Transportation or architectural barriers, removal of, 217, 218, 223, 441, 445
Travel expenses
about, 164
business trips with other persons, 169
conventions, 172–174
counting business days, 172
deducting, 184
foreign travel, 170
frequent flyer miles and, 153
incidental rate, 181
local transportation costs, 209
partial days of travel, 182
recordkeeping requirements, 182
reimbursement arrangements, 179–182
special substantiation requirements, 54
temporary assignments, living away from home on, 174–175
within U.S., 166–170

Trucks and vans
depreciation and, 200
excise taxes and, 525
heavy SUVs, 195
Trust fund amounts, 512
Trust fund recovery penalty, 518
Trust fund taxes, 28
Tuition and fees, 418, 419
Turnaround Management Association, 492
Turnover tax, 249
20-year property, 273, 276, 277
Two-and-a-half-month rule, 44–46, 133
200% declining balance rate, 176

Unadjusted basis immediately after acquisition (UBIA), 407, 410, 411, 414
Unamortized costs of failed businesses, 492–493
Unborrowed policy cash value, 433
Undyed kerosene and undyed diesel fuel tax credit, 398
Unemployment benefits, supplemental, 145, 156, 347, 410, 441, 445, 453, 513, 520
Unemployment insurance number, 489
UNICAP (uniform capitalization rules), xi, 49, 247, 279
Uniform capitalization rules (UNICAP)
about, 49
capitalization required, 49
change in accounting method and, 50
Uniforms, cost of, 429
Unincorporated businesses, 4, 30, 35, 248, 373, 420–421, 496
Unrealized receivables, 105, 480
Unrecaptured depreciation, 116, 117, 280
Unrecaptured gain, 102–103
Unrelated business taxable income (UBTI), 330
USDA, 68, 71, 434
Use and occupancy insurance, 349
Use taxes, v, vi, 249, 442, 446, 509, 524–525, 549

Vacation pay, 131, 134, 446, 515
Vans. *See* Trucks and vans
VCSP (Voluntary Classification Settlement Program), 130, 571
Vehicle expenses. *See* Car expenses; Trucks and vans
Venture capital, 486
Vesting in retirement plans, 335
Voluntary Classification Settlement Program (VCSP), 130, 571

Wage differential payments, 513
Wages
reporting, 563–564
worker classification and
Waivers, tax penalties and, 570
Water conservation expenses, 394–395
Websites, costs of, 295, 298
Wellness programs, 387, 388
Whaling captains, deduction for, 424
Worker classification, 5, 128–130
Workers' compensation, 5, 128, 130, 251, 382, 393, 431, 440, 442, 444, 446
Working condition fringe benefits, 151–152
Work opportunity credit, 59, 155–156, 163, 452–453, 460
Work-related personal credits, 454–455
Work sites, temporary, 165, 166, 175
Worthless debt, 227–229, 233
Worthless securities, 109–111, 124, 446, 535, 538
Write-offs. *See* Deductions
Written substantiation, 54
W-2, Wage and Tax Statement
errors, common, 564
reporting health coverage on, 387

Year-end planning, 468